CHILDREN'S
PERIODICALS
OF THE
UNITED STATES

HISTORICAL GUIDES TO THE WORLD'S PERIODICALS AND NEWSPAPERS

This series provides historically focused narrative and analytical profiles of periodicals and newspapers with accompanying bibliographical data.

CHILDREN'S PERIODICALS OF THE UNITED STATES

Edited by
R. Gordon Kelly

Historical Guides to the World's Periodicals and Newspapers

Greenwood Press
Westport, Connecticut • London, England

Library of Congress Cataloging in Publication Data

Kelly, R. Gordon.
  Children's periodicals of the United States.

  (Historical guides to the world's periodicals and
newspapers)
    Bibliography: p.
    Includes index.
    1. Children's periodicals, American. I. Title.
II. Series.
PN4878.K39   1984   051′.088054   83-8574
ISBN 0-313-22117-0 (lib. bdg.)

Library of Congress Catalog Card Number: 83-8574
ISBN: 0-313-22117-0

First published in 1984

Greenwood Press
A division of Congressional Information Service, Inc.
88 Post Road West
Westport, Connecticut 06881

Printed in the United States of America

10 9 8 7 6 5 4 3 2 1

Copyright Acknowledgments

Grateful acknowledgment is given for permission to use the following:

''Letter from the Publisher'' (May 1973). Reprinted by permission of *Ebony Jr*.

The poem used in each issue of *Humpty Dumpty's Magazine*. Permission given to reprint in full by
the Children's Better Health Institute, Benjamin Franklin Literary & Medical Society.

Excerpts from an article by R. Gordon Kelly in *Phaedrus* 4:2 (Fall 1977). Reprinted by permission
of the publisher.

Every reasonable effort has been made to trace the owners of copyright materials in this book, but
in some instances this has proven impossible. The publishers will be glad to receive information
leading to more complete acknowledgments in subsequent printings of the book, and in the meantime
extend their apologies for any omissions.

For my parents, Iole Scudder Kelly and
Robert Morrison Kelly, in grateful memory

Contents

Preface

This volume is intended to provide brief, authoritative descriptions of a broad sample of American periodicals for children. Its entries supplement and extend the handful of profiles of juvenile magazines appended to Frank Luther Mott's venerable five-volume *History of American Magazines*. Each entry consists of an analysis of the selected periodical and a description of its contents; a section that provides sources of additional information about the periodical and locations of libraries holding complete or nearly complete files; and a publication history section that details changes in title, editor, and place of publication throughout the periodical's history. In many instances, these publication histories correct, clarify, or supplement existing sources of information.

Although every effort has been made to present a balanced, representative selection from the history of American periodical publishing for children, several factors have shaped the final form of this volume. Regrettably, no comprehensive bibliography exists. The list of 423 titles appended to this volume is a beginning—but a very limited one. Second, this volume is shaped by the selection and retention policies of libraries, including the Library of Congress, the broad outlines of which are clear enough, even if the details have not been systematically studied. Children's periodicals have not been collected regularly by research libraries, and even the Library of Congress has not retained copies of certain types of children's periodicals. Perhaps forty to fifty titles are relatively widely held in university libraries and state historical societies. For the many dozens of other titles, accessibility is distinctly limited. To that, add the fact that the serious study of children's literature is just twenty years old and that the study of children's periodicals has attracted only a handful of researchers, and the difficulties in the way of compiling a truly balanced and representative selection become formidable. Specialists will quickly point out certain omissions. Religious periodicals, for example, are not as well represented as they deserve to be, given their numbers and historical significance. Regrettably, foreign-language periodicals published in the United States are not represented at all; their history remains to be written.

This volume, with its emphases and omissions, accurately reflects the stage of development of a still-neglected aspect of children's literature. Fifteen years ago, this book could not have been written. Ten years from now, it would be a different, doubtless better book. Nevertheless, until superseded, it takes its place as the richest single source available for information about American periodicals for children. Intended for a broad audience, it is hoped that the volume will prove useful for scholars in literary and cultural history as well as laypersons who seek a more thorough, historically informed description of a particular periodical than is available elsewhere. A system of cross-references to other entries enhances the usefulness of the volume, permitting the reader to identify quickly other relevant titles and information. An asterisk after a magazine title indicates that there is an entry for that magazine in this work. The three appendices—an alphabetical list by title, a chronological listing by date of publication, and a listing by place of publication—bring together information on more children's periodicals than is provided in any other existing source.

There is disappointingly little scholarship on American children's periodicals, and much of what has been done is highly selective—devoted to a mere handful of magazines—and relatively inaccessible. The most detailed study of the development of secular periodicals for children in the nineteenth century, for example, languishes as an unpublished doctoral dissertation. With a few notable exceptions, existing studies seldom offer more than generalized, even cursory, descriptions of the contents of the periodicals chosen for study. Although superseded in part by more specialized studies, the best, most accessible overview of the development of periodicals for children in the United States is to be found in Frank Luther Mott's magisterial *History of American Magazines* (5 vols., Cambridge, Mass.: Harvard, 1938-1968). Mott's account of periodical development is admittedly brief, but his supplemental descriptions of notable periodicals such as *Parley's Magazine,* * *Merry's Museum,* * *The Youth's Companion,* * *St. Nicholas,* * and *Wide Awake* * are basic and essential. The more recent history of American magazines by John Tebbel (1972-1978) adds virtually nothing to Mott's account of children's periodicals.

Other brief but largely derivative overviews are cited in Eleanor Nolen's "Nineteenth Century Children's Magazines" (*Horn Book* 15 [1939]:55-60) and Justin Schiller's "Magazines for Young America: The First Hundred Years of Juvenile Periodicals" (*Columbia Library Columns* 23 [1974]:24-39). The editorial objectives of six commercial children's periodicals (*Guardian and Monitor, Parley's Magazine, Robert Merry's Museum, Every Youth's Gazette*, and *Boys' and Girls' Magazine,* and *Fireside Companion* *) are described in John Crume's "Children's Magazines, 1826-1857" (*Journal of Popular Culture* 6 [1973]:698-706), where Crume explored the extent to which the magazines were used as a means of social control.

Several dissertations, taken together, provide a more comprehensive but less accessible description of the development of American children's periodicals. The most useful of them is Betty L. Lyon's "A History of Children's Secular Magazines Published in the United States from 1789-1899" (Ed.D. diss., Johns Hopkins, 1942), which contains the most comprehensive bibliography of juvenile periodicals currently available, a chronological listing of 145 periodicals, and a wealth of publishing data. Lyon described three stages in the development of the juvenile periodical in the nineteenth century. From 1789 through the 1830s, she concluded, they were shaped by religious, educational, and reform interests. From the 1840s through the Civil War, education became the central concern, and writing for children increasingly came to be regarded as an activity requiring special skills. From 1865 until the turn of the century, secular juveniles were intended primarily for entertainment, and the best magazines made available to children the work of the period's finest writers and illustrators. Lyon concluded that children's periodicals directly influenced the development of literature for children and were an important, if indirect, force helping to advance the cause of education.

E. C. Strohecker, "American Juvenile Literary Periodicals, 1789-1826" (Ph.D. diss., Michigan, 1969), is an effort to describe all of the juvenile literary periodicals of the first quarter of the nineteenth century. Excluding religious periodicals and titles no longer extant, Strohecker described the purpose, editorial policy, contents, and contributors to twenty-five periodicals and in an appendix provided a useful register of editors, printers, publishers, and engravers, together with a chronological and geographical listing of the surviving magazines. He concluded that there was a perceptible shift in the period from instruction toward entertainment.

Two studies purport to evaluate as well as describe historical juvenile periodicals. The more ambitious effort, Goldie Platner Merrill's "The Development of American Secular Juvenile Magazines: A Study of the Educational Significance of Their Content" (Ed.D. diss., Washington University, 1938), assesses a limited number of periodicals in terms of six comprehensive educational aims widely advocated at the time of the study. Although Merrill concluded that the several aims were generally met by all magazines selected (*The Youth's Companion, St. Nicholas, Boy's Life,* * *The American Girl,* * and *Story Parade,* * among others), she did not claim that editors and writers sought consciously and consistently to further the six goals. Her evaluative criteria do not derive from the magazines themselves but were simply imposed upon them. As a consequence, her study tells less about how those who wrote for and produced the periodicals understood what they were doing and more about the relative continuity of educational values in the late nineteenth and early twentieth centuries. J. S. Clarke's "Evaluative Study of American Juvenile Periodicals, 1865-1875" (M.S. thesis, Southern Connecticut State, 1968) similarly imposes contemporary criteria on historical materials. Clarke sought to evaluate the extent to which selected juvenile periodicals contributed to the development of children's literature in the decade after the Civil War—that development understood as a trend away from a didactic style to a more "natural" style of writing. Clarke argued that three-quarters of her sample was free of didacticism, but the definition of didacticism, turning on an elusive concept of "balanced" representation of types of behavior and consequences, begs more questions than it answers. The pertinence of Clarke's evaluation is called into question by the dubious assumptions that lie behind her effort to devise a means of discriminating didactic from nondidactic style and content without paying any attention to how writers and editors understood the relationship between entertainment and instruction in fiction for children.

Periodicals for children, like children's books, are shaped by the concepts of child and childhood held by editors and authors. In "Conceptions of Children in American Juvenile Periodicals, 1830-1870" (Ed.D. diss., Rutgers, 1977), Jill Delano Sweiger documented changes in the concept of the child in *The Youth's Companion, Merry's Museum, Parley's Magazine, The Juvenile Miscellany,* The Child's Friend and Family Magazine** and concluded that by 1870 the view of the child as basically a person with good intentions who makes occasional mistakes had replaced the earlier prevalent concept of infant depravity. Although she found that rewards and punishments changed in the forty-year period investigated, the actual standards of behavior to which children were expected to conform changed little, as did the central importance assigned to family life and the designation of the child as someone fundamentally in need of adult supervision and guidance.

Almost no attention has been given to the subject of illustration in children's periodicals, beyond the widely expressed view that late nineteenth-century periodicals such as *St. Nicholas* were as well illustrated, by the standards of the period, as the best adult magazines. Mary Alice Hunt's study "Trends in Illustrations for Children as Seen in Selected Juvenile Periodicals, 1875-1900" (Ph.D. diss., Indiana, 1973) considers the types of illustration, format, methods of reproduction, and changes in illustration in three of the period's most successful juveniles, *Wide Awake, The Youth's Companion*, and *St. Nicholas*, as well as the relationship between text and illustration. Much remains to be done, however, on the content of illustration in children's periodicals and the beliefs about the nature and function of art that editors and illustrators sought to communicate to children.

Several efforts have been made to describe and evaluate contemporary periodicals for children. The most ambitious of them is Margaret Irene Koste's "Evaluation of Magazines Published for Children in America" (Ph.D. diss., Ohio State, 1962), which examines fourteen periodicals on the basis of criteria derived from child-development research, from aesthetics, and from an acceptance of the view that children's literature ought to promote the development and appreciation of democratic values. Finding that no magazine met all criteria, Koste concluded with recommendations for improvements. A similar study is M. C. Schiffler's "Critical Analysis of Juvenile Periodicals, 1940-1950" (M.S.L.S. thesis, Western Reserve, 1951), which evaluates ten magazines on the basis of format, appearance, organization of content, and literary merit. Schiffler found none of the magazines to be "completely satisfactory." Alice Gray's "Development of Magazines for Young People in the Twentieth Century" (M.S. thesis, Western Reserve, 1950) briefly surveys twenty-one magazines, largely in terms of editorial statements of purpose. Her evaluative statements derive largely from standard reference works such as Laura K. Martin's *Magazines for School Libraries* (Frankfort, Ky.: Kentucky Development of Education, 1977). On the basis of these studies, it seems that the history of children's periodicals in this century can hardly be said to have been begun.

Studies and commentary on individual children's periodicals are both uneven and highly selective. *The Youth's Companion*, the most popular and long-lived American children's periodical, and *St. Nicholas*, generally acknowledged to be the best children's magazine, have been widely discussed; but outside of the histories already cited, extended analyses of individual periodicals are rare. The best of the handful available is John Morton Blum's introductory essay "Our Young Folks" in *Yesterday's Children* (Boston: Houghton-Mifflin, 1959), an anthology drawn from the pages of the forerunner of *St. Nicholas*. Blum argued that in the decade following the Civil War, the traditional New England virtues, summarized in the term *character*, were challenged by the social changes being wrought by immigration, industrialization, and urbanization. In *Our Young Folks*,* writers for children responded to the changes they perceived by urging the continued value of rural living, strenuous physical activity, and the virtues of honesty and self-reliance. Less incisive and less informed is Alice M. Jordan's appreciation of *Our Young Folks* in her collection of essays *From Rollo to Tom Sawyer* (Boston: Horn Book, 1948).

Despite its brevity, J. M. Smith's description of *Rose Bud** *(Horn Book* 19[1943]:15-20), a children's magazine edited by Caroline Howard Gilman and published in Charleston from 1832 to 1834, is useful since so little has been written about short-lived periodicals or about southern writing for children. Mary June Roggenbuck's "Twenty Years of *Harper's Young People*" (*Horn Book* 53[1977]:29-35), emphasizes the extent to which Harper's entry in the field of quality children's periodicals followed the pattern established by *Our Young Folks* and perfected in *St. Nicholas*. Carolyn L. Karcher's "Lydia Maria Child and the *Juvenile Miscellany*," in *Research About Nineteenth-Century Children and Books*, ed. Selma K. Richardson (Urbana, Champaign, Ill.: University of Illinois Graduate School of Library Sciences, 1980), 67-84, discusses Mrs. Child's anti-slavery writings in the children's magazine that she edited.

In addition to the material on *The Youth's Companion* in Mott and Lyon especially, an interesting analysis is Rex Burns's exploration of the concept of success presented in the *Companion* from its founding in 1827 to 1860 (in *Success in America* [Amherst: University of Massachusetts, 1976]). Drawing heavily on Henry Nash Smith's classic *Virgin Land* (Cambridge: Harvard University Press, 1950) for his conceptual framework, Burns argued that *success*, initially defined as individual, moral, financial, and religious achievement, open to all, increasingly was replaced by a concept of success defined in terms of wealth and independence won through competitive endeavor.

Other writing about *The Youth's Companion* tends to be anecdotal and descriptive. Louise Harris's "*None But the Best*" (Providence, R.I.: Brown University, 1966) is an embarrassingly inept account of the *Companion*; Daniel Sharp Ford, its editor from 1857 until his death in 1889; and Charles Asbury Stevens, a prolific contributor during the late nineteenth century. Ford, one of the great children's editors of the period, deserves better. M. A. de Wolfe Howe, who worked as an editorial assistant on the *Companion* for five years following his graduation from Harvard, championed its forgotton strengths in "You Used to Read It, Too" (*Saturday Review of Literature* 21[March 23, 1940]:3-4); Felix Ranlett provided another insider's view in "*Youth's Companion* as Recalled by a Staff Member" (in *The Hewins Lectures, 1947-1962*, ed. Siri Andrews [Boston: Horn Book, 1963]), pp. 85-104).

More has been written about *St. Nicholas* than about any other American children's magazine, but much is repetitious and devoted to uncritical appreciation. A first-rate analysis of *St. Nicholas* during the Progressive Era is Fred Erisman's " 'There Was a Child Went Forth': A Study of *St. Nicholas* Magazine and Selected Children's Authors, 1890-1915" (Ph.D. diss., Minnesota, 1966). More accessible than the dissertation are three articles based upon it. In "L. Frank Baum and the Progressive Dilemma" (*American Quarterly* 20 [1968]:616-23), Fred Erisman examined the differences between the Oz books and a more realistic series, *Aunt Jane's Nieces*, arguing that the Oz series reveals Baum's increasing skepticism about the utility of traditional agrarian values in the urban setting. "The Strenuous Life in Practice" (*Rocky Mountain Social Science Journal* 7[1970]:29-37) discusses the school sports stories of the prolific Ralph Henry Barbour in terms of Barbour's emphasis on physical fitness, teamwork, fair play, and scrupulous honesty. "Transcendentalism for American Youth" (*New England Quarterly* 41[1968]:238-47) analyzes the writing of Kate Douglas Wiggin. Throughout the study, Erisman was interested in the relationship between rural values characteristic of the fiction in *St. Nicholas* and the urban world frequently depicted in the nonfiction.

Mary Mapes Dodge, who edited *St. Nicholas* from its founding in 1873 until her death in 1905, is widely regarded as the preeminent children's editor of the period. A full-scale description and analysis of her tenure as editor is Mary June Roggenbuck's "*St. Nicholas* Magazine: A Study of the Impact and Historical Influence of the Editorship of Mary Mapes Dodge" (Ph.D. diss., Michigan, 1976). Roggenbuck traced the history of *St. Nicholas* under Dodge, emphasizing its well-known contributors, the noteworthy and representative writing in it, and trends in its content. She concluded that the most exemplary period of the magazine's history was the 1880s, when a number of high-quality juvenile novels were serialized in it, and she accounted for Dodge's success in terms of her understanding of children's needs and her highly developed literary taste. One of Dodge's coups, getting Rudyard Kipling to contribute to *St. Nicholas*, is detailed in C. M. Wright's "How *St. Nicholas* got Rudyard Kipling and What Happened Then" (*Princeton University Library Chronicle* 35[1974]:259-89).

Dodge's success in attracting the best writers of the period to *St. Nicholas* has been widely remarked. It is a point of emphasis in Alice M. Jordan's celebratory essay in *From Rollo to Tom Sawyer* and the subject of R. D. Kennedy's essay "*St. Nicholas*: A Literary Heritage" (*Catholic Library World* 37[1965]:239-41), as well as of G. S. Weight's thesis "A Study of the Contributions of Selected Prominent American Authors to *St. Nicholas* Magazine" (M.L.S. thesis, Carnegie Institute of Technology, 1951). An incisive and authoritative discussion of the place of *St. Nicholas* in the development of American literary taste is found in E. C. Saler and E. H. Cady, "St. Nicholas and the Serious Artist" (in *Essays Mainly on Periodical Publishing in America*, ed. James Woodress [Chapel Hill, N.C.: Duke University Press, 1973]), which describes its relationship to the three-cornered literary conflict of the period between "romantics," "neoromantics," and "realists." The role of *St. Nicholas* in encouraging young authors is celebrated by Florence Sturges in her Hewins lecture "The *St. Nicholas* Years" (in *The Hewins Lectures*, ed. Siri Andrews [Boston: Horn Book, 1963]).

"The Reading Ease, Human Interest Value and Thematic Content of *St. Nicholas* Magazine" (*Journal of Educational Psychology* 42 [1951]:152-65) presents the conclusions of two researchers, Barbara Sward and Dale B. Harris, who sought to determine whether significant changes had occurred in seventy-five years following the founding of *St. Nicholas*. Using techniques developed by Rudolf Flesch, they sampled issues of *St. Nicholas* and *Child Life*,* a periodical begun in 1922, and found little variation in the level of reading ease and a consistently high level of human interest value over the seventy-five-year period. A complicated form of content analysis revealed marked continuity in thematic content as well. As in previous studies cited above, contemporary categories, in this case measures of readability and a typology of psychological events, are imposed on historical material with little consideration of the appropriateness of applying such measures. In this author's own work, *Mother Was a Lady: Self and Society in Selected American Children's Periodicals, 1865-1890* (Westport, Conn: Greenwood Press, 1974), the analysis of fiction in *St. Nicholas, The Youth's Companion, Wide Awake*, and *Our Young Folks* proceeds from the assumption that adults writing for children in the late nineteenth-century were engaged not only in efforts to entertain their young audience but in a highly self-conscious effort to transmit their culture, their world view, to American children who would one day be charged with furthering the nation's historical destiny. Stories in several periodicals were shaped by editors' and authors' desires to entertain children but also by their wish that, grown to adulthood, those children would hold and act on certain beliefs and values. Fiction of the right sort, they were convinced, was a powerful means of persuading young children to adopt a correct view of the world and of their place in it. Such an analysis aims not at evaluating the fiction characteristic of American children's periodicals in the late nineteenth century but of understanding its characteristic form by examining the factors that shaped its creation and by viewing the fiction as complex symbolic acts designed to achieve ends that cannot adequately be summarized simply by saying that children's authors sought to please and entertain their readers.

Appreciations of *St. Nicholas* abound. W. D. Hogarth, ''Window to America'' (*Horn Book* 25 [1949]:59-62), described one Englishman's experience of visiting an America made recognizable by twelve years of reading *St. Nicholas*. Anne Parrish's ''Do You Remember'' (*Horn Book* 25[1949]:26-32) is a personal reminiscence and appreciation written in response to an anthology compiled by the noted historian Henry Steele Commager. Commager's account of editing the anthology, ''Super! This Must Go In: Editing the *St. Nicholas* Anthology'' (*Publishers Weekly* 154 [October 30, 1948]:1874-77), is an engaging tribute.

The study of the children's periodical in America, it must be concluded, is a neglected area within the relatively neglected field of children's literature, and although there may be differences in opinion about what is most worthy of study, few would deny that a wealth of opportunities for study exists. In my opinion, the most pressing need is for a comprehensive bibliography of children's periodicals, one that includes religious and special-interest magazines as well as the literary periodicals that have claimed so much attention to date. Once we know more about what magazines there were, we need to have a variety of questions answered. Who wrote for them and with what intent? Insofar as fragmentary data permits investigation, who read them? What was the geographical pattern of their distribution? Some good work has been done as to the content of the best-known children's periodicals, particularly fiction, but much remains to be done, especially in terms of analyzing content of all kinds in terms of categories that emerge from the material rather than by means of contemporary categories indiscriminately applied to it. Moreover, there should be more emphasis on understanding and interpretation and less on evaluation, much of which has a distinctly peevish, not to say parochial, tone to it. We need to know more about the social meanings mediated by children's periodicals, the illustration of children's periodicals, and why children's magazines appear to have declined so much in quality in this century, despite persistent efforts to recapture the lost glories of *St. Nicholas* in the 1880s.

R. Gordon Kelly

Acknowledgments

Without the help of a number of people, this book would have been impossible. It is a pleasure to acknowledge their assistance. Fred Erisman took time from a demanding schedule to write the splendid essay on *St. Nicholas* magazine that was used as a model for contributors to this volume. I am grateful, too, for the help of Peggy Coughlan and Sybille Jagusch at the Children's Book Center, Library of Congress. Pearl Leopard and Katie Helene lent their typing skills to the project with unfailing good cheer. Melissa Hilbish, Laura Barbeau, and Scot Guenter provided invaluable research assistance at a crucial point in the manuscript's preparation. JoEllen Laissue's encouragement and sound editorial sense were indispensable. Throughout the project, Cynthia Harris, Reference Editor at Greenwood, has been extraordinarily patient and helpful. Although I have thanked the contributors individually, I do so again here because it is their book far more than it is mine.

Introduction

When Hartford printer Barzillai Hudson and his partner George Goodwin brought out the first number of *The Children's Magazine** in January 1789, the future of the venture must have seemed uncertain at best. Within three months they would decide to halt publication of the nation's first periodical for children with the April issue. Of the four issues printed, copies of three survive; there is no known copy of the February number. To set *The Children's Magazine* beside its latter-day counterparts—*Cricket,* *Boys' Life,** even *'Teen Magazine**—is one dramatic measure of the nearly 200 years of cultural change that separate us from that first effort to create a periodical expressly for children.

In retrospect, 1789 seems too early by a generation for a successful children's periodical to be established in the United States and Hartford perhaps too far from Philadelphia, then the publishing center of the new nation and hence a more logical site from which to launch a new kind of periodical. Nevertheless, in the fall of 1788 when Hudson and Goodwin presumably concluded their plans for *The Children's Magazine*, there must have seemed sound reasons for cautious optimism. The two men, partners for nearly ten years, were experienced printers, with a thriving and expanding business. In addition to being publishers of the *Connecticut Courant*, the state's third oldest newspaper, they were printers of Bibles and had negotiated a favorable contract with Noah Webster, whose *Grammatical Institute* they had begun publishing in 1783. Unlike a number of subsequent children's periodicals, *The Children's Magazine* does not appear to have been a casualty of undercapitalization or inexperience. Moreover, the partners could hardly have been ignorant of the profits beginning to be made in the printing of children's books, mostly of English origin, by men such as Isaiah Thomas, the foremost American printer of the time. As publishers of Noah Webster, Hudson and Goodwin were doubtless optimistic about the future of textbooks and related educational materials in a region that historically held literacy in high regard. In the first issue of *The Children's Magazine*, they wrapped themselves in the sober mantle of pedogogy. The new periodical, they suggested, was designed to occupy a place between children's (elementary) spelling books and their more demanding reading such as Webster's *American Selection of Lessons in Reading and Speaking Calculated to Improve the Minds and Refine the Taste of Youth.*

Nevertheless, the obstacles confronting even experienced, well-capitalized printers interested in publishing a children's periodical were daunting in 1788— and would remain so well into the nineteenth century. Printing presses required frequent repairs and, depending on the problem, the services of one of several specialized craftsmen. Procuring adequate supplies, particularly paper and ink, much of which was still imported, was a chronic problem. The country's postal and transportation system was primitive and its population small and thinly spread. At the risk of simplifying a complicated issue, childhood was widely, if not universally, regarded as a time for parents, and adults generally, to apply conscientious discipline to the young. The triumph of a more modern, indulgent concept of child nature and the role of childhood in the life cycle still lay in the future. A decade after Hudson and Goodwin's short-lived experiment, Charles Smith's effort to found a weekly children's periodical in New York, *The Youth's News Paper*,* also quickly failed. Like them, Smith was an experienced printer of almanacs and textbooks, but he ceased publication of *The Youth's News Paper* after six issues. The real beginnings of children's periodical publishing can be traced to Philadelphia, which maintained its preeminence in printing and publishing until the Erie Canal, completed in 1825, gave New York access to western markets and a competitive edge that it never subsequently lost. Two children's periodicals made brief, simultaneous appearances in Philadelphia in 1802, the *Juvenile Olio* and *The Juvenile Magazine; or Miscellaneous Repository of Useful Information*,* which survived about a year and a half. Ten years later *The Juvenile Port-Folio and Literary Miscellany** was begun by a precocious fourteen-year-old Thomas G. Condie, whose father was an established bookbinder, bookseller, and inkmaker. Despite his youth, and the death of his father in 1814, Condie was able to keep the *Juvenile Port-Folio* afloat unil 1816. Philadelphia was also a center for religious publishing and the home of the American Sunday School Union, under whose auspices was published the *Youth's Friend and Scholar's Magazine*,* beginning in 1823. A prototype of the nonsectarian Sunday school paper, the *Youth's Friend* claimed a circulation of 60,000 within four years.

The 1820s witnessed a remarkable expansion of periodical publishing in general, and by 1829 the New York *Mirror* noted that "The mania for periodicals has extended itself to children." In Boston John Putnam had established *The Juvenile Miscellany** in 1826, edited by the able Lydia Maria Francis Child and later Sarah Josepha Hale, who would go on to a distinguished editorial career at *Godey's Lady's Book.* Perhaps the most notable juvenile begun in the decade, certainly the longest lived, was *The Youth's Companion*,* founded in Boston by Nathaniel Willis in 1827 and destined to survive until 1929.

On the heels of its success with the *Youth's Friend*, the American Sunday

School Union began publishing a monthly for children of ages six and seven, the *Infant's Magazine*.* Sectarian Sunday school periodicals such as the *Children's Magazine*,* published in New York from 1829 to 1874 by the Episcopal Church, became more numerous and account for about half of the juvenile titles of the period.

Periodicals for children began to appear in the 1830s outside the publishing centers of Philadelphia, Boston, and New York. Brunswick, Maine, played host to a weekly, *The Juvenile Key*, for seven years. Beginning in 1830, *Rose Bud*,* another effort at a weekly periodical, was issued from Charleston, South Carolina, the first of a number of attempts, invariably short lived, to establish periodicals for the South's children.

Along with *The Juvenile Miscellany*, several magazines of the 1830s and 1840s signaled a growing stability and maturity in publishing for children. *Parley's Magazine*,* begun in 1833 as a biweekly, brought the period's most popular author of children's books into periodical publishing. Samuel G. Goodrich, the beloved "Peter Parley" of dozens of books, edited the magazine for only a year or so before ill health forced him to relinquish it, but the magazine survived, perhaps partly on the strength of his name, until 1844, when it merged with *Robert Merry's Museum*.* Goodrich, his health long-since restored, began *Merry's* in 1841 and continued to edit it for eleven years. One of the most successful juvenile periodicals before the Civil War, *Merry's* hosted the work of literary notables such as Lydia Sigourney ("The Sweet Singer of Hartford"), Catherine Sedgwick, and Timothy Shay Arthur. In its latter days, *Merry's* was edited by Louisa May Alcott. The financial success of *Little Women* and its sequel enabled her to resign the editorship, the duties of which she found onerous from the beginning.

The 1830s marked the beginning of reform-oriented periodicals for youth. The *Slave's Friend** was founded in 1836 as a publication of the American Anti-Slavery Society but was suspended two years later. *The Youth's Emancipator*,* published from Oberlin, Ohio, survived less than a year. A far more enduring effort to harness a children's periodical to a reform movement was the *Youth's Temperance Advocate*,* founded in 1839 by the American Temperance Union and backed by its considerable resources, which included an ambitious publishing program. Like Sunday school papers, with which it had much in common, the *Advocate* was inexpensively available at a bulk rate and distributed, in part, through Sunday schools. It ceased publication some time in the early 1860s. Other temperance periodicals include the *Temperance Ledger and Youth's Monitor* (West Chester, Pa., 1833-1834), *Temperance Offering and Youth's Cascade* (Boston, 1845-1846), *Youth's Temperance Enterprise* (Albany, New York, 1842-1844), and *Youth Temperance Visitor* (Rockland, Maine, 1863-1870).

By the 1840s, then, the shape of children's periodical publishing was fairly clear. Both the denominations and nonsectarian agencies such as the American Sunday School Union and the American Temperance Union were adopting the periodical format, especially in conjunction with the burgeoning Sunday School movement, which provided a distributional framework. These periodicals, many of them weekly, were buffered from the vigorous economic competition that beset the "secular" periodicals devoted to instruction and amusement such as *Merry's Museum* and *The Youth's Companion*.

The beginnings of a third kind of juvenile periodical can be discerned in *The Youth's Casket*,* published in Buffalo from 1852 to 1857 by Erastus F. Beadle. One of the great alchemists of his time, Beadle successfully transmuted the boredom of tens of thousands of Union soldiers to gold through the agency of the dime novel. *The Youth's Casket* was a miscellany, offering a familiar blend of stories, travelog, biographies, and poetry. In stories such as "A Burning Village," which describes Indian depredations in New York's Otsego County during the Revolution, are the ingredients of the numerous tales of adventure and violence making up the boys' story papers of the 1870s, 1880s, and 1890s.

The 1860s offer a convenient watershed in the history of American children's periodicals. With the exception of *The Youth's Companion*, few periodicals from the 1840s and 1850s competed successfully with those that, founded in the late 1860s and early 1870s, dominated the field until the end of the century. *Merry's Museum* barely survived to 1872, and Lippincott's moderately successful *Little Pilgrim*,* begun in 1853, suspended publication in 1868, ironically, just as a writer for *Putnam's Magazine* was proclaiming a "new era in this country in the literature for children." In children's periodicals, that new era had already begun with two distinguished, if short-lived, monthlies—*Our Young Folks: An Illustrated Monthly for Boys and Girls*,* begun in January 1865 by Ticknor and Fields in Boston, and *The Riverside Magazine** (1867-1871), begun two years later, also in Boston, by Hurd and Houghton, the forerunner of Houghton Mifflin. Both were ably edited, the former principally by Lucy Larcom with the assistance of John Townsend Trowbridge; the latter by Horace Elisha Scudder. Insisting on the highest standards of writing and moral idealism, Larcom and Trowbridge succeeded in attracting to the pages of *Our Young Folks* well-regarded New England writers such as Harriet Beecher Stowe, Louisa May Alcott, Thomas Bailey Aldrich, and the poets Whittier and Longfellow. The editors quickly built up a substantial circulation of 75,000, but financial losses forced the sale of the magazine to Scribner and Company, which in November 1873 brought out *St. Nicholas: Scribner's Illustrated Magazine for Boys and Girls*.* Like *Our Young Folks, St. Nicholas* built up a subscription list of approximately 75,000, a figure it apparently never exceeded. Under Mary Mapes Dodge, whose tenure as editor ended with her death in 1905, *St. Nicholas* became the preeminent American children's periodical, a judgment that lapse of time has only enhanced.

Between the founding of *Our Young Folks* in 1865 and the coming of *St. Nicholas* eight years later, a number of other literary periodicals for children were begun, making the decade after the Civil War perhaps the richest in the history of American children's periodicals. In 1865 *The Little Corporal*,* edited by the Chicago publisher Alfred L. Sewell, joined *Our Young Folks* to inaugurate the new era in children's magazines. Sewell had successfully directed a fund-raising effort among American children to benefit wounded Union soldiers, and *The Little Corporal*, dedicated to promoting moral leadership and "fighting against wrong," had a pronounced military tone until Emily Huntington Miller replaced Sewell as editor. With a circulation of some 80,000 in 1869, *The Little Corporal* was a popular success, but financial reverses in the early 1870s dictated its sale, and it was absorbed by *St. Nicholas* in 1875. In 1866 William J. Demorest founded *Demorest's Young America*,* designed to counter what he saw as a pronounced and unfortunate tendency toward the fantastic in children's literature. An ardent abolitionist who turned his attention to the temperance movement, Demorest increasingly used his *Young America* as a platform for that reform movement between 1870 and the magazine's demise in 1875. *Frank Leslie's Boys' and Girls' Weekly*,* a prototypical sensational story paper, was also begun in New York the same year. Leslie, an English-born engraver turned publisher, had already been strikingly successful with his *Lady's Magazine, New York Journal*, and *Illustrated Newspaper*. His children's *Weekly*, ostensibly devoted to genteel entertainment, featured serialized fiction of the sort pioneered in Beadle's *Youth's Casket* and subsequent dime novel series and illustrations keyed to the more sensational incidents in the stories. In sharp contrast to *Leslie's*, on the other side of the continent, the Church of Jesus Christ of Latter-day Saints, settled finally in Utah, inaugurated *The Juvenile Instructor*.*

In addition to the founding of *The Riverside Magazine*,* 1867 saw two attempts to establish southern children's magazines, *Burke's Weekly for Boys and Girls** in Macon, Georgia, and *Southern Boys' and Girls' Monthly*,* in Richmond, Virginia. The former published the fast-paced adventure stories of John Crittendon Duval, the "father of Texas Literature," as well as domestic fiction, much of it set in the South; fairy tales; biography; and articles about natural history. A conventional literary miscellany of the period, the *Weekly's* short life doubtless reflected the economic exhaustion of the South immediately after the Civil War. Even less successful was Richmond's *Southern Boys' and Girls' Monthly*, a literary magazine edited by Rev. E. Thompson Baird and his brother William Logan Baird. Devoted to Christian principles, the Bairds attempted to draw exclusively on southern writers, but their efforts to sustain a strictly southern children's periodical foundered on problems with transportation, erratic postal service, and shortages of supplies.

William Taylor Adams, the prolific "Oliver Optic" of boys' series fiction, launched *Oliver Optic's Magazine*ated* in Boston with the backing of Lee and Shepard, perhaps the preeminent juvenile publishers in the years immediately after the Civil War. Much of their success came initially from the popularity of Optic's books. The following year Adams serialized the novel *Ragged Dick* by an obscure fellow Bostonian, recently moved to New York: Horatio Alger, Jr. Begun as a weekly, *Oliver Optic's Magazine* became a monthly in 1871, shortly before the publisher's bankruptcy forced suspension of the periodical. Adams typically sought to combine entertainment with instruction in the pages of his magazine, and his sense of what constituted an exciting but, withall, wholesome adventure story drew attacks from fellow editors such as Edward Eggleston and Emily Huntington Miller (of *The Little Corporal*) and Louisa May Alcott. Yet another Boston periodical founded in 1867 was *The Nursery*,* an early attempt to provide a magazine especially suited for very young children. Under the editorship of Fanny P. Seavers, the new monthly sought to appeal to children from four to ten with a liberally illustrated blend of short fiction, nonfiction, verse, and an occasional song, through all of which can be traced the moral earnestness typical of the better magazines of the period. *The Nursery* survived until 1880, when it merged with a new periodical to become *Our Little Ones and the Nursery*,* edited by the experienced William Taylor Adams. In the 1880s, *St. Nicholas* was joined by *Wide Awake*,* begun in 1875 by Daniel Lothrop, a successful Boston publisher of children's books, who had brought out *The Pansy** the year before. Buoyed by the response to it and to *Wide Awake*, Lothrop added *Babyland*,* another periodical for very young children, in 1877 and *Our Little Men and Women** in 1880.

Yet another effort to found a southern children's periodical was *Acanthus*,* begun in 1877 under Annie Barnes, a children's author who had extensive experience editing publications for the Methodist Episcopal Church, South. Despite the difficulties that plagued earlier magazines such as *Burke's, Acanthus* managed to live up to its own motto, growing in the face of adversity, until 1884.

The 1870s saw the founding of several competitors to *Frank Leslie's Boys' and Girls' Weekly*. *Boys of New York*,* begun by Norman L. Munro in 1875, achieved a circulation of 200,000 within six months. Its serialized stories depicted brave and honest lads, usually of lower class origin, who save the day when disaster strikes their social superiors. This emphasis was sustained by Frank Tousey, who took over from Munro in 1878 and edited it until 1894, when *Boys of New York* merged with *Happy Days*.* More benign, in terms of contemporary taste, was the weekly story paper *Golden Days for Boys and Girls** (1880-1907), containing serials by Horatio Alger, Jr., Frank H. Converse, and "Oliver Optic," as well as shorter fiction, rhymes, puzzles, and news associated with the Golden Days Club. *Golden Days* was edited by James Elverson, a British-born telegrapher who had established the successful Philadelphia weekly *Saturday Night* in 1865. *The Golden Argosy* was a New York juvenile created by Frank Munsey in 1882. Modeled on Elverson's *Golden Days*, it also published serials by Alger and Optic as well as sports and hunting stories, biographies of successful men, and articles on natural history. By 1887 circulation had increased to 150,000. A year later, seeking a wider audience that included more adults, the editors changed the title to *The Argosy*, and the periodical ceased to be an exclusively juvenile publication. In their wake came a host of other story papers, such as *The Boys' Champion** (1881-1883), offering what their detractors deplored as a surfeit of vulgarity, violence, and aggression. At the end of the decade, the house of Harper made a belated entrance into the quality juvenile periodical market, adding *Harper's Young People** to their stable of successful magazines to compete with *St. Nicholas* and *Wide Awake*. Reflecting the standard and values of Harper's other publications, the new magazine drew on their existing contributors and subscription lists and grew rapidly. Initially a weekly, it became a monthly, *Harper's Round Table*, in 1895 before being suspended in 1899. Among the more notable contributors were William Dean Howells, Louisa May Alcott, Sarah Orne Jewett, and Howard Pyle. Although intended for both boys and girls, as were its principal competitors, *Harper's Young People* reveals a pronounced emphasis on feminine roles and domesticity throughout the 1880s that shifted, in the 1890s, to a preoccupation with masculine heroes and athletics.

In the twenty years following the Civil War, approximately sixty juveniles, half of them Sunday school papers, were in circulation in any given year, with new magazines constantly appearing to replace those suspended. From 1885 to 1905 the number rose to seventy-five, of which Frank Luther Mott estimates two-thirds were religious periodicals. These figures suggest what a look at new titles in these decades confirms: the heyday of the quality juvenile periodical was passing. To be sure, the 1880s and 1890s were the golden years of *St. Nicholas's* success, and *The Youth's Companion* was enjoying a circulation of 500,000. By the turn of the century, however, both were in decline; and Daniel Lothrop's highly successful *Wide Awake* had been merged with *St. Nicholas* in 1893, following the publisher's death in the preceding year. *Harper's Young People* ceased publication in 1899. One of the last of the quality literary miscellanies, *Little Folks: An Illustrated Monthly for Youngest Readers*,* was successfully launched in 1897, edited by Charles and Ella Pratt, who brought to the venture twenty years of experience on *Wide Awake* and *Our Little Men and Women*. *Little Folks* was, in effect, a consolidation and an extension of several infant periodicals, absorbing *Our Little Ones and the Nursery* in 1899 and *Little Men and Women—Babyland* in 1900. In part, by swallowing its competitors, it survived until 1926.

The quality juveniles of the late nineteenth century were closely allied with some of the most prestigious publishing houses in the country and with a concept of literary culture rooted especially in antebellum New England. Although both *St. Nicholas* and *The Youth's Companion* survived well into the new century, Dodge's death in 1905 effectively ended an era. The literary miscellany for young people, a junior version of *Scribner's* or *Harper's*, was increasingly an anachronism. The future belonged to juvenile periodicals allied with a movement such as scouting or addressed to an audience narrowly identified (increasingly for the benefit of advertisers) in terms of gender and age and, later, ethnic identification, or specialized interest. The shape of the future could be discerned, in part, in the founding of *American Boy** (1899), *The Boys' Magazine** (1910), *Boys' Life* (1911), *The Open Road* (1919), *The Girls' Companion** (1902) and *The American Girl** (1917). The quality juveniles of the late nineteenth century— *The Youth's Companion, Harper's Young People*, and *Burke's Boys' and Girls' Weekly*—had been addressed to young people generally, although their readership may have been predominantly female. After 1900, however, the working assumption of common youthful interests increasingly gave way to the assumption that interests, after the ages of nine or ten, were inescapably linked to biology; there was not one audience of "youth" but two: boys and girls. To be sure, the point can be exaggerated. Religious periodicals would continue to address youth of both sexes, as would publications as diverse as the classroom supplements published by Scholastic, Inc., or the politically radical *New Horizons for Youth*.*

The Boys' Magazine, edited by Scott F. Redfield in the western Pennsylvania town of Smethport, sought to mold character and foster self-improvement. Walter Camp, who brought together the first All-American football team, brought a strong emphasis on athletics to the magazine between 1911 and 1915, and the fiction generally emphasized the virtues of decisiveness and quick thinking, whether the setting was the playing field, the Wild West, or some dramatic moment in American history. *Boys' Life*, founded as a bimonthly by George S. Barton in Boston, was similarly dedicated to character building as well as to scout craft. Within a year it became the official organ, published monthly, of the Boy Scouts of America, and it has reflected the strenuous idealism of the scouting movement as well as its shifting preoccupations. *The Open Road*, founded in 1919, styled itself "the quality magazine for older boys." Stressing a vigorous manliness, its editors sought to avoid sensationalism without sacrificing adventure and served up a mix of historical fiction, nature adventure, school stories, and western tales. Articles emphasized technological progress, physical fitness, and the more easily achieved forms of self-improvement. After 1927 the magazine sponsored a Pioneers Club for outdoorsmen. *The Open Road* survived the Depression and World War II to merge with *American Boy* and *Mark Trail* in 1953. The merger failed to revive the participants' faltering futures, and *American Boy—Open Road* ceased publication a year later.

For girls, the new century brought *The Girls' Companion* (1902-1949), a weekly paper for young Protestant women edited by David C. Cook, one of the nation's most successful publishers of Sunday school literature. Each issue led off with an illustrated story in which the central character, typically an adolescent girl, found her moral convictions tested in difficult circumstances. Articles encouraged quality and practical homemaking skills and sought to foster an understanding of God through nature. More widely known, and arguably more influential, is *The American Girl*, which appeared in 1920, an outgrowth of *The Rally*. Founded in 1917 as a bulletin of the Girl Scouts of America, *The Rally* was quickly transformed into a magazine and its title changed to embrace the widest possible constituency. Closely tied to the scouting movement throughout its history, *The American Girl* enjoyed a circulation of 650,000 during its heyday in the late 1950s. Publication was suspended in 1979. The twentieth century has been hard on children's magazines, particularly the literary periodicals that enjoyed such success and acclaim in the late nineteenth century. Magazine publishers increasingly have sought to reach specific segments of the youth audience. Only magazines for the very young continued to bear a marked resemblance to their earlier counterparts and to enjoy a measure of success.

An interesting, if short-lived, effort to provide a magazine for black children was *The Brownies' Book*,* published by W.E.B. Du Bois and Augustus Granville Dill. Du Bois and Dill had founded *The Crisis* in 1910. *The Brownies' Book* was an outgrowth of an annual children's issue of *The Crisis*. Dedicated to supporting black culture and emphasizing the importance of education, *The Brownies' Book* published fiction and poetry, biographies of notable black figures, and editorials by Du Bois and literary editor Jessie Redmon Fauset.

Children's periodicals designed to supplement school curricula appeared throughout the nineteenth century, but the most notable successes of the genre have been in the twentieth century. Scholastic, Inc., with total circulation in excess of 10 million in 1980, grew out of a Pittsburgh-area high school sports weekly, *Western Pennsylvania Scholastic*, founded in 1920 by Maurice Robinson. Within two years it had become a national periodical retitled *Scholastic*. Under Kenneth M. Gould, managing editor from 1926 to 1944 and thereafter editor-in-chief until his retirement in 1960, *Scholastic* became a highly successful blend of timely fiction for adolescents, current events, and social studies materials. Its widespread acceptance enabled the company to expand during the 1940s with additional scholastic magazines, for example, *Junior Scholastic*,* aimed at students in elementary and junior high schools.

Literary magazines for young children continued to appear, despite the high mortality rate for such magazines. *Children's Playmate*,* founded as *Play Mate* in 1929, offered a familiar mix of stories, poems, articles, games, puzzles, contests, and regular departments. Changes of ownership in the 1960s and 1970s were symptomatic of increasing problems, however, and *Children's Playmate* is now one of the eight children's periodicals published by the Benjamin Franklin Literary and Medical Society, an organization that is long on health and short indeed on literature. Although the title has been retained, the magazine has been transformed and bears little resemblance to its namesake. Now intended for children of ages five through eight, most of its contents relate to health and hygiene. A similar fate has befallen *Jack and Jill*,* Curtis Publishing Company's very successful literary magazine founded in 1938 and guided for years by the knowledgeable Ada Campbell Rose. *Jack and Jill* entered the 1960s with a circulation of nearly 1 million, but efforts to stay in touch with the changing times, including a reorientation to nonfiction primarily, failed to maintain its readership; and *Jack and Jill* became a juvenile health-care periodical in 1979, following its acquisition by the Benjamin Franklin Literary and Medical Society. About the same time, the society also acquired the ailing *Children's Digest*,* a pocket-sized reprint magazine founded in 1950 by the publishers of *Parents' Magazine* as well as *Humpty Dumpty's Magazine** (1952), also a shrewdly edited publication of Parent's Magazine Enterprises and intended for preschool and beginning readers. A blend of stories, verse, and activities, liberally illustrated, *Humpty Dumpty's Magazine* quickly established a circulation of over a million; but it, too, encountered increasing difficulties in the 1970s before being swallowed up by the voracious Literary and Medical Society.

More resistant to the ravages of change have been the girls' magazines *'Teen,** *Ingenue,** and *Seventeen,** which emerged in response to the growing affluence of the postwar period. *Ingenue* was founded in 1959 and intended to provide somewhat more cosmopolitan fare than *Seventeen*, begun optimistically in 1942. Articles, fiction, and features typically ran in the narrow groove of diet, fashion, personal appearance, and romance. Challenged by changing mores in the 1960s and 1970s, *Ingenue (New Ingenue* after 1973) adapted but continued to advocate the importance of preparing for marriage and family life and the need to begin in the teenage years to establish "meaningful" relationships with males. *'Teen Magazine* antedated *Ingenue* by two years and offers much the same blend of articles and features about fashion, appearance, and how to be an informed consumer, as well as romantic fiction in which conventional or traditional solutions to the heroine's dilemma underscore the essential conservatism of the periodical. *Seventeen*, still going strong after forty years, addresses essentially the same issues and adheres to the same formula, whether of values or content.

Despite the changes that appeared to be working in American society during the 1960s and 1970s, several significant and innovative children's periodicals were established. *Cricket,** a literary magazine for children of ages six to twelve begun in 1973, was self-consciously cast in the mold of *St. Nicholas*. One of the central aims of its creators was "to bridge the gap existing in children's magazine publishing since *St. Nicholas* ceased publication in 1937" (*sic*). The editors sought to provide "literate, mind-widening material" that would entertain and inspire without condescending to its young readers. Like its progenitor, *Cricket* is a wide-ranging miscellany of poetry, folk tales, biography, nonfiction, and fiction. The *Cricket* league sponsors the same sorts of contests that proved so successful for *St. Nicholas* and drew the youthful talents of a host of later successful writers.

Ranger Rick's Nature Magazine,* begun six years earlier in 1967 by the National Wildlife Federation, has doubtless benefited from the heightened concern about ecology and environmental issues that emerged in the 1960s. Brilliantly illustrated, *Ranger Rick's Nature Magazine*, like *Cricket*, aims to treat its readers "as intelligent young people who should not be talked down to or patronized." More recent, and arguably more daring in concept but intended for much the same audience of children of ages eight to thirteen, is *Cobblestone,** a monthly periodical devoted to American history. Begun in 1980 by two former schoolteachers, *Cobblestone* devotes each issue to a single theme, which is explored in short articles, biographical sketches, historical fiction, and poetry.

The 1970s also saw the founding of two periodicals oriented toward minority experience. *The Weewish Tree,** founded by the American Indian Historical Society in 1971, was created to provide reliable information on American Indians, both past and present. Its circulation, however, never surpassed 11,000, and publication was suspended in 1980. Far more successful has been *Ebony Jr!**

Begun by John H. Johnson, the publisher of *Ebony, Jet*, and *Black World, Ebony Jr!* offers fiction, feature articles, games, and activities intended to develop and sustain its readers' awareness of the distinctiveness of black culture and to encourage educational exploration.

CHILDREN'S
PERIODICALS
OF THE
UNITED STATES

A

ACANTHUS

The *Acanthus* is a children's periodical whose existence has been all but forgotten. Only its dates and place of publication—1877-1884, Atlanta, Georgia—are mentioned in Frank Luther Mott's *History of American Magazines*.[1] Little more is found in biographical sketches of its editor, Annie Maria Barnes, who "undertook the publication of a juvenile paper called 'The Acanthus.'...In literary character it was a success, but financially, like so many other southern publications, it was a failure."[2]

The name of the paper was borrowed from the plant whose leaves were often used for decorative purposes by the Greeks and Romans. On the front page these leaves interlace the letters of the paper's title. In a paragraph appearing on the paper's masthead, Barnes observed that this plant's growth is persistent in the face of obstacles, and she drew an analogy between the acanthus and human beings, presumably for the encouragement of her young readers: "So genius, when acted upon by resistance or opposition, redoubles its attempts to overcome every impediment." A motto—"Upward! Onward!"—also appears on the masthead, echoing the lesson to be derived from the plant.[3]

The editor identified her eight-page periodical as a monthly. Although Barnes undoubtedly intended to follow this schedule of publication, too few issues of the *Acanthus* are available to determine how well she succeeded. Only four issues of volume 2 and one issue of volume 5 are known to be extant, and in two of them the editor apologized for delay or interruption in publication. In November 1878 she wrote: "The delay in getting out our last issue was caused by the loss through the mails of a package of MSS. passing between the editor and publisher. We have grown completely heart-sick over the repeated irregularities, and have determined to make no more excuses."[4] Then in July 1881 this apology appeared: "Owing to circumstances beyond the control of the editor, our subscribers have missed two issues of our paper. We are again at our post, however, and will do everything in our power to remedy past irregularities. We hope the excuse is sufficient to warrant a full pardon."[5]

The genre dominating the *Acanthus* is domestic fiction characterized by the didacticism typical of the era. "Nan the Good for Nothing," with the subtitle "The Story of a Black Sheep," is certainly an example of fiction used to teach a lesson. Written by Barnes under the pseudonym "Cousin Annie,"[6] the story is an account of the success of Nan Vanderlyn, the black sheep. She wins the "rose-wood writing desk" for submitting the best essay in a contest conducted by Dr. Peterkin Pettigrew, the school's headmaster. Her two older sisters, who not only dismiss Nan's efforts but also anticipate winning the prize themselves, learn the danger of being so vain as to overestimate oneself and underestimate another. Moreover, Nan learns that if one tries hard enough, one can emerge from a dark past and find undreamed-of success.[7]

Despite the fact that Barnes's stories usually carry with them a moral, they are more skillfully told and less sentimental than several others published in the *Acanthus*. "Going to Heaven by Railroad," which is unsigned, is a maudlin tale of a little girl's witness to a railway conductor concerning immortality.[8] "Ruby Ray, the Little Circus Girl," whose author signs himself "Cousin Tom," is similar in tone. After Ruby Ray is fatally injured while performing on a horse, her father vows at her bedside to give up the life of the circus, a life that Ruby Ray has participated in but has not approved of.[9]

The *Acanthus* published some of its fiction serially. Two installments of "Little Heroes," also by "Cousin Annie," appear in the October and November 1878 issues. When Van, the central character in these chapters, fails to go to church, his behavior is questioned by Dwarfed Dick, a physically and mentally handicapped child. The protagonist, in a fit of temper, canes the "poor deformed, helpless creature," only to be observed by Bob Winston, an admirer who cannot believe that his hero is capable of this "contemptible" act. Although Van leaves Dick and Bob without apologizing, the reader has been told that the perpetrator feels "guilty and confused";[10] before the November installment concludes, an episode begins in which Van's redemption, through a brave deed, is foreshadowed.

The *Acanthus* also contains numerous brief nonfiction articles. Some concern historic incidents or facts. Others offer advice to the young readers concerning their behavior. For instance, in one issue "Aunt Leo" points out ways in which girls may achieve inner beauty and the value of neatness in dress. The next month, in "A Word to the Boys," she warns of the pitfalls to be found in the undisciplined life. Still other articles suggest ways to make items for the home such as lamp shades, window transparencies, rugs, and picture frames.

Verse appears in each of the issues of the periodical. Some selections are unsigned, and others are attributed to long-forgotten poets. Two exceptions are poems appearing in the July 1881 issue. There on the first page are published

"Home Song" by Henry Wadsworth Longfellow and "Fame and Duty" by Friedrich von Schiller. Generally of indifferent quality, the poems in the *Acanthus* often treat one of two themes: the beauty of nature and the truths one may discover by observing it or human relationships within the family and between boys and girls.

The fiction, nonfiction, and poetry are frequently categorized under the titles "Our Dumb Friends," "Our Funny Little Folks," "Our Little Folks," "Our Boys," and "Our Girls." The section designated "Our Dumb Friends" offers reading about animals, their behavior, and the ways in which they should be treated. "Our Funny Little Folks" serves as a title for humorous anecdotes about very young children, and "Our Little Folks" consists of material designed to appeal to this same group.

The *Acanthus* recognized a special group of readers as members of "The Open Eye Club." The membership seems to have comprised those who submitted questions for others to answer. The names of new members are listed as is the name of the president, an office that was earned each month in some way that is not made clear. Another opportunity for subscribers to contribute to the paper always appears on the back page of the paper under the title "The Puzzle Box." Some, although not all, of the puzzles, riddles, and enigmas have been submitted by readers, and prizes are awarded for those solving the previous month's offerings.

Paradoxically, the most interesting reading in the periodical for the contemporary reader appears either on the editorial page or in a column with the title "Our Letter Box." On the editorial page Barnes frequently published accounts of her visits on behalf of the paper to persons and places in Georgia and neighboring states. Through the letters to the editor, the reader discovers other bits of social history in addition to insight into the reception accorded the *Acanthus* by its subscribers.

The editor's use of "Cousin Annie" as her by-line and the use by some other contributors of similar pseudonyms (for example, "Aunt Mary," "Aunt Leo," "Uncle Jimmy," and "Cousin Tom") lend a familiar, informal tone to the *Acanthus*. This familiarity is enhanced when subscribers to the periodical are addressed as "cousins" or refer to themselves as such in their letters to the editor. Indeed, the *Acanthus* might well have become for many of its young readers a part of their extended family, which has traditionally been, in the South, large and complex.

Barnes, who was born in 1857 in Columbia, South Carolina, evidently spent much of her life writing and editing. One biographer stated that when she was eleven years old, she contributed her first article to the Atlanta *Constitution* and that she had become a regular "correspondent" of that paper by the time she was fifteen. Although she contributed to many periodicals, she wrote extensively for the Methodist Episcopal Church, South, becoming the editor of at least one of its publications. Moreover, she was the author of twenty-eight books, many of whose titles suggest that they were intended for children or young people. Her first book was published in either 1885 or 1887; her last appeared in 1927, when she was seventy years old. None of the sketches of her life includes the date of Barnes's death.[11]

Notes

1. Frank L. Mott, *A History of American Magazines* (Cambridge: Harvard University Press, 1957), 3:177.
2. "Barnes, Miss Annie Maria," *A Woman of the Century*, ed. Frances Elizabeth Willard and Mary A. Livermore (Buffalo: Moulton, 1893).
3. *Acanthus*, October 1878, p. 4. Another motto is inscribed on the front page immediately below the paper's title: "Devoted to 'the Good, the Beautiful, and the True.' "
4. *Acanthus*, November 1878, p. 4.
5. Ibid., July 1881, p. [4].
6. Annie Maria Barnes, *Scenes in Pioneer Methodism* (Nashville: Barbee and Smith, 1891), 1:[3].
7. *Acanthus*, July 1881, pp. 1-3.
8. Ibid., November 1878, p. 2.
9. Ibid., October 1878, p. 7.
10. Ibid., November 1878, p. 1.
11. "Barnes, Miss Annie Maria," *A Women of the Century*; "Anna Maria Barnes," *A Handbook of Southern Authors* (1907); "Barnes, Annie Maria," *Who Was Who in America* (1961-1968).

Information Sources

BIBLIOGRAPHY
Annie Maria Barnes, *Scenes in Pioneer Methodism* (Nashville: Barbee and Smith, 1891), vol. 1.; "Barnes, Annie Maria," *Who Was Who in America* (1961-1968); "Barnes, Miss Annie Maria," *A Woman of the Century*, ed. Frances Elizabeth Willard and Mary A. Livermore (Buffalo: Moulton, 1893); Frank Luther Mott, *A History of American Magazines* (Cambridge: Harvard University Press, 1938-1968).
INDEX SOURCES
None.
LOCATION SOURCES
Nos. 8, 9, 11, and 12 of vol. 2 and no. 2 of vol. 5 are at Duke University, Durham, N.C. Photocopies of these issues are available at the University of Georgia, Athens, Ga.

Publication History

MAGAZINE TITLE AND TITLE CHANGE
Acanthus (1877-1884).
VOLUME AND ISSUE DATA
None.
PUBLISHER AND PLACE OF PUBLICATION
Dodson & Scott, Atlanta (1877-1884).

EDITOR
Annie Maria Barnes (1877-1884).

Lalla N. Overby

AMERICAN BOY—THE OPEN ROAD

In November 1919 *The Open Road* began publication, offering itself as "the quality magazine for older boys." It took its title as a metaphor for the lives ahead of young men, lives they must learn to command, enjoy, and fulfill. Selling for 25¢ a copy, subscriptions $3 a year, this new periodical was originally published by the Torbell Co. of Boston, an organization in which editor Clayton H. Ernst also served as vice-president.

In an opening statement Ernst set some high standards for *The Open Road*. Fiction would be chosen for its reality, for its revelation of unchanging truths. Stories would contain action "but never, we hope, distorted or sensational."[1] Similarly, if they employed sentiment, they avoided sentimentality. In summarizing the fiction's goals, Ernst commented: "*The Open Road* stories speak an honest language—we want them to do their share toward solving the great riddles of life."[2] Articles would be written by experienced men, experts in their fields, whether athletes, business people, or explorers. A dedication to high ideals was also evident in the departments augmented in *The Open Road*. Dr. Norman B. Cole offered a monthly column on fitness, "Keeping Fit," and author John Clair Minot's "Looking Over the New Books" critically reviewed the latest offerings for teens.

For the most part, in its early years *The Open Road* worked to achieve these aims. Although some of the historical romances could have been labeled sensational by the more strict, they did carry moral impact, stressing the virtues of the valiant gentleman. "The Mutineers" (November 1919 and following issues) exemplified this, recounting the adventures of a seventeen-year-old sailor shipping out to the China Sea in 1809. Charles Boardman Hawes was named associate editor in 1920 and was responsible for many later tales of adventure in *The Open Road*, among them "The Great Quest" (November 1920 and following issues), "The Esperanto and her Men" (December 1920), "Peter Ronco" (October 1921), and "Out of the Storm" (December 1921).

Aside from historical romances and tales of exotic places, other fiction in *The Open Road* also concerned topics of interest to active young American males. Editor Ernst's "The Mark of the Knife" (November 1919 and following issues) presented a popular view of prep-school life, the birthmarked, orphaned hero becoming a football star and ultimately discovering his true heritage. In stories of school and university life, sports often played a key role, such as J.G.B. Morse's "Touchdown to Go" (November 1920). The old West was an even more popular topic, represented by titles such as Ray Palmer Tracy's "Downfall of Lightning Bill" (December 1920) and "The Piano of Sunrise Gulch" (May

1921). A racist attitude toward blacks pervaded the humor of many "darkey" stories by Charles H. Baker, Jr., among them "Young Lochinvar Is Gone into the West" (April 1921), "The Last Day of Pompeii" (January 1921), and "The Haul of the Wild" (November 1921). Probably the most common fiction in *The Open Road* depicted young men confronting nature, whether in the form of wild animals, such as E. Waldo Long's "Wildcat Band" (July 1920), or in the form of harsh battles with the elements, such as Farnsworth Wright's "Pole Star" (February 1921). In its early years, *The Open Road* did not condone or publish detective stories, editorializing against them, since so often they "don't ring true."[3]

Articles, like fiction, were intended to enlighten and entertain. Frank Wigglesworth was a frequent contributor of pieces about electronics and technology; Everett P. Gordon, pieces about aviation. Glamorous role models retold their experiences, such as "Hunting White Polar Bear with the Eskimo" (December 1919) by arctic explorer Donald MacMillan, and "The War Cruise of the Corsair" (January 1920) by former Princeton football star David Tibbott, an officer in the naval reserve. A major concern was to promote an interest in seeking a viable, worthwhile vocation based on the reader's particular skills and interests. William Orr's "Look Before You Leap" (March 1920) and E. M. Weaver's "Are You a Future Captain of Industry?" (October 1920) exemplify the more general of this type of article; Edward W. Frentz's "Opportunities in Newspaper Work" (June 1920) and Weaver's "Railroading as a Career" (July 1920), the more specific. In 1920 an *Open Road* vocational department was established that regularly polled readers with a questionnaire, posted results, and offered advice.

Encouraging citizenship was also considered vitally important, both in warning threats against Bolsheviks and calls for civic pride by men like Herbert Hoover (May 1920). An article by publisher Ormond E. Loomis, "Where Do You Stand?" (October 1920), called for support of the newly formed National Community Board in its endeavor to create citizenship clubs throughout the land. Loomis served on the board, which explains *The Open Road's* continuing support of the project and the sequel article "Were You Born too Late?" (December 1920) by head of the board Dr. Henry E. Jackson.

In 1925 the magazine's title was altered to *The Open Road for Boys*. By 1936 it boasted half a million readers, although circulation hovered around 320,000. Some changes had occurred over the years, among them the single-copy price dropping to 10¢ and the publishing house moving to Menasha, Wisconsin. Although the basic categories of fiction remained the same, there was a touch of more sensationalism in exotic adventures like I. A. Sowers's serial "Chinese Pirate House" (January 1936 and following issues), the story of an American orphan against Yangtze River cutthroats. Tall tales had made an appearance, and so had detective stories, even with a contest held for the readers, giving them the clues to an imaginary bank robbery in the mythical town of Whizzerville and offering rewards for the most logical solutions. Alfred M. McCoy, all-around athlete and coach at Northeastern University in Boston, started in January 1936 to offer monthly advice on basketball, baseball, and football. C. W. Whittemore's series of tales about cub reporter Marc Taylor and Eldon G. Magnuson's similar series about outdoorsman Gary Wade both appeared in several installments.

Regular departments included ''Read Em and Grin,'' the monthly joke column; ''My Friends Abroad,'' the pen-pal correspondence column conducted by Sven V. Knudsen; ''Sales and Swaps,'' the advertisement column; and ''Stamps,'' Roger Wolcott Minard's monthly look at the popular hobby. By far the most important department was Deep-river Jim and the Campfire Chief's monthly report for *The Open Road* Pioneers Club.

This club was founded in 1927 for outdoor boys and men and took as its pattern the old-time trailblazers; as its code, to meet each obstacle and overcome it; as its motto, ''Be sure you're right—then go ahead.'' Five ranks of membership were attainable; twenty-six trailsman tests were offered. By 1936 more than 70,000 Pioneers were registered; by 1940, more than 100,000. A monthly forum for the club appeared in *The Open Road*, including outdoorsman tips, member activities, and an advice-correspondence column. In February 1936 a monthly sketch of famous pioneers such as Kit Carson, Alexander Mackenzie, and Sam Houston also become a regular feature. *Deep-river Jim's Wilderness Trail Book* was advertised to Pioneers, as were other accouterments such as Pioneer tents and knives.

An increasing sense of militarism filled the pages of *The Open Road* as European totalitarianism increased and the world geared up to the possibility of another major war. A tribute to Finland's soldiers was the cover story in March 1940 and subsequent issues emphasized the air force, navy, and army. Editorials by Ernst reminded readers that ''the freedom earned by pioneers of yesterday must be preserved by pioneers of today''(August, October 1940).[4] Minor changes in departments and a new publishing office were overshadowed by the sense of impending national threat.

After the war *The Open Road for Boys* had a new editor, Don Samson; a new collection of departments; and a new thrust. No longer was the emphasizing of high ideals a major concern—simple entertainment and useful advice to teens experiencing the social traumas of adolescence became the key policies. War stories, sports stories and articles, and westerns were joined by regular departments on stamps, photography, records, movies, and fashion. A regular comic-book-format serial appeared, reworking volume 1's story ''The Mutineers.'' Slang became acceptable, the use of photographs and illustrations increased greatly, and how to win a girl's affection became a discussable issue. Articles such as Ernest Delaney's ''Your First Date'' (February 1947), George Hoyt's ''Gentle Art of Shaving'' (June 1947), and Dick Fleischer's ''Let's Give a Party'' (August 1947) were intended to counsel young men and help them socialize. A column edited by Bill Gates was introduced in August 1947 for reader input on teen concerns, with the questionable title ''Bull Session.''

In 1950 *Outdoors*, a sister magazine published by the same concern as *Open Road*, was absorbed into *Outdoorsman*. Three years later, listing its subscribers at 250,000, *Open Road* merged with *American Boy* and *Mark Trail* to form a new magazine, *American Boy—Open Road*, edited by Philip Steinberg and published by Holyoke Publishing Co. of Dayton, Ohio. This new magazine hoped to live up to the past glories of its predecessors, but it relied on still more cartoons, illustrations, and photography and was produced on lower quality paper. Its intended audience was boys aged ten to seventeen, and it emphasized sports, media stars, and self-improvement. The Pioneers Club was retained but deemphasized, and a "Best Pix by Our Readers"-contest column joined stamp and correspondence departments. The August 1953 issue included an adaption of a "Dragnet" episode with photographs; the February 1954 issue included representative samples such as a photo-essay about Eddie Fisher, another about the Harlem Globetrotters, and an advice column by Charles Furcolowe, "Line Your Pockets With Spending Dough." The magazine ceased publication in October 1954.

Notes

1. *The Open Road*, 1 (November 1919), 2.
2. Ibid.
3. Ibid., 2 (March 1921), 3.
4. *The Open Road for Boys* 21 (August, October 1940), 4.

Information Sources

BIBLIOGRAPHY
None.
INDEX SOURCES
None.
LOCATION SOURCES
The Library of Congress has vols. 1-3; 18; 22; 29; 35, nos. 6-10; 36, nos. 1-8.

Publication History

MAGAZINE TITLE AND TITLE CHANGES
The Open Road (1919-1925); *The Open Road for Boys* (1925-1950); *Open Road* (subtitle varies) (1950-1953); *American Boy-Open Road* (1953-1954).
VOLUME AND ISSUE DATA
The Open Road (vol. 1, no. 1-vol. 7); *The Open Road for Boys* (vol. 7-vol. 32); *Open Road* (subtitle varies) (vol. 32-vol. 35, no. 5); *American Boy—Open Road* (vol. 35, no. 6-vol. 36, no. 8).
PUBLISHER AND PLACE OF PUBLICATION
Torbell Co., Boston (1919-?); Open Road Publishing Co., Menasha, Wis. (?-1939); Open Road Publishing Co., Louisville, Ky. (1939-1953); Holyoke Publishing Co., Dayton (1953-1954).

EDITOR
Clayton H. Ernst (1919-at least 1941); Don Swanson (?-1948?); Philip Steinberg (?-
    1954).
Scot Guenter

THE AMERICAN GIRL

The Girl Scouts were founded by Juliette Gordon Low in 1912. Five years later there were 12,812 scouts throughout the United States. The national headquarters of the Girl Scouts felt the need for some general form of communication between the widely scattered units of this rapidly growing organization. Thus *The Rally* was created—a small pamphlet sent primarily to troop "captains," or leaders. Fewer than 100 individuals subscribed to this twelve-page bulletin, which sold for 10¢ a copy or $1 a year. This seemingly insignificant publication was eventually to become *The American Girl*.

Because troop-organization information was of great importance to early scout leaders, the first *Rally* included reports on various scout activities, leader training camps, and available equipment. Columns that were to become regular features were "News of the Troops," "Good Turns," and "Echoes of the Camps." At first there were no stories or illustrations. That America was at war was all too apparent.

The first page of the first issue of *The Rally*, October 1917, contained an editorial by Josephine Daskam Bacon. Later a consulting editor for *The Rally*, Bacon urged leaders to recruit scouts and scouts to become more involved in war work. Juliette Low wrote asking scouts to raise carrier pigeons for General Pershing, and President Wilson wrote requesting youth involvement in the Junior Red Cross. That first issue also included instructions for knitting sweater sets for use by American and Allied soldiers in Paris.

The Rally staff, headed by editor Gertrude Springer Hill, was interested in producing more than just a dry bulletin for scout leaders—even in the first issue. Scouts were asked to send in troop news—both the good works and the fun variety. "*The Rally* in its present form," said Abby Porter Leland, director, national headquarters, "is only a beginning. In so far as Girl Scouts and Girl Scout leaders make this bulletin their own, by frequent contributions and frankest criticism, will it be able to grow and develop into the bigger and better publication for which we all aspire."[1]

The Rally's first cover illustration appeared on the January 1918 issue. It was a reprint of a photograph that was published in an issue of the French publication *L'illustration*. The photograph was of American Girl Scouts throwing flowers at the feet of soldiers about to leave for duty in France. That same issue, the fourth, contained an editorial urging scouts and leaders to become subscribers so that *The Rally* could continue to exist.

Other early issues of the magazine were similar to the first—containing scout news and suggesting ways for scouts to become involved in war efforts. Issue number 5 contained an editorial by Josephine Daskam Bacon, "Why We are at War." Its purpose was to make young people understand why the United States had a moral obligation to enter World War I. This article was praised by politicians and editors alike, which led to its distribution to several thousand schoolchildren.

The "Official Announcements" section of *The Rally* began in April 1918. Leaders were advised that items appearing there should be given immediate attention. One month later the resignation of Hill was announced. Elsie F. Williams was named acting editor. At this time the Editorial Board stated that the purpose of *The Rally* was "to interest the outside world more and more in what we are doing for our country, and to develop a larger and larger body of readers and subscribers for what we are trying to make the best magazine for patriotic girls of America."[2] Clearly, to be a scout in the early years was to be a patriot.

By August 1918 the format and size of *The Rally* had changed. It was no longer a pamphlet but a full-size magazine with sixteen pages. In addition, a subtitle had been added: *A Scouting Magazine for the American Girl*. Louise Paine Benjamin became the new editor with this issue. She had previously been on the staff of the *Woman's Home Companion*.

The August 1918 issue was significant also because it was the first time that fiction had appeared in *The Rally*. The story written by Josephine Daskam Bacon was "Sister's Vacation: The Story of a Girl Who Liked to Keep House." The other new feature that month was a page called "Scribe's Corner—A Page of Scout Letters"—letters from you, for you, and about you.

In the second year of *The Rally* several more changes were made and departments added. The first serial appeared. It was by Kate Douglas Wiggin, a distinguished author of children's books. A bit of color trim began to appear on the usually black-and-white covers. Topical issues appeared periodically. These issues contained the usual departments, but most articles concerned the theme of the issue—such as gardening, mothers and daughters, and international scouting. *The Rally* finally considered itself "a real girls' " magazine. Scouts were asked to send in their opinions of the magazine. Their opinions were obviously favorable. Circulation nearly doubled—from 3,500 to 6,500 copies—in one year. *The Rally* as well as the entire scout organization was growing rapidly.

The Rally continued to grow as the staff experimented with its contents. More stories and articles appeared with each issue. Four more pages were added. Book reviews began to appear. Girls were constantly being reminded to contribute to the "Scout Scrap Book" page. Articles were almost always illustrated now—usually with silhouettes or black-and-white line drawings.

In March 1920 major personnel changes presaged changes in the magazine. Louise P. Benjamin stepped down to become consulting editor. Edith Curtiss Hixon was named acting editor, and Josephine Daskam Bacon became chairman of publications. The May 1920 issue announced that with the June issue *The Rally* would become *The American Girl*. The price would increase—from 10¢ to 15¢ a copy—but many new features were promised.

The first issue of *The American Girl*, bearing the subtitle *A Magazine for Girl Scouts and Girls Who Love Scouting*, explained the changes taking place:

> *The Rally* was very ambitious. It wanted to grow and grow. Even when its contents were improved and more pages added it wasn't satisfied. It still had a firmly rooted secret desire. . .to be such a big delightful magazine that not only Girl Scouts, but all girls would eagerly read it. . . . And first of all it decided to change its name. . .so that every single girl in our big country might understand that the magazine was for her. . . . There will be just as much scout news as there ever was. But, in addition, there will be new features that will be of interest to every girl. . .a bigger magazine— a better magazine—and yet a magazine that you feel is as much your own as it ever was.[3]

New features included a "Scoutlet Page" ("as a trout is to a troutlet—so a Scout is to a Scoutlet") with its own story—the first by Clara Ingram Judson. *The American Girl* was reaching out to attract even the youngest of scouts. That first issue also included several nonfiction articles on topics such as using libraries, cooking, camping, and building. To make room for the new features, the editors increased the number of pages to twenty-four.

There was to be even more change and growth for *The American Girl* in the early 1920s. Fiction writers included Albert Bigelow Paine, Carolyn Wells, M. W. Niedemeyer, Oleda Schrottky, and the ever-popular Jane Abbott. Marjorie Flack and Joseph Franke did early illustrations. A table of contents first appeared in January 1921 near the back cover. Columns on nature and pets were introduced at this time. Advertising was becoming an important part of the magazine too.

Edith Curtiss Hixon became the editor in February 1921. By June more signs of growth were apparent. An editorial announced that four more pages would be added. Extra stories were promised. Established now as a national magazine, *The American Girl* continued to expand.

The thirty-six-page September issue had the following features in addition to the fiction: "Scribe's Corner," "Our Party Page," "El Comancho" (about nature), "Camp Memories—Picture Page," "More Scout News for You," "Captain's Page" (for leaders), "Movie Column," and "Money-Making Department." The "Movie Column" favorably reviewed William Fox's version of *Connecticut Yankee in King Arthur's Court*. The "Money-Making Department" suggested ways for troops to earn money. Some of these features became regular departments and lasted for many years. Others were short lived. But all were designed to bring continuity to the magazine and to attract new readers.

In October 1921 *The American Girl* adopted the scout motto "Be Prepared" as its own. National headquarters, after all, still wanted *The American Girl* to be primarily a scout publication. The January 1922 editorial subtly touched on this when it stated that "one of the greatest things that *The American Girl* can do for Scouting is to bring together in this way all these eager young people and let them shake hands with each other—in print at least."[4]

The early issues of *The American Girl* also contained plays that could be put on by scout troops at their meetings. "Practical Scout—Indoors and Out" was a new feature. A topical issue, the "Camp Number" of May 1922, was a full forty pages. This was possibly due to increased advertising. Girls were urged to buy from the advertisers, because "then, very soon, we shall be as big as *Boy's Life!*"[5]

To a degree, the changes in *The American Girl* reflected the changes in scouting. *The Rally*, started during the war, was addressed to an older, more serious audience. Scouting was very purposeful. *The American Girl*, however, became lighter with the end of the war, and its editors tried to attract the younger audience. Scouting was worthwhile—but it could also be fun! The August 1922 issue was called the "Humorous Number" and included features such as "Girl Scout Wit" and "More Scout Fun." This issue also included a four-page "Field News Section" attached to the back of the magazine. This special section was in newspaper format and was not illustrated. "Tips for Captains" and "Bird Study for Scouts" were the items included in this short-lived bulletin.

The editorial staff of *The American Girl* still had an identity problem. Their New Year's resolution in 1923 was as follows:

> . . .resolved to give the Girl Scouts the best girls' magazine possible: a magazine that will appeal more and more to our friends who are not Scouts—or, not yet Scouts, shall we say?
> . . .We have resolved to discover new authors and illustrators and to inspire them to give us more thrilling adventures than ever. . .more and more features contributed by the girls themselves. . . .
> It will be a great day for us when *The American Girl* takes her place proudly on the newstands with all the other big grown-up magazines, won't it? Well, that's one of our big hopes for 1923.[6]

In March this desire for growth was again stated—but with more of a scout emphasis. "We sincerely hope that. . .in its pages our own little magazine may carry the true Spirit of Scouting throughout the world. . . .Perhaps someday there'll be a world full of girls in khaki, and then we'll be so big and proud that we will naturally swell in size until the *Saturday Evening Post* will look small beside us!"[7]

Apparently, there was disagreement on the Editorial Board of *The American Girl* about what the magazine really ought to be. In April 1923 Louise M. Price was named editor. One month later Dorothy Culver Mills became acting editor, bringing a new cover and type style to the magazine. Still, all was not well on

The American Girl staff. Did national headquarters want only a scouting magazine? Or did it want the biggest and best magazine ever?

In June 1923 Josephine Daskam Bacon's name did not appear in the credits. In July no editors were listed at all, although the "Editor Speaks" column appeared. Finally, in August 1923 an announcement was made. Helen Ferris would be the new editor. She was already planning the September issue.

Ferris proved to be an excellent choice for the first professional editor of *The American Girl*. She immediately removed the "Field News" from the magazine and had it mailed directly to local scout leaders. She asked the girls to write in telling what they'd like to see in the magazine. The "What-I-Wish-in-My-Magazine" idea became an annual contest for readers. Ferris also began the column "Along the Editor's Trail" in which she talked to the girls each month. Her first message to them said: "We are all listening very carefully these days, to your messages. And we are asking you, as Assistant Editors, to write us what you wish to have in *The American Girl* . . . for all our wishes added together will make our greatest wish—a magazine which every Girl Scout will love."[8]

Evidently national headquarters wanted a scout-oriented publication that would be acceptable to everyone and thus increase circulation figures. But more importantly, it had consented to hiring a qualified professional to make the necessary changes in its publication. Ferris wanted to get the best authors and illustrators for the magazine. She knew that there must be some emphasis on scouting. But she also wanted to include in the magazine everything that might interest the average American girl—sports, books, grooming, nature, fashion, and even the arts. It was Helen Ferris who set the pattern for excellence for *The American Girl*, and it was she who guided its circulation from 7,000 to 42,000 copies in only four years.

Some of the changes in *The American Girl* were obvious immediately. The cover was in three colors and listed special features to be found inside that issue. Besides fiction, early Ferris issues included the first fashion article, poetry, articles by scouts, a stamp column, a drama consultant writing about play production, and a curator writing about nature museums. Mrs. Herbert Hoover wrote several nonfiction articles as did Ernest Thompson Seton. May Lamberton Becker, the "Reader's Guide" of the *Saturday Review of Literature*, began a book column in 1924.

New authors brought to *The American Girl* by Helen Ferris included Elsie Singmaster of the *Saturday Evening Post*; Constance Lindsay Skinner, a writer of pioneer stories; Elizabeth Janet Gray; and Edith Ballinger Price. Promising illustrators included Garret Price and Marguerite de Angeli. In addition, Ferris formed an *American Girl* Editorial Board that consisted of five girls and herself. The board met once a month to decide what kinds of things ought to be included in *The American Girl*.

The first sports page came in January 1925 at the suggestion of the readers. The puzzle page was named "Our Puzzle Pack." The "Beholder" ("Beauty is in the eyes of the Beholder") column also began at that time. It was to be entirely written and illustrated by scouts who would send in a description or picture of something they had seen outdoors. Covers at this time were often by Margaret Evans Price. "Along the Editor's Trail" was changed from editorial comments to a letters-from-readers column. There were many contests then—photo, art, writing, and so on. All were designed to attract new readers. The average age of the winners, ten to fourteen, is almost certainly that of the readership generally.

In October 1925 the subtitle became simply *The Magazine for All Girls*. By now the issues were averaging fifty to fifty-eight pages. The new joke page was called "Laugh and Grow Scout." The current reader's poll showed that girls were most interested in reading mystery, adventure, and sports stories. In earlier years the preference had been for family and boarding-school stories. The new readers—although perhaps younger—were apparently more sophisticated in their reading habits than their older sisters had been.

Articles on women in various careers began to appear. Biographies and autobiographies of famous women were also included. Helen Wills, the foremost girl tennis player at that time, wrote two how-to articles in 1927. Winifred Moses did a cooking column. Helen Rawson Cades, "Good Looks" editor of the *Woman's Home Companion*, began to write for *The American Girl*—usually about fashion. Nonfiction articles, thus, were as timely and as well done as was the fiction.

By January 1928 Helen Ferris had moved on to become the head of the Junior Literary Guild. One of her assistants, Camille Davied, became the new editor and, in general, carried on the excellence begun by her predecessor. A new column "Well, of All Things!" appeared. It was a column in which the readers gave their opinions on topics suggested by the editor. Suddenly, in April 1929, there was another change. Margaret Mochrie, another staff member who had worked with Ferris, became the new editor.

The spirit of Helen Ferris was still evident in *The American Girl* of the 1930s. The list of fiction writers for that period includes some of the finest—Lenora Mattingly Weber, Carol Ryrie Brink, Pearl Buck, Adele De Leeu, Armstrong Speny, and Cornelia Meigs. Lois Lenski was a new illustrator with promise. Nonfiction writers included Lillian M. Gilbreth, Helen Follett, Hazel Hotchkiss Wightman, Eleanor Roosevelt, Arthur Murray, Edwin B. Dooley, Helen Doss, Mary Margaret McBride, and Cornelia Otis Skinner.

Doctors addressed girls' health problems in *The American Girl* of the 1930s. George Carlson became editor of "Our Puzzle Pack." A new current events column was begun by Latrobe Carroll in October 1933. Perhaps it was started because, since the war, there had been very little written on the country and/or patriotism. Little was said about the Depression. The current events column was needed to keep the average American girl "In Step with the Times"—and the column was so named.

In July 1933 Anne Stoddard became editor of *The American Girl*. Changes, if any, were subtle. The contents page was finally moved to the front of the magazine. "Well, of All Things!" became "A Penny for Your Thoughts."

Helen Ferris was engaged to write a new book column that began in October 1933 and lasted for four years.

By 1937, the twentieth year of the scouts' publication, circulation reached 100,000 copies. Articles were about poise and boys, shyness, and decorating. A new feature was a series on American painters. Two other new departments, "What's on the Screen?" and "What's on the Air?" were adapted from other magazines to advise girls about suitable films and radio shows. "Make Your Own Clothes" and "Shopping Scout" were irregular features. The last issues of the 1930s contained—usually—four stories, four non-fiction articles, two scouting features, and departments on books, movies, stamps, jokes, American painters, and current events. Circulation was 125,000 copies, and the subtitle of the magazine was *The Magazine for All Girls Published by the Girl Scouts*.

A two-page subject index appeared at the end of the magazine in December 1940. Material was classified under the eleven program fields of girl scouting. By January 1942 circulation was up to 200,000 copies, despite a shortage of paper. A special issue in October of that year focused on the 25th birthday of the publication. Outstanding stories, poems, and articles published during the previous ten years were reprinted along with a brief history of *The American Girl* by Mildred Adams of the National Board of Girl Scouts.

The first price increase in twenty-three years followed in 1943. The new price was 20¢ a copy. Nonfiction articles during the early 1940s reflected on our war involvements. "Jobs in Aviation for Girls," "Make Your Own Victory Blanket," "Dishes for Meatless Days," "Uncle Sam Wants Weather Girls," and "The Honor and the Glory" were some of the titles. Advertising also indicated the reality of World War II. But although there was some Girl Scout participation in war efforts, the fervor and patriotism of World War I was missing. Perhaps this was due in part to the age of the readers—many of whom were not yet teenagers.

Esther R. Bien became the new editor of *The American Girl* in September 1945 and remained in that position for twenty-two years—longer than any other editor. Her comments to the readers appeared in the column "Stepping Out": "Naturally we can't cover every topic of vital interest to you in one issue," she said, "especially while paper is as scarce as nylon stockings. But keep your eye peeled for a stream of new features with an accent on plenty of down-to-earth career material."[9] In December 1945 Bien reduced the price of *The American Girl* to 15¢ again. With the end of the war, fewer articles on scouting appeared. Fashion was becoming an increasingly important part of *The American Girl*. The last issue of the 1940s contained three stories, four articles, five fashion-and-good-looks features, and two scouting features. Prominent writers after the war included Julia M. Seton, Miriam E. Mason, Phyllis Whitney, Erick Berry, Loula Grace Erdman, Elizabeth Coatsworth, Nan Gilbert, Helen Diehl Olds, Betty Cavanna, Elizabeth Ryder Montgomery, Janet Lambert, Amelia Elizabeth Walden, and Florence Crannell Means. Such an array of talent brought widely diversified kinds of stories to the magazine—westerns, mysteries, gothic, family, adventure, and romance. American girls read all kinds of stories, and *The American Girl* brought them the very best of each kind.

The 1950s brought few drastic changes in *The American Girl*. Bien continued to attract high-quality stories from the most popular writers of teenage fiction. Anne Emery, Rosamund du Jardin, Robert Longstreet, D. S. Halacy, Jr., Beverly Cleary, and Lois Duncan were some of the authors. Nonfiction experts included Maureen Daly (writing), Dave Garroway (television), Chris Schenkel (sports), and Katherine G. Fennimore Cooper (pollution).

"By You" became a new column in 1951. It was similar to Helen Ferris's "Beholder" and consisted of poems, pictures, and drawings sent in by readers. Other features at this time included "Teen Shop Talk," "Recipe Exchange," and "Speaking of Movies." "The Music Stand" appeared to take the place of "Turntable Talk"—with broader coverage to include classical music. The current events column was dropped. The cost of *The American Girl* was now 25¢ a copy.

The 35th anniversary issue appeared in October 1952. Only one statement was made about the anniversary, and it said, in effect, that *The American Girl* of today with its stories and articles and circulation of more than half a million copies was a far cry from *The Rally* pamphlet that preceded it.

"Dear Good Grooming Editor" became a popular 1950s feature. The August back-to-school fashion issues were usually the largest—often eighty-two pages. Articles were about topics such as summer jobs, the Olympics, serving Uncle Sam, water ballet, and littering. "The Painting-of-the-Month Plan" began in 1954. It was similar to the previous series on American painters. The term *cover girl* was first used by the magazine in June 1950, as the covers began to feature models instead of just artwork. Cover girls included Carol Lynley, Sandra Dee (her first modeling job), and Tuesday Weld. Book columns reviewed geography and archeology books as well as teenage fiction. Andy Warhol was an illustrator and a cover artist. Movies reviewed included "My Man Godfrey," "Operation Madball," and "Light in the Forest." "Listening Corner" by Robert Sherman took the place of "The Music Stand."

The 1950s for *The American Girl* were relatively uneventful, but the 1960s brought a measure of confusion and turmoil to the magazine. Edward R. Murrow, Sargent Shriver, Ellen Peck, and Don Herbert (TV's Mr. Wizard), were some of the well-known nonfiction writers of the 1960s who appeared in *The American Girl*. Peter Spier, later a Caldecott Award winner, did several illustrations. Robert McKay, Zoa Sherborne, and Eloise Engel continued *The American Girl* tradition of excellence in fiction. Continuity was maintained in non-fiction as well. Articles were entitled "First Date" and "What Do Boys Look for in a Girl?" "The First Interview," and "Your Career as a Secretary." The traditional August fashion issue reached ninety pages—more than ever before. But there was more to *The American Girl* reader than just fashion in the 1960s. Young people were becoming more involved in politics and government—especially after the death of President Kennedy in 1963. Articles about the elections of 1964 and volunteer work of teens in Appalachia showed that teenagers around the country did care.

When Esther Bien retired in 1967, her place was taken by Pat di Sernia, who became editor and publisher. She requested visits and letters from her readers, made more personnel changes, and added new features such as "It's Happening," designed to tell of new records, movies, and books. A short-lived "Dear Reader" column by editor di Sernia began in April 1968. It was really just a hello from the editor—not a chat with the reader as Helen Ferris's columns were. In the fall of 1968 the price went from 35¢ to 40¢ a copy. A new column, "Buzz, Buzz," had a boy answering letters to girls on their problems. With the appointment of a new fiction editor, more stories began to appear in each issue. Another new feature, "It Really Happened," authored by readers, first appeared in December 1969.

The year 1971 was the 51st year of *The American Girl*. Pat di Sernia continued to serve as editor but had been replaced in 1970 as publisher by Warren W. Haight. The editorial in the January issue said: "Ever since 1920 we've been known as 'The Magazine for all girls published by the Girl Scouts of the U.S.A.' The Girl Scout purpose of helping girls to grow into happy, resourceful citizens is behind our planning of every page. But we have found that some. . .just don't recognize the material that their own magazine offers for troop activities."[10] Evidently, the scouts wanted articles related to their activities. The editors thought the material had been there all the time without specifically being called scout related, but they responded by saying that such articles would be identified in the future.

The November 1971 issue contained no fiction, but there was a new department, "Boythink," by Arthur Field. There were no questions as in the "Buzz" column, only helpful advice to girls about boys. During the next year attempts were made to make the nonfiction articles as relevant to the times as possible. The topics covered included things such as pantyhose, coed dorms, saving the baby seals, and women in sports. But the fiction was often that sent in by readers, and articles relating to scouting were few. Clearly, the features that had made *The American Girl* so praiseworthy were disappearing. So was the editor. In June 1972 there was no editor listed. In July Cleo Paturis was the new editor.

The last decade of *The American Girl* was difficult at best. The artwork was commendable, but the format was ever changing. The contents page was vague—giving no authors or department titles. Only article titles and page numbers were given. Two kinds of paper were used—newsprint green and glossy. There was little fiction.

However, many of the articles were very good. Topics included plagiarism, interior decorating, newsworthy teens, and pollution control. Special "All-By-You" and "Girl's Lib" issues were published. Still, the predominating articles in the early 1970s dealt with diet, beauty, records, and films.

In August 1974 there was another shakeup. Cleo Paturis was now the editor-in-chief, and John J. Frey was the new publisher. *The American Girl* seemed to be returning to a more balanced state. The contents page returned. Scouting received some attention—four pages in the October 1974 issue.

By December of that year regular features of the magazine included "In the News," "Special Girl Scouts in Action," "A Penny for Your Thoughts," and "By You." Although the author was not listed on the contents page, there was a story in the magazine.

But the future of *The American Girl* was not secure. By the late 1970s the cost of the magazine was 75¢. Circulation had declined from a million copies to a little more than 600,000. Production and postal costs, on the other hand, were increasing. Girls were watching television more and reading less. Without warning, *The American Girl* ceased publication with the July 1979 issue.

The American Girl was an exemplary periodical for girls. Although it began as a vehicle for the Girl Scouts, it grew quickly into a magazine that appealed to all girls. Of course, there were problems as the title grew—primarily identity problems. What kind of magazine did *The American Girl* want to become? What it became—at its finest—was one of the most popular youth periodicals of its day. It was known for its excellent articles—both fiction and nonfiction—which were idealistic, timely, and well written. The regular features—included to attract new readers—changed constantly with the times. But it is the stories for which the magazine will best be remembered—realistic stories by the finest writers.

Notes

1. Abby Leland Porter, "Policy and Plans," *The Rally* 1 (October 1917), 5.
2. Editorial, ibid., 1 (May 1918), 4.
3. Editorial, *The American Girl* 3 (June 1920), 4.
4. Ibid., 5 (January 1922), 4.
5. Ibid., 5 (May 1922), 4.
6. "New Year's Resolutions," ibid., 6 (January 1923), 4.
7. Editorial, ibid., 6 (March 1923), 4.
8. "Along the Editor's Trail," ibid., 6 (September 1923), 42.
9. "Stepping Out," ibid., 28 (September 1945), 19.
10. "1971," ibid., 54 (January 1971), 11.

Information Sources

BIBLIOGRAPHY
Gayle Ealy Cawood and M. Jean Greenlaw, "Juvenile Magazines of the U.S.A.: A Complete Overview with History and Trends," *Top of the News* 34 (Summer 1978), 365-74; Lavinia Dobler, comp. and ed., *Dobler World Directory of Youth Periodicals* 3d enlarged ed. (New York: Citation, 1970); Laura Katherine Martin, *Magazines for School Libraries* (New York: H. W. Wilson, 1950).
INDEX SOURCES
Access (Syracuse, New York: Gaylord), since 1975; The December issues of *The American Girl* for the years 1940-1944 contain subject indexes. Separate indexes for some years beginning in 1961 are available by request from Girl Scout Headquarters in New York.

LOCATION SOURCES
The complete run of *The American Girl* is available only at Girl Scout headquarters,
  New York, and the New York Public Library. The Library of Congress has vols.
  1-58 and parts of vols. 61 and 62.

Publication History

MAGAZINE TITLE AND TITLE CHANGES
The Rally (1917-1920); *The American Girl* (1920-1979).
VOLUME AND ISSUE DATA
The Rally (vol. 1, no. 1-vol. 3, no. 8); *The American Girl* (vol. 3, no. 9-vol. 62, no.
  7).
PUBLISHER AND PLACE OF PUBLICATION
The Girl Scouts of America, New York (1917-1979).
EDITOR
Gertrude Springer Hill (1917-1918); Elsie F. Williams (1918); Louise Paine Benjamin
  (1918-1920); Edith Curtiss Hixon (1920-1923); Louise M. Price (1923); Dorothy
  Culver Mills (1923); Helen Ferris (1923-1927); Camille Davied (1928-1929);
  Margaret Mochrie (1929-1933); Anne Stoddard (1933-1945); Esther R. Bien (1945-
  1967); Pat di Sernia (1967-1972); Cleo Paturis (1972-1979). Often, between ed-
  itors, an issue or two would appear without an editor's name.

Nancy Dahlstrom

B

BABYLAND

Babyland was one of the juvenile magazines published by D. Lothrop and Company of Boston. Other Lothrop publications included *The Pansy** (1874-1906); *Our Little Men and Women,** later *Little Men and Women* (1880-1894); and *Wide Awake** (1875-1893). As the title suggests, *Babyland* was designed for the youngest children. Eliza Anna "Ella" Farman and Charles S. Pratt, editors of *Wide Awake*, were also the editors of *Babyland* from its inception in 1877 until 1892, at which time E. Addie Heath, editor of *Our Little Men and Women*, became editor. When *Babyland* was purchased by Alpha Publishing Company in 1895, Mrs. Charles Pratt (the former Ella Farman) and her husband became the editors again.

The Lothrop juvenile periodicals were designed to cater to the needs of the Sunday schools and were closely associated with the nondenominational Chautauqua movement. Materials were chosen for interest as well as for their informative and edifying qualities. Although all of the material in *Babyland* would be considered very moralistic and didactic by today's standards, it was chosen to contain things that would appeal to children. An advertisement that appeared in the back of the first issue of volume 13 summarized the philosophy and purpose of *Babyland* by saying that "With *Babyland* in the home the little tots may look at pictures and hear mother read long before they have learned to read themselves. The poems and stories are short and have to do with dolls, toys, kittens, puppies, and babies. The bright cover [of the annual gift volume] is alone worth more than several bottles of soothing syrup. Baby's eyes will sparkle when he sees it."[1]

Early issues of *Babyland*, which appeared monthly, were syllabicated, but the practice was dropped in later volumes. The print was large and designed for a young audience. Some of the stories were written in a form of baby talk as were stories about Boofer Kitten and Toddlekins, which appeared in serialized form through several volumes.

Each issue had about eight pages and consisted of stories, poems, a cartoon, and a slate picture for baby to draw. The cover was always illustrated with a subject designed to capture the interest and attention of the child. Advertisements for wholesome products such as Cerealine Flakes and Ivory Soap and for other Lothrop publications were found at the back of each issue. The annual gift volumes, which were offered for sale separately, dropped the advertisements.

Fiction and poetry were short, simple, and didactic. Toys and animals were usually anthropomorphic. Fairies were a frequent subject of both fiction and poetry.

Fiction divides into two basic categories: realistic and fantasy. Realistic fiction featured white middle- to upper-class households with stereotyped characters. Good people and their actions were always rewarded, and bad ones were inevitably caught and punished for their misdeeds. The same traits were evident in the fantasy, although the characters were toys, fairies, or animals. Industriousness, devotion to duty, honesty, thrift, love, concern for others less fortunate than oneself, and other Christian virtues were stressed.

Poetry was selected for the dual purposes of appealing to the interests of children and teaching moral lessons. Margaret Sidney's poem "Our Baby" (March 1879) was typical of the poetry found in *Babyland* and other juvenile periodicals of the day. Although most of the poetry in *Babyland* would be considered excessively sentimental today, the poem "Little Boy's Lament" would be appealing. It also gives a good example of the syllabicated format of the early issues of *Babyland*.

LITTLE BOY'S LAMENT

When I be-gin to think some-times
Of all we have to do now,
In books and les-sons, prose and rhymes,
I get so mad! Don't you, now?
I wish I'd lived when things went slow;
Why, dear me! I would rath-er
Be born just seven-ty years a-go,
And be my own grand-fa-ther![2]

Fingerplays and shadow designs for the wall were also included in *Babyland*. Both provided wholesome activities and were educational. Counting and other skills could be taught through the fingerplays. "The Beehive," a fingerplay that is still used in kindergartens, taught the children to count from one to five.

Fingerplays and shadow designs included illustrations showing the children how to do each of the motions or steps in the activity.

Illustrations in *Babyland* ranged from full-page prints to small sketches to accompany the stories and poems to the diagrams for fingerplays and shadow designs. Most of the illustrations were in black and white, although some of the covers were in color.

As with the poems and stories, cartoons and slate pictures usually featured toys or animals. One cartoon that was reprinted "at the request of many children" showed a large foot with pigs for toes and was captioned "Little Pigs Went to Market."[3] Slate pictures were simple drawings for the children to draw on their own slates. They were white on black and designed to resemble the chalk-on-slate picture that the children would draw.

Authors of the works in *Babyland* were not always identified by name. Sometimes initials were used. Margaret Sidney, wife of the publisher and best known for her "Five Little Peppers" stories, which first appeared in *Wide Awake*, was a contributor to *Babyland*. Mary Lockwood, Mary Spring Walker, Charles Higgins, and Lou Burney were also contributors as were most of the regular writers for *Wide Awake* and other Lothrop publications.

In 1898 *Babyland* merged into *Little Men and Women* to become *Little Men and Women—Babyland*, which in turn became *Little Folks* in 1900.

D. Lothrop and Company also published several books by *Babyland* contributors. They include *Cradle Songs* (1882), *Babyland Classics* (1897), and *Babyland Stories for Our Household Pets* (1899).

Notes

1. *Babyland* 13 (January 1889), n.p.
2. "Little Boy's Lament," ibid., 3 (September 1879), 74.
3. *Babyland* 3 (March 1879), 49.

Information Sources

BIBLIOGRAPHY
Frank Luther Mott, *History of American Magazines*, 5 vols. (Cambridge: Harvard University Press, 1938-1968); *National Cyclopedia of American Biography* (New York: James T. White & Co., 1909).
INDEX SOURCES
None.
LOCATION SOURCES
The Library of Congress and the Milwaukee Public Library have the most complete collections.

Publication History

MAGAZINE TITLE AND TITLE CHANGES
Babyland (1877-1893); *Babyland: The Babies Own Magazine* (1894); *Babyland* (1895-1898).

VOLUME AND ISSUE DATA
Babyland (vol. 1, no. 1-vol. 17, no. 12); *Babyland: The Babies Own Magazine* (vol.
    18, no. 1-vol. 18, no. 12); *Babyland* (vol. 19, no. 1-vol. 22, no. 12).
PUBLISHER AND PLACE OF PUBLICATION
D. Lothrop and Company, Boston (1877-1895); Alpha Publishing Company, Boston
    (1895-1898).
EDITOR
Eliza Anna "Ella" Farman and Charles S. Pratt (1877-1892); E. Addie Heath (1892-
    1895); Eliza Anna "Ella" Farman Pratt and Charles S. Pratt (1895-1898).

Carol J. Veitch

THE BAPTIST UNION

From its establishment in 1890 throughout the fourteen years of its existence,
The Baptist Union was concerned with the education of young people. Ideas
about the nature of that education differed, though, depending on the editor.
The *Union* was initially established as *The Loyalist*, under which title it was
published for two months. Its proprietors and editors, J. M. Coon and O. W.
Vas Osdell, sought to encourage interest in young people's work in Baptist
churches and gave space in these early issues to letters of congratulations and
support, affirming the need for just such a paper especially devoted to this kind
of church work.

Control of the journal soon passed to the American Baptist Publication Society
in Philadelphia, which changed the periodical's name to *Young People at Work*.
The first issue was addressed to members of young people's societies in Baptist
churches and acknowledged that it was the era of the young people when their
horizon was broadening.

Although *The Loyalist* was short lived, its columns and features shaped the
form of *The Baptist Union* throughout its history. "Bible Study," "Topic for
Prayer Meeting," "Help's for Sunday School Teachers," "Missions," "News
from the Field," and "Temperance" reveal the editors' emphases. This relatively
narrow focus was expanded in *Young People at Work* with the addition of regular
columns such as "Recent Science," which presented examples of good scientific
work and helpful discoveries; "Spirit of the Press," which reprinted material
from other papers; and "Gleanings in Literature," consisting of excerpts from
the works of authors such as Nathaniel Hawthorne, Horace Mann, Charles Kings-
ley, and Frederick Farrar. Book reviews and letters from readers were also
added.

One of the subjects of current interest covered by *Young People at Work* was
the national convention of Young People's Societies held in Chicago in July
1891. At this meeting the Baptist Young People's Union of America was established, with headquarters in Chicago, and by November the new organization
had taken over the publication of *Young People at Work*.

The first issue under the editorial direction of Frank L. Wilkins expressed the
journal's goal: "The young people's paper, in voicing this young life and sen-

timent in the churches, will talk the vernacular of the young people, hope with them, plan with them (joke with them)."[1]

Although the new paper retained most of the established columns, Wilkins introduced changes in the content and format. He printed stories about current events and initiated a feature section, "Young People's World," that contained biographical, geographical, historical, and scientific articles such as the five-part travelog "Cycling Through the Dales of Yorkshire" (April 1, 1893, and following issues) and a biography of Joseph Islands, missionary to the Creek Indians (April 21, 1894). "Our Juniors," aimed at a younger audience than the periodical as a whole, included puzzles, jokes, and stories.

The work of the parent organization was highlighted in the pages of the journal. For weeks before the annual summer convention, there were features on the host city and the conference agenda. Afterward, the proceedings were reported in detail. During some years the issues about the conference were offered as a special series with a separate subscription rate for those who wanted only the thirteen weeks of coverage devoted to the convention.

In the fall of 1893 Wilkins introduced an important innovation with the establishment of the Christian Culture Courses. Readers were invited to enroll in the following studies: Bible Readers' Course, Conquest Missionary Course, Sacred Literature Course, and Junior Bible Course. Each week from October through April, a lesson in each course appeared. Readers were assured that only 20 minutes a day would be adequate for the course study. At the end of April examination blanks were printed, and those who had completed the course could fill out the exam, send it in, and receive a certificate if the work had been done satisfactorily. Each fall a new series of lessons under the same general headings was begun, and the Christian Culture Courses continued throughout the journal's existence. Numerous editorials promoting them stressed the necessity of continuing education for readers.

Under Wilkins's editorship, the appearance of the journal changed as the scope of coverage expanded. Sketches and photographs were included to illustrate articles. More white space was used, which resulted in a more readable layout. In 1895 the first full-page pictures appeared, and some color was used, especially in the "special numbers" of the paper, another Wilkins innovation. These special editions, such as the "Woman's Number," "Educational Number," "Seed Number," and "Bicycle Number," were made up largely of topical feature articles, stories, and columns. For example, the "Seed Number" (February 22, 1896) contained informative articles such as "Easily Grown House Plants" as well as poems such as "Daffodils" by William Wordsworth and "Old Fashioned Roses" by John Whitcomb Riley.

The title *The Baptist Union* was adopted in 1894, in an effort to honor the denomination to which it was related and distinguish the paper from the local young people's society as well as from "every other order of young people's effort, denominational or interdenominational."[2]

After Wilkins resigned in 1896 to return to pastoral work, the editorship fell
to Hazlitt Alva Cuppy, director of the University of Chicago Press. When Rev.
E. E. Chivers was appointed to succeed Cuppy a few months later, an editorial
of thanks revealed that it had, in fact, been Mrs. Cuppy, not her husband,
"whose facile pen has enriched the columns of our paper, and whose careful
supervision has maintained its standard" in the interim.[3]

During Chivers's tenure, the established columns, Christian Culture Courses,
and thorough convention coverage remained important parts of the journal. Chivers also continued to print travelogs, biographies, and historical features, but he
also began to include more consideration of current events and politics. Articles
were devoted to topics such as Admiral Dewey's exploits (October 7, 1899) and
"The South African Crisis" (October 28, 1899). A nineteen-part series, "The
Christian and His Citizenship," was prepared by Rev. Samuel Zane Batten
(October 30, 1897, and following issues). A "World at Large" column of short
news stories was introduced. Biographies of political figures such as Napoleon,
"whose despotic measures must be viewed with repugnance" (June 2, 1900),
and Charlotte Corday (March 31, 1900) were included. Author W. E. Glanville
praised Corday, noting "Her method aside...it may be said that her noble-
minded patriotism, her unsullied self-sacrifice and her unflinching courage, entitled her to the honors which we involuntarily pay to those elect ones who give
themselves without stint for the overthrowing of oppression and the welfare of
our common humanity."[4] A feature, "The Presidential Contest of 1900" described the candidates and platforms but did not endorse anyone (August 25,
1900).

Biographies of artists like Jean Baptist Camille Corot (August 18, 1900) and
authors like Robert Burns (April 7, 1900) also indicate a more "secular" emphasis for the journal. Illustrated visits to various places, including the Baptist
Young People's Union of America headquarters (April 15, 1899) and a factory
"The Making of a File," (March 13, 1900), were also included for the readers'
general education.

In July 1898 the paper went to a smaller format to give it a more "up-to-
date" look. Editorials were moved to the front page, and a new question-and-
answer column provided information ranging from a description of the type of
government in the New Hebrides Islands to the names of several recommended
papers for boys: *The Youth's Companion*,* *St. Nicholas*,* and *American Boy—
Open Road*.* That same year a companion periodical, *Junior Baptist Union*,
was begun, and the "Junior Union" section was replaced by "Junior Work and
Workers," a column designed to provide practical advice for church members
engaged in work with that age group.

Citing the need for more time for study, mental development, and family life
and noting that strain was undermining his physical health, Chivers returned to
a pastorate in 1901. His successor, W. H. Geistweit, was quick to introduce
changes in the journal's emphasis. He enlarged the editorial department and
returned its emphasis to religious issues, reducing the attention to current events.

A new column, "Monday Evening Conference," dealt with questions concerning daily life and Christian service. The "Prayer Meeting" section was given more prominence.

However, Geistweit retained staples such as Christian Culture Courses, special numbers, and complete convention coverage, and he was not able to ignore current affairs entirely. He justified an editorial about the attack on President McKinley by saying that "We have nothing to do with politics, nor the discussion of state questions in this paper; but we have everything to do with that which makes character, and with the forces that make the society in which we live."[5]A column listing brief news items, "Pen Points of Men and Things," was added in 1902.

Although general features continued, stress was placed on Christian Culture Courses, columns, and the work of the Baptist Young People's Union of America. The use of color declined, as did the number of illustrations, and by 1903 some issues included none at all. Perhaps some of these changes were prompted by financial considerations. The 1904 decision to cease publication of a weekly journal in favor of a monthly magazine, to be called *Service* was based in part on the belief that the monthly version would be better from a business point of view.

The announcement of the pending change promised that the new magazine would have fine illustrations, enlarged space, new departments, and a month's Christian Culture Course lessons collected in a compact "book" size. The final issue of *The Baptist Union* pledged that its successor would keep its spiritual tone, since there were already "secular magazines a-plenty."[6]

Throughout its history, *The Baptist Union* was clearly aimed at a specific audience: Baptist young people. The regular columns and lessons related to ongoing activities of the youth groups in prayer meetings, Sunday school, and Bible study. Feature articles were usually nonfiction and informative. Topics ranging from biography, geography, and history to current events predominated, although the emphasis on such features varied with the several editors. In addition to those articles of information about secular matters, numerous articles were printed dealing with moral questions and advising young people how to handle various problems. "Purity is Power" (April 26, 1891), "How to Cure Gossip" (October 23, 1980), "The Match That Is Made in Heaven" (October 24, 1896), and "Be True to Yourself" (August 31, 1901) are representative of articles that remained a staple throughout *The Baptist Union's* history.

One of the most pressing moral issues that concerned its editors was temperance. At the outset, a special issue, "The Curse of Intemperance" (November 6, 1890), focused on the subject, and although the space devoted to the topic decreased as time went on, concern never disappeared entirely. In 1897 a full-page ad by the Charles E. Hires Co. put forth evidence to prove that Hires Root Beer was no more intoxicating than soda water despite some claims to the contrary. A 1901 editorial, "Mrs. Nation and the Lawless Liquor Traffic," deplored her methods but insisted that saloon keepers must be stopped somehow (September 23, 1901).

Although most of each issue was nonfiction, some space was reserved for fiction. Most of the time one installment of a serial appeared in an issue although the pages for the juniors often contained short works. The fiction was uniformly didactic, trying to educate the reader in the proper Christian life. "Won but not One" by Mrs. Emily L. Blockall (October 3, 1891, and following issues) portrayed the disastrous consequences of marriage between people of different denominations. "Donald McDonald" by Sophie Bronson Titterington (January 24, 1903, and following issues) showed how its hero overcame various obstacles toward leading a productive life after an accident had seemingly destroyed all hope for the future. Poetry rarely appeared except in special numbers, usually at Christmas and Easter. Education, not entertainment, was the chief aim.

Notes

1. *Young People at Work*, 1:1 November 1891.
2. *The Baptist Union*, January 6, 1894, p. 8.
3. Ibid., March 3, 1897, p. 174.
4. Ibid., August 25, 1900, p. 280.
5. Ibid., September 14, 1901, p. 827.
6. Ibid., September 10, 1904, p. 819.

Information Sources

BIBLIOGRAPHY
None.
INDEX SOURCES
None.
LOCATION SOURCES
The most complete sets of bound volumes are at the University of Chicago and at the American Baptist Historical Society, Rochester, N.Y. Partial sets are in the Library of Congress and New York Public Library and at the Historical Commission of the Southern Baptist Convention, Nashville, Tenn.

Publication History

MAGAZINE TITLE AND TITLE CHANGES
The Loyalist (1890); *Young People at Work* (1890-1891); *Young People's Union* (1891-1894); *The Baptist Union* (1894-1904).
VOLUME AND ISSUE DATA
The Loyalist (vol. 1, no. 1-vol. 1, no. 8); *Young People at Work* (vol. 1, no. 9-vol. 1, no. 47); *Young People's Union* (vol. 1, no. 48-vol. 3, no. 52); *The Baptist Union* (vol. 4, no. 1-vol. 14, no. 37).
PUBLISHER AND PLACE OF PUBLICATION
J. M. Coon & O. W. Vas Osdell, Chicago (1890); American Baptist Publication Society, Philadelphia (1890-1891); Baptist Young People's Union of America, Chicago (1891-1904).

EDITOR
J. M. Coon and O. W. Vas Osdell (1890); Philip L. Jones (1890-1891); Frank L. Wilkins (1891-1896); Hazlitt Alva Cuppy (1896-1897); E. E. Chivers (1897-1901); W. H. Geistweit (1901-1904).

Kathy Piehl

THE BOYS' AND GIRLS' MAGAZINE, AND FIRESIDE COMPANION

The children who opened the first issue of *The Boys' and Girls' Magazine, and Fireside Companion* (later *Forrester's Boys' and Girls' Magazine, and Fireside Companion*) found on the left a full-page illustration of an eagle, looking imperiously over snow-covered crags, and on the right a smaller woodcut of an old man, seated under a tree and surrounded by four children who appear to be listening attentively. In addressing himself to "My Young Friends," Mark Forrester admitted that others might write more interesting stories "than I can, with my plain ways and trembling hands." But he confidently asserted, "Your magazine will delight you with the stories it tells, and profit you by its instructions." In it there will be:

> stories of peril and adventure; of travel in strange lands, and voyages over far distant seas; of dangers braved by courage, and difficulties overcome by perseverance; with lives of men whose names live after them;—pleasing descriptions of rural scenes, and the various incidents of country life; of the curious history and habits of beasts, birds, fishes, and insects with some particulars respecting shells and fossils, suggested by a ramble along the seashore;—histories of wonderful inventions, which, in their progress to perfection, are producing silent revolutions throughout all parts of the habitable globe, and are intimately connected with the common matters of life;—descriptions of the marvelous works of nature and of the curious productions of art, on which the ingenuity of man has been exercised with success;—memorials of imprisonment, and of the perils encountered and the sufferings undergone in the prosecution of escapes from captivity;— narratives of strange and terrible convulsions, of cities buried by volcanoes, or swallowed up by earth quakes:—these, and many other narratives, to amuse you and teach you what strange things have happened, and do happen in the world, will find a place in your Magazine.[1]

For ten years Mark Forrester, and later Francis Forrester, together with Uncle [Miles] Hawthorne, cousin Mary Forrester, and other Forresters, kept the thirty-two-page monthly afloat with stories, tales of exotic places, nature lore, and articles on science and technology, mostly of their own writing. In the initial number, Forrester made no mention of his reasons for undertaking a children's magazine at the advanced age of seventy-two, but in a later issue, in his column "Chats with Readers," he described the situation that prompted him: "A long time ago I used to think that old men were of very little use in the world." They tended to be sour and crusty and a trial for those around them. Having become elderly himself, he confessed that he "used to be considerably troubled with *the blues*." Concluding that idleness, if not the cause of, certainly exaggerated "the blues," he "set about doing something to make other people happy, during all my leisure moments." A busy usefulness proved the salvation of this New Englander, as it had been for the sons and daughters of Puritanism generally. "Acting on this plan, I commenced the 'Boys' and Girls' Magazine.'"[2]

The first issue set the form for the magazine; and for its ten-year history, it ran in well-worn grooves, in part because it had the editorial continuity of a family undertaking and in part, too, because it exemplified the type of children's miscellany that was well-established by 1848 when the magazine was begun. Editor Forrester followed his address to his readers with a story that in title and substance was utterly conventional: "Honesty Is the Best Policy: A True Story." This was followed by a brief article on the royal eagle depicted on the frontispiece, the first of a long succession of such natural history pieces, and by a dialog between an old man selling a monthly children's magazine, several children eager to buy, and a skeptical parent who is finally won over.

A longer article on magnetism—its properties and uses—heralded a series of essays on natural science topics and bespoke the editor's intense interest in the ways and wonders of nature, his devotion to rational inquiry, and his enthusiasm for the practical application of scientific principles. Over and over, in various ways, he admonished his readers to be attentive to the world around them. He concluded his survey of magnetism by saying, "I have told you but little about magnetism. Perhaps enough to waken your attention. Live to grow wiser."[3] "Wisdom" has a moral as well as an intellectual dimension, and Forrester was equally concerned that knowledge of the world be turned to useful purposes and that attentiveness be not simply pleasurable contemplation but the basis for an active attention to detail, an important aspect of the work ethic.

"The First Snow-Storm" urged readers to appreciate the snow-altered landscape and described with evident relish—and some nostalgia—the elaborate snowmen and fortifications made possible by the first snowfall. This was followed by "A Residence Among the Indians," the first of a series of articles by [Uncle] Miles Hawthorne of his personal experiences as well as the first in a far greater series of articles on foreign ways of life. The attitude that informed Miles Hawthorne's accounts is worth noting. Confessing childhood fears of Indians, fears based on stories still circulating in New England about Indian atrocities, he admitted that age and experience reshaped his views. "As I grew in years, and in knowledge, and, with the excellent opportunities I have had, examined their true characters and dispositions, my foolish youthful fears vanished, and I was led to look upon the poor Indian as a human being like myself, gifted with reason, though ignorant; the nobleness of whose nature would compare favorably with many other wiser nations."[4] This view, he added, was based on having spent a "considerable portion" of his life among them.

Uncle Miles's tantalizing account of the first steamboat passage up the Missouri River to the mouth of the Yellowstone must have been the high point of the issue for many a boy reader, who may well have skipped hastily and easily over succeeding selections: a gentle poetic tribute, "The School Mistress"; a didactic tale about "wishes"; a page-long piece, "The Little Girl and the Shell"; Robert Herrick's "To Daffodils"; and "The Story of a Little Lamb." "Napoleon Bonaparte," the first of a succession of biographical articles, dealt not with the great man's military exploits but with some childhood anecdotes. "Catching Wild Ducks" served as a pretext for a warning about those ("decoy ducks") who wittingly or not lead others into situations of danger or disrepute. Finally, in "A Chat with Readers and Correspondents," Forrester promised "to devote one or two pages of each number to my correspondents, and in proposing questions and riddles to learn you to think." The importance of this exercise was clear: "You should never make up your mind to anything, or conclude that you are right, until you have carefully examined the subject on all sides."[5] Conundrums, anagrams, rebuses, and puzzles became the staple items of Forrester's "chat," a feature maintained throughout the life of *The Boys' and Girls' Magazine*. There the editor acknowledged correspondence, announced those who had submitted successful answers, and encouraged those whose answers were incorrect to try again. A judicious selection of letters praising the magazine and its grandfatherly editor duly appeared from time to time. The tone of the magazine was generally personal—with letters from "Elizabeth," moral tales from "Cousin Mary," and the adventures of Uncle Miles all rendered in the first person; but nowhere was the reader taken aside and addressed so directly and engagingly as in these monthly chats with the editor.

In the second issue Mark Forrester began a series of autobiographical articles, "Life of the Editor"; provided an article about the magnetic telegraph promised in the inaugural issue; continued Uncle Miles's account of his experiences among the western Indians; and with "Elizabeth's" letter from the Azores, offered the first of numerous travel accounts that became a staple of the magazine and doubtless catered for seafaring New England's, and especially Boston's, sense of being in touch with the four corners of the world. Elizabeth's letters were followed by Nephew John's from China (May 1848) and by a host of articles, stories, and vignettes of exotic places: Algiers (July 1848), "Tahita" (January 1849), and so on; and exotic peoples, for example, "Customs of the Kirgis," a wild nomadic Siberian tribe (April 1851), and "The Malays," dreaded pirates of Asia (April 1848).

Natural history remained an important part of the magazine. For several years, the frontispiece remained a full-page picture of the subject of the month's natural history sketch. The eagle of the first issue was replaced by the deer, which was followed by, among others, the seal, harvest mouse, walrus, whale, shoveller, camel, northern hummingbird, tiger, and dozens of others. The illustrations accompanying the natural history essays were the principal illustrations in the early years of *The Boys' and Girls' Magazine*. A representative issue (volume 1, number 4), contained, in addition to a handsome depiction of the harvest mouse, the following woodcut illustrations: a half-page cut of a Malay village and a subsequent vignette of three children at play, a picture of Indians hunting buffalo (for Uncle Miles's series), and three cuts illustrating an article, "The City of Cairo and the Sphinx." The number and relative quality of illustration improved in the magazine's final years, but it was not as heavily illustrated as the post-Civil War magazines tended to be.

In addition to emphasizing travel, natural history, science and invention, and biography (Napoleon, as mentioned earlier; Lord Nelson; and many others), *The Boys' and Girls' Magazine* offered stories, narrative sketches, and anecdotes intended primarily to instruct. In his initial address to his readers, Forrester rang the familiar changes on amusement and instruction, but the emphasis given the latter can be judged from the titles of representative stories—"Can't and Try," "The Spirit of Obedience," "Strive and Thrive"—as well as from the opening sentence of "The Spirit of Obedience": "Now, my dear children, I am going to tell you a story about some children, to illustrate what this means."[6] The content of the magazine's moral instruction can be gleaned quickly from a selection of representative titles: "Filial Piety" (July 1848), "Neatness and Order" (July 1849), "Hear Both Sides" (July 1849), "Do Not Despise Small Things" (September 1849), "Patience" (March 1850), "The Idle Are Always Unhappy" (February 1851), "Thou Shalt Not Steal" (April 1851), "Alexander and Frank; or True and False Courage" (July 1856).

The values that inform these stories and homilies are the traditional work-related virtues of New England—diligence, thrift, prudence, neatness, conscientiousness, honesty—as well as more general, time-honored qualities of character such as courage. "Wishy and Worky—A Good Story," a serial begun in March 1849, can stand for the earnest moralizing in fiction and anecdote found throughout the magazine's ten years. In the well-established formula of the contrast between an exemplary character and a deficient character, "Wishy and Worky" describes two apprentices, the former a lackadaisical, easily distracted lad and the latter a model of energetic purposefulness, who diligently seeks to improve each moment of the workday. The serialized story is a sermon in narrative and a hymn to the work ethic. An anecdote in the editor's "chat" following the first installment of "Wishy and Worky" neatly illustrates one work-related value repeatedly emphasized in the magazine. As Forrester told it, a penniless boy comes to Paris to seek work. He is repeatedly rebuffed in his efforts. As he leaves, discouraged from another fruitless interview, he notices a pin on the pavement, picks it up, and saves it. "This little act of prudence was observed by the person who had just turned him away, and it occurred to him that a boy, while under the anxiety of mind naturally attending disappointment like this, who could notice so small a thing as a pin possessed admirable traits of character for a person of responsibility and trust." The boy is hired on the spot and eventually becomes a partner. "Never neglect small things. Fix on your mind this old but sterling proverb, 'Little things are little things, but to be faithful in little things is something great.' "[7]

At the end of 1852 Mark Forrester left the editor's chair, to be replaced by Francis Forrester, who, in his greetings to his readers, offered no explanation for the older Forrester's resignation but promised to provide the same mix of articles and essays. Aside from some minor changes in typography—more variety and a lighter face—the magazine remained essentially unchanged. Francis appears to have included more fiction, and his "Francis Forrester's Curious Sayings" was an innovation, although an obtrusively moralistic one. With the December 1857 issue, the magazine ceased publication. Money, as usual, may have been part of the problem. In his final "Chit-chat with Readers and Correspondents," Francis Forrester urged his readers to renew their own subscriptions and to solicit at least one new subscription in order to double the rolls. If a doubling of subscribers was, in fact, necessary to meet the magazine's expenses, the effort was doomed to failure. *Forrester's* merged with *The Student and Schoolmate** in January 1858.

Notes

1. *The Boys' and Girls' Magazine, and Fireside Companion* 1 (January 1848), 3.
2. Ibid., 5 (February 1850), 92.
3. Ibid., 1 (January 1848), 10.
4. Ibid., p. 13.
5. Ibid., p. 32.
6. Ibid., 5 (May 1850), 154.
7. Ibid., 3 (June 1849), 190.

Information Sources

BIBLIOGRAPHY
None.
INDEX SOURCES
None.
LOCATION SOURCES
Library of Congress; American Antiquarian Society, Worcester, Mass. Available on
    microfilm in the American Periodical Series, University Microfilms International,
    Ann Arbor, Mich.

Publication History

MAGAZINE TITLE AND TITLE CHANGES
The Boys' and Girls' Magazine, and Fireside Companion (January 1848-December 1850);
    Forrester's Boys' and Girls' Magazine, and Fireside Companion (January 1851-
    December 1957).
VOLUME AND ISSUE DATA
The Boys' and Girls' Magazine, and Fireside Companion (vol. 1, no. 1-vol. 6, no. 6); *Boys' and Girls' Magazine, and Fireside Companion* (vol. 7, no. 1-vol. 20, no. 6).

PUBLISHER AND PLACE OF PUBLICATION
Bradbury and Guild, Boston (January 1848-December 1849); William Guild, Boston
    (January 1850-December 1850); William Guild, Boston, and W. C. Locke & Co.,
    New York (January 1851-December 1851); William Guild & Co., Boston (January
    1852-December 1852); F. and G. C. Rand, Boston (January 1853-December
    1856); Binney and Allen, Boston (January 1857-December 1857).
EDITOR
Mark Forrester (January 1848-December 1852); Francis Forrester (January 1853-Decem-
    ber 1856); "Father" Forrester (January 1857-December 1857).

R. Gordon Kelly

THE BOYS' CHAMPION

The Boys' Champion, a weekly newspaper-magazine for boys aged twelve to
fifteen, survived from October 1, 1881, until February 17, 1883, absorbing Leon
Leroy's *New York Boys* in 1882 (volume 1, number 34, May 20, 1882). Published
by the Champion Publishing Company in New York, *The Boys' Champion* was
edited by staff members, and like so many other publications of this kind, it
appeared in tandem with a dime novel series, the Champion Library. Contributors
to the weekly also wrote novels for the same company. Relying on its fiction,
both the serial and the single-issue short story, *The Boys' Champion* is an example
of what Frank Luther Mott called "the blood and thunder, bang-bang-bang type
of cheap weekly for boys."[1] There is little difference between *The Boys' Champion* and Frank Tousey's *Boys of New York*,* many of the same authors appearing
in each: Paul Braddon, Howard De Vere, Lieut. E. H. Kellogg, Police Captain
Howard, and Orrin Goble.
    Each issue of these papers consists of eight pages of five-column print with
three or four crude, but dramatic, illustrations.[2] The paper sold for 8¢ an issue;
the subscription price was $2.50 a year or $1.50 for six months. Besides the
five or six serials running concurrently, regular short fiction appeared by "Harry,"
"Pickle," and later Frederick Lee. Lee began to appear in number 37 (June 10,
1882) at a time when several shorter features crowded the pages, for example:
"Our Critic's Corner" (a review of Amateur publications replacing "Amateur
Theatricals," one-act plays generally sporting with blacks), "Punishments for
Crimes, in Various Countries," and columns of various sorts from the syndicated
press. Other regular features included "Funny Things," a column of tepid jokes
and anecdotes; "Things to Remember," information about how to mix powder
for stuffing birds, measure the height of trees (the Canadian way), preserve belts,
and detect copper in pickles and green tea; "The Puzzle Department" ("The-
dom"), a collection of charades, acrostics, and other word games; "Reciter's
Corner," a poetry column containing "one or more excellent pieces of poetry
or prose for the study and use of those who like declamation" (examples include
Hamlet's "To be or not to be" soliloquy; poems by Burns, Scott, Southey, and

Mrs. Hemans; parodies of Shakespeare; and a host of verse by forgotten de-
claimers); and "Our Mail Box," short answers to readers' questions in which
editors tell readers the best remedy for pimples or freckles, inform a seventeen-
year-old boy that he should be "5 feet 4 inches high, and weigh 111 pounds,"[3]
and encourage others with their writing (one reader—S.R.M.—received the
advice: "Try to get the same number of syllables in each line, and your poems
may find a place").[4] Then there are the advertisements for the Champion Library;
a Three-Mile Whistle; a Cinderella Slipper with a Silver-Plated Thimble; and
books such as *The Way to Skate, The Way to Dance, The Way to Make Love*,
and other pastimes.

Several gimmicks are designed to boost sales. As early as the fifth number
(October 29, 1881) the editors offered $5 in gold for the best amateur production
for "Reciter's Corner." A more forthright appeal to readers began in number
11 (December 10, 1881) with the offer of five "Solid Silver Hunting-Case
Watches" to be given away with each issue. From number 11 to number 36
(June 3, 1882) each issue contained a coupon on its first page; five coupons
contained a secret sign known only to the editors, and those five would gain the
purchasers of *The Boys' Champion* a solid silver watch. When this offer expired,
the editors announced that "we have kept our word and given away the watches
as we said we would," and soon they intended to make a present to every
reader.[5] This promise dangled before readers for several weeks without anything
more concrete appearing. Finally, like *The Boys' Champion* itself, it disappeared
without warning.

Despite such appeals, the real selling point of *The Boys' Champion* was its
fiction. The editors, in describing their paper as "an instructive and entertaining
journal for young America," attempted to point out the "improving" nature of
their publication, but a note in the fifth number (October 29, 1881) is somewhat
more candid: the editors assured their readers that this paper "will be kept
absolutely pure in tone." Furthermore, the aim of the paper "is to furnish boys
with a class of entertaining stories, containing enough excitement to make them
interesting, but free from anything that could be taken exception to save by a
carping critic."[6] Some months later they assured one reader, M. Wendelsohn,
that "All the stories published in this paper have a basis in fact."[7] After reading
these stories, no one could believe this last statement, but a recent reader of *The
Boys' Champion* suggested that they were harmless: "Although these stories
were mildly sensational, they were not vicious."[8]

Certainly, the emphasis was more on entertaining than instructing, as a brief
summary of a typical *Boys' Champion* serial indicates. "The Life and Adventures
of Old Sagacity" by Police Captain Howard ran in the first eight numbers of
the paper (October 1, 1881–November 19, 1881). The story begins with three
exclamatory "Spats!" The scene is a dark room with a man sleeping at a desk.
The spats prove to be blood dripping from the ceiling, and as the man comes
to consciousness he realizes with horror that his wife is upstairs. Racing to her
room, he finds her "stretched on the floor, clad in her night clothes only" and

a pool of blood "a couple of feet" each side of her lifeless body. "He saw the ghastly, red-lipped knife wound whence a stream of blood was still flowing."[9] The man goes out of his mind and the first chapter ends. Why his wife was murdered we never do learn. It is enough that in chapter 2 this same fellow emerges from a mental hospital as Old Sagacity, detective *extraordinaire*. He spends his time (how he makes a living is anyone's guess) tracking criminals to large houses, finding secret entrances, chloroforming the villains, and removing their shoes and socks. While Old Sagacity engages in chiropody, a Mr. Asa Ellwood finds himself blackmailed by Lionel Moore. The nefarious Moore asks not for money but for the hand of Ella Ellwood, daughter of Asa. Ella, of course, has a young man she would prefer to marry, but what is a young girl to do when her father's response to her refusal to marry Moore is: " 'Then farewell forever!' ...Ella saw him hastily place to his lips and swallow the contents of a bottle labelled: Poison!'"[10] After much convoluted goings-on with counterfeiters and blackmailers and illegal whisky producers, Old Sagacity corners Moore in an apartment. The chloroform comes next. Off come Moore's shoes and socks, and now we learn why Old Sagacity has this obsession with feet: the murderer of his wife, it turns out, was barefoot and left footprints in the blood, footprints revealing a missing big toe on his right foot and two webbed toes on his left. Lionel Moore proves to have these unique feet and Old Sagacity allows him to regain consciousness before stabbing him to death: "with the fury of a madman" Old Sagacity "plunged the glittering blade again and again into the body, reserving a fatal thrust for the last."[11]

This is sensational, but is it not also vicious? The brutality in *Old Sagacity* is a feature of virtually every story in the paper. Most evident is the blood. In "The Demon Rider" by "Texas Joe," Comanches raid a farmhouse and kill the farmer's wife (mind you, she is the wife of the villain!): "It was Red Horse himself who seized her before she had got more than a dozen steps from the door. The next moment his knife had drank her blood; then her scalp was torn from her head, and her lifeless and mutilated body was thrown back into the burning building."[12] Perhaps more execrable, however, are the stories by Nicodemus Dodge and Phineas Budge that appear as regular "comic" serials in *The Boys' Champion*. For example, "Montague Mumps," which ran from June 10, 1882, to August 5, 1882, concerns the humiliation and brutal treatment of an ugly but vain person. Mumps is hideously ugly, but he fancies himself a lady killer, a masher. He thinks he has "mashed all the girls in New York" and that a trip to the country might offer him new conquests. Arriving at a country station, Mumps accepts the invitation of the stationkeeper to stay in his house for $20 a week. The stationkeeper has five daughters and three sons. This crew spends the next nine issues baiting Mumps: his face is lacerated by bees and sharp hay, his body is "plastered...from head to foot" in mud, he is tricked into riding the horse reputed to be "the most vicious brute in that part of New Jersey,"[13] he must wear girl's clothes when his are stolen, he is the butt of endless jokes, and he is placed in a smokehouse where he is smoked "like a ham, until he was black as a nigger.''[14] There is much more, and through it all Mumps continues to believe, encouraged by the girls, that he is succeeding in his manly pursuits.

In another story, "Bob Bliffers; or One of the 'Bhoys' " by Phineas Budge (September 30, 1882-December 16, 1882), a rheumatic old sea captain with a wooden leg receives a treatment of bees from the hero, Bob. Dressed in "an airy, fairy costume of night-shirt and wooden leg," the captain howls in pain while the bees "kissed him on the ear, and caressed him between the eyes; they made love to all of his anatomy that was visible. . . . Wasn't it fun, though? Oh, you bet it was! Fun for the bees, and a regular orgy for our hero." (Sex in *The Boys' Champion* is another subject.)[15] The insensitivity evident here also features in the weekly column "Funny Things." The most egregious example is an item in the fifth number: "If you want to study the immense variety of the human face in expression, you should bend your gaze upon the mobile countenance of a deaf and dumb man when he reaches under the plank walk for a lost nickel and picks up a raw bumble-bee by the stem.''[16]

This reflects the entertainment in *The Boys' Champion*. Any instruction in the paper has little to do with values; boys learn the virtue of vengeance, bravery, and swift and violent justice. The introduction to Leon Lenoir's "Ninety-Six; or The Boy Partisan" (November 5, 1881) states that the story concerns "deadly wrong, unflinching courage and revenge," and this sums up nearly every plot, whether the story is a western, detective story, African adventure, historical romance, or wonderful invention tale. A boy would also learn that Indians are fiendish savages and that blacks are dimwitted (one exception to this is "Black Bob; or The Negro Boy Detective" by Police Captain Howard, which ran from February 11, 1882, to April 8, 1882). As for prose style, the writers are masters of the dime novel cliché: "Eight rifles vomited forth their sheets of flame, and eight leaden messengers of death were sent into the solid mass of advancing fiends" ("Nemo; or The Mysterious Unknown" by Paul Braddon).[17] True, boys did learn to "avoid the contraction of the habit of irresolution,''[18] they did learn facts about the manufacture of paper and the amount of salt in the sea, and they did learn the fastest time in which the hundred-yard dash had been run. Despite all of this, *The Boys' Champion* did not last. The competition in the sensational and overwritten was too great.

Notes

1. Frank Luther Mott, *A History of American Magazines* (Cambridge: Harvard University Press, 1938), 3:111, 178.

2. R. Gordon Kelly's assessment of the illustrations (and the stories too) in *Frank Leslie's Boys' and Girls' Weekly* applies equally well to those in *The Boys' Champion*: in the *Champion* "the careless rendering of figures, the stark tonal contrasts, and a visual preoccupation with physical injury provide the pictorial counterparts of a literary style that is frequently dominated by restless action, unconvincing motivation, meretricious diction." R. Gordon Kelly, *Mother Was a Lady* (Westport, Conn.: Greenwood Press, 1974), 29-30.

3. *The Boys' Champion*, January 21, 1882, p. 8.

4. Ibid., June 3, 1882, p. 8.

5. Ibid., June 3, 1881, p. 4.

6. Ibid., October 29, 1881, p. 8.

7. Ibid., March 4, 1882, p. 8.

8. Yolanda D. Federici, "American Historical Children's Magazine of the Nineteenth and Early Twentieth Centuries," *The Boys' Champion* (Westport, Conn.: Greenwood Press Microform Department, n.d.).

9. *The Boys' Champion*, October 1, 1881, p. 3.

10. Ibid., p. 8.

11. Ibid., November 19, 1881, p. 3.

12. Ibid., November 26, 1881, p. 3.

13. Ibid., June 17, 1882, p. 1.

14. Ibid., June 24, 1882, p. 5.

15. Ibid., September 30, 1882, p. 5.

16. Ibid., October 29, 1881, p. 3.

17. Ibid., October 22, 1881, p. 2. Compare this with a passage from one of the Buffalo Bill dime novels quoted by Russel Nye in *The Unembarrassed Muse* (New York: The Dial Press, 1971), 207: "There was no time to use his Winchester, but the two six-shooters leaped from his belt, and the scout was soon surrounded by a sheet of flame as his deadly revolvers vomited leaden hail into the scarlet foe. The fight was short, sharp, and decisive, and was soon at an end, with seven scarlet bodies weltering in their blood under the midnight sky."

18. *The Boys' Champion*, February 4, 1882, p. 4.

Information Sources

BIBLIOGRAPHY
Yolanda D. Federici, "American Historical Children's Magazines of the Nineteenth and Early Twentieth Centuries" (Westport, Conn.: Greenwood Press Microform Department, n.d.); R. Gordon Kelly, *Mother Was a Lady* (Westport, Conn.: Greenwood Press, 1974); Frank Luther Mott, *A History of American Magazines*, 5 vols. (Cambridge: Harvard University Press, 1938-1968); Russel Nye, *The Unembarrassed Muse* (New York: The Dial Press, 1971).
INDEX SOURCES
None.
LOCATION SOURCES
The complete *Boys' Champion* is available on microfilm from Greenwood Press, Westport, Conn.

Publication History

MAGAZINE TITLE AND TITLE CHANGES
The Boys' Champion (1881-1883).
VOLUME AND ISSUE DATA
The Boys' Champion (vol. 1, no. 1-vol. 2, no. 73).
PUBLISHER AND PLACE OF PUBLICATION
Champion Publishing Company, New York (1881-1883).

EDITOR
None listed.

Roderick McGillis

BOYS' LIFE

When *Boys' Life* started in 1911, it competed especially with several other popular magazines aimed at the same young male market, including *St. Nicholas,* The Youth's Companion,** and *American Boy—Open Road.* Boys' Life* alone survives—and if it were not for the Boy Scouts, it probably would not survive either. Its continued publication of wholesome articles and stories about things perennially of interest to boys has led some observers to characterize *Boys' Life* as a sociological dinosaur that has not changed with the times. Its circulation figures negate the dinosaur image, however. As the flagship publication of the Boy Scouts of America, *Boys' Life* is the largest American juvenile periodical. Although its 1982 circulation of 1,542,000 is down from its peak number of 2,650,000, *Boys' Life* still has the 22nd largest circulation of all American periodicals. Of its 1,542,000 readers, 1,200,000 are scouts who get their subscriptions through their troops for $4.20 (compared with the $8.40 regular subscription rate, itself a great bargain), and the proportion of Boy Scout subscribers did not change significantly during the decade of the 1970s. About 3,400,000 boys, 2,100,000 adults, and 778,000 girls read it, although its main appeal, clearly, is to the nine- to fifteen-year-old boy.[1]

Boys' Life was started in New England in 1911 and purchased by the Boy Scouts of America to provide material on the scouting program and a source of good reading for boys. Originally, it came out twice monthly. The first publisher and editor, George S. Barton, identified two objectives in the March 1911 issue:

> First—To furnish the Boy Scouts with a paper which they may consider their own, and which will keep them in touch with good, clean, stirring stories of adventure.
>
> Second—To place in the hands of all boys a paper of which they may be proud, and one which they will not be afraid to have their parents see them reading.[2]

Barton went on to say that he intended to publish "absolutely the best stories that can be obtained," good, healthy stories of adventure that would do their part toward building character in boys.[3] Barton also promised to include a long, complete story of 10,000 words or more in each issue and articles on athletics (in season), a continuing feature on strength and body building, and two departments—stamps and amateur journalism.

In more than seventy years of publication, *Boys' Life* has deviated little from its original purposes. The scope of the magazine was a good deal narrower in its earliest years, but some features remain unchanged, such as the scout-craft items. Those of the 1980s reflect contemporary times and interests but are not substantively different from those of 1911. The feature "Things All Scouts Should Know" in the first issue showed: how to make a camp night-light using only candle ends, a tin can, and sand or earth; how to make a washstand for camp; the correct way to flatten nail points; how to tie down the cork of a bottle; and how to roll a jersey or sweater for packing or for strapping on one's belt.[4] Scout-craft items in the 1980s tend to deal with things such as constructing a bluebird house, searching for a lost child, earning money for the troop, earning merit badges, and using layered cardboard for constructing strong, lightweight furniture.

Although the materials and the specific projects may reflect changes in the times, the underlying nature of these features has changed little over the years. A January 1982 issue has the feature "Super Skier Tim Luke"; an article about canoeing in Manitoba; an illustrated piece, "The Fastest Cars on Earth," about seventeen automobiles that set world land-speed records; a story about a cattle drive that climaxes with a stampede; a feature about aluminum gliders; another feature about ways to make money; seven cartoon features (including a Bible story and "Scouts in Action"); six features about scouting; and fifteen columns, including items about humor, bicycling, nature, records, books, history, stamps and coins, pets, and card tricks. All of these areas of interest are thoroughly consistent with the magazine's original purposes.

Advertising is another indication of a publication's outlook, and the space and classified advertisements in *Boys' Life* issues provide an intriguing perspective that is in many ways unchanged after seventy years. One difference is that relatively little advertising appeared in the first 1911 issue—4.5 out of 48 pages, or 9 percent (compared with 30 percent advertising to 70 percent text in later decades). Advertisements in the first issue were for the International Cornet School (learn to play while you're young!), the Ames Premium Company (earn Brownie cameras, watches, scout uniforms, baseball gloves, or snare drums by selling the company's soaps and toilet articles), the Harding Uniform Company, the Hamilton .22 caliber hunting rifle, leather shoes, *Scouting for Boys* (the 344-page handbook by Sir Robert Baden-Powell, originator of the Boy Scout movement), scout uniforms, and an opportunity to get a "free" moving-picture machine for selling twenty-four packages of Bluine.

Music instruction and musical instruments frequently are advertised in the early issues. The Conn and King companies regularly promoted their band instruments throughout the early years. In the 1930s more family-oriented products appeared in the ads, such as Old Dutch Cleanser, Shredded Wheat, and Beech-Nut Peanut Butter. Ads for family-oriented products disappeared during the post-World War II period and were replaced gradually by ads for numerous items of interest to boys and girls. Charles Atlas's "Dynamic Tension" method of body building, conceptually and methodologically not very far removed from George Barton's clothesline-and-broom-handle body-building method of the earliest years of *Boys' Life*, is still being promoted in the 1980s. Clearly, some things in *Boys' Life* never change.

After the 1940s band instruments disappeared from the advertising pages for several decades, only to reappear in the form of a few King Company ads in the 1980s. The more typical ads of the 1980s are for Activision Stampede (a video game), MPC Model cars, the Columbia Record and Tape Club, guitars, board games, athletic shoes, Chapsticks, boarding academies and military schools (twenty-six in the January 1982 issue), numerous summer camps, and three or more pages of classified-style boxed ads for "gifts and gimmicks." These pages also include ads for several folding knives, baseball and football cards, and kits and supplies for constructing and launching model rockets. A full-page, four-color ad on the slick, inside back-cover page (November 1980) promotes "Dungeons and Dragons," the popular fantasy, role-playing adventure game.

Premium offers also have not changed over the years. The first issue featured a two-page (inside back-cover and facing-page) spread advertising the Ames Premium Company's prizes "Given away for very little work."[5] Seven decades later, premium offers, most frequently those of the Olympic Sales Club, are still featured on two-page spreads. The Olympic Sales Club asks the boys to sell all-occasion greeting cards, note paper, and personalized stationery. Each sale earns $1 or one "prize point," which can be redeemed: a Huffy Motocross bike for seventy-two prize points, a bike speedometer for nine, a portable television for seventy-five, a mess kit-canteen outfit for twelve, an electronic "Space Invader" game for thirty-one, or a backpack for seven.

The thematic content and emphases of the articles and features reflect the philosophy and outlook of the Boy Scouts of America even more directly than the advertising does. Environmental education, for instance, has been a dominant theme in *Boys' Life* for many years, reflecting the parent organization's emphasis on outdoor activities. Indeed, the magazine was doing articles on conservation, wildlife, and taking care of the environment decades before "ecology" became a popular issue. Conservation emerged as a distinct and continuing emphasis during the 1950s.

For conservation articles, Robert E. Hood, editor of *Boys' Life* since 1964, has made an effort to use writers who are authorities in their fields (such as wildlife science and environmental education), who also know young people and thus can write with both expertise in the subject and sensitivity to the audience of young readers. George Laycock and Durward Allen have been frequent contributors. A Laycock piece about the California condor, "Last of the Giant Gliders" (January 1982), concludes with several paragraphs about the efforts of diverse groups to save the big birds, groups including the U.S. Fish and Wildlife Service, the National Audubon Society, and the California Fish and Game Commission.

Similarly, another Laycock feature is about the giant white trumpeter swans that live in Yellowstone National Park and a handful of other wildlife refuges. Like many of the features on various species of wildlife, this one makes the point that conservation efforts rescued these beautiful, large waterfowl from possible extinction (November 1980).

Still other conservation features include Laycock pieces about the wild turkey (July 1981), giant snakes of the world (September 1981), and a "how-to" piece on tree planting as an excellent troop project (September 1981). A young reader may quickly and completely forget the many facts that are presented in these articles about interesting animals, plants, and physical features of the land. But he is likely to absorb and assimilate the underlying message that species of wildlife should not be killed off and our environment should not be spoiled by human indifference or ignorance.

Another important category is the sports story. Baseball players have featured prominently in these stories over the years. Stories by and about Ken Boyer (July 1965), Roy Campanella (March 1958), Joe Cronin (October 1966), Willie Mays (March 1966), Stan Musial (March 1955), Phil Rizzuto (March 1964), Jackie Robinson (June 1948; April 1951), and Warren Spahn (August 1966) provide biographical data about the players and numerous hints about how to play the various field positions or arrange a set of catcher-pitcher signals.

Football players have been featured almost as frequently as baseball players and even more frequently during the 1970s and 1980s. A feature about Dan Fouts, quarterback of the San Diego Chargers (November 1980), makes the point that young Dan set out to be a pass-catching end, but his father talked him into playing quarterback. Such pieces about athletes of all ages in almost all sports appear in virtually every issue of *Boys' Life*. Young high achievers also feature prominently, such as thirteen-year-old "Super Skier" Tim Luke of Golden, Colorado, who is also a championship soccer player and swimmer (January 1982). Fiction stories about football are used too, for example, "Master Mind" by B. J. Chute, a frequent contributor of sport stories (June 1967); "Talking Turkey" by Andrew Hall (November 1954); and "Bench Captain" by William Herman (November 1967).

Similarly, basketball players feature prominently in many *Boys' Life* short stories. These stories emphasize quick thinking, strong team play, competition, and the feelings of achievement that derive from trying hard in a game of physical skill. As in all *Boys' Life* stories, the characters generally are well-drawn, admirable students in urban and suburban high schools—although junior high and middle-school-age characters appear frequently. Girls and women are almost totally absent from the stories, however; events concern only boys, their teacher-coaches, their across-town rivals, and sometimes their fathers. The boys learn new skills, solve problems, learn to work as teams, and in whatever ways the short time spans of these stories permit, they grow up. Among the basketball stories are "Kid Brother" by B. J. Chute (October 1964), "Hoop Hokum" by Jackson V. Scholz (August 1957), and "Lobsters Don't Make Champions" by Charles Coombs (January 1954).

The short stories, often of 1,500 or fewer words, and the occasional continued story or serialized story in cartoon format, usually are briskly written pieces that engage the reader early. An example is "Banjo" (May 1981) by Robert Newton Peck, author of several widely read adolescent novels. The two boys at the center of this story are Alvin Dickinson and his friend Ferguson Hale Byler, who is called Banjo, because he always carries a banjo and because friends just don't call a boy by a name like Ferguson. One day the two boys (both of them are some indeterminate age between ten and thirteen) fall into an abandoned mine shaft and realize that they are hurt—Banjo has broken his leg, possibly some ribs, and a banjo string—and are not likely to be found, because Alvin has told his mom that he was going to the library. Banjo's banjo will still play with three strings, however, and his tunes eventually attract the attention of Jake Horse, a hermit-prospector. Using a rope sling, Jake pulls the boys out of the shaft and quickly, almost tenderly, gets a splint on Banjo's broken leg to immobilize it, while chatting about his own banjo. At the end of the story, Banjo realizes that his banjo now has an intact fourth string; Jake's undoubtedly is functioning with only three strings. Like most *Boys' Life* stories, this one is readable, good (but not exceptionally distinguished), engaging, and has well-drawn, admirable-but-human protagonists.

Other well-known authors of books for juveniles and young adults have published stories in *Boys' Life*. Jane and Paul Annixter had a story in the 1960s. Some of America's most popular authors for the adult market also have written stories for *Boys' Life*, including Isaac Asimov, Pearl S. Buck, John Knowles, and Isaac Bashevis Singer. On occasion, *Boys' Life* seems to have made an effort to seek out well-known contributors. Bobby Fischer, for example, contributed a chess column even before he gained fame as a world-class chess player. Many Norman Rockwell paintings were reproduced on *Boys' Life* covers from 1914 through the 1920s and 1930s. Numerous well-known professional athletes have been featured since the 1950s and 1960s.

Another continuing characteristic of *Boys' Life* has been its readability. In the more than seventeen years he has served as editor, Robert E. Hood has never believed in using word lists, Fry graphs, or other kinds of readability formulas. Instead, his goal has been to stretch the boys, to "pull them along" with the articles and stories in which they are interested. The editorial staff does make an effort, however, to keep sentences short and simple.[6] Short sentences can sometimes result in choppiness, but in *Boys' Life* there is almost always sufficient variety in sentence length to prevent monotony. The editorial staff also makes an effort to define technical and less familiar words in context and to use English rather than Latinate terms when choices are available. All of these policies make *Boys' Life* a model of clarity and readability. Both the copy chief and executive editor bear down on the writing style in the articles, features, and stories—not to achieve any conformity in style but to ensure that the prose is lively and clear.

The copy department also serves as the first line of defense against error, checking every manuscript line by line, not only for matters of grammar and usage but also to verify the facts presented. If a writer of an article reports that a baseball player hit thirty-two home runs and a reference source says thirty-one, further checking is going to be necessary before the article is published. The careful work of the copy department ensures that the material published in *Boys' Life* is accurate.

The legibility of *Boys' Life* is also a strong point. Articles and features are set in serifed type in a three-column format, with a sans-serif typeface being used for the titles and internal heads. Graphics and color photographs are excellent; the design, pleasing. Much color is used. Two or three items an issue will have color photographs or illustrations across two facing pages for a more intense, attention-grabbing splash of color. The use of color also serves a purpose other than aesthetic. Readership surveys have shown that the use of color increases the readership of a feature 10 to 20 percent.[7]

The biographical and historical content in *Boys' Life* nonfiction has been another continuing strong point, encouraging youth to understand their heritage. People who live and work in some danger, who travel to faraway places, or who have served their country in some patriotic or heroic way are frequently featured. Young people appear often. A piece about Buffy Gebel's life in the circus, where his father is superstar Gunther Gebel-Williams (November 1981), is an example of a feature about a child or youth. Such features typically are highly informative, as are the articles and features on topics such as famous fighter planes of World War II (November 1981), the early "How I Learned to Fly" by Orville Wright (February 1928), and the many articles and stories of military heroism that appeared during the World War II years.

Selections about health, diet, career information, and hobbies are equally informative: bicycling, stamps and coins, the outdoors, pets, magic (and card tricks), records, music, puzzles, and "how-do" columns appear regularly. "About Books" usually reviews several recently published books, sometimes three or more within a category—books on cooking, baseball, animals inventors, and the like. The column "History" deals primarily with military history—Civil War naval engagements and World War II air battles, for instance.

The "Think and Grin" joke pages, featuring jokes sent in by readers, are filled with little-boy humor. From Terrence Gochee of San Antonio, Texas: "*Amazon*: What has four eyes and sleeps in a waterbed? *Nile*: The mighty Mississippi." Cartoons are sprinkled throughout the issues, and letters to the editor, addressed to a burro named Pedro, frequently display humor aimed at nine-year-old boys. "Dear Senor Hayguzzler, Have you done anything on Yeti or (the) Abominable Snowman? Jay Price, Sante Fe, NM" The response from Pedro reads: "We're waiting for new information. I asked Sir Wilfred, the explorer, if he had found one. He said, 'Not Yeti.' "[8]

The size of the magazine has changed from time to time over the years. *Boys' Life* began as a 6 1/2- by 9 1/4 inch magazine that sold for 5¢. In 1912 a smaller, almost digest-size format was adopted and the price was increased to 10¢. This price held until 1926, although the size increased in 1921 to the 10 1/2- by 14 inch *Life* magazine format that would be retained for nearly sixty years. Not until the September 1970 issue did *Boys' Life* go to the smaller format of *Time* and *Newsweek*. In 1932 the price dropped again to 10¢, where it held throughout the Depression, rising to 20¢ again in the latter part of the World War II years. The 1982 single-issue price is 80¢.

Despite the high degree of continuity that has characterized *Boys' Life*, important changes have occurred: the increasing variety in material, increasing use of color, and decreasing length of articles and stories. In the earliest issues, 10,000-word stories of adventure were not uncommon; as late as the 1950s and 1960s, 3,500-word articles were used. By the 1970s and 1980s, however, selections rarely exceeded 1,500 words. The influence of television, the apparent decline in boys' reading ability, the decreasing age of the readership (a larger proportion of younger, Cub Scout subscribers), and the editor's desire for each issue to contain an increasingly large variety of material are some of the reasons for the trend toward shorter reading selections. The variety of different things in each issue is clearly greater in the *Boys' Life* of the later years. Each issue features articles about many subjects, reflecting Robert Hood's belief that the magazine must be a smorgasbord, or a little supermarket, and provide material for boys who have many interests, some of which may eventually lead to careers.

The nearly total absence of girls and women is noticeable in the stories, articles, and photographs. It is not unusual to have several issues in a row in which no females appear. When girls and women do appear, however, they are usually shown in active roles—but this is because the females are shown most frequently in things such as full-page ads for Adidas athletic shoes. One wonders why girls and women are almost completely invisible in a publication that taps so many *other* important aspects of a boy's life.

Minority persons are almost as invisible in *Boys' Life* as females are. An occasional black scout is shown, such as the black youth on the cover of the February 1981 issue, but an examination of the first three decades of *Boys' Life* fails to reveal a single Hispanic surname, and nearly a decade of the 1970's issues must be searched before finding a Spanish-surnamed scout. In this case, Mark Martinez of an El Paso, Texas, troop that hiked part of the historic Mormon Battalion trail in southern New Mexico was shown in a photograph of part of his troop (March 1981). Six months later, another Spanish surname appeared— in a feature about Keith Hernandez, "baseball's new super hitter" (September 1981). The omission of Hispanic persons and the absence of females might not be so noticeable if it were not for an additional factor: ubiquitous sexist language. Sexist forms are used consistently, with no apparent effort to modify even those that are easy to convert to nonsexist usage.

Scouts who are *not* high achievers are similarly ignored. Handicapped scouts do not appear, except for an instance or two of truly remarkable paralyzed and otherwise physically handicapped scouts being featured, and there are very few instances of any attention being given to the ordinary, everyday youth who does a good (but not outstanding) job in school, athletics, and scouting. Unremarkable activities and people do sometimes get mentioned in "Scouting Around" or in an article about one of the National Jamborees—but only rarely. The emphasis remains on conspicuous achievement.

Another category of material excluded from *Boys' Life* is anything that might conceivably be considered unwholesome. Divorce, single-parent families, drug abuse, teenage alcoholism, child abuse, poverty, and the like do not exist in *Boys' Life*; nor does sexuality. The first article to deal with drug abuse appeared in the November 1981 issue and does not seem to signal a trend toward more realism. Consequently, *Boys' Life* cannot serve the therapeutic function of helping its readers come to grips with such problems in their own lives. This is a matter of editorial intent and policy. Although Robert Hood is not certain, he believes that *Boys' Life* readers generally are the American boys who are managing to resist the temptations of contemporary life and who want something to cling to. "I can't promise you that none of our readers are also flipping through *Playboy* and smoking pot, but I know those things aren't as prevalent as among boys who don't read *Boys' Life*. The subject of sex, I haven't dealt with at all. It's too big to handle."[9] Seventy years later, *Boys' Life* is still completely consistent with George S. Barton's original desire to provide thoroughly wholesome material for American boys.

In contrast, the trend in adolescent novels read by the same age group that reads *Boys' Life* has been toward realism; hence much has changed during the past decade. The use of drugs is common. Sexual relations are a regular part of teenage relationships. Sports, dances, and even friends frequently mean much less to teenagers, whose mood may be pessimistic, despairing, or hostile.[10] However, some observers believe that although contemporary adolescent fiction uses characters, settings, and life-styles that were not included in earlier adolescent novels, "the dominant themes not only uphold but also reinforce traditional beliefs and values. Instead of providing adolescents with subversive or unconventional ideas, these books legitimize the existing social order and provide sensitive, moral role models for readers.[11]

Boys' Life serves the same purpose more directly and didactically than does most of the reading material currently intended for this age group. The avoidance of contemporary problems of boys' lives also stem from the thoroughly positive and optimistic tone of *Boys' Life*. There is so much that is positive and optimistic as to leave no room for the negative, pessimistic, and problematic. Thus in many ways, *Boys' Life* is the *St. Nicholas* of a later era: popular, natural, entertaining, and informative—and also as thoroughly permeated with the traditional values of white, middle-class America as it is with the values of its parent organization. It serves well its purpose of providing good reading "for all boys," although its destiny is tied to that of the Boy Scouts of America. The significance of *Boys' Life* as a historical record of the Boy Scouts is enormous (especially as no complete history of the Boy Scouts now exists). Its significance in juvenile literature is almost as great; it embodies the idealistic, largely middle-class view of American boyhood.

Notes

1. Tom Overton, "Boys Are Still Boys," *Houston Post*, November 8, 1981, p. 7-, B8.

2. George S. Barton, "Round the Campfire," *Boys' Life* 1 (March 1, 1911), 21-22.

3. Ibid., p. 21.

4. Ibid., pp. 33-34.

5. Ibid., p. 46.

6. Robert E. Hood, personal communication, 22 December 1981.

7. Overton, "Boys Are Still Boys," pp. 1, 7-B8.

8. *Boys' Life*, January 4, 1982, p. 4.

9. Bob Greene, "Boy at His Best," *Esquire* 95 (June 1981), 18.

10. Robert C. Small, Jr., "The Young Adult Novel as a Mirror of the Teenage World," *Texas Tech Journal of Education* 7 (Winter 1980), 36.

11. Maia Pank Mertz, "The New Realism: Traditional Cultural Values in Recent Young-Adult Fiction," *Phi Delta Kappa* 60 (October 1978), 104.

Information Sources

BIBLIOGRAPHY

Best Jokes from Boys' Life (New York: G. P. Putnam's Sons, 1970); *Boys' Life Book of Basketball Stories* (New York: Random House, 1966); *Boys' Life Book of Horse Stories* (New York: Random House, 1963); *Boys' Life Book of Mystery Stories* (New York: Random House, 1963); *Boys' Life Book of Outer Space Stories* (New York: Random House, 1964); *Boys' Life Book of Wild Animal Stories* (New York: Random House, 1965); *Boys' Life Book of World War II Stories* (New York: Random House, 1965).

INDEX SOURCES

ACCESS (Syracuse, N.Y.: Gaylord), since 1975; *Subject Index to Children's Periodicals*.

LOCATION SOURCES

Boys' Life is widely held but some of the more extensive collections include: Tuskegee Institute, Tuskegee, Ala.; Library of Congress; St. Paul Public Library, Minneapolis-St. Paul; Kansas City Public Library; Ohio University, Athens; Brigham Young University, Provo, Utah; St. Louis Public Library.

Publication History

MAGAZINE TITLE AND TITLE CHANGES

Boys' Life: Boys' and Boy Scouts' Magazine (1911); *Boys' Life Magazine: The Magazine for Boys and Boy Scouts* (1911); *Boys' Life: A Real Boys' Magazine* (1912); *Boys' Life: For All Boys* (1954-).

VOLUME AND ISSUE DATA

Published twice monthly for the first volume year; monthly since 1912.

PUBLISHER AND PLACE OF PUBLICATION

George S. Barton, Boston (1911-1912); Boy Scouts of America: New York (1912-1954); New Brunswick, N.J. (1954-1979); Irving, Tex. (1979-).

EDITOR

George S. Barton (1911-1913); Walter P. McGuire (1913-1917); none listed, but during this time James E. West was chief scouting executive and Daniel Carter Beard, as associate editor, was filling much of the editor's role (1918-1923); James E.

West (1924-1943); Elbert K. Fretwell (1944-1946); Irving Crump (1947-1953); Harry A. Harchar (1953-1964); Robert E. Hood (1964-).

Alice Denham

THE BOYS' MAGAZINE

From 1910 to 1921 *The Boys' Magazine* offered young men a monthly publication that combined the adventure and suspense of dime-novel fiction with the more acceptable juvenile literature in which proper behavior reaped rewards and stories had obvious morals. With entertainment its primary purpose, *The Boys' Magazine* also sought to mold character, encourage fitness, and develop interest in hobbies and skills.

The thirty-two-page magazine sold for 10¢ a copy, or $1 a year, and was published by the Scott F. Redfield Co. in Smethport, Pennsylvania, a small town in the then thriving Pennsylvania oil fields. Redfield, born in 1880 in Washington, D.C., the son of a newspaper reporter, moved to Smethport and married into a prominent local family. He was involved in real estate and automobile sales before his publishing venture and edited the magazine throughout most of its existence.

The Boys' Magazine presented short stories and serialized longer pieces in which the hero was a teenage or young adult male. It also included articles on exemplary young men, athletics, and hunting, as well as regular departments that were an important part of the periodical in its first eight volumes. George Avison illustrated almost all of the covers and a high percentage of the stories published, although the artwork of other artists, such as A. O. Scott and Clare Angell, was regularly used too.

Most of the fiction was dramatic and exciting, placing the young heroes in perilous situations that called for bravery and clever thinking. Conventional narrative forms predominated: historical fiction, technology and transportation, confrontations with bank robbers, Indian life, prep school or college life, sports, and nature adventures.

The smallest category, historical fiction, included serialized accounts of young men's patriotic efforts during the American Revolution, such as John T. McIntyre's "Young Continentals at Bunker Hill" (January 1910 and following issues) and Everett T. Tomlinson's "Light Horse Harry's Legion" (August 1910 and following issues). One other historical topic for fiction was the taming of the old West, but the majority of stories were given a contemporary setting.

Some of the stories dealt with young men's adventures in aircraft, automobiles, and trains. A positive attitude toward technical knowledge was reinforced in these stories, encouraging the readers to learn how to operate and care for mechanical equipment. The opening issue contained "Skimming the Skies," a serialized tale of two bright young men who not only build and fly dirigibles but also catch thieves. "Gasoline Bronc" (July 1915) by George M. Johnson illustrates the superiority of modern technology: a ranch manager's son uses his motorcycle to break through an Indian attack and bring back help to rescue the surrounded cowpunchers. In several of the railroad stories, such as Roe L. Hendrick's "Return to Duty" (April 1913) and C. H. Claudy's "Dick's Start" (February 1911), near wrecks are averted at the last minute by quick-thinking youths who comprehend the intricacies of dispatching and telegraph communications. Another tale clearly stressing the need to master modern communication skills is "The Surrender of Father" (January 1915) by Maud Mary Brown, a story in which the hero assembles a wireless transmitter and calls in aid to put down a strike in his father's coal mine.

Bank robbers were regularly foiled in *The Boys' Magazine* fiction by brave young men who used their wits. "The Proving of Billy" (February 1915) by Gardner Hunting, "When the Hour Struck" (January 1911) by J. S. Danielson, and "Fixing a Robber" (February 1913) by Harry W. Newcombe exemplify this type of story. Indian stories were also very popular, whether in an entirely Indian cultural setting or in recounting a clash with white traders or settlers moving west. A large number of the Indian stories published in *The Boys' Magazine* were by Ernest Carliowa, a regular contributor.

Slightly more numerous are stories depicting prep school and college life, often emphasizing the team sports offered by such institutions. John Clair Minot wrote a succession of stories recounting the adventures of young university men, including "The Entombed Feud" (January 1910) and "A Husking Checker's Experience" (February 1910). "Fenton's Debt" (January 1912) by E. M. Jameson shows the influence of Burt L. Standish's "Frank Merriwell" series, a bully creating fear among smaller classmates. Serials about football and baseball-team activities included "Left End Edwards" (September 1915 and following issues) by Ralph Henry Barbour and several stories by William Heyliger, including "Fair Play" (March 1915 and following issues), "Five Yards to Go" (January 1913 and following issues), and "The Winning Hit" (June 1916 and following issues). One baseball serial, "The Young Pitcher" (September 1914 and following issues), was written by Zane Grey, best known for his popular western novels. Other sports were also given attention in *The Boys' Magazine*, notably sailing and track.

Nature adventures made up the largest single group of short stories in *The Boys' Magazine*. These stories were of two basic types: stories of young men who battle the elements and stories of young men who confront wild animals. Examples of the first type include Hugh F. Grinstead's "Flood and Its Messenger" (December 1914), Arthur Knowle's "Adrift on an Ice Raft" (January 1913), and Archibald Rutledge's "Vine and the Whirlpool" (February 1913). In the second type of these stories, the animal might be a puma, a panther, or even a bear, but always the young hero narrowly escapes a grisly death. Examples of this type include "A Tussle with a Wildcat" (March 1915) by Ladd Plumley, "The Worthlessness of Buster" (February 1913) by Roe L. Hendrick, and "A Crop of Sweet Corn" (August 1914) by Harrison R. Heath. A fascination with the great outdoors is apparent in many serials as well, notably the string by Hugh Pendexter: "The Young Lumbermen," "The Young Prospectors," "The Young Forest Rangers," "The Young Timber-Cruisers," and "The Young Gem-Hunters."

Although most of the magazine was devoted to fiction, articles also appeared. Usually, they presented an exemplary young man as a role model or offered tips on athletics, hunting, or fishing. Occasionally, articles appeared urging correct moral behavior (such as temperance) or discussing geographical wonders, but they were not very common. John L. Harbour was responsible for many short, inspirational, biographical pieces, such as "Our President's Young Son" (January 1913), concerning Charlie Taft, and "From Messenger Boy to Fifty-Thousand Dollars a Year" (January 1912), the rags-to-riches story of corporation president Belvidere Brooks. Advice articles on sports or hunting were penned by experts, such as baseball professional Billy Evans's serial "Developing a Crack Baseball Team" (July 1913 and following issues) and the reoccurring tips on shooting by Warren H. Miller, editor of *Field and Stream*.

From the start a heavy emphasis was placed on regular departments. Alfred P. Morgan edited a monthly column on electricity and mechanics, Arthur Mallett edited one on stamps and coins, and Donald Grandon edited another on photography. Day Allen Wiley's "Curios Department" disappeared in May 1910, and A. Neely Hall's "Carpentry Department" debuted in March 1910. Both in emphasis and presentation, the most significant department dealt with athletics and was edited by Walter Camp, originator of the first All-American football team. Camp's name and influence were so integral to *The Boys' Magazine* that in November 1911 he was made editor-in-chief, responsible for a monthly editorial on sportsmanship. Redfield made himself editor again in 1915, dropping Camp to the status of contributing editor. An article by Simon T. Dillon, "Boy Scouts Movement" (December 1910), led to the inauguration of a monthly column edited by John Prine Jones. Devoted to the activities of the Boy Scouts of America, this column extolled their work and encouraged membership. Beginning in August 1911, it predated *Boys' Life*,* which did not start publication until the following July.

The departments were converted or disappeared during a reorganizational shakeup of *The Boys' Magazine* that occurred in the premiere 1915 issue. Herbert Hungerford was made "chief booster" and ostensibly took over the editing of the magazine, although Redfield retained the title. Formerly active in the YMCA and creator of the first Boy's Success Club in New York, which developed into the later Success League, Hungerford sought to make the periodical more dependent on reader submissions with an expanded Prize Department. He also enlisted the aid of Orison Swett Marden as contributing editor on success winning and character building topics; Warren H. Miller as outdoor life editor; Spencer Hord of Kodak as photography editor; Jack Glennister, founder of *Boys' Life*, as athletics editor; and Edna Earle Henderson as nature editor.

Circulation was listed as more than 100,000 by April 1915 and more than 110,000 by July 1915, but there were signs the magazine was in trouble. Pulpier, less expensive paper was used, and typeset size was reduced as advertising increased. By volume 9, stories from volume 1 were being reprinted in their entirety. Hungerford's attempt to stimulate circulation by allying the readers with his Success League and later with his "Squarefellow's Republic," a similar program encouraging readers' contributions, ultimately failed, and *The Boys' Magazine*, after raising its price in September 1920 to 20¢ a copy, ceased publication at the end of that year.

Information Sources

BIBLIOGRAPHY
None.
INDEX SOURCES
None.
LOCATION SOURCES
Bound volumes (excluding vol. 10) are in the Library of Congress.

Publication History

MAGAZINE TITLE AND TITLE CHANGES
The Boys' Magazine (1910-1920).
VOLUME AND ISSUE DATA
(vol. 1, no. 1-vol. 11, no. 12).
PUBLISHER AND PLACE OF PUBLICATION
Scott F. Redfield Co., Smethport, Pa. (1910-1920).
EDITOR
Scott F. Redfield (1910-1911); Walter Camp (1911-1915); Scott F. Redfield (1915-February 1920); Herbert Hungerford (March-September 1920); Scott F. Redfield (October-December 1920).

Scot Guenter

BOYS OF NEW YORK: A PAPER FOR YOUNG AMERICANS

On August 23, 1875, Norman L. Munro published his first issue of an eight-page folio-sized newspaper, *Boys of New York: A Paper for Young Americans*, which sold for 5¢ an issue or $2.50 a year. By volume 1, number 26, it claimed a readership of more than 200,000. A typical example of an inexpensive weekly for boys, the paper featured action-packed, serialized stories that were often compiled and published as novelettes in series such as the Riverside Library and the New York Boy's Library; and, later, as Frank Tousey's *Happy Days*,* in one of his libraries such as the New York Detective Library, Pocket Library, and Wide Awake Library. Tousey merged his *New York Boys' Weekly* (1877-1878) with *Boys of New York* and continued to publish the paper weekly until October 13, 1894.[1] Then he announced, "Hereafter this paper will be entitled

Happy Days. All the good features of *Boys of New York* will be retained and new ones added.''[2] One week later the paper appeared under its new title and continued for thirty years.

Under the editorship of Norman L. Munro (1875-1879), publisher of the *New York Family Story Paper*, the paper sponsored article and story contests and featured several columns to which readers contributed. The ''Theatricals Column'' (1875-1877) offered space for announcing the organization of musical and theatrical groups and minstrel shows. In another column readers were permitted to advertise items for sale or exchange. ''Leisure Moments'' (1875-1878), a column of puzzles, charades, and enigmas, also accepted reader contributions. Through the correspondence column boys received advice from the editor on careers and their prospects in business, found recipes for dispensing freckles, and were provided with a wide range of factual information. Munro published from one to five poems or songs in each issue, and some of them came from readers. He also included nonfiction, most of it about sports or nature, in his ''Sports and Pastimes'' column (1875-1877). As editor he experimented in the early years of *Boys of New York* with the column ''Popular Songs,'' another one that featured short plays: ''Our Stage,'' one that contained announcements of baseball games, and a number of other, short-lived, columns.

Munro established as the mainstay of the paper the action-packed, sensational stories with protagonists from the lower classes; throughout its history they made up most of the paper. They were illustrated by engravings that depicted some dramatic and suspenseful episode from one of the stories. Other features he introduced were the humorous adventure stories by Peter Pad (George G. Small) and the column of personal anecdotes that ''Ed'' contributed (1875-1894). They, too, remained regular fare of the paper after the ownership passed to Frank Tousey.

As editor, Frank Tousey (1878-1894) briefly offered ''Singer's Corner'' (1880-1881), consisting of popular song lyrics, and ''Kurious Kweries'' (1878), a puzzles, charades, and enigmas column that was briefly continued by ''Amateur Magician.'' He divided ''Amateur Advertisements'' (1880-1883) from the professional ads that also appeared. Boys were encouraged to use the ''Amateur Column'' (1880-1882) to invite others to join their clubs, to attend their dramatic performances, and for challenges—to egg-sucking contests, cobbling and talking matches, and baseball games. Gradually, Tousey eliminated the columns to which the readers contributed, but he did maintain the lively correspondence Munro had begun.

A few features appeared regularly in *Boys of New York*; they included the columns ''Ed'' and ''From Ear to Ear'' (1878-1894), containing short humor, ethnic and peddler jokes, and brief reports of slips of the tongue and malapropisms. Another regular feature was ''From Everywhere'' (1887-1894), a collection of curious bits of information about every imaginable topic from rat traps to epitaphs to soap mines. Tousey usually published only one poem or song in each issue. The nonfiction he included either provided background information to the stories or ideas for leisure pursuits. In the first category were articles about sunken ships, icebergs, electricity, and how it feels to die ten different ways. Among examples of the second type are instructions how to make a variety of boats, canoes, rafts, and small toys. Various games and sports such as gymnastics and weight lifting were explained in others. Tousey used the same type of sensational illustrations that Munro used to capture readers' interest in stories, but he enlarged one of them and displayed it prominently on the front page of each issue. He included more small engravings throughout the paper; they also depicted the more exciting and climactic episodes of stories.

Throughout its history *Boys of New York* was composed largely of serial fiction and a few short stories. Fast paced and suspenseful, these stories often featured boys from the lower classes as heroes. Scorned and insulted by the upper classes, these selfless, honest, and, above all, daring young heroes managed always to find themselves conveniently at hand when disaster struck one of the high and mighty. They saved rich men's daughters from drowning, burning, and attacks by men and beasts. They were, of course, generously rewarded. Kit Clyde's "Ollie, the Office Boy; or The Struggles of a Poor Waif" (September 22, 1888, and following issues) and P. T. Raymond's "Bowery Prince; or A Bootblack's Road to Fame" (September 12, 1889, and following issues) are typical of the story of the poor boy whose luck and courage serve him well.

These success and adventure stories cast boys as bootblacks, stockbrokers, actors, railroad engineers, divers, explorers, pilots, and ventriloquists. Their adventures took them to ruins in the Yukatan, into the western frontier, across the skies in balloons or air ships, to remote seas and islands, over glaciers, and down Wall Street. The heroes, although assigned different activities, were generally of a single type. Their dialog was stiff and peppered with pious platitudes; their motives, pure. A common thematic thread ran through them; all suggested that risk takers can reap substantial rewards. They preached the gospel of gambling on one's own abilities and luck, of striking out, and of attempting to do the extraordinary.

Boys of New York authors generally specialized in a single type of story. Fire fighters were the protagonists in most of Robert Lennox's stories, which included "Phil the Boy Fireman; or Through the Flames to Victory" (September 1, 1888, and following issues) and "The Phantom Fireman" (December 25, 1888, and following issues). Paul Braddon contributed stories set in the West—tales of Indian massacres, outlaws, and adventures in the woods. Mystery and detective stories written by Police Captain Howard, a New York detective and a U.S. detective, were regularly featured. Historical romances were provided by a number of authors, including Corp. Morgan Rattler who specialized in these as well as stories intended to appeal to youthful Irish immigrants, such as "The Boy from Blarney; or The Strange Adventure of an Irish Jockey" (November 17, 1888, and following issues) and "O'Kelly's Eclipse; or The Wild Irishman's Luck" (January 1, 1887, and following issues). J. G. Bradley chiefly contributed sea stories. "Noname" published the many adventures of Frank Reade, Jr., whose electric contraptions and fantastic air ships must have inspired many a hopeful inventor.

A weekly feature of *Boys of New York* was a humorous serial story by Peter Pad (George G. Small) and, later, Sam Smiley or Tom Teaser (1891-1894). "Those Quiet Twins," "A Rolling Stone; or Jack Ready's Life of Fun," "Jack Ready's School Scrapes," "Smart and Company, the Boy Peddlers," and "The Deacon's Boy: The Worst in Town" suggest something of the character of these stories. They were farcical accounts of boyish pranks—saddling horses backwards, setting booby traps, frightening adult victims with devices like firecrackers—tales of tricks and swindles and domestic quarrels and mishaps. Pranksters sought out their victims among the adult population, frequently picking on black men or knocking the stuffing out of priggish members of the middle class. The dialog included the use of racial and ethnic dialects, and characters tended to be flat stereotypes.

To the boys who spent their days working in factories or scrounging a living blacking boots, *Boys of New York*, with its comic and sensational stories and dramatic illustrations, provided some much needed escape. It also presented a view of the world that could leave them both hopeful and lighthearted. It assured them that through honesty, hard work, and daring they could rise in the world.

Boys of New York survived for 1,000 issues. It was continued by *Happy Days*, a sixteen-page weekly that carried much the same material.

Notes

1. Frank Luther Mott, *A History of American Magazines* (Cambridge: Harvard University Press, 1938-1968), 3:179.
2. *Boys of New York* 20 (October 13, 1894), 4.

Information Sources

BIBLIOGRAPHY
Frank Luther Mott, *A History of American Magazines*, 5 vols. (Cambridge: Harvard University Press, 1938-1968).
INDEX SOURCES
None.
LOCATION SOURCES
Library of Congress and Hess Collection, University of Minnesota, Minneapolis. Vols. 1-19 (incomplete) are available on microfilm from Datamatics, New York; and Greenwood Press, Westport, Conn.

Publication History

MAGAZINE TITLE AND TITLE CHANGES
Boys of New York: A Paper for Young Americans (August 23, 1875-October 13, 1894); continued as *Happy Days: A Paper for Young Americans*.
VOLUME AND ISSUE DATA
Boys of New York: A Paper for Young Americans (vol. 1, no. 1-vol. 20, no. 1000).

PUBLISHER AND PLACE OF PUBLICATION
Norman L. Munro and Company, New York (1875-1878); Tousey and Small, New York
    (1878-1880); Frank Tousey, New York (1880-1894).
EDITOR
Norman L. Munro (1875-1878); Frank Tousey (1878-1894).

Constance Gremore

THE BOYS' WORLD

The Boys' World was created by one of the largest publishers of Sunday school literature, David Caleb Cook. In 1875 Cook began publishing religious books and supplemental teaching aids for Sunday schools. Although Cook was a Methodist, his publications had an interdenominational slant and became popular in many of the mainstream Protestant churches. Business expanded, and in 1882 he moved his company from its original location in Chicago to nearby Elgin, Illinois. After the success of *Young People's Weekly*, which began in 1887 and reached a circulation of 250,000, Cook decided to develop separate Sunday school periodicals for girls and boys, appealing to their divergent interests, yet constantly maintaining an overriding sense of proper Christian behavior. Accordingly, on Easter Sunday in 1902, Cook Publishing Co. launched *The Girls' Companion** for young women Sunday school students and offered their male counterparts a companion publication, *The Boys' World*.

That first issue, April 5, 1902, set a pattern that *The Boys' World* would follow throughout the periodical's existence. Fiction, practical articles, educational looks at nature and geography, inspirational pieces about role models, regular columns, and even the weekly puzzles were all intended to strengthen a sense of Christian moral commitment in boys in their teens. David C. Cook, Jr., who joined the Editorial Board in December 1913, had this to say about the periodical's purpose: "It seeks to picture American boy life in which adventure and achievement are combined with honesty, justice, sympathy, and genuine religious faith. It endeavors to lead boys to feel that neither mere knowledge nor material success is true success, unless limited with greatness of character and high motives."[1] Aware of the secularization American society had been going through, especially since its expanding industrialization in the nineteenth century, the editors of *The Boys' World* sought to "bridge the chasm between the everyday life of the boy and the Church, and make religion vital and real by showing its relation to everyday living."[2]

The publisher himself served as editor-in-chief of this eight-page weekly, which sold for 25¢ a year for packets of five or more, 50¢ a year otherwise. George E. Cook handled the position of managing editor, and Elizabeth Ansley was associate editor.

Each issue opened with a 1,800-2,200-word illustrated story written to specific formulaic requirements. The main characters were teenage males, usually contemporary Americans or Canadians. The story opened with action or conversation on the part of the boys, who during the course of plot development would undergo some test of moral strength or confront some unexpected crisis. After emerging victoriously from the conflict, the hero or heroes would gain insight into the obvious moral superiority of a true Christian life-style. This message might not be blatantly stated but was usually integral to the story. Maude Morrison Huey's "A Story's Double Mission" (January 22, 1910) is an example of this genre. Honest Londy Gleason secretly stops a practical joke his chums plan for their spinster schoolmarm. Knowing that she is excited about a short-story contest she entered, they send her a bogus letter of congratulations for winning. When she reads them her prizewinning story about upright, honest school students, they feel pangs of guilt but are later relieved to learn that Londy intercepted their missive and that the schoolmarm really did win the contest. All vow to be more like Londy in the future.

Excitement and adventure serve often as significant ingredients in these first-page stories. Frequent contributor Nora Colter used both in "The Conversion of Andy Whiting" (September 10, 1910), the tale of a mischievous boy who later finds himself in an emergency, driving a cart of nitroglycerine through the Pennsylvania oil fields by night. Andy does not blow up, but an oil tank does in "The Danger Point" (November, 12, 1910) by Mrs. Frank Lee, another frequent contributor. This story shows the dangers of alcohol upon the clear mind a young man requires for industrial work.

Although these tales often contain elements of surprise and danger, the central focus remains a lesson for the readers to experience vicariously. The lesson might range from a reminder to think of those less fortunate and help them—such as in Elizabeth Clarke Hardy's "Easter Lily in the Blue Bowl" (February 26, 1910) and Dennis H. Stovall's "Mystery of the Coal Oil Can" (September 28, 1912)—to an admonition that hard work and perseverance will be recognized and rewarded—such as in Mabel Way's "R.F.D. No. 4" (January 8, 1910) and Stovall's "Golden Candlestick" (April 5, 1913). One popular theme, allowing for the development of suspense, demonstrates the need for calm, logical, and resourceful thinking when confronting a sudden accident or calamity. The volumes of *The Boys's World* are replete with such tales, among them H. F. Cable's "Mechanical Sense of Oliver Boyd" (January 6, 1912), in which an ingenious youth fashions a sail for a railway handcar to deliver an urgent call for evacuation when the telegraph lines are down, and Hugh F. Grinstead's "Blowing Up of the Samson Dam" (June 6, 1914), in which the lives of more than a thousand hang in the balance, dependent on young Fred Turner's decision.

Along with the opening stories, *The Boys' World* also printed shorter stories, from 900 to 1,400 words, and serials, from two to eight chapters, each chapter from 1,700 to 2,000 words. Although the lengths might vary, these stories followed the same guidelines as the opening pieces, and many fell into the categories of cowboy, Indian, school, sports, holiday, and historical stories.

Many contributors, like Colter, Lee, and Cable, wrote regularly for the periodical, and often they developed specialties. Coe Hayne was responsible for many of the cowboy stories, and a pair representing his work are "The Long Trail" (June 23, 1912) and "The Mystery of the Guarded Ranch House" (August 8, 1914). E. Pauline Johnson, always including her Indian name "Tekahion-wake," penned tales depicting Indians as noble savages, such as "The Brotherhood" (February 5, 1910), "The Potlatch" (October 8, 1910), and "Silver-Craft of the Mohawks" (November 12, 1910).

In the early years of the magazine, the majority of stories set at school deal with prep-school or boarding-school life, reflecting the impact Burt L. Standish's "Frank Merriwell" series of books had on juvenile literature in this period. "Thompson's Trek" (January 7, 1911) by Bunny MacPherson exemplifies the camaraderie such a life can generate; "The Fixing of Simp" (June 15, 1912) by H. Bedford Jones emphasizes the importance of cleanliness and proper dress in a young gentleman's life. Athletic stories concentrate on honesty, good sportsmanship, and the upholding of amateur ideals, whether on a sailboat as in Alice Follansbee Chase's "Winning of the Cup" (July 23, 1913), a race track as in A. E. Swoyer's "Loser of the Quarter Mile" (May 23, 1914), or the most popular location, a football field, as in Coe Hayne's "Protest" (September 21, 1912, and following issues).

Religious holidays, such as Thanksgiving, Christmas, and Easter, provided an opportunity for *The Boys' World* to present seasonal stories with Christian messages. In "Easter Dawned on Roaring River" (April 11, 1914) by Coe Hayne, young Jean, trapped on the roof of a clubhouse being washed downstream in a flood as the sun rises on Easter morning, bravely sings hymns and explains the Easter story to the frightened youths trapped with him. The boys are later rescued and not only sign Jean's antialcohol petition but agree to start attending his Sunday school class. Other holidays that also receive regular attention are usually of a patriotic nature, such as Washington's Birthday, Memorial Day, Independence Day, and for the significant Canadian audience, Dominion Day.

Occasionally, stories set in the past would be included, but they usually either showed a conversion of a pagan to Christianity or an episode in American history intended to instill a sense of national heritage. Virginia Baker wrote many of the history stories in serial form, an example of the first format being her "Young Viking" (June 11, 1910, and following issues), in which young Thorolf accepts Christ; and an example of the second, her "Luke Hill's New Year's" (December 31, 1910, and following issues), in which a Quaker boy in old Pennsylvania helps Indians, earning the admiration of William Penn himself.

The Boys' World published several articles in every issue, intended to edify and enrich its young readers. Often they promoted ideals of hard work, whether in agriculture, such as Secretary of Agriculture James Wilson's "Farm Boy's Opportunity in Hay" (June 11, 1910), or in industry, such as J. Mervyn Hull's "Knowing the Business" (August 13, 1910). Many titles could speak for themselves: "How One Boy Found a Practical Way to Make Himself Felt in the World" (January 28, 1911) by George M. Miller, "Be on Time" (June 14,

1913) by Thomas W. Lloyd, and "Finding Your Proper Work Place in Life" (March 8, 1913) by Thomas Alva Edison.

Other articles strove to build character. Themes encouraging pacifism and respect for elders were common, as were admonitions against gambling, smoking, and swearing. More practical pieces discussed skills that would interest young men, such as "The Fine Art of Woodworking" (September 13, 1913) by David D. Avery and "The Inner Science of Baseball for the Amateur" (June 14, 1913) by James Callahan.

The Boys' World had an eye to the future of technology, with articles such as George F. Runnice's "Building a Railroad in China" (April 2, 1910), John L. Cowan's "Potash from Seaweeds" (October 12, 1912), and Dennis H. Stovall's "Sending Pictures by Telegraphs" (October 19, 1912). A sense of nationalism—what some might call imperialism—was evidenced in articles dealing with Latin American countries. In "Punishing a Bully and Saving a Rich State for the World's Good," H. F. Cable wrote, concerning intervention in Nicaraugua, "This is, of course, but one step forward to the time when the United States will indirectly control all that lies between us and our great Isthmus of Panama."[3] In "Our Conflict with Mexico Explained by the Character of Its People," R. H. Little compared the Mexicans to naughty children requiring punishment for insulting our people, our navy, and our flag.[4]

Foreign lands often received better press in *The Boys' World*, which devoted many articles to geography and some to foreign cultures. However, the largest category of articles was that which presented role models for the young readers to emulate. J. L. Harbour wrote many of these biographical sketches, such as "Up from the Ranks" (January 15, 1910), the rags-to-riches success story of railroad man W. C. Brown; and "A Great Master of Electricity" (January 7, 1911), the educational growth of Professor Charles Steinmetz.

Regular columns provided continuity for *The Boys' World*. "Science for Boys" weekly explained a Bible lesson through the workings of nature and then commented on areas of science popular with boys, such as botany and astronomy. "Athletics" proposed to promote fair play and improvement both in sports training and participation. "Some Brave Deeds" and "Some Successful Boys" honored contemporary teens who exemplified the ideals of *The Boys' World*. "Boys Clubs" filled in details on secular and religious organizations; beginning in 1914, "What Working Classes Are Doing," a column by Henrietta Heron, the editor of *Young Men's Class Weekly*, printed pictures and letters updating what Sunday school classes were doing throughout America for community and self-improvement. "Kinks and Quirks" provided a weekly puzzle corner; "This and That," a weekly potpourri with tidbits about geography, natural science, and current news. The letters column, "The Round Table," gave prizes for the best letters submitted, and, as in *The Girls' Companion*, the last page of each issue included a summary of the main truths of the International Lesson Series and the Joint Diocesan Series, two Sunday school Bible study plans. Similarly, it presented Bible quotes with homilies from a variety of junior religious societies. Between one and two pages of each issue were devoted to advertisements.

In December 1913 David C. Cook, Jr. (also known as David Charles Cook), joined the editorial staff, and subtle changes could be seen in the periodical's editorial policy. Perhaps influenced by the popularity of more secular boy's magazines, stories with detectives and smugglers made appearances, but the underlying Christian moral message remained the same. If reports in the periodical itself can be relied on, by February 1914 over half a million boys read weekly this "first and only really and exclusively boys' Sunday School paper published."[5] *The Boys' World* continued in publication until April 24, 1949, when it and *The Girls' Companion* were merged into a new publication, *Sunday Pix*, with a circulation that would climb well past the million mark. In 1968 *Sunday Pix* converted to *Bible-in-Life-Pix*, a periodical still in existence.

Notes

1. David C. Cook, Jr., *How to Write Stories for Boys* (Elgin, Ill.: David C. Cook Publishing Co., 1914), 6.
2. Ibid.
3. H. F. Cable, "Punishing a Bully and Saving a Rich State for the World's Good," *The Boys' World*, January 8, 1910, p. 3.
4. R. H. Little, "Our Conflict with Mexico Explained by the Character of its People," ibid., May 23, 1914, p. 2.
5. *The Boys' World*, February 21, 1914, p. 1.

Information Sources

BIBLIOGRAPHY
None.
INDEX SOURCES
None.
LOCATION SOURCES
Bound vols. 1-4 are in the New York City Public Library. Bound vols. 9-13 are in the Library of Congress. A more complete collection is in the private archives of the David C. Cook Publishing Co., Elgin, Il.

Publication History

MAGAZINE TITLE AND TITLE CHANGES
The Boys' World (1902-1949).
VOLUME AND ISSUE DATA
(vol. 1, no. 1-vol. 48, no. 17).
PUBLISHER AND PLACE OF PUBLICATION
David C. Cook Publishing Co., Elgin, Il. (1902-1949).

EDITOR
David Caleb Cook (1902-1927); David Charles Cook (1927-1932).

Scot Guenter

THE BROWNIES' BOOK

The Crisis, the very successful magazine of the National Association for the Advancement of Colored People, had by 1919 reached a circulation of more than 100,000. It was in that year that W.E.B. Du Bois, historian, sociologist, political activist, and editor of *The Crisis*, joined with Augustus Granville Dill, the magazine's business manager, to publish a periodical for children entitled *The Brownies' Book*. Since 1910 *The Crisis* had produced an annual *Children's Crisis*, which featured stories, poems, and illustrations of special interest to black young people; this annual was "easily the most popular number of the year."[1] *The Brownies' Book*, an heir to this publication, was printed monthly from January 1920 through December 1921. Du Bois "conducted" the magazine; Dill served as business manager; and Jessie Redmon Fauset, literary editor of the parent publication, also served as literary editor of the juvenile periodical. Du Bois, Dill, and Fauset had more in common than their involvement in the NAACP—all were Ivy League-educated blacks attracted by a classical intellectual tradition,[2] but repelled by the racism that culture often fostered.[3]

In the October 1919 issue of *The Crisis*, Du Bois announced the forthcoming publication of the children's magazine for "The True Brownies." Although he believed that the adult monthly must accurately report the horrors perpetrated against blacks, he worried about the cynicism and anger these isolated truths might engender in young people. For the readers of *The Crisis* he articulated this dilemma: "To educate (children) in human hatred is more disasterous to them than to be hated; to seek to raise them in ignorance of their racial identity and peculiar situation is inadvisable—impossible." Du Bois saw but one alternative—to publish thereafter a "little magazine" that "would be a thing of Joy and Beauty, dealing in Happiness, Laughter and Emulation...designed especially for the Children of the Sun."

It will seek to teach Universal Love and Brotherhood for all little folk—black and brown and yellow and white.
Of course, pictures, puzzles, stories, letters from little ones, clubs, games and oh—everything!
Deftly intertwined with this mission of entertainment will go the endeavor:
(a) To make colored children realize that being "colored" is a normal, beautiful thing.
(b) To make them familiar with the history and achievements of the Negro race.

(c) To make them know that other colored children have grown into beautiful, useful and famous persons.

(d) To teach them delicately a code of honor and action in their relations with white children.

(e) To turn their little hurts and resentments into emulation, ambition and love of their own homes and companions.

(f) To point out the best amusements and joys and worth-while things of life.

(g) To inspire them to prepare for definite occupations and duties with a broad spirit of sacrifice.[4]

The magazine sold for 15¢ a copy or $1.50 a year. It was printed on good quality paper, and each issue used a thirty-two-page format.[5] The cover usually featured a seasonal sketch. This was followed by a frontispiece, a full-page photograph of a black child or an example of black art, that gave a realistic attention to the black experience that line drawings simply could not achieve. In fact, most issues of *The Brownies' Book* contained seven or eight pages of photographs—pictures of black children in a variety of national and international settings, snapshots of graduating students, club members, listeners at a story hour, beautiful black babies, as well as an occasional photo of a more famous contributor to black culture.

Generally, stories and poems in *The Brownies' Book* used a literary style familiar to readers of *St. Nicholas** and *The Youth's Companion.**[6] Although main characters were usually black or brown, a variety of settings, class affiliations, and emotional predicaments were presented. The fiction clearly reflected an appreciation of cultural pluralism; racial and sexual stereotyping was conscientiously avoided. The magazine contained stories in which a white character could be substituted for the black protagonist, as well as stories that definitely focused on the experiences and meaning of being "colored." Fiction highlighting animal characters, traditional Indian legends, African myths, and Hispanic tales appeared regularly. Humor figured significantly throughout the juvenile periodical as topics such as a child's search for racial identity were playfully addressed in story or poem. Frequent contributors to the magazine included Hilda Rue Wilkinson, Marcellus Hawkins, Laura Wheeler, A. O. Stafford, Augusta Bird, Peggy Poe, and other authors and illustrators recognizable to readers of *The Crisis*. The works of Mary Effie Lee, Yetta K. Stoddard, Annette C. Browne, and Bertie Lee Hall appeared regularly. Langston Hughes and Pocahontas Foster, still high school students, were first published in *The Brownies' Book*. More than 90 percent of the contributors were black.

One piece of nonfiction was generally included in each issue—stories on nutrition (February 1920) and the Girl Reserves (January 1921), for example. Advertisements were reserved for the back flap and were usually limited to special offers for agents and/or subscribers. In the January 20, 1921, issue circulation was described as "less than 5000 copies per month. In order to keep the magazine at its present high standard—as we are determined to do—we must have at once 12,000 subscribers.''[7] Apparently, this goal was never reached. Du Bois and Dill also used the back flap to advertise "Books for the Children's Library," which they published; they included *The Complete Poems of Paul Laurence Dunbar*, Mary Ovington White's *Hazel*, and Du Bois's *History of the Negro*.

Another regular feature, a two-page current-events section, "As the Crow Flies,"[8] was written by Du Bois himself. Here, in the persona of a proud and lovely black bird (I like my black feathers, don't you?), he flew across the world commenting on oppression, rebellion, and his hopes for a more just and peaceful planet. Not only did Du Bois describe a history and political philosophy not evident in the popular press, but he made unsubtle and uncompromising comments about items given considerable media coverage elsewhere. For instance, before explaining to his readers the platforms set forth at the 1920 Republican and Democratic conventions, he quipped: "Will you believe it, I found my dear United States quite torn up because of two meetings, one in Chicago and one in San Francisco. They were not very important meetings because neither of them was seriously interested in questions of Work and Bread and Butter and Justice and Joy which are the things which really matter.''[9] Elsewhere he detailed the human and financial costs of war, publicized strikes, and chided young readers to remember the hungry and deprived peoples of the world. Du Bois's view of communism was clearly at odds with that found in other children's magazines of the day. In describing a "new kind" of Soviet government he wrote: "In this government the working people have all the power. Nobody can vote who does not work. Other nations declare that the Russian workers have been tyrants and have killed many of the rich and well to do. This is denied by the Russian workers.''[10]

Du Bois's black perspective is also evident in his reportage. For example, in a brief note on the death of William Dean Howells, Du Bois remembered the literary critic as one of the first to give Paul Laurence Dunbar recognition (June 1920).

Clearly, Du Bois wanted his readers to share the perspective of and be moved to action by "the crow." At one point he lamented: "There is no place like home—none, none so good and none so bad: good because it belongs to us; bad because it is Ours to make better and this means Work and Eyesight. I, the crow, am Eyesight. I am Eyes. I see!''*[11] In this column Du Bois used a voice and presented a message that was serious and substantive. He saw his audience as interested in world affairs, capable of understanding their import, and (eventually) responsible for the betterment of the human condition. He also saw the importance of sharing with "the true brownies" the joys and disappointments of his own fight for justice.

Another column in *The Brownies' Book*, "The Judge," was apparently written by Jessie Fauset.[12] In this section a kindly, wise guardian of the law engaged a fictional family in discussions about childrearing. The importance of choice was a recurrent concern. When faced with the choice of how to spend a dollar, the Judge suggested to children that they consider "which is best for me, for mother, for the family, for my people, for the world."[13] Elsewhere, the Judge responded to a fictional child who complained of the humiliation of being whipped. The magistrate explained the inequities apparent in the parent-child relationship and concluded: "If you are trained when you are little not to overdo, then you may grow up to live a sane, temperate, well-balanced and efficient life."[14] But in the next month's column the Judge reconsidered. He declared that his heart wasn't in the last lecture about whippings and instead he wished to give parents "a piece of my mind."

> ...a regular use of continuous blows will not make men or women of your children. This is a world full of sorrows, and the sorrows of your children, although they may seem trivial to you, are just as tragic to them as any of your own. When therefore you increase their sorrows, do it with Thought and Object.
> ...What you want to do is to strengthen, not weaken your children; make them serious, not frivolous; make them thoughtful, not rattle-brained.[15]

In support, the fictional child added, "After-all, there's nothing in the world but feeling, is there Judge?" The Judge replied, "I don't know. That is a vast question."[16]

In other columns the Judge provided reading lists (July 1920), weighted heavily toward the European classics; suggested a philosophy of wealth (February 1921); and commented on the value of writing clearly (May 1920). It was in the Judge's column that the failure of The Brownies' Book was finally announced.

As "The Judge" was the voice of the Editorial Board, "The Jury," another regular feature, voiced the opinions of readers by printing letters from subscribers. Readers seemed to view the magazine as a community journal and expressed their appreciation for the kind of company it provided. A fifteen-year-old boy from Charlottesville, Virginia, complained that his town is too small and he "longs for larger things. It's killing me."[17] Another child from Toronto wanted to know about black libraries and expressed his hopes of going to Africa someday (March 1920). Frequently, photographs of readers were presented in this section. Similar snapshots were printed in another department called "Little People of the Month," which described the achievements of various "Brownie" readers.

The "Grown-Ups Corner," another regular feature, provided further justification for the existence of The Brownies' Book. Not only did adults write to celebrate the fine quality of the journal, but they also appeared to see it as fulfilling a real need. A mother from New York City wrote: "My little girl has been studying about Betsy Ross and George Washington and the others, and she says 'Mama, didn't colored folks do anything?' When I tell her as much as I know about our folks she says: 'Well, that's just stories, Didn't they ever do anything in a book?'"[18]

Perhaps in response to similar comments, each issue of *The Brownies' Book* contained a biography of a famous black; the name of each highlighted figure was followed by the subtitle "A True Story." These sketches included diverse figures such as Katy Ferguson (January 1920), Sojourner Truth (April 1920), Toussant L'Ouverture (May 1920), Phyllis Wheatley (August 1920), Frederick Douglass (September 1920), Samuel Coleridge-Taylor (December 1920), Alexander Dumas (January 1921), and Denmark Vesey (February 1921).

Another regular department, "Playtime," like the biographies, was edited by guest columnists. Directions for Mexican and Scandinavian games, reading games, and family entertainment were presented in detail. Again, the ideology of the editors found concrete expression here—play is an activity *all* children enjoy, and that as individuals, families, and communities, readers will be enriched by the sharing of play experiences.

Although the creators of *The Brownies' Book* might well be accused of propagandizing, I suspect this criticism would have been warmly received. In a speech presented to the NAACP in 1926, Du Bois addressed this issue as he explained his passion for publishing.

> I stand in utter shamelessness and say that whatever art I have for writing has always been used for propaganda and for gaining the right of black folk to love and enjoy.... I do not care a damn for any art that is not used as propaganda. The apostle of Beauty thus becomes the apostle of Truth and Right, not by choice but by inner and outer compulsion.... If a colored man wants to publish a book, he has to get a white publisher and a white newspaper to say it's great; and then you and I can say so. We must come to a place where a work of art when it appears is reviewed and acclaimed by our own free and unfettered judgment.[19]

Thus even as Du Bois and Dill announced the discontinuance of the little magazine, their regret must have been mingled with satisfaction. "The fault has not been with our readers. We have had an unusually enthusiastic set of subscribers. But the magazine was begun just at the time of industrial depression following the war, and the fault of our suspension therefore is rather in the times, which are so out of joint, than in our constituency."[20]

In sum, *The Brownies' Book* gave to black children a visibility, literature, political philosophy, and direction nowhere apparent in other juvenile periodicals, past or present.

Notes

1. *The Crisis*, October 1919, p. 285.
2. Du Bois graduated from Fisk in 1888 and received an undergraduate degree cum laude from Harvard in 1890. He spent 1892 in Germany studying at the University of Berlin and then returned to Harvard, where his doctorate was awarded in 1895. Dill, a student of Du Bois's, received a B.A. from Harvard in 1908. Jessie Fauset was a Phi

Beta Kappa graduate of Cornell with postgraduate work at the University of Pennsylvania and the Sorbonne.

3. For a penetrating discussion of how this conflict was actualized in Du Bois's life, see Arnold Rampersad, *The Art and Imagination of W.E.B. Du Bois* (Cambridge: Harvard University Press, 1976).

4. *The Crisis*, October 1919, p. 285.

5. As stated earlier, the first issue of *The Brownies' Book* was published in January 1920. Du Bois's anticipated November 1919 publication date was delayed by a printer's strike.

6. Although the issue of dialect rarely arose, the editor's attitude toward nonstandard English seems to be summarized in the following excerpt from a biography of Sojourner Truth (April 1920): "Being uneducated she spoke in a dialect or broken English, which I shall not attempt to reproduce here, though her speech, evidently, lost nothing by its use."

7. *The Brownies' Book* 2 (January 1921), back cover.

8. After the demise of *The Brownies' Book*, the crow occasionally reappeared in the pages of *The Crisis*.

9. *The Brownies' Book* 1 (July 1920), 235.

10. Ibid., 1 (May 1920), 159.

11. Ibid., 1 (October 1920), 320.

12. Elinor Desverney Sinette, "The Brownies' Book: A Pioneer Publication for Children," *Freedomways* 5 (Winter 1965). 139-40.

13. *The Brownies' Book* 1 (January 1920), 12.

14. Ibid., 1 (February 1920), 51.

15. Ibid., 1 (March 1920), 81.

16. Ibid.

17. Ibid., 1 (April 1920), 5.

18. Ibid., 1 (February 1920), 45.

19. B. Joyce Ross, ed., *J. E. Spingarn and the N.A.A.C.P.*, Studies in American Negro Life (New York: Antheneum, 1972).

20. *The Brownies' Book*, 2 (December 1921), 354.

Information Sources

BIBLIOGRAPHY
Elinor D. Sinnette, "The Brownies' Book: A Pioneer Publication for Children," *Free-
domways* 5 (Winter 1965), 133-42.
INDEX SOURCES
None.
LOCATION SOURCES
Bound volumes are in the Schomberg Collection of the New York Public Library. Mi-
crofilm copies are available from Greenwood Press, Westport, Conn. Herbert
Aptheker, ed., *Selections from the Brownies' Book* (Millwood, N.Y.: Kraus-
Thomson Organization, 1980), includes complete reprints of "As the Crow Flies"
and "Taboo," an essay by Du Bois printed in the May 1921 issue. Du Bois's
fiction from *The Brownies' Book* will be included in another volume of the Ap-
theker series.

Publication History

MAGAZINE TITLE AND TITLE CHANGES
The Brownies' Book (1920-1921).
VOLUME AND ISSUE DATA
The Brownies' Book (vol. 1, no. 1-vol. 2, no. 12).
PUBLISHER AND PLACE OF PUBLICATION
Du Bois and Dill Publishers, New York (1920-1921).
EDITOR
W. E. Burghardt Du Bois (1920-1921).

E. Wendy Saul

BURKE'S WEEKLY FOR BOYS AND GIRLS

Two brothers were responsible for the publication of *Burke's Weekly for Boys and Girls* as well as its successor, *Burke's Magazine for Boys and Girls*. Thomas A. Burke served as editor of the papers printed on the presses of J. W. Burke & Co. in Macon, Georgia. The men must have begun the enterprise with high hopes. In the first issue, July 6, 1867, an editorial sounds a note of confidence and optimism: "We promised the boys and girls of the South the handsomest and best juvenile paper published in this country, and we think we have kept our word. As far as *looks* are concerned, we think that the point will be conceded at once. . . . We are proud, too, of our table of contents."[1] The heading, which the editor described as "peculiarly beautiful and appropriate," is an engraving, with the periodical's title displayed on an outdoor scene dominated by figures of a boy and girl reading a paper.[2]

An aggressive subscription campaign is signaled in the initial issue. The "boys and girls" are urged to send in "long lists of subscribers," with the promise that once these subcriptions are received, *Burke's Weekly* will be "just as good a paper as you can ask for."[3] Although the cost of a single subscription is $2, clubbing is encouraged; in fact, those ordering as a group need not receive their papers at one post office. Finally, premiums are offered to those readers obtaining subscriptions, and more than half a column is devoted to explaining related policies and procedures. Readers are told that they may find descriptions of the premiums in the advertising columns of the paper and in a catalog, which contains "*a list of the very best Juvenile books published in this country.*"[4]

Editorial remarks introducing "Our Letter Bag," a column devoted to letters from readers, suggest that a prospectus for the paper had been published earlier in other periodicals. Here, too, is additional evidence of the buoyant spirit in which the publication of *Burke's Weekly* began: "Letters have come to us from half a dozen States, assuring us that the boys and girls are delighted with the idea of a Weekly of their own, and will send us scores of subscribers. Indeed, the number already received has far exceeded our expectations."[5] Extracts from letters follow these remarks, with a concluding observation that they are but a few of the many letters received from "little friends."

The principal feature of this first issue of *Burke's Weekly* is the opening chapter of Rev. Francis Robert Goulding's "Marooner's Island; or Dr. Gordon in Search of His Children." The serial is a sequel to Goulding's *Robert and Harold; or The Young Marooners on the Florida Coast*, an "immensely popular book going through more than ten editions in America and England, as well as being translated into several foreign languages."[6]

"Marooner's Island" ran throughout the first year and into the second year of the paper's publication. It recounts Dr. Charles Gordon's efforts to find four children, whose small boat had been "dragged seawards" from Tampa Bay by a devilfish, "one of the most powerful and most dreaded monsters of the deep."[7] The action of the plot is repeatedly interrupted by digressions in which Dr. Gordon instructs the other members of the search party on a wide variety of subjects, for example, mangroves, palmettos, gannets, and mosquitoes. In addition, each member of the party is invited to relate the circumstances of his life. Although a contemporary reader finds the digressions unacceptable, the editor considered them part of the intrinsic value of the work. In the December 19, 1868, issue he praised Goulding's works for their instruction and amusement and announced that readers could look forward to another serial by the same author: "Sal-o-qua; or Boy-life Among the Indians" would begin with the first issue of 1869.

In contrast to Goulding's slow-moving stories are those of John Crittendon Duval, described as "The Father of Texas Literature" by J. Frank Dobie.[8] The story "Jack Dobell; or A Boy's Adventures in Texas" runs serially in *Burke's Weekly* from August 10, 1867, to March 7, 1868. Two weeks before publication of the first installment, the editor described the story as "one of the most thrilling...it has ever been our good fortune to read";[9] and in the issue of December 21, 1867, as one that compares favorably with Mayne Reid's best stories. Letters from readers echoed this appreciation of Duval's fast-paced stories of high adventure, and the editor responded to the readers' interest by publishing more Duval. The third volume includes two of the author's stories: "The Adventures of Big-Foot Wallace, the Texas Ranger and Hunter" and "A Hunt on the Wakulla; or Jack Dobell in Florida." Although the fourth volume of *Burke's Weekly* is not available for examination, in the first and only volume of *Burke's Magazine for Boys and Girls* appear two other Duval serials: the concluding installments of "The Young Explorers; or Boy-Life in Texas" and the entirety of "The Indians at Dirt Dauber's Nest: A Tale of the Seminoles."

Burke's Weekly also offers its readers serials that might be classified as domestic fiction, although the plots are often all but lost among the lessons and other digressions. Three of them that prove particularly interesting reflect their authors' perceptions of the South in the nineteenth century. "Ellen Hunter: A Story of War," written under the pseudonym of Byrd Lyttle, appears in the first volume. Its purpose, according to the author, is to depict for young readers the circumstances surrounding the Civil War. Mrs. S. E. Peck's "Lillian Lisle; or Life at the Old Farm House," which runs for thirty-five installments in the second and third volumes, is filled with instructions for keeping house. In fact, the story is dedicated to "those little girls, who, reared in affluence, are now compelled to assist their mothers in household work."[10] Published in these same volumes is "Mountain Hall: A Story of the Old Dominion," written by Rev. Thomas Ward White under the pseudonym Philip Barrett. This serial, which is still incomplete at the conclusion of the third volume, is set in antebellum Virginia.

Stories of adventure and domesticity are not the only kinds to run serially in the Burkes' papers. Fantasy in the form of fairy tales is often published in this manner. In the first issue of *Burke's Weekly* appears a chapter of "The Little Woman in Green" by Theodosia Ford, a frequent contributor who is identified as the headmistress of a school of "young ladies."[11] This is the story of Ellie, a child whose kindness is rewarded by visits to Fairyland, where "only the pure, the loving, the true," can go.[12] She travels to meet the Queen of Fairyland on the wings of the little women, whom she and her ill-tempered sister Mary first meet as they walk home from school.

Poetry is another genre well represented throughout the issues of *Burke's Weekly* and *Burke's Magazine*. The subjects treated cover a wide range, but the activities of children and animals are favorite topics, frequently embellished with moral instruction. The verses are at times unsigned, but the lack of a signature does not necessarily mean that the poet is unknown; indeed, the authors of a few poems can be readily identified. Many of the verses, however, are acknowledged: some with the names of forgotten versifiers but others with those of recognized poets. The poetry of southerners such as Paul Hamilton Hayne, Margaret Junkin Preston, Francis Orray Ticknor, and Mary Harris Ware is represented in the papers as is that of William Blake, Alfred Tennyson, George McDonald, and William Cullen Bryant.

Burke's Weekly and *Burke's Magazine* are both generous in their publication of expository articles, with many offered serially. Typical is the first in a series of "Biographical Sketches" that is printed in the initial issue of *Burke's Weekly*. There are recounted the exploits of Serg. William Jasper, a Revolutionary War hero. It is in the use of this genre that the change in the character of the paper is most apparent during its second year of publication. During this time many columns are devoted to long-running series with titles such as "Trades and Professions of Animals, Birds and Insects" and "Biographies of Ancient Persons: For Young Folks." Less material is directed toward readers under the age of nine or ten. "Our Chimney Corner," the page reserved for riddles, conundrums, enigmas, and other puzzles, remains intact, but the brief stories obviously designed for young children appear infrequently. In the February 13, 1869, issue the editor observed that although he received letters, not many of them were from these younger readers. The assignment of a page, "Our Little Folks," to the younger readers, beginning on February 27, 1869, may have been an attempt to encourage this segment of the paper's audience. Furthermore, the choice of material for the third volume, which begins with the July 3, 1869, issue also reflects a fresh awareness of this same group of readers.

Exactly why the Burkes changed their periodical from a weekly to a monthly is unknown; certainly, the reasons must have been discussed in the last issue or issues of *Burke's Weekly*. Early evidence that the paper had frequent financial concerns, if not serious problems, may be inferred from its aggressive subscription campaigns as well as the editor's defense (January 2, 1869) of the subscription rate. Moreover, in the issue of February 19, 1870—more than halfway through the third volume—the editor stated frankly that the periodical was "not yet a source of profit to its publishers."[13]

Whatever the circumstances, *Burke's Magazine for Boys and Girls* began publication as a forty-eight-page monthly in January 1871. Its contents were little different from those of the second volume of *Burke's Weekly*. One notable offering not previously mentioned is "Pictures from Froissart" by Paul Hamilton Hayne. The publication of these sketches, begun in *The Riverside Magazine for Young People*,* was taken up by the Burkes after the Boston periodical ceased publication. Another feature worth noting is "Fireside Amusements," a series of articles discussing games and their rules. The first five installments contain material "adapted from an English work," and the last six further develop the original purpose.[14] Of interest, too, are the appearances of several brief stories by Annie Maria Barnes, a writer who would later edit a children's paper of her own: the *Acanthus*.

The publication of the juvenile paper was abandoned with the December 1871 issue. On the last page appears the evidence that the ending was bitter: "For three years and a half, we have striven to give the boys and girls of the South a periodical of their own. We thought such a publication was needed, and would meet with a cordial support. We were mistaken. Either Southern boys and girls do not want a Southern juvenile publication, or we have not succeeded in making one to their liking."[15]

After so confident a beginning, why did the papers or paper fail? It would seem that a periodical publishing a wealth of prose and poetry and countless engravings would enjoy success. In his autobiography John Burke stated that the paper, "pronounced on all hands to have been one of the best papers for young folks ever published," ceased publication "for want of patronage."[16] Perhaps the periodical's seeming inability to define clearly its audience is in some way related to this lack of subscribers. However, back of the paper's inherent problems were difficulties related to the times in which the Burkes introduced their juvenile paper. At the close of the Civil War a disrupted economy was a major obstacle to "normal publishing" in the South. Furthermore, circulation of the paper, largely dependent on the postal service, was often hindered because of late or lost mail.[17] Thomas Burke would certainly have attributed some of his problems to the siren call of the northern press, which he castigated on his editoral pages more than once.

The Burkes were not without experience. Before the war Thomas Burke had edited and published *Horn of Mirth* (1849-1850), "a humorous monthly"; and with his brother, the *Mistletoe: A Magazine of the Sons of Temperance* (1849), a short-lived publication dedicated to temperance and the arts and sciences.[18] In addition, according to his brother's autobiography, he had edited the *Augusta Evening News* and the *Savannah News*.[19] As for John Burke, who was a Methodist minister, he became the publisher for the Methodist Episcopal Church, South, and according to one source, he served for a time as the "public printer for the state of Georgia."[20]

Notes

1. *Burke's Weekly for Boys and Girls*, July 6, 1867, p. 4.
2. Ibid.
3. Ibid.
4. Ibid.
5. Ibid., p. 5.
6. Robert M. Willingham, Jr., "Francis Robert Goulding," in *Southern Writers: A Biographical Dictionary*, ed. Robert Bain et al. (Baton Rouge: Louisiana State University Press, 1979), 185-86.
7. *Burke's Weekly for Boys and Girls*, July 6, 1867, p. 1.
8. John C. Duval, *The Adventures of Big-Foot Wallace*, ed. Mabel Major and Rebecca S. Lee (Lincoln, Nebr.: University of Nebraska Press, 1936), xxx.
9. *Burke's Weekly for Boys and Girls*, July 27, 1867, p. 29.
10. Ibid., February 2, 1869, p. 249.
11. Ibid., August 3, 1867, p. 36.
12. Ibid., July 13, 1867, p. 15.
13. Ibid., February 19, 1870, p. 268.
14. *Burke's Magazine for Boys and Girls* 1 (February 1871), 62.
15. Ibid., 1 (December 1871), 572.
16. John William Burke, *Autobiography: Chapters from the Life of a Preacher* (Macon, Ga.: J. W. Burke & Co., 1884), 148.
17. Louis T. Griffith and John E. Talmadge, *Georgia Journalism: 1763-1950* (Athens, Ga.: University of Georgia Press, 1951), 90-92. Griffith and Talmadge discussed several problems editors and publishers faced immediately after the Civil War, including closed post offices. Thomas A. Burke finally called upon his readers to send their subscriptions by registered mail.
18. Bertram H. Flanders, *Early Georgia Magazines: Literary Periodicals to 1865* (Athens, Ga.: University of Georgia Press, 1944), 108-11.
19. Burke, *Autobiography*, p. 148.
20. Flanders, *Early Georgia Magazines*, p. 109; and "Burke, John William," *Herringshaw's Encyclopedia of American Biography of the Nineteenth Century*, 1907.

Information Sources

BIBLIOGRAPHY

"Burke, John William." *Herringshaw's Encyclopedia of American Biography of the Nineteenth Century*, 1907; John William Burke, *Autobiography: Chapters from the Life of a Preacher* (Macon, Ga.: J. W. Burke & Co., 1884); John C. Duval,

The Adventures of Big-Foot Wallace, ed. Mabel Major and Rebecca S. Lee (Lincoln, Nebr.: University of Nebraska Press, 1936); Bertram H. Flanders, *Early Georgia Magazines: Literary Periodicals to 1865* (Athens, Ga.: University of Georgia Press, 1944); Louis T. Griffith and John E. Talmadge, *Georgia Journalism: 1763-1950* (Athens, Ga.: University of Georgia Press, 1951); Robert M. Willingham, Jr., "Francis Robert Goulding," in *Southern Writers: A Biographical Dictionary*, ed. Robert Bain et al. (Baton Rouge: Louisiana State University Press, 1979).

INDEX SOURCES
None.
LOCATION SOURCES
Scattered issues are in libraries noted in the *Union List of Serials in Libraries of the United States and Canada*. The University of Georgia Libraries, Athens, Ga., has vols. 1-2 of *Burke's Weekly for Boys and Girls* and vol. 1 of *Burke's Magazine for Boys and Girls*; the Atlanta Public Library and the Middle Georgia Library, Macon, Ga., have vol. 1 of *Burke's Weekly for Boys and Girls*; and the Ina Dillard Russell Library of Georgia College, Milledgeville, Ga., has vols. 2-3 of *Burke's Weekly for Boys and Girls*.

Publication History

MAGAZINE TITLE AND TITLE CHANGES
Burke's Weekly for Boys and Girls (July 6, 1867-December 24, 1870); *Burke's Magazine for Boys and Girls* (1871).
VOLUME AND ISSUE DATA
Burke's Weekly for Boys and Girls (vol. 1, no.1-vol. 4, no. ?); *Burke's Magazine for Boys and Girls* (vol. 1, no. 1-vol. 1, no. 12).
PUBLISHER AND PLACE OF PUBLICATION
J. W. Burke & Co., Macon, Ga. (1867-1871).
EDITOR
Thomas A. Burke (1867-1871).

Lalla N. Overby

C

CHILD-GARDEN OF STORY, SONG AND PLAY

Child-Garden of Story, Song and Play was begun as a publication of the Kindergarten Literature Company of Chicago in 1892 and was edited by Andrea Hofer Proudfoot and her sister Amalie Hofer. It promoted the Froebellian kindergarten movement in the United States. The Froebellians believed that children learn by doing. Play is the most valuable form of self-expression, and early educational experiences should help to develop all aspects of the child. The mother and the home are very important in the education of the young. Trained kindergartners helped mothers work with their children in early educational experiences. Programs in some of the early kindergartens were for children through the ages of seven or eight with summer programs of nature study and other activities for children as old as twelve.

In June 1900 *Child-Garden* became the national organ of the League of American Mothers, organized by Proudfoot to "promote the best interests of childhood by helping to develop and encourage in mothers those attributes which are highest and sweetest and best in their natures."[1] The league was identified closely with the Froebellians and continued to promote the kindergarten concept.

Each monthly issue of *Child-Garden* had a section for the children and a section for the mothers. The periodical was designed for white middle- and upper-class families. This slant was evident in both sections of the periodical.

"Elsie's Hard Time" (June 1901) is representative of the realistic fiction found in *Child-Garden*. Elsie is bored until her mother finds a project for her to do that encourages her to think of someone less fortunate than she is. Even the fantasy was written to present a virtue or an appreciation of nature. In "The

Sunbeam Fairies'' by Myrtle L. Champlin (June 1901) children learned the virtue of service to others as well as an appreciation for clouds and sunsets.

Although the realistic fiction was generally didactic, it was also very ethnocentric. People of non-WASP middle- and upper-class backgrounds were depicted in stereotyped, usually derogatory fashion. The Eskimos in "Allen's Trip with Jack Frost" by Ella Scatterday (December 1900) "are very ignorant, and live in miserable little, dirty houses made of ice and snow. They ride on sleds and have dogs to pull them about.''[2] A two-part story by Margaret W. Arnold, "The Picaninny" (March and April 1901), depicted Rasmus and the other black cotton plantation workers as "busy, happy-hearted negroes."[3] Semiliterate dialect was used when the Negroes were talking, although standard English was used throughout the rest of the story.

No violent stories, including folktales, were included in *Child-Garden*. Proudfoot, the editor, believed that these stories were harmful to the proper development of children.

Poetry was also chosen for its ability to convey the didactic message or was about subjects such as fairies, the seasons, nature, and other topics considered suitable for young readers. Appreciation for nature, hard work, and home life were recurring themes.

Authors were sometimes named at the end of their works. Some regular contributors were designated by their initials; other works, especially fiction, did not provide the names of authors. Illustrations were included for some titles and ranged from small sketches to full-page illustrations.

Some issues contained songs that were used in the kindergartens. They included the musical score as well as the lyrics. Each issue also featured a section where children's original stories and poems were published. Contributors for this section ranged in age from about four or five to twelve or thirteen. They were signed with the child's name and age.

In the section aimed at mothers, Elsa Hofer Schreiber's column "What We Do in Kindergarten" presented information about the month's kindergartner programs and gave suggestions for follow-up at home. This column was later edited by other kindergartners and was entitled "Froebellian School Primary Work." Lessons and activities were discussed in detail and included topics such as the principle underlying the work, artwork, domestic science, work in geography, number work, and nature study.

After *Child-Garden* became the official publication of the League of American Mothers, this section contained articles on home training that Proudfoot said were not to "give set opinions but...to call forth the free discussion of fathers and mothers."[4] A "Monthly Catechism" for parents sharpened the focus of discussion and could be used as part of the program for local mothers' leagues. Many of the issues that were discussed in this column are as relevant today as they were in the early years of the twentieth century as this sample from the December 1900 "Monthly Catechism" shows.

Monthly Catechism

1. Should my child get more Christmas gifts than he can use and esteem?
2. How many should he get?
3. Shall I take the children to the shop to see me buy or help choose?
4. What is the educative value of toys, and what should be my standard in choosing them?
5. What is the value of choosing?
6. Shall my child give Christmas presents, and shall they be bought or made, or both?
7. What idea have I given my child of Santa Claus?
8. How may I use this myth to make the Christmas spirit seem real to my child and still keep it so impersonal that he will not feel defrauded on discovering the delusion?[5]

Proudfoot also provided guidelines for setting up local mother's league chapters to promote on the local level the ideals of the national organization. Local leagues could write to Proudfoot at *Child-Garden*, and these exchanges of letters were frequently printed in *Child-Garden* as examples for other mother's league chapters.

Advertisements in *Child-Garden* were closely monitored by Proudfoot and her editorial staff to eliminate those that "are descriptive of disease or any untoward conditions."[6] These advertisements, which were admittedly more lucrative to the publication, were aimed, according to Proudfoot, at selling useless products to gullible mothers.

Child-Garden was edited from 1892 to May 1896 by Andrea Hofer Proudfoot and Amalie Hofer. From June 1896 until *Child-Garden* ceased publication in 1903 Proudfoot was the sole editor.

Notes

1. Lida H. Hardy, "A Letter from the President of the League of American Mothers," *Child-Garden of Story, Song and Play* 9 (June 1900), 246.
2. *Child-Garden of Story, Song and Play* 9 (June 1900), 5.
3. Ibid., p. 126.
4. Andrea Hofer Proudfoot, "Home Training," ibid., 9 (December 1900), 28.
5. "Monthly Catechism," ibid., p. 29.
6. Andrea Hofer Proudfoot, "Your Reading Time and How to Make the Most of It," ibid., p. 31.

Information Sources

BIBLIOGRAPHY
None.
INDEX SOURCES
None.

LOCATION SOURCES

Minneapolis Public Library and Carnegie Public Library, Pittsburgh, have the most
    extensive holdings. Some bound volumes are in the Library of Congress and other
    university and public libraries.

Publication History

MAGAZINE TITLE AND TITLE CHANGES
Child-Garden of Story, Song and Play (1892-1903).
VOLUME AND ISSUE DATA
Child-Garden of Story, Song and Play (vol. 1, no. 1-vol. 11, no. 7).
PUBLISHER AND PLACE OF PUBLICATION
Kindergarten Literature Company, Chicago (1892-1898); Kindergarten Literature Com-
    pany, Morgan Park, Il. (1898-1903).
EDITOR
Andrea Hofer Proudfoot and Amalie Hofer (1892-1896); Andrea Hofer Proudfoot (1896-
    1903).

Carol J. Veitch

CHILD LIFE

Rand McNally inaugurated *Child Life: The Children's Own Magazine* in a
specimen issue dated December 1921. A stylish sixty-four-page monthly, *Child
Life* was beautifully illustrated, well designed, and well printed on coated paper.
It carried a modest amount of commerical advertising from companies such as
American Flyer (toy trains), John M. Smythe (perhaps Chicago's premier furniture dealer at the time), A. C. McClurg (Chicago publishing house), the Santa
Fe Railroad, and Bradley Knitting Company (makers of children's clothing).
Format and advertising both made clear that *Child Life* was intended for a well-
to-do, cultivated segment of the children's periodical audience, although the cost
of an issue, 25¢, did not make it substantially more expensive than a number
of other literary juveniles of the period. For ten years, *Child Life* remained a
stylish miscellany, deviating little from the format established in the early issues
and notable especially for its beautifully drawn, richly colored covers that must
be reckoned among the best of any American children's periodical. To describe
the cover of the January 22 issue, for example, as depicting a child (not Little
New Year, although the hint is there) setting the hand of a clock whose hours
are marked with the signs of the zodiac is hardly to begin to suggest the charm
and affecting simplicity of the drawing and its strong coloring in red, blue, and
beige.

Under its first editor, Rose Waldo, who served through 1931, *Child Life* offered
features for children from the age of about five to the traditional cut-off age of
fourteen or fifteen. For each issue Rose Waldo wrote a short poem rather than
an editorial column. Even the specimen issue, where the precedent for an editorial
statement is almost universal in American juvenile publishing, she chose to offer
her readers a versified invitation to accompany her to "Child Land": "Our trip's

so full of interest, / So full of earnest thought, / In every land we visit / We
learn just what we ought,'' a sentiment that conjoins the time-honored aims of
pleasure and instruction.[1]

During Waldo's tenure as editor, *Child Life* was organized under a dozen or
so headings. ''Nursery Nuggets'' was exactly what the title suggests: short poems
and stories for very young children. This feature was followed by ''Happiness
Hall'' for older children and consisted typically, too, of a story and poem or
two. In January 1933, for example, ''Happiness Hall'' offered a poem about
frogs and a conventional story-with-a-moral, ''How Billy and Helen Found the
Baby New Year,'' in which two children make their way to the center of a
woods at midnight on New Year's Eve, having been too credulous of an uncle's
teasing. There they find a grouse, nearly frozen in the snow, which they rescue
and bring back to their family, who are thoroughly alarmed by their inexplicable
absence. In terms of structure, rural setting, language, and the lesson learned
by the children, the story could have appeared in any of the quality literary
miscellanies produced for American children from 1870 on.

''Fairy Fancies,'' ''Nature Stories,'' and ''Types of Children'' are other *Child
Life* features, conventional categories for which there was ample precedent in
its nineteenth-century predecessors. ''Common Sense Food for Tiny Tummies,''
however, has a distinctly modern air about it. *Child Life* also devoted a good
deal of space to the arts. ''Little Artists'' presented short articles on famous
painters. ''Rosa Bonheur'' (January 1933) is interesting for the choice of Bonheur
over a more recognizable male artist and reproduced two of her paintings, a
portrait of a lion and ''The Horse Fair.'' ''Plays and Pageants'' reprinted one-
act plays; ''In Film Land'' offered articles on films and Hollywood personalities,
and ''In Music Land'' introduced readers to famous composers or interesting
topics, for example, ''The Music the Colonists Brought to America'' (January
1922). Finally, there was ''Outdoor Sports and Indoor Pastimes,'' which in
January described the game of Fox and Geese, printed the first pattern in a quilt
project that would extend throughout the year, and provided a cut-out toy; and
''Joy Givers Club,'' which was open to readers under age twelve and published
their original creations, either writing or drawings. From time to time, other
features were added and became staple items, for example: ''Our Heroes''; ''Just
Like This,'' a single-page story interspersed with six drawings illustrating moments (''just like this'') in the story; and ''Animated Botany,'' a full-page
drawing, featuring anthropomorphic plants. In May 1922 ''The Forgetful Tulip''
presented a conversation among apple blossoms, tulips, and daffodils, correcting
common human mistakes or misapprehensions: tulips, readers learned, originated
in Persia, not Holland. Virtually all of the material in *Child Life* in the years
under Rose Waldo was written by women, and the magazine's principal readership was doubtless girls. The editor's own contribution to *Child Life* are monthly
poems on her ''Greeting Page.'' ''Fireside Fun'' (November 1922) is typical—
and short enough to be given in full:

Sweet summer is done, and early fall fun;
Now our winter joys begin:
    In the fire light glow
    We are happy, you know,
That Jack Frost drove us in.

It gives us delight on days long and bright
To travel through interesting lands;
    But the joy that is best
    Is in our home nest
Doing work with our busy hands.

And isn't it sweet, when our work is complete,
To bring it to Mother to view,
    Then watch Daddy's eyes
    Open wide with surprise
When he sees the fine things we can do?

It really is true it's what we can do
That makes us more happy than elves,
    And the pleasure we take
    In things that we make
Is the joy of expressing ourselves.[2]

With the December issue of 1931, Rose Waldo left the editorship of *Child Life* and was replaced by Marjorie Barrows, who held the position through 1938. During this period *Child Life* was still published by Rand McNally, but under Barrows's direction a number of important changes were made. *Child Life* began to appear on a cheaper grade of paper, and the quality of its illustrations declined. A different mix of advertising suggests that Barrows and her staff were seeking a somewhat different audience. In addition to World Book Encyclopedia and Corona typewriters (''Do you know...how much a typewriter can help even a six-year old in reading, writing, spelling, and building priceless habits of clear and ordered expression?''[3]), advertisements for household staples predominated: Heinz foods, Kleenex, Lifebuoy soap, Lux, Kellog's cereals, Cream of Wheat, and Phillips' milk of magnesia. Gone now were the old headings such as ''Nursery Nuggets'' and ''Happiness Hall.'' Taking their place were omnibus categories: ''Stories and Poems,'' ''Things-to-Do,'' ''Special Features,'' ''Pages of Special Interest to Parents,'' and ''Read-Aloud Pages'' for the very young children who remained part of the magazine's intended audience. The new activities section, ''Things to Do,'' expanded the section that, in Rose Waldo's day, had included indoor and outdoor activities. A typical issue's activities in the 1930s might include a puzzle (finding the hidden objects in a picture); notices of the pen and pencil club, hobby club, and ''Good Citizens' Leagues''; and a variety of games, stunts, and tricks. For parents (but principally mothers), typical features included the ''Child Life Pantry,'' for example, ''Food for the Run-about,'' that is, the child between the ages of two and four (March 1937); ''The Well-Dressed Child'' by Carolyn T. Radnor-Lewis, who was then managing editor of *Harper's Bazaar*; and ''Mother's Service Bureau,'' which proferred advice on consumer products. In the March 1937 issue, for example, World Book Encyclopedia (''interestingly written,'' ''authoritative'') and ''Baby-Glo'' windows were featured; both firms happened to be long-time advertisers in the pages of *Child Life*. The mother's section also typically included recipes, frequently with an eye on the seasons or holidays, and ''Our Book Friends'' conducted by Muriel Fuller, which briefly reviewed a handful of children's books each month.

In December 1941 Rand McNally relinquished control of the magazine to Child Life, Inc., a company organized by Clayton Holt Ernst. Wilma McFarland, who had replaced Marjorie Barrows as editor in 1939, remained in that position under the new management until 1946. At that time, *Child Life* was still a monthly and still sold for 25¢, but its page count was down to forty-eight, and its contents were arranged under the three headings ''Stories, Poems, and Plays''; ''For You to Do''; and ''Keeping Up with Child Life,'' which included book reviews, children's fashions, brief articles about movies or music or dance, and usually a recipe or two, directed now to the child reader rather than to mothers. Articles about hobbies and collecting continued to appear, and ''The Hollow Tree,'' which reprinted readers' poems and prizewinning letters about trips readers would like to take, continued the practice, begun under Rose Waldo, of publishing children's creative work. During the postwar period a distinctive emphasis on travel appeared in *Child Life*. The June 1947 issue, for example, not only included ''Helen Belkin Takes You on a Tour of New England'' (nine sites, including a covered bridge and the Puritan village at Salem), but an article ''Alice Rogers Hager Tells You About When You Fly,'' which describes in detail what the child passenger would encounter in traveling by air in 1947. (For stay-at-home readers, the same issue provided plans for making a ''Flying Wing'' paper airplane).

Monthly publication of *Child Life* ceased in December 1949; thereafter it was published on a ten-month schedule, which combined June and July, August and September, in two issues. By 1953 *Child Life* numbered forty pages, and the yearly subscription rate was $3. It had become a magazine intended for children under age twelve, with about half of each issue given over to simple activities: solving puzzles, finding hidden objects in a picture, following the dots to fill in a picture, coloring in ''jigsaw'' pictures, and the like. Illustrations, too, were greatly simplified, and the magazine bore little resemblence to its namesake in the 1920s. Under Adelaide Field, who served as editor from 1952 to 1964, *Child Life* was organized in terms of ''Story Time,'' ''Feature Time,'' and ''Playtime.'' ''Feature Time'' consisted of some carryover from earlier days—a letters column, for example, and record and book reviews, as well as jingles and games that frequently overlapped features in ''Playtime.'' By 1962 *Child Life* had much in common with *Highlights for Children*.* Both were intended for the same age group; both by then included brief notations to parents and teachers about the meaning and intention of stories, in particular; and both appeared to lean heavily on experts for editorial assistance. At the end of Adelaide Field's tenure at *Child Life*, separate editors were carried on the masthead for books, science, sports, music, and social science. Later, in the middle 1960s, a "Parent-Teacher Key" reproduced almost exactly the categories employed in *Highlights*. There was the same emphasis, and roughly the same distribution of emphasis, although *Child Life* managed on fewer categories: four levels of reading skills—"Reasoning Skills," "Science," "Creative Skills," and "Appreciation of Wit and Humor." Although *Child Life* was then billed as the "Oldest Continuously Published Independent Children's Magazine in the United States," the continuity lay principally in the title; by November 1966, the last issue published by Child Life, Inc., the magazine had little in common with Rand McNally's elegantly conceived literary miscellany.

From December 1966 to mid-1973 *Child Life* was published by Review Publishing Company. During this time editorial turnover was high, but Beurt R. SerVass and Rita Cooper appear to have been the principal figures managing *Child Life* before August 1973, when the magazine passed to the Saturday Evening Post Company. In their hands, and under new editors, it underwent two substantial changes. In April 1974 it became a sixty-four page, digest-size miscellany, with much the same mix of stories, articles, and activities as before. With the smaller format came dramatic changes—and improvements—in layout and especially illustration. In October 1976 the periodical was again transformed, becoming *Child Life Mystery and Science-Fiction Magazine*. Some continuity remained, however, in a three-fold division between stories, features, and activities and in the retention of long-popular features such as jokes, riddles, and hidden pictures. Also retained was "Tips for Teachers," which continued the practice of advising adults on the use of *Child Life* as a classroom supplement. Since 1980 *Child Life* has been published by the Benjamin Franklin Literary and Medical Society, an Indianapolis organization that has also bought up long-established children's periodicals such as *Jack and Jill** and *Humpty Dumpty's Magazine*.* Its new owners have reduced its size to forty-eight pages and have redirected its emphasis to health-related issues.

Notes

1. *Child Life* 1 (December 1921), 5.
2. Rose Waldo, "Fireside Fun," *Child Life* 1 (November 1922), 659.
3. *Child Life* 16 (March 1937), 127.

Information Sources

BIBLIOGRAPHY
None.
INDEX SOURCES
None.
LOCATION SOURCES

Library of Congress.

Publication History

MAGAZINE TITLE AND TITLE CHANGES
Child Life: The Children's Own Magazine (December 1921-November 1940); *Child Life*
(December 1940-December 1947); *Child Life: The Magazine for Young Children
and Their Mothers* (January 1948-to at least June 1950 [July-August issues not
found]; *Child Life: Stories, Games, Pictures, Puzzles* (December 1950-September
1951); *Child Life* (October 1951-August/September 1976); *Child Life: Mystery
and Science Fiction Magazine* (October 1976 to at least December 1978); *Child
Life: Mystery, Adventure, Science Fiction* (January 1980-May 1980); *Child Life:
Children's Health Publication* [also subtitled *For Twixt and Teen/Incorporating
Young World*] (June-July 1980); *Child Life: Children's Health Publication* (Au-
gust/September 1980-).
VOLUME AND ISSUE DATA
Child Life (vol. 1, no. 1-)
PUBLISHER AND PLACE OF PUBLICATION
Rand McNally, Chicago (December 1921-November 1941); Child Life, Inc., Boston
(December 1941-November 1966); Review Publishing Co., Indianapolis (Decem-
ber 1966-June/July 1973); Curtis Publishing Co., Indianapolis (August/September
1973-December 19, 1978); Benjamin Franklin Literary and Medical Society, In-
dianapolis (January 1980-).
EDITOR
Rose Waldo (1921-1931); Marjorie Barrows (1932-1938); Wilma McFarland (1939-1946);
Janet Newton (January 1947-June 1947); Anne Samson (July 1947-1951): Adelaide
Field (1952-June/July 1964); Beurt R. SerVass (November 1964-August/Septem-
ber 1967); Rita Cooper (October 1967-March 1970); Beurt R. SerVass (April
1970-June/July 1970); Beth Wood Thomas (August/September 1970-April 1971);
Rita A. Cooper (May 1971-June/July 1971); John N. Allen (August/September
1971-December 1971); E. Catherine Cummins (January 1972-February 1972);
John N. Allen (March 1972-August/September 1972); E. Catherine Cummins
(October 1972-August/September 1974); June Norris (October 1974-March 1976);
Peg Rogers (April 1976-at least through December 19, 1978); John D. Craton (at
least from January 1980-).

R. Gordon Kelly

THE CHILDREN'S BOOK OF CHOICE AND ENTERTAINING
READING FOR THE LITTLE FOLKS AT HOME

*The Children's Book of Choice and Entertaining Reading for the Little Folks
at Home* began publication in January 1855 in Nashville, Tennessee, and continued until April 1860. The editors, who were listed only as "Uncle Robin"
and "Aunt Alice" in the first issue, continued to be associated with it until the
final issue, when "Uncle George" (George C. Connor) announced the change
of title to *Youth's Magazine**, under his editorship, beginning with the May
1860 issue. Publisher for both periodicals was Graves & Marks of Nashville.

In "Uncle Robin's Introductory" the purpose of the *Children's Book* was set forth: "to teach and encourage you to cultivate these excellent virtues—to be good, to honor and obey your parents, to make you intelligent that you may become good, great, happy and useful, and therefore honored and respected....The first great step in this whole matter is to teach you to love to read; the second is to provide something useful and entertaining for you to read—good food for little minds."[1]

Another facet of the purpose of the magazine was mentioned by Aunt Alice, writing of herself: "When she looked far away at the children of the Northern States, she saw them with several pretty monthlies, prepared and published, specially and solely to meet their wants; but those of the South and Southwest, as far as she knew, had not one published for them."[2]

During its first year the publication consisted of thirty-two pages an issue, and the subscription price was $1 for the year. In December 1856 the editors begged each reader to secure one new subscription during Christmas week as a New Years gift to the *Book*, because "we cannot afford new and rich pictures unless we have twice as many subscribers."[3] Premiums, consisting of "libraries" (Kriss Kringle's Library, the Little Folk's Library, Parley's Cottage Library, and Youth's Pictorial Library) of varying numbers of titles were offered by Graves & Marks to ministers and teachers securing subscriptions to the *Book*. Few advertisements appeared in the publication: in early editions announcements for Edward H. Fletcher, a New York publisher, were carried, and the back cover of the September 1856 issue gave the "List of Juvenile Books" sold by Graves & Marks Co.

The cover of the *Children's Book* would be considered attractive for its time. It featured a family scene of parents and at least seven children all reading, listening, writing, or being otherwise occupied in intellectual pursuits. In the December 1855 issue a special Christmas scene was prepared for "Uncle Robin's Chapter of Varieties," showing all of the family reading copies of the *Children's Book*.

Several features appeared regularly in the monthly: "Aunt Alice's Chat with Her Nephews and Nieces," which usually consisted of advice on conduct—"be generous to orphans; say a verse of Scripture every morning at the table; value honest labor; idleness is a disgrace and a sin";[4] a story such as "The Unkind Brother" (July 1856); or one whole piece devoted to an alliterative, alphabetical verse (July 1859). "The Newspaper" (edited by Uncle Robin for the little folks) gave excerpts from news stories around the country and was designed to "interest and improve the children." Its contents dealt with the electoral college (December 1856), origins of words (September 1857), a table of the dates of the settlement of the colonies (November 1857), and the "Wild Girl of Wisconsin" who preferred to live in a cave (December 1857). "The Miscellaneous Reading Department" consisted of subjects such as the oldest Bible in the world (August 1855), Poor Richard's Maxims (August 1858), and an easy method for calculating 6 percent interest (August 1859). In "Correspondence" the editors both spoke to the readers and published letters from them. In November 1857 Uncle Robin stated that he "liked to receive and read the letters; they are proof of the love of the *Book*";[5] but in March 1859 he asked if the letters were falling off because he corrected their faults and carelessness or if the parents were unwilling to pay the postage. Much of the material carried in "Correspondence" was testimonial: one parent wrote that she was "thankful" for a person like Aunt Alice to help her educate her children (July 1857), and a correspondent from Knoxville, Tennessee, stated that "the paper is like a ray of sunshine on our family."[6] Correspondence was recorded from all sections of Tennessee and from Arkansas, Alabama, Kentucky, Mississippi, and even Texas.

Like its contemporaries, the *Book* always contained a section of puzzles and games to entertain and instruct the children, consisting of miscellaneous enigmas, charades, riddle verses, anagrams, and conundrums; and much space was devoted to the solutions and directions for solving the puzzles.

Some materials appearing in the *Book* were credited to other periodicals such as *The American Messenger* (March 1856), *The Children's Friend** (September 1856), the *Child's Paper* (October 1856), and the *Fall River Monitor* (June 1859). A few items in the periodical appeared twice in its pages in its short life, such as Dr. Watts's "Cradle Song," printed first in December 1855 and again in November 1858. Other articles were printed at least in part for a second time, and close examination of the *Book* and its successor, *Youth's Magazine*, reveals that many articles originally included in the former publication eventually reappeared in the latter.

Foremost among the literary offerings of the *Book* were the Bible stories from both the Old and New Testaments, many of which were accompanied by engravings: "The History of Moses," published in serial form (December 1855 and following issues), and "The History of Our Savior," in many installments (March 1856-July 1859). In addition, many other materials were directed at the Sunday schools: "Short Stories for the Young" contained "the best of the stories told at the National Conference of Sabbath School Teachers in Philadelphia, condensed for young readers."[7]

Many stories that were not of a biblical background were at least didactic, such as "What Perseverance Accomplished" (November 1858), "The Hole in the Elbow" (April 1859), and "Laughing During Prayers" (Jaunary 1860). As is to be expected, fables played a large part in the literary content of the *Book*: "The Frog and the Ox" and "The Miller and His Ass" were accompanied by an explanatory note about Aesop, which concluded that Bible stories are better than fables because they are older (September 1857).

A more worldly type of story was found in the magazine at times: "Adventure in the Backwoods" (March-April 1860), "The Lighthouse Heroine" (January 1860), and "Ellen Manning, the Child Woman" (January 1857). Chapters from two published books were included: *Harry's Vacation* (January 1855) and *The Marooners* (July 1857). "The Youthful Hero" was actually the story of the

Dutch boy who plugged the hole in the dike with his finger, here used to prove the influence of one individual in doing good (June 1859).

Although most of the verse contained in the *Book* was cautionary—"Employment, That Is Enjoyment" (December 1855) and "On Whiskey" (November 1858)—or about a dying or dead child—"Early Lost, Early Saved" (June 1858) and "Waiting for God to Come for Me" (November 1858)—some poems were more useful: "The Grammar School," a verse on the parts of speech (January 1855) and "The Use of Flowers" (August 1859). Signed verses were by E. H. Sears (September 1859), Laura Elmer (February 1860), Jane Taylor (March 1859), and Mrs. L. H. Sigourney (January 1860). It is noteworthy that Clement C. Moore's famous poem appeared as "Christmas Times," without the author's name (March-April 1860).

Frequently, songs and music were offered in the *Book*: "To a Bird" was a song with its music and an engraving (March 1859); "The Children's Hosanna," "Christ's Kingdom," and "The Wisdom of God" appeared with their music (August 1858); and "The Battle Is Won, the Victory Is Ours" was a commencement song in January 1860. An article about Hoffman, illustrating the power of music, was included in March 1859, and Dr. Watts's "Cradle Hymn" appeared as verse only in November 1858.

Nature and science interests were served by articles such as weather (March 1856), the sloth (November 1857), a curious attack of ants (June 1859), pulling teeth (July 1859), a flea under the microscope (January 1860), and seashore studies (March-April 1860).

Readers of the *Book* were introduced to a variety of places and times in its geographical and historical articles: "A Story of the Time of Charlemagne" (January 1855), "Dr. Kane of the Arctic Regions" (November 1857), "The St. Lawrence River" (June 1858), and "Hadji in Syria" (July 1859). It also contained much factual miscellaneous information: curious calculations—properties of *five* and extraordinary *seven* (March 1856), origins of Christmas customs (December 1857), and a list of states with dates of settlement and dates of admission to the Union (January 1860).

Biographical sketches were included about persons such as Columbus (September 1858); Diogenes (October 1856); William Tell (April 1857); Henry Clay (August 1858); and Joan of Arc (June 1858).

The demise of the *Children's Book* was announced in "Uncle George's Chat," where after having apologized for the lateness of the current issue (March and April were bound together), he stated that henceforth *he* would address his "nephews and nieces" monthly. "The next number will be much larger and better and will be called the *Youth's Magazine*."[8] In the advertisement for *Youth's Magazine*, which followed "Uncle George's Chat," a note to parents said that "there will be a department devoted to the 'little ones' that they too may be taught early the ways of virture. The *Magazine* will thus meet all the wants of the family circle. Father and mother, brothers and sisters, young and old, will find it interesting. . . . We are positive it will please the most fastidious."[9]

Notes

1. *The Children's Book of Choice and Entertaining Reading for the Little Folks at Home* 1 (January 1855), 3.
2. Ibid., 1 (December 1855), 251.
3. Ibid., 2 (December 1856), 256.
4. Ibid., 2 (June 1856), 52.
5. Ibid., 3 (November 1857), 260.
6. Ibid., 4 (April 1858), 461.
7. Ibid., 5 (July 1859), 107.
8. Ibid., 6 (March–April 1860), 472.
9. Ibid., p. 474.

Information Sources

BIBLIOGRAPHY
None.
INDEX SOURCES
None.
LOCATION SOURCES
Duke University Library, Durham, N.C.; University of North Carolina, Chapel Hill, N.C.

Publication History

MAGAZINE TITLE AND TITLE CHANGES
The Children's Book of Choice and Entertaining Reading for the Little Folks at Home (January 1855–March/April 1860). Superseded by *Youth's Magazine.*
VOLUME AND ISSUE DATA
The Children's Book of Choice and Entertaining Reading for the Little Folks at Home (vol. 1, no. 1–vol. 5, no. 3).
PUBLISHER AND PLACE OF PUBLICATION
Graves, Marks & Company, Nashville (1855–1860).
EDITOR
"Uncle Robin" and "Aunt Alice" (1855–1859); George C. Connor (1860).

Mary D. Manning

CHILDREN'S DIGEST

One of the offspring of *Parents' Magazine, Children's Digest* is a relatively young periodical. Founded as recently as October 1950, it remained remarkably stable for twenty-eight years, only to undergo some drastic changes since 1978. It began, as its title implies, in frank imitation of *Reader's Digest*. A pocket-sized, reprint magazine for children of ages seven to twelve, it appeared monthly except for June and August. By 1978 it had become a high-quality magazine of excellent materials and tasteful format. Then a series of rapid changes occurred. Between 1978 and 1981 there were four editors; George Hecht retired as chairman of the board; *Children's Digest* merged with another of *Parents'* offspring, *Children's Playcraft*; and there were two changes in publishers. These events resulted in wholesale changes in *Children's Digest*'s content and format. Literature is virtually absent from the June-July 1981 issue by Children's Health Publications. Beginning to disappear in 1979 and to be replaced by nonfiction, it includes in this issue only two short stories and a few poems, all blatantly as didactic about health, nutrition, safety, and exercise as the rest of the magazine. Furthermore, this literature is not reprinted but is solicited from amateurs—both children and adults. Finally, this 7½- by 10½-inch, newsprint issue has few illustrations and little color. After only thirty-one years there is hardly anything about *Children's Digest* that distinguishes it from other Children's Health Publications or that recalls it as it was in its earlier days.

As *Parents'* new child, it reflected the philosophy and shrewdness of George Hecht, the founder of *Parents' Magazine* in 1926 and chairman of the board of its publishing company until November 1977.[1] It was "a nice mixture of his zeal for child welfare—and profits."[2] Bountiful and colorful in its 132 pages of offerings, it appealed to both parents and children. Its four-color cover, two colors inside, tinted green paper, and special flat binding made it attractive. Advertised as "selected reading to delight, instruct, and entertain," it offered "the cream of new stories for boys and girls; reprints of the best-loved classics"; educational and humorous comics; book reviews by Phyllis A. Whitney; poetry and songs; and a hodgepodge of crafts, puzzles, games, and jokes.[3] Nearly half of each issue in the first years was not literature but comics, jokes, and other materials more certain to attract children than the "best stories" and "famous classics" announced on the magazine's spine. In this fashion, Hecht covered all fronts and ensured the magazine's financial success. Nothing in the magazine, on the other hand, was without educational function or in poor taste. Many of the comics, for example, were *True Comics*—about great men and great deeds. Purchased by Hecht in 1941 in hope of giving competition to the less savory comics then on the market, this comic magazine was his one financial failure at the time. Strips in the first issues of *Children's Digest* included "Cavalcade of England," "The First Telescope," "Marco Polar Bear," "Smoking Fists," and "Cities of Destiny." There were also humorous ones such as "Tizzie" and "Buster Bunny," teaching morality and deportment. Indeed, the literature was no more didactic and no less entertaining than these special features. Many examples of fantasy and folklore appeared, much less realistic fiction, and almost no nonfiction. Teaching subtly and delighting the imagination, many of the poems and stories were among the best that children's literature had to offer at the time, for example, Carl Sandburg's *Rootabaga Stories* and Lucretia P. Hale's *Peterkin Papers* (both December 1951), L. Frank Baum's *American Fairy Tales* and Robert McCloskey's *Homer Price* (both April 1952), and Seumas MacManus's *Donegal Wonder Book* and Astrid Lindgren's *Pippi Longstocking* (both July 1958).

Harold Schwartz, editor of *Children's Digest* during its first seventeen years, effected a few changes in the late 1950s and early 1960s. The magazine gradually shrank in size, stabilizing at ninety-eight pages. Increasingly, comic strips disappeared, and each issue included one picture book and some of its original illustrations. The science, history, biography, morality, and deportment originally taught by the comic strips, furthermore, now appeared as undisguised nonfiction in, for example, "What Was the Gordian Knot?" from *The Book of Knowledge* (July 1956), "Martin and Abraham Lincoln" from the book of the same name (February 1957), "Soap and Water Through the Ages" from *Story Parade* (January 1960), and "Why Do Zebras have Stripes?" from *The Answer Book* (December 1962). By the early 1960s the ratio of nonfiction to fiction in each issue was one to two, with scientific (especially natural science) and historical articles being three-fifths and one-third, respectively, of each issue's nonfiction. The changes in the inscription on the magazine's spine from "Best Stories • Famous Classics • Picture Stories" in the late 1950s to "Great Stories • History • Science • Biography • True Adventure" in the early 1960s reflected the magazine's evolution.

By the late 1960s *Children's Digest* was a mature magazine. Under its second editor, Elizabeth Redousakis Mattheos (1967-1977), it was stable, polished, and inviting. Each issue's collection of "Stories and Poetry," "Articles," and "Fun and Activities" (clearly organized under these rubrics) exhibited, with few exceptions, considerable merit. Reprints were from works such as Padraic Colum's *Legends of Hawaii* and Louis Wolfe's *Stories of Our American Past* (both January 1969), Roy Chapman Andrew's *All About Dinosaurs* (February 1969), I. G. Edmond's *Ooka the Wise* (January 1974), Lewis Carroll's *Alice's Adventures in Wonderland* (May 1975), Kenneth Grahame's *Wind in the Willows* (November 1974), C. S. Lewis's *Voyage of the Dawn Treader* (October 1977), J.R.R. Tolkien's *Hobbit* (February and March 1974), and Richard Peck's *Day No Pigs Would Die* (January 1974). There were typically four to five stories and one poem. Usually, one story was a folktale; one a picture book; one, a Tintin comic strip adventure by Hergé; one, a fantasy; and one, realistic fiction—most often historical fiction. In "Articles" were book reviews (by Barbara Nolen until 1972 when Ingeborg Boudreau began) and two essays or book chapters. The ones about science—especially natural science (especially animals)—comprised more than half of the articles. Biographies were nearly a third. The next largest category concerned practical matters of the how-to-do-it variety. Historical articles, rather than being one-third as they were in earlier issues, were slightly more than one-tenth of the magazine's nonfiction during these years. "Fun and Activities" most often offered a crossword puzzle, jokes, riddles, and an explanation of how to make, do, or cook something. Between 1973 and 1978 issues alternated between ninety-eight and seventy-four pages. Beginning in 1975 issues sometimes did not include picture books; after July 1978 none was ever used. Despite these losses, however, *Children's Digest* retained its particular format and high standards until the late 1970s. Under Mattheos's editorship, moreover, several of the magazine's features were outstanding.

First were the picture books. Many excellent ones were reprinted. Some of them were Ludwig Bemelman's *Madeline's Rescue* (December 1971), William Steig's *Amos and Boris* (September 1972), Judith Viorst's *The Tenth Good Thing About Barney* (March 1973), Laurent de Brunhoff's *Babar's Birthday Surprise* (March 1974), Charlotte Zolotow's *My Grandson Lew* (July 1975), and Maurice Sendak's *Pierre* (May 1976). Picture books whose illustrations rely heavily on color or some element other than line were not used. The illustrations were line drawings, little affected, other than brightened, by the wash of a primary color here and there added.

Editorial taste was equally apparent in a second feature, Hergé's Tintin adventures. In *Children's Digest* a complete adventure existed in ten parts, coming one an issue, the whole in one year, for example, *Prisoners of the Sun* in 1969, *Tintin in Tibet* in 1971, *The Castle of Doom* in 1973, and *The Pharaoh's Revenge* in 1975. One can be certain that the source of many a child's attraction to *Children's Digest* was the monthly Tintin installments. Their creator Hergé, a pseudonym for Georges Remi of Brussels, published twenty-two books of Tintin's adventures, all written and drawn by him, each having taken about two years to complete.[4] Full of mystery, suspense, provocative clues, traps, other potential disasters, unusual characters, and exotic places, they combine ingredients powerfully compelling to most readers. Most important, however, is their boy hero whose intelligence, bravery, perseverance, and competence allow him always to achieve his goals. Without exception, furthermore, his goals demonstrate his superior moral character—his devotion to justice, equality, and fairness. As a hero, Tintin is thus a powerful idol and role model.

A third outstanding feature of these years was the use of novels. Nearly always, as was the case with all novels previously mentioned, a chapter or two were printed with hints about the remainder of the book, obviously inviting a complete reading. Besides the titles already given, other excellent examples were Scott O'Dell's *Island of the Blue Dolphins* (March 1972), Roald Dahls' *Charlie and the Chocolate Factory* (February 1973), Jean Craighead George's *Julie of the Wolves* (March 1974), and Madeleine L'Engle's *Wrinkle in Time* (October 1975). Only once during these years was the policy to excerpt, not condense, violated.[5] From February to July 1977 an entire novel—*Treasure Island*—was printed in condensed installments.

A final feature was Ingeborg Boudreau's contribution. Over the years in the "Parent/Teacher Pages," she commented, for example, on Isaac Bashevis Singer (February 1972); books about reproduction and birth (January 1973) and aging (February 1973); Sendak (July 1974); Mother Goose (April 1975); Jules Verne (February 1976); and "Children's Books—A Bicentennial View" (September 1976). In her book reviews ("Take off with Books" until 1975; "Exploring with Books" thereafter), she was also provocative and entertaining, writing each month one essay on a theme, "Four Faces of Humor" (November 1973), for example, and "Animal World" (September 1976).

Prices increased from 75¢ an issue in 1976 to $1.25 in 1979, circulation decreased from about 800,000 in 1970 to less than 450,000 in 1977, and the excellence achieved under Mattheos faded away. Her first successor, Anita Malnig (1977-1978), made almost no changes except for eliminating the "Parent/ Teacher Pages" and the book reviews. The same was less true of Karen Craig (1978-1979), who began "Book Nook" or book reviews by child readers in July 1978; added a "Playcraft" section in September 1978 after the two magazines merged; eliminated Tintin in January 1979 (returned it from April 1979 to May 1980 and never thereafter); and reorganized the format to "Stories and Articles," "Features," and "Activities." During 1979 she provided only three pieces of literature an issue, reprinting mostly nonfiction from the "soft" sciences. Representing a significant change in the attitudes of the late 1970s, articles about anthropology, psychology, and sociology were as numerous as those about natural science and technology. This change was even more evident under Lois Cantwell (1979-1980), who reprinted but most often hired a freelance writer to create pieces such as "Kids Rights" from *I Am Not a Short Adult* (July 1979), Jean Thomas's "Why Brothers and Sisters Fight" (November 1979), Patricia Farewell's "How You Can Beat Inflation" (January 1980), and "Teasing: How to Handle It; How to Stop It" (May 1980), and June Tau's "Teaching Your Teacher About You" (October-November 1980). Indeed, the whole magazine under Cantwell's editorship was increasingly "kid centered," from each issue's beginning with a letter opening "Dear Kids" and closing "Lois," through its many child-written features, to its articles relevant to children. In each issue's very apparent efforts to attract and please children, furthermore, one suspects a somewhat desperate struggle for survival.

In 1980 the magazine was sold to Benjamin Franklin Literary and Medical Society, a nonprofit organization that also publishes *Turtle: Magazine for Preschool, Children's Playmate,* Humpty Dumpty,* Jack and Jill,* Child Life,* Health Explorer*, and *Jr. Medical Detective*—all now called Children's Health Publications. Very similar in their formats, somewhat less so in their contents, these magazines are all now depressingly uniform. Stressing health, safety, nutrition, and exercise, they perform a worthy function for today's children. But in their lack of originality, attractiveness, and subtlety, they surely appeal to only the most avid readers. Only *Cricket** now provides children with the classics of literature and nonfiction once reprinted for them in *Children's Digest*.

Notes

1. "*Parents*' New Child," *Time*, October 9, 1950, pp. 49-50.
2. Ibid., p. 50.
3. Advertisement of *Children's Digest, Parents' Magazine* 25 (September 1950), 163.
4. "You Asked About Hergé," *Children's Digest* 25 (January 1975), 38.

5. See Rubie Saunders, "It's Magic!" ibid., 25 (October 1975), 5-7, for statement and discussion of this policy.

Information Sources

BIBLIOGRAPHY
There are no critical studies, relevant biographies or histories, or published anthologies or collections. See *"Parents'* New Child," *Time*, October 9, 1950, pp. 49-50.
INDEX SOURCES
Children's Book Review Index; Subject Index to Children's Magazines.
LOCATION SOURCES
Bound volumes and various issues are in university libraries across the country; the entire run is available on microfilm from University Microfilms International, Ann Arbor, Mich.

Publication History

MAGAZINE TITLE AND TITLE CHANGES
Children's Digest (October 1950-July 1978); *Children's Digest Incorporating Children's Playcraft* (September 1978-February 1980); *Children's Digest and Children's Playcraft* (March 1980-November 1980); *Children's Digest: A Children's Health Publication* (December 1980-).
VOLUME AND ISSUE DATA
Children's Digest (vol. 1, no. 1-vol. 27, no. 279); *Children's Digest Incorporating Children's Playcraft* (vol. 27, no. 280-vol. 29, no. 294); *Children's Digest and Children's Playcraft* (vol. 29, no. 295-vol. 30, no. 299); and *Children's Digest: A Children's Health Publication* (vol. 30, no. 300-).
PUBLISHER AND PLACE OF PUBLICATION
Parents' Institute, Inc.: Chicago (1950-1958); New York (1959-1962); Parents' Magazine Enterprises: New York (1962-1973), Bergenfield, N.J. (1973-1978); Gruner and Jahr, Inc., Bergenfield, N.J., (1978-1980); Benjamin Franklin Literary and Medical Society, Indianapolis (1980-).
EDITOR
Harold Schwartz (1950-1967); Elizabeth Mattheos (1967-1977); Anita Malnig (1977-1978); Karen Craig (1978-1979); Lois Cantwell (1979-1980); Christine French (1980-).

Virginia L. Wolf

CHILDREN'S FRIEND (1862-1915)

The *Children's Friend* published its first issue in Richmond, Virginia, in August 1862, under the auspices of the Presbyterian Committee on Publication. The initial issue described itself as "a monthly missionary on its errand of love." In the early years it consisted of four multicolumned, folio-sized pages of newsprint-quality paper, which sold for 30¢ a copy.

Many issues of the *Children's Friend* had the subtitle *An Evangelical Sabbath School Journal.* The publication of this magazine had been ordered by the General Assembly of the Presbyterian Church, meeting in Augusta, Georgia, in December

1861, but "owing to various hindrances it has been found impractical until now to comply with this instruction."[1] An editorial delineated some problems facing the endeavor: "At first paper could not be procured here. Next the demands of the war called off so many of the printers that a contract was both difficult and expensive. Then for a few months the safety of Richmond was seriously threatened."[2] Frequently, war-related problems of mailing the publication and of currency exchange were the subject of editorial comment in the early issues.

In the beginning no editor's name was given, but in January 1863 the editorial was entitled "Who Is Editor?" The answer was, "It will do no harm to answer that question; therefore by advice of good friends, his name will be found on this page."[3] There it was: Rev. William Brown, a name that was to appear on the masthead for several issues. At this point contributions to be published in the magazine were solicited and criteria given for their inclusion: "Articles should be short, no more than one column in length. Let them be pointed in style and full of important truth. Here is a place to do good which an angel might covet. Such pieces are greatly needed. Who will write them?"[4]

One of the early goals expressed in the *Children's Friend* was to offer its readers engravings in each issue. The first contained an illustrated masthead "Suffer the Little Children to Come unto Me," but in the editorial it stated that "the engravings now furnished are not all we could wish for nor such as we may hope to secure at a more favorable time."[5] After the war the problem of securing engravings was solved, and each issue usually contained at least one per page—some large, some small.

The *Children's Friend* provided, as did many other religious periodicals of the time, instructional and entertaining as well as religious materials within its pages, although it was understood that every article, regardless of content, was aimed at the instruction of the child in the ways of godliness and salvation. In the early issues most items were overtly admonitory: "Seven Classes of Company to Be Avoided" (August 1862), "Turn the Other Cheek" (August 1862), "Don't Tattle" (September 1862), "Don't Travel on the Sabbath" (April 1863).

At least one Bible story was contained in each number: "Boaz and Ruth" (August 1862), "Christ in the Boat" (September 1862), "The Little Cloud" (March 1863), and "The Wall of Fire" (April 1863). By 1869 the Scriptures were being treated in a special feature, "Philip Barrett's Bible Stories" (July 1869).

After the war much emphasis was placed on missionary stories and the activities of the church's missionaries: "The Jungle Boy" was a story by the wife of a missionary to India (May 1863); "My New Bible" told of an aged "heathen convert" who vowed that no dust would ever gather on his Bible (January 1870); and "Opening Little Sally's Missionary Box" was about a child's successful solicitations from her friends in behalf of the missions (March 1870).

The role that the *Children's Friend* was to play in the formation of Sabbath schools was evident as early as September 1862, when it contained "Advice to Sabbath School Scholars from a Dying Boy," telling others how important was the instruction to be had at the Sabbath school (September 1862), and in the following July, ''A Word for Sabbath Schools,'' the account of an organization of one following a meeting in Charlotte County, Virginia (July 1863).

In April 1871 the Sunday school lessons were instituted as a regular feature, the entire back page being devoted to the ''International Lesson'' at the top and the ''Primary Lesson'' at the bottom, consisting of a Bible story followed by questions for study and discussion (September 1878).

Each issue included stories for entertainment and instruction, some that were written especially for the *Children's Friend*, others that were borrowed from other religious periodicals, and a few that were translated from German or French (October 1862, March 1870).[6] Always these tales were didactic and dull: ''The Beautiful Dress'' (August 1862), ''Two Kinds of Riches'' (September 1862), ''Cross Maria'' (May 1864), ''Brave Bessie'' (January 1870), ''The Idle Boy's Prize'' (June 1871), and ''Joe White's Temptation'' (September 1878).

Fables, being generically didactic in intent, can often be found among the pages: ''The Ant and the Cricket'' (September 1862), ''The Hummingbird and the Butterfly'' (February 1863), and some short ''original'' fables of the editors own invention (October 1862).

The *Children's Friend* incorporated verse into its columns even as early as the first issue, where ''The Contrast'' was included with all seven stanzas interspersed with commentary (August 1862). ''Steer Straight to Me, Father'' (December 1862) and ''The Song of the Decanter'' (March 1863) both dealt with the evils of alcohol, the latter being a ''concrete'' poem printed in the shape of a bottle. ''The Fullness of Jesus'' gave chapter and verse citations for each line of its text (June 1863).

Most of the literary pieces in the *Children's Friend* were unsigned or designated ''selected.'' However, three titles by Mrs. L. H. Sigourney appeared—two poems, ''The Dying Sabbath School Boy'' (March 1863) and ''The Boy and the Bird'' (January 1870), and a story, ''The Lady Bird and the Ant'' (October 1862). Other ''literary'' pieces consisted of a discussion of Wordsworth's poem ''We Are Seven'' (May 1863) and ''Swear Not at All,'' an admonition based on a quote from Cowper (July 1870). In the April 1871 issue ''Our Dog Dash'' was actually a story of the little dog in *Greyfriars Bobby* (April 1871).

The instructional and educational aspects of the magazine encompassed geography, history, natural science, and language. A very early issue devoted three-fourths of a page to an engraving and an article about Pilot Mountain, North Carolina (October 1862); another issue contained a piece about Labrador (January 1870); another, a piece about Chinese rivers and one about Hindoo [sic] children (July 1870); and still another, about the River Ganges (February 1870). In 1871 Greece was the subject of one article and the deserts another (April, December 1871). Historical articles dealt with George Washington as ''Father of His Country'' and with Napoleon (August 1862). Natural science articles were to appear somewhat later: one about the sea gull, another about leopards, and one about eagles (March, July 1870). In the next few years the spotted deer of India (June, 1871), the wild ox (January 1872), the bread-fruit (September 1878), and glass-making (September 1878) were treated. The one piece about language, "Long Words," dealt with the difficulty encountered by "Mr. Eliot" in translating the Bible for the Indians (April 1863).

From its beginning, the *Children's Friend* included music in its offerings, for in 1863 the editorial announced the gift of a font of music type from the Board of Directors of the North Carolina Institute for Deaf, Dumb and Blind (February 1863). In the next issue it printed the song "Children in Heaven" with its music and in the following one, "Stay, Father, Stay; or The Dying Child" (March 1863).

Like many other religious periodicals for children, the *Children's Friend* featured regular columns of enigmas and other religious puzzles, quizzes, and acrostics. The section "Religious Readings" contained announcements and miscellaneous material about other publications. "Uncle Frank's Talks" was often a retelling of Bible stories, and a companion piece, "Search the Scriptures," encouraged careful reading and discussion of biblical passages. The magazine solicited correspondence but stated in May 1864 that the mailbag had become so large that there was no room to print all letters. As a rule, advertisements did not appear in the *Children's Friend*, but one exception was the announcement of "Bibles for Learning Catechism," which were offered in July 1870.

Over the years of the publication of the *Children's Friend* several changes can be identified: following the Civil War emphasis shifted to the role of the Sunday school, providing lessons and activities for children and teachers' use; longer articles began to replace the short, filler-length items of the early issues; songs, hymns, and music began to play an important part of each number; and the foreign missions and activities and stories about missionaries made up a large part of the contents for many years.

The theme of the stories, verse, and articles in the *Children's Friend*, however, remained staunchly as established: the value of good example by parents in rearing their children in ways of morality and of children in converting wayward adults. Because of its format, as music, stories, and engravings increased in the pages of the *Children's Friend* and as regular Sunday school lessons were included, less correspondence and less reader-participation were evident. In spite of its problem-filled beginnings during the Civil War, the *Children's Friend* persevered and lasted into the twentieth century, a distinction not shared by many of the midcentury religious publications for children.

Notes

1. *Children's Friend* 1 (August 1862), 3.
2. Ibid.
3. Ibid., 1 (January 1863), 23.
4. Ibid., p. 3.
5. Ibid., 1 (August 1862), 3.

6. Publications from which material was reprinted in the *Children's Friend* were *The Child at Home* (December 1862); *Juvenile Missionary Magazine* (June 1863); *Confederate Baptist* (June 1863); *The French Sunday School Magazine* (March 1870); *Young Pilgrim* (March 1870); *Mother's Treasury* (June 1871); and *Child's World* (September 1878).

Information Sources

BIBLIOGRAPHY
None.
INDEX SOURCES
None.
LOCATION SOURCES
Tulane University, New Orleans; Harvard University, Cambridge, Mass.; Duke University, Durham, N.C.; Free Library of Philadelphia; Union Theological Seminary, Richmond, Va.; University of Virginia, Charlottesville, Va.

Publication History

MAGAZINE TITLE AND TITLE CHANGES
Children's Friend (August 1862-June 1915).
VOLUME AND ISSUE DATA
Children's Friend (vol. 1-vol. 2; n.s. vol. 1-vol. 51).
PUBLISHER AND PLACE OF PUBLICATION
Presbyterian Committee on Publication, Richmond, Va. (1862-1878); thereafter in conjunction with the Reformed Church (1878-1915).
EDITOR
Rev. William Brown (January 1863); no others identified until Rev. E. T. Baird (1896), who served as an editor of *Southern Boys' and Girls' Monthly*,* 1867-1868; Rev. J. K. Hazen (1878), of the Reformed Church in America, New York.

Mary D. Manning

THE CHILDREN'S FRIEND (1902-)

The Children's Friend, now named the *Friend*, is eighty years old, having first been published in Salt Lake City, Utah, in January 1902. Its history goes back another twenty-five years to 1878, when a group of Mormon women were waiting for a train in Farmington, Utah. Women leaders of the Church of Jesus Christ of Latter-day Saints (Mormon) had come from Salt Lake City to visit the local leaders of the church's women's organization. The hostess was Aurelia Spencer Rogers, who used the time that was available during the train wait to make a proposal. She had been giving serious thought to the behavior of the town's children, particularly the boys of whom she said, "Certainly some of the larger ones well deserved the undesirable name of 'hoodlum.' "[1] She thought that an organization could be founded to help teach these boys how to behave. One of the visitors was Eliza R. Snow, probably the most influential of early Mormon women. She promised to take the proposal back to Salt Lake for consideration by the president of the church, John Taylor.

He agreed to the proposal and wrote a letter to the Bishop in Farmington instructing him to ask Aurelia Spencer Rogers to preside over such an organization for the local children. This organization was called the Primary Improvement Association (later shortened to Primary Association or, informally, just Primary). In an interesting bit of sexism, it was originally conceived of as a boys' organization, but as Rogers began thinking about the matter, she decided it would be better to include both sexes. She sent a letter to Snow in which she stated that although the little boys might need the Primary, the singing there "needed the voices of little girls as well as boys to make it sound as well as it should."[2]

President Taylor agreed to this amended plan. The first meeting was held on August 25, 1878. Before the meeting, Rogers and two women appointed as her counselors or helpers visited each family and personally invited the 115 boys and 100 girls living in the town of Farmington, Utah. In her official report, Rogers wrote that the meeting was "not quite a success." The children arrived at different times. They ranged in age from four to fourteen. Rogers and her two helpers were the only adults present.[3]

However, imperfect as it was, the organization was still filling a need, and soon it was extended to other communities and eventually throughout the entire church. By the late 1800s it was decided to divide the children into classes by age and to prepare lesson material for each age level. Louise Bouton Felt from Salt Lake had been called by the president of the church to be the general president of the Primary. She was instrumental in getting the lessons prepared, but met with disappointment when she asked the church to publish them. Times were hard. The church could not offer financial assistance, and no investor thought that the lessons would be marketable enough to provide a profit. Several women now made up the general board of the Primary, and they conceived the idea of publishing the lessons in a monthly magazine that would be sold to the teachers and officers throughout the church. The church gave permission but still offered no financial support. Felt pledged her home as collateral and also provided room for the editing and mailing of the magazine. Her close friend and living companion, May Anderson, was the first editor.

Volume 1, number 1, appeared in January 1902. It was professionally laid out and printed on good quality paper. The size was 8 ½ by 5 inches, and it was obviously aimed at the adult women who would be directing the children. On page 1 was a poem, "Our Work and Our Wealth"; on page 2 was something like an editorial entitled "Greeting—Beloved Sisters"; and on page 3 was "Suggestions for Officers." In the rest of the magazine there were historical anecdotes of kindnesses performed by the church leaders or of blessings received by the early pioneers. There was a talk on obedience, as well as stories or essays under titles such as, "Avoiding Quarrels" (February 1902), "Arbor Day" (April 1902), "Blessed are the Merciful" (April 1902), "Forgiveness" (June 1902), and "Perseverance" (December 1902). The first volume (1902) totaled 412 pages. By 1912 the magazine had grown to 668 pages, still in the 8 ½- by 5-

inch format, but there was a marked shift in the focus of the magazine. The format and organization were such that adults probably began to share it directly with children. Drawings and photographs were included, and each issue contained seven or eight poems, as well as a "memory gem." Many poems and stories were also included as parts of the lessons that by now were moved to the back of the magazine. Much of the material must have been written or adapted by the editor since no authors were listed except with the poems. Story titles show the moralistic tone: "Lack of Faith Brings Trouble" (June 1912), "Instructions to the Elders" (September 1912), and "Lesson in Obedience" (February 1912). But in contrast was an innovation entitled "Just for Fun Page," headed by photos of a smiling boy and girl and featuring jokes, for example,

Mother: Johnny how is it you stand so much lower in your studies in January than you did in December?

Son: Oh, everything is marked down after the holidays, you know![4]

Some of these jokes were reprinted from *Harper's Weekly, Leslie's Weekly*, and *Ladies Home Journal*.

In the January issue there was a surprise tribute to editor May Anderson, who would continue to edit *The Children's Friend* even when she was called by the church leaders to be the general president of the Primary. She held this job until 1939. Through 1971 the woman serving as Primary president was the official editor. They all shared in making the magazine more child centered.

By 1922 the magazine was clearly intended first for children and second for adults. It opened directly with an illustrated poem appropriate for children. This was followed by stories, for example, the serialized "Dreams of Janet" by Elsie C. Carrol and "Shoe Box," by Jessie Wright Whitcomb, was printed in the December 1922 issue. Picturegraph stories were a kind of puzzle, for example, "Dorothy and Donald See a Real Bear" (September 1922) and "Dorothy and Donald Find a Friend." (June 1922). About half of each issue was this kind of material written for children to read themselves. Then came a two-page "Parents' Department," a five-page "Officers' Department," an eighteen-page "Lesson Department," and a concluding two pages of photos and news featuring children from various geographical areas. By now the Primary Association had grown far beyond the boundaries of Utah, and one article was about fifty children who attended Primary in Japan. It was illustrated with a photo of the primary president in a Japanese kimono. She was apparently the author of the article and an American living temporarily in Japan.

Author's names were now affixed to some of the stories, although they were not included in the table of contents or the index. Not everything was religious. For example, "A Little Court Lady" by N. Hudson Moore (January 1923) told about Francoise-Marie de Bourbon, born in May 1677. The gist of the article was how much better off were ordinary children of the day compared to royalty of the 1600s. An interesting detail was that windows were so scarce that they had to be moved from room to room along with the king. Another feature was "Things to Remember During the Year 1923," a reprint from the American Humane Education Society on kindness to animals.

By 1932 the format of the magazine had changed to accommodate larger pages, 8½ by 12 inches, and the total number of pages was reduced proportionately. The advantage of the larger page was that it could accommodate more interesting layouts. Cartoons, puzzles, and practically full-page illustrations for lead stories made the magazine much more attractive to children. Another innovation was two-color covers. Perhaps to pay for this expense, the back cover (both inside and outside) was sold as advertising. However, the ads, unlike those in children's magazines today, were not for products that children would buy. They were aimed at the adult readers of the magazine and came from institutions such as Beneficial Life Insurance, the Deseret News Press, and Brigham Young University. Since they were all church-related businesses, the ads may have been a form of church support. A few truly commercial ads, for example, one from Troy Laundry in Salt Lake City, were much smaller. The only child's product advertised was "allovers," what today we would call "coveralls," but again the ad was directed at the mothers who would be buying these products for their young children.

In the 1940s *The Children's Friend* encouraged Primary children in their war efforts of collecting tin and paper. Adele Cannon Howells was the general Primary president, and she established departments in the magazine to display children's drawings and other creative efforts. She set up pen-pal exchanges and encouraged the publication of stories to help children learn to love literature. Participation by children was one of her values, and in 1946 she founded a radio show, "Children's Friend of the Air," in which children dramatized some of the stories from the magazine.

A special feature in 1952, the 50th anniversary of the magazine, was the printing of full-color reproductions of paintings done by Arnold Friberg, for which the magazine was awarded first place in the national offset Lithography Competition. Crafts, word play, stories, jokes, songs, plays, and poems were all a standard part of the magazine. By now, the lessons for the primary organization were printed separately in teacher's manuals used over and over again. However Primary teachers still rely heavily on the magazine for music and for stories to supplement the basic lessons.

December 1970 was the last issue of *The Children's Friend* published by the Primary Association. At this time the Church of Jesus Christ of Latter-day Saints took over the publication of various periodicals sponsored by the different branches (called auxiliaries) of the church. They were consolidated into one for adults (the *Ensign*), one for youth (the *New Era*), and one for children (the *Friend*). The *Friend* is very much like *The Children's Friend* and is still commonly referred to by that name. In contrast to earlier times when much of the work was done by one or two people, helped out by volunteers, today there is a managing editor, an associate editor, an assistant editor, an editorial assistant, a designer, an assistant designer, and a secretary. The magazine is promoted and presumably subsidized through the church. Subscriptions are only $6 a year, even though the magazine is printed on good quality paper with about one-third being in full-color and the other two-thirds in two colors. There are no advertisements.

According to Lucile C. Reading, managing editor, much of the content comes from freelance writers (between 500 and 600 unsolicited manuscripts a month). Payment is comparable to that of other children's magazines with the exception of *Cricket*.* In a July 2, 1981, letter Reading observed that "Most of the material we buy needs rather drastic editing. I see a great need to develop good writers for children's magazines."[5] Probably the large number of submissions she receives and the "amateur" quality of many of them relates to the fact that parents are encouraged to read the magazine with their children, just as they were on the "Parents' Page" in 1922. As parents go over and over the stories and games with several children (Mormons traditionally have big families), they begin to think of similar stories and poems themselves and without training or guidance simply write and mail them. Artwork is usually done on assignment by freelance illustrators.

The majority of the 200,000 subscribers are members of the Latter-day Saints (Mormon) Church. In countries where English is spoken, such as Australia, New Zealand, and England, church members also subscribe. In seventeen other non-English-speaking countries, excerpts from all three of the church magazines are translated and combined into one periodical. This kind of exposure probably makes the *Friend* one of the most international children's publications in the world. Being mindful of this unique role, the current editors make an effort to include stories from other countries in nearly every issue.

Today's magazine is much less didactic than issues in the early years, and many of the features are not obviously about religious or moral teaching. However, there is an underlying set of assumptions that would probably be troublesome to children unfamiliar with Morman traditions and beliefs.

Notes

1. Aurelia Spencer Rogers, *Life Sketches of Orson Spencer and Others, and History of Primary Work* (Salt Lake City: George P. Cannon and Sons, 1898), pp. 206-208. Quoted in Susan Oman and Carol Madsen, "100 years of Primary," *Ensign*, 8 (April 1978), 33.

2. *Ibid.*, p. 33.

3. *Ibid.*, p. 33.

4. *The Children's Friend*, 11 (January 1912), 29.

5. Lucile C. Reading, personal correspondence with Alleen Pace Nilsen, July 2, 1981.

Information Sources

BIBLIOGRAPHY

Susan Oman and Carol Madsen, "100 Years of Primary," *Ensign* 8 (April 1978), 32-39; anon., "The Children's Friend," mimeographed history available upon request from current editors.

INDEX SOURCES

None.

LOCATION SOURCES

Bound volumes are in the special collections of Brigham Young University Library, Provo, Utah.

Publication History

MAGAZINE TITLE AND TITLE CHANGES

The Children's Friend (1902-1970); *Friend* (1971-present)

VOLUME AND ISSUE DATA

The Children's Friend (vol. 1 no. 1-vol. 68, no. 12); *Friend* (vol. 1, no. 1-).

PUBLISHER AND PLACE OF PUBLICATION

General Board of the Primary Association of the Church of Jesus Christ of Latter-day Saints, Salt Lake City, Utah (1902-1971); Church of Jesus Christ of Latter-day Saints, Salt Lake City, Utah (1971-present).

EDITOR

May Anderson (1902-1940); Adele Cannon Howells, Janet M. Thompson, and Mary R. Jack, managing editor, joined in the later years by Gladys Daines (1941-1970); Lucile C. Reading, managing editor (1970-). A church authority is listed as the official editor, but the actual work has been done by the managing editors listed above.

Alleen Pace Nilsen

THE CHILDREN'S HOUR

The Children's Hour, a successful yet short-lived magazine for American children published between 1867 and 1874, bears from start to finish the imprint of its editor and publisher, Timothy Shay Arthur. A major contributor to the publication, sometimes pseudonymously or anonymously, Arthur early in the history of the magazine fixed upon a group of authors who remained the favored writers for *The Children's Hour* throughout its short life span. Accordingly, the publication maintains an unusual consistency of format, subject matter, and prevailing ideology. The magazine in several ways looks back to antebellum juvenile magazines, especially in the omnipresent and typically overt didacticism that underlies its verse, nonfiction, prose fiction, and even its illustrations. A sentimentalized, idealized conception of childhood and a resolutely authoritarian stance toward innocent young readers are manifest from the first to the last issue, as is the belief that American children should be taught the rightness of the laws of nature and of the ascendant social institutions of the day. It was from the models provided by the socially dominant—parents, educators, public leaders— that the young could learn, according to the conservative point of view espoused by the writers for *The Children's Hour*. In the final analysis, the magazine was not only literally bought out by *St. Nicholas** but, more broadly speaking, eclipsed by that juvenile publication and others beginning after the Civil War that attended to the imaginative as well as the moral schooling of the children of the American Republic.

The Children's Hour was but one of many publishing enterprises launched by Arthur. Early in his career he was the editor of several Baltimore newspapers. Later he attempted a literary magazine, *Arthur's Ladies Magazine*; a successful weekly (later monthly), *Arthur's Home Gazette*; and a magazine for farmers and mechanics, *The Workingman*. Indeed, the editor sometimes took advantage of the front and back pages of his monthly issues of *The Children's Hour* to advertise, along with chests of tools and "beautiful dolls," his concurrent pub- lishing projects. But Arthur was better known for his didactic fiction, which denounced the evils of gambling and celibacy (versus marriage) and advocated temperance. In 1854 his *Ten Nights in a Barroom and What I Saw There* came out, a title that was second only to *Uncle Tom's Cabin* in sales during the decade. Other works include *Married and Single; or Marriage and Celibacy Contrasted* (1845) and *Pride and Prudence; or The Married Sisters* (1850). Some of the subject matter—namely, temperance—and the techniques of storytelling found in these works—especially the use of sharply contrasting characters to illustrate his themes—mirror those found in Arthur's and others' contributions in *The Children's Hour*.

In the first volumes of the magazine, the primary writers, beyond Arthur himself, who regularly contributed one signed story an issue, are now-forgotten names such as May Leonard, Kate Sutherland, Ada M. Kennicott, and Virginia Townsend, who was also a collaborator with Arthur in other publishing projects. (Throughout its history, not all but certainly a high percentage of the contributors were women). Perhaps the only author of wider popularity is the sentimental poet Alice Cary, who along with her sister Phoebe supplied much of the verse found in *The Children's Hour*. The poetry of Henry Wadsworth Longfellow, to whose poem the title of the magazine refers, is printed only twice in the fifteen volumes of the periodical. In later issues this core of writers is joined by Clio Stanley, Rosella Rice, and Anna Wilmot. Some of these names may well be *noms de plume* for Arthur, who beginning with volume 5 often included a temperance piece of his own under the name "Solomon Soberside," or for other frequent contributors like Townsend. Several pseudonyms such as "Aunt Fanny," "Aunt Mary," "Uncle Herbert," and "Irene L." appear frequently, and ap- proximately one third of the articles in an issue are unsigned.

Ranging from two-page anecdotes to stories serialized over six issues, the subject matter of *The Children's Hour* falls into three chief categories: poetry, short nonfiction essays, and fiction. There are, however, other components worthy of mention, most conspicuously the maxims and pithy reflections that fill out columns at the conclusion of many of the longer pieces. Starting with volume 7 musical lyrics, with accompanying scores, are featured (although Christmas carols always had been a standard item in the holiday numbers). The engravings in the magazine should also be mentioned. An editorial note in the March 1868 issue points out that *The Children's Hour* for 1867 contained more than sixty engravings, and that number held constant in later volumes. Usually, the engravings illustrated the printed matter, but interestingly, it sometimes works the other way: in volume 7 there can be found an illustration entitled "Visit to Grandpa's," which is accompanied by a two-page explication of the picture.

The poetic selections in the magazine tend to be about the close at hand, namely, the domestic and natural worlds, although occasionally a more public subject can be found, for example, "The Pilgrim Fathers" (1870). It is hard to find a poem that is not intended to instruct young readers in appropriate behavior and values. In volume 5 (1869), "Sugar-Making" and "My Gardener," a riddle in rhyme, are exceptions. They are purely informational and lack any moral import. Far more representative of the poetic fare in *The Children's Hour* is Alice Cary's "Pretty Is as Pretty Does," which appeared twice (1867 and 1870, where it was set to music) or Kate Sutherland's "It Takes Two to Make a Quarrel" (1867). Even the poems about nature typically present their material as fable, for example, "What a Bird Taught" (1867), "The Three Bugs" (1868), "The Glow Worm Fable" (1868), and "The Snow-drop and the Crocus" (1867).

The nonfiction in the magazine likewise shows a disproportionate emphasis on natural subjects. Stories about dogs abound; there was, in fact, a series by that rubric in the first two volumes of *The Children's Hour*, along with separate pieces such as "The Shepherd's Dog" (1869). Uncommon flora and fauna are described in the final pages of most issues, for example, the patience plant, argus pheasant, brown beetle, scorpion fly, crested crane, blacktailed deer, and sea flower. A second but far less well-represented category of nonfiction concerns historical or biographical topics. Volume 1 (1867) contains an anecdote about Jenny Lind's charity, a story about the influence of his mother on Benjamin West's career ("The Kiss That Made a Painter"), and a tale of John Quincy Adams's love for his mother. Later volumes include, for example, a fictionalized tale about George Washington (1867) and a curious story, "Roman Children" (1871), which concludes with a chauvinistic comparison between the "ignorant" classical Rome and "our own dear land [where children] are far better off than those in Italy."[1]

The major portion of each issue of *The Children's Hour* is devoted to fiction, and like the poetry, most of the thinly fictionalized tales are meant to instruct the reader. In later volumes the editor's temperance campaign is waged through stories such as "The Little Wanderer," in which young Freddy, who has been kicked by a drunkard, finally dies (1870). The serials, which ran through all six issues of a volume of the magazine, are sentimental, melodramatic *exempla* with titles like "The Fireside Angel" by Arthur (1868) and "Hope Darrow" by

Townsend (1869). These serialized narratives stress charity, perseverance, manliness, and patience, as do the shorter pieces of fiction complete in one issue. Occasionally, a story is told for its own sake, for example, "Daisy Lee's Visit to Central Park, New York" by Aunt Lizzie (1871). The fiction included in *The Children's Hour* is, by and large, previously unpublished work. Curiously, what little fantastic reading there is amidst the multitude of tales of good and evil, for example, "About Two Little Girls, Nellie and Bella" [1869], is borrowed: the Grimms' tale "The Wood-pecker and the Dove" (1867) and "The Wonderful Bean," a highly domesticated variant of "Jack and the Beanstalk" (1867). Another borrowing is "The Father of Lights" from George Macdonald's "Ronald Bannerman's Boyhood," called in the magazine "one of the best juvenile books of the season" (1871); this excerpt teaches love of God by elaborating on the parellel between the Deity and the sun in a conversation between a father and son.

T. S. Arthur's editorial statement in volume 3 (1868) summarized his ideas about children and their reading that shaped his children's magazine: he described the periodical as "a pleasant companion, friend, and counselor of the little ones; and a helper in the work of storing up things good and true and beautiful in their minds through a healthy culture of the imagination, and an attractive illustration of those principles that lie at the foundation of all right living."[2] As the survey above illustrates, domesticity, moderation, religious faith, decorous behavior, and respect for authority were cultivated throughout the magazine's seven-year history. Ultimately, Arthur's publishing criteria and his philosophy were successful at the time, although the magazine was superseded in quality and reputation by its successor *St. Nicholas** and by its contemporaries *Our Young Folks** and *The Riverside Magazine.** In volume 9 (1871) Arthur proclaimed confidently: "*The Children's Hour* is pronounced by the secular and religious press, by fathers and mothers all over the land, by ministers of all denominations, the purest and best magazine for children in the world. Young and old everywhere read it with delight and profit."[3] His enthusiasm is seconded by the substantial body of "reader response" included in the publication, in the form of letters, questions, and submissions from the young readership. Finally, I found it telling that one of the most skeletal allegorical tales I read in *The Children's Hour*, a story called "Bad Company" in volume 2 (1867), was annotated "very good" in a childish hand in the copy I read in preparation for this essay.

Notes

1. *The Children's Hour*, 10 (1871), 112.
2. Ibid., 3 (1868).
3. Ibid., 9 (1871), p. 8.

Information Sources

BIBLIOGRAPHY
Samuel C. Chew, *Fruit Among the Leaves* (New York: Appleton-Century-Crofts, 1950);
    Dictionary of American Biography, ed. Allen Johnson (New York: Charles Scrib-

ner's Sons, 1927) vol. 1; James D. Hart, *The Popular Book* (New York: Oxford, 1950); R. Gordon Kelly, *Mother Was a Lady* (Westport, Conn.: Greenwood Press, 1974).
INDEX SOURCES
None.
LOCATION SOURCES
Volumes 1-5 and 7-10 are in the Hess Collection at the University of Minnesota, Minneapolis; volumes 1-6, 9, 11, and 13 are in the Library of Congress; and volumes 1-3 and 8-15 are in the Free Library of Philadelphia.

Publication History

MAGAZINE TITLE AND TITLE CHANGES
The Children's Hour: A Magazine for the Little Ones (1867-1874).
VOLUME AND ISSUE DATA
The Children's Hour: A Magazine for the Little Ones (vol. 1, no. 1-vol. 15. no. 6).
PUBLISHER AND PLACE OF PUBLICATION
T. S. Arthur and Son, Philadelphia (1867-1874).
EDITOR
Timothy Shay Arthur (1867-1874).

Carol Billman

THE CHILDREN'S MAGAZINE: CALCULATED FOR THE USE OF FAMILIES AND SCHOOLS (1789)

Although *The Children's Magazine* survived for only four months, America's earliest periodical for children made a confident debut in January 1789. Promising to bridge the gap in the young scholar's progress from "a Spelling-Book to such reading as is found in the *American Selection, Scott's Lessons* and *The Art of Speaking*," the unnamed editors of the magazine (its publishers, Barzillai Hudson and George Goodwin) offered families and schools the further inducements of "a *new book* every month," "cheapness," and contents suitable and interesting in "subjects, style, and manner."[1] A close look at the last inducement, "suitable" contents, reveals some of the differences in eighteenth- and twentieth-century ideas of appropriateness, while suggesting that the magazine's publishers were sometimes less concerned with appealing specifically to child readers than with finding enough material to make up forty-eight pages a month.

The January preface outlines the magazine's format: "An abridgement of Geography will appear in the beginning of each number—and the remainder will contain instructive essays on morality, religion, manners, &c—familiar letters, dialogues, and select pieces of poetry."[2] Each of the three extant issues (no February copy has survived) is basically faithful to the prospectus, and none of the reading is more difficult than the early pieces in the previously cited *American Selection*, although the poetry is more sentimental than select, and what is intended by "dialogues" is not clear.[3] No *dialogs*, in the sense that the eighteenth-century reader understood the word, are included; but dialog does occur in some of the essays, and the tone of the familiar letters is certainly meant to be conversational. Rounding off the January prospectus is an invitation to the magazine's "friends to assist them with communications, adapted to the general design."[4]

Curiously and speedily enough, the January issue itself contains just such a communication from a friend who received advance word of the periodical. The contribution is in the form of a letter to the editors of the magazine. The purported author of the letter is "one among many school-boys, who have been extremely rejoiced at the thought of having a *Magazine*, which we young folks might call *our own*."[5] The "School Boy," as the letter writer styles himself, goes on to enumerate the virtues of his school's master, Mr. Shepard. Not the least of these virtues is his donation of a dollar toward the cost of a subscription plus paper and pens for the little club of boys who wish to write for the periodical. The boys chip in money as well. Whether or not the letter is authentic, the publishers of *The Childen's Magazine* clearly intended the School Boy, his friends, and Mr. Shepard to serve as models for the kinds of response the publishers wished to elicit: subscriptions and free manuscripts. Accordingly, in March the School Boy's "True Story" of a thoughtful boy's rescue of an elderly gentleman sees publication. The end of the story cautions against expecting rewards for good deeds and reminds readers that "there is so much pleasure in performing a good or a kind act," but the climax of the story is the earlier revelation that the elderly gentleman eventually dies and leaves the youth "a very handsome legacy."[6] Profit making and pedagogy go hand in hand in the pages of *The Children's Magazine*.

The periodical's claim to gratify the interests and attend to the capacity of child readers met with some success in its monthly feature "An Easy Introduction to Geography." Due credit should be given here, however, to William Guthrie's *New System of Modern Geography* (London, first published in 1770 and followed by many more editions), a source from which the magazine borrowed or, in its phrasing, "abridged" heavily.

Perhaps less interesting, yet still adapted to the child reader's capacities, is January's religious essay, "A Discourse on the Goodness of God, Psalm CXLV, Verse 9." Here the reader is told, in an extract from Dr. Fortin, "Since God is so good, we ought in return to love Him.[7] "Rules for a Life of Business" by Archbishop Synge appears in March. Both the Old and New Testaments are cited repeatedly in this mini-manual of how to succeed in a Christian manner. The advice and precepts may strike twentieth-century readers as inappropriate for those of tender years, but contemporary readers doubtless considered Synge's remarks to be useful instruction for lads destined to be merchants and men of affairs. Literate and able to afford subscription prices, this is the class to which the magazine chiefly addressed itself.

The Children's Magazine also included material for the sisters of future men of affairs. Not surprisingly, these selections stressed the importance of kindness, humility, generosity, good housekeeping, and proper management of servants. The two latter concerns are most apparent in a series of letters from Miss Truelove to Phyllis Flowerdale, a servant girl whom Miss Truelove has befriended and whose education she surpervises. In the April issue pride in her learning leads Phyllis to the gaucherie act of offering to be a bridal attendant for Squire Gilbert's daughter. The news spreads quickly throughout the village and leaves Phyllis to face not only the mockery of the locals but also the disapproval of Miss Truelove, who relents and graciously forgives her on the condition that she has learned her place.[8] Miss Truelove's letters originate from *"New-York,"* where she has gone to visit Lady Racket; however, the letters read as if *"New-York"* has been substituted for "London" and suggest a British source. But the publishers of *The Children's Magazine* were under no obligation to follow any particular model and therefore presumably shared, or at least did not object to, the class consciousness expressed by Miss Truelove.

Miss Truelove's consciousness of superiority pales, however, in comparison with the self-assurance displayed by Mr. and Mrs. Andrews of "Moral Tales," stories that also betray a British influence. The Andrews believe it is their duty to reform the village to which they have moved some miles outside of London, but they, like "all persons in higher stations, who have any humanity in their dispositions, are ready to make proper allowances for their inferiors."[9] Sections on "The Unkind Daughter" and "The Dutiful Daughter and Grand-Daughter" have some discernable relationship to children, particularly female child readers, but "The Complaining Husbands" and "The Jealous Wife" focus on issues that are adult by the standards of both today and yesterday. If they held much interest for child readers, that interest would have been in the stories' explanations of why adults sometimes behaved badly and what can be done to prevent or improve that behavior: Mrs. Perkins, for example, responds to her husband's neglect of home by failing to keep house properly—a man must be hired to *shovel out* the dirt in the house's lower apartment.[10] "The Jealous Wife" may have intrigued child readers with its intimations of adult sexuality, but what were children to make of the following response to the wife's complaint of childlessness:

> She [Mrs. Andrews] added that it was very true, that a family of good children is an honor and a blessing, but the best of them, according to the old proverb, are *careful comforts*; and that whoever would look round the world, and see how miserable numbers of parents were made by their children, might find reason enough to reconcile them to the want of them.[11]

Fittingly, the above remark appeared in the fourth and last issue of *The Children's Magazine*. Later magazines for children would show more skill in defining and building an audience, would consciously formulate and consistently follow a particular editorial policy, and would publish more recognizably American material. *The Children's Magazine* did, nevertheless, identify children as an audience worthy of consideration, and for that, more than one schoolboy must have been grateful.

Notes

1. *The Children's Magazine*, 1 (January 1789), iii.
2. Ibid., p. iv.
3. Noah Webster, Jr., *An American Selection of Lessons in Reading and Speaking Calculated to Improve the Minds and Refine the Taste of Youth*, Pennsylvania State Copyright, May 11, 1785. Numerous editions followed the first.
4. *The Children's Magazine*, 1 (January 1789), iv.
5. Ibid., p. 11.
6. Ibid., 1 (March 1789), 105.
7. Ibid., 1 (January 1789), 27.
8. Ibid., 1 (April 1789), 181-85.
9. Ibid., 1 (March 1789), 114.
10. Ibid., p. 117.
11. Ibid., 1 (April 1789), 164.

Information Sources

BIBLIOGRAPHY

Rosalie V. Halsey, *Forgotten Books of the American Nursery* (Boston: Charles E. Good-
     speed, 1911); Betty L. Lyon, *A History of Children's Secular Magazines Published
     in the United States from 1789-1899* (Ph.D. diss., Johns Hopkins University,
     1942); Frank Luther Mott, *A History of American Magazines*, 5 vols. (Cambridge:
     Harvard University Press, 1938-1968); Lyon N. Richardson. *A History of Early
     American Magazines, 1741-1789* (New York: Thomas Nelson and Sons, 1931);
     Edwin Charles Strohecker, *American Juvenile Literary Periodicals, 1789-1826*
     (Ph.D. diss., University of Michigan, 1969).

INDEX SOURCES

None.

LOCATION SOURCES

Few copies are extant; no known copy of the February 1789 issue exists. The Library of
     Congress; Congregational Library, Boston; John Carter Brown Library, Provi-
     dence, R.I.; American Antiquarian Society, Worcester, Mass.; and New York
     State Library, Albany, N.Y., each has one or more numbers. January, March,
     and April issues are available on microfilm in the American Periodical Series from
     University Microfilms International, Ann Arbor, Mich.

Publication History

MAGAZINE TITLE AND TITLE CHANGES

The Children's Magazine: Calculated for the Use of Families and Schools (January 1789-
     April 1789).

VOLUME AND ISSUE DATA

The Children's Magazine: Calculated for the Use of Families and Schools (vol. 1 no. 1-
     vol. 1, no. 4).

PUBLISHER AND PLACE OF PUBLICATION

Barzillai Hudson and George Goodwin, Hartford, Conn. (1789).

EDITOR
None listed, see above publishers.

Janice M. Alberghene

CHILDREN'S MAGAZINE (1829-1874)

There were two dominant strains in educational theory during the nineteenth century—the modern, liberal theory stemming from Rousseau and the Romantic writers saw children as beings of infinite possibility and inherent good, who should be nurtured and cherished and allowed to develop their innate capacities to the fullest; the traditional idea of childrearing saw children as inherently evil, the result of original sin. Only through unceasing and unremitting efforts by the parents, teachers, and children could their souls be saved from eternal damnation and, on a more work-worldly level, could they make their way in the world of work. *Children's Magazine* (1829-1874), published by a conservative Episcopal Church for its Sunday school audience, adhered strictly to the traditional views. The child must be constantly exhorted to, first, strict religious observance and, second, unremitting hard work at home and school. Even those pastimes looked on today as promoting good mental and physical health were frowned on as a frivolous waste and the first steps on the pathway to hell. A small boy who spends the morning ice-skating is scolded by his Sunday school friends for idleness. He should have been reading an improving book or meditating on religious lessons.

The fare offered in *Children's Magazine* to urge the child onto this difficult road consists of examples from the lives of other children—both good children, who may act as models, and bad children, far more common, who pose a warning; stories from the Bible; stories from religious history, particularly of the Protestant Church; and improving educational material: scientific, historical, and geographic. In presenting this material, some in fictional and some in factual form, the editors frequently interrupted a story to speak directly to the readers in an admonitory tone, charging them to examine their own conscience and exhorting them to follow the maxims contained in the stories.

The severity with which the children were addressed may surprise the modern reader. Admonished constantly to think about death, both their own and that of others, on one occasion they are advised to wander daily through the graveyard, "a good place for a child" to confront the imminence of death. They are graphically told what may happen to them after they die. The story of "Basil and His Difficulties" is a typical moral *exemplum*, containing both the motif of death and the model child:

> Poor little Basil! no wonder he wept! for the grave by which he stood was the grave of his mother. His father had died many years before, and he and his mother had lived on in poverty, but in the happiness of mutual

love, earning daily sufficient for their daily wants. But now she has gone, and Basil had to face the cold world alone. The next day he was to be apprenticed to a shoemaker in the neighboring town. This had been fixed for him, and he was obliged to submit.[1]

So Basil is apprenticed to Mr. Hardman and works twelve hours a day as a shoemaker's apprentice. His "difficulties," however, lie not in the hardships and deprivations of his new life, but in the temptations set by the other boys in the shop. Hardman's son Bob urges Basil to join in play when the father is not looking: "You are very good to want to talk to me, but you had better not, as your father told you to mind your work," replies Basil, after some meditation on the diplomacy of this response.[2]

Later he is tempted to other indiscretions by Bob's brother Dick, who sees in Basil a willing dupe to cover for Dick's nightly excursions on the town, an indulgence of the older apprentices. But Basil's real problems come in trying to say his prayers in a family where godliness is as scarce as cleanliness:

The dinner being ready, they stopped their game, and he followed his companions into the dirty kitchen, where the rest of the family were assembled, one elder girl and two or three children. And now Basil had another difficulty. He had always been taught to ask God's blessing on the food he was about to eat, and he waited, expecting it as usual; but they all instantly began to eat without such a thought. Happily, Basil was not yet helped, so that he had time, unobserved, to say a few words to himself, and to think that another day he would do it unnoticed before he came into the room, for he doubted whether it would be right for him a little boy, to attract attention by doing differently from all the others at table.[3]

So Basil ends his first day of difficulties.

Death is a common theme in *Children's Magazine* stories, the deaths of mothers and young children particularly. Fannie Graham, who misbehaves in school and neglects her homework and the care of her little brother, is redeemed from her delinquency when her friend's mother dies. Her own mother has gone to bed with a headache, and Fannie believes that if she doesn't behave better her mother will die too. In the story of little Mary Redfield, it is Mary herself who is to die: "She lay quietly a long time, as if meditating, and then looking up to her mother, said cheerfully: '. . . I think, mother, it is better that I should go now: if I should grow to be older, I might become more wicked, and perhaps not reach heaven at all.' "[4] Bible stories, with their attendant sermon, were staples of the Sunday school periodical, and *Children's Magazine* included at least one in every issue, along with stories of early Christian martyrs, like Perpetua, a wealthy Roman woman who suffered martyrdom in the arena during the reign of the Emperor Severus. Perpetua's end is both pathetic and exemplary.

The earlier issues of the magazine (1829-1830) rely heavily on the biblical sermon, but later issues (1854-1861) are broadened to include articles on history, geography, and science ("The Wonders of the Microscope," "The Mahogony Tree," "Thunderstorms," "The Great Wall—Tartars," "Egypt and The Sphinx"). These articles, more instructional than moralistic, suggest the growing popular interest in science after the middle of the century; but they also sustain the earlier moralistic emphasis, summed up in the poem, "A Dialogue About a Little Bird" which advocates knowledge and abhors sin.

An interesting addition to the usual stern moral fare is the monthly report of a missionary to the Ojibwa Indians, who describes the establishment of a mission house, St. Columba, "one hundred and fifty miles above the Falls of St. Anthony on the Mississippi River in Minnesota." These "Chippewa Pictures" show Indian life during the gradual incursion of the American settler:

It was just after this season that the cornerstone of St. Columba was laid. The cold had driven the children within doors for a school-room. We had invited some of the Indians to remain near us during the winter, instead of going abroad upon their hunts, promising them work. A number of families therefore followed our advice, and for the first time they began to clear land for cultivation. They also brought the wood to us upon their backs for our fires. The children also chopped firewood the first part of each day, and the second part attended school in the principal room of the Mission House. It was now that the daily Ojibwa service began to assume a definite form. The parents came in to hear their children taught, and at the close of the school we invited all to attend and unite in the worship of the GREAT SPIRIT.[5]

The life of the missionary is as harsh as that of the early settler in the cold of the Minnesota winter: "The snow is deep, and the thermometer, seldom above zero, often sinks below it. St. Columba, as I have told you, is one hundred and fifty miles above the Falls of St. Anthony, and west of the *Father of Waters*. We are living beyond white settlers, and the imperfectly marked summer road, which ends here completely, is now reduced to a trail. No double teams can reach us. We begin now to realize, for the first time, how far away we are from our friends."[6] Indian life is portrayed by the missionary in a sympathetic manner. He seems genuinely concerned with giving an accurate and informative picture of their ways. At times, however, the writer betrayed the condescending attitude of the American toward the Indian and his complete lack of understanding of Indian customs and values. The Indian was frequently referred to with the epithet "savage." On one occasion, describing an assembly of the men of the Ojibwa tribe, the missionary declared that the Indian warriors were awarded a feather to be worn in their hair for each scalp that they took. In actual practice, the feather was awarded for "counting coup," accomplished by one mounted warrior striking another with his lance.

Although the missionary's primary concern was with the Christianizing of the Indian, his image of Indian life would have given the young reader a glimpse of the Indian living at one with his natural environment, an interesting contrast to the predominant *Children's Magazine* motif of the Protestant Christian drive to transform the environment through a life both stern and earnest.

Notes

1. *Children's Magazine*, January 1854, p. 9.
2. Ibid., p. 9.
3. Ibid., p. 13.
4. Ibid., 28 (January 1856), 12-13.
5. Ibid., 29 (June 1857), 125.
6. Ibid., p. 122.

Information Sources

BIBLIOGRAPHY
None.
INDEX SOURCES
None.
LOCATION SOURCES:

American Antiquarian Society, Worcester, Mass.; Boston Public Library; Boston Atheneum; Brown University Library, Providence, R.I.; Colorado College Library, Colorado Springs, Colo.; Columbia Law Library, Columbia University, New York; Columbia University Library, New York; Hartford Seminary Foundation, Hartford, Conn.; Harvard University Library, Cambridge, Mass.; Henry Huntington Library, San Marino, Calif.; Historical Society of Philadelphia; Iowa State Library, Des Moines, Ia.; Juanita College, Huntingdon, Pa.; Kansas City Public Library, Kansas City, Mo.; Minnesota Historical Society, St. Paul, Minn.; New York Public Library; New York State Library, Albany, N.Y.; New York University Library, New York; State University of Iowa Library, Iowa City, Ia.; Syracuse University Library, Syracuse, N.Y.; University of Michigan Library, Ann Arbor, Mich.; University of Notre Dame Library, Notre Dame, Ind.; Western Kentucky State College, Bowling Green, Ky.

Publication History

MAGAZINE TITLE AND TITLE CHANGES
Children's Magazine (1829-1874).
VOLUME AND ISSUE DATA
Children's Magazine (vol. 1, no. 1-vol. 46, no. 12).
PUBLISHER AND PLACE OF PUBLICATION
General Protestant Episcopal Sunday School Union and Church Book Society, New York (1829-1874).

Meredith M. Klaus

CHILDREN'S MAGAZINE (1903-1913)

For its first two years, 1903-1905, *Children's Magazine* was called *Holiday Magazine for Children*. Its motto was taken from Shakespeare: "Now I am in a holiday humor,'' conveying the strong presence of adult guidance in the magazine. The shift to *Children's Magazine*, and later to another motto (Stevenson's ''The world is so full of a number of things/I'm sure we should all be as happy as kings'') is emblematic of a more gradual change the publication underwent before its demise in 1913. From 1903 until 1909 the magazine had a New York address—the Holiday Publishing Company, apparently affiliated with Moffat and Yard. With a move to S. E. Cassino of Salem, Massachusetts, publishers of *Little Folks*,* *Children's Magazine* exchanged its first identity as a vehicle for a pragmatic yet lively interaction between adults and children for that of a more distinctly literary periodical with very little overt editorializing. In each phase there were signs of real excellence. In the early years its best features were its nonfiction, games, and puzzles. Later, it published quality fiction representative of American literary realism.

The editors were from upper middle-class backgrounds, and the magazine clearly participated in what has been called the genteel ideal.[1] It differed from *St. Nicholas** in its progressive pedagogical aims and attempts to reach a mass audience, at least in the New York years. The promotion campaign stressed the low price—initially 5¢ a copy and 50¢ a year for twelve issues. Advertisements seemed aimed at mothers and teachers, emphasizing books, baby food, housecleaning products, children's clothing at bargain rates, and practical prizes for subscriptions. Initially, its stated purposes were educational: to impart a taste for literature and art and to stimulate a desire for wholesome fun and work. Its writers and artists, the editors promised, were inspired by genuine love for children. The stress on work seemed equivalent to the stress on play; the founding editor's connection to Ernest Thompson Seton, with his dream of ending juvenile delinquency through organized activity, seems as important as any claims the magazine made in its pages.[2] Features would offer ''real literature for the little ones in school and home'' and would include articles of geographical and historical interest as well as natural history, introductory science, and contemporary events.[3] The periodical was to be content oriented as well as generally instructive and entertaining.

Katherine Newbold Birdsall, who was born in 1877, worked for the periodical from its beginning and is listed as editor after 1903. She had already written some children's books of a practical nature: *Jacks of All Trades* and *How to Make Money* (a theme she would emphasize in *Holiday*). After 1910 she left the magazine for *Over Sea and Land Magazine* and edited *The Young People's Bookshelf*. One of Birdsall's most prominent effects on *Children's Magazine* was her creation of ''Aunt Kate's Cosy House,'' a column devoted to the virtues of home life and apparently intended to attract girl readers in the same way her articles about Seton's Woodcraft Indians appealed to boy readers (soon to have the Boy Scouts available to them). The articles about Seton's nature lore had at first encouraged girls to join Woodcraft ''bands'' or to form their own groups to emulate ''the best things of the best Indians.''[4] Such attempts to be inclusive apparently did not work, however, and ''Aunt Kate'' began offering household projects and exemplary stories for girls. Her readers were invited to write in and to become members of "a Club of clubs" to enhance home life (badges were offered in return for subscriptions and later for a low price). "Aunt Kate" received mail from boys as well as girls wanting to be listed in the Club's Honor Roll for good behavior at home. Recipes, games, things to make, and ways to pass rainy days were interspersed with letters from children and their mothers.

Birdsall edited the magazine until it was taken over by S. E. Cassino, but two other editors are listed during the New York period. For two years (1904-1906) she was assisted by Walter Whitman Storms, former editor of *The Inland Educator: A Journal for the Progressive Teacher* (Terre Haute, Indiana) from 1899 to 1900. The magazine's varied attempts to involve children in experiments, puzzle solving, design, storywriting, exercise, and other activities may reflect Storms's background. From 1907 to 1909 Birdsall's partner was Vivian Burnett, who had worked on *McClure's Magazine*. Shortly after he joined *Children's Magazine*, Birdsall or her business associates pressured him to enlist his mother's support and the use of her name.[5] Although Frances Hodgson Burnett objected to the commercial aspect and exploitation of Vivian in this way, she allowed the magazine to advertise itself as "Frances Hodgson Burnett's *Children's Magazine*" and to list her as editor for a short period. She also published two of her stories in the magazine. "The Good Wolf" and "Barty Crusoe and His Man Saturday" are among a handful of fantasy tales the magazine published during its New York years.

The format of *Children's Magazine* was relatively unchanged from a slick paper, thirty-page quarto profusely illustrated with photographs, line drawings, and reproductions of paintings. Rebus, cartoons, and puzzles were also frequent. Often story contests involved the cover design, a seasonal drawing of children at play—fishing, marching in a patriotic parade, or skiing. Cover illustrators included Anthony H. Euwer, George Hittrick, Florence Choate, and Harold Sichel, many of whom also produced the ornate monthly calendar featured on the inside cover.

During Birdsall's tenure, departmental features were numerous, varied, and, at least during the early years, popular. In addition to "Cosy House" and "The Seton Indians," they included "Sam Loyd's Puzzle Page"; a column on gardening that carried out the magazine's seasonal theme; a Children's National Humane Society column called "The Bark" in which animals narrated brief accounts of how to care for them safely; "By the Sea," a feature encouraging donations to the Fresh Air Fund; and various cartoon items: Arthur A. Folwell's "The Wumpies" (a busy society of white males attended by one black male); "The Dollivers" (a largely female doll society equipped with one black female servant) and Gellett Burgess's "Goops." Other regular columns included nature writing by various authors, usually seasonal—for example, about Christmas greens or birds that could be observed in the Northeast that month; and "Thinkabit," analytic puzzles with readers' answers to be published the following month. All of these features stressed knowledge, habits of observation and inquiry, a love for the natural world, a mutual interchange between adults and children, and various kinds of social responsiblity. They did this with brevity, humor, and clarity, often inviting children to participate by laughing, searching, or building. Few features used what now would be considered heavy-handed methods; one that did, "Uncle Sam," a patriotic column that offered too-obvious lessons in civics, was discontinued after a year.

Part of the appeal of the magazine during the Birdsall editorship was the rich diversity of features. With its strength in informational writing, seconded by fiction, it seemed to pay little attention to the quality or frequency of poetry in its pages. The verse that did appear was often trite and didactic; during the Cassino period poetry was better represented by clever nonsense verse and child-experience poems, as well as by stories of children's visits to Tennyson and Longfellow. If Birdsall emphasized work-as-play, the Cassino years stressed word-as-play instead.

One of the earliest nonfiction articles, serialized in volume 1, suggests the standard that Birdsall hoped to meet, for it was advertized in the first issues, along with a forthcoming story by Jack London ("Keesh, the Bear Hunter") as the kind of story readers would enjoy in the new periodical. "Child of the Arctic" (published as *Snow Baby* in its book form) was the story of Marie Ahnighito Peary, the daughter of Commander Peary and the first white child born in the Arctic. Written by Josephine Peary and based on her diaries and her daughter's recollections of early childhood, the work is more thorough and honest than many contemporary biographies for children today. It gives a realistic portrayal of the not-always-comfortable meeting of two cultures. Although no comparably detailed biographies were to appear in subsequent issues, several outstanding nonfiction articles were published in 1904. "How Two Boys Crossed Niagara Falls in a Basket" by Julia D. Cawles (March, 1904) offers a crisp account of two children's loan of their kite to workmen needing it to span the river and of the boys' reward—a ride in the tool box they helped to equip as a pulley vehicle. The boys' terror, despite their agreeing to the "reward," is vividly revealed in dialog. Another article representative of the quality nonfiction of the early years was "China, Land of Kites" by Maude Barrows Dutton, beautifully illustrated with pictures from the American Museum of Natural History (April 1904).

In fiction the magazine seemed able to attract a variety of good authors throughout the two periods. Few names are repeated often during Birdsall's tenure, and none but Burnett is well known today. But in attracting and keeping Gertrude Smith as a regular contributor, the magazine was assured of its appeal to young children. "Mudder and Georgie," a sequence depicting a girl playing with her grandfather, uses effective language play when the two characters pretend to be, respectively, a mother with her mischievous boy. During the Cassino years, Smith continued to be published in the magazine; her "Reggie and Roggie" rebus stories were regular features in the later years. A strength of Birdsall's editorship was the use of occasional stories about immigrant or minority children (but not black children). One good example is "The Comical Pig" by Edith W. Wyede (August 1905), in which a Jewish peddler—helped by his wife—learns the unspoken wish of his little son to keep one of the toys he peddles from his sack. The story shows the child accompanying his mother to work (she is a domestic) and—without preaching—depicts the poverty of the family.

The tendency to include stories about various kinds of Americans was even more noticeable during the Cassino years, no doubt because the Massachusetts publisher seemed genuinely and almost solely interested in literature. After a year's transition, the contents of the periodical had altered, so only poetry, fiction, and a small sampling of nonfiction appeared. The numerous features that had elicited reader participation disappeared, despite an initial pledge to keep "Aunt Kate's Cosy House." The editors narrowed the age range, focusing on younger readers; the addresses to adults within the periodical came to an end, as did the emphasis on subscription sales for useful premiums. Words were bigger and stories longer, despite the omission of material designed for children over age ten or eleven. The magazine adopted an uncluttered look, even omitting standard items such as the table of contents, letters to the editor, and the names of the staff. It no longer solicited manuscripts, and sometimes reprinted material to which Cassino held an earlier copyright.

At least two authors of real merit are preserved in the Cassino volumes, both realistic and regional writers. Lucia Chase Bell wrote stories of the far West, specifically of a California girlhood. Elizabeth Robinson regularly offered tales of her pioneer youth, such as "How We Kept Thanksgiving (When I Was a Little Girl)" (November 1911). Both of these writers created active, interesting girl narrators and protagonists. Robinson's stories seem to be precursors of the Laura Ingalls Wilder tales; in many respects, they seem just as good.

The stories of the later period, in keeping with the expressly literary aims of the editors, often use mythic or folklore forms. They are also rich in wordplay, repetition, and other characteristics of traditional literature. Seasonal emphasis, as in the Birdsall editorship, was retained.

Finances apparently plagued both phases of the short-lived magazine. Cassino remaindered several thousand back numbers in 1911. Ten years later, an effort to revive the magazine was unsuccessful.

Notes

1. R. Gordon Kelly, "Terms for Order in Some Late 19th Century Fiction for Children," *Children's Literature* 1 (1972), 59.

2. John G. Samson, ed., *The Worlds of Ernest Thompson Seton* (New York: Knopf, 1976).

3. *Holiday Magazine for Children* 1 (August 1903), 1.

4. Ibid., p. 32.

5. Ann Thwaite, *Waiting for the Party: The Life of Frances Hodgson Burnett, 1849-1924* (New York: Scribner's, 1976), 218.

Information Sources

BIBLIOGRAPHY

Vivian Burnett, *The Romantick Lady* (New York: Scribner's, 1927); R. Gordon Kelly, *Mother Was a Lady* (Westport, Conn.: Greenwood Press, 1974); idem, "Terms for Order in Some Late 19th Century Fiction for Children," *Children's Literature* 1 (1972) 58-61; Ann Thwaite, *Waiting for the Party* (New York: Scribner's, 1974).

INDEX SOURCES

None.

LOCATION SOURCES

The Library of Congress has the most complete holdings, although their set is missing vol. 16 as well as vols. 3-4 and 6-11. Some listed sources have destroyed their holdings (for example, Oberlin). Duke University, Durham, N.C., has vols. 1-3 and 5-6.

Publication History

MAGAZINE TITLE AND TITLE CHANGES

Holiday Magazine for Children (August 1903-November 1905); *Children's Magazine* (December 1905-June 1913).

VOLUME AND ISSUE DATA

Holiday Magazine for Children (vol. 1, no. 1-vol. 5, no. 5); *Children's Magazine* (vol. 5, No. 6-vol. 16, no. ?)

PUBLISHER AND PLACE OF PUBLICATION

Holiday Publishing Co., New York (1903-1909); S. E. Cassino Co., Salem, Massachusetts (1909-1913).

EDITOR

Katherine Newbold Birdsall (1904-1909); Walter Whitman Storms (1904-1906); Vivian Burnett (and Frances Hodgson Burnett) (1907-1909); none listed (1909-1913).

Nancy Lyman Huse

CHILDREN'S PLAYMATE

In June 1929 Arthur R. Mueller, a printer and lithographer in Cleveland, Ohio, published the first edition of a children's magazine, which he called *Play Mate: For the Little Folks*. The opening page was inscribed with this verse: "The book is full of pastimes/As jolly as can be,/And all of those who read it/Will be Play Mates, you see." The *Playmate* concept—to entertain young people, provide outlets for their participation, excite imaginations, and inform—still permeates the magazine.

Mueller started *Play Mate* as an adjunct to his printing business. For the first two years he and Evelyn Betz, his secretary and bookkeeper, published the magazine. Then Esther Cooper was named editor; Fern Bisel Peat, art editor; and Evelyn Betz, business manager. Since both of the editors worked out of their homes, Betz had to serve as coordinator, forwarding the manuscripts from the Mueller office to the Cooper home in Richmond, Indiana, and then arranging for the artwork.

Mueller sold his business and the magazine in 1961 to Joseph T. Ondrey and Ralph Niederst with the right to use the Mueller name. Ondrey continued publishing the magazine at his Mueller Printing Company until 1968, when Beurt SerVaas, owner and president of Review Publishing Company, who had previously acquired *Child Life*,* purchased it and moved the magazine to Indianapolis, Indiana. In 1972 Curtis Publishing Company acquired Rival Publishing Company through a merger, and the Saturday Evening Post Company published the magazine until October 1979, when the Benjamin Franklin Literary and Medical Society, Inc., whose director is Cory SerVaas, M.D., wife of Beurt SerVaas, started to publish it. In April 1980 the Franklin Society exercised its option to purchase the magazine, and in August 1980 it began publishing *Children's Playmate* as a child health-care magazine. It is now one of the series published by the Children's Better Health Institute of the Benjamin Franklin Literary and Medical Society, Inc., with each magazine structured for a different age group: *Turtle* (two-six), *Humpty Dumpty's Magazine** (four-seven), *Children's Playmate* (five-eight), *Jack and Jill** (seven-ten), *Child Life* (eight-eleven), *Children's Digest** (nine-twelve), *Health Explorer* (ten-thirteen), and *Jr. Medical Detective* (eleven-fourteen). Beth Wood Thomas has served for most of the Indiana period as executive director of the group as well as the editor of *Children's Playmate*. For three and a half years (December 1973–August 1976) Julie Nixon Eisenhower acted as assistant editorial director of *Children's Playmate*.

The audience for the earliest *Play Mate* magazine was the age group four to fourteen; later it became six to twelve; under SerVaas, first three to eight and then five to eight. The editors found the age span three to eight too wide to serve—at best one or two read-aloud or rebus tales could be included for the preschoolers. To serve this group more adequately, then, a magazine *Turtle* for preschoolers two to six was added, and the *Children's Playmate* age group was changed to five to eight.

The magazine was first published in a 6½- by 9 ½-inch format with heavy cover; when the magazine was moved to Indianapolis, it became digest size (September 1968) with larger print, more interspersed color, and a more diversified cover design, usually featuring animals. In June-July 1977 the editors reverted to the original format to conform to the other magazines in the group. For economy, the covers became self-covers, and the former fifty-page magazine became a forty-eight-page issue printed on inexpensive soft pulp paper.

The magazine was published monthly until September 1959, when to ease publishing pressures it became a ten-issue publication with bimonthly issues during the summer. Since 1981 it has been published nine times a year, with bimonthly issues from April through September. Originally, the magazine cost $1.50 for twelve issues; it increased gradually to $5.00 for ten issues in 1970 to $10.95 for nine issues in 1981. No national advertising appears in the magazine, nor are there newsstand sales.

A generous portion of both conventional and traditional art—about a 50-50 ratio with editorial content—has been used over the years to illustrate and embellish and suggest. Ed Cortese, executive art director for the magazine, said, "Art plays a key role in encouraging children of this age bracket to read."[1] Illustrations by artists such as Joe and Beth Krush, Al Michini, and Joseph Csatarie are found throughout the pages, along with work of staff artists.

Very early issues used covers depicting a young boy and girl dressed in rich basic colors and a few color pages of cutouts in the center of the book, with more sprightly illustrations done in black and white generously interspersed. In later years the color became more subdued and cover figures more varied and more abstract, with animals and elves shown romping on the covers. Inner pages used colored type and, intermittently, blocks of basic colors as background, with second colors superimposed.

For the past years, economy has forced a more conservative use of art; and the new health commitment, a different cover policy. Type is now in black and less color is found inside, but lavishly colored full-spread covers are used. The covers display animals carrying a multitheme approach, with seasonal aspects and usually some phase of health or exercise portrayed, often with much detail. Peter Rabbit rides a bicycle carrying a basket of Easter eggs along a road where spring flowers are sprouting; bears in football jerseys jog down the road, and a turkey and a goose cast their November ballot for the Thanksgiving meal entree, against a red, white, and blue banner reminding folks to vote today. Every cover carries the notice "Children's Health Publication," and the editorial page now lists several medical doctors and other health consultants.

Children's Playmate today has a circulation of some 250,000. Much of today's material is staff written or is "recycled" material from other society magazines or is noncopyrighted material, but freelance material is also used. Beth Wood Thomas, the current editor, stated that 1,000 to 1,200 unsolicited manuscripts a month are received by the eight health magazines.[2] Ten percent of them are considered worthy of publication, and fewer than one-half are actually used. Some of the freelancers have become regular contributors over the years. Frances B. Watts has been publishing in the magazine since 1957; other frequent contributors include Fred Crump Jr., Roberta L. Fairall, Julia F. Lieser, and Lois J. Funk. Payment is modest, approximately 4¢ a word and $135 for a cover art display.

From the start the magazine has invited reader involvement; children were encouraged to send in letters about themselves, which the *Playmate* clown, Mr. Gee Whiskers, put in jingle form and published along with the sender's name and town. Children were urged to seek pen pals through the pages, send snapshots, and use "Everybody's Mailbox." With a few variations in form, this policy has been retained by all editors. Children send in riddles and enter storywriting and coloring contests. A recent column "All Yours" invites children to submit original drawings that are reproduced in the magazine. *Playmate* displays a marked degree of continuity over the years. Special columns and features have been retained and offer a sense of security for the young readers, who appreciate familiarity. Regular features include a page for easy recipes, a two-page richly illustrated poem, and serials such as "The Adventures of Beauregard Bunny," "Mystery in Spoof," and "Sue and Steve Shannon's Thrilling Space Adventure."

Other features have come and gone: cover poems of inspiration in the early days, an "Ask Gina" column, and a sixteen-page insert of colored comics. During the past few years this feature has been reduced to a two-page cartoon featuring the adventures of "Woof-Woof and Flip Flea," which provides a quiet, sophisticated humor with its incongruous characters and sly turn of events. Separate columns devoted to activities for boys and girls have been replaced by an arguably less sexist approach.

To keep step with the times, features on television personalities and their families and on space exploration have taken their place alongside the present emphasis on health care and good nutrition, and with the fables, folktales, word-building exercises, and puzzles with math and alphabet and phonics concepts. Rebus stories, embeddings, and cutouts are popular. Today's magazine often includes a song, has a regular easy science experiment to challenge those with such bent and an "All About" feature intended to inform readers about topics ranging from ostriches to Christopher Columbus to Hannukkah and greeting cards.

Over the years some stories have been built around simple themes such as the excitement of discovering that a woman on the bus is concealing a kitten in her bag; here children share the emotional response. Others recognize the need of children to belong and offer incidents to illustrate how children can learn to build satisfying friendships; others urge the need to cooperate, put away toys at night, and be kind and courteous and alert to dangers; still others give reassurance in various forms or recognize achievement—all a warm affirmation of traditional social values. Lively tales with animals allow children to relate these solutions to human situations—"Beaver the Best-Hearted Dog," "Bumble, the Oddball," "Gilly, the Gadabout Groundhog"—or share the adventures of "Trigger and the Trucker Mouse" and empathize with "The Girl Who Couldn't Eat Vegetables."

The early *Play Mate* title page listed sections for "Stories," "Articles," "Verse," "Pages to Amuse You," "Departments," and "Playmate Contests." Under the Thomas editorship, the sections were combined, with equal space for "Stories" and "Poems," "Features" and "Articles," and "Things to Do"; today's health publication has only two sections: "Health" and "More Fun." More than 50-70 percent of today's content is concerned with health, especially preventive medicine. The editorial policy is "to present material in a positive . . . light and to incorporate humor and a light approach wherever possible without minimizing the seriousness of what is being said."[3]

Articles, then, shun the didactic but attempt to be informative and appealing. Puzzles are now good food puzzles. Stories demonstrate telephone safety and the fact that glasses can be attractive. Articles explain why one needs sleep, how to avoid fire hazards. Games are built around concepts such as bicycle-safety rules, poison hazards, and aerobic exercises. Rhyme and rhythm, humor and wit, and pictures abound, so children will be entertained but will become informed as they enjoy. It is the society's conviction that good health habits and behavior patterns can be taught, that the teaching should start with the very young and should be sustained over a period of years, and that one of the best ways to teach children is through their magazines.

Early editions of the magazine included a page designed to involve parents directly; there they were urged to instill ideals of good workmanship in their children, to read to them in order to encourage superior intellectual development, to avoid disparaging effort, and to refrain from perpetual scolding and nagging. This didactic approach was soon abandoned, but in 1981 the editors reintroduced adult involvement in their health-care magazine. They now address parents and teachers to explain what the focus and emphasis of the issue is and what specific activities and stories achieve this. They note aims such as providing alternatives to the usual sugar-laden party menus, teaching caution and safety rules, avoiding bicycle accidents, and teaching the child not to touch strange animals. They explain, furthermore, that they use games and puzzles with important messages in them about health, safety, and nutrition, because children learn more readily when they are playing and enjoying themselves. They add that rhythm and rhyme and short poems make appealing teaching tools, that all is "fun with a purpose." The promise of jolly pastimes and entertaining playmates, made some fifty years ago in the first edition, remains, and *Children's Playmate* continues to woo children to the adventure and joy of reading and learning—today with an emphasis on health care.

Notes

1. Personal interview with Beth Wood Thomas, June 10, 1981.
2. Ibid.
3. "Editorial Requirements," Children's Better Health Institute, Benjamin Franklin Literary and Medical Society, Inc., p. 1.

Information Sources

BIBLIOGRAPHY
Children's Better Health Institute, Benjamin Franklin Literary and Medical Society, Inc., "Editorial Requirements." Bill Katz, ed., *Magazines for Libraries*, 2nd ed. (New York: Xerox, 1972).
INDEX SOURCES
Subject Index to Children's Magazines.
LOCATION SOURCES
Bound volumes are in the office of the Benjamin Franklin Literary and Medical Society, Inc., Indianapolis.

Publication History

MAGAZINE TITLE AND TITLE CHANGES
Play Mate (1929-1934); *Children's Play Mate* (1935-1952); *Children's Playmate* (1953-).

VOLUME AND ISSUE DATA
Play Mate (vol. 1, no. 1-vol. 6, no. 7); *Children's Play Mate* (vol. 1, no. 8-vol. 24, no. 7); *Children's Playmate* (vol. 24, no. 8-).
PUBLISHER AND PLACE OF PUBLICATION
A. R. Mueller Printing Co., Cleveland (1929-1961); Joseph Ondrey, Cleveland (1962-1968); Review Publishing Company, Indianapolis (September 1968-1972); Curtis Publishing Company, Indianapolis (1973-September 1979); Benjamin Franklin Literary and Medical Society, Inc., Indianapolis (October 1979-).
EDITOR
Esther Cooper (1932-1953); Rosemary Hart (1953-1961); Bonnie Ranville (D'Ettorre) (1962-August 1968); Rita Cooper (September 1968-March 1969); Beth Wood Thomas (April 1969-).

Evelyn Schroth

THE CHILD'S FRIEND AND FAMILY MAGAZINE

The Child's Friend, later *The Child's Friend and Youth's Companion* and finally *The Child's Friend and Family Magazine*, was edited intially by Eliza Lee Cabot Follen and published in Boston from October 1843 until February 1858 by the American Sunday School Union, as one of the pamphlets providing a focus for a curriculum for young Christians, both confessed and prospective. It is remarkably similar in content to *Children's Magazine* (1829-1874)* and other Sunday school material of that era and even later. Most of the contents is overtly moralistic—stories from the Bible intended to instill religious principles, as well as fictional episodes, usually stories about children, demonstrating a particular moral lesson. There are also occasional articles about history, geography, and natural science interspersed in the religious material, for the Sunday School Union was more than simply a religious institution.

The American Sunday School Union, founded in 1824, was an offshoot of the Sunday school movement in England, initiated by Robert Raikes in 1780.[1] According to an apocryphal account written for *The Child's Friend* by Nathaniel Hawthorne ("A Good Man's Miracle"), Raikes was inspired to found the first Sunday school while walking through a poor section of London.[2] According to Hawthorne's version, Raikes was struck by pity for the children in the street, who were spending idle time fighting, swearing, thieving, and gambling. Upon being told that things were even worse on Sunday, when none of the children had work, he began his first Sunday school to provide a moral environment for them at least one day of each week and to instruct them in their letters so that they might become better citizens and proper Christians.

In actual fact, and somewhat less dramatically than the Hawthorne version, Raikes began his career as a reformer working in prisons and only gradually became more concerned with the pitiful condition of street children. Although his first Sunday school was a failure, he publicized his efforts more successfully, and the institution proliferated throughout England.

Early Sunday schools in America, like those in England, were founded by benevolent citizens who wanted to provide education for poor children. They had both the evangelistic mission to convert the underprivileged to Christianity or to exploit such religious principles as they might already have and to provide a basic literacy for this group. Thus the "First Day" societies were founded in Philadelphia and Boston, and similar local societies grew up in many places on the Eastern Seaboard. As the momentum of the benevolent movement grew in the early years of the nineteenth century and as the young nation had resources increased beyond mere subsistence level, the basis for a national society was created. In 1824 The American Sunday School Union was founded, modeled in part on its English predecessor and in part on the American Bible Society (1816).

The Union suffered from the problems of communications of that time, making it difficult to maintain an organized and uniform pattern of instruction or to ensure the quality of instructors. The volunteer instructors were sometimes poorly prepared and often little older than their pupils. However, the society was caught up in the enthusiasm of westward expansion, and as settlement spread across the Mississippi Valley, the Union found a determination to provide both education and religion to the primitive western communities. In 1830 a platform was written "to establish a Sunday-School in every destitute place throughout the valley of the Mississippi."[3] Large contributions came from New York and Pennsylvania, and the drive established hundreds of schools in the West. For many, these Sunday schools were the only means of instruction for children.

In many ways the Sunday school pioneered for the public schools, forming "an interim organization for semi-popular education until the State was ready to take up its duty."[4] Concerned over illiteracy on the frontier, the Union sought to bring order into this society. Furthermore, the Union offered a model for later public schools by its mere existence—a school with a building, books, teachers, and pupils—and conditioned the public for the support of such an institution. Sunday schools had collections of books in many places where public schools and general libraries did not exist until decades later. A reader published by the Union sold 100,000 copies between 1850 and 1854.[5]

The Child's Friend began publication at the height of vitality of the Union in 1843 and continued until that vitality had begun to wane in 1858. During most of that time the editorship was in the hands of Eliza Lee Cabot Follen, who stepped down as active editor only in 1850, when she became seriously ill and was forced to leave Boston for a year in Hamburg. Apparently, the change in climate and scene was ineffective, because after her return she remained too ill to work on the pamphlet. Her job was taken over by a friend, Harriet L. Brown, in January 1851. The last editor was Anne Wales Abbot, 1857-1858.

The magazine provided the material needed by the enthusiastic, young volunteer teachers to instruct their charges in the generalized Christian morality endorsed by the Sunday School Union. To a modern reader, the morals seem impossibly repressive and stultifying, although they are typical of the schoolroom lessons of the time, as Henry Steele Commager commented in his examination of the McGuffey readers.[6]

The contents of *The Child's Friend* were appropriate to its purpose, short selections, each with its moral lesson—stories from the Bible, stories about children, edifying tales from foreign lands—and at the end of some issues, a few notes from the editor to the Sunday school teacher, giving the editor's views on educational theory. Thus in one issue we find, along with a biblical lesson called "The Justice of Jesus," a "Hymn" by Harriet Martineau, some notes on a meeting of the Teacher's Social Union, and Mrs. Follen's advice in "Methods of Teaching."[7] She believed that memory is the first quality formed in the mind of the child, "before imagination or reason," and that the teacher should depend mainly on this quality in the child's instruction. She pointed out that this has been the primary method of instruction in New England schools and the result, "the greatness of New England." Some conversation, she remarked, should ensue, after the memorized lesson has been recited, in which the teacher shows the child the point of the lesson. This would presumably have prevented the mere random memorization of Bible verses that was one of the banes of the Sunday School Union classes, deplored by the more skillful and industrious teachers.[8]

Some of the tales in *The Child's Friend* are simple morality tales, much like those found in the oral tradition, like the tale of two spoons, one of silver, one of iron. The silver spoon lords it over the iron one, but the iron staunchly defends itself as more useful and therefore the more valuable of the two. Others endorse the general morality of the Sunday school—kindness to the poor, thoughtfulness of the feelings of others, loyalty to obligations, as in the story of "The Wishing Cap," where two little sisters make woolen petticoats for poor children while their brothers chop and stack wood for the stoves of poor families. They wish for a wishing cap, so they can help all poor children. They are told to begin with small tasks, enough of which can reform the world.

Some stories, however, contain moral impositions that most today would find repellent.[9] In "Ernest's Birthday," Ernest is given as a present a "Birthday Book," containing a list of all bad things he has done during the year—not much of a positive reinforcement. In "The Little Red Shoe" a little girl is proud of her appearance in her new red shoes, until one of them gets wet and fades. She is forced to wear shoes of two colors and learns the emptiness of vanity. These and similar stories develop a sense of guilt in the child that most modern teachers would prefer to avoid.

Notes

1. Information on the history of the American Sunday School Union is largely taken from William Bean Kennedy, *The Shaping of Protestant Education* (New York: Association Press, 1966).
   2. *The Child's Friend* 1, no. 5 (February 1844), 151.
   3. Kennedy, *The Shaping of Protestant Education*, p. 15.

4. Frederick A. Packard, *Popular Sketch of the Rise and Progress of Sunday-Schools in the United States* (Philadelphia: The American Sunday School Union, 1845).
5. Kennedy, *The Shaping of Protestant Education*, p. 24.
6. Ibid., p. 29.
7. *The Child's Friend* 1, no. 4 (January 1844).
8. Ibid., p. 209.
9. Ibid., 9, no. 2 (November 1847), 66, 70, 82.

Information Sources

BIBLIOGRAPHY
None.
INDEX SOURCES
None.
LOCATION SOURCES
American Antiquarian Society, Worcester, Mass.; Boston Public Library; Boston Atheneum; Bowdoin College, Brunswick, Maine; Brown University, Providence, R. I.; Burton Historical Collection, Detroit, Mich.; Harvard University, Cambridge, Mass.; Iowa State Travelling Library, Des Moines, Ia.; Library of Congress; New York Public Library; University of Michigan, Ann Arbor, Mich.; University of Minnesota, Minneapolis, Minn.; Wellesley College, Wellesley, Mass.; Yale University, New Haven, Conn. Also available on microfilm in the American Periodical Series, University Microfilms International, Ann Arbor, Mich.

Publication History

MAGAZINE TITLE AND TITLE CHANGES
Child's Friend; Designed for Families and Sunday Schools (1843-1845); *Child's Friend* (1845-1851); *Child's Friend and Youth's Magazine* (1851-1855); *Child's Friend and Family Magazine* (1855-1858).
VOLUME AND ISSUE DATA
Child's Friend; Designed for Families and Sunday Schools (vol. 1, no. 1, October 1843-vol. 4, no. 6, September 1845); *Child's Friend* (vol. 5, no. 1, October 1845-vol. 15, no. 6, September 1851); *Child's Friend and Youth's Magazine* (vol. 16, no. 1, October 1851-vol. 25, no. 6 (?)); *Child's Friend and Family Magazine* (vol. 26, no. 1 (?) October 1856-vol. 31, no. 5, February 1858).
EDITORS
Eliza Lee Cabot Follen (October 1843-September (?) 1851); Harriet L. Brown (October (?) 1851-December (?) 1856); Anne Wales Abbot (January (?) 1857-February 1858).
PUBLISHER AND PLACE OF PUBLICATION
Leonard C. Bowles, Boston (1843-1858).

Meredith M. Klaus

COBBLESTONE

Cobblestone, an American history magazine for young people of ages eight to thirteen, published its first issue in January 1980. Founded by Hope Hamilton

Pettegrew, publisher, and Frances Brown Nankin, editor, *Cobblestone* is an attractive monthly publication, designed to be both informative and entertaining. Its purpose is to make history alive and relevant for young people.

The idea for the magazine grew out of Hope Pettegrew and Frances Nankin's changing attitudes toward history as adults and from their experiences as elementary schoolteachers. "We both recognized that there was a dearth of periodicals on American history for children," said Nankin. "It was our feeling that the upper elementary schools are quite negligent in teaching history. That was certainly our experience as kids. When we came to American history as adults and discovered how exciting it can be, we were amazed at what we had missed."[1] In addition, both women thought that children should be given a realistic picture of American history without the myths about perfect forefathers who never told lies, so that children would not become disillusioned.

Pettegrew and Nankin met each other for the first time on Labor Day 1978 at a dinner party given by Audrey Sweeney, a mutual friend (now administrative assistant for *Cobblestone*). Much to their surprise, they discovered that they had the same ambition: to publish an American history magazine for children. Also, they both had recently left teaching: Nankin was expecting her first baby and Pettegrew wanted more time to be with her teenage daughters. They were ready for a new venture.

Between them they had relatively little publishing experience. Only Nankin had previously written and published a book (*My First Book of Words*, Walker and Company). However, both of their husbands had had experience in publishing—Pettegrew's husband is a corporate director of advertising for Yankee Publications and Nankin's husband is a former newspaper editor—so this helped the women to make contacts. Also, their location in Peterborough, New Hampshire, was an advantage since at least twenty-five magazines are published in the area and the nearby MacDowell Colony attracts artists, musicians, and authors. There were numerous individuals the women could turn to for expertise, advice, and inspiration.

For a year and a half they met in coffee shops and the town library of Peterborough, researching the market, computing costs, and mapping out the first issue. When they approached banks about a loan, their applications were turned down. "Two relatively inexperienced women trying to launch a children's history magazine just didn't impress them as a good risk," said Pettegrew.[2] In June 1979 they became a corporation, drew up a prospectus, and sought local investors. After raising only $110,000 and sending out 100,000 direct mail proposals, they began publication. Since then the list of subscribers has grown from the original 2,500 to more than 33,000 (September 1981).

Each issue of *Cobblestone* focuses on a single theme, such as a person ("Thomas Edison," February 1980), an event ("The Boston Massacre," March 1980), a place ("The Grand Canyon," June 1980), an institution ("Old-Time Schools in America," November 1981), or an idea that has some relation to the month of the publication ("America at Play," July 1980).

Pettegrew and Nankin decided to devote each issue to a single theme, because "As teachers, we know that children learn by reinforcement. Just to have a hodge-podge of articles is meaningless to them in a lot of ways. We also see this as a mini-unit for teachers."[3]

By having a single theme for each issue, the magazine's founders hope to give children an in-depth view of history. The October 1980 issue, for example, includes articles about Thomas Nast, the father of political cartooning; Victoria C. Woodhull, the first woman presidential candidate; the method by which we elect our president; the origin of electioneer techniques that began in 1840; the history of the League of Women Voters; the drawing of caricatures; and anecdotes about past presidents; as well as an introductory essay, written by the editor, that gives an overview of the theme discussed in the issue.

In addition, the magazine tries to have children see a historical event from a variety of angles and points of view. The March 1980 issue, for example, contains two differing eyewitness accounts of the Boston Massacre. The April 1981 issue on the Civil War includes articles about both the South and the North, so youngsters will know what happened in their region during that conflict and will be exposed to both sides of the argument.

In choosing themes, Nankin uses three criteria. During any twelve-month period the themes must progress through a variety of areas so that they cover a long period from the early Spanish explorers to the present, touch upon different areas around the country so that the entire United States is covered, and deal with a variety of human experiences, not just wars and battles, people or inventors.[4]

To help her generate themes and plan each issue of the magazine, Nankin has an Advisory Board, comprised of individuals who share the same basic interest in children and history but who come from different backgrounds. The primary members of the board are Robert S. Fay, Ed.D., a teacher and writer; Marvin Hoffman, Ph.D., a principal and writer; William Riley, Ph.D., a historian; and John Pierce, the managing editor of *Yankee*.

Every six months Nankin asks the Advisory Board to suggest the themes they would find exciting for *Cobblestone*. From these suggestions she plans another twelve issues. Thus the magazine is almost always mapped out eighteen months in advance of publication. Periodically, Nankin also has "wish meetings" where board members brainstorm particular themes to determine what they'd like to see in issues having those particular themes. Following the meetings she and her assistant map out the proposals, taking into consideration the feasibility of each of the ideas.

"We also try to do things that there's not a wealth of material on," said Pettegrew. "Everyone's written on Abraham Lincoln and George Washington and Benjamin Franklin. Not that we wouldn't cover anything like that. We also want to get the children interested in other things in history. There's more to our history than those few people we all think of immediately."[5]

Certainly, the first issue of *Cobblestone* had an unusual theme for its focus: "The Philadelphia Mummers." Nankin chose this theme because the first issue would come out in January 1980. It would be the beginning of a new year and a new magazine, so she and Pettegrew said, "Let's celebrate with a parade."[6] Looking around the country, Nankin decided to focus on Philadelphia, because, historically, it is one of the centers of American history. The custom of mumming on New Year's Day came to Philadelphia with the early English settlers, and Philadelphia's mummers are famous for their annual parade. Also, since George Washington was used in some of the mummers' plays instead of Saint George, the issue could include a biography of him—something that readers would expect to be in the magazine.

Each issue of *Cobblestone* contains a variety of reading material, both non-fiction and fiction. The carefully chosen and well-edited text and its accompanying illustrations (a blend of photographs, engravings, art reproductions, maps, charts, drawings, and cartoons) convey the editor's belief that "History is not simply a chronology of events that people happen to remember. It's a discussion of all the disciplines—literature, art, science, politics."[7] The first issue of the magazine noted in bold-faced type the scope of the magazine's contents: play, dance, music, nonfiction, making things, biography, poetry. Although every issue may not include all of these categories, each seeks to present a rounded view of history.

"Our message to young people is 'You and I make history. People make history.' " said Nankin.[8] It is therefore not surprising that the majority of the nonfiction articles are biographical, and they can be grouped into four categories. Approximately one-third of the biographies are about famous, well-known Americans of the past. Articles such as Linda R. Wade's "Thomas Jefferson: Our Expansion-Minded President" (September 1980), Charlotte Van Vleck's "Willa Cather: Nebraska's Pioneer" (December 1980), Peg Mims and Walter Oleksy's "The Woman Called Moses" (February 1981), Kathleen Burke's "For the Love of the Prairies; The Story of Buffalo Bill" (August 1981), and Laurel Sherman's "King of Steel" (September 1981) encompass a wide variety of human accomplishments and include persons from different regional, ethnic, and social backgrounds. Most of these biographies stress the importance of childhood experiences in which skills are learned, habits are formed, aptitudes are developed, friendships are made, and goals are formulated. They show clearly how these experiences shaped the person's life and played a significant role in the individual's adult life. They also extol the virtues of bravery, individualism, self-confidence, and persistence.

Another one-third of the biographies deal with lesser known or obscure individuals in American history. Otis Hays, Jr.'s "Bird Woman" (September 1980) focuses on Sacajawea, the sixteen-year-old Shoshone Indian who acted as a guide for the Lewis and Clark expedition; Louise Purdy Monk's "Deborah's Namesake" (November 1980) relates the story of Deborah Simpson, who disguised herself as a man and fought in the American Revolutionary War; Tim Clark's "Old Leather Man" (January 1981) tells of a man dressed in leather who walked a 366-mile circuit through the countryside of Connecticut and eastern

New York and appeared in towns with clocklike regularity every thirty-four days; Robert Feeman's "First Prisoner of the Civil War" (April 1981) deals with Thaddeus Lowe, a balloonist who used aeronautics to spy on the Confederates; and Darren Sextro's "Mount St. Helens' Harry Truman" (May 1981) sketches the life of a man who refused to leave his home beneath a volcanic mountain. The recurring theme in these biographies is that every person is a part of human history.

The remaining biographical articles are of two types: profiles of groups of people and biographies of animals. Charlotte Gemmell's "Builders of the First Transcontinental Railroad" (May 1980) is about the Irish, Chinese, and other workers on the Union Pacific and Central Pacific Railroads; Robert C. Euler's "People of the Blue-green Water" (July 1980) is about the Havasupui who live in Grand Canyon; and Tim Jones's "Sourdoughs" (August 1980) is about the Klondike prospectors. All of these contributions record the history, life-styles, and contributions of people who shared a common enterprise or culture. Vera Saban's "Roman Nose, The Horse That Joined the Klondike Stampede" (August 1980), Walter Oleksy's "Eagle That Went to War" (April 1981), and Eloise Paananen's "Astrocreatures: Real Pioneers" (July 1981) all show how animals have played important, often heroic, roles in our history too.

Historical articles constitute the second largest group of essays. Some of them focus on places. Typical are Glen Swanson's "Farmington: 300 Years of History" (January 1981) and Dianne MacMillan's "Boston Light: America's First" (June 1981). Processes are described in Lila Watz's "How We Choose Our President" (October 1980) and Karen O'Connor's "Getting the Goods to Market" (September 1981). Kathleen Burke's "John Brown's Raid at Harper's Ferry" (February 1981) and "The Story of America's Industrial Revolution" (September 1981) deal with events or historical periods. The origin and history of things such as games, foods, words, institutions, and traditions in our country today are related in David Lee Drotar's "Wild and Crazy Sport" (July 1980), Loretta Holz's "*Fraktur*: A German-American Tradition" (November 1980), and Virginia C. Holmgren's "Our Spanish Heritage" (March 1981). Although most of the historical articles are about the past, a few look forward as does Herbert Bixler's "Railroads Tomorrow" (May 1981). All of these articles try to familiarize children with precedents and give them a better perspective on the events that have led up to the present state of affairs so today's problems will seem less unsolvable, less frightening.

"I like to imagine that *Cobblestone* is helping to shape a generation of leaders who will have a clearer vision of the total picture of human events," stated Nankin. "If we can give our readers a clear picture of how things we take for granted today got started, we are also giving them a very important tool. Knowing why people decided to do things in a certain way at a certain time helps us decide, considering our present need, what changes need to be made."[9]

To make history relevant and alive for children, the magazine includes some eyewitness accounts of events, such as Robert Louis Stevenson's account of his train ride from Iowa to California in "Across the Plains" (May 1980), explorer John Wesley Powell's journal entries regarding his expedition down the Colorado River in "In Search of a River's End" (June 1980); and astronaut Eugene Cernan's recollections of the Apollo 17 mission in "Memories from the Moon" (July 1981). A few of the eyewitness accounts are those of young people, such as "Frog-Holes and Other Summer Tales" (July 1980), which is a collection of short sketches written by children about their summer activities; "Searching for Rachel" (November 1980), which records Adina Rachel Hoffman's search to find out more about her aunt who died in a concentration camp; and "May 18th, 1980: Eyewitness Accounts by Cobblestone Readers" (May 1981), which contains drawings, poems, and first-person reports regarding the Mount St. Helens' eruption. These latter accounts not only reinforce the idea that the children themselves are participating in history, but they also encourage children to record present-day events that may be of interest to people in the future.

Because *Cobblestone* wants children to experience history, a large number of articles are activity centered. Bill Young's "Making a Telegraph Sender and Receiver" (February 1980) and "The Game of Goose" (July 1980), Vivian Day's "Let's Draw a Buffalo" (August 1980) and "Making a Family Chart" (November 1980), and Ruth Pittman's "Making a Soddie" (December 1980) and "Cocido Español" (March 1981) encourage children to apply scientific principles, use their imaginations, conduct research, develop skills, and enjoy some aspect of their culture.

Reader involvement is also encouraged through regular departments. "Dear Ebenezer" publishes letters that children (and adults) write to the magazine's mascot Ebenezer. "Ebenezer's Teasers" includes quizzes and puzzles on the material in each issue. "Digging Deeper" lists books for kids and books for grownups and suggests places to visit.

So far, few scientific articles have appeared. Bruce Porell's "How Do You Ask a Bird What It Knows?" (April 1980), Linda Wong's "Monitoring a Mountain" (May 1981) and Louise Riotte's "Space Suits for the Moon" (July 1981) are some of the exceptions, although scientific material is presented in other nonfictional and fictional selections.

Stories, plays, poems, and, occasionally, folk songs constitute the magazine's fiction. Lucinda Winslow's "Free Wheeling" (February 1980), which dramatizes a day in the life of enterprising, thirteen-year-old Thomas Edison aboard the Grand Trunk Railroad, and Ann Keefe's "If There Had Been Television in 1869" (May 1980), which is a television news script for an on-the-spot coverage of the linking of the Union Pacific and Central Pacific Railroads, help children recreate an event or adventure. The majority of the stories, which are historical fiction, also attempt to show children not just what happened, but how people (or animals) felt and what they thought about events and places. Barbara Brenner's "Joseph Mason's Journal" (April 1980) is written to help children imagine how it must have been like to work every day with John James Audubon.

Marguerite Henry's "Over the Rimtop" (June 1980) tells about Brighty, a lonely burro, who climbs to the rim of Grand Canyon in search of companionship.

The name of the magazine was derived easily and by accident. "A friend of mine was going into business and mentioned Cobblestone as a possible name for her real estate office," said Pettegrew. "I thought the name said a lot in one word. It suggests history and a road, and the magazine is a journey through history. When Fran heard the name, she said, 'That's it!' "[10]

Pettegrew and Nankin almost put as their subtitle for the magazine "a journey through history" but decided on *A History Magazine for Children* instead. Eight months later they changed the subtitle to *A History Magazine for Young People* after receiving letters from junior high teachers asking them to make this change.

"Cobblestones are also durable," said Nankin, "and one aspect of these issues is that they're timeless. They're living testimony to what has happened."[11] Readers who want to keep past issues bound together may order a slipcase from *Cobblestone*, which also publishes a yearly index listing the authors and subjects covered in any particular year.

The magazine's mascots, Ebenezer, a town crier, and Colonel Cracker, a crow, were also easy to choose, as was their illustrator, D. B. Johnson, a cartoonist living in Lebanon, New Hampshire. Comical Ebenezer and his mischievous crow, with whom children can easily identify and communicate, appear throughout every issue in regular departments that are named after them: "Dear Ebenezer," "The View from the Crow's Nest," "Ebenezer's Atlas," "Cracker's Barrel," and "Ebenezer's Teasers." Thus the editor speaks indirectly to her readers through these mascots.

Cobblestone, like a number of other children's magazines, offers children lively, imaginative reading, but as a bonus, it also gives them history and inspires an interest in their heritage.

Notes

1. Maria Lenhart, "History Magazine for Young People Tells It Like It Was," *The Christian Science Monitor*, January 18, 1981, p. 21.
2. Frances Nankin and Hope Pettegrew, interviewed by Janet D. Vine (Peterborough, New Hampshire), 11:30 a.m., July 7, 1981, hereafter cited as "interview."
3. Alice Fuld, "Success Delights 'Cobblestones' Founders," *The Keene Sentinel*, November 3, 1980, p. 8.
4. Interview.
5. Ibid.
6. Ibid.
7. Ibid.
8. Ibid.
9. Frances Nankin, personal correspondence with Janet D. Vine, October 6, 1981.
10. Interview.
11. Ibid.

Information Sources

BIBLIOGRAPHY

Georgina Fiordalisi, "Jamestown Native Starts New History Magazine," *The Post-Journal*, November 1, 1980, p. 3T; Alice Fuld, "Success Delights 'Cobblestone' Founders," *The Keene Sentinel*, November 3, 1980, p. 8; Pat Graves, "Cobblestone," *Leisure*, April 23-30, 1981; Maria Lenhart, "History Magazine for Young People Tells It Like It Was," *The Christian Science Monitor*, January 18, 1981, p. 21; "Unusual Magazine Makes History Fun," *New York Times*, August 23, 1981, p. 44.

INDEX SOURCES

None.

LOCATION SOURCES

Issues of the magazine may be obtained from *Cobblestone*, Peterborough, New Hampshire. Some issues are in various public libraries.

Publication History

MAGAZINE TITLE AND TITLE CHANGES

Cobblestone: The History Magazine for Children (January 1980-July 1980); *Cobblestone: The History Magazine for Young People* (August 1980-).

VOLUME AND ISSUE DATA

Cobblestone: The History Magazine for Children (vol. 1, no. 1-vol. 1, no. 7); *Cobblestone: The History Magazine for Young People* (vol. 1, no. 8-).

PUBLISHER AND PLACE OF PUBLICATION

Cobblestone Publishing, Inc., Peterborough, N.H. (January 1980-).

EDITOR

Frances Brown Nankin (January 1980-).

Janet Diana Vine

CRICKET: THE MAGAZINE FOR CHILDREN

Cricket: The Magazine for Children, published monthly by Open Court Publishing Company, was introduced to the public in September 1973 and since that time has attempted to maintain its declared high standards of giving its readers, six to twelve years of age, the very best in reading matter. Consisting of about 100 pages an issue, it sells for $1.75 a copy on the newsstands or $15.00 a year by subscription (1981) and carries no outside advertising.

From the beginning *Cricket* has boasted a distinguished Editorial Board consisting of Lloyd Alexander, Eleanor Cameron, Sheila Egoff, Virginia Haviland, Paul Heins, Walter Scherf, Isaac Bashevis Singer, and Kay Webb. At its inception the senior editor was Clifton Fadiman; Marianne Carus is now editor-in-chief, and John Rowe Townsend serves as executive editor of the United Kingdom edition. An avowed aim of the magazine was to "attempt to bridge the gap existing in children's magazine publishing since *St. Nicholas** ceased publication in 1937 [*sic*]."[1] The emphasis would be on "quality, with original stories, poems, articles, and illustrations by foremost writers and illustrators."[2] Fadiman was quoted as stating: "There is no substitute for the written word and the well-drawn line. . . . We want *Cricket* to act as neutralizer against the cheap, the sensational, and the violent."[3]

The theme of "crickets" is carried throughout each volume by using little creatures in margins, as well as in articles, stories, and illustrations, to explain difficult words and concepts and to give a running commentary on that page's content, author, and illustrations. Beside Cricket, there are Ladybug, Muffin (a British beetle), Slugge (a snail), H. A. Rey (a flea), Earthworm, Ugly Bird, Mimi (a spider), Anna and Marianne (ants), Charlie the youngest cricket, and Everybuggy, the magazine's designation for everybody. Although this device was early criticized as being "gimmicky," it has helped endear the magazine to its young readers through this personalization of the creatures: they are as real and as important as any other facet of the content.[4]

Within the pages of *Cricket* "various subjects and genres are represented, including poetry, folktales, biography, nonfiction articles, and fiction from animal stories to adventure, fantasy, science fiction, and modern realism."[5] Here are to be found some of the best poets of the last half of our century as well as some older ones: Harry Behn (March 1974), Richard Wilbur (March 1974), David McCord (September 1974), Aileen Fisher (September 1975), John Ciardi (September 1978), and Karla Kuskin (September 1974).

A variety of folk literature has been presented in the magazine: a Vietnamese tale, "What a Tailor Should Know" (March 1974); an African tale, "The Clever Warthog" (September 1974); a Lithuanian tale, "The Popplesnitch" (September 1978); a Yurek Indian tale, "When Eel Gambled" (September 1979); a Scottish hob-goblin story, "Good Luck Bogle" (September 1980); and a Celtic myth, "The Finding of Oisin" (September 1980). Biographical sketches have been included on Mozart (September 1975), Thomas Jefferson (March 1974), and "The Real Robinson Crusoe" (September 1976).

Cricket has offered its readers nonfiction articles on an impressive array of subjects; historical topics treated include the Ice Age (September 1974), "Codes in the Revolutionary War" (September 1976), "The Great Corliss Engine" (September 1976), "Quill Pens and Berry Ink" (September 1979), and "Mummies Made in Egypt" (September 1980). Interesting scientific topics that have been explored are owls (March 1974), blinking (September 1974), crickets (September 1976), and sea turtles (September 1980). Sports and other activities were the subject of some articles: "The Dance," a story in pictures from jumping rope to ballet performances (September 1976); "Who's Minding the Fort?" the story of the origin of lacrosse (September 1977); and "Bouncing Games" (September 1980).

Selections dealing with crafts have concerned homemade playdough (March 1974), gardening in a bottle (September 1975), making cardboard furniture (September 1976), and unusual Halloween decorations (September 1980).

Many popular stories for children have appeared in whole or in part in *Cricket*: Arnold Lobel's "A Swim—A Frog and Toad Story" (September 1974) and "Ice Cream" (September 1976), *Mandy's Grandmother* by L. Skorpen (September 1975), and *Emma* by W. Kesselman (September 1980). Among the outstanding authors whose stories have been featured are Mary Stolz and Jane Yolen (September 1974), George Selden (March 1974), Astrid Lindgren (September 1975), Natalie Savage Carlson (September 1979), William J. Smith (March 1974), and Hilda Van Stockum (September 1977).

In each issue stories introduce characters and situations from other lands: "The Chess Player" (September 1974), "Janet Reachfar and the Kelpie" (September 1976), "Listen to the Angels Laughing" (September 1977), and "The Dancing Man" (September 1980).

"Meet Your Author" is a monthly feature giving a sketch of an author whose work appears in that issue. Among the authors who have been included are F. N. Monjo, author of "Letters to Horseface" (September 1975); Russell Hoban, author of "Tisbury Toads" (September 1976); and Arnold Lobel, author of "The Crickets" (September 1977). Two variations of this feature have been "Meet Your Poet"—John Ciardi, who wrote "A Bit of This, a Bit of That" (September 1978) and "Meet Your Artist"—Trina Schart Hyman, art director of *Cricket* (September 1975).

In analyzing the artwork of *Cricket*, Selma K. Richardson stated: "The excellence in literary content is complemented by the many illustrations, often by notable illustrators, which add much diversity and liveliness to the magazine."[6] The covers of *Cricket* were mentioned by another critic: "The very beautiful cover illustrations are worthy of framing."[7] This is especially true of the September 1977 issue, which had a full-page cover illustration of Pieter Brueghel's "Village Fair" and then discussed his work and his life in an unusual article inside.

Other regular features of *Cricket* help account for its success and popularity. "Cricket League" is the department of the magazine that sponsors monthly contests among the readers in three areas of creativity: stories, poems, and artwork—each subdivided into younger and older levels. Each month challenging, imaginative topics, often related to some area of that issue's content, are announced, and three months later the award-winning entries are published. Some story topics have been "my happiest/funniest/worst birthday party"; "midsummer's eve"; "a long, long time ago"; "a pet's adventure"; and "the best Christmas present I ever gave." Poetry subjects have been "the other side of the fence"; "a body of water"; "the time of day I prefer"; "I know a secret"; and "the time capsule." Artwork has been solicited on subjects such as "a daring rescue," "what I like best at the fair"; "crazy cakes"; "vehicles"; "the music lesson"; and "through the window." At times the subjects are left open for the children's free choice. In an editorial note it was stated that an average of 600 contest entries are received each month (September 1976).

"Cricket's Bookshelf" is devoted to book reviews, several of which are contained in each issue, usually focused on a single theme: grandparent stories (September 1975), Scandinavian stories (September 1976), whales (September 1977), and terrific or terrible teachers (September 1979).

Other regular features of the magazine are "Crossbird Puzzles," usually following a seasonal theme; Waldo Weddershin's "Practical Hints"; and the "Letterbox," submissions such as jokes and riddles, and correspondence from readers throughout the English-reading world. Usually, the back cover is a foldout enumerating the enticing features of the next issue.

"Old Cricket Says," the final department of each issue, serves as an editorial forum and has been a source of information about diverse subjects such as "the Battle of Yorktown" (October 1981), "the history of elevators" (November 1981), "toothbrushes" (September 1981), and "curious sayings from folk speech" (September 1976). In the 5th anniversay edition, Old Cricket discussed how winners are chosen in the monthly contests: "Most important in all categories are good, original ideas. We are looking for lively, well worked-out stories with a beginning, middle, and end, careful and clear writing, and a good choice of words. Poems do not always have to rhyme, but they have to have rhythm and meter and a *mood* that touches the person who reads them. . . . We judge drawings on technique, draftsmanship, and the ability to 'solve the problem' set up by the contest topic."[8]

Cricket, through an array of special offers, attempts to make itself an integral part of its readers' lives. Back issues, slipcases for holding a year's issues, posters, t-shirts, sunvisors, and recordings all aim at surrounding the faithful reader with Cricketry. In addition, two paperback libraries of ten books each—Ladybug Favorites (for young readers) and Slugge's Favorites (for older readers)—are available: "our favorites. . .books that never grow old, never lose the touch of magic. . . . We think some of our favorites might become your favorites."[9]

In an early issue Old Cricket explained to readers the magazine's purpose: to give "you funny stories and fairy stories and scary stories and stories about things that happen all around us—stories by American story-tellers and also writers from foreign countries. Nonsense verse and songs to sing and jokes to laugh at and riddles and puzzles and tongue-twisters—stuff about great men and women of the past and present; about science and machinery and plants and animals and *loads of pictures*."[10] All this and more has been done. When one surveys the variety of fare *Cricket* offers to its readers, sustaining its high quality month after month and year after year, it is evident that its avowed purpose of offering "a good range of literate, mind-widening material and not talking down to its readers has been achieved.[11] "Without a hint of condescension, every word is directed to the children," whether it is story or article, illustration or feature;[12] and children, as well as their parents and teachers, have loved every elegantly detailed issue and made *Cricket* their favorite literary magazine.

Notes

1. *"Cricket*—A New Quality Magazine for Children," *Publishers Weekly*, July 16, 1973, p. 91.
2. Ibid.
3. "Critic's *Cricket*," *Time*, December 10, 1973, p. 94.
4. Stephanie Harrington, "In the Company of Crickets," *New York Times Book Review*, November 4, 1973, p. 63.
5. Selma K. Richardson, *Periodicals for School Media Programs* (Chicago: American Library Association, 1978), 111.
6. Ibid.
7. Mary Ann Wentroth, "Added Entries—*Cricket*," *Top of the News* 29 (April 1973), 262.
8. *Cricket*, September 1977, p. 96.
9. Ibid., inside back cover.
10. Ibid., September 1974, p. 96.
11. "Critic's *Cricket*," p. 91.
12. Wentroth, "Added Entries," p. 262.

Information Sources

BIBLIOGRAPHY

Alyce Joyce Chambers, "Recent Trends in Children's Periodicals" (M.A. thesis, Tennessee State University, 1975); *"Cricket*—A New Quality Magazine for Children," *Publishers Weekly*, July 16, 1973, p. 91; "Critic's *Cricket*," *Time*, December 10, 1973, p. 94; Stephanie Harrington, "In the Company of Crickets," *New York Times Book Review*, November 4, 1973, p. 63; Bill Katz, ed., *Magazines for Libraries*, 2nd ed. (New York: R. R. Bowker, 1972); Selma K. Richardson, *Periodicals for School Media Programs* (Chicago: American Library Association, 1978); Mary Ann Wentroth, "Added Entries—*Cricket*," *Top of the News* 29 (April 1973), 262.

INDEX SOURCES

Subject Index to Children's Magazines.

LOCATION SOURCES

New Serial Titles lists twenty-eight libraries—university, public, and state—with holdings from vol. 1, no. 1.

Publication History

MAGAZINE TITLE AND TITLE CHANGES
Cricket: The Magazine for Children (September 1973-)
VOLUME AND ISSUE DATA
Cricket: The Magazine for Children (vol. 1, no. 1-).
PUBLISHER AND PLACE OF PUBLICATION
Open Court Publishing Company, LaSalle, Ill. (September 1973-).
EDITOR
Marianne Carus (September 1973-).

Mary D. Manning

D

DEMOREST'S YOUNG AMERICA

When William J. Demorest began publishing *Demorest's Young America* in November 1866, he proposed to fill a need he saw evident in the offerings of literature to the children of his day. The illustrated monthly that sold for 15¢ a copy was instituted to counteract and compete with a "low and demoralizing class of literature, prepared expressedly to gratify that love of the marvellous, the absurd, and the unnatural that is fostered in the young."[1] *Demorest's Young America* championed a rational conception of reality, focusing on interesting and amusing facts of nature and society. Its goal was to present to the young "an epitome of this curious world in which they have come to live and in which they are to leave their mark for good or evil."[2] Seeking to elevate and entertain his readers at the same time, Demorest's move away from overt didacticism to a more subtle presentation of values was indicative of a trend in American children's literature that developed during this period.

Demorest had entered publishing in 1860, with German and English editions of *The Mirror of Fashion*. Aided by his wife, who styled herself Madame Demorest, he consolidated his efforts into *Demorest's Illustrated Monthly*, which became *Demorest's Monthly Magazine*, a women's fashion magazine edited for twenty-seven years by Jenni C. Croly, who pioneered women's departments in the American press.[3] An ardent abolitionist, Demorest also issued during the war an abolitionist paper, *Phunniest Phun*, and circulated an abolitionist petition that Charles Sumner eventually presented to Congress, precipitating the Emancipation Proclamation.

Many of Demorest's interests and values can be linked to the "gentry elite," a social group that controlled major publications for children at this time.[4] The gentry elite stressed the importance of education, moral vision, self-reliance, and a strong sense of rural naturalism, as did *Demorest's Young America*. However, the gentry elite's disdain for fashionable society was not supported in *Demorest's Young America*, for, after all, its parent magazines were purveyors of fashion. An interesting example of how this irreconcilable difference made the periodical distinct from other publications issued by the gentry elite can be found in the closing chapter of the long-running serial "Mice at Play" (January 1875). Bessie, the heroine, convinces her Aunt Maria, a spiteful spinster, that people ridicule the aunt because she dresses in an old-fashioned manner. Bessie goes to Madame Durant's store, which imports everything from Paris, selects a new wardrobe for her aunt Maria, introduces her to fashionable respectability, and melts her heretofore bitter heart. Madame Durant's store is strikingly similar to the often advertised "Madame Demorest's Emporium," located in New York City. Current children's fashions are also repeatedly advertised in the magazine. Thus, in the case of *Demorest's Young America*, fashion is favorably presented and is even used in the fiction to advance the moral principles of the gentry elite.

The first two volumes of *Demorest's Young America* measured 4½ by 6½ inches and ran thirty-two pages an issue. The next two volumes were expanded to 5½ by 7½ inches; the final five, to 5½ by 9 inches. Despite the changes in size, each monthly issue contained articles, stories, poems, songs, games, and a puzzle page, all intended to edify and entertain the young. From the start an extensive premium system was used to encourage subscriptions at the price of $1.50 a year. Premiums included microscopes, books, musical instruments, popular chromo prints, and if fifty subscriptions were obtained, a sewing machine. This use of premiums to encourage magazine sales was picked up by James B. Upham, who would employ the method to boost *The Youth's Companion** by 1885 to the highest circulation of any magazine—excluding mail-order papers—in the country.[5]

Nonfiction in *Demorest's Young America* supported Demorest's pledge to avoid abstractions and explore the concrete realities children enounter. One category of articles offered direct urgings to conform to the social standards of the gentry elite. Titles such as "Be Industrious" (November 1866), "Be Gentlemen" (October 1867), and "What Smoking Does for Boys" (July 1869) are self-explanatory. A series of articles on "Learning to Cook" for girls eventually led in volume 3 to the creation of the department "The Little Housekeeper." Subscribers were urged to submit contributions of advice for other girls, preparing for their future role as homemakers. Inaugurating the department, Demorest warned, "We do not want mere receipts of indigestible puddings and pies, but we want brief records of what some smart little girls have done, and can do, in the way of housekeeping."[6] The next year a parallel column was introduced for boys, "The Young Farmer," intended to publicize subscribers' tips for helping with farm work. This was soon adapted to "The Farm and the Workshop," then "Our Workshop," with an emphasis on carpentry projects boys could complete. These monthly features joined "The Post Office," a readers' correspondence column, and "Our Editorial Sanctum," Demorest's monthly chance to speak directly to his readers.

History and geography were also given attention in *Demorest's Young America*. Articles such as "George Washington" (October 1871) and Hale Burleigh's "Boyhood of Our Eminent Men" (November 1866) helped propagate the George Washington cult, noting that young Washington "could run, leap, toss bars, and ride a horse better than any lad in the country."[7] "Historical Sketches" (June 1869 and following issues) reconstructed rulers from antiquity in relationship to their children. The series "All Around the World" was a regular geography lesson. "Tyrol and the Tyrolese" (April 1869), "Samoa" (April 1870), and "The Rivers of America" (January 1875) exemplify the varied geographical areas chosen for review.

A certain preoccupation with French culture might have come from the magazine's ties to the world of fashion. "France," a historical serial on French history, started in 1870 and continued for several years. Beginning in volume 2 and appearing erratically until the magazine ceased publication in 1875 were a series of lessons in French pronunciation, grammar, and vocabulary.

Still, the predominating category of articles aimed at explaining the world of nature; chemistry, astronomy, and biology were all given due coverage in representative pieces such as "Nature's Mysteries" (August 1869 and following issues), "The World Above Us" (November 1866 and following issues), and "Garden Weeds" (November 1866). The monthly department "Our Knowledge Box" briefly defined and illustrated various flora and fauna. Volume 4, for instance, opened each monthly issue with a color plate, poem, and brief essay, all concerning a particular species of bird.

While emphasizing a rational attitude and acceptance of nature, *Demorest's Young America* supported the basic Christian precepts accepted by the majority of the gentry elite. "History of the World" (November 1866) retells stories from Genesis. Similarly, "Six Days of Creation" (August 1869 and following issues) is a series of poems and pictures interpreting the Genesis creation story. A cartoon, "The Darwin Theory Illustrated," displays monkeys dressed as humans in a schoolroom run by a clothed baboon (November 1873).

The fiction in *Demorest's Young America* avoided fantasy and emphasized young people learning to make correct moral decisions. The one noticeable exception to the ban on fantasy was the inclusion of selections from Aesop's Fables, which occurred, profusely illustrated, from volume 1 through volume 9. Perhaps the heavy emphasis on morals in these stories made them acceptable, even if they did include flights of imagination such as talking animals. Volume 2 contained an interesting attempt to introduce great literature to the young; a serialized adaptation of *Robinson Crusoe* was presented, written only in words of one syllable. Occasionally, such as in the case of "The Blind Man's Dog" (December 1868), European stories would be translated.

Serialized stories accounted for at least half of the fiction in *Demorest's Young America*. Three major contributors who helped meet this demand were Neil

Forest, May Mannering, and George J. Varney. Forest's offerings included "Patches" (January 1874 and following issues), a tale in which a grandmother's quilt becomes a symbol of Christian piety; and "Fanny" (April 1873 and following issues), a more straightforward account of a sweet little girl who struggles with lisping. Mannering's "Little Fred" (January 1873 and following issues) emphasized the strength of families, and her "Just My Luck" (December 1872 and following issues) moralized that "hard work and farm manners do not make one any less a gentleman in the noblest sense of the word."[8] Varney's pieces included "The Captive Children" (May 1874 and following issues), a dramatic tale of two white children taken by the Indians; and "From the Car to the Farm" (November 1868 and following issues), "Frank's Adventures" (January 1873 and following issues), and "Alf and Eddie" (January 1871 and following issues), all series emphasizing an outdoor life for boys with nature adventures.

Demorest's Young America continually tried to include varied special bonuses for its readers, such as dioramic pictures, foldout puzzles, kites, or paper doll costumes, furniture, and even houses. (Volume 1 included a foldout replica of a French suburban villa.) In an attempt to sustain the periodical by encouraging reader contributions, a club known simply as "OURS" was started for subscribers in November 1872, with a monthly column publishing members' poems, essays, and compositions. A badge could be purchased for 25¢, and officers were elected by democratic vote. Membership rules numbered five: Avoid all intoxicating drinks and discourage their use; abstain from tobacco; use no profanity and do not ridicule others; always be honest; and obey parents, teachers, and guardians.

The first rule of "OURS" indicates Demorest's zealous devotion to the temperance movement; in the latter part of his life he gave his publishing concerns to his sons and devoted himself to securing temperance legislation. A contest to write a temperance story appeared in *Demorest's Young America* in 1870. From then on increasing coverage was given to the movement. Most graphic was the series "The Twelve Steps of Intemperance" that opened each issue in 1874. Written by Rev. Dr. C. F. Weens, the series, accompanied by cartoon frontispieces and flowery poems, traces the downfall of a misguided young man. He succumbs to a first drink on New Year's Eve, becomes an alcoholic, neglects his family, loses his job and money, beats his children, robs to get liquor, and goes to prison for attempted murder. Fortunately, in the November issue he attends a temperance meeting and signs the pledge; in the Christmas issue he is released and reformed.

In 1875 Demorest discontinued *Demorest's Young America* as a separate publication but maintained a "Young America" department in *Demorest's Monthly Magazine*. Although his attempt to create and sustain a successful children's periodical had failed, his movement away from overt didacticism, use of a complex premium system, and introduction of a club as a mechanism to engage reader interest were all techniques favorably adapted in the near future by periodicals such as *St. Nicholas** and *The Youth's Companion*,* in the dawning golden age of American children's magazines.

Notes

1. *Demorest's Young America* 7 (August 1873), 255.
2. Ibid., 2 (November 1867), iii-iv.
3. "Jane Cunningham Croly," *National Cyclopedia of American Biography*, 6:499.
4. R. Gordon Kelly, *Mother Was a Lady* (Westport, Conn.: Greenwood Press, 1974), 58-69.
5. Frank Luther Mott, *A History of American Magazines* (Cambridge: Harvard University Press, 1938-1968), 3:177.
6. *Demorest's Young America* 3 (February 1869), 155.
7. Ibid., 1 (November 1866), 14.
8. Ibid., 6 (December 1872), 368.

Information Sources

BIBLIOGRAPHY
Frank Luther Mott, *A History of American Magazines*, 5 vols. (Cambridge: Harvard University Press, 1938-1968).
INDEX SOURCES
None.
LOCATION SOURCES
Bound volumes are in the Library of Congress.

Publication History

MAGAZINE TITLE AND TITLE CHANGES
Demorest's Young America (1866-1875).
VOLUME AND ISSUE DATA
Demorest's Young America (vol. 1, no. 1-vol. 9, no. 12).
PUBLISHER AND PLACE OF PUBLICATION
William J. Demorest, New York (1866-1875).
EDITOR
William J. Demorest (1866-1875).

Scot Guenter

E

EBONY JR!

Ebony Jr! was the brainchild of John H. Johnson, longtime publisher of popular black magazines such as *Ebony, Jet,* and *Black World* as well as the publisher of black juvenile books. He first started considering a children's magazine after receiving many letters from readers asking where they could acquire black literature for elementary schoolers. He "knew the country needed some type of publication to excite and motivate Black youngsters. It was a matter of finding the right thing."[1]

A precedent had been set in the United States for an ethnic children's magazine with the publication of *The Weewish Tree** in 1971 by the American Indian Historical Society. The 1960s had created a receptive climate for independent expressions from ethnic groups, although the stimulus for the second literary venture came not as a result of the first but from a felt need within the ethnic group.

Constance Johnson, a former reading teacher, heard of plans for a magazine for black children while she was working on her master's degree at Harvard University, where she was specializing in literacy and the black child and editing materials in reading and mathematics. She brought her interests and expertise to *Ebony Jr!* and became its first managing editor. With the publisher and editor, John H. Johnson, she hoped to create a periodical that would help children use and develop reading skills as they gained information about themselves. These purposes and future directions were set out in the publisher's letter printed in the first issue of *Ebony Jr!* in May 1973:

We of *Ebony Jr!* believe that you deserve a magazine which reflects the sounds and sights and colors of your community.

Ebony Jr! is about learning and exploring. It is based on the idea that learning is fun. It is based on the idea that reading is the door to opportunity. It is based on the idea that exploring—exploring new games, exploring new places, exploring new words—is half the fun of growing up committed and productive. For these reasons, *Ebony Jr!* will be a magazine of action. It will be filled with things to do.

Ebony Jr! will also be a magazine of opportunity. It will challenge you and remind you of the great tradition of which you are a part. Your forefathers created great monuments and dreamed great dreams in Africa. They came here with the first explorers and were among the founders and builders of this nation. It is your task to prepare yourself for the next chapter in a great human story which began hundreds of years ago.

I hope you will remember that more will be required of your generation than of any other generation in the history of Black people. I hope you will remember that to be young, gifted and Black today is an honor and an opportunity. *Ebony Jr!* is about your life and your opportunity. I hope you will read it and make it your very own.

John H. Johnson
Publisher[2]

With a circulation of 90,000, *Ebony Jr!* is published monthly except for the two bimonthly summer issues of June-July and August-September. The physical format of the magazine has changed only slightly during its eight years of publication. Page size is 9¾ by 6½ inches. Originally sixty-four pages, *Ebony Jr!* was reduced to forty-eight pages with the June-July 1976 issue, following a price increase from 50¢ a single issue, $6 a year, to 75¢ an issue, $7 a year, that had taken effect in April 1975.

The content of the magazine includes fiction, nonfiction, poetry, current events, profiles of outstanding peers, black history, games, crafts, recipes, humor, and children's contributions designed for an audience of children, especially black children, of ages six through twelve. About one-third of the content is staff written. There are four main divisions in the content of *Ebony Jr!*: covers, stories, features, and games and activities. The brightly colored covers are closely related to the theme of a given issue: "Things to Do for Summer Fun" (June-July 1973), "Big Brothers Aren't So Bad" (April 1974), "The Heart of a New Beginning" (February 1981), "Creating Cartoons" (May 1981). The inside front cover contains a monthly calendar that indicates births, deaths, and accomplishments of blacks as well as events and holidays of interest to blacks.

The back cover has contained the "Ebony Jr! Art Gallery" since the third issue, August-September 1973. Drawings sent in by children are reduced in size and printed with the children's names and ages. The stimulus for this idea came from an activity, "Draw Yourself," which appeared in the first issue of the magazine. Instructions were given for drawing faces and features. Children were encouraged to send in their self-portraits to be published. Over time the activity idea was expanded to include any type of drawing. Child readers are continually encouraged to send in their creative works.

The stories in *Ebony Jr!* have been selected to provide historical and contemporary identity as well as discovery of self. Many reflect real people and real life, past and present. The historical picture-story of Harriet Tubman, "Harriet and the Promised Land," that appeared in the June-July 1973 issue was a reprint of the book written by Robert Kraus and illustrated by Jacob Lawrence and published by Windmill Books/Simon and Schuster in 1968. A more recent figure of the past, "Langston Who? The Langston Hughes I Knew," appeared in the May 1973 issue; and contemporaries, "Meet the O. J. Simpsons," were introduced in November 1974. Some stories reflect real life but have fictional characters with which the child can easily identify. "Tina's Present" in the June-July 1981 issue introduces a child character who has two common problems. Tina talks too much and can't think of a good present for her father on his birthday. Documentaries such as "Rafting on the Rio Grande" in the June-July 1974 issue provide information, and fantasies and traditional stories like "Why Broo Goat Can't Climb" in the June-July 1981 issue stimulate a child's imagination. Occasionally, a skit or a play like "Beckwourth's Surprise" published in November 1974 encourages creative involvement. A few stories have been continued from one issue to the next.

Generally, the stories are carefully written. A concern for vocabulary growth is obvious. New words are printed in darker type within the article and repeated at the bottom of the page with syllabic divisions and definitions. Children were reminded of this unique running glossary through messages on the back covers of the first two issues of the magazine.

Features in *Ebony Jr!* are both long and short term. An examination of single issue features shows great variety in content from "Lleda Llama Leads the Spring Book Parade" in May 1981, containing book reviews about blacks throughout the world, to "Autopedmobiles" in March 1974 and "Swinging Tips from Hank Aaron" in April 1974, both of which are sports related. "Feelings Are Real" in August-September 1979 provides for self-understanding, and "Stevie Wonder—a Musical Giant" in March 1977 provides an outstanding role model of accomplishment even though he is disabled. Poems like "Lightning" in October 1976 are single features as well. The differences between single-issue stories and features is not clearly defined.

Long-term features are often identified by children as favorites. They continue to motivate interest in the magazine from one issue to the next. An *Ebony Jr!* feature that is frequently mentioned in the letters from child readers is "Sunny and Honey," a double-page, four-picture cartoon sequence. A short doll-like figure identified as "I" or "me" is often involved in the sequence. Usually, the message is humorous and often it teaches. The text in the first issues used very simple vocabulary and sentence structure, but this changed to a wider range of words and fuller sentences at times. There seems to be no definite pattern. Michael Davis was responsible for this feature through February 1978, when Buck Brown took it over. "A Letter from Sunny and Honey" appeared for the first time in August-September 1973. The letter has always been located on one of the beginning pages and serves as an introduction to the contents in the issue as well as a glimpse of what will be contained in next month's issue. Often the letter encourages the young readers to write and send creative works. Marginal illustrations of Sunny and Honey introduce other features in recent issues.

Successful efforts to encourage reader's responses have resulted in three continuing features, including the "Ebony Jr! Art Gallery" already described. "From Our Readers" began in February 1974 and contains letters from children with their photographs. "Writing Readers" has featured the creative writings of children since the August-September 1973 issue. The poems, brief stories and articles are accompanied by names, addresses, and photographs of the contributors. In addition, the magazine sponsors a writing contest each year for readers in two age categories. First- and second-place winners in each age category receive a cash prize, in addition to having their stories published in a fall issue, usually October. "Ebony Jr! News," another opportunity for children to contribute, has been a feature from the beginning. Children's answers to newsworthy questions are printed beneath photographs and name identifications.

Phonics exercises have been included in *Ebony Jr!* from its inception, as part of the editor's concern to encourage reading skills. In March 1974 "Phonics with the Loonicans," created by Anne Rowry Jones, became a regular feature. The Loonicans, cartoon characters with huge eyes, accompanied by a short poem or statement, occupy one page, and the opposite page is devoted to a word puzzle or other exercise requiring practice of a specific phonics rule or sound.

Several features proved less popular and were soon dropped. "Mama Write-On's Scribblin' Scope" was an exercise page meant to improve both manuscript and cursive writing. "Ebony Jr of the Month" featured a child who had made outstanding accomplishments.

The fourth and final division of content in *Ebony Jr!* is "Games and Things to Do." There has been great variety over the years in this division with art activities, word puzzles, games, experiments, riddles, dot-to-dots, recipes, sewing, music, crafts, and so on. Some types of activities are repeated in succeeding issues. During the first three years of publication, a visual-discrimination exercise called "Find the Two That Look Alike" appeared in each issue. Almost always a crossword puzzle is included that relates to the theme of the issue. "Metric Madness" began with the February 1978 issue. This includes an illustrated story problem that requires changing standard measures to metric. The formula is given. "Daze-a-Head" is another regular expectation since June-July 1977. This page requires considerable thought. It first included riddles and drawings sent in by readers, but more recently the activities have been related to the issue themes and thus check comprehension. One page in each issue contains the answers for all puzzles and exercises.

Ebony Jr! is a magazine that combines fun and learning through the active involvement of black children. Guidelines for the writers stress the presentation of positive images of blacks in both nonfiction and fiction—past and present. Writers are requested not to include death, violence, and religious material in their manuscripts.

Besides *Ebony Jr!* the Johnson Publishing Company publishes a supplement to each issue called *A Guide for the Use of Ebony Jr!* When initiated, this supplement contained sixteen pages, but it was subsequently reduced to eight pages of exercises and activities designed to increase comprehension of the material featured in an issue. Each reading skill, whether it be context clues, inferences, or comparison and contrast, is clearly defined for the parents and teachers using the guide. Subscribers who want the guide sent with every issue can receive it for an additional cost of $2 a year.

Notes

1. Sherry Ricchiardi, "At 23, She Lands Top Job on Magazine for Black Youths," *Des Moines Register*, May 2, 1973, p. 13.
2. John H. Johnson, "Why Ebony Jr?" *Ebony Jr!* 1 (May 1973), 4.

Information Sources

BIBLIOGRAPHY
James Fraser, "Black Publishing for Black Children," *Library Journal* 98 (November 15, 1973), 3421; Sherry Ricchiardi, "At 23, She Lands Top Job on Magazine for Black Youths," *Des Moines Register*, May 2, 1973, p. 13; Marcia V. Roebuck, Information sheets from *Ebony Jr!* (Chicago: Johnson Publishing Co.).
INDEX SOURCES
Subject Index to Children's Magazines.
LOCATION SOURCES
Bound volumes are in the Iowa State University Library, Ames, Ia.; microform copies are available from University Microfilms International, Ann Arbor, Mich.

Publication History

MAGAZINE TITLE AND TITLE CHANGES
Ebony Jr! (May 1973-).
VOLUME AND ISSUE DATA
Ebony Jr! (vol 1.-).
PUBLISHER AND PLACE OF PUBLICATION
Johnson Publishing Company, Inc., Chicago (1973-).
EDITOR
John H. Johnson (1973-).

Rosalind E. Engel

F

THE FAMILY PIONEER AND JUVENILE KEY

Brunswick, a small coastal town in southern Maine, is the seat of Bowdoin College. In 1819 Joseph Griffen, at the request of the president of Bowdoin, went to Brunswick to inaugurate the college printing office. This office printed a local newspaper, the catalogs for Bowdoin, and the textbooks and monographs for distinguished college professors, including the early French language works of Henry Longfellow. The printing office eventually broadened into a book and stationery store and from time to time served as a publishing house. One venture into publishing was during the seven-year period of 1830 to 1837 when a children's weekly magazine came forth from the presses. For more than two years it bore the title of *The Juvenile Key* and was subtitled *A Child's Newspaper*; it was subsequently retitled *The Family Pioneer and Juvenile Key*.

The fact that this magazine was issued from a printer's office plus the involvement of children in its production makes it a unique amateur publication. The masthead stated that the magazine was published by Z. J. (Zerui'ah-Juan) and J. W. (Joseph Warren) Griffen, his two eldest children. This credit may have been Griffen's way of saluting his children or it may be accounted for by the recent sale of some of his publication rights.

Griffen made it explicitly clear that the children were heavily involved in the publication. Several issues stated: ''The publishers of The Key, by whom most of the type work is performed, are children, one seven and one nine.'' Besides the typographical work, they were also involved in the makeup, promotion, distribution, and, at a later date, editorship of several issues.

There is little doubt that J. Griffen was the editor, although the masthead never attested to this fact. ''Oliver Oldwise'' was the stated editor of the first few issues, but that apparent alias was subsequently replaced by the statement that the weekly was published "At the Office of J. Griffen."

The Juvenile Key first appeared on September 18, 1830. It was a 7- by 9-inch, four-page magazine that was hand delivered by the Griffen children to each of the 200 recipients. The cost was 75¢ for a year's subscription. Wishing to entice a readership to the weekly, Griffen did not require payment from the subscribers for the first three months of publication. He also offered free binding of the issues upon the completion of the volume if it was presented to the printer's office within thirty days. However, in the 12th issue an editorial speaks of economical realities that the publisher was facing; he "must raise some money to pay for stock." Subscribers were presented with bills. "We shall now see whether our young patrons have been so far entertained and excited to industrious and economical habits, as to be in readiness to pay the hard earned wages of the printers."

Volume 1 was completed on August 27, 1831, ending with issue number 52 and page number 212. The additional four pages were due to a pagination error. The editorial of the last issue of this volume hinted at economic problems by stating that in the future, if anyone wished to receive the weekly he or she must apply for it "with the necessary accompaniments to pay their expenses."

The holdings of volume 2 at Bowdoin College are incomplete making number 50, issued on April 6, 1833, the last issue available for study. One can only surmise that the Griffens completed volume 2 with the additional two issues. This second volume of *The Key* took eighteen months to complete.

Joseph Griffen was a man of sobriety and an advocate of peace, who opposed war, capital punishment, slavery, and the use of alcohol, tobacco, and holiday fireworks. He was a strong believer in the practical parts of religion "which brings peace on earth and good will to men." His partisanship toward one political party and one religious denomination was never shown in his weekly magazine, which in itself was unusual for the times. His zealousness, however, in choosing professional literature that exhibited qualities of high morality and early habits of industry, cannot be questioned. Titles such as "Proud Temper Cured," "Two Apprentices," and "Brave Souls" attest to the didactic nature of the stories. The stories always occupied the first page and on numerous occasions shared that page with a pictorial representation of the "strong arm of justice." Most stories were two pages and some appeared as sequels.

Geographical data, an entry entitled "Wit and Sentiment," a few pen and ink drawings, and "News of the Day" completed the format of *The Key*. The news included "Important News from Europe," specifically England and the Netherlands, as well as domestic news. The children were apprised of murders, tragedies, catastrophies, untimely deaths, and disasters, the lurid details of which were presented in unusually full detail. Interestingly, in describing fatal accidents, there was often a phrase that did not appear to be in keeping with the sentiments of the text: a man who burned to death due to careless smoking took his "last whiff," a man who was brutally murdered "left a deathly sight," another had "his head smattered to atoms." This occasional liveliness and light touch in an otherwise pious publication was not typical of the times and was not seen in *The Key's* contemporaries.

There was little evidence of an exchange of items between *The Key* and other magazines, despite Griffen's editorial pleas for material. Occasionally, he re-printed stories from *The Youth's Companion** and *The Dover Enquirer*. *The Youth's Companion*, according to Griffen, plagiarized two original articles from *The Key*. Mutual recrimination ensued.

Early in 1833 a weekly paper, printed by Griffen, ceased publication, leaving an available market in Brunswick. Griffen took this opportunity to publish a weekly magazine that included items of interest to the whole family and yet retained the format of *The Key*, ensuring the continued readership of the youth. The four-column, four-page, weekly was of a larger format and was renamed *The Family Pioneer and Juvenile Key*. There were fifty-two issues in each of the four volumes and each had a circulation of 350. The cost was $1 a volume, payable in advance, with an additional cost of 25¢ for binding. Although the masthead of the first issue held the publication date of March 17, 1833, the distribution of this issue was withheld supposedly until volume 2 of *The Juvenile Key* could be completed.

The young printers were retained in their original capacity as typesetters and were joined in 1834 by their younger brother George, aged six years. In volume 5, 1835, the "young publishers" now thirteen and fifteen years of age, were totally responsible for several issues including setting type, proofreading, editing, and preparing the format.

As in *The Key*, the first-page stories of the sequel were pious articles that demonstrated Griffen's moral character as stated in this quote, "It was the endeavour of the editor of *The Family Pioneer and Juvenile Key* to operate upon the public mind, especially that of the young, by the publication of interesting narratives, setting youth in a clear light, and not only pointing out the evils of an intemperate use of intoxicating drinks, but also the dangers of temperate drinking. The abolition of negro slavery, and of the death penalty for crime, were also strongly advocated in the columns of *The Pioneer and Key*."[1]

In *The Pioneer*, the news of the day encompassed both deaths and marriages. Advertisements from local merchants were carried in one column of the fourth page, but this was gradually increased to cover the entire fourth page and even-tually some of the third. In time, the fourth page eventually became known as the *Brunswick and Topsham Advertiser*. Medicinal potions, local dry-good stores, want ads, tenements to let, and the occasional lost and found ads were all laid out to attract a reader's attention. J. Griffen himself advertised the wares of his stationery and bookstore.

The editorial issue of May 23, 1837, stated that due to "having much book work on hand which must be completed during the coming summer," there would be a delay in the first issue of volume 7 "until a fortnight from next Saturday." The issue never came. The magazine was finished. No one profited monetarily; but the editor and the young publishers, a father and his children, must have achieved a sense of satisfaction for a job well done.

Note

1. Joseph Griffen, ed., *History of the Press of Maine* (Brunswick, Maine: The J. Griffen Press, 1872), 78.

Information Sources

BIBLIOGRAPHY
Joseph Griffen, ed., *History of the Press of Maine*, (Brunswick, Maine: The J. Griffen Press, 1872); Clement F. Robinson, "The Juvenile Key," *The Fossil* (April 1957), 254-58.
INDEX SOURCES
None.
LOCATION SOURCES
Bound volumes are in the library of Bowdoin College, Brunswick, Maine.

Publication History

MAGAZINE TITLE AND TITLE CHANGES
The Juvenile Key (1830-1833); *The Family Pioneer and Juvenile Key* (1833-1837).
VOLUME AND ISSUE DATA
The Juvenile Key (vol. 1, no. 1-vol. 11, no. 50); *The Family Pioneer and Juvenile Key* (vol. 3, no. 1-vol. 6, no. 52).
PUBLISHER AND PLACE OF PUBLICATION
Joseph Griffen, Brunswick, Maine (1830-1837). Masthead stated Z. J. and J. W. Griffen.
EDITOR
J. Griffen. Several issues of the first volume used the pseudonym "Oliver Oldwise."
                                                                    Mary Lou McKeown

THE FLY; OR JUVENILE MISCELLANY

The first number of *The Fly*, a specimen issue, appeared October 16, 1805, printed for its pseudonymous publishers Simon Scribble & Co. by Boston's Josiah Ball. Precisely *who* Simon Scribble and Co. were remains a mystery, but what they were is clear enough: a society of young gentlemen with literary interests and a decided taste for the theater. In their initial address to their public, they promised instructive and amusing essays, historical and biographical sketches, poetry, tales, epigrams, anecdotes, "and a variety of incidental matter"—the staples, in short, of the literary miscellany of the period, intended "to present a valuable combination of useful and interesting subjects, particularly designed for the improvement of YOUTH of both sexes."[1] A three-column, four-page fortnightly, *The Fly* was handsomely printed and priced at $1 a year. Subscribers were invited to leave their names with Josiah Ball or with either of two circulating libraries in Boston, clear evidence of the audience sought. Rural subscribers were obliged to pay the cost of postage. At the end of six months, as had been their plan, the editors announced a shift to weekly publication and a new title— *The Juvenile Magazine; or Weekly Messenger*—but the new magazine did not appear.

The showpiece of the specimen issue was the "Speculator," an essay very much "in the style" of Addison's "Spectator," Johnson's "Rambler," and their American counterparts, the "Lounger" and the "Gleaner." The Spectator sought further anonymity in the pseudonym "Peter Quince, Junior, Esq." Internal evidence suggests that "Peter Quince" was one individual and not a group. A second informal essayist, the "Inspector General," was apparently the vehicle for several of the company. The Inspector General appeared in the third number and replaced the Speculator in the fourth and subsequent numbers, and was replaced, in turn, by the "Scribbler" in the final issue of April 2, 1806. In his second essay, the Speculator rang the changes on the importance of reading for self-improvement, especially the reading of history and biography.

The Fly provided little in the way of history, but biographical sketches were a staple, beginning with an account of John Robinson, "Father of New England," in the specimen issue. For a Boston magazine, the choice of Robinson, who elected to remain in Leyden rather than accompany the Pilgrims to the New World, was perhaps unusual, there being other candidates for the title. Subsequent subjects for biographical sketches in *The Fly* must have seemed eccentric, even at the time: Thomas Abthorp Cooper, "The American Roscius," and Augustus Roy Fletcher of Glenorchay, Scotland.

Even before the biography of Cooper appeared, however, readers of *The Fly* could not have missed Simon Scribble & Co.'s passionate interest in the theater. It was an interest that, given especially the place—Boston, in the last decade of the nineteenth century, is the most distinctive feature of this short-lived and, in other respects, utterly conventional periodical for youth. "Theatricus" debuted in the specimen issue, providing reviews of Boston theatrical performances and announcements of performances to come, and reappeared in each subsequent issue, avoiding the revolving door that claimed the Speculator and the Inspector General.

The specimen issue concluded with a selection of verses, which appear to have been commissioned for the issue, and a brief cautionary tale, "The Contending Brothers." Subsequent verse offerings appeared beneath the epigraph "The mind to virtue is by verse subdu'd,/And the true poet is a public good," a sentiment that summarized the editors' conventional sense of the power and purpose of poetry.[2]

In later issues of *The Fly*, the Inspector General predictably explored the folly of "fashion," a term that for the next half-century and more served as a covering term for the increasingly visible urban *nouveau riche*, as well as the temptation to profanity (not "manly" at all) and the dangers of gambling (as a waste of time, especially). Fiction, printed under the heading "Instructive," included "Downfall of Pride," "The Fruits of Industry," and similar narrative efforts designed to define appropriate and inappropriate behavior and to instance the rewards and punishments that Necessity bound to each. The only significant addition to the features of the specimen issue of *The Fly* was "The Inquirer," a column inaugurated in the fifth number: "nothing tends more to blend instruction with amusement, than the mode of question and answer."[3] For his first question, the Inquirer asked his readers to consider the following: two Arabs sit down to eat, one bringing five loaves, the other three, to the table. A stranger asks to join them and at the end of the meal puts down eight coins in payment. The man who brought three loaves to the table suggests dividing the coins, and the ensuing dispute is finally settled by recourse to a magistrate who gives seven of the eight coins to the man who brought the five loaves. "Was this sentence just?" The answer appeared in the following number. In later columns, less easily answered questions appeared: "Is poverty the mother of vice?" "What is contentment?" The column also provided readers a forum for their own queries: "How many years did Diocletian reign?" "Who reigned after him?"[4] In a periodical that did not try to establish an editorial persona as was later to characterize some of the most successful ventures in children's publishing, the Inquirer became the principal focus for correspondence with readers, whose solutions to mathematics problems, cryptograms, and puzzles were regularly printed.

With the exception, then, of its attention to the world of Boston theater and its apparent base in a literary society of cultivated young gentlemen, *The Fly* was a conventional miscellany devoted to instruction and amusement, the former taking precedence, which meant, in practice, moral instruction, cultivation, and refinement rather than intellectual growth. Like the vast majority of children's periodical editors, Simon Scribble & Co. expressly avoided politics. Rejecting a reader's submission, they wrote: "*Junius the Younger* is received, but it contains a manifest allusion to *party*, and is therefore inadmissable. It would be a dangerous experiment for *The Fly* to get entangled in the *cobwebs* of political dispute."[5] Instead, *The Fly* took its stand on relatively safer ground, urging on its readers such time honored New England virtues as thrift and industry and finding in "the Follies of the present day" ample fields for its young Speculators, Scribblers, and Inspectors General to adapt the familiar essay of Addison and Steele to matters properly Bostonian.

Notes

1. *The Fly; or Juvenile Miscellany* 1 (October 16, 1805), 1.
2. Ibid., p. 4.
3. Ibid., 1 (December 11, 1805), 19.
4. Ibid., 1 (February 5, 1806), 38.
5. Ibid., 1 (November 13, 1805), 11.

Information Sources

BIBLIOGRAPHY
Jayne K. Kribbs, *An Annotated Bibliography of American Literary Periodicals* (Boston: G. K. Hall, 1977).

INDEX SOURCES
None.
LOCATION SOURCES
Tufts University, Medford, Mass.; American Antiquarian Society, Worcester, Mass.;
    Yale University, New Haven. Available on microfilm in the American Periodical
    Series, University Microfilms International, Ann Arbor, Mich.

Publication History

MAGAZINE TITLE AND TITLE CHANGES
The Fly; or Juvenile Miscellany (October 16, 1805-April 2, 1806).
VOLUME AND ISSUE DATA
The Fly; or Juvenile Miscellany (vol. 1, no. 1-vol. 1, no. 13).
PUBLISHER AND PLACE OF PUBLICATION
Josiah Ball, Boston (October 16, 1805-April 2, 1806).
EDITOR
Josiah Ball.

R. Gordon Kelly

FORWARD

Forward is one of those many denominational periodicals whose publications
began in the decades immediately following the Civil War.[1] The first issue of
the paper was published in January 1882 in Philadelphia, Pennsylvania, by the
Presbyterian Board of Publication and Sabbath-school Work under the auspices
of the Presbyterian Church in the United States of America.

In an announcement, which appears beneath the masthead of the small, fifteen-
page paper, the audience is identified as young people—''say, sixteen or seventeen or eighteen''—who believe themselves too mature for ''children's papers.'' The announcement states that *Forward* ''will be made as attractive and
instructive in its articles and engraved illustrations'' as possible. Readers are
assured that the periodical ''will seek to be helpful, to be elevating, to lead
heavenward, whilst also sprightly and wide awake to topics of present interest
to young men and young women.''[2] The paper is to be published twice a month
with a subscription price of 50¢ a year for single copies or 40¢ for five or more
copies sent to the same address.

Although his name does not appear on the masthead of this initial issue, James
Russell Miller was editor of *Forward* at its inception.[3] A respected Presbyterian
clergyman, he wrote more than twenty-five books dealing ''with the spiritual
and practical side of life'' in a style described as ''simple, clear and strong.''[4]
Miller was appointed editorial superintendent of the Presbyterian Board of Publication and Sabbath-school Work in 1880. He remained in this position as well
as that of editor of the young people's paper until shortly before his death in
1912.

With time *Forward* improved the quality and variety of its offerings; however, the contents of the first issue are not extremely different from those of many issues to follow. The lead story, "Uncle Tim's 'For'c'stle' and the Walrus-Fight" by Rev. Edward A. Rand, gives an account of a visit by Ned and Frank Waters to Uncle Tim, a retired seaman. The visit provides a frame for facts about the walrus and for a lesson concerning the use of alcohol. Although certainly not the only messages delivered by *Forward*'s didactic stories, the use and misuse of alcohol are often the themes upon which object lessons are built. For instance, this same issue reprints from *Our Young People* a story illustrating the proverb "Woe to him that putteth the bottle to his neighbor's lips" and prints, presumably for the first time, two anecdotes that also treat the subject: "A 'Bacca'-Fed Baby" and "Jack and His Hard Lump."[5]

A sermon, "The Life Worth Living" by Dr. Leroy J. Halsey, is the only other prose appearing in the first issue that is attributed to a specific author. It is possible, however, that at least some of the other selections were written by Miller, including "The Leaning Tower of Pisa" and "The Boyhood of Jesus." Both of these articles are well written, something that cannot always be said of the fiction or nonfiction appearing during the early years of the periodical's history. Just as its title indicates, the first selection describes Pisa and its principal attraction, concluding with the admonishment that lives should be built "straight up and down morally."[6] Similar articles describing places and events of historic interest appear frequently in later issues of *Forward*, sometimes with a didactic conclusion. The second selection draws upon the author's travels in Palestine and his reading: he infers what day-to-day life was like in Nazareth when Jesus was a boy. These two articles as well as the lead story are generously illustrated with engravings.

Two poems appear in this first issue. "Do You Think to Pray?" which is unsigned, proposes that daily prayer will enable the believer to cope with the difficulties of life. The second, "All Members Have Not the Same Office," is by Eva Travers and is reprinted from the *London Christian*. The smallest service for Christ "finds recompense beyond our highest thought" serves as the theme of the poem, whose title is taken from Paul's letter to the Romans.[7]

Brief paragraphs containing bits of informative and inspirational material fill much of the remaining space. The final page, however, is reserved for the announcement of new publications from the Presbyterian press. Each title is followed by a brief annotation that indicates the contents and price of the book.

There are columns not found in the first issue of *Forward* that later appear regularly and fill an evident need of the periodical's readers. They carry titles such as "Christian Endeavor," "Department of Young People's Work," and "Department of Religious Education." The first of them consistently offers program outlines and suggestions to the Endeavor societies; the other two report news of young people's denominational activities.

On December 15, 1895, *Forward* appeared in an enlarged format, and the announcement was made that the periodical would be published weekly, containing the work of new writers and artists as well as "interesting" serials.[8] Then, on July 4, 1897, the format was enlarged again. An announcement appeared in this issue that identified the audience as much the same—young persons above fourteen—and described the periodical's proper subject as "everything that belongs to the life of the young man or young woman."[9]

Evidence of these decisions may be seen in subsequent issues of *Forward*. For instance, in the January 3, 1903, issue appeared the first of five installments of "A Mountain Summer," written by Mabel Earle and illustrated by J. E. McBurney. Here, themes based on Christian morality recur, although the structure of the story is more complex than in earlier stories complete in a single issue. Edna Graham is spending the summer with her aunt, the proprietor of a hotel in a western mining town. The principal plot involves nineteen-year-old Edna's efforts to establish a Sunday school; she succeeds, largely it would seem, because she chooses the superintendent of the mines to be the superintendent of the Sunday school. A subplot deals with the resolution of difficulties stemming from false accusations made against two other characters, Uncle Herman and his nephew Adolph Rothmann.

"Li'l Cotton Blossom," written by E. E. Garnett and illustrated by F. Adams, appears in its entirety in this issue of *Forward*. The story treats a subject that is unusual for the periodical at this time: the relationship of members of the black and white races. Belle Marchant—or Li'l Cotton Blossom—and Silas, her father's black employee, are at odds after the child tells her father that she has reason to believe that Silas is abusing Ole Steady, the mule that turns the crank of the plantation's cotton press. Animosity deepens between Silas and the young girl, who reminds one of Elsie Dinsmore; but following a series of events that climax in Silas's rescue of Belle's dog, the two are happily reconciled.

Besides fiction, this issue introduces the first of several columns under the general title "The Girl Beautiful." Minna Stanwood offers the reader a recipe for a beautiful face: "Be good, do right, feel pleasant, smile!"[10] Another column, "This and That," contains bits of interesting information as well as humorous anecdotes. (Although the tone of *Forward* is usually optimistic, humor is in short supply.)

Worth noting also about this issue is the inclusion of fillers from other magazines, such as *Our Young Folks** and *The Youth's Companion*.* From its first issue *Forward* has drawn from these or similar sources but never to the degree that the periodical loses a life of its own.

Finally, by 1903 advertising had begun appearing in the paper—and not just for books from the Presbyterian press. This issue features ads for a variety of items: from shoe polish to clothes pins to gold-eye needles.

Before another decade had passed, *Forward* had lost its first editor. J. R. Miller died in 1912, and after what seems to have been a transition period, John Thomson Faris became editor of the periodical. Neither available biographical material nor the paper itself indicates an exact date; however, Faris, who had been associate editor of the Presbyterian Board of Publication and Sabbath-school

Work since 1908, assumed the responsibilities of editor in 1912.[11] Whether the position encompassed the editorship of *Forward* is not clear. He was not designated editor on the masthead until 1915, but neither did Miller's name appear on the masthead of the early issues of *Forward*. Faris, who was also a Presbyterian clergyman, published extensively. He was the author of fifty-six books concerning religion, history, and travel;[12] and an examination of *Forward* reveals that he contributed to the paper many of the essays contained in his travel books.

With the passing of still another decade, the fictional characters became more sophisticated than those in *Forward* of 1903. In the January 4, 1913, issue the principles of Christian morality are more subtly offered, although one of the oldest themes is used once again—the cost of intemperance. But this time the problem is treated with sympathy for the alcoholic as well as his family.

An example of the increased sophistication of characters is seen in "The Girl with the Beautiful Eyes," the lead story in this issue of the periodical, written by Elizabeth Earl and illustrated by Will Thomson. On the one hand, Kate Foulkes, the new girl in town, has beautiful eyes and a "deep, sweet voice"; on the other hand, she relishes praise and is considered "silly and conceited." Playing foil to Kate is fair and square Bess, whose own popularity is soundly established. The girls share a frightening experience and thus become friends, despite Kate's undesirable qualities. Upon Kate's insistence, Bess finally explains to her new friend that she would be liked better if she would give others a chance to see that "she is really quite splendid inside."[13]

Intemperance or alcoholism occurs as a theme in the story "Between Midnight and Morning," written by Frederick Hall and illustrated by J. Lawrence Stone. Tom, the son of an alcoholic, is so ashamed that he decides to run away from home even though he has completed only his first year in high school. As he is waiting to jump a freight at Birch Crossing, he sees a body on the track—the body of Joe Carrington, the brother of the village doctor. Joe, too, is an alcoholic, and when Tom witnesses Dr. Carrington's love and concern for his unconscious brother, the would-be runaway returns home to help his mother find aid for his father.

The principal material filling the remaining pages of this issue is an installment of a serial and two feature articles typical of *Forward*. The seven-part serial, written by Minna Stanwood and illustrated by Elmer P. Cook, is entitled "The Popham Pews." One of the articles, "At the Moon's Inn" by Harriet Malone Hobson, discusses the ancient customs of the Armenians. The other, "Joining the Continents" by W. Thorburn Clark, is an account of Cyrus Field's perseverance in laying the first Atlantic cable.

The most obvious change that occurs in *Forward* during the next ten years is the reduction in the number of brief articles and miscellaneous fillers. The editorial page still features contemporary proverbs and short inspirational articles, but the rest of the paper is dominated by stories and articles of some length. Remaining space is given to regularly printed columns.

In the January 6, 1923, issue the front page is devoted to the beginning of a ten-part serial: "The Lookout on Starvation Peak," written by E. E. Harriman and illustrated by George A. Newman. The first installment introduces Brett Cable, a young stenographer who works for the supervisor of the National Forest Service. Hearing that a veteran forester has failed to conquer the heights of Starvation Peak, thus prohibiting the construction of a lookout tower, Brett suggests that the failure was caused by a lack of spirit, spirit that he himself has. When the supervisor learns that Brett has been a mountain climber, he asks him to try to do what the veteran had failed to do. The installment ends after the reader is introduced to the men whom Brett has chosen to go with him.

Two other selections of fiction are complete in this issue. "The Half-Breed Pack," with F. W. Calkins as author and Paul Gill as illustrator, is a tightly written piece reminiscent of the Androcles story. In "The Half-Breed Pack" the chief characters are a Russian wolfhound and a rancher's daughter; because she had once befriended him, the dog returns the kindness when a pack of animals— half dog and half wolf—attempt to attack Lura, her sister, and a companion. "The Girl Who Did Not Understand," written by Frederick E. Burham and illustrated by Mariann Oldham, is a slight, sentimental story about a girl named Fanny, who returns after graduation from college to care for her father. She is insensitive to his feelings toward the crude pieces of furniture that he had made for her mother. However, all ends well once she is made aware of the price of her insistence that the furniture be thrown away.

The first issue of 1923 also offers two feature articles. One, "The Pribilof Islands' Summer Visitors" by Charles A. David, gives an account of seal life and seal hunts on these islands. The second is the thirteenth chapter of the series "Studies of Familiar Hymns" by Louis F. Benson. Through the years *Forward* has treated other subjects that lend themselves to this format, for example, famous men, honorable young men, churches, and cities.

In January 1923 *Forward* could look back on forty years of publication, no small achievement when one considers the transistory nature of many children's and young people's papers. At least two factors contributed to the periodical's longevity: it was, as Frank L. Mott wrote, a "high-grade" paper of its "class," offering "excellent content in good format";[14] second, it enjoyed the support of a denomination.

Forward consistently spoke to that audience identified by its first editor: young people in their late teens. Although its tone was usually positive, it offered its readers little humor and practically no fantasy. Poetry appeared in early issues, but prose dominated the pages of the paper. It consistently published prose— fiction and nonfiction—that reflected what its editors, both churchmen, perceived to be the teachings of the Christian church. Although with time the teachings were often skillfully interwoven with the action, they remained central to the editors' concept of *Forward*'s purpose.

Notes

1. Frank Luther Mott, *A History of American Magazines, 1741-1930* (Cambridge: Harvard University Press), 3:174.

2. *Forward*, January 1882, p. 6.

3. Although Miller's name does not appear on the masthead of early issues of *Forward*, John T. Faris, his successor, entitled a series of memorial paragraphs "In Memory of *Forward*'s Founder." This material was published in the paper on August 17, 1912, about six weeks after Miller's death.

4. "Miller, James Russell," *National Cyclopaedia of American Biography* (1900), vol. 10.

5. *Forward*, January 1882, p. 7.

6. Ibid., p. 4.

7. Ibid., p. 13.

8. Ibid., December 15, 1895, n.p.

9. Ibid, July 4, 1897, p. 212.

10. Ibid., January 3, 1903, p. 3.

11. "Faris, John Thomson," *National Cyclopaedia of American Biography* (1958), vol. 42.

12. Ibid.

13. *Forward*, January 4, 1913, pp. 1-2.

14. Mott, *History*, 3:180; 4:274.

Information Sources

BIBLIOGRAPHY

"Faris, John Thomson," *National Cyclopaedia of American Biography* (1958), vol. 42; "Miller, James Russell," *National Cyclopaedia of American Biography* (1900), vol. 10; and Frank Luther Mott, *A History of American Magazines*, 5 vols. (Cambridge: Harvard University Press, 1938-1968).

INDEX SOURCES

None.

LOCATION SOURCES

Library of Congress; Free Library of Philadelphia; Garrett Biblical Institute, Evanston, Ill.

Publication History

MAGAZINE TITLE AND TITLE CHANGES

Forward (1882-1957)

VOLUME AND ISSUE DATA

Forward (vol. 1-vol. 76).

PUBLISHER AND PLACE OF PUBLICATION

Presbyterian Board of Publication and Sabbath-school Work, Philadelphia (1882-1957).

EDITOR
James Russell Miller (1882-1912); John Thomson Faris (1912-1939); P. H. Miller (1940-
    1946); no editor listed 1947-1956.

Lalla Overby

FRANK LESLIE'S BOY'S AND GIRL'S WEEKLY

One of the most popular and successful illustrated periodicals for children of
the late nineteenth century was *Frank Leslie's Boy's and Girl's Weekly*. The
periodical was the brainchild of Frank Leslie, a prolific publisher and a towering
figure in the annals of American illustrated journalism.

It is difficult to separate Leslie's various periodical endeavors from the man
himself, for his imprint is clearly present in both title and content. Frank Leslie
was himself the product of fictional origins, for he was born Henry Carter in
1821 at Ipswich, England. His family were prosperous glove manufacturers, and
it was expected that young Henry would succeed, in time, to ownership of the
family business. However, Henry had other interests, most notably drawing,
which in turn led to his mastery of engraving. His interests were not shared by
his family, and they were adamant that he desist from his drawing and learn the
glove business. Undaunted, he pursued his interests secretly and adopted the
name "Frank Leslie" as a pseudonym.

He eventually broke with his family and secured employment with the *Illustrated London News*, quickly moving up in the organization to become head of
the engraving department. It was there that Frank Leslie learned all aspects of
the illustrated-paper publishing business. Always looking for new opportunities
and recognizing that his position at the *Illustrated London News* was limiting
his talents, he decided to immigrate to the United States in 1848. He worked
for *Gleason's Pictorial* until 1854, when, at the age of 33, he began his own
publishing house.

His early successes included *Frank Leslie's Lady's Magazine, New York Journal*, and his most enduring venture, *Frank Leslie's Illustrated Newspaper*. These
financially profitable publications enabled Leslie to branch out into other potential
markets, one of which was the overlooked children's market. Initially published
as *Frank Leslie's Children's Friend, Frank Leslie's Boy's and Girl's Weekly:
An Illustrated Journal of Amusement, Adventure and Instruction* first appeared
on October 6, 1866.[1]

The scope of the periodical was prominently stated in the first issue:

FRANK LESLIE'S BOY'S AND GIRL'S WEEKLY will be published
in the form of a handsome paper of eight pages, of three columns each.
It will be adapted to the tastes and capacities of boys and girls; but will,
nevertheless, contain, as an important feature, a page for children of tender

years, so that it will be a welcome visitor in every family, having something of interest for all its members. It will contain stories, travels, adventures, sketches of natural history and scenery, illustrations of manners and customs of all nations, biography, anecdotes, sports for the parlor and the field, arithmetical and geographical exercises, poetry, and whatever else may serve to instruct and entertain the young. Every number will have five or more illustrations, besides comic and minor engravings.[2]

Frank Leslie's Boy's and Girl's Weekly enjoyed immediate popularity. Originally it was limited to eight pages and sold for 4¢ a copy or $1.50 a year, but changes in size were quickly undertaken. With issue number 3, the size was increased to twelve pages and the price increased to 5¢ a copy and $2.00 a year. However, with the next issue the periodical expanded to sixteen pages of three columns each. The issue price stayed at 5¢, but the subscription cost increased to $2.50 a year.

Apparently, everyone, including Leslie, was surprised at the overwhelming success of the periodical. In a modest statement in issue number 4, he described the broader scope necessitated by this new-found popularity:

The great, and to a certain extent, unexpected general success of *Frank Leslie's Children's Friend*, which was only intended for children of tender years, has determined the publisher to enlarge his original design, and produce a paper which, while it includes all his young family friends, takes the entire range of our youthful classes.

We therefore present to the public a serial which will be dear to all as a household companion, and shall spare neither labor nor expense in making FRANK LESLIE'S BOY'S AND GIRL'S WEEKLY the amusing companion and the pleasant instructor of the young.

For this purpose we shall make it as generally interesting as possible, and all that can attract the young will be found garnered in its pages.

Healthy Fiction, Romantic Adventures, Parlor Amusements, Science Made Easy, Natural History, Incidents of Ancient and Modern History, Anecdotes illustrating character, selected specially for youth; Instances of modern progress, Customs of Foreign Lands, Magic and entertaining Conjuring, Easy Lectures on Hard Subjects, Enigmas, Conundrums, and Fireside Amusements for Winter Evenings—in short, FRANK LESLIE'S BOY'S AND GIRL'S WEEKLY will be a selection of reading matter, with numerous illustrations, admirably calculated to please the youthful reader. To accomplish this end, the different departments have been entrusted to writers eminently qualified for their task. Arrangements have also been made with authors celebrated for this specialty to write upon the most suitable subjects.[3]

Despite the apparent humility, Leslie's minions were actively engaged in a variety of efforts to increase circulation. The periodical promoted the development of clubs of new subscribers and awarded substantial cash awards and other prizes such as silver watches, tool chests, and sewing machines to energetic subscribers. Readers were also encouraged to submit games, riddles, and other literary amusements. Successful entries would also receive prizes.

Availability was undoubtedly another factor in the success of *Frank Leslie's Boy's and Girl's Weekly*. Given an already established network of distribution for the Leslie publishing empire, the *Boy's and Girl's Weekly* had access to all newsstands where the other Leslie periodicals were sold. In addition to this market, Leslie hired young people to sell his publications in the newly developed and rapidly expanding railroad network in this country. Railway stations and the trains themselves all served as extensions of Leslie's marketing acumen.

Technology also played a part in advancing the popularity of *Boy's and Girl's Weekly*. New developments in composition, typesetting, and binding encouraged mass production and cheap prices. Leslie's imaginative use of picture-and-text combinations were innovative and appealed to the mass audience. His own innovation for the rapid production of complex engravings by dividing an engraving in thirty-two segments and using thirty-two engravers, each working on a separate part of the engraving, reduced the process of reproducing engravings from two weeks to overnight. All of these technological innovations enabled him to supply the mass-market juvenile audience with popular literature.

Although the financial and technical successes of *Frank Leslie's Boy's and Girl's Weekly* are without question, there remains some doubt about whether Leslie succeeded in accomplishing the moral, societal, and literary goals he outlined for the periodical. In retrospect, it would be wise to divide the content into serialized fiction and "other contents." Other contents would be elements such as games, riddles, history, natural history, and true adventure stories. There is little doubt that they served to satisfy the objectives put forth by Leslie.

However, in the area of serialized fiction, there is reason to question the compatibility of sensationalized fiction of the dime-novel variety, accompanied by engravings of the most hair-raising segments of the episode, and the espoused goals of the periodical. R. Gordon Kelly, in one of the few studies of American children's periodicals, commented on *Boy's and Girl's Weekly*: "The brutality and violence evident in the *Weekly* have no counterpart in the other magazines studied. . . . In the *Weekly*, the careless rendering of figures, the stark tonal contrasts, and a visual preoccupation with physical injury provide the pictorial counterparts of a literary style that is frequently dominated by restless action, unconvincing motivation, meretricious diction, and covert morality that contradicts the passages of overt moralizing casually interspersed in the narratives."[4]

Lest we judge *Boy's and Girl's Weekly* too harshly, the fact remains that for eighteen years it was a very popular periodical. In its pages can be found the "Jack Harkaway Stories" by Samuel Bracebridge Hemyng; Far West stories of Indian chiefs by W. O. Stoddard; and contributions by George L. Aiken, Roger

Starbuck, Captain Tom Singleton, and Oswald A. Gwynne—all successful writers. Although the mass audience for which it was intended was distinct from say *St. Nicholas*,* that in no way diminishes its wide appeal.

Granted, the stories may have been sensationalized, but this was characteristic of a large portion of Victorian literature. Likewise, the images represented tended to be those stereotypical images associated with the Wild West or darkest Africa or the exotic Orient. Such images and writing styles were abundantly represented in adult periodicals and books of the period. Like popular literature of all periods, it may not have been the "best" literature available, but it was widely read and enjoyed.

To characterize its contents as brutal is to deny the realistic brutality of the world and the dangers faced in everyday life. Morality, too, was present, in its typical Victorian manner: maidens were pursued, but they were not caught and defiled by dastardly villians; chivalry and manly behavior were not dead in its pages. The often continued plots of poor young men overcoming tremendous obstacles to gain fame and fortune was, until recently, the American dream and reflected the vitality and opportunities associated with this country. Indeed, it must be kept in mind that Leslie himself was this type of an individual. He came to America to make his fortune, he overcame obstacles, and through hard work, he succeeded.

Frank Leslie was an entrepreneur and he knew his various markets. A motto attributed to him portrays his philosophy: "Never shoot over the heads of the people."[5] His aim was straight, and he succeeded in the competitive mass marketplace, despite many unsuccessful attempts by others to imitate his products.

Leslie died unexpectedly on January 11, 1880, of a "fibrous tumor in the neck." The business was willed to his wife, who did not have the same interest in this title as in some of the other Leslie periodicals. Consequently, quality lessened; attempts to increase circulation by changing formats failed; and the inclusion of sport news (baseball and tennis) could not attract sufficient readers. As a result, the February 9, 1884, issue was the last number to be published by Leslie. It was abruptly sold to the Franklin Company with stories unfinished and riddles unsolved.

Notes

1. "Frank Leslie," *Frank Leslie's Boy's and Girl's Weekly* 15 (February 7, 1880), 416.

2. Ibid., 1 (October 13, 1866), 8.

3. Ibid., 1 (November 3, 1866), 39.

4. R. Gordon Kelly, *Mother Was a Lady* (Westport, Conn.: Greenwood Press, 1974), p. 29.

5. John Tebbel, *A History of Book Publishing in the United States* (New York: R. R. Bowker, 1975), 2:500.

Information Sources

BIBLIOGRAPHY
R. Gordon Kelly, *Mother Was a Lady* (Westport, Conn.: Greenwood Press, 1974);
Madeline B. Stern, ed., *Publishers for Mass Entertainment in Nineteenth Century
America* (Boston: G. K. Hall, 1980); John Tebbel, *A History of Book Publishing
in the United States*, 3 vols. (New York: R. R. Bowker, 1975).
INDEX SOURCES
None.
LOCATION SOURCES
Vols. 1-36 are available on microfilm from the Library of Congress and Michigan State
University, East Lansing, Mich.

Publication History

MAGAZINE TITLE AND TITLE CHANGES
*Frank Leslie's Boy's and Girl's Weekly: An Illustrated Journal of Amusement, Adventure
and Instruction* (1866-1883); *Frank Leslie's Boy's and Girl's Weekly: An Illus-
trated Record of Outdoor and Home Amusements* (1883-1884).
VOLUME AND ISSUE DATA
*Frank Leslie's Boy's and Girl's Weekly: An Illustrated Journal of Amusement, Adventure
and Instruction* (vol. 1, no. 1-vol. 34, no. 870); *Frank Leslie's Boy's and Girl's
Weekly: An Illustrated Record of Outdoor and Home Amusements* (vol. 34, no.
871-vol. 36, no. 905).
PUBLISHER AND PLACE OF PUBLICATION
Frank Leslie Publishing House (also known as Frank Leslie's Publishing House), New
York (1866-1884).
EDITOR
No editor is listed in the periodical itself, and it is presumed that Frank Leslie exerted
editorial control and direction himself from 1866 to 1880, when he died. From
1880 to 1884 it is presumed, although with less assurance, that Mrs. Leslie (who
legally changed her name to Frank Leslie after her husband's death) was the editor.

Edward J. Jennerich

G

THE GIRLS' COMPANION

The Girls' Companion was created by one of the largest publishers of Sunday school literature, David Caleb Cook. Cook began publishing supplemental teaching aids for Sunday schools in 1875, including weekly papers and religious books. Although Cook was a Methodist, his publications were interdenominational and became popular in many of the mainstream Protestant churches. In 1882 he moved his company from its original location in Chicago to nearby Elgin, Illinois. After the success of *Young People's Weekly*, which began in 1887 and reached a circulation of 250,000, Cook decided to develop separate Sunday school periodicals for boys and girls, appealing to their divergent interests, yet insisting on a common, overriding sense of proper Christian behavior. Accordingly, in 1902 *The Boys' World** was launched for young gentlemen Sunday school scholars, and their female counterparts were offered *The Girls' Companion*.

The first issue, April 5, 1902, set a pattern that would be adhered to throughout the periodical's existence. Fiction, practical articles, educational looks at nature and geography, inspirational pieces on role models, regular columns, and even the weekly puzzles and contests were all intended to strengthen a sense of Christian moral commitment in girls between the ages of eight and twenty. The publisher himself served as editor-in-chief of this eight-page weekly, which sold for 25¢ a year in packets of five or more, 50¢ a year otherwise. He was assisted by two able women who were also major contributors: managing editor Belle Kellogg Towne and associate editor Harriet Lummis Smith.

Each issue opened with a 1,500- to 3,000-word, illustrated story that always met certain formulaic requirements. The central character was a contemporary young girl in the age range of the intended audience. This heroine would undergo some test of moral strength or confront some unexpected crisis and would emerge victorious or at least gain insight into the obvious moral superiority of a true Christian life-style. One popular variation on this theme presented the heroine as a person with certain faults, who acknowledged and overcame them, often under the influence of a mother, an aunt, or a comparable role model.

Towne's offering for the first issue, "A Brave Mountain Girl," is one example of this genre. Minty, the heroine, is ridiculed by other rural children because her father is serving a jail sentence. Reacting quickly to a sudden landslide, she rescues a trapped five year old, causing her schoolmates not only to accept her but to honor her. Moreover, her father is restored to his former mining job by the head of the company, the grateful father of the rescued child. Bravery brings success not only to an individual, but to one's loved ones as well.

Later volumes illustrate the variety of opening stories presented, all adhering to this formula. In "The Minister's Joshua" (September 1903) by Susan Hubbard Martin, a happy-go-lucky carefree girl with a gift for music realizes the time has come to buckle down and accept responsibility when her small church's organist retires and the minister calls for a volunteer. "An Old Soldier" (May 1906) by Mary S. Daniels is a Memorial Day story in which the heroine befriends a lonely old GAR veteran who has become a hermit and is instrumental in his eventual reconciliation with his long lost daughter. Themes can often be simple domestic lessons, as in Harriet Lummis Smith's "Molly Mortimer's Trip to the Beach" (July 1907), a tale that hinges on obeying a mother's directions when caring for younger siblings. Still, there is room for properly handled adventure too: "A Daughter of the Muskoka Wilds" (January 1911) by Rose E. Wakefield relates how a northern Canadian girl saves two visiting city girls adrift in a boat during a storm. Subsequently, they secure a maid's position for the heroine so that she might attend school in the city, and two years later she is able to return to her Muskoka wilds and become the area's much needed schoolteacher. Perseverance, bravery, gentility, charity—all are important themes that repeatedly occur in these opening stories.

Although these opening stories were the main offering of fiction in each issue, there were usually two or three other shorter pieces. Often they would follow the same formula, and always they would have a clear moral message. Serialization of longer stories occurred regularly, to encourage continued reader interest, and often tucked away in the middle pages of The Girls' Companion would be a chapter in a continuing serial, such as "From A to Z Company" (January 1911 and following issues) by Arthur T. Crane, the story of a girl who must accept new family members in an extended household; and Gale Darling's "Hope Fuller" (August 1907 and following issues), the story of a poor but diligent girl who works her way through college.

Beginning in November 1907, each week The Girls' Companion published a short story following the formula of the opening stories but specifically designed to exemplify the morals inherent in the Sunday school lesson for the forthcoming week, following the organized lesson-plan system provided by the David C. Cook Publishing Co. At first this feature was rotated to regular contributors, but in January 1908 Alonzo Macmillan took control of the project, only to be replaced a few months later by associate editor Harriet Lummis Smith, who continued to author the column for many years. Smith was a prolific writer, also often writing for other children's periodicals of the day, such as the nonaffiliated *Boys' Magazine.**

The true Christian girl should be not only moral but practical, and every issue of *The Girls' Companion* included some articles to encourage homemaking skills as well as gentility. "Pretty Things for a Girl to Make," which appeared off and on, was a column on handicrafts for the home, often devoted to seasonal decorations. Articles on sewing and cooking occasionally appeared. Social acumen was also acknowledged as a legitimate concern and was given attention in various columns printed irregularly. "When Mother Entertains" presented tips on helping make the home beautiful, a pleasure for guests to visit. "The Young Hostess" offered much the same advice, and "The Well Dressed Girl" explained that its goal was "to assist. . .in forming correct ideas of how the body should be clothed."[1] "When You Are a Guest" discussed etiquette in others' homes. Along with such social concerns, *The Girls' Companion* also regularly encouraged practicality in "Light Hearted School Girls," a catch-all advice column, and in articles emphasizing the importance of a proper education.

In the area of education *The Girls' Companion* devoted much attention to articles concerning both nature and geography. Perhaps a holdover from the popular nineteenth-century concept of understanding God through understanding nature, a fascination is apparent in *The Girls' Companion* for biology, botany, and the beauties of an unravished countryside. Indeed, one column, "In the Fields," lists as its motto "As you get close to Nature's heart, you draw nearer God."[2] "Nature Studies" became one of the more constant features, examining plants, insects, trees, and animals. Two of the most important contributors of nature articles to *The Girls' Companion* were David Hall and John Carver.

Carver also was responsible for many of the articles of geographic interest in *The Girls' Companion*. Throughout its existence, the periodical constantly tried to present information about distant countries and cultures, often with a trace of underlying missionary emphasis. Aside from frequent articles on foreign societies, two reappearing columns, "Girls from Far and Near" and Mary S. Daniel's "Our Travel Class," both conveyed knowledge, often accompanied with photographs, of a world that must have seemed distant to the subscribers in their Sunday school classrooms.

Role models were presented for the young girls to emulate, not only in the fiction, but in regular columns as well. "Bits of Biography" tended to examine successful authors, often women such as Louisa May Alcott or Alice French. Other repeated features indicate by their titles the salutary influence they were designed to instill: "Girls Who Love Music," "Girls in the Business World," "Girls Who Excell in Sports," "Girls Who Make the Mark," and "How Girls

Earn Money." Two weekly columns, "In the Realm of the Girl" and "Girls Who Are Brave," were planned, respectively, to show the heights attainable and the feats of valor possible for any persevering Christian girl. The former column included representative titles such as "A Successful Girl Writer," "The Success of an American Girl Artist," "A Blind Girl's Success," and "The First Woman Lawyer in Italy." The latter documented true acts of bravery, such as "A Chain of Life Savers," "Operator Sticks to Her Post," "Girl Saves Her Mother," and "Heroine of an Ocean Collision." In 1906 a *Girls' Companion* Brave Deed Medal was initiated to be awarded to Sunday school members for extraordinary courageous behavior, and its first recipient was twelve-year-old Gladys Hamilton, who saved the life of a drowning boy.[3]

Various miscellaneous features also often appeared in *The Girls' Companion*. "The Girl on the Farm" was still another column conducted by Harriet Lummis Smith, this one extolling the superiority of a rural background over an urban one, a common theme that had continued in children's periodicals since the nineteenth century. "Swinging Into Health" was a regular feature on physical fitness, intended "to help you in making your body a fit home for young girls." "Aunt Cheery Speaks Her Mind" offered a mythical elderly aunt a chance to pass along the moral wisdom of her years to interested young girls. By 1910 *The Girls' Companion* was presenting personal-experience essay contests, limited to 1,800 words, on topics such as "How I Am Helping in Our Organized [Sunday School] Class" and "What I Have Learned as a Wage Earner." "The Companion Correspondence Club," the weekly column devoted to letters submitted by subscribers, was conducted by managing editor Belle Kellogg Towne and served not only as an advice column but also as both a travelog and a meeting place for pen pals.

Since it was a Sunday school publication, part of *The Girls' Companion* was also devoted to Bible reading and Sunday school lesson preparation. "The Book of Life" was an intermittent column offering advice on preferred methods of Bible study. The Bible Searchers Club was initiated "to encourage companioning with the Bible." Open to those who agreed to own their own Bible, read it daily, and study their Sunday school lesson in connection with it, the Bible Searchers Club conducted a prize contest four times a year. This contest involved answering twenty-five scriptural questions gleaned from the assigned Bible readings for the three-month period. *The Girls' Companion* also regularly offered a Hide-and-Seek Lesson Puzzle Contest, in which biblical verses were derived from picture clues.

From the start *The Girls' Companion* also promoted the I.A.H. Circle, a religious society that claimed 200,000 members when the periodical began. It appears that David C. Cook ran this society, membership in which was signified by receiving a special silver ring. Subscribers to *The Girls' Companion* were encouraged to also become members of the Girls' Companion Branch of the I.A.H. Circle, and "Lead a Charmed Life." What I.A.H. stood for could apparently be divulged only to members. Each week *The Girls' Companion* also summarized the main truths of the "International Lesson Series" and the "Joint Diocesan Series," two Sunday school Bible study plans. Similarly, it faithfully presented the "Diamond Points," weekly biblical quotes with homilies, from a variety of junior religious societies.

David C. Cook died in 1927 and was succeeded as editor by his son, who himself died in 1932. If reports in the periodical itself can be relied on, by Thanksgiving 1907 a half million girls were reading *The Girls' Companion* each week. *The Girls' Companion* continued in publication until April 24, 1949, when it and *The Boys' World* were merged into a new publication, *Sunday Pix*, with a circulation that would climb well past the million mark. In 1968 *Sunday Pix* was converted to *Bible-in-Life Pix*, a periodical that is still in existence.

Notes

1. *The Girls' Companion*, January 14, 1911, p. .5.
2. Ibid., April 21, 1906, p. 5.
3. Ibid., November 24, 1906, p. 6.

Information Sources

BIBLIOGRAPHY
None.
INDEX SOURCES
None.
LOCATION SOURCES
Bound vols. 1-11 are in the Library of Congress. A more complete collection is in the private archives of the David C. Cook Publishing Co., Elgin, Ill.

Publication History

MAGAZINE TITLE AND TITLE CHANGES
The Girls' Companion (1902-1949).
VOLUME AND ISSUE DATA
The Girls' Companion (vol. 1, no. 1-vol. 48, no. 17).
PUBLISHER AND PLACE OF PUBLICATION
David C. Cook Publishing Co., Elgin Ill. (1902-1949).
EDITOR
David Caleb Cook (1902-1927); David Charles Cook (1927-1932); David C. Cook III (1933?-1946); no editor listed 1947-1949.

Scot Guenter

THE GOLDEN ARGOSY

With promises of $2,500 from a Maine stockbroker and $1,000 from a friend, Frank A. Munsey packed the manuscripts on which he had spent his life savings and traveled to New York in hope of starting a new children's periodical modeled after Philadelphia's *Golden Days*.*[1] He arrived in the fall of 1882. On December

9, 1882, Munsey brought out the first issue of his eight-page weekly, *The Golden Argosy*, but only after his financial backers had broken their promises to him. He was forced to take his idea to E. G. Rideout, who agreed to publish the weekly, employing Munsey as editor. After five months Rideout's company went bankrupt, and Munsey himself became the publisher.[2]

Functioning as office boy, editor, publisher, and contributor, Munsey managed to put out the magazine week after week, with the assistance of a $300 loan from a friend in Maine. He offered premiums to attract subscribers. With volume 2 he boasted of readers in South America, England, and Canada. He invited every subscriber to work as an agent selling subscriptions for a cash commission of 40¢ each or in exchange for valuable premiums.

After several years of financial struggle, Munsey was able to get some credit from his suppliers. Taking advantage of this situation in 1886, he launched a campaign to increase the circulation of *The Golden Argosy* by advertising and printing 100,000 sample copies, which he distributed in New York and Brooklyn.[3] The first installment of his own "Afloat in a Great City" was featured on the front page. New subscriptions began to pour in; for the first time the weekly began to make a modest profit.

Munsey then increased the size of the paper from eight to sixteen pages and raised the price from 5¢ to 6¢ a copy and from $1.75 to $3.00 a year with volume 5. Next he flooded the country with more than 11 million sample copies. He incurred a debt of more than 100,000 dollars in doing so, but in May 1887 he had increased circulation to 150,000.[4] Suddenly, in the fall of 1887 circulation abruptly stopped growing. Other juvenile periodicals found themselves in similar situations, and Munsey concluded that the only way to increase readership was to broaden the audience.

With volume 7 (1888) he added covers and many illustrations, some colored, expanding the magazine from sixteen to about thirty-six pages. He reduced the size of the pages, printed it on heavier paper, and raised the price from 6¢ to 10¢ a copy. He included more humor and cartoons but continued to feature many of the same authors used in the past. The paper continued to be published as a family weekly through March 1894. From April 1894 to September 1917 it came out monthly and then appeared weekly until September 28, 1929. Munsey hoped to attract new readers by changing the title to *The Argosy*, explaining in the first issue that "the old title led people to suppose the paper [was] intended solely for small children. Nothing could be further from our purpose as you and all readers know. Without doubt, however, this "Golden" has kept manly boys and young men from reading the paper simply because they did not like to be classed... with the small boys who read fairy tales and nursery stories."[5]

This statement sounds different from the one in which Frank Munsey made his original appeal to readers, distinguishing *The Golden Argosy* from other juvenile periodicals. He explained,

> Its advantage over all other publications can easily be seen. In the first place there are but few YOUTHS' PAPERS published that have a HIGH

MORAL TONE. In the second, of these few, some seem designed for readers ranging from childhood to old age; thus filling the paper with reading matter that boys and girls (from the ages of TEN to TWENTY) care nothing about. When they buy such a paper for themselves they practically get but half a paper that they wish to read.[6]

He went on to criticize those publications that offered only stories, pointing out the profit to be gained from reading the informative articles that appeared in *The Golden Argosy*.

As the first editor and, later, publisher, Munsey established the scope and character that *The Golden Argosy* retained while it remained a children's periodical. In fact, the masthead of the paper never specifies that from 1883 to 1887 Malcolm Douglas did much of the editorial work.[7] Munsey himself refurbished much of the nonfiction borrowed from older publications and contributed a number of his own stories during those early years.[8]

When it first appeared in December 1882, Munsey announced:

One of the prominent features of this publication will be its stories, and we desire to call attention to them. Every one will be especially written for us, and will be correct in all descriptions. Through these stories as well as in other ways, we shall attempt to stimulate ambition and good resolution in our readers. By this we do not wish to give the impression that the stories will be flat and uninteresting. On the contrary, they will be filled with strong, stirring adventure and interesting scenes that will make them as fascinating as a true portrayal of life will allow. They will be finely illustrated by engravings which will bring out the force of the stories.[9]

The paper generally included three serialized stories and several other short stories by prominent authors. Success stories were common. Horatio Alger's "Struggling Upward; or Luke Larkin's Luck" (March 3, 1886, and following issues) and Mary A. Denison's "Only a Boy; or Little Bec, the Flower Girl" (May 8, 1886) were typical of the success story that inspired many a young reader of *The Golden Argosy*. In these stories protagonists were often orphans or boys who had recently come from farms or small towns to New York, where they hoped, by honest toil, to establish careers. Humble, they gratefully accepted entry-level jobs and quickly distinguished themselves as outstanding workers. Often a jealous relative of the owner or a dishonest co-worker attempted to soil the hero's reputation, but truth invariably prevailed. The accuser was humiliated and punished by dismissal or, sometimes, imprisonment or insanity while the hero earned promotions, financial rewards, and esteem. The importance of hard work, honesty, and attention to duty were among the more frequently rewarded virtues in *The Golden Argosy* stories.

Another type of story that frequently appeared was the hunting story. The illustrations accompanying it often depicted the protagonist in some perilous situation. Bernard Redlands's "A Hunt in Poland" (March 12, 1887), Lt. R.H. Jayne's "Perils of the Jungle: A Tale of Adventure in The Dark Continent" (July 24, 1886), and George H. Coomer's "Boarded by Polar Bears" (January 8, 1887) suggest something of the character of these tales. The heroes might hunt anywhere in the world, and they managed to kill many wild, ferocious beasts.

School stories were also published regularly in the paper. They generally emphasized the importance of loyalty to friends, honesty and truthfulness, and diligence in study. High scholastic achievement was applauded only if the scholar loved or valued learning; those who learned merely for the sake of earning a high rank in class constantly had to be on their guards against the temptation to cheat.

Oliver Optic (William T. Adams), who had himself edited a number of juvenile periodicals, including *The Student and Schoolmate,** *Oliver Optic's Magazine** and *Our Little Ones,** was a regular contributor to *The Golden Argosy*. He often wrote stories about boats and boating such as "The Cruise of the Dandy" and "The Young Pilot of Lake Montoban." Like most of the heroes in the paper's stories, his had solid morals and high ideals, and after many adventures and near disasters, their virtue was rewarded.

Other regular contributors included Horatio Alger, who wrote success stories; Edward S. Ellis, who specialized in stories about the West; Arthur Lee Putnam, who often wrote about telegraph boys, newsboys, and bootblacks; Matthew White, Jr., who served as an editor for Munsey for forty-seven years; and Frank A. Munsey himself.[10] A number of women authors published stories in *The Golden Argosy* also; among them were Annie Ashomore, Laura E. Richards, Ida D. Monroe, Mary A. Denison, and Julia Freeman.

As editor, Munsey introduced a number of regular columns. Some of them only survived a short time. "Amateur Journalism" (1882) lasted but a few issues. It was designed to acquaint readers with some of the papers boys and girls were publishing throughout the country; it provided critiques and encouragement to those interested in writing, editing, and publishing. "Argosy Yarns" (1882-1883) by D.O.S. Lowell was intended as a regular feature of the paper but appeared only occasionally. In it old legends—usually Greek—were retold. "Puzzledom" (1882-1886) featured a variety of word puzzles, many of which were supplied by readers. The correspondence column (1882-1888) was a great information source for readers and included statistics, unusual facts, and personal advice. It was sometimes combined with the "Exchanges" column through which readers could offer goods and issues of *The Golden Argosy* they wished to trade. "Personal and Other Items" (1882-1883) was a compilation of miscellaneous factual information and anecdotes, and "The Funny Side" (1884-1886) was a humor column. "Golden Thoughts" (1882-1888), a collection of short inspirational quotations remained a feature of the paper throughout its history.   Munsey always included a number of short editorials in each issue. They might be anecdotes that functioned as parables or more direct lessons. Among them were warnings against smoking and the dangers of candy, bad habits, and practical jokes. Readers received short lessons about the value of friendship and how to avoid dishonest debts. Hard work, honesty, perseverance, hope, and respect for parents, among other virtues, were strongly encouraged. Munsey also regularly published short poems by William Cullen Bryant and Oliver Wendell Holmes as well as some by lesser known poets.

The nonfiction Munsey included covered a wide range of topics, with sports and natural history most often featured. Articles about how to make or do things also seem to have been especially popular. Provided most consistently, however, were the brief biographies of persons who, no doubt, were to serve as role models to readers. They included religious and political leaders, generals, judges and lawyers, scientists, journalists and editors, and even actors. Nearly all were biographies of men, although girls also read *The Golden Argosy* and were sometimes protagonists in stories.

Matthew White, Jr., assumed the editorship of the paper in 1887, making only minor changes.[11] The stories and biographies changed little, and several of the regular columns—"Golden Thoughts" and the correspondence and exchanges columns—were also retained. The stories he included tended to be less didactic, and he featured more adventure tales. He also used more serialized stories than short ones. Nonfiction articles tended to be longer, and a greater diversity in subject matter was offered; in addition to the usual articles on sports and things to make were articles on coins, ships, armaments, and animals. He continued to publish poems and increased the number of illustrations in each issue. He also added a new feature—cartoons.

The Argosy superceded *The Golden Argosy* on December 1, 1888. With the establishment of the new magazine, Munsey acted on his belief: "Of all the deadly schemes for publishing, that of juvenile publishing is the worst. It is hopeless. . . . One never has a circulation that stays with him; for as the boys and girls mature they take adult periodicals. It is a question of building new all the while. Then again, the advertiser. . . wants to talk to money-spenders—not dependents—not children."[12] The weekly paper for boys and girls became a 10¢ magazine for all ages. It received a face-lift. The puzzle column was reinstated but featured more complex puzzles. A humor page was added. Its host of authors and regular features continued to be offered to a broader audience.

Notes

1. Edited by Edward S. Ellis and published by James Elverson. George Britt, *Forty Years—Forty Millions: The Career of Frank A. Munsey* (New York: Farrar, Rinehart, 1935), 61.

2. Frank A. Munsey, *The Founding of the Munsey Publishing House* (New York: De Vinne Press, 1907), 17.

3. Ibid., pp. 22-23.

4. Ibid., pp. 25-30.
5. "To Our Readers," *The Argosy* 7 (December 1, 1888), 34.
6. *The Golden Argosy* 1 (December 9, 1882), 4.
7. Britt, *Forty Years*, pp. 66-67.
8. Munsey, *The Founding*, pp. 19-20.
9. *The Golden Argosy*, 1 (December 9, 1882), 4.
10. Britt, *Forty Years*, pp. 66-67.
11. Ibid.
12. Munsey, *The Founding*, pp. 21-22.

Information Sources

BIBLIOGRAPHY

George Britt, *Forty Years—Forty Millions: The Career of Frank A. Munsey* (New York: Farrar, Rinehart, 1935); Frank Luther Mott, *A History of American Magazines*, 5 vols. (Cambridge: Harvard University Press, 1938-1968)); Frank A. Munsey, *The Founding of the Munsey Publishing House* (New York: De Vinne Press, 1907).

INDEX SOURCES

None.

LOCATION SOURCES

Library of Congress. American Antiquarian Society, Worcester, Mass.; vols. 1-6 are available on microfilm from Datamatics, Inc., New York.

Publication Information

MAGAZINE TITLE AND TITLE CHANGES

The Golden Argosy: Freighted with Treasures for Boys and Girls (1882-1886); *The Golden Argosy* (1886-1888). Superceded by *The Argosy*.

VOLUME AND ISSUE DATA

The Golden Argosy: Freighted with Treasures for Boys and Girls (vol. 1, no. 1-vol. 4 no. 14 [170]); *The Golden Argosy* (vol. 4, no. 15 [171]-vol. 6, no. 52 [312]).

PUBLISHER AND PLACE OF PUBLICATION

E. G. Rideout and Co., Publishers, New York (1882-1883); Frank A. Munsey, Publisher, New York (1883-1888).

EDITOR

Frank A. Munsey (1882-1883); Malcolm Douglas (1883-1887); Matthew White, Jr. (1887-1888). None listed after vol. 1, no. 39.

Constance Gremore

GOLDEN DAYS FOR BOYS AND GIRLS

During its twenty-seven-year history (1880-1907), the visually attractive miscellany *Golden Days for Boys and Girls* strove to entertain and edify active, diligent, middle-class youngsters. Appearing on a weekly basis, it enjoyed a wide circulation—in both the United States and Canada—thanks largely to the business acumen and determination of its founder, publisher, and sole editor,

James Elverson (1838-1911). Frank Luther Mott observed that, like Elverson's other weekly, the Philadelphia *Saturday Night* (1865-1902), *Golden Days* continued to make "large claims" but remained unwilling to face its "evident failure."[1] His judgment is all the more severe because it is unsubstantiated. In fact, Elverson's accomplishment as the lone editor of these miscellanies is truly commendable. For the modern reviewer *Golden Days* offers an outstanding example of the ways in which a periodical's repeated ideas and marketing devices become idiosyncratic reflections of the man at the helm.

A British native, Elverson came to the United States at the age of nine; after five years of formal education he found employment at the Magnetic Telegraph Company in Newark, New Jersey, where he distinguished himself as a young man eager to rise quickly: from operator, manager, and instructor to director of the American Telegraph office in Washington, D.C., during the Civil War. A shrewd businessman, too, Elverson was constantly reinvesting his profits. Using such gains and espousing the goal of municipal reform, he established his first weekly, *Saturday Night*, in 1865. The journal became a family story paper by the next year. Relying on his own ingenious marketing skills, he boosted the paper's circulation to a remarkable 300,000 and, after buying out the interest of his associate, acquired sole proprietorship in 1879. Tireless as well as inventive and solvent, Elverson then began *Golden Days*, with all of the confidence of a promoter in the fine old tradition of Thomas Boreman and John Newbery. Boreman had flattered potential young purchasers of *The Gigantick Histories* (1740-1743) by promising to publish the names of subscribers in its subsequent volumes. Newbery had enticed children with toys, friendly letters from Jack-the-Giant-Killer, and promises of books as free gifts—with only tuppence to pay for the binding; he had even slipped advertisements for his patent nostrum, Dr. James' Fever Powder, into the narrative of *Goody Two-Shoes* (1765). Elverson was equally adept: his decision to distribute 3 million copies of the first issue of *Golden Days* "free to all" was so successful that by the next week he had secured over 50,000 subscribers. As the masthead declared, he maintained subscription rates at a modest "$3.00 per annum in advance." In a very straightforward way the Salutatory of the inaugural issue (March 6, 1880) announced his allegiance to useful entertainment for the young. Always respectful of "the conscience of the public," Elverson described his intention to produce "a hightoned, unobjectionable paper" that would contain "warm, interesting and vivid narratives, prepared by the most popular and competent writers." After reiterating his belief in "Sunday church and Sunday schools," he concluded his editor's catechism with this summary: "In short, our creed is mirth, honesty, study, work, play, manliness and the golden rule, 'Do unto others as you would that others should do to you.' "[2]

Elverson knew how to do more than allay the fears of cautious, monitoring parents: he knew how to interest children. Just as Newbery had changed from the instructive lecturing of parents and nurses about the rational upbringing of children to the chatty friendliness of Jack-the-Giant-Killer, Elverson—after he had received the nod from parents—enticed young purchasers through his affordable prices. He set out to attract all kinds of readers—those wanting only one issue, at "six cents each," and others who were "Golden Days Club" members taking out multiple subscriptions at reduced rates. For large and small purchases alike Elverson's claim was the same: "We pay postage on all United States and Canada subscriptions." He ran a column, "Exchange Notices," as a form of free classified advertisements for juniors, where subscribers who abided by the rules could exchange—but not sell—stamps, postal cards, and clothbound collections of authors like Alger, Henty, and Scott. Elverson would not permit the advertisement of "notices containing offers of or for shotguns, airguns, pistols [and] poisons"; he informed his readers peremptorily that such notices "will not be inserted."[3] In Mary Waggaman's serialized story, "Tom's Administration," which began in *Golden Days* on November 30, 1889, the fifteen-year-old hero who assumes the direction of his beleaguered family's finances is the quintessence of ledger-book common sense: "He had gone through profit and loss, and was steering triumphantly through a second course of bookkeeping that was a very model of red ink balance lines and faultless entries."[4] One might apply these words with similar force to the purposive and profitable direction of Waggaman's editor.

Elverson offered his young subscribers an alluring variety of literary fare: serialized stories, narrative vignettes complete in one issue, tidy rhymes, forays into puzzledom, and small inserts of encyclopedic information to make full use of the four-column format of each page. Although the illustrations were usually unsigned, they were displayed engagingly; rarely reproduced as mere blocks, the artwork took the form of ellipses, circles, and parallelograms and often spilled over into more than a single column. The masthead used in each issue set the prevailing tone; in addition to picturing a girl and boy contentedly poring over a copy of the magazine, it spread emblems of instruction and delight above, below, and behind its letters: a globe and compass are prominent, but so are a cricket bat and ball, a palette and brushes, a quiver of arrows and a bow, a fishing pole and a bird cage. *Golden Days*, one assumes, was addressed to bookish yet active youngsters who enjoyed being informed but could not be called stodgy. Many became Golden Days Club members and cheerfully appropriated names like "Bo Peep," "Dauntless," "Heres Howe," "May B," "Myself," "Seer," "Shadow," "The Raven," "Yankee," and "C. Saw." Their activities were reported in a column called "Club Chat." But one wonders how waggish the festivities were when one reads the account of "the sixth regular meeting of the New York Puzzle Club": "The literary exercises consisted of three interesting contests. The first, known as the "Club Prize Contest" for best rhymed fiat, was won by Shadow and May B. The second break, a Con Game, was mastered by Myself and Seer. The third struggle—Word Building—landed Dauntless and The Raven as winners. Social enjoyment held sway during the remainder of the evening."[5]

Although there is a disingenuous cast to this report, Elverson featured stories
in *Golden Days* intended to reflect faithfully the idiom of different social classes.
The emphasis was placed squarely on socioeconomic contrasts, not on the exploration of language and sound for its own sake. Dialogue was definitely a tool
and sometimes laboriously wielded. In William Perry Brown's "Sea Island Boys:
A Story of the South," for example, the social gulf separating carefree and
casual Paul Roanoak and painfully correct Jacob Ehrich is made clear when,
after Paul has suggested they be friends, Jake considers the possibility aloud:
"Certainly we will, if you will only meet me half-way. Your folks are high-
toned but hard up. My folks are not toney, but they have money. Isn't that about
the size of it, Paul?"[6] Unsurprisingly, the aristocratic but impoverished Roanoaks
are attended by an old and fiercely loyal Negro servant, Uncle Ham, who takes
occasion to reprimand "Marse Paul" for his egalitarianism: "Whuffo' make
you go an' take up wif dat low-bo'n trash, Jake Ehrich? Don't you know yo'
folks don't like hit? De squire will jess raar, dat he sho'ly will!"[7] In "Tom's
Administration," social class contrasts the speech of the genteel hero with that
of the less fortunate little lamplighter, Jack O'Lantern, who is actually knocked
down and injured by Tom's friends, the tobogganing "jolly seminary boys."
Tom wants a doctor to be called to minister to the lad, but plucky Jack gasps
in attempted reassurance: "No cop, no sawbones, no—....I ain't hurt much, I
reckon....Don't make no row."[8] Although Jack lives in "a 'shady' locality
indeed,...in depths into which [Tom] had never been permitted to venture,"
the lamplighter persists in voicing his deferential amazement that "a fine fellow
like [Tom]" would consider helping a poor urchin.[9] In "Cattle Jack," the dialect
switches to the Carolina mountains and helps to promote the theme of brains
over brawn, an issue closely related to the socioeconomic one in Elverson's
view. After he has realized that his favoring of one son, the huntsman par
excellence, over his more quiet sibling has been a great blunder, the rustic father
announces his change of heart in idiomatic solemnity at the story's close: "Well,
ef I do say it myself,...yes, ef I do say it—Jack has grit, en' you kin carry grit
en' sense where you can't carry guns, en' when you ain't got guns. He knowed
what to do when we didn't, en' he shill go to school soon es he likes. Yes sir,
ef I hev to see arfter the cattle myself, Jack shill go to school."[10]

As well as delineating social strata, dialogue used as a conclusion often served
to convey the satisfying theme of each story. Many of the shorter accounts,
contained in a single issue, promote one specific, highly edifying idea, but they
are strictly tailored to this end, with the result that they become predictable and
a little smug. A story like "Harry and Himself" by Sidney Dayre (November
30, 1889) is so full of admonitions that it never knows when to stop castigating
the central character whose greed and weakness have led him to claim a package
found on a streetcar as his own and to be reluctant as well as deceitful in returning
it to its owner. Dayre simply cannot resist salting poor Harry's discomfort, when
he closes with this righteous prodding: " 'I'll tell you what,' said a boy, con-
fidentially, as they went in at the sound of the bell, 'if I thought as much of

myself as you do, I'd try to be something worth thinking of .' ''[11] For another reason, the spoken conclusion of Agnes Carr Sage's "Who Won the Brush? The Tale of a Thanksgiving Hunt" (November 29, 1890) is unsatisfying; the widow's pious gratitude—'' 'Such generous kind young ladies, and such a dear, blessed holiday as it has been, after all!' ''—merely underlines the sharp contrast between a hunting story where "our young Dianas" have been preoccupied with a fox and this prayerful but too-neat ending. The dailogue throughout the story has been forced to be so practical and informative that it has lost any ring of truth and merely become stylized utterance. Nancy Vernon's speech is meant to characterize her as an eager equestrienne—especially when her "more sensitive" friend is questioning the morality of the fox hunt in ponderous terms. Nan rushes to defend her sport with what is supposed to be the exaggerated enthusiasm of adolescence: "Nonsense! That is where the fun comes in. It will be the next thing to seeking Master Reynard in his native haunts, and will be a clever imitation, at least, of the glorious English hunts of which Papa has so often told me. Oh, I know it will be deliciously exciting, and if I am not in at the death, I shall be the most disappointed girl in all Long Island.''[12] In fact, her speech is overdone: slightly too full of pedantic detail and girlish exclamations. Moreover, the hunted fox is not torn to pieces by the dogs, but spared as a domestic pet—a narrative feature which nonviolent yet sport-loving Elverson, disallower of advertisements for guns and pistols, would heartily endorse.

The influence of Elverson's controlling hand is discernible in all features of the magazine. Storytellers were valued for their tight management of narration, few deft strokes of characterization, suitable moral rectitude, and engagingly varied locales. The early issues of the 1880s did boast stories by raconteurs such as Horatio Alger, Jr., Frank H. Converse, and "Oliver Optic," although soon the contributors came from the ranks of the lesser known like George Coomer, Cuthbert Bede, and Clara J. Denton (January 4, 1890). Despite the diminution of literary art in the magazine stories, Elverson continued to choose his writers to conform to an exacting yet prosaic system of values. Hence it comes as no surprise that, unlike Samuel Goodrich, this edifying go-getter did not inspire a host of imitators. *Golden Days* ceased publication when its editor was in his 70th year. It did not outlive Elverson, possibly because his staunchness made this children's miscellany inimitable.

Notes

1. *A History of American Magazines* (Cambridge: Harvard University Press, 1938), 4:87.
2. *Golden Days for Boys and Girls* 1 (March 6, 1880), 8.
3. Ibid., 26 (November 4, 1905), 832.
4. Ibid., 11 (November 30, 1889), 2.
5. Ibid., 26 (November 4, 1905), 832.
6. Ibid., p. 818.
7. Ibid.

8. Ibid., 11 (November 30, 1889), 1.
9. Ibid.
10. Ibid., p. 3.
11. Ibid., p. 4.
12. Ibid., 12 (November 29, 1890), 1.

Information Sources

BIBLIOGRAPHY
Frank Luther Mott, *A History of American Magazines, 1865-1885* (Cambridge: Harvard
    University Press, 1938) vol. 3.
INDEX SOURCES
None.
LOCATION SOURCES
Complete runs of the magazine are in the Free Library of Philadelphia and the Library
    of Congress; incomplete collections are at the University of Minnesota, Minne-
    apolis; the University of Washington, Seattle; the Boston Public Library; and the
    St. Louis Public Library. Microfilm copies are available from Greenwood Press,
    Westport, Conn.

Publication History

MAGAZINE TITLE AND TITLE CHANGES
Golden Days for Boys and Girls (1880-1907).
VOLUME AND ISSUE DATA
Golden Days for Boys and Girls (vol. 1, no. 1-vol. 28, no. 27).
PUBLISHER AND PLACE OF PUBLICATION
James Elverson, Philadelphia (1880-1907).
EDITOR
James Elverson (1880-1907).

Patricia Demers

GOLDEN HOURS: A MAGAZINE FOR BOYS AND GIRLS

"Whatsoever your hand findeth to do, do it *with your might*." So advised
Solomon Owl in his regular letter to young readers in an 1876 issue of *Golden
Hours: A Magazine for Boys and Girls*. But there were two magazines under
the name of *Golden Hours* during the late nineteenth century. The first, the
subject of this paper, was published by the Methodist Episcopal Church as a
Sunday school paper, one of four magazines authorized by the General Conference in 1868. Under five editors, it appeared from 1869 to 1880. At that time
the Methodist Church supported two publishing centers in New York and Cincinnati. From 1863 to 1867 sales from both centers were $2,535,199 (New York)
and $2,399,508 (Cincinnati).[1] The time was ripe for a new religious periodical
for children.

The second magazine under the name of *Golden Hours* was begun as "a paper
for young ladies in 1888" and published by Norman L. Munro until about 1910.

W. C. Dunn was editor of this *Golden Hours* during its first ten years. In 1904, according to Frank Luther Mott in his *History of American Magazines*, this periodical became a family monthly selling for 25¢ a year.[2]

I. W. Wiley (1825-1884) served as the first editor of the Methodist *Golden Hours* from its birth in 1869 until he was elected bishop in 1872. Wiley had been a medical missionary in China (1850-1854) and had been editor of the Methodist women's magazine, *Ladies Repository*, since 1864. He continued as editor of this publication until 1872.[3] *The Religion of the Family* (1872), Wiley's best known book, was a collection of his articles from this magazine.

Golden Hours: A Magazine for Boys and Girls was 7 by 9 inches and contained forty-eight pages in its first issue. The editor gave an explanation of why *Golden Hours* was born: "We wish to make a magazine for Christian homes, for children who believe in Jesus and love his religion. We do not mean that all the articles in the magazine are to be about religion, but the magazine...is to stand for the right, the true and the good."[4]

The editor also told his young readers what kind of magazine to expect and what it would contain. "In each number we will give an illustrated Bible lesson. Two pieces of music, a hymn and an instrumental piece will be given each month. The Editor's portfolio will furnish you indoor and outdoor amusements, plays, enigmas, riddles, charades, rebuses etc.; notices of new books for children and young people and a monthly gossip of correspondence, proverbs, anecdotes, witty sayings and cheerful chitchat."[5]

Editor Wiley was assisted in putting out this publication by S. W. Williams from 1869 to 1872. Then Williams was co-editor with Erastus Wentworth until 1876. Of S. W. Williams, nothing is known beyond his work in *Golden Hours*.

The first issue seemed to have more nonfiction presented in a narrative form than later numbers. Even the fiction had a didactic religious tone. For example, in a story called "The Orphans," a dying mother tells her children, a girl, ten, and a boy, eight: "My dear children, God can make me well; but if he should not, he knows always what's best for us and you must not murmur. That God who has watched over you from infancy will not forsake you when I am gone, and you must put your trust in him."[6]

A Bible enigma in the first issue's Editor's Portfolio includes:

The initials and finals of—
1. an Asiatic city having a synagogue
2. a Scribe
3. a city of the tribe of Judah
4. a noted capital of the Israelites
5. a queen of Ethiopia
—will give the name of a patriarch and his dwelling place.[7]

A book review of *Little Women* by Louisa May Alcott in the first issue of *Golden Hours* commented: "Louisa Alcott is a very sprightly and fascinating writer, and her sister, Mary Alcott, always makes beautiful pictures to illustrate the books. Their books and stories are always very interesting and instructive about every-day life. They are not religious books, should not be read on Sunday and are not appropriate for the Sunday School. This is the character of the book before us. It is lively, entertaining and not harmful.''[8]

''Editor's Gossip'' outlined the values underlying *Golden Hours* in setting out the qualifications of an ideal reader: ''WANTED: A BOY WITH TEN POINTS— 1. Honest; 2. Pure; 3. Intelligent; 4. Active; 5. Industrious; 6. Obedient; 7. Steady; 8. Obliging; 9. Polite; 10. Neat.''[9]

The first year's table of contents to *Golden Hours* shows that 165 selections (both prose and poetry) were published, with 70 illustrated. Of them, only four were reprints credited to other publications. Contributors to the first year's *Golden Hours* included forty-eight authors, with 12 articles of the 165 published penned by the editors themselves. A note from the editors to prospective contributors in the first issue said: ''We will give preference to short articles, to articles plainly written, to history, fact, science and travel rather than to tales or fiction.''[10] None of the first year's contributors would be known to readers today except for Hans Christian Andersen, represented by ''The Daisy.''

When Wiley was elected bishop in 1872, Erastus Wentworth (1813-1886) was appointed to work with S. W. Williams. Wentworth's publications include *Music: Its Moral and Social Influence* (1843); *Arithmetical Problems Arranged for Drill and Review* (1872); *The First Half Century of Life and Work of the Troy Conference of the Methodist Episcopal Church* (1882).[11] Wentworth served as *Golden Hours* editor with Williams until 1876.

A new feature begun in September 1872 under Wentworth's editorship was the inclusion of readers' letters in the ''Editor's Gossip'' department. At this time the magazine was printed on thinner, poorer quality paper and contained fewer, simpler pictures. Temperance articles were run in 1872-73 and were commented upon in a reader's letter printed in February 1873. ''I write you this to ask if you will organize, through the 'Golden Hours,' a temperance society for boys and girls, with perhaps several branch departments.''[12]

During the next several years the paper quality and number of illustrations fluctuated (1872, poor; 1873, good; 1874, poor again). Religious content went down, including music. Whereas thirteen songs were published in the 1872 issues, only five were included in 1873. By 1875 no music at all was listed in the table of contents.

As for circulation, a statement in the ''Editor's Portfolio'' announced in 1872 having ''several thousand readers monthly over the past four years,'' but continual pleas to subscribe and find new readers were common in these columns too. Thus the circulation figures of this magazine are hard to judge due to the fact that it was distributed in Sunday schools as well as through mail subscriptions.

In volume 7, 1875, there were thirty-one writers in the magazine beside the editors. Hans Christian Andersen, whose story ''Five in a Pea Shell'' was published, is the best known author today among these contributors. This year's

Golden Hours contained 150 selections, with 51 of them illustrated. In addition, 55 poems were published in 1875, but no music was offered. The illustrations were of good quality and primarily black-and-white line drawings. The editors, E. Wentworth and S. W. Williams, announced the addition of "one Lady Editor," H. V. Osborne to the staff in the July issue.

In August 1875 a new feature replaced "Games for Children's Evenings." It was called "Owldom," written by Solomon Owl. The August "Editor's Portfolio" told readers that "some stories in little words and big letters for the very little folks who are just beginning to read" would appear in *Golden Hours*. "The Ped-Dler and the Mouse" is an example of this "easy-reader"-type story. Many of these stories listed H. V. Osborne as author, evidence that these new features reflected her influence on the magazine content.

But these changes in mid-decade in content may not have been solely due to the new editor but to the expansion of Sunday schools and a potential mass audience. In 1870 there were 16,440 Methodist Episcopal Sunday schools with 1,197,674 students. This figure had grown in 1872 to 17,132 Sunday schools and 1,259,464 children enrolled. At the demise of *Golden Hours* in 1880, there were 20,835 Sunday schools with an enrollment of more than 1,500,000 students.[13] The changes noted above in *Golden Hours* might have made it more appealing to new Sunday school members. One year's subscription in 1870 and 1871 was $2. The July issue of 1878 announces a subscription rate of 75¢ for six months.

The last change of editors of this Methodist monthly for children came in 1876. H. V. Osborne, of whom nothing is known beyond her writing in *Golden Hours*, was co-editor with Daniel Curry (1809-1887). Curry, an 1837 graduate of Wesleyan University in Middletown, Connecticut, had been editor of two other Methodist magazines, the *Christian Advocate* from 1864 to 1875 and the *National Repository* from January 1877 to December 1880.[14] Simultaneous to his appointment to *Golden Hours*, Curry was asked to edit the *Ladies Repository* to try to broaden its audience beyond church members. Later, he served as editor of the *Methodist Review* from 1884 until his death in 1887.

Writing contests for readers were introduced by these editors, with the winning stories published in the April "Owldom" department. The story for beginning readers was an established feature now. But no music or book reviews were included in the 1876 issues.

Popular authors of this era whose work did appear in *Golden Hours* were Rev. R. H. Howard, Paul du Chaillu, Mrs. E. S. Martin, J. F. Hurst, and once, Mrs. E. G. Farnsworth. Most of the contributors were not well-known writers, and only a few became regular monthly writers during the eleven-year life span of *Golden Hours*.

The 1880 census report of newspapers and periodicals by S.N.D. North (volume 8) listed *Golden Hours* among 120 publications (including 5 Methodist) in Cincinnati, population 313,374. *Golden Hours* was not identified as Methodist but was classified as a Sunday school paper. The subscription rate for *Golden Hours*, according to this source, was $2 a year.

The cause of the death of *Golden Hours* is not clear. Most likely the General Conference decided against continuing it. There isn't any evidence within the magazine content of deterioration in quality, but it had become more secular. The 1880 census counted 217 children's papers published in the United States, "the greater part of which were of this class of Sunday-school papers."[15] This count included lesson sheets and tracts as well as periodicals.

The principal purpose of the editors of *Golden Hours* was to further the religious education of their readers. How their personalities, families, and talents influenced their carrying out of this purpose is wrapped in the mystery of the past. The product was for the most part a credit to its creators and sponsors—"golden hours" for the young.

Notes

1. James Penn Pilkington, *The Methodist Publishing House: A History, Beginnings to 1870* (Nashville: Abingdon Press, 1968), 463.

2. Frank Luther Mott, *A History of American Magazines* (Cambridge: Harvard University Press, 1957), 4: 273.

3. Nolan B. Harmon, ed., *Encyclopedia of World Methodism* (Nashhville: Abingdon Press, 1974), 2562. All biographical information about the editors was obtained from this source provided by the librarian, Agnes Fair, of the Methodist Publishing House.

4. *Golden Hours: A Magazine for Boys and Girls* 1 (January 1869), 47.

5. Ibid.

6. Ibid., p. 6.

7. Ibid., p. 44.

8. Ibid., p. 45.

9. Ibid., 1 (April 1869), 239.

10. Ibid., 1 (January 1869), 47.

11. See *The National Union Catalog, Pre 1956 Imprints* (London: Mansell, 1968-1980), 663:535, for list of publications.

12. *Golden Hours*, 5 (February 1873), 96.

13. Addie Grace Wardle, *History of the Sunday School Movement* (New York and Cincinnati: The Methodist Book Concern, 1918), app. 1, p. 213.

14. See *The National Union Catalog, Pre 1956 Imprints* 407:462, for a listing of Curry's editorships and publications; and see Nolan B. Harmon, ed., *Encyclopedia of World Methodism*, p. 616, for biographical data.

15. S.N.D. North, *The Newspaper and the Periodical Press*, Report of the Tenth Census (Washington, D.C.: Government Printing Office, 1884), 8:115-25.

Information Sources

BIBLIOGRAPHY

Nolan B. Harmon, ed., *Encyclopedia of World Methodism* (Nashville: Abingdon Press, 1974); R. Gordon Kelly, *Mother Was a Lady* (Westport, Conn.: Greenwood Press, 1974); Frank Luther Mott, *A History of American Magazines* 5 vols. (Cambridge: Harvard University Press, 1938-1968); S.N.D. North, *The Newspaper and Pe-*

riodical Press, Report of the Tenth Census (Washington D.C.: Government Printing Office, 1884), vol. 8; James Penn Pilkington, *The Methodist Publishing House: A History* (Nashville: Abingdon Press, 1968); Addie Grace Wardle, *The History of the Sunday School Movement* (New York and Cincinnati: The Methodist Book Concern, 1918).

INDEX SOURCES
None; table of contents in each volume.

LOCATION SOURCES
Complete or almost complete sets of bound volumes are in the Ohio Wesleyan University Library, Delaware, Ohio (vols. 1-8, 10-11); and in the New York Public Library (vols. 1-12). Other libraries have incomplete holdings and are listed in *Union List of Serials*.

Publication History

MAGAZINE TITLE AND TITLE CHANGES
Golden Hours: A Magazine for Boys and Girls (1869-1880).

VOLUME AND ISSUE DATA
Golden Hours: A Magazine for Boys and Girls (vol. 1, no. 1-vol. 12, no. 12).

PUBLISHER AND PLACE OF PUBLICATION
Hitchcock and Walden, Cincinnati, Chicago, and St. Louis; Carlton and Lanaham, New York (1869-1880)

EDITOR
I. W. Wiley and S. W. Williams (1869-1871); Erastus Wentworth and S. W. Williams (1872-1874); Erastus Wentworth, S. W. Williams, and H. V. Osborne (1875-1876); Daniel Curry and H. V. Osborne (1876-1880).

Martha Rasmussen

H

HAPPY DAYS

Happy Days continued Frank Tousey's *Boys of New York** and was published weekly from October 20, 1894, until September 12, 1924, when the paper announced, "This will be the last issue of *Happy Days* published. Due to lack of support from the reading public, it no longer pays to issue it."[1] From start to finish, the publishers seem to have regarded this inexpensive, sensational weekly as strictly a commercial venture. The paper was filled with serial stories that Tousey later compiled and sold as "libraries" of pulp novels. *Happy Days* provided material for the Young Sleuth Library, Wide Awake Library, Boys' Star Library, and others. It was also used as a vehicle for advertising the many "how-to" books Tousey offered to the public. They included everything from instruction manuals for doing magic tricks and writing letters to books about how to become a scientist or speaker.

The eight-page *Boys of New York* was expanded to sixteen pages under its new title, and the size of the pages was correspondingly reduced. It was printed in the same almost microscopic print and featured the dramatic and prominently displayed engraved illustrations of its predecessor. Throughout its history *Happy Days* featured the same writers. "Tom Teaser" and "Sam Smiley" provided the humorous stories. The same host of authors who produced the sensational fiction for Tousey's other publications contributed to *Happy Days*, among whom were C. Little, P. T. Raymond, Frank Forrest, Albert J. Booth, and Gaston Garne.

Without significantly altering the content of the paper, in 1897 Tousey attempted to expand his audience by changing the subtitle to *A Paper for Young and Old*. He also offered premiums to subscribers. Few new authors' names were added to the list of contributors after 1900, and as the century progressed, the paper clearly lost ground. The price was raised. The number of illustrations was reduced. Old stories and illustrations were rerun, and nonfiction from old issues was reused until *Happy Days* consisted of little but recycled material. In 1922 Harry E. Wolff assumed publication, making a short-lived effort to respond to popular interest in radio and motion pictures, but the attempt to revitalize the paper failed. In 1924 it ceased publication.

Under Frank Tousey's editorship *Happy Days* attempted to encourage the kind of reader involvement with the paper that was characteristic in the early days of *Boys of New York*.* Not only was the lively correspondence column retained from the earlier paper, but in the first volume, readers were invited to submit biographies and photographs of themselves. They were asked, "Have you ever had some stirring event occur in your life? Have you ever performed some brave action? Have you ever done a noble act of charity? Have you ever been the means of saving life? Have you ever done anything you think worthy of being published?"[2] Like their counterparts in the paper's stories, readers rescued children from burning buildings, saved friends from drowning, defended their property from tramps and gypsies, and killed wild beasts. Many claimed narrow escapes from death.

Aspiring artists as well as young heroes were encouraged to contribute. *Happy Days* offered cash prizes in drawing contests sponsored in 1895-1896 and 1898-1899. Using the circle in a form provided in the paper, readers were to create a funny face using a limited number of strokes. Entries were judged by comic artist Thomas Worth and authors "Tom Teaser" and "Sam Smiley." Examples of the better submissions were published until the winners were announced.

All regular readers had opportunities to exchange coupons clipped from the paper for sets of rare stamps or items such as watches and cameras offered at minimal cost. By 1895 *Happy Days* had begun to sponsor coupon contests, giving away bicycles, pianos, and other valuable prizes to those who submitted the largest numbers of coupons. At various times premiums were also offered to subscribers and those who persuaded others to subscribe.

These opportunities encouraged readers to become, like the heroes in the paper's stories, active, enterprising, and willing to gamble on their own abilities. Like *Boys of New York*, this publication appealed primarily to boys of the lower and lower middle classes who hoped to rise in the world. Shipwrecks, fires, factory and railroad accidents, and encounters with thieves and kidnappers provided the protagonists in the popular serial stories opportunities to become heroes. They ventured into the arctic, explored underwater worlds in primitive diving suits, crossed continents on their bicycles, fought to preserve high ideals at work and in school, and thwarted the evil plans of masked members of secret societies.

A number of stories focused on the successes of young entrepreneurs, like "Halsey and Company, the Young Bankers and Speculators: a Story of How Two Boys Made Their Fortunes on Wall Street" by H. K. Shackleford (July 13, 1895, and following issues). Sea stories such as "Under the Black Flag; or

A Buried Treasure of the Seven Seas: a Thrilling Story of the South Pacific''
by J. G. Bradley (April 13, 1895, and following issues) were regularly featured
as were tales of Indian uprisings and life in the West, circus and sports stories,
detective and ghost stories.

The Frank Reade, Jr., stories by ''Noname,'' which featured various mechanical contraptions and air ships, appeared regularly, along with Robert Lennox's fire-fighter stories. Added to the list of those who had been regular
contributors to *Boys of New York* were Cornelius Shea, Old King Brady, and
Fred Fearnot.

The action-packed, fast-paced stories with their flat characters did present to
Happy Days' readers a world full of opportunities. There were frontiers to be
conquered on all sides—in the open territories of the North and West, in business
and the entertainment industries, in the seas and skies, and even in crowded
cities.

Although most of the paper was devoted to stories, Tousey also included some
nonfiction. In 1894 an occasional column, ''Our Knowledge Corner,'' featured
substantial articles on topics such as the perils of sea travel and the development
of electrical science. From 1896 to 1898 Philat's ''All About Stamps'' and
Nevertire's ''Bicycle Talks'' appeared. Francis W. Doughty contributed many
longer articles between 1896 and 1900. Frequently illustrated, these informative
articles covered topics of general and historical interest. Doughty wrote about
coins, balloons and ships, and natural phenomenon like comets, wind, and the
moon. He wrote ''What the Architect Does'' and ''English Sports in the Olden
Times.'' Shorter articles of unspecified authorship offered instruction in knot
tying, paper folding, and making wooden cannons or presented information about
a wide variety of topics such as Alaska, glass making, penal settlements, and
mud-bath treatments.

''A Little Fun,'' a column of shorter humorous anecdotes, and ''Interesting
Items'' appeared throughout most of the publication life of *Happy Days* (1894-
1923). Continued from *Boys of New York*, the humor column poked fun at the
ignorant and included short dialogues in which children outwitted their parents.
''Interesting Items'' remained a compilation of bits of curious factual information, reporting on everything from kangaroos to steam engines to the household
expenses of the Sultan of Turkey. The column by ''Ed'' (1894-1924) used self-
mockery and hyperbole in the humorous personal and family anecdotes that
appeared week after week. ''Ed'' offered advice on matrimony, described encounters with the butcher, or related his struggles in learning to swim or garden.

Under the editorship of Luis Senarens (1923-1924), *Happy Days* offered previously published serial stories and columns by ''Ed.'' Intermittently, ''From
Ear to Ear'' and ''Interesting Items'' appeared along with reprints of the stories
that had kept the paper going for many years. Senarens introduced a new feature,
''Radio News and Hints'' (1923-1924), which, alongside the recycled illustrations of persons in antiquated dress, appeared out of place. He made a brief,
desperate attempt to save the paper in 1923 by publishing photographs and stories

from popular motion pictures, but, in 1924, *Happy Days* reverted to offering only old material until its cessation in September of that year. It failed to respond to the changing interests of successive generations of boys. It took no note of how events, such as a world war, might have tempered the optimism of its readers. It could not compete with the sensational appeal of the new media.

Notes

1. *Happy Days* 60 (September 12, 1924), 8.
2. Ibid., 1 (December 12, 1894), 4.

Information Sources

BIBLIOGRAPHY
Frank Luther Mott, *A History of American Magazines* (Cambridge: Harvard University Press, 1938-1968), vol. 3.
INDEX SOURCES
None.
LOCATION SOURCES
Bound vols. 1-60 are in the noncirculating Hess Collection, University of Minnesota, Minneapolis. Volumes for 1894-1910 are available only from Datamations, Inc., New York.

Publication History

MAGAZINE TITLE AND TITLE CHANGES
Happy Days: A Paper for Young Americans (1894-1897); *Happy Days: A Paper for Young and Old* (1897-1924).
VOLUME AND ISSUE DATA
Happy Days: A Paper for Young Americans (vol. 1, no. 1-vol. 7, no. 158); *Happy Days: A Paper for Young and Old* (vol. 7, no. 159-vol. 60, no. 1563).
PUBLISHER AND PLACE OF PUBLICATION
Frank Tousey, New York (1894-1922); Harry E. Wolff, Publishers, Inc., New York (1922-1924).
EDITOR
Frank Tousey (1894-1922); Luis Senarens (1923-1924). The name of the editor is generally not listed.

Constance Gremore

HARPER'S YOUNG PEOPLE: AN ILLUSTRATED WEEKLY

At its first appearance on Tuesday, November 4, 1879, *Harper's Young People: An Illustrated Weekly* became the fourth periodical published by Harper Brothers, a firm long established at Franklin Square in New York City. Like *St. Nicholas,** the already successful juvenile periodical published by Scribner's, *Harper's Young People* was from its inception closely tied to its publisher's other interests and reflected the standards and values of its adult publications. The new juvenile joined *Harper's Weekly, Monthly,* and the *Bazaar,* drawing heavily upon their reputations, editorial strength, stable of contributors, and subscription lists. Indeed, the immediate "unprecedented success" of the new magazine has been attributed to "someone's bright idea of sending the first thirty issues free to all subscribers of the other three journals, along with subscription blanks."[1] With such support, the new weekly grew rapidly. Beginning as an eight-page paper, within six weeks it increased both page and type size, improved the quality of its illustrations, and increased the number of pages, assuming the sixteen-page format to which it adhered until April 30, 1895, when it transformed itself, without missing a number or interrupting a serialized story, into *Harper's Round Table*.

That Harper Brothers should have established a juvenile periodical in the late 1870s seems almost inevitable. The firm was well known as a publisher of children's books, a field it entered before the Civil War. From the 1850s it was active in producing and distributing school texts, readers, and spellers. It developed several popular educational series, like Dr. William Rolfe's English Classics for School Reading, and after 1879 these publications were regularly advertized in the back pages of *Harper's Young People*, along with their new juvenile fiction, often targeted for Christmas, and children's classics such as Jacob Abbott's Rollo books, an old Harper's property.

Despite a secure foothold in the children's market, Harper's did not develop a unique or innovative juvenile periodical. Both the format and tone of *Harper's Young People* resembled the established *St. Nicholas*. Harper's new publication featured similarly fine illustrations (often a full page), semieducational articles, and pleasing genteel fiction with emphasis upon domestic realism, history, and fantasy, often by authors who also published in *St. Nicholas*. Both magazines specialized in holiday-oriented stories and features, beginning each year in time for Christmas gift subscriptions and advertizing a gala Christmas issue. That two such periodicals—one weekly, the other monthly—could coexist in the same market for twenty years only underlines the popular appeal of the values they supported and the vision of childhood and youth they represented through the 1880s and 1890s.

From its inception the editorial policy of *Harper's Young People* appealed directly to the tastes and standards of prosperous, upwardly mobile people who wanted the best for their children and feared the corrupting influence of less genteel branches of the popular press. An announcement of the new juvenile periodical, published in *Harper's Weekly* in 1879, noted that "In this age of the press, half of the influences which mould [*sic*] mind and character must be drawn" from what boys and girls "read in hours of recreation. But much of the reading now offered to them is void of intellectual stimulus, much of it appeals to and cultivates a vicious taste, and some of it seems to aim at corrupting the heart."[2] *Harper's Young People* dedicated itself to the "belief that this great juvenile public ought to have the best." Similarly, an advertisement addressed to "Parents and Guardians" in *Harper's Bazaar* noted that the "evils of sensational literature for the young" are "seen in every neighborhood throughout the land, and the want of an antidote has been long felt. This the publishers of *Harper's Young People* propose to supply by placing at a price within the reach of all a weekly illustrated journal filled with matter fitted to attract, amuse, and instruct the rising generation, avoiding on the one hand the objectional features of sensational juvenile literature, and on the other that austere moralizing tone which repels the youthful reader."[3]

Year after year, the editors assured their subscribers that they spared "Neither pains nor expense" in preparing the magazine. Early, bombastic statements recommended the magazine as a medium for advertizing and announce its intention to be "the most entertaining, *instructive*, high-toned, and popular weekly paper" for young "Americans."[4] As it matured in the 1880s, its editors described *Harper's Young People* as a vehicle for genteel taste, useful skills, and decorous fun. The annual prospectus for 1884 stated that "no other publication of its kind is so lavishly adorned with the finest engravings and cuts. Its presence in a family assists the children to the formation of correct tastes in art, and helps them to grow in the love of the beautiful."[5] The editors serenely noted, among contributors to the magazine, the "most accomplished writers for the young" and added that the "heroic element is made prominent in *Harper's Young People* because its conductors recognize the fact that nothing more truly incites children to noble conduct than reading about and hearing of brave and self-denying acts on the part of others of their own age."[6] The editors emphasized that they spoke to all members of the domestic circle. For boys, there were "descriptions of manly sports" and articles giving "practical directions concerning tools and their uses." For girls, there were "suggestions for needle-work" and instructions for making "gifts for home dear ones" and "advice for every-day deportment." Since "even nonsense" has its "place and time in the wisely managed household," the periodical also included riddles and jokes, as well as "bits of rhyme and musical jingles" for the "wee ones in the nursery." *Harper's Young People*, its editors concluded, was "the home paper," whose "sunny face never wears a frown."[7]

This representative statement with its emphasis upon life in the family parlor as a source of good taste, morality, and appropriate role definitions indicates the *Young People*'s line of descent from the domestic periodicals and omnipresent giftbooks of earlier American generations. Although primarily addressed to readers "from 6 to 16," the *Young People* saw itself as a family publication in harmony "with the moral atmosphere" of "every cultivated Christian household."[8] Its tone often suggests the editors' awareness of a right-thinking Christian parent looking over the child subscriber's shoulder. Items such as "Piano Lessons and Practice" and "The Care of Children's Teeth" (March 6, 1888) are obviously addressed to parents. It is, therefore, not surprising to find letters from adults on the contributors' page, like one from "Pater" who praised the magazine's "good, healthy tone" and its success in showing children how to become "good, wholesome *American* young men and women."[9]

In its twenty-year career, *Harper's Young People* had several editors. The first was Kirk Munroe, the author of many boys' adventure stories, followed by "a Miss Van Duyne" and in 1885 by A. B. Starey.[10] No other member of the Editorial Department left as clear and personal an imprint as Margaret Elizabeth Munson Sangster, who as the "little Postmistress" conducted the regular contributors' page, "Our Post-Office Box," for many years. When she took over this position in 1882, Sangster had edited the childrens' page of the weekly *Hearth and Home* for three years, from 1872 until the periodical closed in 1875. (Her predecessor in this position was Mary Mapes Dodge, who left it to become editor of *St. Nicholas*.) While at *Hearth and Home*, Sangster took a second editorial position on *The Christian at Work*, which she held for six years until 1879, and when *Hearth and Home* closed in 1875, she became editor of *The Christian Intelligencer*, a position she held for some years while working for *Harper's Young People*.[11]

Sangster's "Post-Office Box" department, like the "Letter Box" of *St. Nicholas*, was designed to encourage reader participation and loyalty to the magazine. Casting herself as the "friend of every child who writes to her," the "Little Postmistress" commented cheerfully upon the letters she printed, praising good deeds and good jokes, and encouraging the illusion of personal friendship. Sometimes, assuming the role of a schoolmistress, a profession she admired,[12] she assigned topics to her young correspondents or commented on their penship and spelling since "part of a polite education consists in the elegant and straightforward use of the pen."[13] Urging boys to write, she asked them to send "your favorite book, your favorite game, your pleasantest amusement, and your favorite motto."[14] She was especially receptive to mail from abroad, a gesture that emphasized Harper's international status and encouraged children to cultivate a practical knowledge of geography and politics. She also used her department to collect funds for childrens' charities, such as the Boys' Club in St. Mark's Place, New York, and the "Young People's Cot" in St. Mary's Free Hospital at 34th Street, New York.

An active church member all of her life (originally Methodist; Presbyterian in her adult years), Sangster believed she had a special "mission to girlhood."[15] Like many other American Protestants of her generation, she saw the home as the center of Christian experience and women as domestic missionaries promoting faith within the family circle. In her replies to letters sent to her as "Little Postmistress" and in the short fictional pieces sometimes included in her column, Sangster characteristically portrayed a home and family gently dominated by well-behaved girls who woo disruptive boys from their rude impulses. One such piece describes "The Little Housekeepers Club of Brier Junction," a society whose object is "for us to learn how to keep house" and whose motto is " 'Little children, love one another.' " In the course of the story, an inevitable skirmish between the sexes breaks out:

"When we break any of our by-laws," said the President, "we must pay a fine of two cents."

"We haven't any by-laws!" shouted Fred. "Ho! ho!"

"You are very rude, Cousin Fred," said Ethel, offended.

And Irene remarked, with dignity, "If the boys make fun, we will not have them in with us."

"Don't let us forget our motto," pleaded gentle May; and peace was restored.[16]

As the "Little Postmistress," Sangster was undoubtedly successful in becoming a personality for the readers of the magazine. It is a measure of her influence that her portrait was printed on the cover of one issue of *Harper's Young People* (January 25, 1887), the only editor so honored by the periodical. Throughout the years of her connection with it, her interests helped to set its tone, assuring an emphasis upon "girl life" and activities or relationships in the home.

In 1889 Sangster succeeded her friend Mary Louise Booth as editor of *Harper's Bazaar*. She continued to write occasionally for *Harper's Young People* and even had a column in *Harper's Round Table*, but the juvenile publication was no longer her primary interest. Her changed place in the Harper's structure may have helped to effect the shift in focus at *Harper's Young People*, away from attention to girls and domestic life toward boys' activities, sports, and "manly" pursuits.

To some extent, editorial and authorial functions overlapped at *Harper's Young People*; Sangster published verse, fiction, and advice columns while conducting the contributors' department, and Kirk Munroe's fiction was often featured while he was an editor. Some other authors who regularly published in the magazine wrote principally for children, among them J. T. Trowbridge; James Otis [Kaler], often described as "the author of *Toby Tyler*," which first appeared as a serial in the magazine; Sophie Swett, who contributed many "down East" stories; and Lucy Lillie, whose romances—*Rolf House* (1886), *Jo's Opportunity* (1886), and *The Household of Glen Holly* (1888)—were serialized. No contributor was more revered than Louisa May Alcott, whose story for the Christmas issue always evoked a flurry of editorial excitement. Many other contributors, however, wrote principally for the adult market, among them, Rose Terry Cooke, Mary E. Wilkins, Harriet Prescott Spofford, Sarah Orne Jewett, and Nora Perry. William Dean Howells appeared regularly in *Harper's Young People* after he joined the house of Harper in the mid-1880s. The autobiographical account of his youth, *A Boy's Town* (1890), was serialized in the magazine, and his august reputation was also invoked to adorn the special Christmas number. This mixture of so-called juvenile and adult writers suggests what a reading of their stories reveals: in *Harper's Young People* fiction suitable for the juvenile market is defined by content. Stories in which children or young adults figure prominently and display bravery, charity, or other "noble" qualities are appropriate for young readers. Fiction that treats adult life, has a darker moral cast, or presents a critical view of social or economic issues does not appear in the magazine. *Harper's Young People*'s fiction is often sentimental, and poverty, physical suffering, and human tragedy are present, but such trials are easily resolved. There is no "social problem,'' ''other half,'' race conflict, or unbridgeable gulf between rich and poor in Harper's juvenile publication. A writer like Howells, whose adult fiction criticizes established American institutions, is not characteristically represented in his contributions to *Harper's Young People*.

Within its first year *Harper's Young People* established the format to which it adhered with few variations until the 1890s, when the editors began to experiment with a different emphasis that finally led them to rename the magazine. Through the 1880s a typical issue begins with a lead story that provides the subject for a large front-page illustration. It includes at least one chapter of a serial (that runs typically two to three months), another short story, some short factual items, the full-page ''Post-Office Box'' department, and a final page of jokes. There are several large drawings and one or two cartoons. Many issues include poetry, sometimes printed on a full page with accompanying illustrations; songs with music; and, again, illustrations. Fictional items outnumber factual at least three to one. Most of the fiction deals with contemporary life in a realistic manner, employing standard English throughout and a vocabulary of reasonable difficulty. A few stories and poems employ misspellings intended to simulate nonstandard English, but this is not common. When it occurs, it is designed to render rural American speech, as in Sophie Swett's down-East stories, the Irish-English associated with an urban servant class, or the ''baby talk'' of two and three year olds.

In its serials, *Harper's Young People* favored romances in which young heroes or heroines leave home to visit strange places, but the dominant tone of each issue is usually determined by the nearest holiday. This is especially true of Thanksgiving and Christmas, which occupy the first three months of each year. The treatment of these holidays and their lessons merits consideration. In a typical year in the 1880s, Christmas is introduced in November with the story of a poor boy, lame Rick, who sells his pet turkey to buy food for an even poorer family's Christmas dinner. This charitable act is discovered by a rich neighbor who gives money so Rick may be educated (Sophie Swett, ''How Rick Made Himself a Christmas,'' November 17, 1885). A week later, in a Thanksgiving story, a brave boy saves his younger cousin from drowning and thus effects a reconciliation between their parents. Both families gather for Thanksgiving dinner at the old homestead (Julia K. Hildreth, ''Friends at Last,'' November 24, 1885). In the next issue two young daughters of a rent collector learn from their father of a poor family with a blind mother, who cannot pay the rent. The little girls sing carols on a ferry-boat to earn money for the impoverished family and so shame the landlord into helping his tenants (John R. Coryell, ''Little Miss Santa Claus,'' December 1, 1885). Similar stories appear in succeeding issues (Lucy Lillie, ''The Lonely Lady's Christmas,'' December 8, 1885; William O. Stoddard, ''Christmas on the North Fork,'' Supplement, December 1, 1885), culminating with Louisa May Alcott's ''A Christmas Turkey and How It Came'' (December 22, 1885), in which the children of a man who wastes money on drink work to earn the money for the family's Christmas celebration. The youngest, Kitty, gives some holly to a poor street child and is at once rewarded with the chance to help a rich boy who has hurt himself. The boy's sister gives Kitty presents for her family, and she arrives home to find that her father has bought a turkey and promised never to drink again. Similar tales of charity appear in verse (Margaret Sangster, "Her Gifts," December 1, 1885; and C. D. Weldon, "The Happiest Christmas," December 15, 1885) and advice columns (Mrs. W. J. Hays, "A Christmas Chat," December 1, 1885). The theme is reinforced by articles on making Christmas presents and accounts of holidays in far-away places (Lt. Frederick Schwatka, "Two Thanksgivings in the Arctic," November 24, and December 22, 1885). After the holidays, the holiday theme is continued, as in Mrs. W. J. Hays, "The Minister's Barrel" (December 29, 1885), D.T.S., "The Chorister of Westminster Abbey" (January 5, 1885), and Agnes Sage, "Twelfth Night Revels" (January 5, 1885). It is taken up again in February, where the theme is "What St. Nicholas Forgot and St. Valentine Remembered" (Charles S. Pratt, February 13, 1883), and so on throughout the year. Fiction without a holiday setting reiterates the role of the noble child (as in J. T. Trowbridge, "Ned Thurlow's Trial" (November 6 and 13, 1888), as do advice columns (as Aunt Marjorie Precept, "About Being the Captain," October 30, 1883; and Margaret Emma Ditto, "Which—The Right; or The Rest of the Boys," March 19, 1899). The emphasis upon childish generosity, and especially the ritualization of the holidays as an occasion for expressions of humanitarian concern, reflect the dominant social attitudes of the magazine. There is, in such stories, tacit recognition of the gulf between the very poor and the "comfortable," who have jobs and some money—although they are not rich—and who know how society functions. This group has a duty to mediate between the "deserving" poor and the very rich, who are remote and indifferent but not deliberately unkind. Careworn adults, who have their place in the "system," are not free to promote justice, and so it is the noble, middle-class child whose spontaneous charity corrects society's wrongs and whose good-heartedness is inevitably, often financially, rewarded. The child is cast as an instinctive, although necessarily weak, reformer. With the little personal adjustments he or she effects, the social fabric is stable. This affirmation of the status quo constitutes a substantial part of the "patriotism" that the editors repeatedly claim for their publication.

The line between fiction and nonfiction is sometimes hard to draw, since the *Young People* often fictionalized "fact," presumably to make it more attractive. This might occur in the fictional framing of instructions for making gifts (Alice M. Kellogg, "Brightie's Christmas Club," November 10, 17, 24, 1885) or the presentation of geographical information with a fictional thread ("The Spotted Wolf: A Boy's Adventure in Northern Russia," November 11, 1884). Clearly, nonfiction is the account of natural science, physics, or machines, geographical description, current events, and numerous articles about "things to do"—games, crafts, sports, hobbies, puzzles, pets—designed to reflect and enlarge children's interests. The treatment of natural science is often sophisticated, as in Sarah

Cooper's deftly descriptive articles; Charles Morris, "An Animal in a Box," that is, turtles (December 15, 1885); Charles C. Abbott, "Recent Studies of the Intelligence of Birds" (November 6, 1888); and William M. Davis, "What We Know of the Moon" (January 22, 1895). Physics and machines also receive detailed, sophisticated treatment, as in John Russell Coryell's discussion of Edison and recording "The Talking Machine" (February 5, 1889) and John Ashdown Audsley's "A Simple Electrical Machine" (January 15, 1895). Geographical items are less technical, as in Sherwood Ryse, "Snow-Skating" (January 26, 1884) and "A Garrison on the Tops of the Alps" (November 13, 1894). Many such items take the semifictional approach of treating "child life" in other lands. The implication is that a younger child will read geographical items, but machines, tools, and electricity are for the scientifically oriented teenage boy.

Harper's Young People includes occasional accounts of historical events (Capt. Howard Patterson, "The Blowing Up of the Ironclad 'Albermarle,' " February 5, 1893), but they are not frequent; neither are accounts of historical figures, although they may accompany a reproduction of a famous painting, as the full-page picture "after Vandyck" is paired with Eliot McCormick's account of "The Children of Charles I" (June 19, 1883). Reports of contemporary life range from an interview with the girl who played Little Lord Fauntleroy on the New York stage (Lucy Lillie, "Little Lord Fauntleroy," (January 29, 1889) to the biography of "A Little Kansas Heroine" who saved her baby brother from fire (November 13, 1888). There are series on prominent Americans, such as the "Early Days of Successful Men" articles that include Admiral Gherardi (November 6, 1894) and General Miles (November 20, 1894). Much the most numerous and diverse factual items are those that describe "things to do," since they respond to the changing interests or fads of the young readers. There are descriptions of games (James Otis [Kaler], "King's Court," February 20, 1883), sports (Henry P. Wells, "Fishing and Fishing Tackle," July 2, 1889), pets (Sherwood Ryse, "Dogs and Their Management," June 26, 1883), crafts (R. B. Williams, "A Homemade Scroll-Saw," January 29, 1889), and hobbies, such as the long-running department on stamp-collecting and the popular camera club of the 1890s. Almost every issue included instructions for making a gift, Valentine, handkerchief, pincushion, or some other small item. Woodworking is also recommended as in Charles Henry Webb, "Carpentry for Girls" (May 29, 1888). Many articles assume the "how-to" formula (Frank Beard, "How to Sketch from Nature," June 18, 1883; F. Chasemore, "How to Make a Boat with a Screw-Propeller," January 19, 1889; Edward Fales Coward, "Private Theatricals and How to Get Them Up," November 13, 1894). The suggestion of these items is that the child wants to acquire many different skills and pursue an active, useful life. Sports are recommended to prepare the body for a healthy life, and crafts and hobbies are presented as enjoyable paths to useful knowledge.

By far the most innovative contributions to *Harper's Young People* in the 1890s were by Howard Pyle who, both as author and illustrator, brought to the magazine an imagination not dedicated to useful sobriety or bounded by local color realism, sentimentality, and the religion of the home. His career again illustrates the relationship between *St. Nicholas* and Harper's juvenile publication. In 1876, as a young art student in New York City, Pyle repeatedly sent material to Mary Mapes Dodge, who rejected it either because *St. Nicholas* was "overstocked," or because Pyle's work was unconventional.[17] Eventually, Charles Parsons, the art director for Harper's magazines, became interested in Pyle and gave him work on the *Weekly*. Meanwhile, Pyle, struggling to define his own interests and hoping to support himself as an author and illustrator without living in New York, developed various independent projects. His first major entry in the juvenile field, *The Merry Adventures of Robin Hood* (1883), was published by Scribner's. Looking for further inspiration, Pyle "took Thorp's Northern Mythology out of the Mercantile Library" and found it "a rich mine to select from, though a dull book to read."[18] From it he adapted fairy tales that soon began to appear with Pyle's illustrations, first in *St. Nicholas* and then, as he cemented relations with Harper's, in *Harper's Young People*, where they were frequently published throughout the 1880s. These jovial fantasies, cast in a lightly archaic English, imitated and mocked the familiar moral tale. Pyle also conceived "the idea of writing humorous verses, printing them by hand and decorating them with pen-and-ink drawings on the same page."[19] These pieces first appeared in *Harper's Young People* and then as a book, *Pepper and Salt; or Seasoning for Young Folk* (1886), published by Harper's. Of his many books and stories, Pyle's best known is *Men of Iron* (1891), a boy's story of the court of Henry IV of England, which first appeared as a serial in *Harper's Young People*.

Pyle's work is remarkable both for his personal, witty style as a writer and his sophisticated taste in illustration. Whereas most juvenile writers are soberly instructive or uplifting, Pyle makes fun of obvious "morals" and the view that "history" for children should be a parade of heroes in stories such as "How Boots Befooled the King" (December 1, 1885) and "Ill-luck and the Fiddler" (October 15, 1889). As an illustrator, he avoided the unnaturally sweet-faced children, satisfied adults, and cosy domestic situations most often represented in *Harper's Young People* and drew cunning magicians and medieval children with flinty eyes. He was immensely versatile, the master of several distinct illustrative styles. As an illustrator of historical works, Pyle was known for accuracy in costume and the ability to capture character (even the wooden George Washington), but his sardonic eye also records cracks in the plaster and peeling paint in great houses where historic events take place. In a different vein, his decorative borders for music or verse (often his own or his sister Katherine's) reflect the simplified patterns of art nouveau. The long, profitable association with Harper's and *Harper's Young People* helped to establish Pyle's preeminence as an illustrator in the juvenile field and gave the magazine a measure of visual distinction unmatched by its competitors.

Pyle was, however, only one of a talented group of illustrators gathered at Harper's under Charles Parsons, who, according to the artists that worked for him, played as great a role in shaping the Harper's periodicals as did his better-known colleague, George William Curtis, first incumbent of the "Easy Chair." At a time when photographs were not often used in journalism, Harper's, especially its *Weekly*, relied upon a team of illustrators to produce speedy, accurate drawings of current events. Parsons developed a corps of artists, capable of working together to produce large, clear, descriptive pictures. These illustrators' role as "visual reporters" forced them to develop similar techniques, a realistic style, and an eye for contemporary manners. Their work is exemplified in the drawing of W. A. Rogers, whose drawings capture the jolly, informal aspect of American life. His pictures, even political cartoons designed to criticize institutions or individuals reflect a tolerantly amused view of life. Rogers' style was well adapted to the pleasantly conservative outlook of *Harper's Young People*, in whose pages young Booth Tarkington saw Rogers's illustrations for *Toby Tyler* and correctly concluded that the artist was "humorous" and "friendly," "as kind and sunny as he was keen."[20]

Harper's Young People's "girls' stories" were equally well illustrated, often with drawings by Alice Barber or Jessie Shepherd, whose clear, elegant pictures show fashionably clad young ladies of the period reading, exercising, or visiting each other, as such well-bred girls should. These illustrations combine careful depiction of contemporary costume, such as might be found in the fashion pages of *Harper's Bazaar*, with individual characterization suitable to the accompanying story. Because it attracted gifted artists and reproduced their work carefully, *Harper's Young People* is a rich storehouse of visual information about the lives and activities of prosperous, largely urban, Americans in the 1880s and 1890s. Its illustrations are, of course, limited by its fiction, and like its stories, its drawings do not reflect serious social problems, human suffering, and the darker side of life. Poor children are ill-dressed, but they have clean, bright faces, and even the sick are seemly.

Harper's Young People was an illustrated weekly, and the number and quality of its illustrations played an important role in defining the character of the periodical. Like *Harper's Bazaar* it featured beautiful pictures and implied that possessing them, even if they were magazine illustrations, indicated the subscriber's cultural interests. The editors' devotion to "profuse" illustration on which "no expense" is spared suggests their belief that the public wanted a picture paper. In every issue there were three or four large illustrations; in the special issues near winter holidays, there might be twice as many. A full-page engraving "after" the work of a well-known European painter was often printed. These reproductions are crude to the modern eye and jarring beside realistic scenes from commonplace life drawn by Harper's regular illustrators. Yet the inclusion of such reproductions suggests that art, in itself, was important to the magazine and its subscribers. In any case, *Harper's Young People* offered its version of the nonutilitarian beautiful to a sizeable popular market at a comparatively low price (4¢ an issue in 1879, rising to 10¢ a month or $1 a year in 1899).

The arts are also represented in poetry and music, of which every issue of *Harper's Young People* contained some examples. Both verse and music were often set apart on a full-page spread, surrounded by an illustration or an appropriate motif. Pyle's verses are usually hand lettered and decorated as are those by some less well-known writers. Such items, especially frequent in the holiday issues, are apparently presented as special attractions, representing the extra pleasures that the arts may offer a sober, industrious people.

It is characteristic of the period that writers and editors of *Harper's Young People* thought in terms of "girls' stories" and "boys' stories" when composing the magazine. Throughout its first decade, the magazine emphasized feminine roles and domesticity, although there was always material intended for "boy readers," such as the articles about sports and games (Arthur Brisbane, "The Rugby Game of Football," December 8, 1885); exercises to develop chest and shoulder muscles; and fiction with boy heroes. In the 1890s the focus of *Harper's Young People* changed and items for boys predominated. In volume 16, a series on eastern boarding schools for boys was introduced, along with descriptions of interscholastic sports accompanied by photographs of their teams. Topics in civics were expanded with articles such as Henry Cabot Lodge, "A Day in the Senate" (December 25, 1894). These shifts culminated with a change in title from *Harper's Young People* to *Harper's Round Table*. In the first issue with the new title, the editors explained that they were enlarging the magazine by adding two departments ("Interscholastic Sport," to be conducted by "The Graduate," an "experienced writer and student of scholastic athletics"; and "Bicycling," to be "under the editorship of an expert wheeler") and changing the typeface to add 200 words to each page of the paper. This increase, suggesting greater expense to the publishers, also implies a need to enlarge circulation. At the same time, the editors reiterated traditional concerns of the magazine, noting that the name was changed not only because its "Order of the Round Table," a subscribers' club founded four years before, had grown, but also because the periodical was for the domestic circle "as they sit about the family round table of an evening," and "its purpose is to introduce and maintain in the family of the 19th century some of the manly qualities of chivalry, honesty and uprightness which have made the Table Round of King Arthur so famous in history."[21]

The domestic aspect of *Harper's Round Table* faded swiftly, and a new format evolved emphasizing boys' adventure stories, athletics, and hobbies. Photographs increasingly replaced the hand-drawn engravings of the 1880s, and hand-drawn illustrations acquired sepia tones that mimic photography. The magazine also experimented with two-color illustrations (December 17, 1895); full-page reproductions of European masterworks disappeared as the magazine took on the appearance of a boys' newspaper. Volumes of *Harper's Round Table* continued the numbering of *Harper's Young People*, so it is the first issue of volume 18 (November 3, 1896) that bears a new masthead, with a drawing of seven boys posed to suggest the interests inscribed on an unfurled banner above them: "Athletics, Literature, Science, Travel, Sport."

A few months later *Harper's Round Table* announced its change from weekly to monthly publication. The editorial statement noted that modern tastes differ from those of a decade before, but the magazine would remain a "story paper" for all youth that loves romance, adventure, and honest ideals."[22] Margaret Sangster returned as editor of an advice department, "The Pudding Stick," addressed largely to girls; and Sophie Swett's "down-East" stories appeared frequently in the remaining issues of the magazine, but it became increasingly a boys' publication. As if designed for a "nation of joiners," its emphasis was on group activities. The regular departments became "clubs" (for example, the "Camera Club") devoted to conventionally "boyish" hobbies like stamp collecting, photography, and bicycling. A special page in each issue reported the meetings of various *Round Table* "chapters," listing members and sometimes indicating a "special purpose" such as "international correspondence."

In its last year (1898-1899) *Harper's Round Table* had four regular departments: "Editor's Table" (a contributor's page), "Stamps and Coins," "Problems and Puzzles," and "Camera Club." It serialized Kirk Munroe's "Forward March" and frequently published other fiction based on military life, such as Julian Ralph, "My Borrowed Torpedo Boat" (March 1899). The Christmas story, Percivale Riesdale's "Revolutionary Santa Claus" (December 1898), combined the Christmas theme with an account of army life during the American Revolution. The Wild West was a setting for autobiographical pieces by W. F. ("Buffalo Bill") Cody, "Crossing the Plains" (November 1898) and "Rounding Up Indians" (January 1899). January's "things to do" was devoted to "An American Boy's Workshop." The April issue carried a long, factual article by Franklin Matthews, "The Making of Big Guns," and in August a major article was George Orton's "Year's Work in Interscholastic Athletics" with photographs of captains and outstanding players. Before it closed, the Harper's juvenile publication had essentially abandoned its domestic orientation and its potential "girl readers" to become a monthly magazine for boys betwen ages ten and sixteen.

This radical recasting of the periodical suggests that, in the 1890s, *Harper's Young People* had a diminishing subscription list. As J. Henry Harper noted in his history of the house of Harper, "One reason why we determined to discontinue" the juvenile publication "was the fact that we found it necessary to create a new audience for the little weekly every three or four years, as it took about that time for an average subscriber to outgrow the constituency for which it catered."[23] There was, however, little change in format or content throughout the first twelve years of the magazine, which suggests that for that period the magazine's style and attitudes were acceptable to several new groups of young readers and their parents. It may be more important that a generation of parents who had young children in 1879 (ranging, perhaps, from nursery age to eight years) had disappeared by the 1890s, when all of their children would be too old to read *Harper's Young People*. However, the search for new subscribers only partially accounts for the shifting orientation of Harper's juvenile periodical.

As a part of the Harper's organization, it was subject to the financial and administrative difficulties experienced by the house as a whole. Changes in ownership and the direction of the firm, stemming from the deaths of original partners and the dispersal of family holdings, led to a major reorganization of the company in 1899. At that time publication of the juvenile periodical ceased. It had, J. Henry Harper noted, "run from 1879 to 1899, making twenty volumes, a library in itself of juvenile literature."[24]

Notes

1. Eugene Exman, *The House of Harper* (Evanston and London: Harper and Row, 1967), 139.

2. J. Henry Harper, *The House of Harper* (New York and London: Harper and Row, 1912), 457.

3. *Harper's Bazaar*, November 15, 1879, p. 738.

4. *Harper's Young People*, December 16, 1879, p. 56.

5. Ibid., November 4, 1884, p. 14.

6. Ibid.

7. Ibid.

8. Ibid., October 26, 1880, p. 775.

9. Ibid., April 3, 1883, p. 350.

10. Frank Luther Mott, *A History of American Newspapers* (New York: D. Appleton), 3:178.

11. Carlin T. Kindilien, "Margaret Elizabeth Munson Sangster," *Notable American Women, 1607-1950*, ed. Edward T. James et al. (Cambridge: Belknap Press of Harvard University Press, 1971), 3:234-35. See also Margaret Elizabeth Munson Sangster, *From My Youth Up* (New York: Fleming H. Revell Co., 1909).

12. Sangster, *From My Youth Up*, pp. 59-60.

13. *Harper's Young People*, October 30, 1883, p. 830.

14. Ibid., October 15, 1889, p. 866.

15. Kindilien, "Margaret Elizabeth Munson Sangster," p. 234.

16. *Harper's Young People*, January 6, 1885, p. 158.

17. Charles D. Abbott, *Howard Pyle: A Chronicle* (New York and London: Harper & Brothers, 1925), 44.

18. Ibid., p. 93.

19. Ibid., pp. 102-3.

20. Booth Tarkington, "Introduction to *A World Worth While*, by W. A. Rogers, (New York and London: Harper & Brothers, 1922).

21. *Harper's Round Table*, April 30, 1895, p. 450.

22. Ibid., November 1897, p. 1268.

23. Harper, *The House of Harper*, p. 461.

24. Ibid.

Information Sources

BIBLIOGRAPHY

Charles D. Abbott, *Howard Pyle: A Chronicle* (New York and London: Harper & Brothers, 1925); Eugene Exman, *The House of Harper* (Evanston and London: Harper and Row, 1967); J. Henry Harper, *The House of Harper* (New York and London,

Harper and Row, 1912); Carlin T. Kindilien, "Margaret Elizabeth Munson Sangster," *Notable American Women, 1607-1950*, ed. Edward T. James et al. (Cambridge: Belknap Press of Harvard University Press, 1971); Frank Luther Mott, *A History of American Newspapers* (New York: D. Appleton, 1930), vol. 3; Mary June Roggenbuck, "Twenty Years of *Harper's Young People*," *Horn Book*, 53 (February 1977), 29-35; W. A. Rogers, *A World Worth While* (New York and London: Harper & Brothers, 1922); Margaret Elizabeth Munson Sangster, *From My Youth Up* (New York: Fleming H. Revell Co., 1909).

INDEX SOURCES

Vols. 5-20 are indexed annually.

LOCATION SOURCES

Bound volumes are in many university and major public libraries. Various issues of *Harper's Round Table* (vols. 1-18, no. 939, n.s. 1-2, no. 12, November 1879-October 1897, and n.s., November 1897-October 1899) are available on microfilm from Greenwood Press, Westport, Conn.

Publication History

MAGAZINE TITLE AND TITLE CHANGES

Harper's Young People: An Illustrated Weekly (November 4, 1879-April 23, 1895); *Harper's Round Table* (April 30, 1895-October 1899).

VOLUME AND ISSUE DATA

Harper's Young People: An Illustrated Weekly vol. 1, no. 1-vol. 16, no. 808; *Harper's Round Table* (vol. 16, no. 809-vol. 20, no. 12). The Union List of Serials indexes all volumes under the last title, *Harper's Round Table*.

PUBLISHER AND PLACE OF PUBLICATION

Harper & Brothers, Franklin Square, New York (November 4, 1879-October 1899).

EDITOR

None listed regularly, but the following are known to have edited the periodical: Kirk Munroe, "A Miss Van Duyne," and A. B. Starey.

Jane Benardete

HIGHLIGHTS FOR CHILDREN

Highlights for Children was founded in June 1946 by Garry Cleveland Myers and his wife Caroline Clark Myers. When Myers died in 1971, his wife succeeded him as editor, serving until 1980, when Walter B. Barbe, the Myerses' longtime associate, assumed the editorship. During the thirty-five years of the Myerses' tenure, *Highlights* underwent few significant changes of content or format. Although founded after World War II, *Highlights* owes less to the postwar era than might be assumed merely by noting the date of its founding. In concept, *Highlights* was an extension of *Children's Activities*, which Garry Myers established in December 1934. He remained editor-in-chief until May 1946; the following month the first issue of *Highlights* appeared. *Children's Activities* was carried on by others, but after its demise in the late 1950s, *Highlights* added to its copyright page the phrase "Incorporating Children's Activities." Both *Chil-*

dren's Activities and the later *Highlights* were organized in terms of, and informed by, psychological principles that Garry Myers espoused as a young man and to which he remained devoted throughout his life.

Born in 1884, Garry Myers took a Ph.D. in psychology at Columbia University in 1913. Thereafter he served in the Sanitary Corps as an officer responsible for the education of recruits. During the 1930s he was head of the Division of Parent Education, Cleveland College, Western Reserve University, and the author of more than a dozen works, including *Developing Personality at School* (1931), *Learning to be Likable* (1935), *Marriage and Parenthood* (1934), *The Modern Parent* (1930), *The Modern Family* (1934), and *Training the Toddler in Safety* (1936). He was also associated with the Child Training Association in Chicago, which published *Children's Activities*, and served as editor-in-chief of *Weedon's Modern Encyclopedia*. In these works, Myers sought to reach the widest possible general audience by adopting a plain and simple style: short sentences, short paragraphs, and a minimum of technical psychological terms. His monthly column in *Highlights*, "Friendly Chats with the Editor," drew heavily on these writings from the 1930s and on the theme of works such as *Building Personality in Children* and *The Modern Family*.

Myers's summary of parental goals in the first chapter of the latter work can serve as a useful gloss on his aims in *Highlights*. Parents, he suggested, want (or *should* want) the child to be strong in body, happy, able to express himself or herself freely, and to have his or her questions answered. Myers especially stressed the importance of security and becoming as free as possible from fear, and he wanted the child "to be kept from strong feelings of inferiority, to develop personality, to have enthusiasm, to give vent to his imagination, to build, invent, create, plan and carry through his plans, to have curiosity—to be always inquiring, always investigating, always learning something."[1]

Garry Myers was acutely concerned with personality and with "building personality in children," the title of one of his earliest and most characteristic books. As M. V. O'Shea correctly pointed out in the preface to that work, *personality* was, for Myers, an extraordinarily broad term, covering all of an individual's attitudes toward others, all feelings about the self, all characteristic reactions to situations in which the individual is placed, and everything the individual says and does as well as his or her appearance, posture, and unconscious mannerisms. A more inclusive definition of personality would be difficult to imagine. Given the encompassing nature of personality and given further that practically everything affects the child for good or ill, Myers concluded that everyone in contact with a child should be sensitive to his or her needs. Preeminent among these needs was security. Myers thought it crucial to build social confidence so that the child would not suffer from fears of inferiority or other "social fears." Myers's chapter titles suggest those aspects of behavior and appearance that most concerned him: "Clothes and Personality," "Posture and Personality," "The Eyes and Personality," "The Voice and Personality," "Speech and Personality." Building personality meant, among other things, adopting a posture or a manner of looking others in the eye when talking or listening, which was justified on the grounds that adopting such behaviors made one likable in the eyes of others. Social fears, in Myers's view, were more threatening to personality development than physical fears, and in the pages of *Highlights*, a good deal of attention is paid to the subject of manners, broadly construed.

The first issue of *Highlights* established a format from which Garry and Caroline Myers were to deviate little. "Fun with a purpose" was their motto, and for years the starkly simple cover page bore the title, the motto, and a silhouette of a boy and girl taking turns looking at the stars through a telescope and evidently enjoying themselves. Published as a forty-eight-page monthly, except for July and August, *Highlights* cost $4 for a year's subscription. The Myerses organized the contents of the first issue under two headings: "Stories and Features" and "Things to Do." A third category, "Verse," was soon added, and these three remained the organizational categories throughout the magazine's life. By 1964 *Highlights* had garnered a number of awards: a certificate of Merit (1963) and a Service Award (1964) from the National Association of Gifted Children; Certificates of Recognition (1958, 1960, 1961) and a Brotherhood Award (1962) from the National Conference of Christians and Jews; and an award from the National Safety Council (1960) "for exceptional service to safety." Garry Myers's pride in these awards is evident in the prominence they are given, and he must have taken great satisfaction in the recognition afforded his emphasis on safety, social equality, and the development of creativity and reasoning ability.

Besides giving overall direction to *Highlights* from its founding until his death in 1971, Garry Myers contributed several regular features: "A Friendly Talk," his monthly editorial chat with readers that for years ran on page 2; "Goofus and Gallant," a cartoon feature contrasting bad behavior (Goofus) and good (Gallant); and "The Bears," another cartoon feature in which a family of bears confronted or solved their common difficulties or problems. For both cartoon features, Myers wrote only the copy; a staff artist did the drawings. In this context, it should be noted that *Highlights* was liberally, if simply, illustrated from the start and that a staff artist was designated in the masthead from the first issue. As the magazine prospered, two and frequently three staff artists were employed.

As noted earlier, much of the material that appeared in the editor's monthly chats were rewritten from books such as *Building Personality in Children*. Garry Myers's simple, direct style required relatively little modification for the pages of *Highlights*. The following examples do not exhaust the topical range of Myers's chats, but they encompass the principal features of his style: "We all want to have other persons like us. One good way to make them like us is to learn their names and say these names properly."[2] On the virtues of looking into people's eyes, Myers wrote: "When a dog likes you he looks right into your eyes as you talk to him."[3] On listening, he offered the same counsel: "You want everybody to like you, so you are going to listen carefully as they speak to you or to the group of which you are a part.''[4] Some chats are topical. In October 1947 Myers discussed having the right kind of Halloween fun, for example. In December 1947 his theme was unselfishness at Christmas: "It will be wonderful if you can make yourself prove to your playmates that you are thinking more about them and their happiness than your own.''[5]

"Goofus and Gallant," which Garry Myers transferred to *Highlights* from *Children's Activities*, consists typically of three illustrated pairs of morally contrasted behaviors: "Goofus doesn't make his own bed"/"Gallant makes his bed.''[6] In many instances, Goofus has a slight but discernible deviltry about him, and Gallant appears, if not smug, perceptibly confident of his winning ways. "The Bear Family," also written by Myers, was frequently the last item in the early years of *Highlights*. "The Bears' Thanksgiving" (November 1946) exemplifies Myers's approach. "Poozy (one of the bear children) cracks nuts for Piddy," hitting his finger in the process. He goes to his mother, who praises him for his bravery while she puts the Thanksgiving turkey in the oven. The family goes to church, and on their return "All the bears help get the dinner." End of story.

Although neither the Bear family nor Goofus and Gallant appeared in the first issue of *Highlights*, that issue otherwise represents the mix of features that became the *Highlights* formula. Some types of articles had long been staples of children's periodicals. "The Leak in the Dyke," a retelling of the familiar Dutch tale, was followed by a mildly adventurous story of two American children hiking in the Mexican mountains with their Mexican friend; a brief biography of Thomas Jefferson; an article about the Bible ("The World's Best Seller"); and an article on insect babies. A full-page picture invited readers to find hidden objects in it, and several features encouraged children to do things: learn to arrange flowers, build a model log cabin; play finger games, and make clothespin dolls. "Please help Sammy Spivens" introduced a feature that was to run for years. Readers were asked to write to *Highlights* suggesting ways that Sammy might root up his "weeds," his bad habits, or telling of their own weeds and what they were doing about them. The showpiece of the first issue is an article about the American flag. Written for Flag Day, June 14, the essay gently discards the Betsy Ross story as historical myth and goes on the describe depictions of the earliest American flags that survive in the paintings of Peale and Trumbull and to discuss the history of flags and the variations among the first versions of the Stars and Stripes. At the conclusion of the essay, however, the author, Jane Porter, admonished her young readers not to forget Betsy Ross: "For us, the important thing is to remember and respect the Flag and what it stands for. The Betsy Ross Story may help us to do that.''[7]

Through such articles and features, then, Garry Myers began to make good on the editorial promise stated in the first issue: "This big book coming to you month after month will help you be a happy, useful citizen now and a happy, useful citizen as long as you may live." It will make you smile, laugh, and feel good, Myers went on, but it "will also make you try harder to do right, even when you are tempted to do wrong.... Boys and girls who read *Highlights for Children* will learn and feel that it is a manly or womanly thing to help their mothers, to be mannerly, to be kind to animals and younger children, to be respectful to older persons, to be thoughful, to read the Bible, to pray and go to Sunday school and church."[8]

Throughout the first ten years of its existence, few significant changes were made in *Highlights*. The amount of space given to verse increased, and more illustrations were used; but Garry Myers's concept of what *Highlights* should be and do remained very stable. An issue from 1955 looks remarkably like an issue from the late 1940s, with two exceptions. The magazine was reduced to forty-two pages from the original forty-eight, and its educational mission is emphasized in the listing of a twenty-two member Advisory Board, followed by a guide intended to help parents and teachers in using *Highlights* with children. The Advisory Board was broadly representative. It included religious leaders drawn from the major faiths; for many years, the dean of the Washington Cathedral, for example, served on the board. The majority of those named, however, were drawn from the ranks of psychologists, child-development specialists, and educationists. The inclusion of Gladys M. Rossdeutscher, a pianist on the faculty of the Eastman School, is a reminder of the Myerses' commitment to music. One of the staple features in *Highlights* for years was an article about some noted composer, often accompanied by a short excerpt from one of his best-known works.

Below the Advisory Board, the contents of a given issue are arrayed against a thirteen-item list: reading (three levels of difficulty); conduct; living with others; health and safety; moral or spiritual values; appreciation of music and other arts; nature and science; our country, other lands; stimulation to think and reason; stimulation to create; encouragement of group participation; smiles and laughter. At a glance the reader can see what article or feature promotes which objective(s), the emphasis broadly, from issue to issue, being on reading (especially) and stimulation to think and reason. After several years the last two categories, "encouragement of group participation" and "smiles and laughter," were dropped. The creation of an Advisory Board appears to have had no substantial impact on the direction of *Highlights*, however. Its aims had been clearly established from the outset; and the guide for parents and teachers simply made overt and explicit the emphases on reading and on reasoning that were evident from the beginning. Garry Myers had always included "Ph.D." with his name on the masthead of *Highlights*, and the Advisory Board served, in part, to affirm and legitimize the authority—moral, spiritual, and educational—that, by implication, *Highlights* had laid claim to from the start and that informs the dedication that came into use in the 1950s: "This book of wholesome fun is dedicated to helping children grow in basic skills and knowledge, in creativeness, in ability to think and reason, in sensitivity to others, in high ideals and worthy ways of living—for CHILDREN are the world's most important people."

Garry Myers's concern with reading is evident throughout *Highlights*, but he never appears to have had the literary aspirations that would have made it a showcase for distinguished writers, especially of children's fiction. Stories are typically short, and it must also be said that the magazine was intended primarily for younger children. Nevertheless, Robert Frost's "The Runaway" appeared in *Highlights* for November 1965. The preceeding month Maia Rodman (Wojcie-chowska), author of the Newberry Medal book *Shadow of a Bull* (1964), con-tributed the story "From Up Above"; and from time to time other well-known authors found their way into *Highlights*.

Articles about science and nature were a staple in the early years of *Highlights*, but following the addition of a science editor in the late 1950s, more attention was paid to science, both in terms of explaining basic principles of matter and energy, for example, and in keeping readers abreast of important applications of science: "Let's Talk About Computers" (June-July 1965) by a systems en-gineer at General Electric; and "The Laser" (October 1970) by Alan B. Graf-inger, also of General Electric. Jack Myers, a professor of botany and zoology at the University of Texas and the son of the founder of *Highlights*, was science editor throughout the 1960s, during which time his series "Things You've Won-dered About," written in the familiar, chatty style of the magazine generally, explored a wide variety of devices, principles, and phenomena: the pendulum (December 1960), atoms and elements (June-July 1965), and simple electro-chemical experiments (June-July 1979), for example. Typically, the Myerses sought experts whenever possible, duly noting an author's credentials: an article about mosquitoes (May 1960) by a professor of zoology; "The Moon" (January 1955) by David Dietz, a science editor who had won a Pulitzer Prize for his science writing; and an article about otters (October 1965) by a former staff member of the Chicago Natural History Museum.

Meanwhile, Sammy Spivens, Goofus and Gallant, the Bear Family, and the editor's friendly chats remained virtually unchanged. Said Garry Myers on the subject of growing up in his January 1970 chat: "If you are over nine or ten, boy or girl, you can prove you are growing up by sewing missing buttons on for yourself and by washing some of your own clothes. Another way to feel you are getting big is to change your garments, especially your socks and underwear, as often as you know you should. Nice fresh-looking and fresh-smelling clothes make you feel good and think well of yourself. They also make your friends and playmates like you better."[9] Forty years before, in the pages of the books of advice and social analysis that poured from his pen in the 1930s, Myers had said the same things in essentially the same accents. Judging from *Highlights*' success throughout the 1960s and 1970s, these sentiments were still helpful, at least to parents, while their offspring presumably puzzled over the full-page drawings containing hidden figures and objects or worked out on the various mind-teasing puzzles and problems to which several pages of every issue were devoted.

Notes

1. *The Modern Family* (New York: Greenberg, 1934), 3-4.
2. *Highlights for Children* 2 (March 1947), 2.
3. Ibid., 2 (April 1947), 2.
4. Ibid., 2 (May 1947), 2.
5. Ibid.
6. Ibid., 5 (June 1950), 28.
7. Ibid., 1 (June 1946), 5.
8. Ibid., p. 2.
9. Ibid., p. 5.

Information Sources

BIBLIOGRAPHY
None.
INDEX SOURCES
None.
LOCATION SOURCES
Library of Congress.

Publication History

MAGAZINE TITLE AND TITLE CHANGES
Highlights for Children (June 1946-).
VOLUME AND ISSUE DATA
Highlights for Children (vol. 1, no. 1-).
PUBLISHER AND PLACE OF PUBLICATION
Highlights for Children, Inc., Columbus, Ohio.
EDITOR
Garry Cleveland Myers (1946-1971); Caroline Clark Myers (1971-1980); Walter B. Barbe
    (1980-).

R. Gordon Kelly

HOLIDAY MAGAZINE FOR CHILDREN

See *Children's Magazine*.

HUMPTY DUMPTY'S MAGAZINE

Some months before the first issue of *Humpty Dumpty's Magazine* was to come out in 1952, Alvin Tresselt, who was already well known as an author of children's books, became its managing editor. Inasmuch as Humpty Dumpty himself was listed on the masthead as editor-in-chief, one of Tresselt's first writing tasks was to explain the presence of a healthy Humpty on the staff of the magazine. (Even the youngest subscribers would know that Humpty Dumpty had been hopelessly injured in a fall.) Alvin Tresselt turned to modern medicine and ingenuity, devised an American doctor, and came up with a poetic explanation that appeared on the first page of every issue throughout *Humpty Dumpty's* history until the last 1980 issue.

> Humpty Dumpty
>   sat on a wall,
> Humpty Dumpty
>   had a great fall;
> All the King's horses and
>   all the King's men
> Couldn't put Humpty
>   together again.
> But a clever young doctor
>   with patience and glue
> Put Humpty together
>   —better than new;
> And now he is healthy
>   and back on the scene
> Busily editing
>   this magazine!

The idea for a magazine especially for preschoolers originated with George Hecht, publisher and president of Parents' Magazine Enterprises, and was named, almost by accident, after dozens of suggestions had been rejected, by Mrs. Hecht during a casual conversation over dinner. The magazine's purpose was to give parents (and, to a certain degree, teachers) interesting material for prereading and beginning-reading children. The magazine's editorial policy was consistent with this broad purpose throughout the editorships of Harold Schwartz, its first editor; Alvin Tresselt, who served as editor from 1963 to 1969 after being managing editor for the magazine from its inception; and Ruth Craig, who followed the pattern established earlier of serving as managing editor before moving into the editor's position.

Humpty Dumpty's began with a first-year circulation of 250,000, thanks to the built-in links with *Parent's Magazine* and the work of its distributors and sales force. Circulation grew steadily and reached 1.25 million within two years. The 1.25 million figure seems to be the magazine's plateau, although circulation did go higher occasionally and dip to 900,000 from time to time also. It stayed around the 1.00 million mark during most of the 1970s.

Former editor Tresselt credits several writers with being at least partly responsible for the magazine's early success. Martin Gardner, for example, had the knack of being able to devise activities for young children. From 1955 through 1963 Gardner created about half of the pages of each issue, many of which were designed for the children to color, paste, fold, or cut. Gardner also originated the "Humpty Dumpty, Jr." stories that appeared each month throughout most of the 1950s and were written by Jay Williams in the early 1960s. Another strong influence has been Lillian Moore, a reading consultant for the Board of Education in New York City, who contributed a story each month for an extended period and provided the editorial staff with expert knowledge about reading acquisition.

Each issue of *Humpty Dumpty's* typically has a beginner-reader story (two of them during Alvin Tresselt's editorship), two or three read-aloud stories (intended to be read aloud to the child by a parent or by an older brother or sister), some poetry, and some learning-and-doing activities to teach manual skills and visual differentiation of sizes and shapes. The reading-readiness emphasis is apparent in many of the ''What's Wrong with This?'' pictures and hidden-faces illustrations that teach young children to see likenesses and differences. Tell-me stories (typically one an issue) are stories for parents to read themselves and then tell to the children in their own words. The tell-me stories frequently are folktales and legends.

The ''beginner reader'' stories, which are picture stories for very young readers, did not appear after the winter 1980 issues. A typical one is ''A Halloween Surprise'' (October 1978), consisting of seven full-page picture panels, with six or seven word texts at the bottom of each picture.

Another feature, ''Humpty's Science Fun,'' teaches science concepts. One of them, ''Keeping Warm,'' explains and illustrates the concept of insulation in three pages, the first of which has only three sentences of text: ''To keep warm in winter, cats and dogs grow heavy coats of fur. The animals stay warm because their thick fur keeps their body heat from escaping. The fur acts as *insulation*.''[1] The following page of ''Keeping Warm'' gives another example and illustration of insulation, that of a winter coat helping to keep a boy's body heat from escaping. The third and final page shows how a heavy glove acts as insulation to prevent body heat from melting an ice cube in your hand and to keep your hands warm. Text and illustrations thus provide enough instances of the insulation concept to enable a child to generalize the idea to other kinds of insulation.

Similarly, a feature in a later issue discusses the different ways that people and animals deal with cold winter weather. In five illustrated pages, several concepts are introduced: migration (of geese and robins), hibernation (of raccoons and skunks), and the growing of extra fur to keep warm. A final kind of winter protection is mentioned: the changing from brown to snowy white of the weasel and the snowshoe rabbit (January 1981). The post-1980 editorial policy evidently is encouraging (or demanding) more parental involvement with such features that deal with more than a single concept. This pedagogically sound approach—providing good, clear assistance to help the young child attain a concept—is typical of *Humpty Dumpty's* thrust. The same characteristic, however, frequently mitigates against the literary quality of selections. Stories do not always seem as interesting, vital, or high in quality as they ought to be.

Despite the sometimes undistinguished stories, *Humpty Dumpty's* has been characterized by informative material presented clearly and accurately to young readers. Two representative issues, selected randomly from bound library volumes, have the following types of material. The January 1971 issue has one story for beginning readers, three read-aloud stories, one tell-me story, and one story in words and pictures (large panels). The second (February 1971) issue contains one nature story, five games and puzzles, six cutouts, one song, and one each of coloring-fun, mix and fix, and science-fun activities. Also, a one-page feature by Anne Walentas, former editor of *Humpty Dumpty's*, discusses special material contained in the issues in "A Guide for Teachers and Parents," intended to help those who work with children get the most out of the magazine.

Animals frequently are featured in the stories, in every situation from the life of the family dog to the life of the lion. Many of the animal stories are fantasies, but a few elves, fairies, and talking insects appear. All editors of *Humpty Dumpty's* have scrupulously avoided stories and characters that are too "cutesy."

Legends and folktales, on the other hand, appear fairly frequently, especially in the tell-me story category. The folktales are not necessarily old but are stories told in a folktale vein. Some of the writers capture the feeling of old folktales by using slightly archaic phrasing, which also gives the tales a slightly formal tone. Wilbur Wheaton, for example, wrote "Cassim's Black Bag" (September 1962) in that way. The story is about a magic bag that sprouts watermelons and eventually creates a watermelon surplus in the town. Its opening paragraphs read: "On the Street of Merchants in old Bagdad there once lived two brothers who sold watermelons for a living./Now from morning till night Cassim, the older of the two, tried hard to become rich. He never sold a watermelon unless he was paid twice as much as it was worth. And, of course, he never gave one away. But all of his efforts were to no avail. Cassim became poorer with each day."[2]

Stories may have a moral (even animal stories may have a moral and frequently make the point in a lighter vein than do the stories with human characters). Occasional stories make psychological points also, for instance, "Who Am I?" In this story (January 1962) Tim's mother returns from the hospital with a new baby, and Tim has difficulty figuring out whether he is still a baby himself, a big boy, or someone in between.

Humpty Dumpty's children generally are well behaved and shown at their best, sometimes even performing nearly heroic deeds. In "Andy and the Runaway Horse" (November 1962), for example, Andy runs to the corner and pushes the traffic-light button in time to stop cross traffic before a runaway horse can reach the intersection. Jonathan, in a beginning-reader story (March 1962), seems to be the only person in the vicinity who has the presence of mind to turn in a fire at the alarm box. These two stories bring out the point that Andy and Jonathan were able to perform these feats because they were avid question askers. Jonathan, in fact, is called "Jonathan Why," which ought to encourage young children's inquiring tendencies.

Poetry always has been an important feature. A poem may have no more than four lines encapsulating a small aspect of the child's world, a bit of humor, or an evoking of the mood of a day or a season. An example of a word picture giving a new insight into a child's world is the poem "Storm," written by Adrien Stoutenberg in free verse (February 1963). "In a storm/ the wind talks/ with its mouth wide open./ It yells around corners/with its eyes shut./ It bumps into itself/and falls over a roof/ and whispers/oh. . .oh. . .oh. . ."[3]

Because of *Humpty Dumpty's* emphasis on fresh, clear, direct, and uncluttered language, some of the stories have a poetic feeling, especially in the rhythm of the prose and the economy of language, for example, these opening lines from "Someday Never Comes" (March 1963):

> "When may I ride on a train?" asked Gregory one morning.
> He'd been asking that for a month now.
> "Maybe someday," said his mother who was scrubbing out the goldfish bowl.
> "And when may I raise chickens?" Gregory asked.
> He'd been asking that for a week.
> "Maybe someday," mother murmured.
> Gregory helped put the pebbles back.
> "Well then, when do I ever get to ride on an elephant?"
> He'd thought that up just now.
> "Oh, heavens!" Mother laughed. "I don't know—maybe someday."
> "That's what you always say," cried Gregory. "But someday never comes!"[4]

Beginning with the December 1980 issue, *Humpty Dumpty's* became one of six children's health periodicals published by the Benjamin Franklin Literary and Medical Society. Organized in 1976, this organization aims to disseminate medical and nutritional information to the health professions and to the general public and to promote and advocate good nutrition, health, and safety practices. It accomplishes this goal in a variety of ways, one being its publications: *Turtle Magazine* (for preschool children ages two to six), *Humpty Dumpty's Magazine* (for beginning readers ages four to seven), *Children's Playmate** (ages five to eight), *Jack and Jill** (ages seven to ten), *Child Life** (ages eight to eleven), and *Children's Digest** (ages nine to twelve). *Turtle Magazine* features bedtime or naptime stories to be read to the small child, whereas *Humpty Dumpty's* and *Children's Playmate* emphasize easy-to-read stories for the beginning readers. The post-1980 *Humpty Dumpty's* also is characterized by content and vocabulary on a slightly higher reading level. Still another change has been the shift from digest size to a slightly larger 6 ½- by 9 ½-inch format.

Humpty Dumpty's post-1980 content has clearly been consistent with the goals of the sponsoring organization. Its articles, activities, and stories have almost all focused on health, safety, or nutrition. This includes good hygiene, proper care of the body, good nutrition, and an awareness of those things that are bad for a growing child or an adult—including the dangers of using alcohol, tobacco, and drugs. Even the poems deal with these topics. Jimi Samuels "Roller Rules" (March 1981), for example, gives six verses of good advice on skating safety: dress to cover elbows and knees, watch for cracks and stones, and remember to put the skates away afterward.

Articles, features, and activities have successfully avoided taking on a preachy or moralizing tone. Nevertheless, the message sometimes is heavy handed, as in "A Different Tale of Cinderella" (March 1981), which is the tale of Cinderella as told by food and nutrition experts. In this version, an apparently contemporary Cinderella dusts, sweeps, and cooks for her wicked stepmother and stepsisters. They have her make strudel, fried cakes, and rich pastries for them every day— but Cinderella is allowed to eat only berries from the forest, fresh vegetables from the garden, and milk she milks from the cow. The wicked stepsisters get fat and develop tooth decay, poor skin, and low energy levels. When the Prince comes around to the house looking for the beautiful girl he danced with, he recognizes Cinderella by her slender figure and clear skin. So the Prince and Cinderella wed. But although she finds herself in the lap of luxury, she always eats simple healthful foods, takes long walks, and, naturally, lives happily ever after.

This version of Cinderella makes the point about nutrition very well. But many children feel some resentment and discomfort when the very familiar fairy stories and folktales are changed in any way—a point for any editorial staff to consider when deciding to rewrite familiar works.

In the rest of the post-1980 issues virtually everything carries out the health theme. In one of them (March 1981) the "Connect the Dots" activity reveals who will share the fresh, crunchy vegetables with a leprechaun. The recipe for Shamrock Salad emphasizes fresh fruits and vegetables. A two-page article, "Kite-Flying Safety," is followed by a two-page coloring activity. "Whistling Winds" discusses various kinds of winds and storms, making several points about swimming and boat safety. "Roller Rules" deals with roller-skating safety in verse. "How to Brush Your Teeth" is reprinted from an American Medical Association source. A final piece deals with exercise to build healthy muscles.

In short, although *Humpty Dumpty's* has undergone a significant change in content since becoming a project of the Benjamin Franklin Literary and Medical Society, it still serves well its original purpose of providing interesting reading material for young children just beginning to read. Stories and other materials present their themes in a positive manner, although they do make young children aware of those things (drugs, alcohol, tobacco, and poor nutrition) that are bad for growing children and adults. Materials in the post-1981 *Humpty Dumpty's* have a slightly higher reading level than do those in earlier issues—which may turn out to have long-term benefits for the magazine, permitting the publication of higher quality, more interesting material.

I do not wish to imply, however, that the effects of the change of publisher on the post-1980 *Humpty Dumpty's* have been entirely salutary. Children need and deserve to have sources of unrestricted reading material. The new *Humpty*

Dumpty's, although colorful, clear, factually correct, devoted to an unquestionably "good" cause, and frequently interesting, is now severely limited in subject matter. How much of an overall constraint this will constitute remains to be seen.

Notes

1. *Humpty Dumpty's Magazine* 26 (October 1978), 65.
2. Ibid., 11 (September 1962), 117.
3. Ibid., 12 (February 1963).
4. Ibid., 12 (March 1963).

Information Sources

BIBLIOGRAPHY

Publications Portraits of Highlights for Children, Child Life, Jack and Jill, and Humpty Dumpty's (New York: The Writers Institute and Hawthorn Books, 1963).

INDEX SOURCES

The Children's Catalog, Subject Index to Children's Magazines.

LOCATION SOURCES

Bound volumes, especially 1970-, are in many university and large public libraries. Microform copies also are available from University Microfilms International, Ann Arbor, Mich.

Publication History

MAGAZINE TITLE AND TITLE CHANGES

Humpty Dumpty's Magazine for Little Children (1952-1980), *Humpty Dumpty's Magazine* (1981-).

VOLUME AND ISSUE DATA

The January 1981 issue began vol. 29 with issue no. 283; issues have been numbered consecutively throughout the publication history. A nine-issues-a-year (instead of ten) schedule began in 1981.

PUBLISHER AND PLACE OF PUBLICATION

Parents' Magazine Enterprises, New York (1952-1980); Children's Health Publications, Benjamin Franklin Literary & Medical Society, Inc., Indianapolis, (1981-).

EDITOR

Harold Schwartz (1952-1963), Alvin Tresselt (1963-1969), Anne Walentas (1969-1971), Thomas S. Roberts (1971-1972), Ruth Craig (1973-1980), Michaela Muntean (1980), Christine M. French (1981-). Some issues in the 1952-1973 period appeared without an editor's name; Alvin Tresselt, Rubie Saunders, and Ruth Craig (as managing editor or editorial director) filled the editor's role during those times.

Alice Denham

I

INFANT'S MAGAZINE

Infant's Magazine was published monthly by the American Sunday School Union from 1829 to 1842 and was designed "to supply children under six or seven years of age with a monthly reward book suited to their age and capacity and to assist parents and teachers on the work of education by exciting a taste for reading."[1] Consisting of sixteen pages illustrated with numerous, small woodcuts, the publication sold for ½¢ a copy or 18¢ a year.

Unsigned biblical and didactic material fill the magazine's pages. "An Address to Infant Scholars" (January 1829) exhorted children to learn to be good, useful, and happy, so that friends and parents would love them dearly. Happiness was promised to those who behaved well and were religious.

An early feature, "A Dialogue Between Edward and His Father" (January 1829), blended natural science and religion. The first dialog was devoted to snow—how it looked, how it covered, how it compared in weight to feathers, and how life went on in lands covered by snow the entire year, such as Lapland. When Edward wonders why the animals and people did not freeze to death in the perpetual cold and snow, his father assures him that by the goodness of God, bodies were made to suit the lands in which they lived. Similarly, "The Stars" and "Goldfish" (February 1829) bring biblical examples to bear on the teaching of natural science.

Infant's Magazine also instructed its readers on safety. "Sliding on the Ice" (January 1829) cautioned children not to slide on the ice lest they break an arm or a leg or, worse, fall through the ice and drown. This lesson in prudence combined information about ice skating in Holland with religious instruction. All weather changes come from God: "He has promised the earth remainth-seed time and harvest, and cold and heat, and summer and winter, and day and night not cease'' (Genesis 8:22).

Throughout its years of publication, *Infant's Magazine* encouraged children to read the Bible and honor the word of God. ''The Bible'' (January 1829) provided a brief story demonstrating that prayer enabled one to understand and be able to lead a good life. ''Infant School Conversations'' (February 1829), for example, used a question-and-answer format to dramatize the efficacy of prayer. Children discussed what Mary and Martha might have done when their brother Lazarus was ill, concluding that only frequent prayer offered a cure for sickness and prevented wickedness.

Wise use of time was a frequent theme. In ''Little Jane'' (February 1829) a child fidgets and wants to see pictures while her grandmother is reading from the Bible. The homily stresses the importance of listening to the Bible and learning from it the path to salvation.

Another important theme is the acceptance of others' infirmities and imperfections. ''Little Catherine'' (February 1829), for example, hoped never to be like a lame woman that she had seen, forgetting that her own grandmother had been lame. Her mother reminds her that God never discloses what will befall anyone and that only through repentence and a holy heart could one live in God's presence.

Obedience to parents was everywhere expected and demanded. ''Thomas and Ellen'' (January 1829) describes two children who observe a moth buzzing itself to death against a candle. The anonymous author of the sketch proceeds to draw a parallel between the moth and children who fail to heed their parents and as a consequence are injured, sometimes fatally. Similarly, ''Lucy and Willy'' (November 1842) find themselves in grave difficulty, because they walk where they have been forbidden to go and become hopelessly mired in the mud.

Important biblical figures such as ''Adam'' (January 1829), ''Cain, the First Murderer'' (February 1829), and ''Moses'' (November 1842) were introduced in each issue with appropriate scriptural quotations. However brief, the stories appear to be calculated to capture the children's interest of the period. To reinforce learning and actively involve the children, each story was accompanied by fourteen questions such as ''Who was Adam?'' and ''How was his body made?''

Didactic and religious poems were an important part of each issue. ''The Cow—A Song for Infant Schools'' (January 1829) rhythmically tells how God, through the lowly cow, provides milk and cheese, skins for boots and shoes, horns for combs, and hair for mortar.

Infant's Magazine is a significant document of the nineteenth-century Sunday School Union Movement. For that period it was well illustrated and thoroughly written and provided those American children who read it with everyday instruction, counsel, knowledge of the Bible, and directions for successful living in a form that encouraged participation and reflection on the part of its readers.

Note

1. Mabel F. Altstetter, "Early Magazines for Children," *Peabody Journal of Education* 19 (November 1941), 131-36.

Information Sources

BIBLIOGRAPHY
None.
INDEX SOURCES
None.
LOCATION SOURCES
Bound volumes at the American Antiquarian Society, Worcester, Mass. Microfilm and
    Zerox copies are available for a fee.

Publication History

MAGAZINE TITLE AND TITLE CHANGES
Infant's Magazine (1829-1842).
VOLUME AND ISSUE DATA
Infant's Magazine (vol. 1, no. 1-vol. 14, no. 11).
PUBLISHER AND PLACE OF PUBLICATION
American Sunday School Union, Philadelphia (1829-1842).
EDITOR
Paul Beck (1829-1842).

Marguerite Davern

INGENUE

Ingenue, a girls' magazine published by Dell from 1959 to 1973, was designed
to compete with *Seventeen* by offering somewhat more sophisticated or cosmopolitan fare. In practice, this consisted initially of an emphasis on fashion,
with a trip to Paris offered as a prize in a survey lottery; direct preparation for
adult female roles (wife and homemaker, not parent); and a wide umbrella of
features about the popular arts. The first issue included "Facts about Teen
Marriages," which discouraged them; the last issues spoke with acceptance of
masturbation and premarital sex and, in the youth counselor's column, presented
ways to deal with problems such as incest and alcoholism. The counselor,
Margaret Ross, had written for the magazine from its inception and had changed
from being an adamant naysayer on the topic of sex among teenagers to an
adviser on "When to Give It the Green Light" (December 1971). The answer
included much caution but did not say no and was a follow-up to a candid
November column informing readers that women do not ask for rape and should
always report it.

Matters related to sexuality reflect most directly the way *Ingenue* changed
during the 1960s, but in other areas the magazine also mirrors the decade. By
April 1961, for example, the "ingenues" were being urged to develop inter-

national interests, to join civic organizations, and generally to cultivate a political conscience. Although Jackie Kennedy was held up as a role model, readers were also given stories about the Peace Corps, features about Washington, and even "Yes, a Girl Can Be President" (January 1964). The emphasis on political and social change generated articles such as "Red China's Teens" (March 1965), "I Marched in Montgomery" (June 1965), and "Germaine Greer on Women's Liberation" (February 1972). They may stand out simply because they are so different from the welter of articles that regularly appeared on diet, fashion, popularity, acne, understanding boys, and school (the latter comparatively rare). Another and subtler form of change occurred in the magazine's approach to the female adult role. It moved, with the era, from a decorative and idealized concept exemplified by an early feature, "Maison Ingenue," which presented ideas for home furnishings (such as a display of various hope chests), to a certain practicality about the woman's inevitable job outside the home. It printed statistics about women's work lives: readers could expect to work twenty-five years if they married (June 1962).

All of these responses to the climate of the 1960s, however, did not deflect from the magazine's most basic message: girls should prepare for marriage—marriage sooner rather than later, to judge by the fashion, food, and health sections that defined girls' lives primarily in terms of their relationships to boys. Essentially, *Ingenue* had the structure of a traditional woman's magazine throughout its life and the tenure of all of its editors. Perhaps, true to its name, it turned a disarmingly receptive face toward political and social ferment and in its detached innocence was unafraid to include "radical" writers along with its potpourri of ultrafeminine features. For example, in the December 1962, issue the readers were told, "Demonstrate Your Female Rights" (to be admired, pampered, protected, helpless, and courted). Alice Thompson, the first editor (1959-1961), placed more emphasis on fashions and cooking than did Sylvie Schuman and her successors, but the magazine departed very little from its original concept. Thompson had held up France as an ideal in the title and in many features, because there "the woman who creates and runs a home is considered a fine artist."[1]

Sylvie Schuman, editor from 1961-1968, presided over the magazine's response to the 1960s and emergent issues such as feminism and black activism. (Fewer antiwar features appeared, although the student underground was represented once or twice). Schuman had been executive editor under Alice Thompson, and she also wrote occasional articles and fiction. As editor, one of her first acts was to simplify departmental headings from the old pattern of "A Happier You" (the counselor column), "A Prettier You," and so on to forthright labels such as "Problems" and "Beauty." She also initiated a column describing a specific college each month and altered the initial "V.I.P. Juniors" column relating the accomplishments of several teenagers (often boys) to a "Teens Who Did Something" feature highlighting the achievements of one girl each month. In 1968 Schuman left *Ingenue*. For a few months Helen Meyer (the publisher) was listed as editor and then was succeeded by Joan Wynn, who stayed until Dell was sold to Doubleday, and *Ingenue* was one of a number of casualties of the merger.

In its regular departments, *Ingenue* of the 1960s included categories such as "Fiction," "Fashions," and "Fun," in addition to "Problems" and "Beauty." Many other headings were rephrased with a light tone: "It's Your Turn" was the letters column; "Star Stuff" featured movie stars or rock groups; "Your Lively Arts" covered movies, dance, and records, as well as a short-lived column in which famous people recommended their favorite books. In August 1960, for example, Mary Martin listed her favorites: *A Lost Lady*, *Precious Bane*, *Dance to the Piper* (Agnes DeMille's autobiography), *War and Peace*, and *A Passage to India*. In general, fiction did not seem to be an important part of *Ingenue*; only one attempt was made, with the printing of a Katherine Mansfield story, to use classic literature. A column on classical music, however, was used for most of the magazine's life.

The magazine responded quickly to its readership, especially in the use of language for headings and captions. The column called "Volunteens" in the first issues was quickly changed to "*Ingenue* Cares." Surveys and question-naires, as well as letters from readers, served as editorial aids. Early on, for example, the magazine printed a survey for readers to pass on to boys they knew. When the boys indicated they neither preferred girls who dressed in pink nor avoided those who exhibited brains, *Ingenue* adjusted its advice to readers, true to its implicit promise to enhance good relationships or success with boys. A column by Justin Mason, "Boy Talk," was added, and several articles dis-cussed boys' feelings about the draft.

Graphically, the magazine was revamped more than once to offer a clearer, more compelling format. Photographs, line drawings, and romantic illustrations were employed liberally. The "Fashion" and "Beauty" sections, especially, were colorful and extensive, featuring seasonal displays—for example, girls standing on boys' shoulders at the beach. A party and recipe section picked up on the seasonal theme, as did the "makeover" feature showing a girl's trans-formation by way of hair, makeup, and clothing. Cover photos, usually of a young girl, were accompanied by teasing captions advertising stories. "Are You Taking Drugs?" (June 1969) was the cover caption for a mild story entitled "Take a Look at the Drugs in your Medicine Chest." Much like the cover of an adult female counterpart in the magazine world, *Cosmopolitan*, *Ingenue*'s cover usually presented a more racy image than the contents offered.

Except for the guidance column by Margaret Ross, *Ingenue* seldom featured articles about parents' views or problems, nor did it deal with—until the last year or two—the fact that the early marriages and/or sexual relationships with boys implicitly advocated by the magazine's general tone would more than likely include, for many readers, early parenthood. Sibling rivalry and similar family problems were seldom mentioned. History (except for current events), religion, science, and philosophy were also outside the scope of the magazine; only the arts, of all subjects the girls might be studying, constituted material for leisure reading. Poetry, plays, and even humor were conspicuously absent. A few times, an issue containing the readers' fiction and essays appeared, but this was not a regular practice.

After an undistinguished start in fiction, the later *Ingenue* did print stories by writers who have since distinguished themselves in the adolescent market. Nat Hentoff, M. B. Goffstein, and Honor Arundel contributed at least one story each. Most stories concerned adolescent love and the obstacles to it—usually the girl protagonist's need for more self-confidence or some other personal change. A frequent contributor was Hila Coleman, whose story "No Simple Matter" (November 1962) showed a girl being helped by her boy friend to avoid the financial mistakes of her parents. The fiction mirrors the age about as well as the other features do; a July 1971 novella by Honor Arundel, "The Longest Week-end," dealt with the problems and growth of an unmarried mother as she raised her baby in her parents' home. With what might be the classic *Ingenue* (or indeed, nineteenth-century) touch, her experience prepares her for marriage— with the baby's father.

A bit spicier, perhaps, than some of its rivals for teenage readers, and certainly amply supplied with fashion and beauty hints and full of advice for those who were lovelorn or lovefilled, *Ingenue* is at once a mirror of an age and for the most part an unsurprising result of long-held assumptions about its audience. In some ways, the inclusion of articles about 1960s issues is surprising, given its overall character. *Ingenue* did encourage the young girl to think of herself as an American in a larger world, as a member of a community beyond the family. The teenage Twiggy was expected to travel out into the world.

Note

1. *Ingenue*, August 1960, p. 39.

Information Sources

BIBLIOGRAPHY
None.
INDEX SOURCES
None.
LOCATION SOURCES
A few libraries have kept their holdings, but most keep current issues only of popular magazines. Minneapolis Public Library has issues from 1967 to 1972; no library seems to have a complete set. Doubleday, Garden City, N.Y., keeps an archive of the magazine. Jaine Fabian, Dell librarian in New York City, arranged to have the archive available for this study.

Publication History

MAGAZINE TITLE AND TITLE CHANGES
Ingenue for Teen-age Girls (1959-1961); *Dell Teenagers Ingenue* (1961-1973); *New Ingenue* (1973-).

VOLUME AND ISSUE DATA

Ingenue for Teen-age Girls, Dell Teenagers Ingenue, (monthly, beginning in July-August 1959; no volume numbers used).

PUBLISHER AND PLACE OF PUBLICATION

Dell, N.Y. (1959-1972), *New Ingenue*, Twenty First Century Communications Inc., (1973-   ).

EDITOR

Alice Thompson (1959-1961); Sylvie Schuman (1961-1968); Helen Meyer (1968); Joan Wynn (1968-1973); Joanna Brown (1974-   ).

Nancy Lyman Huse

J

JACK AND JILL

Jack and Jill, the last magazine founded by the Curtis Publishing Company, was always its smallest. Clearly, though, Curtis began and sustained its baby using the same editorial philosophy implicit in the history of its two giants, *Ladies Home Journal* and *The Saturday Evening Post*. Founded to reflect and represent women's interests, *Ladies Home Journal* became known as "the Bible of the American Home." *The Saturday Evening Post*, called "An American Institution," had even greater mass appeal. Begun for American businessmen, it was "for many years an accurate reflection of American life."[1] When in 1938 the Curtis Circulation Office considered the possibility of a children's magazine, Ada Campbell Rose was hired, first to research the market and then to edit a magazine not for parents or other adults but "expressly for children readers."[2] Circulation of the new magazine very soon reached over half a million, and profits averaged $200,000 to $250,000 annually. Like its elders, *Jack and Jill* was by 1940 the representative and most successful magazine in its field.

In the 1960s, however, this situation began to change. In 1960 *McCall's* surpassed *Ladies Home Journal* in circulation. In 1961, for the first time in its history, *The Saturday Evening Post* lost money. Of all of the Curtis magazines, it had always been the most stable in its format and editorial policy—and always the most representative of America. Now it was the least responsive to profound differences in the fabric of American life.[3] The flamboyant and very public struggle to change *The Post* ended with its death in 1969, preceded shortly by the sale of *Ladies Home Journal* in 1968. *Jack and Jill*, if less drastically than these other magazines, also exhibited signs of the Curtis Publishing Company's collapse. Between 1959 and 1972 there were six editors, whereas only one preceded and one followed this period. Also during these years the magazine's circulation twice dropped significantly from its usual 1 million, and it increasingly published more nonfiction and fewer well-known authors than it had under its first editor. Despite these changes, however, *Jack and Jill* prospered until the 1970s. After the demise of Curtis in 1969, the magazine had four publishers; steadily shrank in size, quality, and circulation; and became an essentially new magazine in 1980. Even this decade of struggle with rising inflation did not, however, radically alter the magazine or erase the decisive influence of its first editor whereas its sale to its latest publisher emphatically did.

Like Edward Bok of *Ladies Home Journal* and George Horace Lorimer of *The Saturday Evening Post*, Ada Campbell Rose was a great editor. Daughter-in-law of the editor of *Country Gentleman*, another of Curtis's magazines, she brought substantial experience—as a reporter for the Pueblo, Colorado, *Chieftain* (1919-1923); as a textbook editor for Scott, Foresman and Company (1923-1926); as a freelance writer of women's magazine articles (1926-1938); and as a mother of two—to her position as editor of *Jack and Jill*. The magazine she developed displayed the usual genius of a Curtis editor. Knowing her audience (both child and mother), she shaped the magazine to reflect them. That her magazine was child centered was evident in its emphasis on "doing," each issue offering from five to ten activities of the puzzle, riddle, game, drawing, cooking, and "things-to-make" variety. Also regular features were letters from readers ("North, South, East, West"), writing and drawings by readers ("At My Desk"), an editorial modified for children ("Finnie, the Office Goldfish"), and some cartoons ("Boo Boo, the Woods Boy" and "Mollie's Dream"). The print throughout was large and the vocabulary controlled. Besides these direct appeals to children's involvement, abilities, and interests, each issue usually included eight to ten pieces of literature and two or three of nonfiction—each less than six pages, including several illustrations. In the brevity of each item and the variety of each issue, the magazine revealed Rose's understanding of what children ages seven to twelve find appealing. Then, too, the magazine was bright and attractive, liberally illustrated in many colors on good quality paper of 6 3/4 by 10 inches. Many fine illustrators provided work, including Margot Austin, Ed Emberly, Ursula Koering, Beth Henninger Krush, Leo Politi, and Janet Smalley.[4] If "expressly for child readers," *Jack and Jill* also appealed to its older readers, especially on its "Mothers' Page."

On the "Mothers' Page," furthermore, Rose spoke directly to adults. Here she wrote of the nature of children, of the needs she hoped to meet with *Jack and Jill*, of the authors included in that issue, and, in general, of her philosophy as an editor of a children's magazine. In this forum, for example, she explained her efforts "to make the magazine in a way that will suggest as much creative activity as possible, identifying children as "active by nature," praising "home-made" activities as attractive to children, and recommending such activities, therefore, as the source of happiness for children.[5] She also frequently discussed her selection process here. In one issue she pointed out that children are affected by current events and thus need topical features (June 1951). In another, she asserted that "there is a place for authors with varying degrees of experience in a good magazine for children."[6] In yet another issue, she said "there is no satisfaction greater than that which comes with the privilege of providing children with something superlative."[7] Eschewing elitism and recommending pragmatism throughout these pages, Rose nevertheless crusaded for children's right to excellence. Her ideal was Mary Mapes Dodge's *St. Nicholas.**[8] She contended "that a children's magazine is worthy of a good author's best work" (November 1950),[9] lamented "that [children's] books do not come in better quality instead of so much quantity,"[10] and insisted "that it is important for everything in such a magazine [one for children] to be as carefully screened, as accurately checked, and as thoughtfully illustrated as if the materials were being prepared for the most discerning audience of adult readers."[11]

Despite her crusade, Rose actually published much very good but little excellent writing. She selected pieces by writers such as Pearl Buck, Rowena Bennett, Maude Hart Lovelace, Mabel Leigh Hunt, Miriam Clark Potter, Ivy O. Eastwick, James Playsted Wood, Edward Eager, Cornelia Meigs, and Lucy Parr. Many stories by writers never known outside *Jack and Jill's* pages were as good as those written by better known authors. Nancy Ford's Baba Yaga stories, Ann King's "Storm King" serial (June-October 1945), Evelyn Nevin's "Story of an Indian Capture" serial (November-May 1949), and Catherine Magee's "A Typhoon Is Coming" (November 1958) are some examples.[12] All of this fiction was exciting, entertaining, and well written—if very conventional and traditional in its values. Rose's budget was small as was her profit. But although she could pay little, she encouraged the writing and publishing of good children's literature in "Mothers' Page" after "Mothers' Page," and she published the best that she could afford. Those on her staff—Nancy Ford, Ann King, and Jean LaWall, for example—wrote many fine pieces. *Jack and Jill*, moreover, functioned as a place for young authors to begin, and it promoted their competition with one another in the annual serial contest begun in 1950. Rose did very well, considering her budget.

A small budget, however, was not the only factor determining the literary quality of pieces selected. Also sometimes detrimental was the effort to be up-to-date.[13] Rose clearly preferred modern over historical fiction and realism over fantasy. There were one or two folktales or fantasies among each issue's "tiny tales"—the very short stories intended for very young children. But nearly all of the longer stories for older children were realistic fiction, many of them reflecting current events. During World War II, for example, *Jack and Jill* published so many stories about children's efforts to save money and materials for the U.S. Army that it was cited by the Treasury Department for "patriotic cooperation in behalf of the War Finance Program."[14] The events portrayed and the moral stance adopted by some stories were quickly dated. The fostering of whole-hearted patriotism in "Tommy Buys a Tank" (July 1943), for example, troubles the reader today as does the easy acceptance of spanking in stories such as "The Butter Paddle" (February 1949). A rigidity and an innocence in many stories limits them to an era when there was less questioning of authority than there is now. Those stories undoubtedly helped educate children to their future roles in society, but so thoroughly reflecting their era, they also lacked the originality and insight needed to transcend it. Thus they reveal the limits of Rose's talent as an editor. Although she sensed and met the needs of her readers, in her quest for literary quality, she occasionally settled for the current and socially acceptable story.

As suggested before, the emphasis of the nonfiction was on activity. If one counts only articles, mostly about famous people, customs, and animals, only a very small portion of each issue was nonfiction. On the other hand, if the activities are counted, nonfiction occupied very nearly the same space as literature. Stressing industry, investigation, accomplishment, and self-reliance, all of these activities, by their mere presence, instilled traditional American attitudes toward work. Biographical articles, naturally, offered similar messages. Examples were "Booker and the Magic Marks" (April 1947), "An April Poet" (April 1955), "Washington and Lincoln" (February 1956), and "Benjamin West" (October 1957). Also, as these titles suggest, the biographies encouraged patriotism and admiration for famous people. More common than biography were articles about customs—often those used for celebrating holidays, for example, "The First Thanksgiving" (November 1950), "Folk Festivals, Kamehameha Day" (June 1951), and "New Year's Customs" (January 1952). They obviously functioned, like the even more numerous pieces about natural science, to expand the child's awareness of the world. They are surprisingly free of racism, given their time; only tinges of patronization are disturbing. The most numerous kind of articles were about animals. They, especially the series "Animals in the News," supplied information unencumbered by any implicit moral stance.

Having lost her husband and one son in an accident, Ada Campbell Rose retired in 1959.[15] Nancy Ford, who had been with the magazine since 1938, and Jean LaWall continued as senior editors, LaWall alone after Ford's death in 1961. More importantly, Karl K. Hoffman became the publisher.[16] *Jack and Jill's* circulation had slipped by 100,000, and Hoffman was hired to correct this situation, which he quickly did. He changed the editorial direction of the magazine. First, he removed the magazine's book look to make it more attention getting. Next, he cut staff, paper, and contributor costs. Finally, he beefed up the appeals to readers and abandoned Rose's concern with literary quality. Within a year, circulation was back to normal.

The cost-free item was the most characteristic feature of the magazine under Hoffman. The pages of letters, stories, poems, and drawings by children expanded, and he added "Finish This Story"—one begun so that children might write and send in endings to be published. Instead of five or six activities, Hoffman regularly included ten or more. A special feature of these years was "Bedtime Stories Mrs. Benjamin Spock Read to Her Sons," a series of reprinted classics such as Potter's *Peter Rabbit* (October-November 1960) and Jean de Brunhoff's *Story of Babar* (May-June 1961). Attractively advertised by the name of this famous children's doctor's wife, these items, free of copyright, cost the magazine nothing. The same was true of the monthly "Surprise Feature," a television story prepared by the network or later a movie review prepared by the studio. Reaching out for readers perhaps more attracted to television and movies than to magazines, these features were about the stars and shows children loved. Examples were "Pirate Jolly Lou" by Jay North, television's Dennis the Menace (September 1960), "My Television Adventure" by Roy Rogers (May 1961), and "The Jetsons—TV's Space-Age Family" (July 1963). Each of these features publicized a television show or movie on *Jack and Jill's* cover and in four to five pages. In return, the show gave air time to *Jack and Jill*. Hence these items were not only cost free, they were also free advertising.

The four to six stories and one or two other articles were not large budget items. If not reprinted, they were written by the staff or unknown authors. "Rabbitville Gazette" (a comic newspaper); "Diz and Liz," "TV Pup," and "Wampun" (cartoons); and "Perky Puppet" (replacing "Finnie, the Office Goldfish") were regular, staff-written features. Nonfiction stressed entertainment, history, and safety. James Playsted Wood, as contributing editor, wrote some excellent articles, for example, "The First Airmail" (September 1960) and "The First Automobile Race in the United States" (April 1961). He also wrote some very good stories such as "The Elephant at the County Fair" (September 1960) and "Adventure at Night" (June 1961). Most fiction continued to be realism rather than fantasy, Nancy Ford's Baba Yaga stories remaining notable exceptions. Similarly, several were narrowly tied to the mores of the period. The serial stories and the level of fiction achieved by Rose at her best, however, disappeared.

In the 1960s Curtis was in the throes of its new president's efforts to save the company, which included numerous dismissals, wholesale changes, and flamboyant gestures. In 1963 Matthew Culligan's revolution hit *Jack and Jill*. The magazine began to take advertising, and Culligan hired Dr. Frances R. Horwich of "Miss Frances' Ding-Dong School" as director of children's activities and Dr. Frederick J. Moffitt, a retired public school administrator, as editor.[17] Then Hoffman was dismissed. Two years later, after much in-fighting and many clashes among the powers at Curtis, Hoffman was recalled. *Jack and Jill* was losing money and circulation. Once again, as was hoped, Hoffman rescued the Curtis baby. *Jack and Jill* weathered the storm that resulted in the losses of *Ladies Home Journal* and *The Post*. Under Hoffman's direction, it regained its circulation and profits as it had when he took over the first time.

When Moffitt was editor, "The Things to Do and Make," "From Our Readers," and "Regular Features" remained as they were under Hoffman. Nonfiction, once appearing as some of the "Special Features," he grouped under "Articles." This special attention to nonfiction grew in the years that followed, partially due, no doubt, to the popularity of Moffitt's addition of one outstanding feature.

A series of articles about occupations, each told by a child about her or his father's or mother's work, as in "My Father Makes Money" (November 1963) or "My Father Plays Major League Baseball" (January 1964), appeared monthly, beginning under Moffitt and surviving until 1979. These features, however, did not suffice to maintain circulation when the rest of the magazine lacked appeal. Moffitt eliminated the "Surprise Features" about television and the movies. Rather than entertainment, he emphasized stories. Patriotic, moralistic, and somewhat sentimental, these stories implied what was more openly stated on the "Parent-Teacher Page." Speaking in platitudes of childhood (July 1963), writing glowingly of the magazine's "heritage and vision" (November 1963), and patronizing children in his attempt to express understanding (December 1963), these pages repeat fuzzy, rose-colored, empty generalizations. Rose spoke to an audience she knew of childhood as it was then; so did Hoffman but to a different audience in a changed America—a less idealistic, faster-paced, media-fascinated America. Moffitt spoke to Rose's audience in Hoffman's world, and his ignorance of this audience was apparent in what he said—or did not say. In any case, what he said was out of date as he wrote it.

For a few years *Jack and Jill* again enjoyed its circulation of 1 million, decked out in Hoffman's journalistic, colorful, slick, nearly cost-free packaging. But by the time the "Curtis Caper" ended and *Jack and Jill* settled down as a property of the Saturday Evening Post Company in 1971, inflation, paper costs, and magazine prices were on the rise and circulation and profits on the decline.[18] By 1979 an issue of *Jack and Jill* cost 75¢, and circulation had dropped to slightly more than 0.5 million. The magazine, furthermore, reduced to ten rather than twelve issues a year, shrank half an inch, lost as many as sixteen pages in many issues, replaced its high-quality paper with soft newsprint, and eliminated all but a little color.

As editors, Nellie Keys Bell, then Ellen Taggart, and finally William Wagner made the necessary adjustments in content. Under them, the magazine's table of contents resembled Moffitt's version more so than Hoffman's. Bell and Taggart organized the contents as "Special Features," "Stories," "Articles," "Poetry," "Regular Features," "Things to Do and Make," and "From Our Readers." Wagner's only alteration of this format was to eliminate "Special Features" in 1974.

"Special Features" included "My Mother" or "My Father Is" pieces (after 1973 appearing as "Articles") and a new series about different locations, often accounts by children who had lived there. Examples were "I Lived in Australia" (March-April 1971), "Hopcotch and Akido" (May 1971), "I Live on Cortez Island" (June-July 1972), and "I Live with the Eskimos" (November 1972). Many unusual occupations surfaced in the other special feature. Examples were training killer whales (August 1971), being a Secret Service Agent (March 1972), hunting hurricanes (September 1972), being a classical Japanese dancer (November 1972), making Christmas decorations (December-January 1973), flying a Goodyear Blimp (January 1974), teaching deaf children (May 1976), being a Thunderbird (November 1976), and being an Indian Chief (June-July 1977).

A third item more rarely listed as a special feature than the two usual ones was one about television or a movie, for example, "$1,000,000 Duck" (June-July 1971), "Walt Disney's World" (April 1972) and "Movie Magic" (January 1974). Hoffman's effort to ally the magazine with the other media was all but dropped until 1977 when William Wagner regularly featured an article about some aspect of entertainment for children. January 1977 saw one about "Peanuts," February about the Osmonds, March about the Fonz, April about the Raggedy Ann and Andy movie, and so on. Wagner also introduced a new special feature in 1973 when he ran the story contest for children and published the first-, second-, and third-prize winners separately in three issues, August, September, and November. Thereafter, he solicited and printed a reader's story in nearly every issue under "From Our Readers." Then in January 1977 he began annual contests "for Young Poets, Writers, and Artists," publishing and awarding $50 for the first prize, $25 for the second, and $10 for the third.

After 1970 there were from three to six stories, typically five or six during the early part of the decade and fewer in the later part. They were characterized by suspense, excitement, and the other ingredients that make for good entertainment. Fantasy was much more common than at any earlier time, but the very short stories called "Tiny Tales" by Rose and "Read Aloud Stories" by Hoffman were gone. New were the many multicultural stories, for example, "Hai Lu and the Necklace" (May 1972), "The Festival of Lights Friendship"(November 1973), "Desert Rescue" (August-September 1974), "The Geese at Marenta" (April-May 1975), "The Biggest Horse of All" (May 1976), "Messenger to the Gods" (March 1977), and "Talking Bells for Poh" (June-July 1978). None of this fiction was excellent; most of it was good; and all of it was clearly children's fare—fast paced and adventurous. So many titles indicate the nature of the stories that one might quote at length. A few were "Skipjack on Bay" (June-July 1971), "Manchester Bob—the Story of a Brave Dog" (November-December 1972), "The Acrobat's Revenge" (April-May 1974), "Hurricane!" (March-April 1975), "The Secret Compartment of 6B" (January 1976), "Blizzard!" (January-February 1977), "The Night of the Wolves" (February-March 1978), and "Troubles in Small Spaces" (April 1979). Features during these years, moreover, were Baba Yaga and the new "Melba the Brain" stories.[19]

Perhaps the magazine during this decade differed most notably from earlier issues in the quantity of its nonfiction. Steadily increasing from Rose's time, it had by 1970 become two-thirds of each issue, including regularly from four to six lengthy articles and from eight to twelve activities. Of the articles, those about occupations were most numerous with those about animals a close second. Biographies, including the series "Famous People," were third, and the majority of them portrayed athletes. Very nearly as many articles were about entertainment, and no other category was as well represented as these four. Others frequent enough to be noted were geography, technology, practical advice about how to do things, and history, including an "Old Time America" series. If one groups the articles with the activities under "Things to Do and Make," however, the category containing by far the most examples was practical advice. Thus the magazine continued to emphasize American pragmatism. But as the stories were more purely entertainment than they had even been, so was the nonfiction as the numerous articles about television, movies, exotic places, and sports demonstrated.

Besides these items, *Jack and Jill* also printed from three to five cartoons or short, humorous features during these years, continuing "Rabbitville Gazette," "Diz and Liz," and "Perky Puppet" until 1978, 1974, and 1978, respectively, and adding "Kookie Kaper" from 1974 to 1976, "Peanuts" from 1977 until the present, and "Worthless Advice from Uncle Wilbur" from 1978 until the present. "From Our Readers" consisted of from two to four items an issue and less regularly a few more. Letters, stories, poems, nonfiction, and drawings were published.

In October 1979, then, when the Benjamin Franklin Literary and Medical Society took over the publication of *Jack and Jill*, although the magazine had changed in major ways, it still resembled the magazine it was in 1938. Even after its sale to this new publisher, it remained much the same for nearly a year, the chief difference being that items were starred and labeled "health," "nutrition," "safety," or "exercise." Nonfiction dealing with these subjects increased, and fiction decreased. But the enormous alteration in the magazine did not occur until August-September 1980 when the table of contents was divided into "Health," "Stories," "Features," "Things to Do and Make," and "From Our Readers." In January 1981 "Stories" was eliminated, and the magazine's organization has not varied since then. Fiction is still a regular feature, but the two or so stories are generally classified under "Health" or occasionally under "Features." Besides the fiction, the items under "Things to Do and Make" are reduced—from the eight to twelve of the 1970s to only three or four. "From Our Readers," on the other hand, has remained very much the same. The largest section, then, is the new one called "Health." Here fiction and nonfiction are intermingled and identified on the pages where they are printed in full as about one of the magazine's four subjects: health, nutrition, safety, or exercise.

Obviously, *Jack and Jill* in the August-September 1981 issue has diverged greatly from what it was in November 1938. But perhaps the most startling contrast between these two issues is in tone. Rose's desire to stimulate, occupy, and entertain children has almost fully given way to the need to educate. The didacticism of the early magazine is minor when compared with that of the current issue, whose lessons, no matter how worthy, are never more than thinly covered with the cloth of fiction. Overt and insistent, sometimes nearly shrill, this latest issue is seldom fun. The attractive format, very good fiction, outstanding features, and many entertaining activities that characterized *Jack and Jill* throughout most of its history are gone. In this Children's Health Publication, American pragmatism has won out.

Notes

1. James Playsted Wood, *The Curtis Magazines* (New York: Ronald Press, 1971), vii.

2. Ibid., p. 149.

3. Wood expressed this opinion throughout both *The Curtis Magazines* and *Magazines in the United States* (New York: Ronald Press, 1971).

4. See *A Short History of JACK AND JILL* (Philadelphia: Curtis Publishing Co., 1953), unpaged.

5. *Jack and Jill* 14 (November 1951), 68.

6. Ibid., 11 (February 1949), 68.

7. Ibid., 5 (July 1943), 52.

8. See Wood, *The Curtis Magazines*, p. 149.

9. *Jack and Jill* 13 (November 1950), 68.

10. Ibid., 17 (November 1954), 68.

11. Ibid., 21 (November 1958), 68.

12. Nancy Ford, *Baba Yaga's Secret* (Philadelphia: Lippincott, 1959); idem, *Baba Yaga and the Enchanted Ring* (Philadelphia: Lippincott, 1960); idem, *Baba Yaga and the Prince* (Philadelphia: Lippincott, 1961).

13. See *A Short History*.

14. Ibid.

15. Ada Campbell Rose, *Acquainted with Grief* (Philadelphia: Westminster Press, 1972).

16. See Wood, *The Curtis Magazines*, pp. 230-31.

17. Ibid., pp. 268-69.

18. The *Curtis Caper* is Joseph Goulden's term in his book by that name (New York: Putnam's, 1965).

19. Iva Ruckman, *Melba the Brain* (Philadelphia: Westminster Press, 1979).

Information Sources

BIBLIOGRAPHY

Matthew Culligan, *The Curtis-Culligan Story: From Cyrus to Horace to Joe* (New York: Crown Publishers, 1970); Curtis Publishing Company, *Stories from JACK AND JILL* (New York: Wonder Books, 1960); Nancy K. Ford, *Baba Yaga and the Enchanted Ring* (Philadelphia: Lippincott, 1960); idem, *Baba Yaga and the Prince* (Philadelphia: Lippincott, 1961); idem, *Baba Yaga's Secret* (Philadelphia: Lippincott, (1959); Otto Friedrich, *Decline and Fall* (New York: Harper and Row, 1969); Joseph C. Goulden, *The Curtis Caper* (New York: Putnam's, 1965); *The JACK AND JILL Christmas Book* (Philadelphia: Curtis Publishing Company, annual 1968-1972); Ada Campbell Rose, *Acquainted with Grief* (Philadelphia: Westminster Press, 1972); idem, ed., *JACK and JILL Mystery Book* (Philadelphia: Curtis Publishing Co., 1959); idem, *JACK AND JILL Round the Year Book* (Philadelphia: Curtis Publishing Co., 1958); idem, *JACK AND JILL Stories and Other Features from JACK AND JILL* (Philadelphia: J. C. Winston Co., 1948); Iva Ruckman, *Melba the Brain* (Philadelphia: Westminster Press, 1979); *A Short History of JACK AND JILL* (Philadelphia: Curtis Publishing Co., 1953); James Playsted Wood, *The Curtis Magazines* (New York: Ronald Press, 1971); idem, *Magazines in the United States* (New York: Ronald Press, 1971).

INDEX SOURCES
Subject Index to Children's Magazines.
LOCATION SOURCES
Bound volumes are in many university and major public libraries. Vols. 1-42 are available
    on microfilm from University Microfilms International, Ann Arbor, Mich.

Publication History
MAGAZINE TITLE AND TITLE CHANGES
Jack and Jill (1938-).
VOLUME AND ISSUE DATA
Jack and Jill (vol. 1, no. 1-vol. 43, no. 6).
PUBLISHER AND PLACE OF PUBLICATION
Curtis Publishing Company, Philadelphia (1938-1970); Holiday Publishing Company,
    Indianapolis (1970-1971); Jack and Jill Publishing Company, Indianapolis (1971);
    Saturday Evening Post Company, Indianapolis (1971-1979); Benjamin Franklin
    Literary and Medical Society, Indianapolis (1979-).
EDITOR
Ada Campbell Rose (1938-1959); Nancy Ford and Jean LaWall (1959-1961); Jean LaWall
    (1961-1963); Douglas Benney (1963); Dr. Frederick J. Moffitt (1963-1965); Karl
    K. Hoffman (1965-1970); Nellie Keys Bell (1970-1972); Ellen Taggart (1972);
    William Wagner (1972-).

Virginia Wolf

JOHN MARTIN'S BOOK: THE CHILD'S MAGAZINE

John Martin's Book: The Child's Magazine was established in 1912 and issued
monthly until February 1933. During its twenty-year history the magazine was
published by John Martin's House, Inc., and edited by its president Morgan
Shepard under the name John Martin. In 1923 Helen Waldo joined him on the
masthead, first as associate editor and in 1924 as editor.

Morgan Shepard was born in 1865 in Brooklyn, New York, but spent nine
of his formative childhood years on a Maryland plantation where some of his
fondest memories were of his mother telling him stories of martin birds. In 1881,
at the age of sixteen, he embarked on a series of adventures that included fighting
in a Central American revolution. After returning to the United States, he worked
his way west by punching cattle, herding sheep, oiling engines, and picking
grapes. In California he worked as a streetcar conductor and newspaper reporter
and as a banker in San Francisco for thirteen years—a job at which he reportedly
felt completely "submerged." He then went into the publishing business and
later traveled abroad to study book printing, book binding, and jewelry design.
He returned to San Francisco and began a designing firm, which was destroyed
in the San Francisco earthquake of 1906. Under the name John Martin, Shepard
began writing children's verse and, to supplement his income, long letters to
children telling whimsical stories illustrated by funny drawings.

At the end of two years he was mailing 2,000 letters monthly. In 1912 the letters were turned into a monthly magazine known as *John Martin's Book*, which had attained a circulation of approximately 40,000 by 1925. Although Shepard characterized the magazine as a financial failure, it continued publication for a little more than twenty years.[1] In addition to the magazine, John Martin's House, Inc., published compilations of stories, games, and features from previous volumes of the magazine in annual *Big Books*; volumes of John Martin's verse for children such as *God's Dark and Other Bedtime Verse* and *A Book of Prayers for Little Men and Women*; books of features from the magazine such as *Peter Puzzlemaker* and *Make and Do Books*; and novelty items such as prayer posters and psalm folders based on art from the magazine.

The magazine was directed at the middle-class child between the ages of three and twelve. Its original aim was to specialize in the young child, but its scope gradually expanded until by 1921 the major focus was on the child over ten with only one-third of the magazine devoted to children under six years. By 1927 the portion of the magazine devoted to the young child had been moved to the back of the book and consolidated into a section called "Johnny Junior," to avoid the "baby" look objected to by older readers. "Johnny Junior" eventually gave way to a small section entitled "Cuddle Tales for Bedtime," a collection of read-aloud stories, simple games, and puzzles that featured many of the characters from the early years of the magazine.

The editorial philosophy of *John Martin's Book* was frequently stated in the magazine as an inducement for parents to subscribe for their children. The "John Martin Creed," as printed in 1917, was:

> To be pure but merry, wise but not priggish. To be happy and diffuse happiness; to teach without preachment, guide without coercion. To credit the child with the qualities of humor, imagination, and divination. To provide the *best* that the heart and mind can give without affectation or patronizing sentimentality. To be to the child a perfectly *natural friend* who loves and understands him. To work blithely and play joyously, to live hopefully and helpfully; and to love all childhood in spirit and sincerity. Finally, never to lose sight of its aim to influence the formation of the manners, tastes and ideals of our future *Men and Women*.[2]

The editors claimed their publication as:

> the only and best magazine that is developed scientifically and sympathetically for children in the impressionable years between three and twelve. It is the only magazine that gives the child a perfect book in magazine form. It is a big book, printed in colors, indestructible, beautiful and appealing in art and literature. In presenting a child with *John Martin's Book* you give fun, fancy, good work-to-do, and good thoughts-to-think.

A delightful gift, which lasts a year, while its instruction, attractively presented, brings an influence for good that will last a life time.[3]

By 1926 the magazine could grandiloquently claim about itself:

It stands for childhood ideals and fancies, fun and nonsense, thoughts and dreams, work and play unspoiled by stilted systems, prudery, sentimentality or sect obstinacy. It stands for the best art, the best literature, the best English and the best and happiest influence for the child, all of which must be given in the child's own way.... It stands firmly as a constructive influence upon the mind and character of the child. It demands American ideals, pure and unshadowed by intellectual sophistries. It is not merely a pleasure provider but a daily living guide in morals, manners, tastes and ideals. It makes finer, happier and more useful men and women.[4]

In addition to these appeals to parents not to deprive their children of its sterling influence, the magazine frequently took the opportunity, especially from the mid-1920s onward, to address parental concerns and needs through letters and advisory columns discussing various childrearing concerns and the provision of school and camp directories as well as extensive book reviews.

The magazine's content included a broad spectrum of stories, poems, games, puzzles, and "make and do" features in each issue. A large cast of continuing characters peopled its pages, allowing for the inclusion of a great deal of variety while maintaining an aura of familiarity. Readers could look forward to a letter from Toofy the Bear, the continuing escapades of the W. Chuck Family, the cartoonlike Chubbies and Mr. Scoodle-Do, mischievous Jolly Polly, and Wise Owl. The fiction included hero tales, Greek myths and legends, Bible stories, gentle domestic stories, adventure serials, and a great deal of verse—all of which promoted the virtues of consideration for others, fearlessness, honor, truthfulness, obedience, thrift, patriotism, and reverence.

The nonfiction leaned heavily toward biographical sketches, instructional stories, and historical essays. "The purpose is to build character, ideals and standards; to entertain while supplying a broad cultural background. We supplement school by stories of history and nature, with biographies, myths and legends, stories of real life, of customs and children of other lands, helping the young reader to orient their knowledge by finding familiar facts and subjects outside their textbooks."[5]

The extensive "do and make" pages were designed to "satisfy the craving for activity and creation while contributing to manual skill and coordination."[6] Each issue of the magazine contained a wide variety of games, puzzles, and activities for children of all ages. Many were designed to increase language and observation skills with crossword puzzles, puns, riddles, fill-in-the blank stories, word games, mazes, and find-the-mistake puzzles. The featured activities were easily carried out with materials found in most homes and many of them were

designed to teach scientific principles. In addition, the magazine heavily promoted patriotic, humanitarian, and educational causes such as the Red Cross,
aid to French refugees, polio victims, and Children's Book Week.

From the beginning readers were encouraged to think of themselves as be-
longing to a special club of "John Martiners," complete with secret sign and
long letters from John Martin. By the mid-1920s the magazine was soliciting
letters, poems, stories, and drawings from its readers for the "Around the Table
Club" and was sponsoring a pen-pal exchange in the "Geography by Mail"
department. These features were a true indication that the focus of the magazine
had shifted from the very young child to the more mature child of ten to twelve
who wanted to participate actively in the magazine.

The most outstanding and interesting aspect of the magazine, however, was
its visual appearance which was a complete departure from *St. Nicholas** and
*The Youth's Companion.** Morgan Shepard's European training in book design
and his desire to appeal to the young child combined to create a magazine with
a new look. The sophisticated use of graphic design elements drawing upon the
liberal use of white space and imaginative typography and layout; the use of
flat, bold shapes and primary colors; and a mix of art styles all contributed to a
look that is very contemporary.

The magazine maintained a remarkably consistent look, which changed very
little until its size changed to a larger format in 1928. Even though the magazine
then more nearly reflected the style of the times, it never completely lost its own
distinctive graphic image. This is no doubt due to the strong editorial control
exercised by Morgan Shepard and to the fact the majority of its artistic contributors remained with the magazine throughout its history. Besides the work of
its regular contributors—George Carlson, Harold Sichel, H. L. Drucklieb, Mary
and Nelson Grofe, Marjorie Hartwell, Anne Appletree, Jo McMahon, and Stephen Walton Wilcox—the publication featured well-known illustrators such as
Justin Gruelle, Henry Pitz, Kate Seredy, and Robert Lawson.

Illustrations were carefully matched to story or feature with the romantic
realism of Henry Pitz illustrating stories of King Arthur and other heroic tales.
Woodcuts after the style of C. B. Falls dramatically pointed up poems, alphabets,
nonsense rhymes, and other features for small children. Elaborate decorations
surrounded poems, songs, and stories of a sensitive nature. Humorous stories
called for cartoonlike figures, with charcoal and line drawings illustrating animal
and nature stories. E. H. Shepard's Winnie-the-Pooh illustrations influenced the
drawings for domestic stories featuring young children. The magazine's covers
reflected a strong folk-art influence, which also carried into the magazine itself.
The bold and colorful designs are as fresh and inviting today as they were seventy
years ago.

Throughout its twenty-year history, *John Martin's Book* remained true to its
ideals and standards—to provide good and wholesome reading, games, and
activities, and uplifting and inspiring sentiments to its readers. It was straightforward in promoting the causes it felt would benefit the child, and succeeded

in providing information and meeting pedagogical needs while always remaining
entertaining, amusing, and sympathetic to the child's interests and needs.

Notes

1. *New York Times*, May 17, 1947, p. 16. Obituary, Morgan Shepard.
2. *John Martin's Book: The Child's Magazine* 15 (January 1917), page preceding back cover.
3. Ibid.
4. Ibid., 33 (January 1926), page preceding back cover.
5. Ibid., (January 1927), three pages preceding back cover.
6. Ibid.

Information Sources

BIBLIOGRAPHY
William Burke and Will Howe, *American Authors and Books*, rev. Irving R. Weiss (New
     York: Crown Publishers, 1963); *New York Times*, May 17, 1947, p. 16, col. 2.
INDEX SOURCES
None.
LOCATION SOURCES
Los Angeles Public Library (vols. 37-43); Library of Congress (vols. 19-42); North Texas
     State University, Denton, Tex. (vols. 38-47); Massachusetts Historical Society,
     Boston (vols. 15, 29, 36); St. Paul Public Library, St. Paul, Minn. (vols. 30-47);
     Ohio University, Athens, Ohio (vols. 37-47); Brigham Young University, Provo,
     Utah (vols. 35-47); Salt Lake City Public Library (vols. 15-47). Microfilm copies
     are available at the Research Library Group, New Haven. (vols. 1-47).

Publication History

MAGAZINE TITLE AND TITLE CHANGES
John Martin's Book: The Child's Magazine (1912-1926); *John Martin's Book: The Mag-
     azine for Young People and Johnny Junior for Little Folk* (1927-February 1928);
     John Martin's Book: The Child's Magazine (March 1928-February 1933).
VOLUME AND ISSUE DATA
John Martin's Book: The Child's Magazine (vol. 1, no. 1-vol. 34, no. 12); *John Martin's
     Book: The Magazine for Young People and Johnny Junior for Little Folk* (vol.
     35, no. 1-vol. 37, no. 2); *John Martin's Book: The Child's Magazine* (vol. 37,
     no. 3-vol. 47, no. 2). (*Note*: Vol. 46 contained only five numbers with July-
     August a combined issue no. 1.)
PUBLISHER AND PLACE OF PUBLICATION
John Martin's House, Inc.: Garden City, Long Island, N.Y. (1912-August 1918); New
     York (September 1918-September 1929); editorial and general offices: New York;
     and publication offices: Concord, N.H. (October 1929-February 1933).
EDITOR
Morgan Shepard (1912-1923); Morgan Shepard and Helen Waldo (1923-1933). (*Note*:
     The name of the editor did not appear on the masthead until 1923. It then appeared
     as John Martin and Helen Waldo, associate editor [April 1923-April 1924]; John
     Martin and Helen Waldo, editors [May 1924-February 1933]. Helen Waldo ap-

peared as the managing editor in the Statement of Ownership, Management, and Circulation as early as 1918.)

Anne Menzies

JUNIOR NATURAL HISTORY MAGAZINE

In 1936 the American Museum of Natural History, which had published *The American Museum Journal* from 1900 to 1919 and had been publishing *Natural History* since 1919, decided to publish a natural history magazine for children. *Junior Natural History Magazine* was founded in the belief that natural history is so interesting to children that it does not have to be dressed up or put into story form. *Junior Natural History* was first published in March 1936 and continued for twenty-seven years until June 1963, when it was replaced by *Nature and Science*. The periodical generally had sixteen to twenty-four pages with little advertising, except for an occasional small book announcement for a publishing company or museum bookstore. The first issues in 1936 sold for 10¢ each; by 1963 they were 15¢ each. The magazine's editor, Dorothy L. Edwards (Shuttlesworth), wrote in a straightforward and lucid style, and her intention was to provide a well-illustrated publication.

Edwards, also a published author of children's books, remained the magazine's editor until 1963. The final issue of *Junior Natural History* in June contained a tribute to Dorothy Edwards Shuttlesworth, writer; Capt. Nelson R. Perry, roving reporter and photographer; George F. Mason, writer and artist; and Matthew Kalmenoff, museum artist, for their consistent efforts to enrich the magazine during its twenty-seven years of publication.

The magazine's covers reflect its emphasis on illustrations. The early ones contained a drawing, usually of an animal or a plant. A brief description of the subject appeared on the contents page. Photographs were used on later covers. Some examples include "Flamingoes" on the July 1936 cover; "Sea Horses" in August 1936; and "Praying Mantis" in October 1936. In March 1950, for instance, the cover had a photograph of a tarsier; in April 1950, an angel fish; and in March 1962, a red squirrel. In some later issues the color theme of the cover was carried throughout the magazine. If, for instance, the cover was in brown, so would be the print and illustrations of ensuing pages. Other issues featured red, blue, gray, or green. For the final cover in June 1965, George F. Mason prepared a last drawing, "Goodbye."

Throughout the magazine's history, Mason was noted for his fascinating presentations, including "Wild Animal" (1948) and "Wildwood Animal Cartoons" (1950), and for his lucid informational illustrations, such as "Shrimp Boats," "Changing Scenes in Alaska," "Insect Music," "How Insects Survive the Winter," and "Glaciers" (all 1962) and "Power of Water," "Eagles," "Windstorms," "Money Drips from Trees," "Animal Families," and "Back Cover Memories" (all 1963). Readers' interest in the text was whetted by titles such as "A Pet for the Month" (1936), "What Is Its Name?" (1938), "Transportation Means Many Methods to Many People" (1962), and "Animal, Vegetable, or Mineral—What Do You Think?" (1963). The readers' participation was enlisted by various picture and word puzzles, crosswords, questionnaires, and missing word games. These mental exercises had titles such as "How to Make It," "What's My Name?" and "Fun With Funetics." Each issue offered a "Pen Pal" column, listing the interests of particular children, and the magazine also published stories, photographs, and poems about natural history submitted by children. Occasionally, there was a natural history poem by an adult as well.

A series of articles written by specialists discussed the intricacies of the museum and its operation. Examples include "In Museum Workshops—Preparation of Insects" and "Mounting of a Bird" (both 1949).

An interesting two-page spread was "The Animal's Picture Page" (1938), which featured a particular animal with large, eye-catching photographs accompanied by a description of the animals' habits and habitat. All issues gave facts about flowers of the states, gems, stamps picturing a country's flora or fauna, birthstones, or data relative to the names of months and special holidays. Most issues included a small section devoted to brief reviews of current and interesting books about natural history.

To alert children to the wonders of a zoo, the magazine frequently featured photographs and announcements of special events such as births of animals, exotic additions, and unusual occurrences. In 1948-1949 a one-page column provided information about conservation, covering topics such as "Watersheds," "Forests," "Protection of Wildlife," and "Disappearing Waterfowls."

Realizing the keen interest that some children have in pets and their care, Marguerite Gubik, V.M.D., was enlisted to write a series of articles such as "Good Care for Horses" and "Christmas Pets" (both 1948) and "Good Manners for Fido" (1951).

The column "Careers in Science" hoped to prepare children for vocations, by providing them with appropriate knowledge. Articles included "Oceanography" by Dr. John Armstrong, "Mamology" by Donald Carter, and "Herpetology" by Dr. Charles Bogert (all 1948) and "Social Anthropology" by Dr. Margaret Mead (1949).

Children were taken on literary flying carpets to fascinating, exotic corners of the earth through exciting photographs and features such as "Bandits of the Australian Bush" by Gittel Branda and Sylvia Green (1949), "Collecting Sea Treasures of Australia's Tropics" by Fred Lard (1950), "Pearls" (1962), and "An Expedition to Ecuador" (1963) by Russel Ryman.

In the 1960s the magazine began to reflect interest in the solar system stimulated by the space program, publishing articles by the National Aeronautics and Space Administration (NASA); Bell Laboratories, "Amazing Laser"; and the United Nations Educational, Social, and Cultural Organization (UNESCO), "A Sputnik's Eye View of the Earth" (all in 1962). However, articles on the solar system had appeared earlier. James Perry Wilson's succinct articles "Our

Neighbor the Moon,'' "Mars," "The Asteroids," "Jupiter," "Saturn," and "Comets" were published in 1948 as were Catherine E. Perry's articles "Once Upon a Midnight Clear," "Spectral Class," and "Once Upon the Seas" in 1962 and "Fathers of Astronomy" in 1965.

Throughout the magazine's history the most qualified writers in their fields were invited to contribute. Some of the magazine's many excellent articles were "Smoke Hunter's Holiday" by Raymond L.D. Timars and William Bridges (1936), "An Undersea Expedition" by Eunice Thomas Miner (1936), "Snuffy, The Shrew," by Kenneth M. Lewis (1936), "Vanishing Wilderness" by Francisca La Monte and William L. Welch (1936), "Salamanders" by William G. Hassler, (1937), "Nature's Gardening" by Harriette Wilburn (1937), "Footprints in the Snow" by Kenneth M. Lewis (1938), "Whaling Adventure" by Jeanette Edwards Rattray (1948), "Snails Are Fun" by Bill Birky (1950), "Feathered Swimming Champ" by Grace Gannon (1962), "Fascinating Ostrich" by Richard Weiss (1963), and "Lakes in Arid Lands" by Don C. Miller (1963).

Throughout *Junior Natural History* one finds a variety of subject matter but never a monotonous repetition of topics. The magazine's style was always suitable for its intended audience. Carefully edited, *Junior Natural History* covered an impressive range of subjects, and set high standards for its contributors. The magazine succeeded in its mission to provide American children with reliable information about the natural world and about the major discoveries made in the field of natural history since the 1930s.

Note

1. Frank Luther Mott, "General Science and Medicine," *A History of American Magazines*, 5 vols. (Cambridge: Harvard University Press, 1938-1968).

Information Sources

BIBLIOGRAPHY
Harry C. Strauss, "Views on Science Books," *The Hornbook Magazine* 54 (April 1978) 189-90; Zena Sutherland, *The Best in Children's Books* (Chicago: University of Chicago Press, 1974).
INDEX SOURCES
Subject Index to Children's Magazines.
LOCATION SOURCES
Bound volumes are in the Library of Congress, some university libraries and the American Museum of Natural History, New York.

Publication History

MAGAZINE TITLE AND TITLE CHANGES
The Junior Natural History (March 1936-April 1937); *The Junior Natural History Magazine* (May 1937-May 1946); *Junior Natural History Magazine* (June 1946-November 1953); *Junior Natural History* (December 1953-June 1963).
VOLUME AND ISSUE DATA

The Junior Natural History (vol. 1, no. 1-vol. 2, no. 2); *The Junior Natural History Magazine* (vol. 2, no. 3-vol. 11, no. 3); *Junior Natural History Magazine* (vol. 11, no. 4-vol. 18, no. 9); *Junior Natural History* (vol. 18, no. 10-vol. 28, no. 4).
PUBLISHER AND PLACE OF PUBLICATION
American Museum of Natural History, New York (1936-1963).
EDITORS
Dorothy L. Edwards Shuttlesworth (March 1936-October 1952); Marion B. Carr (November 1952-June 1963).

Marguerite Davern

JUNIOR SCHOLASTIC

Junior Scholastic was born of the success of its parent publication *Senior Scholastic* (1920-), the national weekly high school magazine, and introduced into the growing family of Scholastic Publications on September 18, 1937.[1] Intended to address a younger audience, "Upper Elementary Grades and Junior High School," *Junior Scholastic* echoes the values, tone, and content of its older, well-established parent. In fact, Maurice R. Robinson, the creator of *Scholastic* publications; Kenneth M. Gould, the first managing editor and then editor-in-chief of *Scholastic Magazines*; and Jack K. Lippert, editor of both *Senior* and *Junior Scholastic* and then, following Gould, editor-in-chief, served as the new magazine's governing administrative and editorial voices for the first thirty-five years.[2] Other evidence indicating a close association between *Junior Scholastic* and its parent publication include replication of physical characteristics such as the use of soft newsprint, 8 1/2- by 11-inch paper; shared editorial control (Robinson, Gould, Lippert, and Jim Brownell all served as editors of both magazines); and overlapping content to the extent that reviewers frequently refer to *Junior Scholastic* as "the modified version of *Senior Scholastic*."[3] Yet the "modifications" such as feature title changes; the insertion of vocabulary glosses, more skill-building items, and simplified puzzles; and the greater use of supporting visuals such as photographs, maps, comics, and drawings did not make easy reading for the average elementary school student: "*Junior Scholastic* vies with the news sheet in classroom use, but by its reading space and format and more extended consideration of topics, earns a place on the library magazine rack. It has an age adaptation only a little below its senior partner, although its cover suggests that it is intended for young children."[4]

This contrast between the magazine's often youthful cover and its generally mature and serious content, and its sophisticated advertisements, frequently strikes the older reader's awareness. The first issue (September 18, 1937), for example, pictures a preteenage, well-dressed, smiling girl and boy resting on their bikes, standing before a white picket fence, suggesting carefree innocence. The issue's contents, however, include articles such as "The Fast Pace of Discovery" that notes the impact of invention on tradition, commenting under the subheading "Science and Slaughter" that "[i]nventions change the way we live, but not all inventions make life better for us. A new death-ray, long range machine guns, aerial torpedoes—these are inventions that destroy and kill,"[5] while it infuses factual content with moral and philosophical probes: "The above picture shows the mechanical cotton picker, one of the recent important inventions. The picture to the right shows a chemist in his laboratory, working on artificial cotton. If the chemist succeeds, there may be no use for the cotton picker. Something to think about."[6] Other articles cover "Why Is Japan Fighting China?/The Japanese Want More of China's 'Good Earth' "; "Work Wanted/Many Men and Women Cannot Find Jobs"—definitely not carefree topics. Sophisticated advertisements—beginning in 1940, steadily increasing during the 1950s, receiving peak exposure by the 1960s, and slowly changing to an exclusively younger age appeal (toy sports cars, drawing pens, sports file cards, dolls, and shampoo) as 1980 approached—ranged from Brownie reflex cameras by Kodak, Royal portable typewriters, and Arrow sports shirts (all 1946); "Hamilton: The Watch of Rail Road Accuracy," "Greyhound—See All the World Here in America," and Wilson sports equipment (all 1950s); to "Clearasil Personality of the Month," "8 Hit Records for $1.00," "Bell Telephone Careers," and nylon stockings (all 1960's).

Generally, the title, tone, content, print size, and the amount and type of drawings and photographs, in addition to the advertisements, follow a pattern of growing sophistication until the beginning of the 1970s, a time that coincides with the retirement of Jack Lippert. Over the years, however, the distribution of the departments and features introduced with the first issue, while undergoing changes in level of reading difficulty and emphasis and variations in length, maintain continuity. Basic departments include history, science, domestic and international news, and sports; basic features include puzzles, biographies, quizzes, jokes, maps, word games, and a short story or a play. The majority of editorial changes, especially expansions and emphases, can be seen as responses to the social and political issues current upon publication as well as to the magazine's fluctuations in popularity.

During the first two years of publication, for example, "Headline News" gained increasing space as events in other countries augmented a growing American concern over the territorial thrust of Hitler's Germany. In the October 1, 1938, issue, selections about the diplomatic relations between England, France, and Germany are presented along with supplementary material, "German Refugees Seek Haven in U.S.A.," that points out that Germans were coming to the United States "not to seek a fortune as do many immigrants, but rather to escape religious persecution as did the first Americans,"[7] and a short story by Caroline Dale Snedeker about a Quaker girl who suffered religious persecution in early America, "A Story of Persecution in Boston." This technique of focusing an issue on a "theme" topic supported by supplementary articles, features, and stories or plays continues to provide a cohesive framework.

In fact, issue covers usually reflect the week's theme topic, following a discernible pattern of mirroring "Headline News" during times of international crisis or national concern, while shifting its focus: to film stars (September 25, 1939, pictures Gloria Jean, eleven-year-old star of *The Underpup*; May 17, 1950, uses a scene from the movie *Treasure Island*; and September 8, 1977, has a scene from *Star Wars*); to young athletes and sports events (February 19, 1940, "The Center Jump"; April 26, 1961, "Take Me Out to the Ball Game," about national baseball leagues; September 30, 1964, "Olympic Games"; January 31, 1972, "Olympic Power in the Far East"; and October 27, 1977, showing Tracy Austin ready at the net); to significant events in the art world (January 14, 1965, "Alexander Calder: The Ways of Sculpture" pictures entries in his exhibit at New York's Guggenheim Museum); and to seasonal photographs and drawings (Halloween, Thanksgiving, Christmas, Valentine's Day); during "peaceful" periods. Frequently, a geographic section of the United States or of a foreign country is highlighted, explicated by a feature news article and supplemented by a biography or story of an important person and a photographic interview with a native teenager ("World Friendship Series" enjoyed great success during the 1950s through the 1960s). Rarely, however, does an issue appear without some discussion of domestic affairs: "there is constant emphasis in the *Scholastic* publications on domestic problems such as housing, health, and unemployment."[8]

The time during which domestic affairs received the least attention coincided with the duration of World War II. War coverage provided extended discussion of the "causes," motives, aims, intentions, values, politics, history, and geographic location of the Axis as well as the Allied forces—"the armies of world slavery and the armies of world freedom."[9] A new column, "Via Air Mail," printing letters from young readers around the world appeared; the stamp-collecting department received more space;[10] the use of maps and charts increased. The January 5-10, 1942, edition, "War in Far East," presented a "Revised Schedule of Theme Articles" "to correspond with the war situation"; and the February 2-7, 1942, issue boasted an increased editorial staff: Jack Lippert, managing editor, was now supported by Charles S. Preston as associate editor and Margaret Sylvester Ronan and Nancy F. Genet as editorial assistants. The increase in staff was warranted; circulation had increased rapidly, and by 1942 *Junior Scholastic* had reached 141,514 readers; by 1944, 256,001.[11]

Lippert oversaw many changes in *Junior Scholastic* as he moved through positions of increasing editorial responsibility, succeeding Gould as editor-in-chief of *Scholastic* publications in 1965, serving as senior vice-president and publisher in 1968, and returning as a special consultant after his retirement in 1973. First among these various changes was the increasing emphasis on foreign affairs stimulated by World War II. During the postwar period, the new emphasis was apparent in the added subtitle *Your World View Magazine for Home and School* (1945); the growing department "Good Neighbor News," reviewing Pan American events; the extension of the "World Friendship Series"; and the expanded, typically full-page "Victory Quiz" section (later called "Citizenship

Quiz'' in the 1950s and 1960s; ''Skillsquiz'' in the 1980s) intended as a test of reading comprehension. Additionally, Lippert increased the use of comic-strip presentations in ''Builders of America,'' a series that dealt with a famous person such as Junipers Serra or Clara Barton and was designed to ''vivify our national ideals,''[12] and in the series ''Seeing History Through American Achievements,'' thereby increasing the magazine's appeal to a younger audience.

As early as 1941 Lippert had begun to expand the magazine's contents to include ''Teacher's Pages''—a regular feature of *Senior Scholastic* since 1936. Initially, these one or two pages, attached to the front of the student edition, previewed the major points of the feature articles, suggested discussion questions, and offered justification for the point of view taken in the different departments and for the structure of teaching materials such as the various quizzes and puzzles contained in each edition: ''Confucius is often quoted as having said, 'A picture speaks for a thousand words.' Teachers are eager for their pupils to get as much out of a learning situation as possible. With this in mind, and guided by the wholesome precept that in learning we should see—think—and apply, this Picture Quiz of World Events from September, 1944, to May, 1945, was developed.''[13] Eventually, the ''Teacher Edition'' swelled (frequently adding an additional twenty pages to the student copy during the 1950s and 1960s) to include items such as professional essays on pedagogical theory and on student opinion (''What It Takes to Be a Good Teacher,'' March 31, 1947), educator surveys (''Why Can't They Read and Write?'' reported the results on the National Council of Teachers of English ''Articulation Survey,'' March 17, 1947), and news of curriculum trends, as well as information on academic meetings, national conferences, and ''educational travel'' tours. Until the mid-1970s, when inflation had reduced industry profits and had increased production costs, the teacher's pages received extensive coverage. Then after circulation reached an all-time high of 1,833,770 in 1971 and steadily plummeted to 902,939 in 1980, the pages shrank to their first issue numbers.

In the first issue of the fall 1945 term (September 17) Lippert announced the junior division of the Scholastic Writing Awards Program, open to all pupils from the sixth to the ninth grades, similar to the Scholastic Literary Awards Program sponsored by *Senior Scholastic* since 1925. Four classifications—essay, poetry, ''My Community'' article, and short story—with submission guidelines and requirements were described. The best work, so judged by ''a jury of distinguished writers,'' was published in *Junior Scholastic* or mentioned in the magazine's ''Junior Writers'' column. Writers so honored received a Certificate of Merit and a *Junior Scholastic* Achievement (JSA) button and earned a place in the final, ''grand national'' *Junior Scholastic* Awards Program, wherein participants become eligible for ''cash prizes of $25, $15, and $10, in each of the four classifications.''[14] By 1946 the Scholastic Awards Program offered certificates of merit, cash prizes, and scholarships in seventy fields (see the October 7, 1946, issue for more details), and participants received national recognition;

universities and art and technical schools sponsored the program and offered the scholarships.

With great regularity, from 1950 through the mid-1970s, the final May issue of the magazine, usually subtitled *Student Awards Issue* or *Student Achievement Issue*, was devoted to citing student winners, describing winning entries, and publishing all major writing awards. Again Lippert had intensified reader involvement. In fact, in the years following the introduction of the Scholastic Awards Program, circulation reached 352,963 in 1947—surpassing *Senior Scholastic* for the same year (271,113)—and climbed at the approximate rate of 100,000 additional readers each year until it reached 1,400,265 in 1962—the peak figure for the 1960s.

Gradually, however, commitment to the Awards Program waned (compare program coverage in the May 17, 1961, issue with May 18, 1970, and with May 19, 1981); inflation had eroded the available publication space. Similarly, after experiencing an upsurgence during the 1940-1970s—following the appearance of the "Bib and Tuck" stories, a regular biweekly feature designed to "bring your readers a delightful experience in national civics and government"[15]; other selections of short stories and plays primarily aimed at teaching moral lessons and reinforcing traditional values; and the "JS Language Page," offering poetry, book reviews, world games, and grammatical instruction—fiction collapsed under the increased economic pressure. By the end of the 1970s most stories and plays had resumed their prior role of providing a vehicle for history lessons (compare "The Makers of the World: A Pageant Play of Old and New Adventure," September 18, 1937, with any of the fiction found in the "History" department from 1977 to 1981).

From 1945 to 1948 no individual breakdown of the *Junior Scholastic* editorial staff was published; only the name and positions of the executive officers were provided. Then Patricia G. Lauber appeared as associate editor from 1949 to her appointment as editor in 1953. With her appointment came a formal statement of *Junior Scholastic*'s "Editorial Platform" that provides a concise summary of the guiding principles and assumptions underlying the 1950-1970 publication period:

SCHOLASTIC MAGAZINES are published to promote the education for enlightened citizenship of students in the schools of the United States.

We believe profoundly in, and strive to inspire faith in . . . the worth and dignity of the individual; . . . high moral and spiritual values; . . . the democratic way of life, with its basic liberties and responsibilities for all; . . . the American system of constitutional, representative government; . . . free competitive enterprise and free labor working for abundant production; . . . cooperation and understanding among all peoples for the peace of the world.

We are unalterably opposed to communism, fascism or any other system in which men become the slaves of a master state.

We aim to present the clearest explanation of current affairs, the best contemporary thought and creative expression, and the most helpful guidance for adjustment to life, adapted to the understanding and interests of youth. Good citizens honestly differ on important public questions and the young people of today need training under wise teachers to participate in solving these problems as the adult citizens of tomorrow. We therefore believe that all sides of these problems should be impartially discussed in the schools and in classroom magazines, with deep respect for facts and for logical thinking.[16]

Articles on the dangers of communism were not solely the concern of the 1950s ("We Must Teach the Dangers of Communism," December 1, 1954); the topic proved to be of recurring interest to *Scholastic* editors. For example, a series of articles on different aspects of the history, philosophy, and current news of the Communist movement appeared during the fall of 1961 through the spring of 1962 (for example, "Communism No. 7: Stalin's Reign of Terror," February 7, 1962). A special issue, "The Many Faces of Communism" (November 17, 1969), and various articles such as "Growing Up Under Communism" (October 27, 1977) reflect the consistent concern given this topic in later years.

Special issues, such as the one cited on communism, emerged as the most important, consistent feature of the magazine. These issues covered critical national events such as presidential elections ("Candidates for President and Vice-President" and "What Are We Voting for: The Issues of the Campaign" in the October 6, 1948, issue illustrate the typical format and presentation of "differing points of view") and crucial international events—consistent choices from decade to decade. In fact, generally, few editorial innovations or noteworthy changes in format emerged, other than expansion, during the 1950s, following the 1953 statement of editorial principles. After a year as editor, Patricia Lauber moved to editing the new *Junior Scholastic Summertime*, leaving Sturges F. Cary to assume editorial responsibility for *Junior Scholastic* with the March 17, 1954, edition; Jack Lippert as executive editor still retained administrative control. Cary continued Lippert's worldwide focus on the news. Under his editorship, special issues intensified the magazine's editorial self-consciousness first evident in "Remember Pearl Harbor: Review of Year's War in the Pacific" (December 7-12, 1942), a month-by-month summary of *Scholastic* news reporting. Using the same "remember-when" formula, Cary ran a "Top Ten" special-issue series such as the one summarizing "*Junior Scholastic*'s Choices of the Most Important Advances in Science and Industry During 1937-1957" and solicited reader participation: "Do you agree with our 'Top Ten' choices? Send your letter to..." (September 27, 1957). Such requests for student feedback were sincere—Cary printed the results. The highest circulation figures since the magazine's conception (1,400,265) added to the excitement of *Junior Scholastic*'s 25th anniversary celebration in 1962.

By 1963 LeRoy Hayman succeeded Cary after serving an apprenticeship as *Junior Scholastic*'s managing editor. Hayman's tenure as editor was brief; he continued the publication of the special issues edition with "Your Key to Understanding World News," containing demographic data and numerous charts and maps, and appearing annually in late September or in October throughout the 1960-1981 period. Next, Jim Brownell occupied the editor's chair in February 1968, after similarly serving as managing editor of *Senior Scholastic* under Roy Hemming. In fact, Brownell's successor, Lee Baier (November 4, 1975-), followed this same pattern—moving up after holding the managing editor position.

In 1971 Brownell was to see circulation figures rise to the highest figure on record—1,833,770—for the entire publication period 1937-1980 and then fall to 1,351,422 in 1974 before dropping to 902,939 under Lee Baier in 1980. Thus the economic crisis of the mid-1970s-1981, the shrinking age group of *Junior Scholastic* readers, and the influx of increasingly sophisticated forms of juvenile entertainment coincided with Baier's editorship.

The *Junior Scholastic* staff rallied to the vagaries of fortune. Beginning with Cary and continuing into the 1980s, special issues were frequently devoted to student interest questions such as "New Careers in the Space Age" (February 8, 1961) and "Running Away—Is That the Answer?" (October 28, 1976). Although serious international news still ranked as a priority feature, with ever increasing frequency, special issues focused on topics such as "Drugs: Will They Turn You on or Will They Turn on You?" (April 27, 1970), "Organized Crime" (February 28, 1974), "T.V. in Your World" (March 14, 1974), and "Superstition: Stuff 'n Nonsense?" (October 31, 1980), endeavoring to stimulate reader interest.

As circulation sagged, pages dwindled, returning to the customary fifteen-page publication of 1937; only rarely during the late 1970s did even special issues swell to thirty-five pages of text—suggesting the prosperity of the 1960s. The "World Friendship Series" and the "Frontiers of Science" series disappeared; the sports page, the "Quizword Puzzle" page, the map and chart sections were condensed. By the December 13, 1979, issue, the popular department "JS Televiewer," usually a page or more during the 1960s, appeared as a brief entry, "TV Tips," under the single column "Calendar." This last special issue of the decade, however, reviewed the major events of the 1970s using the "remember-when" formula introduced by Lippert in December 1942. In the review, "1972—Terror at Munich," "1974—A President Quits," "1975—South Vietnam Falls," and "1978—Camp David Triumph" shared the spotlight with "1970—Earth Day," "1971—Hey Ma, I'm Voting," "1973—Out of Gas," "1976—Happy Birthday, USA!" "1979—Three Mile Island," and "1977—Saturday Night Fever and Roots," reflecting the distribution of international-national news, social commentary, and attention to the "arts" maintained throughout the first forty-two years of the magazine's publication.

Notes

1. For an extended picture of the growth of Scholastic publications, see "—40 Years Young," *Junior Scholastic*, October 26, 1960, p. 5.

2. The March 28, 1969, issue of *Junior Scholastic* (p. 4) includes a comprehensive obituary and tribute to Kenneth M. Gould—further suggesting the extensive sense of "family" among the editorial and administrative publication staff.

3. Selma K. Richardson, *Periodicals for School Libraries* (Chicago: American Library Association, 1978), 194-95.

4. Laura Katherine Martin, "Magazines for Elementary Schools," *Magazines For School Libraries* (New York: H. W. Wilson, Co., 1950), 41.

5. "The Fast Pace of Discovery," *Junior Scholastic*, September 18, 1937, p. 3.

6. Ibid.

7. "German Refugees Seek Haven in U.S.A.," *Junior Scholastic*, October 1, 1938, p. 7.

8. Martin, *Magazines for School Libraries*, p. 41.

9. "The Mediterranean: The Sea Between Us and the Axis," *Junior Scholastic*, December 7-12, 1942, p. 5.

10. Martin, *Magazines for School Libraries*, noted that "[c]ertainly increased interest in geography created by a truly worldwide war accelerated interest among stamp collectors, but since both *Open Road For Boys* and *Junior Scholastic* maintain stamp departments, a magazine devoted entirely to philately is not necessary in most schools," p. 95.

11. All references to circulation figures are taken from *Ayer & Son's Directory of Newspapers and Periodicals* (Philadelphia: West Washington Square, 1937-81).

12. Martin, *Magazines for School Libraries*, p. 41.

13. "Contents Review," *Junior Scholastic*, May 21, 1945, p. 1-T.

14. *Junior Scholastic*, September 17, 1945, p. 3-T.

15. "Contents Review," ibid., October 14, 1946, p. 1-T.

16. "Our Editorial Platform," ibid., September 16, 1953, p. 3.

Information Sources

BIBLIOGRAPHY

Ruth Ethel Cundiff, ed., *101 Plus Magazines for Schools, Grades 1-12* (Nashville: Tennessee Book Company, 1964); Judith S. Duke, *Children's Books and Magazines: A Market Study* (New York: Knowledge Industry Publication, 1979); Carolyn W. Field, ed., *Subject Collections in Children's Literature* (New York: R. R. Bowker, 1969); Laura K. Martin, *Magazines for School Libraries* (New York: H. W. Wilson, 1950); Miriam Snow Mathes, *Basic Book Collections for Elementary Grades*, 7th ed. (Chicago: American Library Association, 1960); Grant Overton, Percival Hunt et al., *Enjoying the Arts: A Group of Essays on Appreciation (reprinted from Scholastic)* (Pittsburgh Scholastic Corporation, 1933; Anne Pellowski, *The World of Children's Literature* (New York: R. R. Bowker, 1968); Selma K. Richardson, ed., *Periodicals for School Media Programs* (Chicago: American Library Association, 1978); *Scholastic, the War for Freedom: Background Facts to Help You Understand the War* (Dayton: Scholastic Corporation, 1942); Marian H. Scott, ed., *Periodicals for School Libraries: A Guide to Magazines, Newspapers, and Periodical Indexes* (Chicago: American Library Association, 1973); Ernestine Taggard, ed., *Here We Are: Stories from Scholastic Magazine* (New York: Dodd, Mead, 1952).

INDEX SOURCES

Readers' Guide to Periodical Literature (New York: H. W. Wilson, 1937-81); *Subject Index to Children's Magazines* (Madison, Wis.: Cavanagh, 1961-70).

LOCATION SOURCES

Bound volumes are in some university and major public libraries. Bound volumes for 1937 (vol. 1, no. 1) through 1978 (vol. 82, no. 16) are in the Library of Congress. Current issues are in most county and in many junior high school libraries.

Publication History

MAGAZINE TITLE AND TITLE CHANGES

Junior Scholastic (1937-1945); *Junior Scholastic: Your World View Magazine for Home and School* (1945-1966); *Junior Scholastic* (1966-1970); *Jr. Scholastic* (1970-1974); *Junior Scholastic* (1974); *JS: Junior Scholastic* (1974-).

VOLUME AND ISSUE DATA

Junior Scholastic (vol. 1, no. 1-vol. 16, no. 16); *Junior Scholastic: Your World View Magazine for Home and School* (vol. 17, no. 1-vol. 58, no. 8); *Junior Scholastic* (vol. 58, no. 9-vol. 67, no. 4); *Jr. Scholastic* (vol. 67, no. 5- vol. 74, no. 4-); *Junior Scholastic* (vol. 74; no. 5); *JS: Junior Scholastic* (vol. 74, no. 6-).

PUBLISHER AND PLACE OF PUBLICATION

The Scholastic Corporation: Pittsburgh (1937-1943), Dayton (1943-1956); Scholastic Magazines, Inc., Dayton (1956-1980); Scholastic Inc., Dayton (1980-).

EDITOR

M. R. Robinson, president and editor (1937-1940); Kenneth M. Gould, editor-in-chief; Jack Lippert, managing editor (1940-1944); Charles Preston, editor (1944); only the executive staff—Robinson, Gould, and Lippert—appear in contents (1945-1949); Patricia G. Lauber, associate editor (1949-1952), Editor (1953); Sturges F. Cary, editor (1954-1963); LeRoy Hayman, editor (April, 1963-February 1968); Jim Brownell, editor (1968-September 1975); Lee Baier, editor (1975-).

Mary Lou Luttrell Kraft

THE JUVENILE INSTRUCTOR

From its beginnings in 1866 through various name changes to its present format, this Sunday school magazine has existed primarily as an instrument for instruction in the tenets of the Church of Jesus Christ of Latter-day Saints. Moreover, the history of this magazine is intricately related to the struggles that attended the establishment of a strong Mormon settlement in the Great Basin of the American West. Through periodicals like *The Juvenile Instructor** (1866-1929), *The Instructor* (1930-1970), *The Children's Friend** (1902-1970), *The Friend* (1971-), and *The New Era* (1971-), elders, counselors, quorum apostles, and presidents of the Latter-day Saints movement have tried to make their young members aware of the history of their church—a history that in a very particular way accounts for the fervency of beliefs such as service to the community, a strong missionary impulse, and willingly contributed tithe.

Upholding its motto "Holiness to the Lord," *The Juvenile Instructor* was originally a privately published magazine that, as its front page declared, was "designed expressly for the education and elevation of the young." Its success and longevity are directly attributable to the zeal and journalistic experience of its founder and editor, George Quayle Cannon (1827-1901). This Liverpool native surely qualifies as one of the church's most active members.[1] Businessman, counselor, and politician, Cannon was reelected four times as the territorial delegate to Congress, and served as first counselor to a series of church presidents: Taylor, Woodruff, and Snow. In addition to acting as Brigham Young's private secretary, he had also worked as a compositor on two early Illinois newspapers, both edited by his uncle John Taylor, *Times and Seasons* (1839-1846) and *Nauvoo Neighbor* (1843-1845). Trekking further west because of continued persecution, the disciples of Joseph Smith and followers of Brigham Young thankfully adopted the name "Deseret" for their newly organized state in 1849. Meaning "Honey Bee" in *The Book of Mormon* (*Ether*, chapters 2 and 3), the name conveyed the resilient determination of early church members to place their trust in industry and remain confident of sweet rewards. Although Congress changed the Mormon designation to Utah Territory the next year, and although the territory was reduced in size under successive administrations until it was granted statehood in 1896, the name *Deseret* has a lasting significance in the growth of Mormonism and the effectiveness of its publication activities.[2] The history of this church was not only related through its journals and magazines, it relied on them for its continuance and outreach.

After their establishment in the Great Basin, the church elders, in 1850, initiated *The Deseret News*, the first newspaper west of the Mississippi. As one of its early editors and a firm believer in a "properly conducted paper," George Q. Cannon started the Deseret Book Company, a church publishing outlet mainly providing materials for the Sunday school program.[3] From this source, in 1866, he began *The Juvenile Instructor*, which he edited until 1901. The year after its inception Cannon was appointed the first general superintendent of the church's youth-oriented Sunday School Union. Initially printed by *The Deseret News* and then emanating from a press in the basement of the Cannon home, *The Juvenile Instructor* was a semimonthly publication until 1907. During his editorship of the magazine Cannon was imprisoned for 175 days in 1888, on the charge of plural marriage. The marriage question was a vexing problem for Mormonism in this settlement stage. It was the reason why, in 1882, Congress denied Cannon his seat and why statehood was not granted until almost the close of the century.

In the face of persecution, threatened imprisonment, and withheld recognition, Mormonism has always espoused an active commitment to the education of young "Saints." Convinced that "the young must have their taste for knowledge gratified," Cannon set out to satisfy the youthful palate with short, easily digested surveys of Mormon history, summaries of the governing scriptures, and little vignettes of everyday life that would illustrate salient beliefs.[4] *The Juvenile Instructor*, therefore, introduced its readers to the four central books that declared the old but newly revealed truths of Mormonism: *The King James Bible* as the record of God's dealings with peoples on the eastern continent; *The Book of Mormon* as the direct translation of ancient records given to Joseph Smith; *The Doctrines and Covenants* and *The Pearl of Great Price*, both texts also based on the revelation to Smith. The perspective on all aspects of life was resolutely Mormon. American history was reflected through the experiences of a persecuted group. The moral attitude of many of the stories or miniature homilies was conveyed in their titles: "Seek Wisdom," "The Evil Results of Misguided Ambition," and "Death from an Extra Glass of Wine." Except for some accounts of American history borrowed from Jacob Abbott in volumes 3 and 4, no widely known writers contributed to this periodical. Under the pseudonym of "Uncle George," editor Cannon took a large part in the early issues of *The Juvenile Instructor*. To today's reader, most of these doctrinally burdened narratives must seem turgid, maudlin, and, on occasion, unsettling. In the November 1, 1866, issue, for instance, one of the editor's contributions is "Little George Loses a Companion: A True Story." At the outset, the boy hero is very proud of his new suit of clothes, a gift from a kindly benefactress. But the cautionary note is sounded early: "The Lord does not judge men and women and children by the clothing they wear, by the fine carriages they ride in, and by the fine houses they live in, but he judges them according to their goodness, their truthfulness and their obedience to his laws."[5] Like a flavoring clove stuck in the middle of this story is the retelling of Samuel's choice of the shepherd boy David as king of Israel. Returning to the main narrative, the reader learns of little George's diligent progress as a scholar and of the death of his nameless companion, "the poor cripple-boy." The ending is as abrupt and grim as the sound of the hammer nailing the coffin shut: "Little George felt that he had lost a dear friend, which caused a gloom to pass over his spirits, and put a check upon all his joy at being dressed in good clothing. The little cripple-boy had to be buried in the afternoon, and all the boys were permitted to go and see him lying in his coffin before he should be nailed up and shut from their sight forever."[6]

Continuing after Cannon's editorship as the "Organ of the Deseret Sunday School Union," this illustrated monthly gradually included less truncated stories where the control of rapportage was skillful. By the 1920s the magazine was printing "True Pioneer Stories." In the January 1929 issue, the last year for *The Juvenile Instructor*, the "Pioneer" banner headed a very informal interview with the Utah composer and teacher Brother William C. Clive. The chattiness, however, held a purposive message, as the reporter, H. H. Jenson, clarified from the start: "So let Brother Clive's story be a lesson to the young folk of today that hard work will make anyone a musician and that whenever you are asked to give of your time, do so cheerfully, for in the end it will pay, even though appreciation may not come exactly when you expect."[7]

Under the uninterrupted editorship of President Heber J. Grant, the magazine's title was shortened to *The Instructor* in 1930. As well as fostering a respect for the lives of service led by some "Pioneer Saints," *The Instructor* laid increasing stress on the proselytizing activities of Mormonism. Its pages contain reports of far-off missions, newly established "wards" and "stakes," and different manifestations of the Aaronic priesthood. Praise of the refuge that the church offers from worldly, intemperate pursuits occurs with remarkable frequency. In the first issue of the newly named magazine, "The Sketch" by George Smith Dibble establishes this high encomiastic tone. Marveling "at the grandeur and magnificence" of the Salt Lake City Temple, an artist is moved to sketch a group of awestruck tourists. An unnoticed observer approaches, and in the ensuing dialogue the reader finds out that the observer, a Dutch immigrant, has been saved by two Mormon missionaries in Holland. Before long, the Dutchman becomes the main speaker, describing his previous life in carefully disinfected, staid terms; his attitude is retrospectively righteous: "My thoughts were of worldly pleasures rather than of spiritual things. I indulged in tobacco and strong drink and squandered the time, which should have been spent in the company of my dear wife and children, with worthless associates."[8] After the imposition of the elders' hands cured his critically ill son, the man and his family joined the church and moved to Utah. While "his clean face mirrors the joy of his soul," the Dutchman proceeds to eulogize his new life: "No longer is my money wasted on such things as tea, coffee and tobacco."[9] The conversation, soon a monologue, is a transparent pretext for this lengthy paean. For the critical reader and nonmember, this heavy burdening of the story line, along with a suspension of disbelief, is almost too much to tolerate. More story and less sermonizing, the reader sighs. Earlier Sunday school moralists like Mrs. Barbauld, Hannah More, Sarah Trimmer, and Mrs. Sherwood were able to clothe their doctrinal messages in attractive, well-told stories. The meeting of an artist and a stranger is a situation rich in narrative possibilities. From the famous artist-observer dialogue in "The Roman Road," Kenneth Grahame extracted many ennobling and aesthetic insights. But the delicate touch of *The Golden Age* is nowhere to be found in *The Instructor*. Although any comparison of this sort is manifestly unfair, the remark does reflect the limited appeal of this unrelenting high-mindedness for a nonmember.

The inauguration of *The New Era* in 1971 to replace *The Instructor*—as well as *The Friend* replacing *The Children's Friend*—could be viewed as a recognition by the church hierarchy that their message, undiluted and ever confident, needed to be repackaged to reach the children of the 1970s and 1980s. Advertised as the "official monthly publication of the Church of Jesus Christ of Latter-Day Saints for youth and young adults," *The New Era* began under the editorship of Doyle L. Green. The current editor of both *The Friend* and *The New Era* is M. Russell Ballard. President Joseph Fielding Smith's "Message" in the first issue begins with grandfatherly reminiscences of his own youth but adroitly eases into the theme of modesty in dress. Enjoining "proper deportment and modesty at all times," he exhorted his readers not to become wayward "daughters of

Zion.''[10] Prefaced by consistently praising letters to the editor, *The New Era* offers its readers announcements of enough activities and mission opportunities to keep any potential for waywardness entirely occupied in church-oriented business. It is a glossy, full-color magazine with excellent photography and graphic design. Each fifty-page issue boasts either a ''Mormonad'' or ''Mormonisms'': poster art with a gospel message. Two memorable examples are ''Teaching the gospel without love is like serving soup with a fork'' (September 1980) and ''Living the gospel is like brushing your teeth: trying to do it all on Sunday just doesn't work. It's an every-day thing'' (July 1981). Proselytizing vigor and example are still prominent features; even as tourists, Mormons pass the word (''Train to Newcastle,'' July 1981). Reminders of the key events in the Latter-day Saints story continue to appear as well, but on the occasion of the church's sesquicentennial, the article ''Fair-Minded Gentiles'' (September 1980) transcends the usual account of mobbings and murders to include honorable mention of helpful nonmembers—among them, surprisingly, Charles Dickens. *The New Era* is starting to draw on many non-Mormon sources, it seems: the July 1981 issue contains a poem by Gerard Manley Hopkins.

From George Cannon of *The Juvenile Instructor* to Russell Ballard of *The New Era*, the edifying content of Mormon publications for the young has undergone considerable revision to suit the world as it is. Careful honing of journalistic techniques has slowly nudged Latter-day Saints publications away from the dinning of history and doctrine, of chapter and verse, and has ushered in the era of the pictorial narrative showing ''Saints'' in action.

Notes

1. A biography of Cannon written by his son Joseph, Jr., appeared in *The Instructor* from January 1944 to November 1945. See also *The Juvenile Instructor* 35 (January 15, 1900); Wendell J. Ashton, *Voice in the West: Biography of a Pioneer Newspaper* (New York: Duell, Sloan & Pearce, 1950), 148-50, 152-53.

2. Leonard J. Arrington and Davis Bitton, *The Mormon Experience: A History of the Latter-day Saints* (New York: Knopf, 1979), pp. 269-70.

3. As quoted by Monte Burr McLaws, *Spokesman for the Kingdom: Early Mormon Journalism and the Deseret News, 1830-1898* (Provo, Utah: Brigham Young University Press, 1977), 103.

4. As quoted from *The Deseret News*, January 7, 1879, by McLaws, *Spokesman*, p. 102.

5. *The Juvenile Instructor* 1(November 1, 1866).

6. Ibid.

7. Ibid., 64 (January 1929), 10.

8. Ibid., 65 (January 1930), 3-4.

9. Ibid.

10. *The New Era* 1 (January 1971).

Information Sources

BIBLIOGRAPHY

Leonard J. Arrington and Davis Bitton, *The Mormon Experience: A History of the Latter-day Saints* (New York: Knopf, 1979); Wendell J. Ashton, *Voice in the West:*

Biography of a Pioneer Newspaper (New York: Duell, Sloan & Pearce, 1950); Chad J. Flake, ed., *A Mormon Bibliography, 1830-1930* (Salt Lake City, Utah: University of Utah Press, 1978); Monte Burr McLaws, *Spokesman for the Kingdom: Early Mormon Journalism and the Deseret News, 1830-1898* (Provo, Utah: Brigham Young University Press, 1977); Frank Luther Mott, *A History of American Magazines* (Cambridge: Harvard University Press, 1938-1968); Joseph Smith, Jr., trans., *The Book of Mormon: An Account Written by the Hand of Mormon upon Plates Taken from the Plates of Nephi* (Salt Lake City, Utah: The Church of Jesus Christ of Latter-day Saints, 1977).

INDEX SOURCES

Chad J. Flake, ed., *A Mormon Bibliography, 1830-1930: Books, Pamphlets, and Broadsides Relating to the First Century of Mormonism* (Salt Lake City, Utah: University of Utah Press, 1978).

LOCATION SOURCES

Bound volumes are in Henry E. Huntington Library, San Marino, Calif.; Yale University, New Haven, Conn.; Harvard University, Cambridge, Mass.; Princeton University, Princeton, N.J.; Utah State Historical Society, Salt Lake City, Utah; Utah State University, Logan, Utah; Brigham Young University, Provo, Utah; Church Historical Department, Church of Jesus Christ of Latter-day Saints, Salt Lake City, Utah.

Publication History

MAGAZINE TITLE AND TITLE CHANGES
The Juvenile Instructor (1866-1929); *The Instructor* (1930-1970); *The New Era* (1971-).
VOLUME AND ISSUE DATA
The Juvenile Instructor (vol. 1, no. 1-vol. 41, no. 24; vol. 42, no. 1-vol. 63, no. 12); *The Instructor* (vol. 64, no. 1-vol. 105, no. 12); *The New Era* (vol. 1, no. 1-).
PUBLISHER AND PLACE OF PUBLICATION
Deseret Sunday School Union: Salt Lake City, Utah (1866-1970); Corporation of the President of The Church of Jesus Christ of Latter-Day Saints, Salt Lake City, Utah (1970-).
EDITOR
The Juvenile Instructor: George Q. Cannon (1866-April 1901); Lorenzo Snow (May 1901-October 1901); Joseph F. Smith (November 1901-November 1918); Heber J. Grant (December 1918-1929). *The Instructor*: Heber J. Grant (1930-June 1945); George Albert Smith (July 1945-April 1951); Milton Bennion (July 1945-December 1949); George R. Hill (January 1950-September 1951); David O. McKay (May 1951-December 1970). *The New Era*: Doyle L. Green (January 1971-March 1976); Dean L. Larsen (April 1976-July 1978); James E. Faust (August 1978-March 1979); M. Russell Ballard (April 1979-).

Patricia Demers

THE JUVENILE MAGAZINE

During the nineteenth century at least four American children's periodicals bore the title *Juvenile Magazine*. The earliest of them was begun in Philadelphia by Arthur Donaldson, a teacher whose concern over the lack of schooling open to the city's black children led him to found a school of his own. *The Juvenile Magazine* was designed to supplement the textbooks and lessons used in his school, to publicize his efforts and his educational philosophy, and to provide a forum for condemning slavery, for describing the achievements of blacks, and for arguing the need to educate black children.

The first issue of Donaldson's periodical appeared in May 1811, with a subtitle calculated to appeal to those adults who would be the buyers (if not the consumers) of his new venture: *The Juvenile Magazine, Consisting of Religious, Moral and Entertaining Pieces in Prose and Verse. Original and Selected. Designed Principally for the Religious Improvement, Moral Instruction, and Literary Aid of Youth; and Particularly Calculated for Schools*. Presenting himself as a teacher with several years experience, Donaldson disavowed membership in any religious society, thus obliquely asserting that *The Juvenile Magazine* would be nonsectarian. That it would be religious was clear from the subtitle. That it would be unobjectionably Christian was equally clear from Donaldson's choice of a first selection, "Christ's Sermon on the Mount." This was followed by poems by Edward Young and William Cowper, including the former's "Indignant Sentiments on National Prejudices and Hatred; and on Slavery" and the latter's "Christian Freedom." In the first issue of *The Juvenile Magazine* Donaldson included a biographical sketch of Benjamin Banneker, "The African Astronomer and Mathematician," and closed the thirty-six-page issue with the powerful "Complaint of an African Woman for the Loss of Her Husband." There was strong meat in this first issue of *The Juvenile Magazine* and none of the "amusements" typically found in later miscellanies: no illustrations, puzzles, conundrums, and the like, which usually appeared in even the most serious children's periodicals.

In the first issue Donaldson promised a title and general index at the end of six months, but he found it necessary to suspend publication after the second number and did not resume *The Juvenile Magazine* until July (or, as he styled it, "Seventh Month") 1813. The fourth and final issue appeared the following month, August 1813.

When he resumed publication, Donaldson doubled the length of his periodical to seventy-two pages. This issue contains an account of his school, the demands of which, particularly for operating money, almost certainly account for his decision to suspend publication in 1811. In addition to describing his school, he listed the names of his students and provided a census of schools for black children in Philadelphia and a list of black churches in the city. Roughly one-third of this issue amounts to publicity for his efforts on behalf of unschooled black children and a thinly disguised plea for money so that he might add grammar, geography, and "some higher branches of learning," to the basic instruction offered in reading, writing, and "ciphering." The remainder of the issue is devoted, in roughly equal parts, to an outline of arithmetic and historical, biographical, and literary selections about Africa and slavery: a brief history of

Africa, a biographical sketch of Anthony Benezet, excerpts from John Woolman's "Reflections on Holding Slaves," and a stirring poem "The Negro's
Complaint," which concludes with the lines: "Slaves of gold! whose sordid
dealings/Tarnish all your boasted powers,/Prove that you have human feel-
ings/Ere you proudly question ours."[1]

Donaldson devoted the fourth and, as it turned out, final issue of *The Juvenile
Magazine* entirely to historical, biographical, and literary selections, including
sketches of John Woolman and the poet Phyllis Wheatley, a chronology of slavery
in the New World, and "A Family Conversation on the Slavery of the Negro,"
cast in conventional dialog form; he concluded with an account of the character
of Christ ("the wisest and most virtuous person that ever appeared in the world")
and advice on living a holy life by the archbishop of Cambray.[2] With that,
Donaldson let *The Juvenile Magazine* fall silent. That same year he separately
published *Education for People of Color* and followed this a year later with the
textbook *The Orthographer*, which contained 8,000 words, 5,000 names from
Scripture, and reading lessons. Donaldson's only other publication appears to
have been the broadside "To the Tories," which appeared in Philadelphia in
1776 on the eve of the Revolution. It is tempting, although the evidence is
slender, to imagine Donaldson as an ardent republican whose youthful commitment to Enlightenment ideals of liberty and education found expression a
generation later in revulsion at the fruits of slavery: ignorance, prejudice, and
rejection.

Notes

1. *The Juvenile Magazine* 1 (July 1813), 72.
2. Ibid., 1 (August 1813), 40.

Information Sources

BIBLIOGRAPHY
Jayne K. Kribbs, *An Annotated Bibliography of American Literary Periodicals, 1741-
     1850* (Boston: G. K. Hall, 1977).
INDEX SOURCES
None.
LOCATION SOURCES
Boston Public Library; Historical Society of Pennsylvania, Philadelphia. Available on
     microfilm in the American Periodical Series, University Microfilms International,
     Ann Arbor, Mich.

Publication History

MAGAZINE TITLE AND TITLE CHANGES
The Juvenile Magazine (May-June 1811; July-August 1813).
VOLUME AND ISSUE DATA
The Juvenile Magazine (vol. 1, no. 1-vol. 1, no. 4).
PUBLISHER AND PLACE OF PUBLICATION
Arthur Donaldson, Philadelphia (May-June 1811; July-August 1813)

EDITOR
Arthur Donaldson (May-June 1811; July-August 1813).

R. Gordon Kelly

THE JUVENILE MISCELLANY: FOR THE INSTRUCTION
AND AMUSEMENT OF YOUTH

As the number of women's magazines grew in the Federalist period, so did the number of magazines for children. As the *Mirror* remarked in 1829, "The mania for periodicals has extended itself to children."[1] Cornelia Meigs has called *The Juvenile Miscellany* "the first children's magazine in America that was (in spite of its name) really childlike."[2] One of the best-known children's periodicals of its time, it was edited by Lydia Maria Child, who drew to its pages a number of prominent writers including Lydia Sigourney, Hannah Gould, and Sarah Josepha Hale. The predominance of women writers is significant. The periodical was by no means directed only toward girls; in fact, its intended audience was wide. But women authors, especially in the Northeast, were becoming more numerous, probably because writing was one of the few respectable professions for women who needed to work. Women writers gradually came to dominate both children's fiction and children's periodicals. Lydia Maria Child was a typical author of her time; she wrote to earn a living, as well as taught school, and turned to children's writing only after having completed two historical novels for adults, *Hobomok* (1824-1825) and *The Rebels; or Boston Before the Revolution* (1825). Her views on children and their education, formulated during her teaching at a private school in Watertown, Massachusetts, from 1825 to 1828, were also typical, for she was a thoroughgoing Rousseauist. She believed strongly in the power of rational discussions with children about behavior and education. Demonstrating to them the intricacies of science, nature, and social conduct would point inescapably to the glory and benevolence of God in creating and ordering his universe.

The Juvenile Miscellany was founded by Child, who was then Miss Francis, as a bimonthly publication. As its title implies, it was filled with a wide variety of writing of children—poetry, short stories, dialogues, lessons on botany, geography, puzzles, and a smattering of pictures. Child's overriding vision for the *Miscellany* was enunciated in the journal's opening number in her "Address to the Young":

I seldom meet a little girl, even in the crowded streets of Boston, without thinking with anxious tenderness, concerning her education, her temper, and her principles....If I am able to convince you, that you *can* do, whatever you *try* to do, in the acquisition of learning; if I can lead you to examine your own hearts, and pray to your Heavenly Father, to remove from thence whatsoever is evil, I shall be very happy. Believe then, one who loves you much—If you will *persevere*; if you will be *attentive*; if you will learn to *think for yourselves*; you can overcome all obstacles in the path of knowledge; and if you really *wish* to be good, there is a kind Parent, in the heavens, who will help you in every endeavor you make, to be virtuous and religious.[3]

The point of view expressed here is not controversial; in fact, it was accepted childrearing practice by most middle-class families in the Northeast, whose children were the primary audience for the *Miscellany*. There is no evidence that the *Miscellany* had much circulation outside of Boston. Many of the stories feature Boston settings, and although one "C. G."—Caroline Howard Gilman— was a regular contributor with an address of Charlestown, South Carolina, to her by-line, she had recently moved from Boston; most of the other contributors came from New England. There are many historical sketches and biographies in the *Miscellany* that concentrate on the history of New England and its heroes. Although in later years the *Miscellany* featured a regular travel column, describing the anonymous contributor's trips to Baltimore, New York, and other East Coast cities, Boston and New England remained the *Miscellany's* primary setting.

Child's ideas of childrearing were consistent with those expressed, both in essay and in fiction, by the more famous British Rousseauists Maria Edgeworth, Letitia Barbauld, Hannah More, and Thomas Day. Much of the fiction in the *Miscellany* closely resembles that of Edgeworth, More, and Day—the characters are children, either clearly well behaved, industrious, charitable, and inquisitive or naughty but capable of seeing the error of their ways through rational discussion with an all-wise adult who never loses her temper and nearly always knows the answer to any question posed by the children. In the *Miscellany*, the adult is almost never a man; there are aunts and mothers and anonymous speakers but rarely fathers and uncles. This emphasis on female nurture is a by-product both of the industrial revolution, which took men away from their families to work, leaving the children with female caretakers, and of the sentimentalization of the mother's role in the romantic and Victorian periods, which made her the proprietress and disseminator of all higher feelings of religion, sensibility, and morality. No doubt the domination of the teaching of and writing for children by women also contributed to the surfeit of female paragons in the pages of the *Miscellany*.

The *Miscellany* appeared at a time when the field of children's literature was beginning to come to the attention of writers in America. Until the 1820s most of the literature read by American children was imported from England, where more attention had been given to children's reading by the Rousseauists and where writers of children's literature flourished financially. Their works were widely imported and accepted by the American juvenile reading public. But although their ideas were accepted, their British settings and dialects were not. As the Revolutionary War and the War of 1812 gradually faded into history and the United States began to prosper during an era of peace, Americans began to turn, with their increased leisure time and discretionary income, to the question of what American children should read. There was money to buy books, and increasing numbers of literate children to read them, especially in the Northeast, where an emphasis on literacy was one of the most visible legacies of the Puritans. Having fought two wars to establish their independence from England, Americans did not want their children brought up on English reading. With the first fifty years of independence celebrated in 1826, Americans were beginning to develop a sense of their own history and the worthiness of their own language as a vehicle for serious literary expression, serious enough, in fact, to educate American children.[4]

As Anne Scott MacLeod has pointed out, Americans of the 1820s took child nurture very seriously, because the future of the Republic rested with children.[4] Social conditions were changing rapidly with the industrial revolution and continued immigration from Europe. The Republic was an experiment; and raising children to think and speak for themselves was a new idea. No one, including the Americans who were raising the children, knew how or if the experiment would succeed. The emphasis on controlling children, either by punishment or by rational discussion, does not indicate that the children of the time really behaved that way, but rather that parents and educators were particularly worried about children who, for all of their independence, were particularly unruly, as many foreign commentators were quick to note. *The Juvenile Miscellany* dramatized in its articles the many pitfalls of overly independent thinking and action. Independent thinkers had to be taught to think the right way if the Republic and the ideals of their parents were to survive in the fashion the older generation desired. Independence was acceptable as long as it did not degenerate into chaos and anarchy. The exchanges between adults and children in the *Miscellany* clearly embody the idea of parental control: adults always know best, and the most commendable children obediently follow their advice.

The *Miscellany* featured a number of these adult voices, whether in omniscient narration or dialogue between adults and children, the dialogue being a favorite form in the journal. The *Miscellany* generally opened with a serialized story, realistic fiction nearly always about a good child or children and dealing with a variety of their mishaps, whether in the form of other children who are not so well behaved or in natural and domestic disasters. Then followed, at least early in the *Miscellany's* history, a biographical sketch of a notable contemporary or historical figure: Captain John Smith (May 1827), Baron von Steuben (September 1827), and Columbus (March 1828). There were poems, some companion pieces that continued from one issue to the next, such as "Letter from Summer to Winter" (September 1826) about Summer's excellencies, answered by Winter in the next issue (November 1826). There were also some regular columns, such as a dialogue between James and Aunt Maria about various natural phenomena, for example, "The Effects of Oil upon Water" (March 1828) and "Paper and Printing" (July 1828). The dialogue sometimes became technical when investigating scientific phenomena, but the child who read the *Miscellany* was spared no detail. Eliza and her mother were featured in another dialogue series about proper behavior, whether in the conduct of Eliza's schoolwork or her behavior in company. There were original fables, such as "The Butterfly and the Snail," the moral of which is that "people who have great talents were sometimes apt to fly from one thing to another,—and therefore do not accomplish much; but patience and perseverence were always successful."[5] There were also stories or essays about virtues, for example, "Filial Obedience" (January 1828) and "Self-knowledge" (November 1826). Essays and sketches about historical occurrences, monuments, and natural phenomena also appeared. Although the stories and sketches were probably written by Americans, it is difficult to determine authors' identities since few contributions were signed, although some were initialed. Lydia Sigourney contributed sketches about the asylum for the deaf in her home city of Hartford, Connecticut, and Hannah Gould's contributions, mostly sentimental poems, were also signed. But there is little distinctly American about the contributions; they resemble strongly the works of the British Rousseauists. In the later issues of Child's editorship were Scripture studies, emphasizing the religious basis of the *Miscellany*. Always there were puzzles at the end of a number, answered in the puzzle column at the end of the next issue.

The contents of the issues were varied, as was the audience for which the *Miscellany* was arranged. Some stories were for very young children, some for teenagers, and there were stories and sketches of interest to both sexes as well as to each individually. Although there were always some illustrations, at least one as the frontispiece for every issue, they were neither abundant nor distinguished in technique.

In 1833 Child published her essay "An Appeal in Favor of That Class of Americans Called Africans," in which she supported the abolition of slavery. It was a courageous gesture, for public sentiment opposed her. Subscriptions fell off, and Child was forced to abandon the publication of the *Miscellany*. She bid her child readers farewell in the August 1834 issue: "May God bless you, my young friends, and impress deeply upon your hearts that all true excellence and happiness consist in living for *others*, not for *yourselves*."[6] In September, 1834 Sarah Josepha Hale, later the editor of the popular *Godey's Lady's Book*, took over the editorship of the *Miscellany*, promising to bring it out monthly (although at half the length of the former bimonthly issues) and with more pictures, three instead of the former two.

The format and quality did not differ as much as Hale claimed; there were still the morally improving dialogues, sentimental poems, and informational articles. Hale added a regular column at the end of each issue called "The Editor's Table," describing the derivation of each month's name and including a list and description of recommended books for the readers. Frequently, an excerpt from a new book was included in the issue; it would seem that such a method of advertising also made a ready source of articles for the *Miscellany*. Contributors included Felicia Hemans, Hale herself, Emma Willard, Mary Howitt, and a number of other authors identified only by initials. Hale issued the

Miscellany on a monthly basis until March 1836, when the month's issue was missed due to a delay in printing. In April Hale promised a new bimonthly schedule, with twice as many pages, but her plans never materialized; and the *Miscellany's* publication terminated with the April issue.

Notes

1. Cited in Frank Luther Mott, *A History of American Magazines* (Cambridge: Harvard University Press, 1838-1968), 1:492.

2. Cornelia Meigs et al., *A Critical History of Children's Literature* (New York: Macmillan, 1953), 275.

3. *The Juvenile Miscellany* 1 (September 1826), iii-iv.

4. Anne Scott MacLeod, *A Moral Tale* (Hamden, Conn.: Archon Books, 1975), 32-37.

5. *The Juvenile Miscellany* 2 (September 1827), 94.

6. Ibid., 6 (August 1834), 323.

Information Sources

BIBLIOGRAPHY

Alice M. Jordan, " 'The Juvenile Miscellany, and Its Literary Ladies," in *From Rollo to Tom Sawyer and Other Papers* (Boston: Horn Book, 1948), 46-60; Carolyn L. Karcher, "Lydia Maria Child and the Juvenile Miscellany," in *Research About Nineteenth-Century Children and Books*, ed. Selma K. Richardson (Urbana-Champaign, Ill.: University of Illinois Graduate School of Library Sciences, 1980), 67-84.

LOCATION SOURCES

Widely scattered holdings in major public libraries; vols. 1-3 are available on microform in the American Periodicals Series, University Microfilms International, Ann Arbor, Mich.

Publication History

MAGAZINE AND TITLE CHANGES

The Juvenile Miscellany: For the Instruction and Amusement of Youth (September 1826-March 1936).

VOLUME AND ISSUE DATA

The Juvenile Miscellany (vol. 1-4, n.s. vol. 1-6; series 3, vol. 1-6; series 4, vol. 1-4).

PUBLISHER AND PLACE OF PUBLICATION

John Putnam, Boston (1826-1827); John Putnam and Waite, Green, and Company, Boston (1827-1828); Putnam and Hunt, Boston (1828-1831); Carter and Hendee, Boston (1831-1834); E. R. Broaders, Boston (1834-1836).

EDITOR

Lydia Maria Francis Child (1826-1834); Sarah Josepha Hale (1834-1836).

Ruth K. MacDonald

THE JUVENILE PORT-FOLIO AND LITERARY MISCELLANY

When the first issue of *The Juvenile Port-Folio and Literary Miscellany* appeared in Philadelphia on October 17, 1812, its editor, Thomas G. Condie, was only fourteen yers old. There were other adolescents among the editors of early American juvenile periodicals, but Condie was, from the first, remarkably professional in his management of the publication.[1] Through the early issues of the magazine, he was helped by his father, an established bookbinder, bookseller, and inkmaker who was responsible for "the publishing or pecuniary department" of *The Juvenile Port-Folio* and may have advised his son in other aspects of the undertaking. In his address "To the Readers of the Juvenile Port-Folio" at the end of volume 2, Condie recorded his father's death of a "severe and lingering *Pulmonary Consumption*" and spoke of the "irreparable loss" of "an indulgent parent; to whose judicious observations, more than the Editor's own judgment, the public are [*sic*] indebted for the manifold improvements the work has undergone since its commencement."[2]

His father's guidance may have helped Condie anticipate some economic hazards of publishing and so prolonged the life of his periodical. Condie was aware of the problems caused by a shifting subscription list. He announced in the first issue of *The Juvenile Port-Folio* that the price was "only Twelve and a Half Cents per month, payable in advance" but that "No subscription will be received for less than three months."[3] He took advantage of the opportunity to bind annual volumes, offering to have them "Neatly stitched in boards" or "Half bound, titled and fileted with gold" or with "red morocco backs," each with an appropriate charge. A list of subscribers was printed at the end of each volume. During his first year it grew from 300 to more than 600. Condie anticipated a further increase to 700 for the first number of the second volume, but his hopes were not fulfilled; in the second year his list decreased to less than 500 subscribers. In the two following years there were even fewer subscribers, and by 1816, when Condie closed *The Juvenile Port-Folio*, there were only 432 subscribers.[4] The young editor blamed this decline upon the unfavorable economic conditions that prevailed throughout the War of 1812. Despite the "embarrassed state of money concerns" and the "general stagnation of trade," which he noted in the summary note to his readers at the conclusion of *The Juvenile Port-Folio*, the youthful Condie succeeded in producing 208 weekly numbers before converting the periodical into its successor *The Parlour Companion*.[5]

Early as he was, Condie was not alone in the field of juvenile publishing. From the first issue of *The Juvenile Port-Folio* until its last, there were "at least three separate juvenile titles being circulated concurrently" in the United States.[6] It is noteworthy that Condie brought out more issues of his publication than did any of his contemporaries.[7]

Like many later writers and editors for the juvenile market, Condie thought that fiction for young people should be selected with clear moral and intellectual standards in mind. In his opening statement, "To the Juvenile Public," he assured his readers (and their parents) that the material in his periodical would be selected "with particular attention to those subjects, that are adapted to the improvement, edification, and rational amusement of youth." He added that "a preference would be given to those pieces, which are characterized by elegance of expression, chastity of thought, and value of information."[8] At the beginning of his second year he reiterated his intention "to inculcate sound morality;—to dispel the mist of prejudice and ignorance;—to polish and refine the manners;—to promote rational cheerfulness and good humour;—to advance the blessings of social life;—to instruct the rising generation in the knowledge of themselves, and the world;—in a word, to blend agreeable amusement with useful instruction."[9] Like later editors in the juvenile field, Condie attempted to establish a personal relationship with his readers and rejoiced that "liberal and ingenious youth, of both sexes" deemed the publication "their peculiar property" and took "a very great interest in its success."[10] The age of Condie's readers is difficult to determine, since there was at the time no conventional distinction between infancy, childhood, and adolescence: the term *child* or *juvenile* might cover all three. To judge from materials in the periodical, however, it seems likely that the "youth" Condie addressed were in their teens and mature enough to be treated, perhaps jestingly, as adults: "The Ladies," he wrote, might find *The Juvenile Port-Folio* "an entertaining companion, studious of their favour, by courtly manners and valuable information," and "the Gentlemen" would "find in it a manly and correct conduct."[11]

Condie's title naturally invited comparison with one of the best-known periodicals of the time, *The Port-Folio* by Oliver Oldschool (Joseph Dennie), which was established in Philadelphia in 1806. Dennie was a flamboyant figure whose personal fame might well have inspired a young journalist. However, the form of *The Juvenile Port-Folio* resembles that of *The Port-Folio* after 1812, when political articles, of the kind for which Dennie was known, were eliminated. Both Condie's weekly and *The Port-Folio* were literary miscellanies, containing fiction, moral and philosophical essays, items of historical interest, statements of useful knowledge, anecdotes, and a selection of poetry. In general, both publications reflected admiration for the urbane style of the later eighteenth century; the English essayists, especially Johnson; classicism; rationalism; and sentimentalism in fiction.

On the masthead of *The Juvenile Port-Folio* there is a figure of a woman in neoclassic dress, perhaps a muse, wound in a billowing scarf on which is printed "A lasting wreath of various hue,—deck'd with each fragrant flower." The motto suggests Condie's intention to publish a varied collection or compendium of literary selections. Each issue, composed of four pages printed in double columns, begins with a long piece of fiction, which might appear in serial form through several numbers. These stories, comprising nearly half of each issue, are conventionally sentimental. Their tone is captured in titles such as "The Old Soldier: An Affecting Narrative" (October 17, 1812), "Virtue in Distress" (October 31, 1812), or "The Pensive Mendicant" (March 5, 1814). They employ familiar plots, featuring seduction and heartbreak, injustice, misfortune, and misunderstanding: tears flow, pledged lovers are separated, and disaster hovers. Morality abounds, and, at length, selfishness, cruelty, and injustice are punished. Neither sophistication, restraint, nor originality characterizes Condie's major fictional selections. At the end of the first year, the editor noted that the narratives were "of too pathetic, serious and moral nature."[12] However, no greater diversity of tone appeared in later fictional selections, although the "specifically stated moral at the conclusion of each tale" was eliminated.[13]

In every issue the long fictional selection is followed by a page or more of miscellaneous short pieces, some about useful factual subjects, such as "The Manufacture of Paper" (October 31, 1812); some concerned with moral reflections on subjects like "Punctuality," "Bets and Oaths" (both March 13, 1813), and "Sentiment and Feeling" (September 17, 1814). This section might include anecdotes, historical notes, jokes, and other short observations, but invariably the items represent a variety of style and tone. In the June 18, 1814, issue, for example, there is ironic wit in the item "Modern Manners," but a companion piece, "Economy," is soberly instructive. The design of *The Juvenile Port-Folio* calls for such heterogeneity, since it aimed to be a collection of interesting, amusing, and improving observations. In the first two volumes special sections headed "Leisure Hours," "Laconicks," "Court of Honour," "On Education," and "Risibles" appeared. "Gleanings" included even shorter items that Condie described as "Uncollected, miscellaneous pieces and sentences" that "from their brevity cannot well be inserted under separate heads."[14] Short or long, however, the items Condie chose were designed to instruct, amuse, and improve, to please a cultivated reader, and to reflect various interests and moods.

The final page of each four-page issue was invariably devoted to verse. Once again, Condie presented a varied selection. All of the poems are short, and in any week several themes and styles were represented. There is often a sentimental verse and a witty or satiric one. Patriotic items appear regularly, as well as an annual ode to George Washington. Clearly, in this department as in other sections of the weekly, Condie intended to assemble an amusing collection that might appeal to various tastes, interests, and moods in his readers.

Some of the selections Condie printed are attributed to well-known authors, among them Robert Burns, Charles James Fox, Samuel Johnson, and Thomas Paine. Others are signed with initials or pseudonyms, the most frequent of them being "C," "Equitus," and "Virtuoso."[15] Condie's editorial comments indicate that many of the items he printed were contributed by subscribers, and that some of them were original pieces by the "Literary Youth" he had invited to communicate with him (October 17, 1812). He was, however, alert to the temptations of plagiarism and therefore left many items unsigned. At the end of volume 1 he stated that among the "many hints for improvement" of *The Juvenile Port-Folio* were the "early and frequent" requests that the editor identify the authors of all pieces submitted as original. Condie refused, noting that printing the names "would lead his readers into great error, as at least *three fourths* of what is communicated to him as original, are [sic] copied from other works." Other pieces, he added, that "pass for original...are copied from European publications, but...adapted to the country (*Americanized*)." Such reworking he called "a species of literary cobbling."[16]

Overall, Condie's selections, although conventional, provide an amusing variety reflecting a lively journalistic taste and catholic interests. Despite the loss of subscribers in the second year of *The Juvenile Port-Folio*, Condie seems to have had no difficulty holding a faithful core of readers. His decision to convert his publication into *The Parlour Companion* does not seem to have grown from a desire to change the publication radically. Indeed, Condie assured his readers that he would retain the established format and not increase his periodical in either "bulk or price." The new title may have been inspired by Condie's own maturity and consequent desire to be known as the editor of a domestic, rather than a juvenile, publication. "Many a 'region of thought,' " he wrote, closing *The Juvenile Port-Folio*, "remains still unexplored:—The changeful scenes of Fashion, Opinion, and Manners, will always present subjects for their speculation. The image of Error, as discordant as that of Nebuchanessar, still rears its imposing front. Vice still employs her seduction; and though many a valorous band has fought against the influence of prejudice, it still remains bold and unvanquished."[17]

Notes

1. Edwin Charles Strohecker, "American Juvenile Literary Periodicals, 1789-1826" (Ph.D. diss., University of Michigan, 1969), 28.
2. *The Juvenile Port-Folio and Literary Miscellany* I, 4.
3. Ibid., 1 (October 17, 1812), 1.
4. Strohecker, "American Juvenile Literary Periodicals," pp. 150-51.
5. "To the Readers of the Juvenile Port-Folio," *The Juvenile Port-Folio and Literary Miscellany*, 4. Condie's later life and career is not known. I am indebted to my colleague Professor Phyllis Moe for information that *The Philadelphia Directory and Stranger's Guide* for 1825 (Philadelphia: Thomas Wilson, April 1825) lists Thomas G. Condie as an attorney-at-law, residing at 193 Lombard Street with David F. Condie, physician (presumably his brother). The two Condies shared a residence until 1829, when David moved to 138 Catherine Street and Thomas resided at 196 South Fifth Street. Although David Condie continued to live in Philadelphia for many years, Thomas Condie's name disappeared from the city directories after 1833 (see Desilver's *Philadelphia Directory and Stranger's Guide* for 1833 for the final entry).
6. "American Juvenile Literary Periodicals," Strohecker, p. 13.
7. Ibid., p. 15.
8. *The Juvenile Port-Folio and Literary Miscellany* 1 (October 17, 1812), 1.
9. Ibid., 2 (January 8, 1814), 1.
10. Ibid.
11. Ibid., 1 (October 17, 1812), 1.
12. "To the Readers of the Juvenile Port-Folio," ibid., I, 4.
13. "American Juvenile Literary Periodicals," Strohecker, p. 142.
14. *The Juvenile Port-Folio and Literary Miscellany* 1 (February 13, 1813), 71.
15. A list of all signed articles in *The Juvenile Port-Folio* appears in Strohecker, "American Juvenile Literary Periodicals," pp. 288-94.
16. "To the Readers of the Juvenile Port-Folio," ibid.," I, 4.
17. Ibid., IV, 4.

Information Sources

BIBLIOGRAPHY

Frank Luther Mott, *A History of American Magazines*, 5 vols. (Cambridge: Harvard University Press, 1938-1968); Albert H. Smyth, *The Philadelphia Magazines and Their Contributors, 1741-1850* (Philadelphia: Robert M. Lindsay, 1892); Edwin Charles Strohecker, ''American Juvenile Literary Periodicals, 1789-1826'' (Ph.D. diss. University of Michigan, 1969).

INDEX SOURCES

None.

LOCATION SOURCES

American Antiquarian Society, Worcester, Mass. Vols. 1-4 are available on microfilm in the American Periodical Series, University Microfilms International, Ann Arbor, Mich.

Publication History

MAGAZINE TITLE AND TITLE CHANGES

The Juvenile Port-Folio and Literary Miscellany (1812-1816)

VOLUME AND ISSUE DATA

The Juvenile Port-Folio and Literary Miscellany (vol. 1, no. 1-vol. 4, no. 49).

PUBLISHER AND PLACE OF PUBLICATION

Thomas G. Condie, Jr. Printed by John Bioren, Philadelphia (1812-1816).

EDITOR

Thomas G. Condie, Jr. (1812-1816).

Jane Benardete

K

KEEPING POSTED

The first American Jewish children's magazines began publication in the last decades of the nineteenth century.[1] They were preoccupied with conscience and suffered to a certain extent from cultural lag. They had more in common with the early catechistic tracts and the overtly moralistic Christian Sunday School Movement periodicals than they did with the excellent secular children's magazines that were their own contemporaries. The earliest magazine was *Young Israel*, which first appeared in 1871. *The Sabbath Visitor* appeared a few years later and continued for some twenty-five years. *Helpful Thoughts* and its successor, *The Jewish Home*, were great improvements but still far from models of literary sophistication or examples of sensitivity to children's reading interests and needs.

The only Jewish children's magazine of significance in the early decades of the twentieth century was *The Young Judaean*,* which began publication in 1910. It was, essentially, the ambitious house organ of National Young Judaea, a Zionist youth organization. *The Young Judaean* was bursting with energy, innovative techniques, and a sense of purpose, making it very exciting—and a radical improvement in the Jewish children's magazine field.[2]

In 1940 *World Over** was begun under the sponsorship of the Jewish Education Committee of New York and edited for many years by Ezekiel Schloss and Morris Epstein. Despite its limitations, *World Over* was for a long time an excellent magazine, unquestionably the best Jewish children's periodical in the United States and the "standard" in the American Jewish children's magazine field.[3]

In October 1953 *Growing Up* began publication. It was the children's magazine of the American Council for Judaism, although its sponsorship was never formally indicated or officially acknowledged.[4] Nor were the names of an editor or Editorial Board published for the first few years. The magazine was begun because some Reform congregations found *World Over* too Zionistic in orientation (and *The Young Judaean* was certainly not a logical alternative). A general concern for ethics and moral education, consistent with the goals of the American Council for Judaism, dictated the contents of the periodical.

Two years later the first issue of *Keeping Posted: A Jewish News Bulletin for Young People* appeared. The new magazine was a project of the Commission on Jewish Education of the Union of American Hebrew Congregations (UAHC) and the Central Conference of American Rabbis (CCAR), the chief lay and rabbinic organizations of the Reform movement in America. *Keeping Posted* was probably, in its turn, a response to the existence (and therefore potential influence) of *Growing Up*. Certainly, the availability of a magazine published by the "official" movement siphoned off some of the less ardent subscribers to *Growing Up* and may have been largely responsible for that periodical's short life.[5] *Keeping Posted* was also designed to appeal to an audience older than *World Over's* readership, so the two were never really in competition.

The earliest issues of *Keeping Posted* focused largely on current events and the transmission of news items of Jewish interest to youngsters in the religious schools of Reform Jewish congregations around the country. From the beginning it was intended as an unabashed educational tool designed to supplement the classroom learning of seventh- to tenth-grade students. Although attempts were made periodically to encourage individual subscriptions, the magazine has been for the most part ordered and distributed through religious schools.

In its first three years of existence, *Keeping Posted* was prepared by Rabbi Samuel M. Silver, who was at that time public relations director for the UAHC. The masthead lists an Editorial Committee. One of the names is that of Rabbi Eugene B. Borowitz, who became involved in the preparation of *Keeping Posted* shortly after he became Director of Education for the Union in 1957. His influence was quickly evident. With the beginning of volume 4 (October 1958), Borowitz assumed the editorship of the magazine. There was no longer an Editorial Committee, but the publication now had a managing editor, Kathleen J. Schwarzschild, who presumably worked out of her own home, since all editorial correspondence was to be directed to her in care of an address in Jackson Heights, New York. Under Borowitz, *Keeping Posted* developed the format, style, and tone that characterized it for many years. As an educator, Reform rabbi, and theologian, Borowitz was able to fuse different disciplines and areas of interest in the evolution of the magazine.[6]

Volume 5 (October 1958-May 1959) names Edith Brodsky as managing editor. *Keeping Posted* had become a more substantial magazine, and the managing editor received mail at the magazine's office in the UAHC building in Manhattan. A year later Brodsky's title was changed to editor, with Borowitz listed as editor-in-chief. When Borowitz left to assume a position on the faculty of the Hebrew Union College-Jewish Institute of Religion (HUC-JIR), the rabbinical school of the Reform movement, Edith Brodsky—then Mrs. Maurice Samuel—became sole editor. She remained in charge of *Keeping Posted* until 1977 and was chiefly responsible for its growth, prestige, and progressive changes of direction over the years. Samuel's primary professional activity was the magazine. It flourished under her very able editorship.

When she left *Keeping Posted* in 1977 to devote her energies to adult Jewish education,[7] Aron Hirt-Manheimer became editor. He was already associated with the Union as editor of *Reform Judaism*, a monthly newspaper whose circulation includes all members of Reform congregations. Hirt-Manheimer has continued the standard of excellence established by Eugene Borowitz and Edith Samuel. *Keeping Posted* had by this time evolved into a "minicourse" series and could no longer really be considered a magazine.

What did it look like in the early years, and how has it changed? Volume 2 (1957-1958) proclaimed on its masthead that it is "published fortnightly from October to May," but it consisted of only nine issues (six issues of four pages, and three with eight pages each). In the years following (until volume 16, 1970-1971), *Keeping Posted* appeared fifteen times between October and May, with the 1st and 15th issue each sixteen pages long and the others eight pages.

The magazine was printed in black ink on a heavy, coated white stock. Colored ink was rarely used in the first volumes and then only in the page 1 logo. By 1958 additional feature titles were listed in color, and a single color attempted, not very successfully, to highlight and contrast textual material in each issue. With volume 7 (1961-1962) two colors plus color reductions began to be used much more boldly and effectively. Bright blocks of color focused attention and provided variety. As the year progressed *Keeping Posted* looked more and more like a magazine and less like the news bulletin it had started as.

In the beginning there was no separate cover or artwork other than the competent photographs that illustrated particular items in the text. The 1st issue in volume 5 (October 1959) and the 1st and 15th issues in subsequent volumes had distinct covers, although for a while the artwork competed with text for the reader's attention. By volume 10 (1964-1965) the first pages of these double issues were really "covers," and a box on page 2 described the "cover art." The type size was large, almost too large for the young teenagers for whom the contents of the magazine were intended. The open, two-column format and the large headings for relatively short articles gave the magazine a clean and attractive look.

Beginning with Borowitz's takeover, *Keeping Posted* provided a variety of ways in which readers could respond to questions and contests in the magazine and see their names, photographs, and opinions in print. In "Counsel Corner" Borowitz would pose a question that was then answered by students from various congregations around the country. In "Let's Face the Issue" a controversial topic was raised in a particular religious school, and the opinions of the ninth or tenth graders participating in the discussion would appear together with a photograph of the group. "The Reader Writes" elicited responses to specific material, for example, a sociodrama that dealt dynamically with the definition of what makes a person a good Jew, "The Three Sons." The first of a long series of articles on single themes that ran throughout a volume was begun in 1960-1961 with the publication of "Giants of Justice," biographies of fourteen American Jews whose lives and actions "exemplified the value of social ethics." Ethical concerns, often presented in symposium format, were a hallmark of the magazine.

Photography and cartoon contests, as well as a "What I Learned from My Rabbi" contest invited additional reader response. "The Arts and You" presented media reviews by students.

Other regular features were "Challenges," questions for thought, study, and discussion; "Keeping Posted Around the World," a survey of international Jewish-content news happenings, including relevant obituaries; and "Chuckles," jokes with Jewish human-relations themes.

With volume 7 (October 1961) *Keeping Posted* dropped its "news" subtitle and added instead a Hebrew equivalent for the magazine's name, *Davar b'ito* (using Hebrew characters). The translation was not exact, "but a phrase in Proverbs 15:23 conveys the same idea: a *timely* word. Look up the way the phrase is used in Proverbs and you'll understand why we chose it. Our new name tells you that KP—*Davar b'ito* takes the study of *Ivrit* seriously. We'll do our best to help you learn it!"[8] A Hebrew column now began to appear in each issue, giving the Sephardic pronunciation first and the Ashkenazic second (a concession to the pronunciation confusion that quietly disappeared as the controversy itself ceased to have significance).

No stories or poems were published by *Keeping Posted*. Special occasional features included "A Word from the Wise," with contributions by famous people (Abraham L. Sachar and Herbert Lehman, for instance); a "Letter from Jerusalem," written by rabbinical students visiting or studying in Israel; and a series about Jewish philosophers contributed by noted experts in the field, such as an article on Martin Buber by Maurice Friedman (author of major scholarly works about Buber). The quality of the writing and the credentials of the contributors were both impeccable. These formative years set a standard for the excellent informational articles that became characteristic of *Keeping Posted*.

The extensive use of material by readers and the many photographs of young people must have made *Keeping Posted* a strongly attractive periodical in spite of its artistic limitations. The editorial philosophy seemed to be: give teenagers a publication that feels like their own, and they will be willing to accept the additional intellectual contents without protest. The magazine was clearly successful, but it is impossible to determine if students read the high-level articles voluntarily or enjoyed them more than they would have in a straight educational format because they liked other parts of the magazine.

One mark of the magazine's success was the launching by the Conservative movement of a magazine for Jewish teenagers, *Our Age*. The periodical began publication in November 1959 as an eight-page biweekly. It resembled a textbook too much to have stimulated the kind of enthusiasm or pleasure that would make it a serious competitor to *Keeping Posted*.

In Borowitz's last year with *Keeping Posted* (volume 7), the magazine expanded its horizons. Robert S. Oksner began contributing marvelously entertaining cartoons to each issue, beginning with volume 7, no. 6 (January 1962). Oksner was already a very successful cartoonist, having just been "cited as the nation's top comic book artist in 1961 by the National Society of Cartoonists."[9] (Oksner's cartoons ran in *Keeping Posted* until 1970.) Concurrent with Oksner's first issue, the magazine began to be printed on a heavy, uncoated stock, excellent for reproductions. Greater attention was now paid to the work of Jewish artists. Color and black-and-white reproductions of paintings, graphics, and sculpture were an important part of the May 1962 issue.

With volume 7 (1962-1963), Edith Samuel became sole editor of *Keeping Posted*. The masthead includes Ralph Davis as production manager, Hannah Grad Goodman as author of the Hebrew column, Irv Koons as cartoonist, and the eminent HUC-JIR professor Rabbi Jakob Petuchowski, presumably as advisor on the religious content.

The basic format established by Borowitz and Samuel was maintained throughout the 1960s. It seemed to work well, and the magazine flourished. Features were added or changed. "Fun in Yiddish" replaced the earlier "Chuckles." A stamp column and "The Act in Social Action" appeared regularly. "What Do You Think?" begun by Borowitz, could now be found on page 3 of every issue. It presented a controversial theme, usually derived from a news item, and asked readers to draw their own conclusions about the ethics of the decision. Books and movies were reviewed periodically, and occasional special features on poetry appeared. Eight articles by the Jewish musicologist Judith K. Eisenstein in volume 8, dealt with the history of Jewish songs "complete with the tunes and chords."

An extremely popular series, "Chasidic Tales Retold," was written by Rabbi Herbert Weiner, author of *9½ Mystics* and *The Wild Goats of Ein Gedi*. It appeared in each issue in volume 12 (1966-1967). Volume 13 contained fifteen installments from *Certain People of the Book* by Maurice Samuel; a series on "Arabs and Jews" by Joel Carmichael ran through volume 14; and "Folkways and Minhagim" by Rabbi Bernard Zlotowitz was featured in volume 15.

Most of the articles in *Keeping Posted* were written by staff members, congregational rabbis, HUC-JIR faculty members, and high school students. Very few contests were offered, and the amount of reader-written and reader-solicited material decreased greatly with the passage of time. Some of the issues were inviting, but others had a pedestrian quality.

The first issue of volume 16 (October 1970) presented the "new" *Keeping Posted* in the format that has continued to the present. A bright orange cover by Peter Max announced the issue's theme, "moment of awareness: discovering Jewish identity." The magazine had been radically transformed in an attempt to stimulate reader interest in a period of "identity crisis" and to respond to the changed mood of the decade. It became a sixteen-page monthly, completely restyled and redesigned, now much slicker and more sophisticated. The blurb on the back cover of volume 15, no. 15, heralded the reshaping of KP: "The new, new *monthly* KP will be a feature magazine dealing with the concerns of contemporary Jewish youth, topical but not dated, theme-oriented, with provocative, readable Jewish material by top writers. You'll find in the new KP poetry, art, stories, letters, cartoons, reviews, photos—all of it designed to enhance, enliven and deepen Jewish education."[10] The strong focus on current events was gone, as were all of the old features and input from readers. Poetry is used when it is effective.

Each issue since 1970 has had a thoughtfully designed two-color cover that announces the specific subject being considered. The text is illustrated with many photographs, some very sensitively chosen, and with reproductions of art and illuminated manuscripts by medieval and modern Jewish artists (as well as a number of pieces on biblical themes by non-Jewish artists). From time to time unsophisticated sketches can also be found. The only cartoons relate directly to the issue's theme and are often political. The general layout and presentation of text are beautiful.

Keeping Posted's intended audience no longer includes junior high school students but is geared to high school and even adult readers. (In May 1961 the back cover of volume 6, no. 15, had made an appeal to the "more and more adults" who were "reading KP. They find it fun to read, handy for keeping up on the Jewish news, and a fine stimulant for discussion and debate. Keep up with *Keeping Posted* at home and at college." This early desire to capture a mature audience crystallized a decade later.)

Each issue is devoted to a single subject. The topics covered are specific explorations within the following general categories: America; archeology; art and culture; law, ethics and issues; Holocaust; Israel and Zionism; Jewish movements; Jews of foreign lands; Judaism and Christianity; literature and language; love, marriage, and family; traditional texts and holidays; and theology and mysticism. Each issue is written by experts in that field. Contributors include the ecologist René Dubos; the legal experts on church-state relations Samuel Rabinove and Leo Pfeffer; writers Hugh Nissenson, Mark Van Doren, Albert Memmi, and Hillel Halkin; Holocaust scholars Philip Friedman, Albert Friedlander, and Lucy Dawidowicz; the outstanding expert on Soviet Jewry William Korey; and, among others, leading biblical and rabbinic scholars in both the Reform and Conservative movements (including Harry Orlinsky, Leonard Kravitz, Martin Cohen, Robert Gordis, Roland Gittelsohn, Samuel Sandmel, Ezra Spicehandler, Jacob Neusner, Solomon Freehof, and Bernard Bamberger).

Throughout most of *Keeping Posted*'s existence, some sort of teacher's guide or parent's guide had accompanied the magazine. The "new" *Keeping Posted* (from 1970) offers a special eight-page teacher's edition, prepared by Alan D. Bennett, bound together with the regular contents of each issue.

Keeping Posted's philosophy has changed. It has become a monthly teacher-centered, information-oriented, pamphlet-textbook publishing program. It is, in fact, no longer a magazine. Aron Hirt-Manheimer, who has edited the publication since 1977, designates each issue a "minicourse," and a catalog of "minicourses" (including virtually every issue since October 1970) is available for "youth and adult Jewish studies by all branches of Judaism." The tone and effectiveness of each issue vary, but a general high standard is maintained.

Notes

1. A more extensive analysis of these early Jewish children's periodicals appears in Naomi M. Patz and Philip E. Miller, "Jewish Religious Children's Literature in America: An Analytical Survey," *Phaedrus* 7, 1 (Spring-Summer 1980), 21-23.

2. In recent years *The Young Judaean* has become a tired, inexpensively printed, routine house organ for the Young Judaea clubs.

3. *World Over* became static and dull for many years. In the spring of 1977 Ezekiel Schloss was succeeded by Stephen and Linda Schaffzin as editors. Some of their innovations have already become cliché, but the verdict is not yet in on *World Over*.

4. The American Council for Judaism was founded in 1942 as a protest by some Reform Jews against the Reform movement's increasing support for Zionism. It considers Judaism a religion and not a nationality or ethnic group and was for years an articulate defender of the non- and anti-Zionist position in American Jewish life. It has become increasingly ineffective and isolated since 1967.

5. By 1963 *Growing Up* had become moribund, reflecting the increasingly unpopular and beleaguered position of its sponsor.

6. A partial listing of books by Borowitz underscores this: *A Layman's Introduction to Religious Existentialism, The Mask Jews Wear, Choosing a Sex Ethic, Understanding Judaism, Reform Judaism Today.*

7. Edith Samuel died on December 23, 1980.

8. *Keeping Posted* 7 (October 1961), 2.

9. Ibid., 7 (January 1962), 10.

10. Ibid., 15 (May 1970), 16.

Information Sources

BIBLIOGRAPHY
Naomi Patz, "The Jewish Children's Periodical: Study, Evaluation and Proposal" (M.A. thesis, Hebrew Union College-Jewish Institute of Religion, New York, 1979).
INDEX SOURCES
Annual index from vol. 5 (1959-1960), originally published as a supplement and thereafter as part of the teacher's edition to *Keeping Posted*, UAHC, New York; catalogue of "minicourses," indexed by general subject areas in alphabetical order (1981-1982), includes virtually all single-theme issues (those since 1970) and replaces an annual index, UAHC, New York; Miriam Leikind, ed., *Index to Jewish Periodicals* (Cleveland: College of Jewish Studies Press), from vol. 16 (1970) on.

LOCATION SOURCES
Library of Congress; Carnegie-Mellon University, Pittsburgh. Bound volumes are in major
   Judaica collections, including the three campuses of Hebrew Union College-Jewish
   Institute of Religion, New York, Cincinnati, and Los Angeles; and the Jewish
   Theological Seminary, New York.

Publication History

MAGAZINE TITLE AND TITLE CHANGES
Keeping Posted: A Jewish News Bulletin for Young People (1955-1960); *Keeping Posted:
   A Jewish News Magazine for Young People* (1960-1961); *Keeping Posted/Davar
   b'ito* (in Hebrew characters) (1961-).
VOLUME AND ISSUE DATA
Keeping Posted: A Jewish News Bulletin for Young People (vol. 1, no. 1-vol. 5, no. 15);
   Keeping Posted: A Jewish News Magazine for Young People (vol. 6, no. 1-vol.
   6, no. 15); *Keeping Posted/Davar b'ito* (vol. 7, no. 1-).
PUBLISHER AND PLACE OF PUBLICATION
Commission on Jewish Education of the Union of American Hebrew Congregations and
   the Central Conference of American Rabbis, New York (1955-1958); UAHC for
   the Commission on Jewish Education of the UAHC and the CCAR, New York
   (1958-1959); Union of American Hebrew Congregations, New York (1959-).
EDITOR
Rabbi Samuel M. Silver (1955-1958); Rabbi Eugene B. Borowitz (1958-1962); Edith
   (Brodsky) Samuel (1962-1977); Aron Hirt-Manheimer (1977-). Vol. 17, no. 1,
   lists Myrna Pollak as editor.

                                                                    Naomi Patz

L

THE LITTLE CORPORAL

Wars tend to foster a militaristic spirit in areas of life that are not directly associated with the military. This phenomenon is especially evident in those aspects of American culture that are associated with children's play and entertainment. During World War II, for example, sales figures for war toys increased dramatically. Children's radio programs during this period often had war themes, and comic books featured war heroes. A similar trend occurred during the Civil War. Children in this era frequently played war games. They organized themselves into miniature armies complete with commanding officers. Having observed this type of behavior, Alfred L. Sewell, a Chicago publisher, decided to create a children's magazine that would draw upon children's interest in the military. Thus shortly after the Civil War ended, Sewell began publishing *The Little Corporal*.

The idea to create a children's magazine grew out of Sewell's involvement with the Northwest Sanitary Fair. Opened in Chicago on May 30, 1865, the fair was organized to raise funds for soldiers who had been wounded during the war. Sewell was involved with the initial planning of the fair, and he came up with an unusual method of contributing funds to the fair's coffers. He printed album pictures of an eagle named "Old Abe" and began selling the pictures to schoolchildren. Old Abe had served as the mascot for the Eighth Wisconsin Volunteer Infantry, and after the war he became a national hero. In an attempt to increase sales of Old Abe's portrait, Sewell rewarded children for selling pictures to their friends and neighbors. A child who purchased one picture became a corporal in Sewell's Army of the American Eagle. A child who sold two or more pictures could achieve a higher rank. Sewell's scheme worked surprisingly well. Thousands of children became members of Sewell's army, and by the end of the fair Sewell had raised more than $16,000. As his fund-raising project reached its conclusion, Sewell conceived of a plan to convert the Army of the American Eagle into an army of magazine subscribers.

The members of Sewell's Army of the American Eagle received the first issue of *The Little Corporal* in July 1865. Throughout the pages of this issue, Sewell urged his readers to maintain their affiliation with his army by subscribing to the magazine. Sewell promised that in addition to being entertaining, his magazine would provide moral leadership. As stated in its motto, *The Little Corporal* intended to be found "Fighting Against Wrong, and for the Good, the True and the Beautiful." Sewell informed his readers that they, too, could join in the fight for justice by sending in $1 for a year's subscription to his monthly magazine.

The Little Corporal met with approval from both adults and children. Newspapers from across the nation greeted the magazine with praise, and some even declared it to be the best children's publication in the country. This favorable publicity, along with a vigorous effort to increase circulation by offering children premiums if they persuaded their friends to subscribe, caused the magazine's circulation figures to increase rapidly. By the end of its first year, *The Little Corporal* had a respectable circulation of 35,000. When the first *American Newspaper Directory* was published in 1869, the magazine's circulation was reported to be 80,000. According to Herbert E. Fleming, an authority on Chicago publications, Sewell's magazine was "the first periodical from Chicago to secure wide attention."[1]

Sewell made extensive use of military terminology during the first few years of the magazine's ten-year history. He often referred to his readers as soldiers or volunteers. Long-term readers were called veterans. When a reader's subscription expired, Sewell urged the child to reenlist for another campaign. The editorial pages often included announcements that were similar to this strongly worded appeal: "Hark to the voice of *The Little Corporal*. He calls again for volunteers. He wants no cowards, no skulkers; all such may seek some other standard. But all those who are willing for another year to battle for the right, the good and true—to help to purify and glorify, by true living and doing, our free and freedom loving America—to all such, Attention! Fall into line!—right! right! right! FORWARD!"[2]

The early issues of *The Little Corporal* contained a wide variety of features and articles. Poems by Luella Clark, Julia M. Thayer, Emily Bugbee, and others were regularly published. Original music composed by George F. Root appeared in the magazine each month. A page of puzzles was usually included in each issue. Horace Greely contributed a series of articles, "Counsel to Boys" (April 1867 and following issues), and Dr. Worthington Hooker, a professor at Yale, wrote a science column under the pen name of "Uncle Worthy." Much of the fiction published in the early issues was written by Emily Huntington Miller. Another author who frequently contributed short stories was Edward Eggleston.

Sewell and Eggleston had first met at the Northwest Sanitary Fair. At the time Eggleston was a minister in Winona, Minnesota. He was involved with the Minnesota branch of the Sanitary Commission, the sponsor of the fair, and his duties required that he make frequent trips to Chicago. He often saw Sewell during these visits, and they became close friends. When Sewell established *The Little Corporal*, he asked Eggleston to serve as one of his chief contributors. Eggleston had published very little at this point, but since he enjoyed writing, he agreed to send Sewell some stories.

For years Eggleston had collected information about the history and lore of the American Indians, and he decided to draw upon this background in his stories for *The Little Corporal*. Eggleston's series of Indian tales was entitled the "Round Table Stories." He provided Sewell with a new story each month from August 1865 through June 1866. In some of these stories Eggleston recounted various Indian legends. In others he wrote about battles and Indian leaders. For the most part Eggleston portrayed Native Americans as brutal savages, and he was generally unsympathetic toward them. Children, however, enjoyed the tales, and the "Round Table Stories" quickly became one of *The Little Corporal*'s most popular features.

Sewell was so impressed with Eggleston's literary talents that he offered him an editorial position on the magazine. At first Eggleston turned down the proposition, but Sewell persisted, and Eggleston eventually decided to leave the ministry and work for Sewell. In May 1866, Eggleston moved his family to Evanston, a town a few miles north of Chicago, and the following month he assumed his new duties as assistant editor of the magazine. Sewell informed the magazine's readers of Eggleston's arrival in an editorial announcement in the June issue: "I have the great pleasure of announcing this month that Edward Eggleston will hereafter share my editorial labors. Mr. Eggleston is so well known as a writer for children, and my readers have, during the past year, been so delighted with his Indian stories, that the mere statement that he is now one of the editors of *The Little Corporal* will cause rejoicing throughout our entire camp. He is to give us his whole time and energies."[3]

During the first few months of Eggleston's tenure as assistant editor, he did give *The Little Corporal* his whole time and energy. In addition to his editorial work he created a new series of Indian stories, "Evenings at the Nest" (July 1866 and following issues). He also wrote the "Chicken Little Stories" (July 1866 and following issues), a series of fanciful stories intended for the magazine's youngest readers. Besides these two series he contributed numerous short stories and articles. In fact, a few issues were comprised almost entirely of his work. To keep the readers from knowing this, he used a variety of pen names, including Ease, Captain Jack, Professor Willie, Private Queer, Keystone, and Clef de Voute.

Eggleston soon realized that he could not support his family on the small salary that Sewell paid him. Sewell repeatedly promised Eggleston a raise, but the magazine failed to bring in enough money to permit Sewell to keep his promises. Forced to seek other sources of income, Eggleston began lecturing and writing articles for other publications. In December 1866 *The Sunday School Teacher* offered him an editorial position, which he accepted. Since his new responsibilities prevented him from working on *The Little Corporal*, he resigned from the magazine. On February 12, 1867, he sent Sewell a formal letter of resignation, in which he told Sewell that he hoped "still to be one of your band of contributors."[4] For the next two years he occasionally sent Sewell articles. However, as his fame increased he discontinued his relationship with *The Little Corporal*.

For five months Sewell continued to edit *The Little Corporal* on his own. This proved to be a difficult period for Sewell. He had never closed his original publishing business, which meant that he usually attended to *The Little Corporal* after his regular work was done. Before Eggleston's arrival, Sewell had been able to manage his two businesses without many problems. However, during the nine months that Eggleston had worked for him, he had become dependent on an assistant. After Eggleston left, Sewell found that he was no longer able to run the magazine alone. When his health began to deteriorate due to the long hours he was forced to work, he began searching for a new assistant editor. He asked Emily Huntington Miller, one of his regular contributors, if she would be interested in the position, and she agreed to take the job. In July 1867 Sewell announced that Miller would be joining him the following month. The August issue contained Miller's first editorial, in which she gave readers a little information about herself and then closed by saying: "My best thoughts, my best efforts, my best wishes, shall always be at *The Little Corporal*'s service; and as the editor has invited me to share with him the love and esteem he has won from the children, I trust that they will extend to me, as I now send to them, a hearty welcome."[5]

Unlike Eggleston, Miller increased her commitment to *The Little Corporal*. With each issue she assumed more responsibility, and within a few years she was making major editorial decisions. She was instrumental, for example, in changing the format of the magazine. Sewell had originally published *The Little Corporal* as an octavo with small print and few illustrations, but in 1869 it became a quarto; the size of the print was enlarged and more illustrations were added. Her enthusiasm for the magazine affected her husband, John Edwin Miller, who abandoned his career as a teacher and became the magazine's co-publisher in 1870.

As the Millers' involvement with the magazine increased, Sewell began devoting more time to his publishing business and other projects. In January 1870 he founded a short-lived periodical called *The National School Festival*, which contained projects and exercises designed for use by teachers. The Great Chicago Fire, which occurred in October 1871, forced Sewell's withdrawal from *The Little Corporal*. The fire destroyed his publishing business, from which he derived most of his income. Leaving *The Little Corporal* to the Millers, he moved to Evanston, where he founded a newspaper and wrote *The Great Calamity*, a book about the Great Chicago Fire.

The Little Corporal suffered serious losses from the fire. The office was destroyed, equipment was ruined, and records were lost. The Millers, however, were able to rebuild the magazine, although it never fully recovered from the fire. Emily H. Miller became *The Little Corporal*'s editor, and her husband assumed the position of publisher and looked after the magazine's business affairs. In an effort to improve the magazine's financial footing, the Miller's raised the yearly subscription rate from $1.00 to $1.50. The magazine's faltering circulation received a boost in April 1872 when *The Little Corporal* absorbed *Work and Play*, a small children's magazine.

Under Emily H. Miller's editorship, the tone of *The Little Corporal* changed. She made less use of militaristic terms than Sewell had done. Also, the nature of the articles and stories that she selected for publication differed from those that had previously appeared in the magazine. She allotted less space to nonfiction than Sewell had, although she continued to publish a few articles about science and history. Nor did she publish as many adventure stories as Sewell did. Instead, she filled the magazine's pages with domestic fiction, stories portraying family life and conventional moral values. Much of the fiction was published in serial form, including several of Miller's own stories. The poetry she published also dealt with domestic themes. She tended to rely on a small group of regular contributors of which Sarah Woolsey, who wrote under the pen name of Susan Coolidge, was the most famous. Other contributors included Lucia Chase Bell, Harry Castlemon [Charles Emerson Fosdick], Ellis Gray, Olive Thorne Miller, Josephine Pollard, and Mary E. C. Wyeth.

In addition to publishing the regular stories and articles, Miller published letters from child readers, a puzzle page, and an editorial column. She encouraged children to write to a fictional character named Prudy, and their letters were published in a regular feature, "Prudy's Pocket" (January 1872 and following issues). Occasionally, Prudy's response to a child's question or comment appeared after a letter. The puzzle page was called "Work and Play." Private Queer, another fictional character, was listed as being in charge of this feature. "Eyes and Ears" (July 1873 and following issues), the title of Miller's editorial column, included advice, amusing anecdotes, and interesting bits of information.

The Millers published *The Little Corporal* for nearly four years after the Great Chicago Fire, but they were unable to turn it into a profitable venture. Numerous competing children's periodicals sprang up after the Civil War, and these publications drew subscribers away from *The Little Corporal*. By 1875 the magazine's financial condition was so precarious that the Millers decided to allow *The Little Corporal* to be absorbed by *St. Nicholas*.* In June 1875 *St. Nicholas* published Emily H. Miller's final words to the readers of *The Little Corporal*:

After ten years of faithful service, the "Corporal" has been put upon the retired list. We have had a long, brave march together, and it is hard parting company. You will miss your leader, and we shall miss the words of courage and devotion that came from the gallant army, East and West, North and South. But remember, you are none of you mustered out of service. Your new leader, *St. Nicholas*, enrolls his soldiers by the same pledge under which you first enlisted—''For the Good, the True, and the Beautiful''—and the ''Corporal'' feels safe and satisfied in leaving you to his guidance.[6]

The Little Corporal quickly faded into obscurity. Nonetheless, it was one of the first children's magazines in America to have a national readership. Its early success encouraged other enterprising publishers to launch their own children's magazines, and in this way it helped strengthen the overall position of children's periodicals in nineteenth-century America.

Notes

1. Herbert E. Fleming, ''The Literary Interests of Chicago,'' *American Journal of Sociology* 2 (November 1905), 404.
2. Alfred L. Sewell, ''The New Year,'' *The Little Corporal* 3 (December 1866), 93.
3. Alfred L. Sewell, ''Editorial Announcement,'' ibid., 2 (June 1866), 94.
4. Edward Eggleston, ''Letter from Mr. Eggleston,'' ibid., 4 (March 1867), 45.
5. Emily Huntington Miller, ''Salutatory,'' ibid., 5 (August 1867), 28.
6. Emily Huntington Miller, ''To the Army of *The Little Corporal*,'' *St. Nicholas* 2 (June 1875), 516.

Information Sources

BIBLIOGRAPHY
Herbert E. Fleming, ''The Literary Interests of Chicago,'' *American Journal of Sociology* 2 (November 1905), 404-6; William Randel, *Edward Eggleston* (New York: Twayne Publishers, 1963).
INDEX SOURCES
None.
LOCATION SOURCES
A nearly complete file is at The Chicago Historical Society.

Publication History

PUBLISHER AND PLACE OF PUBLICATION
Alfred L. Sewell, Chicago (1865-1870); Alfred L. Sewell and John Edwin Miller, Chicago (1870-1871); John Edwin Miller, Chicago, (1871-1875).
EDITOR
Alfred L. Sewell (1865-1871); Emily Huntington Miller (1871-1875).

Mark I. West

LITTLE FOLKS: AN ILLUSTRATED MONTHLY FOR YOUNGEST READERS

An illustrated monthly for youngest readers established in 1897, *Little Folks* was one of a number of children's magazines published in New England during the early part of the twentieth century. It was published by the S. E. Cassino Co., first in Boston and later in Salem, and initially edited by Charles Stuart Pratt and Ella Farman Pratt, both experienced juvenile editors.

Little Folks was intended for very young readers, with readable type set in a one-column format. The subject matter and reading level of the articles vary, but they seem aimed primarily at lower elementary school readers. Issues are liberally illustrated, occasionally in color, with photographs and drawings. Articles with a seasonal emphasis appear regularly as do poetry, stories (frequently continued from issue to issue), tales for younger readers using words and pictures, riddle rhymes, music, biographies, and activities. The February 1901 edition features winners of a photography competition.

Although many subjects are covered in different issues of the magazine, a consistently high moral tone is maintained. Sex roles are clearly defined and appropriate behavior prescribed for each. In "Ned Longley's Note-Book," for example, Ned is encouraged by his father to write about important things. The January 1904 issue has Ned discussing President McKinley's virtues. He noted that McKinley treated his wife kindly—"of course he would be; all men that amount to much are good to their wives."[1]

An article, "My Childhood Birds" (May 1904), encourages children to take an interest in birds, implying that that interest was greater during the author's childhood. "How We Kept Thanksgiving—When I Was a Little Girl" (November 1900) provides another nostalgic contrast of past and present.

Stories generally have a family orientation and emphasize approved values such as obedience, cheerfulness, and cooperation. Janey, Josey, and Joe appear in a series of family stories, "The Lovable Tales of Janey and Josey and Joe." In the November 1900 issue the main premise of the story "Aunt Susan Mehetible's House" is that the children cannot bear to have one go on an overnight visit away from home. A Christmas story, "The Bethlehem Partner" (December 1903), emphasizes good works, when a Sunday school class adopts a poor newspaper boy. Other stories are essentially vehicles for factual information about other times or places. "What Betsy's Father Found" is an example of a story with a pioneer background (December 1903). "The Thanksgiving Spareribs" (November 1900) combines a family story with a far West setting and describes an earthquake tremor. "Mahaily Jane's Half Holiday" (December 1903) is a humorous family story of a black girl's visit to her grandmother, illustrated with photographs and written in dialect. A number of stories combine science and nature study with a narrative format. "The Green Heron Baby" (November 1904) is written as fiction, but contains scientific information. In "Delia's Nature Studies" (December 1903) science is mingled with the story of a girl and her dolls.

Some stories for very young children appear. They are often in larger print and amusingly illustrated. "The Brown Bunny" (December 1903) is told entirely through pictures.

Poetry appeared on a regular basis. In December 1903 a "Ladybug Poem" was presented as a takeoff on a Mother Goose rhyme. "In the Thanksgiving Firelight" (November 1905) by Carolyn S. Bailey, the emphasis on holiday material combines with poetry. "The Rhyme of the Christmas Tree" (December 1900) features a poem with words arranged in the form of a Christmas tree.

"Bobby's Clothes" (November 1908), a humorous poem, concludes with the lines "But listen! There's a moral boys/Be careful of your clothes!"[2]

The "Little Folks Play Department," begun in November 1908, features plays, articles about play production, cut-out paper pictures, and other activities for children. In December 1911 a paper-doll page was inaugurated. One paper-doll character is Sambo, complete with watermelon and banjo. A cartoon of an Oriental doll in the February 1912 issue refers to "those terrible Japs," but stereotypes of this kind are relatively rare.

In 1908 the editors began to rely more heavily on premiums to encourage subscriptions. Prizes, including books and coasters, were advertised for those obtaining new subscribers to the magazine. In March 1909 the publisher encouraged mothers of readers to send for samples from various advertisers and described the difficulties faced by the magazine, including the problems of obtaining appropriate and well-written material, the cost of postage, and the need for direct renewal of subscriptions.

The December 1920 issue was subtitled *Something to Do for Boys and Girls*. Print was smaller, with some two-column pages. This issue included things to make, short book reviews, nature study, and animal stories, as well as the regular features found in earlier copies.

Although the magazine did not have the exceptional writers and superior quality of *St. Nicholas*, it provided its young readers with a variety of material for their enjoyment on a monthly basis. No information on the readership is available, but its appeal seems to have been to white, middle-class children whose parents would have found the magazine a wholesome form of entertainment for their children.

Notes

1. "Ned Longley's Note-Book," *Little Folks* 8 (January 1904), 87.
2. "Bobby's Clothes," ibid., 12 (November 1908), 20.

Information Sources

BIBLIOGRAPHY
None.
INDEX SOURCES
None.
LOCATION SOURCES
Bound volumes containing issues from 1903 to 1908 are in the Rare Book Room of the Boston Public Library; bound volumes from November 1900 to October 1904 are in the Buffalo and Erie County Public Library, Buffalo, N.Y.

Publication History

MAGAZINE TITLE AND TITLE CHANGES
Little Folks: An Illustrated Monthly for Youngest Readers (1897-1926).
VOLUME AND ISSUE DATA
Little Folks: An Illustrated Monthly for Youngest Readers (vol. 1, no. 1-vol. 30, no. 12).
PUBLISHER AND PLACE OF PUBLICATION
S. E. Cassino Co., Boston and Salem, Mass. (1897-1926).
EDITOR
Charles Stuart Pratt and Ella Forman Pratt (1900-1908); M. O. Osborne (1908-December 1920).

Beverly W. Talladay

THE LITTLE PILGRIM

The title *The Little Pilgrim*, would probably lead today's child reader to think of Thanksgiving and the earliest colonists at Plymouth, Massachusetts. Contemporary readers of the nineteenth-century periodical *The Little Pilgrim*, however, would have had John Bunyan's *Pilgrim's Progress* as their most immediate association with the magazine. The first three issues of the magazine—October, November, and December 1853—have relatively modest mastheads ("The Little Pilgrim" is printed in decorated letters), but starting in January 1854 the masthead design involves not only the names of the magazine and its editor but an illustration of a young boy, staff in hand, making his way with an appealing, hopeful expression. He looks like a child playing at being Bunyan's Christian, but the boy is not in the service of a sectarian publication. Thoroughly commercial, yet thoroughly genteel, *The Little Pilgrim* was both a product and promoter of the age's sentimental piety and therefore shared the middle-class's concern with finding a match between Christian values and profit making. A close look at the magazine's promotional techniques and contents shows that its editorial and publishing team of Sara J. and Leander K. Lippincott tried to create such a match in a variety of ways, not the least of which was through the persona of the eponymous figure of the Little Pilgrim himself.

The prospectus in the first number of the magazine testifies to its editor's desire to offer good value for good money: "It is not our intention to give woodcut illustrations—usually but poor embellishments—but to expend the money they would cost in procuring contributions of the highest character, by some of the best writers of the day."[1] In accordance with this stated aim, the prospectus further explains:

It is not our intention to discuss profound religious doctrines or political problems with our young readers. But our aim shall always be to inculcate a high religious morality. "Whatsoever things are true,... honest,...just,...pure,...lovely," we shall heartily advocate; and ever

strive to present, in fair and attractive forms, the divine truths contained
in that blessed epitome of Faith, Freedom, Love, Temperance, and Peace—
Christ's Sermon on the Mount.[2]

Despite, or perhaps because of, this attention paid to the aim of *The Little
Pilgrim*, the actual contents of the magazine are only briefly sketched. Readers
are advised that "it is our purpose to have our paper composed *entirely of original
matter*," much of it in the form of the editor's European sketches, stories, poems,
and editorial articles.[3] As *The Little Pilgrim* appeared over the years (monthly,
through December 1868), the material it featured was more varied in form and
content than the prospectus promised. A typical issue of the magazine included
the aforementioned European sketch or tale, poems, editorial articles, an animal
story, a story of child life, a contribution from a child subscriber, a fairy tale
(at first a thinly disguised cautionary tale but later an actual work of fantasy),
"Anecdotes and Sayings of Children," obituaries of former subscribers, and a
page of puzzles—a rebus, riddles, enigmas, and charades. The story of child
life was sometimes presented as a reminiscence by the author herself or by one
of her characters; other times it had a distinctly regional cast. In addition to
running these staples, *The Little Pilgrim* occasionally carried special columns
for "little ones," ran a short series on the history of ancient Rome, and another
series on stories from ballads. The disavowal of political commentary notwith-
standing, some discussion of the Civil War can be found in the pages of the
magazine.

Such discussion was probably inevitable, considering the reportorial eye and
abolitionist sentiments of the magazine's editor, Sara J. C. Lippincott. Known
to *The Little Pilgrim*'s readers as Grace Greenwood, she had already won praise
for her writings in *Godey's, Graham's, Sartain's, Saturday Evening Post*, and
Home Journal, but her writing for the abolitionist journal *National Era* incurred
the wrath of Southerners and cost Greenwood her job as editorial associate for
Godey's Lady's Book. The incident only increased her popularity in other quarters: *Greenwood Leaves*, a collection of her magazine pieces, as well as a
collection of stories for children called *The History of My Pets*, came out a few
months after Greenwood's dismissal from *Godey's*. A trip to the continent (1852-
1853) resulted in *Haps and Mishaps of a Tour in Europe* (1854). The interests
and experiences that went into writing the latter two books emerged again in
The Little Pilgrim's European sketches and in countless animal stories. Similarly,
the publication history of the first and second volumes of *Greenwood Leaves*
can also be seen as predictive of *The Little Pilgrim*. Here we see at work the
shrewd marketing instincts that later created and maintained an audience for the
children's periodical. Greenwood advised Ticknor and Fields, the publishers of
her books, to delay the first volume of *Greenwood Leaves* until *Lady's Book*
announced her appointment as editorial associate, and she waited to make a
second collection of *Greenwood Leaves* until she thought that no more copies
of the first would sell.[4]

Greenwood's awareness of her reputation as an effective promotional device is evident in the magazine prospectus cited earlier. There she is careful to tell the public that many of the stories and poems would be furnished "from our own pen."[5] Not content, however, to rely on her reputation alone, Greenwood announced in succeeding issues the names of authors whose works would soon appear and the names of well-known authors to whom she had written or intended to write for contributions. The May 1854 issue, for example, contains the following inquiry: "Do our friends realize that *The Little Pilgrim* presents a list of contributors such as *no other publication of any kind, or size, in this country can equal*; and that this list contains some of the *best and most prominent of living authors—English and American?*" Among the twenty authors cited are Nathaniel Hawthorne, John Greenleaf Whittier, James T. Fields, Louise E. Vickroy, Lydia Sigourney, Anna H. Phillips, and Lucy Larcom.[6] Unlike Whittier, whose "Barefoot Boy" was printed by *The Little Pilgrim* (January 1855), Hawthorne never published in the magazine: "we have learned that himself and family have been suffering from illness, and this, added to the cares and duties of his office, has kept him from using his pen in the way of story-writing."[7] No such problems prevented the appearance of work by Henry Wadsworth Longfellow ("The Rope-Walk," October 1855), Hans Christian Andersen ("The Five Peas," August 1855; "A Visit to Ole, the Tower Keeper," May 1867; and "The Pen and the Inkstand," May 1867); and Charles Dickens ("A Child's Dream of a Star," June 1868). *The Little Pilgrim* also printed several poems by Louisa May Alcott, but they were published in 1858, ten years before her big success with *Little Women* and three years after her more modestly received *Flower Fables* (1855). Although fresher and more fanciful than the usual periodical fare, Alcott's poems, like many of the stories and poems produced by Greenwood's list of "*best and most prominent of living authors*," are not representative of their author's finest work. Greenwood's featuring of celebrated writers did ensure, however, that she could support her periodical's claim to excellence.

The degree to which practical considerations shaped Greenwood's perception of excellence is indicated by her reversal of position regarding the appropriateness of word and picture games—riddles, enigmas, and charades—and of illustrations. In the April 1854 issue Greenwood announced that riddles, enigmas, and charades would not be published, "except in cases of unusual excellence. . . . We do not consider them in keeping with the refined and high-toned literary character which we aim to give our journal."[8] The statement does not square with the magazine's previous publication of "A Curious Plantation" (later "Our Curious Plantation"), a series of puns organized around the theme of planting. The "Plantation" puns appeared for a number of years. This example by a child contributor is typical: "Plant yourself and what will come up? *Yew*."[9] Nor does the statement square with the eventual incorporation of word and picture games as regular features of *The Little Pilgrim*.

Greenwood also reversed herself on the issue of illustrations. The first number of the magazine loftily eschews woodcuts, but one month later, in a notice of upcoming articles, readers are given the confidential information that the next month's *Little Pilgrim* will have an illustration—and so it does, an engraving by Devereux of Robin Hood in the woods. This illustration, as well as the many that succeeded it, surely had the effect of enhancing *The Little Pilgrim*'s appeal to subscribers. At any rate, Greenwood pulled out all the stops when she addressed her readers regarding the magazine's new illustrated masthead in January 1854:

> Are you not all charmed and delighted, dear readers, with our new heading? Was there ever in the world, think you, so comely a little pilgrim as Mr. Darley has sketched for us? We are sure you cannot refuse to greet, with a most hearty welcome, this little stranger. The freshness and youth of his round, sunny face, must win quick responses from the freshness and youth of your generous hearts; and his sweet, wondering eyes draw tender, loving looks from yours—especially *yours*, ye little maidens. Is he not beautiful to behold?[10]

Presented as an object of both admiration and identification, the Little Pilgrim thereby became a potent symbol for enlisting reader loyalties. He was there to help Greenwood find the 50,000 subscribers that she had announced as her goal.[11] Moreover, the Little Pilgrim became indissolubly linked with Greenwood herself. The December issue mentioned above carried Greenwood's poem "Love Me, Love My Pilgrim." Appended to the poem was the following comment: "Editorial friends will best prove their love and constancy by copying the above. G. G."[12]

Linking both herself and her readers to the figure of the Little Pilgrim was part of Greenwood's larger strategy of creating a community or family of subscribers. She often addressed both child and adult readers with notices regarding the contents of upcoming issues and the forming of clubs of subscribers. For an example of the former, see her puff for "The History of Ancient Rome." This was billed as "a new and interesting feature—one that will especially add to its value as the teacher's auxiliary in schools."[13] Greenwood was no less outspoken in urging her readers to "get up" clubs (that is, organize group subscriptions); yet she rarely mentioned the club organizer's financial incentive of earning a reduced rate or even a free subscription. One notable exception to her genteel silence is her regret that "Some of our friends either do not read our terms as carefully as they might, or else they are in a fair way to become skin-flints and misers as they grow older."[14] More typical of Greenwood's commentary on clubs is this response to a letter from a seventy-two-year-old club founder: "Oh, little girls with rosy cheeks—Oh, little boys, with stout young legs, do not your cheeks grow redder, do not your stout legs twitch with shame, that this dear, brave old lady has done so much, and you so little, for your friend *'The Little Pilgrim'?''*[15]

What is surprising about the above appeal is not that Greenwood was so personal but that she did not go one step further and say, ''your *brother, 'The Little Pilgrim,'* '' instead of saying ''your friend.'' Starting with the second issue of the magazine, in 1854, Greenwood apprised her readers of family news, a practice that had the effect of inviting subscribers to become members of the family themselves. Greenwood's marriage to Leander K. Lippincott, publisher of *The Little Pilgrim* was duly noted, as was the birth of their daughter: *''A little baby sister was born to him* [the Little Pilgrim] *on the third of December last.''*[16] Two months later, the ''many tender inquiries'' prompted by the baby's birth received the following reply: ''She has large blue eyes, that will be brown if she lives, golden-brown hair that curls, and a wee dimple in her chin; she is good, and sweet, and bright, and her name is 'Annie Grace.' ''[17] Annie Grace inspired poetry—''Lines Affectionately Inscribed to *The Little Pilgrim's* Sister'' (May 1856)—as well as inquiries, and in later years organizers of clubs of ten and more could choose a card photograph of little Annie from among the premiums offered.

Subscriber's to *The Little Pilgrim* could further link themselves to the magazine by becoming contributors to its columns. Both children and adults wrote letters; sent in puzzles, charades, rebuses, anecdotes and sayings of children; composed stories; and shared their grief over the loss of loved ones. This last practice, the publication of obituary notices and elegies, was begun by Greenwood herself with an anecdote in the second issue of the magazine in which she recounted meeting a little girl, a stranger, who stopped her and announced in grief-striken tones, '' 'the baby's dead.' ''[18] Many years later Greenwood had occasion to record the death of her nephew, a lieutenant in the Sixth Regiment of Michigan Volunteers, Port Hudson (August 1863) and two years later she mourned his commander-in-chief, Abraham Lincoln (May 1865), but the Civil War made death increasingly difficult to idealize. The month before she wrote her tribute to Lincoln, Greenwood found it necessary to reply to readers' objections to the magazine's printing of obituaries: ''For ourselves, we do not like to let go the hands of any of our dear little friends, as their fearless feet touch the cold waves of the river of Death.''[19] Six months later, however, Greenwood acceded to her readers' change in taste with a crisply worded notice that the magazine would not be accepting any more obituaries: ''while the few are gratified by their notices in our paper, the many naturally feel that the space might be occupied by matter of more *general interest.''*[20]

Greenwood was equally businesslike when dealing with contributors' stories: ''When articles fail to suit us, we shall be silent, as the gentlest manner of intimating to the writers that their favors are not accepted.''[21] Not surprisingly, the writers, many of them children, did not feel that silence was an adequate response. Undaunted, Greenwood let it be known that ''We carefully read *every* article sent to us—and when we are obliged to decide against one, we burn it immediately.''[22]

The response is vintage Greenwood and, by extension, vintage *Little Pilgrim*. Although both dismissive and inadvertently humorous to twentieth-century eyes, Greenwood's declaration that rejected articles would be burned actually reflects her genteel notions of fair play: destroying the articles ensured that they would not be exploited later for bits and pieces that the editor (or anyone else) could claim as her own. Burning the articles also prevented them from cluttering up the office. These same impulses of genteel fair play and practical common sense determined the following "Inducements for Subscribing to the Little Pilgrim":

1. It numbers among its contributors some of the best writers of both England and America.

2. It inculcates religion without sectarianism.

3. It combines pure morality with pure literature.

4. It contains matter to interest parents and teachers, as well as children.

5. It is composed almost entirely of original matter.

6. It contains more matter for fifty ¢ than many of the juvenile publications for a dollar.

7. It contains beautiful pictures, by the best artists.

8. It is printed on fine paper and new type.

Greenwood didn't just advertise these inducements. She delivered them, issue after issue, to the satisfaction and delight of a whole generation of child readers.

Notes

1. *The Little Pilgrim* 1 (October 1853), 8.
2. Ibid.
3. Ibid.
4. Margaret Farrand Thorp, *Female Persuasion: Six Strong-Minded Women* (New Haven: Yale University Press, 1949), 153-54.
5. *The Little Pilgrim* 1 (October 1853), 8.
6. Ibid., 1 (May 1854), 36.
7. Ibid., 1 (December 1854), 93.
8. Ibid., 1 (April 1854), 28.
9. Ibid., 4 (June 1857), 73.
10. Ibid., 1 (January 1854), 4.
11. Ibid., 1 (December 1853), 20.
12. Ibid., p. 21.
13. Ibid., 1 (June 1854), 44.
14. Ibid., 12 (January 1865), 6.
15. Ibid., 3 (February 1856), 12.
16. Ibid., 3 (Janaury 1856), 4.

17. Ibid., 3 (March 1856), 20.
18. Ibid., 1 (November 1853), 11.
19. Ibid., 12 (April 1865), 48.
20. Ibid., 12 (November 1865), 146.
21. Ibid., 1 (January 1854), 4.
22. Ibid., 2 (April 1855), 28.

Information Sources

BIBLIOGRAPHY

Harriet R. Christy, "First Appearances: Literature in Nineteenth-Century Periodicals for Children," in *Research About Nineteeenth-Century Children and Books*, ed. Selma K. Richardson (Urbana-Champaign, Ill.: University of Illinois Graduate School of Library Science, 1980), 117-32; Caroline M. Hewins, *A Mid-Century Child and Her Books* (New York: Macmillan, 1926); Edward T. James, ed., *Notable American Women, 1607-1950* (Cambridge, Mass.: Belknap Press of Harvard University Press, 1971), 2:407-09; Lina Mainiero, ed., *American Women Writers: A Critical Reference Guide from Colonial Times to the Present in Four Volumes* (New York: Frederick Ungar, 1981), 3:13-15; Margaret Farrand Thorp, *Female Persuasion: Six Strong-Minded Women* (New Haven: Yale University Press, 1949), 143-78.

LOCATION SOURCES

Bound volumes are in many university and major public libraries. Vol. 1, nos. 1-3, and vols. 1-15 (complete run) are available on microfilm from Greenwood Press, Westport, Conn.

Publication History

MAGAZINE TITLE AND TITLE CHANGES

The Little Pilgrim (1853-1868). Either Leander or Sara Lippincott changed the magazine's subtitle so frequently that the various subtitles are probably best understood as descriptive phrases, rather than as actual subtitles. One month the phrase might read, "An Illustrated Journal for Boys and Girls" and the next month it might be "A Monthly for Girls and Boys."

VOLUME AND ISSUE DATA

The Little Pilgrim (vol. 1, nos. 1-3; vols. 1-15).

PUBLISHER AND PLACE OF PUBLICATION

Leander K. Lippincott, Philadelphia (October 1853-December 1868).

EDITOR

Sara J. C. Lippincott/Grace Greenwood, (October 1853-December 1868).

Janice M. Alberghene

M

MERRY'S MUSEUM

As one of the most long-lived children's periodicals of the nineteenth century, *Merry's Museum* is best known for the number of famous children's authors associated with it and is noteworthy for the changes in format and content brought by them. Begun by Samuel Goodrich in 1841 and continuing under his editorship for eleven years, *Robert Merry's Museum*, as it was then called, mirrored Goodrich's philosophy of realistic, educationally beneficial works for children with a Rousseauistic emphasis on science and nature studies. After Goodrich relinquished control of the *Museum*, it continued under a number of editors until 1867, when the *Museum*'s publisher, Horace B. Fuller, approached Louisa May Alcott about becoming its editor. The January 1868 issue of *Merry's Museum for Boys and Girls*, as it was then called, featured Alcott's first appearance as a writer for and editor of the magazine. In the regular column called "Merry's Monthly Chat with His Friends" appeared a story very much like the Christmas breakfast incident at the beginning of *Little Women*. In terms of the *Museum*'s literary noteworthiness, Alcott's contributions are its high point. She did not retain the editorship for long, since the financial need that brought her to take on the responsibility for the *Museum* was satisfied by the success of *Little Women* (1868). Without Alcott's drive and contributions, the *Museum* dwindled in size and frequency and went out of existence in 1872.

Samuel Goodrich founded *Robert Merry's Museum* in 1841. Robert Merry is a character much like Goodrich's better known literary creation, Peter Parley— a kindly, wise old man, full of patience around children and eager to talk to them and tell them stories, an irrepressible *raconteur* with a limitless fund of facts and anecdotes. Like Parley, he has a bad leg; like Parley, a following of children who wanted to hear his stories. A decade earlier, in 1833, Goodrich had created *Parley's Magazine*,* and he borrowed heavily from its format of continuing serialized stories and columns of information in establishing the *Museum*. In fact, by 1844 *Merry's Museum* was competing so intensely with *Parley's Magazine*, which was still in existence under other editors, that Goodrich merged the latter with the former, retitling the joint publication *Merry's Museum and Parley's Magazine*. In the new magazine under Goodrich's editorship, the emphasis was on short articles about various natural phenomena—trees, birds, geographical formations—and historical events—biographies, monuments to people and happenings, and historical sketches. In these studies Goodrich's bias for the realistic and educational as opposed to the fantastic and entertaining is evident. In his autobiography, he commented on his own childhood reading of Perrault's fairy tales; he was, even as a child, horrified by their monstrosity and violence and in later life wondered why it was that adults would expose children to such reading.[1] Goodrich's own stories were firmly grounded in fact and in conventional Protestant theology; the wonders of science and history were presented to children to prove that God is immanent and active in the world, both in human affairs and in the realm of nature. Early in his career as a publisher, Goodrich had been impressed with Hannah More's *Cheap Repository Tracts*, with its emphasis on realism and godly living; he also perceived a need in the young American Republic for authentically American books of an informative, wholesome nature set in America and peopled with American characters. His entrance as a writer into the field of children's literature was motivated not only from an altruistic desire to provide educational and improving books for American children but also to take advantage of a financially lucrative publishing market.

His earliest success was *Peter Parley's Tales about America* in 1827. Thereafter he capitalized on the character of Parley, the kindly, lovely old man who was narrator of the stories and guide to the historical and natural curiosities presented in the book. In all, Goodrich was the editor or author of 170 books, 116 of which were for children, by his own count.[2] Though he did much of the writing for *Merry's Museum* and *Parley's Magazine* himself, he drew many of the series stories and continuing columns from his published books. For instance, a series called "Sketches of the Manners, Customs, and History of the Indians of America," which was featured in the *Museum* in 1841 (January to December), was borrowed from his volume in *Parley's Cabinet Library* about American Indians. The process also worked the other way; following his serial publication of stories in the *Museum*, he brought them out as books, for example *Wit Bought; or The Life and Adventures of Robert Merry* (1843) and *A Home in the Sea; or The Adventures of Philip Brusque; Designed to Show the Nature and Necessity of Good* (1845). These adventure stories were a staple of the *Museum* and made it a livelier publication than *Parley's Magazine*. Always the entrepreneur, Goodrich did not depend on Robert Merry's own attractiveness and the interest in his stories to keep his child subscribers to the *Museum*; in 1841 Goodrich announced that Peter Parley would become a contributor to the magazine, and thereafter the *Museum* featured stories from Parley story collections intermittently throughout his reported editorship.

As Goodrich's editorship continued, he became less and less rigid about excluding the fantastic from the pages of the *Museum*. In 1848 he began a series of Hans Christian Andersen's fairy tales. Although the series was not long lived, it did at least indicate a softening of Goodrich's position on fantasy. Perhaps he was simply responding to a lessening of anxiety on the part of parents and educators about the detrimental effects of fantasy, especially in light of the new collections of fairy tales emerging from the Grimms brothers and other writers like Andersen.

Under Goodrich's editorship the *Museum* featured many engravings of the objects and scenes described in its pages. In his publishing outside the realm of children's books, Goodrich's aim was to encourage the growth of the American arts, including the visual arts. In his adult publications he encouraged the work of engravers such as J. D. Felter, William Baker, and N. Orr.

His children's works, including the *Museum*, also featured numerous engravings designed to please the eye and educate the mind. Goodrich said in his autobiography that he especially chose subjects to write about that were "things capable of sensible representation," which made the process of illustration that much easier.[3] In the early issues of the *Museum* the pictures are simply black and white, but in the September 1842 issue he began experimenting with a tinted frontispiece. That issue featured a picture of a crocodile that might easily have been taken from one of the Parley volumes about the animal kingdom or about reptiles. He continued the watercolor experiment for about two years.

Robert Merry's Museum, as Goodrich wrote and edited it, did not have any fixed, long running columns. Although a series such as "The Wonders of Geology" (January 1842 and following issues) might continue for two or three years, it did not thereby become permanent in the magazine's pages. Early in the *Museum's* life Goodrich began to publish the letters of its subscribers and to answer and comment upon them, using Robert Merry as pseudonym. Early commentary mostly concerned the lack of postage on many of the letters and the poor penmanship and grammar of some of the correspondents; for example, in 1845 Goodrich chastised "J.L.D., of Boston," who "has sent us a second letter, which we cannot insert, *because it is badly written*. We wish all our young correspondents to understand that we publish *only such letters as are neatly written, and such as are post paid*."[4] The column gradually changed in tone and evolved into "Merry's Monthly Chat with His Readers." It was the one legacy that Goodrich left when he passed the editorship to Stephen T. Allen.

The return addresses of the correspondents indicate how widespread was the readership of the *Museum*. In 1849 letters were received from as far away as North Carolina, Virginia, Georgia, and Tennessee, as well as from all of the New England States. The cost of the magazine, $1 a year if paid in advance or $1.50 if paid at the end of the year, put the magazine within reach of large numbers of Americans. At the end of 1850 Goodrich reported that the *Museum* had 13,000 subscribers; by 1854 his successor reported 50,000. It is difficult to know if these figures are accurate, however; Goodrich was a notable entrepreneur, puffing one work in the pages of another, and exaggerating figures if it suited his purposes. In his autobiography, published in 1857, he reported that there were 7 million copies of his works in circulation, with a yearly output of 300,000.[5]

With his encouragement of American writers in his adult works, Goodrich had many connections with the principal American writers of his day, so it is not unusual that such writers also appeared in the *Museum* pages. Lydia Sigourney, Catherine Sedgwick, and Timothy Shay Arthur, for example, all appeared in the *Museum*, although it is difficult to know if they contributed knowingly and willingly; Goodrich might simply have appropriated their pieces from some of his adult publications without their knowledge.

In 1850 Goodrich relinquished his editorship, but he did not cease the connection entirely, remaining a sort of foreign correspondent and editor until 1854, when he sold his interest to Stephen T. Allen, who merged the magazine with others for children. In 1858 the title became *Merry's Museum, Parley's Magazine, Woodworth's Cabinet and the Schoolfellow*. The publication lost much of its former austere, sober nature, although the educational articles and series that characterized the *Museum* under Goodrich's editorship were continued under Allen. Series such as the Rollo stories of Jacob Abbott and some of the Parley stories appeared alongside columns such as "Spring Fashions for 1858" (June 1858). The Robert Merry persona was joined by Uncle Frank, Hiram Hatchet, Aunt Sue, and other pseudonymous editors; these characters, all benevolent, well-informed older people, wrote columns for children. One of the prominent features under the new editorship was a puzzle column, with rebuses, number games, word games, and acrostics that children were encouraged to solve and answer in letters to the columns. Prizes were offered for the cleverest of these answers. One of the most frequent topics in "Merry's Monthly Chat" became the issue of the annual subscription fee, now $1.50 for all classes of subscribers. Readers were encouraged to enlist their friends as new subscribers. Although in 1858 the *Museum* reported 20,000 subscribers, the urgency and frequency of the pleas for payment suggest that many readers were in arrears and that the *Museum* was suffering financially.

The title page reflected a change in editors several times in the 1850s and 1860s. John N. Stearns took over from Stephen T. Allen in 1858; Horace B. Fuller became the publisher and apparently operated the periodical from 1866, when Stearns resigned, until January 1868, when Louisa May Alcott became the editor. He took back the editorship when she resigned in 1870. A wide assortment of pseudonymous aunts and uncles appeared as editors on the title pages, and it is difficult to identify anyone but the main editors during the later years. Contributors are also difficult to identify; no doubt some were children, so even if their names appeared, they must have no continuing literary significance. The *Museum* lost much of its focus in these years, having lost its guiding light in Goodrich. It managed, however, to hold onto many of its child readers into adulthood as the letters to the "Monthly Chat" show, but even under Alcott's supervision, it acquired no new vision. Alcott agreed to edit the *Museum* and to provide stories, one or two a month, in return for $500 a year. She revived "Merry's Monthly Chat with His Friends," where, under the persona of "Cousin Tribulation," she offered in her first number the breakfast scene that was later revised and included at the beginning of *Little Women*.

In *Merry's Museum for Boys and Girls*, as the journal was then called, the incident is narrated in the first person by "Lu," one of four sisters who are little girls rather than the more mature, teenage March sisters that they become in *Little Women*. The incident takes place on New Year rather than on Christmas, and the menu is different —porridge and molasses rather than buckwheat cakes and popovers, as in *Little Women*. The sisters' father is also part of the procession, bringing food and fuel to the poor German immigrant family; in *Little Women* he is off at the Civil War, and his place is filled by the family's household servant. But the Hummel family portrait is identical to the one in *Little Women*— a large number of ill-clothed children huddled together in one bed to keep warm in the unheated hovel; a newborn and its recently delivered mother languishing for want of proper care; and no food in the house. The lesson of self-sacrifice is particularly apparent in this early version of the scene, since the narrator Lu, with guileless childhood narcissism, wishes that she had eaten the breakfast herself when first asked to relinquish it but then regrets her selfishness when she sees her sisters readily assenting to her mother's proposal to bring it to the Hummels. The scene ends with the merriment of the breakfast, the gratitude of its recipients, and their attempts in broken English to express their gratitude, likening the visiting sisters to "angel-children." The reader is assured that "there were not in all the city four merrier children than the hungry little girls."[6] In the same entry in her diary Alcott recorded Fuller's offer of the editorship of the *Museum* and her editor, Thomas Niles's, urging that she try her hand at writing a girls book.[7] Although she did not begin writing *Little Women* until May 1868, the breakfast incident was clearly in her mind then from her earlier column for the *Museum*.

Alcott continued this high moral tone throughout her editorship of the *Museum*, which lasted about two years. Although she announced her decision in the first "Merry's Monthly Chat" to print only those letters from subscribers that were "of general interest" and "particularly attractive," she later seems to have relented from this position by request of her readers. It may be that some of these letters came from Alcott's own hand, since they are lengthy and not at all childlike in diction, although other letters are clearly the productions of children. In later chats Alcott described scenes from her own life, reminiscences of Civil War veterans, a May Day celebration from her childhood, and the like. She continued "Aunt Sue's Puzzle Drawer," a popular column in the *Museum* begun under Allen's editorship, and included there a column of "Notices to Corre-spondents," commenting on their answers to earlier puzzles and encouraging them to submit puzzles of their own and to correspond with the personae of the *Museum*.

Alcott's most noteworthy contributions to the *Museum* are two novels. In the "Monthly Chat" for March 1868, she promised her novel *Willy's Wonder-Book* later called *Will's Wonder-Book*, a story of "some of the lovely and wonderful miracles...in the summer."[8] The series was a collection of vignettes about nature studies, very much in the Goodrich tradition of such studies to inform children about the world around them and to teach them of the God who designed such beauties. Will, the title character, and Polly his sister ask questions of their grandmother about various natural phenomena—plants, insects, trees. In her answers, the grandmother harkens back to the omniscient adults portrayed in children's literature earlier in the century who function as mouthpieces of encyclopedic knowledge. The series "Will's Wonder-Book" continued for eight issues; as a story it shows Alcott's love of nature but little of her skill in portraying fully realized characters in lifelike situations.

More typical of Alcott's talent as a writer of domestic fiction for children is her second juvenile novel, *An Old-Fashioned Girl*, serialized in the pages of *Merry's Museum* from July to December 1869. Perhaps Alcott was trading on her reader's familiarity with the names Polly and Will from *Will's Wonder-Book*, for the "old-fashioned girl" of the title is Polly Milton, and her favorite brother is Will. Although Polly and Will are not as lively or as fully portrayed as Jo March and Theodore Laurence of *Little Women* are, they are still recognizable as real young children, well behaved, although occasionally led astray. In the novel Alcott holds forth against the modern fashion of bringing up girls, who acted like society debutantes rather than the modest young ladies that Alcott valued. She castigated girls' finishing schools, where girls were not taught any useful knowledge but developed a taste for fashionable clothes that were neither becoming nor practical and habits of flirtation and gossip that make them immodest and unmaidenly. The novel is more didactic than *Little Women*, but it was a success with the readers of *Merry's Museum*, who enjoyed it so much that they requested a sequel which would show how the characters in the book grew up and married. Alcott obliged by portraying the old-fashioned girl and her friends six years later, when they are ready for professions and marriage.

Alcott found the chore of editing the *Museum* particularly time consuming, since she wrote much of the material for each number herself. By 1870 she relinquished the editorship of the *Museum* although to whom is unclear. The *Museum* had proven modestly successful to Fuller, its publisher, perhaps because of its earlier reputation; but without an active, skillful editor, it became a semi-annual collection of short stories for children by little-known authors, although Caroline Hewins, Juliana H. Ewing, and Alcott all contributed pieces. There were no puzzles or monthly chats that had been so popular with earlier readers. The *Museum* limped along for two more years, finally disappearing in June 1872.

Much of the writing in *Merry's Museum* would be of little interest to children today, but the parts that would attract them were also the most popular features in their own time, the "Monthly Chat" and the puzzles. The stories and columns were informative and uplifting, certainly, but the narrative style is flat and uninteresting by the standards of today's literature for children. However, in the "Monthly Chat" the children could see their own letters in print and have them answered by Robert Merry or his fictional stand-ins who took over the "Chat" and the editorship periodically throughout the *Museum's* history. Subscribers could contribute puzzles, send in answers, and be praised by name for correct answers. Of its several editors, Samuel Goodrich and Louisa May Alcott are the most noteworthy, but the *Museum* was not the showcase for their best efforts that it might have been. That children continued to subscribe and to read the *Museum* is more a tribute to their own contributions to its pages than anything else.

Notes

1. Samuel Goodrich, *Recollections of a Lifetime; or Men and Things I Have Seen* (New York and Auburn, Ala.: Miller, Orton, and Mulligan, 1857), 1:166-67.
2. Ibid., vol. 2, app.
3. Ibid., pp. 310-11.
4. *Merry's Museum and Parley's Magazine* 10 (September 1845), 288.
5. Goodrich, *Recollections*, vol. 2, app.
6. *Merry's Museum, for Boys and Girls* 55 (July 1868), 35-36.
7. *Louisa May Alcott: Her Life, Letters and Journals*, ed. Edna D. Cheney (Boston: Roberts Brothers, 1890), p. 186.
8. *Merry's Museum, for Boys and Girls* 55 (September 1868), 114.

Information Sources

BIBLIOGRAPHY
Samuel G. Goodrich, *Recollections of a Lifetime; or Men and Things I Have Seen: in a Series of Familiar Letters to a Friend, Historical, Biographical, Anecdotal, and Descriptive.* (New York and Auburn, Ala.: Miller, Orton, and Mulligan, 1857) 2 vols.; Frank Luther Mott, *A History of American Magazines*, 5 vols. (Cambridge: Harvard University Press, 1938-1968); Daniel Roselle, *Samuel Griswold Goodrich, Creator of Peter Parley: A Study of His Life and Work* (Albany, N.Y.: State University of New York Press, 1968); Madeleine Stern, "The First Appearance of A 'Little Women' Incident," *American Notes and Queries* 3 (October 1943), 99-100; idem, ed., *Louisa's Wonder Book: An Unknown Alcott Juvenile* (Mount Pleasant, Mich.: Central Michigan University and Clarke Historical Library, 1975).
INDEX SOURCES
None.
LOCATION SOURCES
Available in libraries with major historical collections; Boston Public Library and New York State Public Library, Albany, N.Y., have early holdings; later holdings are in the Bangor Public Library, Bangor, Maine. Copies are also available on microfilm in the American Periodical Series, University Microfilms International, Ann Arbor, Mich.

Publication History

MAGAZINE TITLE AND TITLE CHANGES

Robert Merry's Museum (1841-1842); *Merry's Museum and Parley's Magazine* (1843-
    1846); *Robert Merry's Museum* (1847-1851); *Merry's Museum and Parley's Mag-
    azine* (1852-1858); *Merry's Museum, Parley's Magazine, Woodworth's Cabinet
    and the Schoolfellow* (1859); *Merry's Museum and Parley's Magazine* (1860);
    Merry's Museum, Parley's Magazine, Woodworth's Cabinet and the Schoolfellow
    (1861-1865); *Merry's Museum and Parley's Magazine* (1866); *Merry's Museum
    and Woodworth's Cabinet* (1867); *Merry's Museum, for Boys and Girls* (1868-
    1872).

VOLUME AND ISSUE DATA

Robert Merry's Museum (vol. 1, no. 1-vol. 4, no. 4); *Merry's Museum and Parley's
    Magazine* (vol. 5, no. 1-vol. 12, no. 6); *Robert Merry's Museum* (vol. 13, no.
    1-vol. 22, no. 6); *Merry's Museum and Parley's Magazine* (vol. 23, no. 1-vol. 36,
    no. 6); *Merry's Museum, Parley's Magazine, Woodworth's Cabinet and the School-
    fellow* (vol. 37, no. 1-vol. 38, no. 6); *Merry's Museum and Parley's Magazine*
    (vol. 39, no. 1-vol. 40, no. 6); *Merry's Museum, Parley's Magazine, Woodworth's
    Cabinet and the Schoolfellow* (vol. 41, no. 1-vol. 50-no. 6); *Merry's Museum
    and Parley's Magazine* (vol. 51, no. 1-vol. 52, no. 6); *Merry's Museum and
    Woodworth's Cabinet* (vol. 53, no. 1-vol. 54, no. 6); *Merry's Museum, for boys
    and girls* (vol. 55, no. 1-vol. 65, no. 2).

PUBLISHER AND PLACE OF PUBLICATION

I. C. and J. N. Stearns, New York (1841-1844); S. T. Allen, New York (1845); I. C.
    and J. N. Stearns, New York (1846); G. W. and S. O. Post, New York (1847-
    1848); D. MacDonald, New York (1849-1850); S. T. Allen, New York (1850-
    1855); J. N. Stearns, New York (1855-1866); Horace B. Fuller, Boston (1867-
    1872).

EDITOR

Samuel G. Goodrich (1841-1850); Stephen T. Allen (1850-1857); John N. Stearns (1858-
    1866); Louisa May Alcott (1868-1870).

Ruth K. MacDonald

N

NEW HORIZONS FOR YOUTH

It was the best of times, it was the worst of times. It was a time of gladness and youth and victory, of sadness and sudden death. It was the time of John and Robert Kennedy and Martin Luther King, of freedom riders and the Bay of Pigs, of the Cuban blockade and the Kennedy assassinations. It was a time when people of various political persuasions were concerned with building fall-out shelters, getting the Communists out of Cuba, granting equal rights to blacks, and defying the House Un-American Activities Committee. It was a time when college students were beginning to become involved in politics, and *New Horizons for Youth* both fostered and took advantage of that awakening. *New Horizons for Youth* was a Communist newspaper published in the late 1950s and early 1960s. Its first editor, Daniel Rubin, was described as "a prominent Communist youth leader."[1] When Rubin later stepped down to the associate editorship, he was succeeded by Lionel Libson, who also campaigned enthusiastically for Communist causes: "I believe this fact and others give support to the Communist Party's contention that their sole aim is to persuade a majority of our people to decide by free choice that Socialism will benefit them. A new and different view of the Communist Party is needed."[2] This was in response to an attack by the editor of *The Daily Iowan*, student newspaper of the State University of Iowa.

Appealing primarily to younger college and more politically aware high school students, *New Horizons for Youth* covered, with its own particular emphasis, the entire range of a conventional adult newspaper. Editorials and articles developed the ideology of communism and socialism and argued against capitalists and imperialists. Historical articles reviewed the ravages of capitalist attacks on labor and social movements: the so-called Palmer Raids of 1919-1920, the struggle of the Molly Maguires with the Pinkertons in their attempts to organize unions among the coal miners, Joe Hill, the *Sacco Vanzetti* case. Modern social problems and protests were probed: the youth movement in Cuba and China, Freedom Riders in Alabama, and coal miners in Hazard, Kentucky. Cultural articles and reviews emphasized exhibits of Socialist art and frequently spotlighted the superstars of that movement—Pete Seeger and Berthold Brecht. An extensive interview with Seeger covered his political blacklisting as well as his opinions about music. Political news was generated by the Bay of Pigs, Cuban blockade, and ongoing activities of the House Un-American Activities Committee. President Kennedy's policies passed in and out of favor with *New Horizons for Youth*. His attempts to alleviate youthful unemployment and his creation of the Peace Corps were favored, but his intervention in Cuba and dialog with Kruschev were denounced.

An example of editorial policy and a statement on the ideology of *New Horizons for Youth* can be found in a two-part article: "The Possibilities of Democracy under Capitalism" (March 1962) and "The Possibilities of Democracy under Socialism" (April 1962). In the first part of the series the editor sees a restriction of the democratic process, because economic decisions are made only by a small minority of people. (*Democracy* is defined in this article as "the rule of the majority," even though the article is entitled "Individual Freedom."[3] "Only a handful of people making the economic decisions on whether and what to produce, whether to hire workers or not."[4] "Individual Freedom under Socialism" argues that in a Socialist economy no motivation to accumulate capital exists. Furthermore, the test for elected officials is "how well they perform the function of organizing for improvement in the lives of everyone."[5] However, the editor warned, encouragement of a Socialist economy is "a long-term process" and does not ensure that democracy will continually expand. It may be blocked, for example, by a single ill-disposed individual, although the writer does not indicate how the individual has seized so much of the power supposedly firmly rooted in the majority by the law of economic forces. When this obstructing individual is removed, the flood of democracy surges forward. Thus with the death of Stalin, according to the *New Horizons for Youth* editor, democracy was restored to the Russian people, "The cult of personality around Stalin was such a period of violation of socialist democracy. With the ending of the cult, it is evident to nearly all observers that there is an unleashing of energy and initiative on the part of millions of Soviet citizens. Now many millions take part in policy formulation at all stages of economic planning of the program for Communism."[6] In spite of the descriptive title, not once is individual freedom mentioned, either in reference to the United States or Russia.

In another article focusing on ideology, Betty Morrison attacked *Senior Scholastic** and Scholastic Magazines, Inc., for their coverage of communism. She complained of a lack of objectivity, arguing that the merits of communism are not honestly discussed: "[Communism] is spoken of as barbaric in its concept and tyrranical in its inception. Yet one-third of mankind is living under the socialist system."[7] Morrison particularly objected to *Scholastic's* treatment of Castro's Cuba. *Scholastic* claimed that Cuba was plotting the overthrow of moderate and democratic governments in Central and South America. Yet as Morrison somewhat pointedly remarked, there was a notable scarcity of such governments in that area. At the climax of her article, however, when Morrison was discussing *Scholastic's* definition of communism, she quoted not from *Scholastic* but from Hitler's *Reichstag Address*, commenting that *Scholastic's* position was "like" Hitler's.

The Palmer Raids, a series of government arrests of members of left-wing groups after World War I, furnish the basis for one of the historical examinations of the struggles of socialism in America. A. Mitchell Palmer, attorney general from 1919 to 1921, reacting to the Russian Revolution, instituted a series of investigations of radical movements in the United States, investigations that culminated in the *Sacco-Venzetti* case. *New Horizons for Youth* discussed the case briefly and then went on to describe the further depredations of the Palmer task force on workers' associations: the Union of Russian Workers, Industrial Workers of the World (IWW) headquarters, and various Communist party meetings.

New Horizons for Youth enthusiastically and continually reported opposition to the McCarran Immigration Act and to the ongoing House Un-American Activities Committee. In the February 1961 issue it reported a youth demonstration in Washington opposing the committee and supporting Congressman James Roosevelt's motion to reduce funding for it. *New Horizons for Youth* reporters were delighted when the American Nazi party demonstrated on the opposite side of the street in favor of the committee.

In California *New Horizons for Youth* hailed the defeat of Proposition 24, denying public employment and the right to assemble on public property to groups on the attorney general's list.

In the same issue "The Lesson of Birmingham" discussed the impetus given to the black liberation movement by the bus sit-ins in Birmingham, Alabama, as well as the virulent opposition of Governor Wallace. *New Horizons for Youth* saw the action in Birmingham as a turning point in the then almost ten-year-old struggle, which had begun with the school desegregation act of 1954.

In February 1962 *New Horizons for Youth* was appalled by the attack of the McCarran Committee on the Socialist newspaper *The Worker*: "The American government, responding to Ultra-Right pressure, has taken another step to limit democratic freedoms. Ultra-Right Senator Strom Thurmond inaugurated this campaign to silence the dissenting press, with a call for prosecution of the 'Workers' "[8] Although the magazine was published from offices in New York, Rubin was active as far west as Iowa. In an editorial he described a lively day spent with the editor of the University of Chicago newspaper, Jay Greenberg. Greenberg and Rubin have a cops-and-robbers chase, pursued around the city by three men disguised as Associated Press reporters who are almost certainly,

according to Rubin, FBI agents who constantly harassed the editorial staff of
New Horizons for Youth. (Given the political climate of the time and the editorial
policy of the magazine, Rubin's assumption is not complete fantasy). He commented on the clumsiness of his pursuers who seemed to behave without subtlety
or apparent purpose.

Later Rubin debated with the editor of the University of Iowa newspaper, Phil
Currie. Currie was critical of Rubin's defense of the Communist party in the
United States at a speech at the university. In pretended sympathy he wrote:

> I understand now. It is not correct to assume that J. Edgar Hoover,...and
> the many newspapers who describe you as affiliated with the Communist
> Party youth movement know what they are talking about....I found that
> out through your convincing example of how those two "FBI" men (they
> said they were from the Associated Press, remember?), equipped with
> newspapers for disguises and a fake hearing aid trailed you and the Uni-
> versity of Chicago editor through that city with no real effort to disguise
> themselves. You had them figured out all the time! You really showed me
> the stupidity of the FBI when you pointed out how crudely disguised and
> how truly silly they were. I was especially shocked to learn that one of
> the men actually swore under his breath.[9]

Rubin's reply in this editorial debate was a fervent reassertion of the innocent
intentions of the Communist party and its efforts to promote civil rights and
guarantee "democratic freedoms": "I believe this fact and others give support
to the Communist Party's contention that their sole aim is to persuade a majority
of our people to decide by free choice that socialism will benefit them."[10]

The second and final editor of *New Horizons for Youth*, succeeding Rubin in
March 1962, was Lionel Libson, who also traveled widely for political causes,
and who also had his problems with official Washington:

> As we go to press, *New Horizons for Youth* is once again being challenged
> under the anti-democratic McCarran Act. On December 18, your editor
> must appear before a hearing of the Subversive Activities Control Board
> in New York City. The hearing is to determine whether I must register as
> a Communist....There is little doubt that my editorship of *NHY* is the
> reason for my being cited....I am being charged with NO act of sabotage,
> espionage, treason, etc. It is the *ideas* expressed in "New Horizons" which
> are on trial.[11]

Shortly after the Kennedy assassination the paper apparently foundered on
financial difficulties. One issue in November or December 1963 mourns the
death of a liberal president, although the paper had frequently excoriated his
foreign policy. The next issue, probably January-February 1964, trumpets com-

ing achievements in civil rights for blacks and greater freedom for all Americans and then is silent.

Notes

1. *New Horizons for Youth* 2 (March 1962), 7.
2. Ibid., 2 (February 1962), 3.
3. Ibid., 2 (March 1962), 7.
4. Ibid.
5. Ibid.
6. Ibid., 2 (April-May 1962), 7.
7. Ibid., p. 5.
8. Ibid., 2 (February 1962), 2.
9. Ibid., p. 3.
10. Ibid.
11. Ibid., 4 (December 1963), 11.

Information Sources

BIBLIOGRAPHY
None.
INDEX SOURCES
None.
LOCATION SOURCES
Library of Congress; University of Iowa, Iowa City, Ia.; Swarthmore College, Swarth-more, Pa.; University of Michigan, Ann Arbor, Mich.

Publication History

MAGAZINE TITLE AND TITLE CHANGES
New Horizons for Youth (1960-1964).
VOLUME AND ISSUE DATA
New Horizons for Youth (vol. 1, no. 1-vol. 4, no. 2).
PUBLISHER AND PLACE OF PUBLICATION
Youth Publications, New York (October 1960-March 1962); Philadelphia (April 1962-February 1964).
EDITOR
Daniel Rubin (October 1960-March 1962); Lionel Libson (March 1962-January/February 1964).

Meredith M. Klaus

THE NURSERY

First issued in 1867, *The Nursery: A Magazine for Youngest Readers* belongs to the post-Civil War generation of children's magazines, a period during which, as R. Gordon Kelly has commented, "the children's magazine came into its own, and American children's literature entered what many were to recall as its golden day."[1] Like its contemporaries *Our Young Folks,** *Oliver Optic's Mag-*

azine,* and *The Riverside Magazine for Young People,** *The Nursery* was published in Boston.

The editor, Fanny P. Seavers, probably saw her "youngest readers" as ranging
between the ages of four and nine or ten. The children who received *The Nursery*
every month were offered a selection of fiction and nonfiction, verse, and an
occasional song. Many of the pieces are printed with syllable divisions and
accent marks to make the reading easier, and some are in very large type for
the beginning reader. The editor made liberal use of illustrations. For little
children there are decorated alphabets and picture stories with illustrations replacing some of the words. The writers who contributed to *The Nursery* often
hid their identity behind pseudonyms like "Uncle Charles," "Trottie's Aunt,"
and "Aunt Clara" or signed their pieces with initials. Much of the writing
appears over the name of Emily Carter. Probably none of the contributors is a
familiar name any longer, for unlike magazines such as *Our Young Folks* and
St. Nicholas,* *The Nursery* did not attract first-rate writers for children. Today
it is impossible to say whether the magazine sought out such talent without
success or whether it was satisfied with the accomplishments of its contributors.

Distinctions between fiction and nonfiction become blurred in *The Nursery*,
since many pieces that are probably fictional are written as if the events described
actually occurred. For example, "Charles Reading the Bible" begins by stating
that "Charles is six years old. He can read to the folks from the good book. He
likes to read, and he likes to play too."[2] However a critic would classify this,
the writer clearly intended that the young reader would believe in Charles's
existence. A similar piece, "Willy Learns His Letters" (1870), printed in large
type, tells the reader that Willy is three years old and continues: "Willy takes
'The Nursery.' He likes to look at the pictures. He gets his mamma to read the
stories to him; but he learns so fast that I think he will be able to read them
himself before long. He is a good little boy."[3] "Only a Little Brook" describes
the death of a little girl in Bath, Maine, who trusts in God to save her soul and
dies peacefully. Presented as a true story, it is meant to encourage the piety and
religious trust of young readers by giving them the example of this nameless
but presumably real child. William C. Godwin's "The Boy Who Did a Kind
Act" is subtitled "A True Story" (1867). It tells of a poor boy who, turned
away by a rich man whom he has asked for a job, does a kind act for an old
horse, is observed by the rich man, and is then rewarded with a job, eventually
becoming rich himself. It thus falls into the subgenre that might be called the
nineteenth-century fairy tale in which a poor child, usually in an urban setting,
is rewarded for his virtue by a rich and powerful man. But it sounds no more
"true" than the stories of Horatio Alger, Jr.

Another group of stories provides factual information, often in a narrative
framework, for example, "The Codfish" (1870), which uses a fisherman to
convey facts about a mainstay of the New England diet. "Daisy's True Story"
(1871) is presented as told by Daisy herself; a little girl, she writes about her
life at Fort Richardson, Texas, where her father is in the army. The articles

about Albert Victor, the four-year-old Prince of Wales, are examples of straight-forward nonfiction. ''The Ostrich and Her Eggs'' (1872) and ''The Great Bell in Russia'' (1872) are two of the many articles that brought information about the wider world to the magazine's readers. ''Works of Art for Children'' (1873) shows readers how to use cones, flowers, grasses, and burrs in artwork. ''The Infant Musician'' (1874) describes the child Mozart.

As one would expect in writing for young children, fiction in *The Nursery* includes many stories about animals, toys, and daily events in the lives of small children. A glance at some tables of contents gives a sampling of such fare: ''How the Cat Saved the Bird'' (1867), ''Edwin's Dream'' (1871), ''Lily's Sleigh Ride'' (1871), ''Letters from Dolls'' (1868), ''The Children's Picnic'' (1870), ''Six Scenes in Lily's Day'' (1870), and ''A Hard Day's Wash'' (1867). In many of these selections the plot, if any, is extremely slight; the pieces are perhaps better described as sketches than stories. In both fiction and nonfiction, *The Nursery's* authors frequently address the child reader directly, assuming a stance of cozy intimacy. For example, ''The Great Tea-Party'' (1867) opens, ''Don't you wish you could have been at Ruth Green's tea-party? It took place the last week in September. The day was fair and warm.''[4]

Poetry shows the same range of subjects as the fiction: ''The Infant's Song,'' ''The Goose,'' ''Mother's Darling'' (all 1867), ''The Proud Doll'' (1872), ''At Play'' (1870), and ''A Little Girl's Good-by'' (1872). Even by the standards of the time, the verse is generally undistinguished. To entertain readers and to involve them further in the magazine's content, *The Nursery* published occasional brief plays, such as ''Muff the Traitor. A Tragedy in Six Acts. By a Papa'' (1869). Some issues have music, often the musical settings for familiar nursery rhymes.

Whatever the material offered to young readers for their amusement, the prevailing tone of *The Nursery* is one of earnestness. The editor and writers took very seriously their mission to foster the moral development of their audience. They did not hesitate to point out lessons, and the direct address so often adopted is well suited to the explicit moral teaching that characterized *The Nursery*. For example, ''The Little Runaway'' (1869) ends, ''Little Merry never ran away to see the big wheel again. He was a great comfort to his friends, though the run-away spirit was in his heart still. But he was afraid of doing any thing his mamma told him was WRONG. Are *you* afraid of doing wrong? I hope so.''[5] Children were admonished to do good to others, to follow the words of Jesus, to keep their feet dry and avoid sitting in drafts, to be contented and courageous and useful, to love their sisters and brothers, to obey their elders, to extend charity to the poor, to treat servants humanely. One story about the results of bad temper (''Why Emma Did Not Play,'' 1872) tucks in a little lesson about proper posture; under an illustration of a boy reading, the story ends, ''While the younger children are playing in the yard, Charles, who dearly loves his book, is having a good time on the parlor sofa. It is a pity that he does not sit up straight, instead of lounging in such an ungraceful way.''[6]

In these stories thoughtless behavior and moral transgressions bring unpleasant consequences. They may be permanent (for example, the boy who hits an old man in the eye with a lump of ice in "The Dove and the Bee" (1867) brings financial ruin on his father: when the old man is in a position to lend the father money he refuses it, on the grounds that a person who cannot bring up his son to treat old people well is not fit to be trusted) or temporary (in the form of minor illness or the disapproval of others). Good behavior is rewarded by the love of family and friends and by happiness in oneself. Occasionally, good behavior brings more material benefits. The story about a little girl who sells her doll at a fair to raise money for poor orphaned children concludes, "I should not wonder if Blue-Eyes were to wake on Christmas morning and find a new doll—one much prettier than Belvidera— in the stocking which she will hang up" ("How Blue-Eyes Sold Her Doll," 1871).[7] The poor boy in "Daniel's Prayer" (1871) remembers his dying mother's injunction about meeting temptation with prayer; he returns the purse he has found to the old gentleman who has lost it and is rewarded with a position in the old man's counting-house and a place in his home. But for the most part the lesson repeatedly found in the pages of *The Nursery* is that the good child is a happy child and is able to make others happy; that is reward enough.

The Nursery was published for thirteen years, from 1867 to 1880, at which time it merged with a new periodical to become *Our Little Ones and the Nursery** edited by William T. Adams ("Oliver Optic").

Notes

1. R. Gordon Kelly, *Mother Was a Lady* (Westport, Conn.: Greenwood Press, 1974), p. 7.
2. *The Nursery* 4 (1868), 21.
3. Ibid., 7 (1870), 22.
4. Ibid., 1 (1867), 121.
5. Ibid., 6 (1869), 7.
6. Ibid., 12 (1872), 140.
7. Ibid., 9 (1871), 16.

Information Sources

BIBLIOGRAPHY
R. Gordon Kelly, *Mother Was a Lady* (Westport, Conn.: Greenwood Press, 1974); Frank Luther Mott, *A History of American Magazines* (Cambridge: Harvard University Press, 1838), vol. 3.
INDEX SOURCES
None.
LOCATION SOURCES
The only complete set of volumes is in the Boston Public Library (vols. 1-28). Harvard University, Cambridge, Mass., has vols. 1-27, and the Brooklyn Public Library, Brooklyn, N.Y., has vols. 1-20. Partial sets are in some university and public

libraries. Copies are available on microfilm from Greenwood Press, Westport, Conn.

Publication History

MAGAZINE TITLE AND TITLE CHANGES
The Nursery: A Magazine for Youngest Readers (1867-1869); *The Nursery: A Monthly Magazine for Youngest Readers* (1869-1880).
VOLUME AND ISSUE DATA
The Nursery: A Magazine for Youngest Readers (vol. 1-vol. 4); *The Nursery: A Monthly Magazine for Youngest Readers* (vol. 5-vol. 28).
PUBLISHER AND PLACE OF PUBLICATION
John L. Shorey, Boston (1867-1880).
EDITOR
Fanny P. Seavers (1867-1880).

Joan Brest Friedberg

O

OLIVER OPTIC'S MAGAZINE

On the February day in 1862 that William Lee and Charles Shepard opened their bookstore in South Boston, they little imagined that their retail and jobbing business would soon expand into a firm that would "be considered the pre-eminent publisher of books for children in the United States during the period following the Civil War."[1] The transition to publishing began when Shepard bought a collection of publisher's stereotype plates that included "The Boat Club Series" and "The Riverdale Story Books" by Oliver Optic (the pseudonym of William Taylor Adams). Although the first books issued by Lee & Shepard were John Ruskin's *The King of the Golden River* and *Willis the Pilot*, it was Oliver Optic's two series of stories that provided the partners with their initial success in publishing and established the firm's new direction. During the remaining years of the Civil War, Lee & Shepard emphasized books for children rather than books for adults, because juvenile literature sold particularly well then. The profits derived from this policy—due in no small measure to the popularity of Optic's books—encouraged the partners to establish a magazine for young people and appoint Oliver Optic as editor.

The capacity of William Taylor Adams to produce an unending flow of exciting Optic stories and his experience as editor of *The Student and Schoolmate** from 1861 to 1866 made him an obvious choice for the position. In addition to providing his literary skills, he also brought to the enterprise a knowledge of young people gained from nearly twenty years of teaching in the Dorchester and Boston schools. He had been teacher, editor, author—all three—until July 1865, when he resigned as principal of the Bowditch School to devote all of his time to writing.

Oliver Optic's Magazine: Our Boys and Girls made its first appearance on January 5, 1867. Initially, it was a weekly of twelve pages, selling for $2.25 a year. After the first six months, circulation was sufficient to warrant increasing the size of the magazine to sixteen pages and the price to $2.50. Weekly publication, Adams observed, would provide his young readers, who supposedly ranged in age from twelve to twenty, with "satisfaction in the frequent appearance of a periodical adapted to their wants and tastes."[2] To fill the fifty-two numbers of this weekly, he produced three serials the first year and thereafter four annually until the end of 1870. The stress involved in directing a weekly magazine so exhausted Adams that he left Boston in June 1870 for a six-month tour of Europe. During his absence Samuel Burnham, recently employed as associate editor, took over the editorial duties. In January 1871 the publishers changed the magazine from a weekly of sixteen pages to a monthly that grew from sixty-four to eighty pages. By 1875 it had a circulation of approximately 11,000.

The survival of the magazine was closly linked to the prosperity of Lee & Shepard. When losses suffered in the Great Boston Fire and the Panic of 1873 brought the publishers to bankruptcy in the fall of 1875, the firm was forced to discontinue *Oliver Optic's Magazine* with the December issue. Although Adams hoped that Lee & Shepard might revive the periodical "when the skies [should] be brighter and the gales more propitious," its publication was never resumed.[3]

In the first issue of *Oliver Optic's Magazine*, January 5, 1867, Adams outlined the editorial policy that would govern the content and format of the magazine. "We intend," he wrote, "to furnish a magazine which shall interest and amuse Our Boys and Girls, while it makes them wiser and better."[4] The material he selected often combined amusement and instruction in a single item. His own stories, for instance, as well as many of the tales he published, were a mixture of fast-paced action and earnest moralizing. In turn, much of the nonfiction offered information packaged in a lively and entertaining manner. If individual pieces embodied the editor's goals, so too did the distribution of material in every issue.

When Optic's boys and girls opened the covers of their magazine, they were treated to an assortment of fiction, drama, poetry, puzzles, information, and advice arranged in an order established at the beginning of the second volume in July 1867. The distinctive format, adapted from the pattern used earlier in *The Student and Schoolmate*, gave a special character to the magazine and provided continuity from issue to issue. Each number opened with chapters of an Optic story and closed with the editor's comments. After the magazine became a monthly, the arrangement was slightly modified by the addition of one or two pieces of music after the editorial. Within this framework were set the remaining items composing each issue. First came an assortment of tales, articles, and verse and then there followed the many special departments so characteristic of the juvenile periodicals of the period. Although three of these sections—the dialogues, declamations, and puzzles—had already appeared in *The Student and*

Schoolmate, the remaining departments were developed for *Oliver Optic's Magazine*.

The occasional short dramas suitable for reading or amateur performance appearing in the early months soon developed into "Dialogues," a regular department conducted by George M. Baker, a member of Lee & Shepard's staff and the resident "drama machine."[5] "The Orator," a feature promoting public speaking, offered selections of prose and poetry in which appropriate gestures were indicated by sketches in the margin and key words and phrases were emphasized by the use of bold-faced type. In "The Playground," a section chiefly intended for boys, Dr. J. H. Hanaford discussed archery, baseball, boating, lacrosse, skating, and swimming. Adams discontinued this department at the end of 1869, replacing it with occasional articles about games and sports. In "Headwork" Adams placed the puzzles, charades, and rebuses that he and his young readers contributed. There were also two sections devoted to correspondence, "Our Letter Bag" and "Pigeon-Hole Papers." When the first department of readers' letters became too crowded, Adams inaugurated "Pigeon-Hole Papers" in January 1871 as a section to "answer questions," "give extracts from very clever letters," and discuss topics "not important enough for the dignity of an article."[6]

From time to time the magazine ran contests to encourage reader participation and to increase subscriptions. Prizes were offered to those forming subscribers' clubs, to those who solved puzzles, and to those who correctly answered the full-page rebus, which appeared annually once the magazine became a monthly. A growing readership also depended, Adams knew, on the visual appeal of his magazine. Conscious of the importance of improving the number and quality of illustrations in each issue, Adams experimented in 1868 and 1869 with the series "Our Picture Gallery," which featured engravings of the work of Thomas Nast, accompanied by short texts explaining the pictures. When the association with Nast ended, Adams found other ways of enhancing the appearance of the magazine. After 1870 many of the serials and some of the articles were illustrated by artists lke C. G. Bush, W. L. Champney, E. B. Green, L. B. Humphrey, and Henry L. Stephens. As further embellishment, Adams frequently added full-page plates taken from books published by Lee & Shepard, a number of which unfortunately bore no relationship at all to the contents of the magazine in which they appeared.

The format Adams devised provided the setting for the magazine's most prominent feature, its fiction for young people. In fact, so substantial was the commitment to fiction that *Oliver Optic's Magazine* published forty-five juvenile novels in serial form as well as many shorter tales. The shorter fiction includes examples of fantasy like Paul Cobden's fairy tales translated from the French, Charles Barnard's stories of mechanical magic, and Mary N. Prescott's "Sweetmeat Castle" (December 11, 1869). More successful than the often strained attempts at fantasy are the factual stories using believable characters in a fictional framework to convey useful information. C. E. Bishop's "Vacation in Petrolia"

(May 1871 and following issues), for instance, explains the process of drilling for oil by describing two boys who visit an oil field with their uncle.

Of the serialized novels appearing in the magazine, twenty-five are by Oliver Optic and the remaining twenty by established Lee & Shepard authors such as George M. Baker, James De Mille, Amanda Douglas, Elijah Kellogg, Sophie May, and Virginia Townsend. This massive amount of juvenile fiction falls into two broad familiar categories: adventure stories for boys and domestic tales for girls. The books for boys, which considerably outnumber those for girls, involve fast-paced action, boyish pranks, suspense, danger, and a demonstration of manly skills. Although both Oliver Optic and Elijah Kellogg write this type of story, Optic is the acknowledged master of the genre with his formula of the bright, competent boy who wins his way through courage, determination, and athletic ability. Like many of Optic's heroes, Phil Farrington shares his author's love of the sea. "In Cringle and Cross-Tree" (January 1871 and following issues), "Bivouac and Battle" (July 1871 and following issues), and "Sea and Shore" (January 1872 and following issues), Phil becomes second mate on a ship attacked by Spanish pirates, makes a second transatlantic crossing more conventionally by steamer, and enjoys further hair-raising adventures aboard a private yacht. The young gentlemen of "The Yacht Club" (January 1873 and following issues), fortunate enough to live on the shores of Penobscot Bay, spend their time sailing in regattas, and eventually join the girls of a rowing club in the cruise "Ocean-Born" (January 1875 and following issues). If Optic's books encourage youthful enterprise and participation in healthful sports, then Kellogg's stories awaken respect for American traditions. In following James Trafton and his friends through their careers at Bowdoin College, five tales of "The Whispering Pine Series," appearing in the magazine from January 1871 to June 1873, depict an American coming of age enjoyed principally by middle-class American males. Kellogg's remaining novels—"A Stout Heart" (July 1873 and following issues), "Sowed in the Wind" (July 1874 and following issues), "Wolf Run" (January 1875 and following issues), and "Brought to the Front" (July 1875 and following issues)—are historical, set in eighteenth-century America. In "The Lily and the Cross" (January 1874 and following issues) James De Mille also turned to the eighteenth-century for his story of French intrigue in Canada.

In contrast to the discovery and conquest of the world emphasized in boys' books, the novels for adolescent girls stress family life, the acquisition of household skills, and self-discipline. Domestic life seen through the eyes of seventeen-year-old Rosalind is the subject of "Seven Daughters" (July 1873 and following issues) by Amanda Douglas. In Sophie May's "The Doctor's Daughter" (January 1871 and following issues), a story compared in its day with Alcott's *Little Women*, Marian Prescott has the opportunity to learn that "with self-renunciation begins life" when she must care for the family during her mother's fatal illness. Despite the emphasis on the duties of womanhood, the girls in these domestic novels are not passive creatures, for they belong, like Jo March, to the new breed of plucky American girl. The heroine of Mrs. E. D. Cheney's "Sally

Williams, the Mountain Girl'' (January 1872 and following issues) is a fearless, strong countrywoman, who journeys along a dangerous mountain trail to rescue a young man from Boston; and George M. Baker's Becky Sleeper in "Running to Waste" (January 1874 and following issues) is an impulsive, tree-climbing tomboy, who adopts more settled ways without losing her courage or her sprightliness.

Unlike the fiction, which is divided into stories appealing either to boys or girls, the nonfiction generally deals with subjects of interest to both: biography, history, travel, natural science, and instruction in crafts and arts. Although much of the information about these topics, particularly in the early years of the magazine, is relegated to single or half-column fillers appearing between longer items, nevertheless some pieces of nonfiction stand out as being of either significant length or special importance. W. S. George's "Eminent Living Men" (January 18, 1868 and following issues) and Thomas Powell's anecdotal "Poets' Homes" (April 4, 1868 and following issues) provide two long-running biographical series. Millinocket's articles on famous Civil War battles, beginning with "Brave Little Bugler" (February 13, 1869), and "How the American Revolution Opened" (July 1874), taken from T. W. Higginson's *Young Folks' History of the United States*, offer patriotic views of America in crisis. The best of the travel articles is "Camp in the Gulch" (January 1874 and following issues), a western adventure by Julian Dale, a federal officer sent to the far West on a scientific expedition. E. A. Samuels, a well-known ornithologist, contributed a series about birds and animals, and George S. Burleigh wrote about marine life in "Sea Things" (September 14, 1867, and following issues). Among the illustrated articles providing practical instruction are Nellie M. Garabrant's "Six Lessons in Wax Works" (August 1873 and following issues) and L. B. Humphrey's exercises in drawing, "The History of the Art Club" (January 1875 and following issues). As a historical document, the article by Adams on Lee & Shepard's new quarters at 41-45 Franklin Street (July 1874) is one of the most important pieces of nonfiction published in the magazine, for it provides "the only detailed description ever made of the quarters and personnel" of Lee & Shepard.[7]

The editorial columns of *Oliver Optic's Magazine* become the battleground where Adams defended both his books and his view of children's literature. He warned against turning all children's stories into educational devices: "do not be afraid of excitement, so long as it is healthy; do not keep young minds always on the high pressure system of instruction."[8] In "Books for the Sunday School Library" (January 1874) Adams, speaking as an advocate for lively stories that capture the imagination of young people, rejected Edward Eggleston's doctrine that juvenile literature should represent life without exaggeration or undue dramatic effect. This "defense of the new freedom in children's literature"[9] soon became a personal defense against the adverse criticism of writers of juvenile fiction such as Emily Huntington Miller and Louisa May Alcott, who deplored the sensationalism of certain boys' books.[9] In "Sunday School Books" (December 1874) Adams answered Miller's unflattering references to Oliver Optic's books by pointing to the "high moral tone" evident in the exemplary behavior of his heroes and by suggesting that, for reasons of professional jealousy, Miller deliberately distorted the evidence.[10] Louisa May Alcott's famous attack on "optical delusions" in "Eight Cousins," appearing in *St. Nicholas** (August 1874), stung Adams to the quick. His reply, "Sensational Books for Boys" (September 1875), pointed to the improbabilities found in her stories and to her often criticized use of slang, complaining that she "said enough to identify the Optic books and then charged them with the faults of all the juvenile books published, her own included."[11]

With few exceptions in the history of American juvenile periodicals has an editor been so personally involved in a magazine as was William Taylor Adams in *Oliver Optic's Magazine*. Not only were his serials the prominent feature of the publication, but his avuncular voice could be heard in special features, letters, and editorial columns, where he assured his young readers of his liveliness and youthful spirits—tempered, of course, with the wisdom of maturity. In his dual role as schoolmaster and storyteller, Adams instructed and amused thousands of young people for nearly a decade in a magazine judged "in some ways the strangest children's magazine published in America."[12]

Notes

1. Richard L. Darling, *The Rise of Children's Book Reviewing in America, 1865-1881* (New York and London: R. R. Bowker, 1968), p. 15.
2. *Oliver Optic's Magazine* 1 (January 5, 1869), 7.
3. Ibid., 18 (December, 1875), 959.
4. Ibid., 1 (January 5, 1867), 7.
5. Raymond L. Kilgour, *Lee and Shepard: Publishers for the People* ([Hamden, Conn.]: The Shoe String Press, 1965), 122.
6. *Oliver Optic's Magazine* 5 (January 1871), 55.
7. Kilgour, *Lee and Shepard*, p. 152.
8. *Oliver Optic's Magazine* 6 (March 1872), 206.
9. Darling, *Rise of Children's Book Reviewing*, p. 33.
10. *Oliver Optic's Magazine* 8 (December 1874), 957.
11. Ibid., 9 (September 1875), 718.
12. Darling, *Rise of Children's Book Reviewing*, p. 213.

Information Sources

BIBLIOGRAPHY

Richard L. Darling, *The Rise of Children's Reviewing in America, 1865-1881* (New York and London: R. R. Bowker, 1968); Raymond L. Kilgour, *Lee and Shepard: Publishers for the People* ([Hamden, Conn.]: The Shoe String Press, 1965); Frank Luther Mott, *A History of American Magazines*, 5 vols. (Cambridge: Harvard University Press, 1938-1968); William Oliver Stevens, "William Taylor Adams," *The Dictionary of American Biography* (New York: Scribner's, 1928), vol. 1; John William Tebbel, *A History of Book Publishing in the United States*, 3 vols. (New York: R. R. Bowker, 1972-1978).

INDEX SOURCES
None.
LOCATION SOURCES
Bound volumes are in a few university and major public libraries. Vols. 1-18 are available
    from University Microfilms International, Ann Arbor, Mich.

Publication History
MAGAZINE TITLE AND TITLE CHANGES
Oliver Optic's Magazine: Our Boys and Girls (January 1867-December 1873); *Oliver
    Optic's Magazine* (January 1874-December 1875).
VOLUME AND ISSUE DATA
Oliver Optic's Magazine: Our Boys and Girls (vol. 1, no. 1-vol. 14, no. 245); *Oliver
    Optic's Magazine* (vol. 15, no. 246-vol. 18, no. 269).
PUBLISHER AND PLACE OF PUBLICATION
Lee & Shepard, Boston (January 1867-December 1875).
EDITOR
William Taylor Adams (January 1867-December 1875).

Phyllis Moe

ONWARD

In 1868 Thomas Mayne Reid (1818-1883)—known to his youthful readers as
Capt. Mayne Reid—conceived a periodical reflecting his own personality. Never
one to display modesty, he offered "A first-class, high-toned magazine, addressing itself to the Young Men and Women of America. Its design is not only
to entertain and amuse, but to instruct, elevate, and conduct the youth along that
path leading to the highest and noblest manhood." Here was born, according
to a blurb penned in Reid's grandiose style, "Mayne Reid's Magazine, *Onward.
A New Monthly Magazine for the Youth of America. Conducted by Capt. Mayne
Reid.*"[1] With the aid of Charles Ollivant, Reid edited *Onward* monthly from
January 1869 until its demise in February 1870.

We cannot know *Onward* without knowing Reid. Born in Northern Ireland,
he early fashioned a dashing career.[2] At various times schoolmaster, store clerk,
journalist, slave overseer, actor, author, gentleman farmer, and editor, he remembered most proudly his experiences as a southwestern trapper and a soldier
in the Mexican War. His years in these climes later provided the substance for
his most distinctive writing.

Reid tried to live up to his own image. Passersby marveled at his egocentric
garb, which featured brightly checked suits, lemon yellow gloves, a crimson
waistcoat, and a golden monocle. Reid spent well beyond his budget, especially
on "The Ranche," a sprawling duplication of a hacienda erected in Bucking-
hamshire, the building of which contributed to his 1866 bankruptcy.

Both self-esteem and financial difficulties pressed Reid to write several score
publications. Of greatest importance were the approximately seventy-five ad-

venture novels, many with intriguing titles like *The Scalp Hunters*, *The Rifle Rangers*, or *The Death Shot*. Numerous books appeared in Beadle and Adams series, British library series, and newspaper versions. Tens of thousands of readers, mostly boys, clamored for his thrillers, so that in 1868 Beadle and Adams paid him a record $700 for *White Squaw*, and he averaged perhaps $1,000 a novel from all sources.[3]

The great nervous energy and desperate necessity inherent in such literary output led Reid to found his new juvenile periodical. Shortly after his release from bankruptcy in early 1867, he had begun a London tabloid, *The Little Times*. A few months following the collapse of this venture, he returned to America, his land of promise. Spirits temporarily revived, he created for American youth *Onward*.

The magazine enjoyed one initial advantage: publication by G. W. Carleton, an astute New York marketer who successfully purveyed an incredible selection of reading material including religious tracts, Artemus Ward, feminine novels, juvenile classics such as *Robinson Crusoe*, Dickens, and frontier adventures. In 1868 Carleton had bought the American rights to all of Reid's romances, so he was the obvious choice of publisher when Reid conceived his new periodical. The editor in the final issue recollected "having selected a publisher of reputed enterprise."[4] Carleton discharged his obligations by energetically promoting the magazine, which he sold for 30¢ a copy or $3.50 a year (Reid in August reduced the price to $3.00). A Carleton advertisement describes the "first-class, high-toned magazine": "Its literature is entirely original....It is embellished with original illustrations printed upon tinted paper, in an attractive manner, and in size, character, and appearance is the cheapest magazine that has been issued in this country."[5] However, it seems that with the July 1869 issue Reid became his own publisher, for he wrote, "As this month the Publishing Agency of the magazine becomes changed, it is requested that all communications...be addressed direct to the proprietor, MAYNE REID."[6] He evidently purchased the magazine rights (much as he soon afterwards rebought old book copyrights), for we find only his office address—not Carleton's—in the bound copies of volume 1 of *Onward*, individual issues of volumes 2 and 3, and outgrowths of the *Onward* project such as "Onward" croquet sets.

Least successful in *Onward* are short entries gathered into four recurrent sections. "Books" and "Books Only Glanced at," both found in only the first four issues, survey dozens of books, including many like Henry Clok's *Diseases of Sheep*, which could not possibly appeal to many young people. The great majority of the notices and reviews briefly convey superficial impressions. We find fully satisfactory reviews only in rare cases where Reid applied his personal background, as when he attacked Ross Browne's ignorance in *Apache Country*.[7]

Also weak is "Trifles," found in all but the final issue. We find here entertaining snippets on nonserious topics: speedy trains, bobolinks, cockneys, British cabbies, yacht racing, chicken farmers, and so on. However, the odd selection and the unvariedly flippant tone soon dull us.

More worthwhile is "Things Worth Thinking of." Most importantly, Reid conveyed in this section of each issue his republican sympathies. Contemporaries saw him almost as an anarchist who hated authority and worshipped egalitarian America. His famous 1870 lecture praises Byron's role in revolutionary struggles, his 1888 novel *No Quarter!* supports Cromwell, and an 1879 letter boasts, "Politically I am among the most advanced of Liberals."[8] In these *Onward* pages he cheered republicans wherever he found them. He also struck against the corruption of British authority, as his celebrated 1863 Thanksgiving lecture had equated English tyranny with American slavery.[9] Disconcertingly, he devoted many heated paragraphs to demands for reform of the New York streetcar system. Other topics include post office reform, magazine writers, yaks, polar expeditions, lifeboats, steamboat racing, and religious creeds. We find here caustic minieditorials by an author impatient with the world's not accepting his advanced ideas. It seems improbable, however, that young readers would share his enthusiasm for the topics "Worth Thinking of."

In contrast to most children's periodicals, *Onward* offers numerous political essays. Reid consistently argued that England suffered moral turpitude, while America offered rebirth. "A People's Beauty" shows well his principles: "I only see [in Americans] a return to the natural and normal condition of humanity, long degraded by despotism; now, under the benign nurture of republican freedom, being rapidly restored to its pristine state."[10] Young Americans, he thought, must accept their responsibility to effect this restoration. Unfortunately, his persuasiveness diminishes with repetitions of his philosophy and tedious length, as in serialized treatments of Civil War battles.

Although humor is not a strong quality of the periodical, several stories are mildly amusing. The most effective ones possess the rough, brash tone of frontier storytelling. Thus "Christmas Day in a Deadwood" (January 1869) recounts a Tennessean's being stuck in a hollow tree with a skunk and a turkey mashed under his feet. Dialectal words like *minnit* and *dassent* here and elsewhere establish the regional flavor of tall tales. None of the humorous stories evidence sophistication, but more discomfiting is their self-consciousness.

Reid entertained a high opinion of the poetry in *Onward*. Advertising *The Poets of Onward* (never published), he asserted "that no periodical. . . has produced such an outpouring of poetry. . . thoughts that breathe and words that burn, reaching to the heart's core."[11] But we sense authentic poetry in perhaps only C. F. Janes's "The King's Dwarf" (April 1869). Here the narrator imaginatively sees shapes in a dying fire and on an iced window. Most of the poems, like so much contemporary journalistic verse, are weakened by singsong versification and trite sentimentality. Sometimes lush tropical climes arouse mournful memories, as they had in Reid's Caribbean verses printed much earlier in *Godey's* and other magazines (Reid even borrowed from his earlier works). "Southern Sunset," for instance, describes the sun declining over a tropical sea and a prisoner releasing the obligatory "scalding tear" as a sentry remembers his Andalusian homeland.[12] Far too many poems attain prosaic depths like "But, when I bend the suppliant knee, / Then dearest, most I think of thee!''[13] The most outrageously bad verse is Reid's ''The Purple Swallow, or Two Loves in a Life,'' which includes the lines: ''God of Heaven! has she perished— / All on earth I ever cherished? / Can her life no more be nourished?''[14] Such words may ''burn,'' but they hardly constitute worthwhile poetry.

One intriguing feature of *Onward* is Reid's tendency to pursue his own enthusiasms. The most interesting example is croquet. An expert player and advocate of the sport, he published *Croquet* (1863), an exhaustive compendium including 126 rules. In the June 1869 *Onward* he wrote in ''Croquet Literature'' that a new treatise is needed to settle players' disputes. Reid himself provided the ''needed'' treatise, ''Croquet: A Treatise with Notes and Commentaries,'' (June-September), complete with an expanded (to 184) rule section. Reid even authored a poem, ''The Croquet Queen'' (June 1869) and in 1869 published his second, *Croquet*, printed from the stereotype plates used for his *Onward* treatise. He also marketed ''Onward'' croquet equipment.

Onward proves far stronger when it turned to natural science. Here Reid has done careful thinking. Always encouraging his young readers to pursue the curious or little known, he equated adventure and scientific curiosity. For example, he promised that ''there is in Mexico a mine of romance, or study, that will last you for the days of your life.''[15] He wanted to print not everything about a given topic but scientific ''points that are salient and simple, valuable only as forming a basis for more extended study''[16]—this makes sound educational sense. Articles cover unusual topics: vultures, antelopes, Niagara Falls flowers, peat, walruses, ice skating, exotic plants. We see the typical procedure in Reid's ''The Maguey'' (January 1869). Advising us to ''Watch well,'' he colorfully described the plant's appearance, cultivation, and uses. Because of his audience, he made his details active and carefully provided definitions and pronunciations of Spanish terms like *tlachiquero*. The magazine could well use more such articles.

Surely, the most popular element in *Onward* was the adventure stories. Titles themselves—''A Beautiful Ghost: The Dying Confession of a Maniac''—often connote excitement. The most entertaining fiction is Reid's. He could write excellent strong action, as when ''The Mad Skater'' expires: ''A piece of rotten ice . . . broke off with a loud crash; and in another moment the detached fragment, bearing his body . . . swept over the falls, to be crushed to atoms in the seething cauldron below!''[17] His best work is the kind of Southwest and tropical fiction that readers expected. For instance, his serialized ''Lost Sister'' offers an exotic South American locale, intrepid heroes and Indian foes, jaguars and other complications, and a naturalist's description of local vegetation. Meanwhile, the illustrations (a major factor in *Onward*) graphically highlight Reid's writing— we see wide-open eyes, exotic settings, dramatic action. Although parodies of Reid like *The Skull Hunters* (1868) ridiculed the excesses of his swirling prose, many readers reveled in his combination of close detail and improbable action.

Reid spent thousands of hours writing and editing copy; most of the writing is his own. He attracted advertisements for insurance, fishing tackle, pianos, steamship cruises—a motley variety. But such labor could not eradicate problems of triteness, declining quality, and topics not relevant for his readers. Retaining optimism to the end, he concluded *Onward* with "A Magazine Mystery" (which cites sixty-two journalists' praises!) expressing bewilderment that the public has rejected his magazine (February 1870).

Following the demise of *Onward*, Reid fell into temporary poverty and melancholia. But he rebounded and eleven years later launched another children's periodical, the *Boys' Illustrated Newspaper*.

Notes

1. *Onward* 1 (March 1869), [iv].
2. The most trustworthy biographical account is Joan Steele, *Captain Mayne Reid* (Boston: Twayne Publishers, 1978).
3. Edmund Pearson, *Dime Novels, or Following an Old Trail in Popular Literature* (1929; reprint, Port Washington, N.Y.: Kennikat Press, 1968), 47; Graham Pollard, "Novels in Newspapers: Some Unpublished Letters of Captain Mayne Reid," *Review of English Studies* 18 (1942), 73. Anyone investigating Reid quickly comes to appreciate Pollard's exasperation with "Mayne Reid's tortuous bibliography" (p. 72).
4. *Onward* 3 (February 1870), 185.
5. Ibid., 1 (March 1869), [iv].
6. Ibid., 2 (July 1869), ii.
7. Ibid., 1 (March 1869), 265.
8. " 'Lord Byron'—A Lecture by Mayne Reid," *New York Daily Tribune*, April 19, 1870, p. 5; Pollard, "Novels in Newspapers," p. 82.
9. Steele, *Captain Mayne Reid*, p. 30.
10. *Onward* 1 (April 1869), 328.
11. Ibid., 2 (December 1869), [548].
12. Ibid., 1 (January 1869), 65-66.
13. Ibid., 1 (April 1869), 312.
14. Ibid., 3 (February 1870), 107.
15. Ibid., 1 (January 1869), 11.
16. Ibid., 1 (April 1869), 281.
17. Ibid., 1 (June 1869). 481.

Information Sources

BIBLIOGRAPHY
"Captain Mayne Reid," *The Spectator*, October 27, 1883, pp. 1374-75; Albert Johannsen, "Captain Mayne Reid," in *The House of Beadle and Adams and Its Dime and Nickle Novels: The Story of a Vanished Literature*, 3 vols. (Norman, Okla.: University of Oklahoma Press, 1950-1962); Edmund Pearson, *Dime Novels, or Following an Old Trail in Popular Literature* (1929; reprint, Port Washington, N.Y.: Kennikat Press, 1968); Graham Pollard, "Novels in Newspapers: Some Unpublished Letters of Captain Mayne Reid," *Review of English Studies* 18 (1942): 72-85; Elizabeth Reid, *Mayne Reid: A Memoir of His Life* (London: Ward

and Downey, 1890), revised with Charles H. Coe as *Captain Mayne Reid: His Life and Adventures* (London: Greening, 1900); Joan Steele, *Captain Mayne Reid* (Boston: Twayne Publishers, 1978); idem, "Mayne Reid: A Revised Bibliography," *Bulletin of Bibliography* 29 (1972): 95-100.

INDEX SOURCES
None.

LOCATION SOURCES
Several research libraries own partial runs. Complete sets are in the Boston Public Library; Indiana University, Bloomington, Ind.; Library of Congress; and State Historical Society of Wisconsin, Madison, Wis.

Publication History

MAGAZINE TITLE AND TITLE CHANGES
Onward: A Magazine for the Young Manhood of America (January-June 1869); *Mayne Reid's Magazine Onward: For the Youth of America* (July-September 1869); *Mayne Reid's Magazine Onward* (October 1869-February 1870).

VOLUME AND ISSUE DATA
Onward: A Magazine for the Young Manhood of America (vol. 1, no. 1-no. 6); *Mayne Reid's Magazine Onward: For the Youth of America* (vol. 2, no. 1-no. 3); *Mayne Reid's Magazine Onward* (vol. 2, no. 4-vol. 3, no. 2).

PUBLISHER AND PLACE OF PUBLICATION
G. W. Carleton, New York (January-June 1869); Publishing Office [Thomas Mayne Reid], New York (July 1869-February 1870).

EDITOR
Thomas Mayne Reid.

Avon Jack Murphy

OUR LITTLE MEN AND WOMEN

Our Little Men and Women was inaugurated by Boston's Daniel Lothrop in January 1880. Published for the first two years of its life as *Little Folks' Reader*, it was intended for very young children and filled a gap in Lothrop's group of successful ventures in children's periodical publishing initiated with *The Pansy** in 1874 and followed a year later by *Wide Awake,** which competed directly with *St. Nicholas.** *Little Folks' Reader* was a sixteen-page, copiously illustrated monthly set in double columns with broad margins and generous spacing designed for easy reading. A miniature literary miscellany, it offered an unexceptional mix of short fiction, verse, and nonfiction material suffused with the moral earnestness characteristic of Lothrop's other publications. In the initial issue, "Two Pairs of Eyes," for example, developed the theme of being observant that would surface again and again in future issues. "The True Story of Dick's Dollar," in the same issue, describes a bootblack who generously donates a dollar to a "Poor Children's Excursion" program so that some child might have a refreshing day in the country as he himself had once had from the same charity. Benevolence began at home—and began early—in the Lothrop magazines. An illustrated feature, "A Little Country Girl," exemplifies the celebration of rural nature that is another basic theme both in *Our Little Men and Women* and in the quality children's periodicals of the period generally. "Walter's Friend," a natural history article, describes a gray squirrel; and "A Request from the Birds" encourages readers to identify imaginatively with the plight of birds in New England's winter and to save crumbs to feed them.

In February's issue an article about oak trees emphasized again the theme of observation and invited readers to isolate and compare the features that distinguished white from red oaks just as an article in the first issue had shown how to distinguish between hares and rabbits. Another article on nature, "Seeing the World," carried the strong implication that everything, in the natural world at least, had its rightful place—pumpkin vines, for example, belonged on the ground, not climbing on poles. A sketch of a "good boy" made clear some of the relevant criteria for making (and judging) *that* important distinction: good boys did not cry or kick dogs or look cross: and his supper is typically "a big cup of new milk, with nice brown bread. No cake. No pie."[1]

A good deal of the material in subsequent issues is clearly intended to enforce basic distinctions and values. "What Happened in a Garden" (April 1880) exalts utility over pride and beauty, relating how "proud" roses and lilies had to move out of a garden to make room for the useful weed that hosted the silkworm. "Brave Little Dimple" (June 1880) celebrates courage and in doing so instances the concept in a concrete, graspable way. "The Story of a Mitten" (January 1881) illustrates the maxim "A place for everything, and everything in its place," which, in this context, clearly has moral import and is not merely prudential.

Natural history was an early staple, as was the theme of children in other lands. In addition to the articles about oak trees, hares and rabbits, and the gray squirrel noted earlier in connection with the attention paid to the child's developing powers of observation, early issues included "Facts About Elephants" (June 1880); "The First Seam," which described the work of the Indian "tailor" bird (December 1880); and "About Leopards" (September 1881), part of a series that described familiar creatures—spiders and owls, for example, of which the child presumably had firsthand experience as well as exotic animals like tigers, elephants, and leopards met in story books. "Little English Ethel" and "A Bonnie Lassie" illustrate another way in which the editors invited their readers to begin to frame their experience, in this case in contrastive categories of nation and race.

Although some attention is paid to seasonal holidays in the early issues, for example, "May-Day Sports" (May 1881) and "Uncle Jack's May Basket"(May 1882), stories or articles related to Christmas, and especially Thanksgiving, that most New England of holidays, are conspicuously absent through 1882. By 1885, however, both holidays were being observed, for example, "How Ned Watched for Santa Claus" (December 1885); and by 1891 the issues for November and December are largely, if not exclusively, given to Thanksgiving and Christmas. Such changes are presumably part of a broader shift in editorial policy initiated in 1883 as Mrs. Frances A. Humphrey began to have, or be given, more responsibility for running *Our Little Men and Women*. During her tenure as editor, Frances Humphrey also managed to write several books for children published by Lothrop: *Queen Victoria at Home* (1885), *Kings and Queens at Home* (1886), *Adventures of Early Discoverers* (1888), and *The Adventures of Columbus* (1887). By 1883 *Our Little Folks*, now *Our Little Men and Women*, had grown to twenty-four pages, and the price had been raised 25¢ to $1 a year. In addition to six full-page illustrations an issue, children (and their parents) could expect: "Fascinating short stories and poems in short words and short sentences. Little tales of children in other countries . . . and true stories of animals and their habits and haunts. No child who reads 'Our Little Men and Women' will need to be watched by the S.P.C.A."[2] The last sentence catches at something that is apparent to anyone who has done much reading in late nineteenth-century children's periodicals: the degree to which cruelty to animals appeared to be a significant problem to middle-class moralists. Numerous stories in the better periodicals of the day address the issue, typically by showing the unpleasant consequences for boys (it was a "boy" problem) whose notion of fun consisted, in part, of pulling the wings off flies and similar depredations against God's creatures.

By 1885, too, there is less anonymity associated with *Our Little Men and Women*, and more and more contributions bear the name, instead of merely the initials, of the author. Frances A. Humphrey's signed series "Kings and Queens at Home" began in January 1885, an issue that also included a serial story "Polly" by Margaret Sidney, the popular (Lothrop) author of *The Five Little Peppers and How They Grew*. Humphrey also inaugurated "Stories about Favorite Authors" in that issue, a useful indication of which writers even very young children might be presumed to have some interest in: Longfellow, Whittier, Larcom, Aldrich, Trowbridge, Stowe, Holmes, Alcott, Hawthorne, Alice and Phoebe Cary, Bryant, and Margaret Sidney. By 1885, too, songs and their accompaniments began to enliven the pages of the magazine. The commitment to moral instruction remained clear and steady, as did basic value-freighted cultural distinctions such as that between rural and urban. "The Strange Adventures of Mopsy and Hans" (January 1890) begins: "Mopsy was five years old and Hans was six when they went into the country. It was then that their wonderful adventures began. While they were in town they lived in a dull little house which looked into a dull little street, and nothing happened to them. . . . In the country there was nothing dull."[3] A setting for seemly adventure—and moral development: that was part, perhaps the largest part, of the significance of country life as represented in the pages of *Our Little Men and Women* and of New England's children's periodicals generally.

Sometime in 1893 Humphrey apparently left the editorship. Her name does not appear as a contributor in that volume, and minor changes in the periodical's format suggest a change in editorial control. In January 1894 that change is explicit in the designation of the editor as "The Editor of *Babyland*," at that time E. Addie Heath.

Notes

1. *Little Folks' Reader* 1 (February 1880), 30.
2. Ibid., 3 (December 1882), 296.
3. Ibid., 14.

Information Sources

BIBLIOGRAPHY
Frank Luther Mott, *A History of American Magazines* (Cambridge: Harvard University Press, 1938-1957), 3:177.
INDEX SOURCES
None.
LOCATION SOURCES
Library of Congress.

Publication History

MAGAZINE TITLE AND TITLE CHANGES
Little Folks' Reader (January 1880-December 1882); *Our Little Men and Women* (January 1883-September 1894); *Little Men and Women* (November 1894-December 1898?)
VOLUME AND ISSUE DATA
Little Folks' Reader (vol. 1, no. 1-vol. 3, no. 12); *Our Little Men and Women* (vol. 4, no. 1-vol. 15, no. 9); *Little Men and Women* (vol. 15, no. 11-vol. 19, no. 12?)
PUBLISHER AND PLACE OF PUBLICATION
D. Lothrop and Company, Boston (January 1880-December 1894?).
EDITOR
Mrs. Frances A. Humphrey (1883-1893), E. Addie Heath 1894-1898?).

R. Gordon Kelly

OUR LITTLE ONES AND THE NURSERY: ILLUSTRATED STORIES AND POEMS FOR LITTLE PEOPLE

When *Our Little Ones and the Nursery: Illustrated Stories and Poems for Little People* was first published in November 1880, its content and format may have surprised some people. *Our Little Ones'* editor was William Taylor Adams, the same person who wrote under the pen name of Oliver Optic, Irving Brown, Clingham Hunter, Old Stager, and numerous other pseudonyms. Oliver Optic, as he was most commonly known, had been attacked intermittently in the 1870s because of the alleged sensationalism, portrayal of criminal life, puns, flashiness, and generally poor writing in his immensely popular books and stories. Among his most vehement critics were Louisa M. Alcott, Emily Huntington Miller, the *Penn Monthly*, the *Christian Union*, and the *Nation*. At the 1897 Boston Conference of the American Library Association he was both attacked and defended.[1]

Adams had many defenders, but he conducted his own defense in his editorial column in *Oliver Optic's Magazine*. His defense of himself makes as interesting reading as do his exciting books and serials.

William Taylor Adams (1822-1897) was a born storyteller. In his lifetime he published more than 100 books and 1,000 stories, borrowing upon the experiences of a full lifetime. He was born in Bellingham, Massachusetts, on July 20, 1822. In his early adult life he was a Sunday school teacher. He was a teacher and principal of a grammar school in Dorchester, Massachusetts, and in the Boylston School in Boston and later at the Bowditch School in Boston. He traveled widely in the United States, Europe, Asia, and Africa. His experience working with children, traveling, and gifts for writing combined to make him one of the most popular and prolific writers for young people of the nineteenth century. Although most of his writing was for boys, some of it was for adults.

In the editing of *Our Little Ones* Adams turned his attention to very young children of approximately three to nine years of age. *Our Little Ones* was published monthly, selling at $1.50 for an annual subscription, or 15¢ for a single copy. It was published in Boston by Russell Publishing Company and in England as an annual by the London publisher, Griffith and Farran. The London publications ceased after three volumes.

As the subtitle indicates, illustrations were of great importance in this fine quality periodical. *Our Little Ones* was one of only a few children's magazines of the period to list all illustration departments in its masthead and to designate an editor, in this case George T. Andrew. In the annual editions of *Our Little Ones*, each illustration page number is listed in the table of contents and accompanied by the quotation that the illustration corresponds to. A complete list of illustrators is included with every monthly issue. Two well-known illustrators were J. H. Moser, who illustrated Joel Chandler Harris's *Uncle Remus*, and Frederick Stuart Church, who illustrated an 1884 edition of Hawthorne's *Wonder Book for Boys and Girls*.[2] The illustrations reflect the content of *Our Little Ones*. Pictures of animals, small children, mothers and fathers, families,, and mothers holding or reading to children were tastefully executed and completely appropriate to the stories and poems they accompanied.

Contributors to *Our Little Ones* included some of the well-known writers for children of the time. Frequent contributors were Rebecca Sophie Clark (writing under the pseudonym Sophie May), Laura E. Richards, Palmer Cox, Margaret E. Sangster, Emily Huntington Miller, and many writers, who used pseudonyms to conceal their identities. Occasionally, Oliver Optic was a contributor. His "Honeysuckle Hall" (January 1881) was a different kind of story from the kind that his older readers were accustomed to. "Honeysuckle Hall" was a gentle story about children trying to earn money to help the poor.

These brief stories and poems reveal much about the social class who read them. Many periodicals of the late nineteenth century exhorted children to believe in God, to work hard, and to be honest and truthful. *Our Little Ones* reminded children that life is more pleasant and easier if one obeys one's mother; if one is kind and loving to animals; if one doesn't run away from home; and if one doesn't hide under lilac bushes, in trunks, in boilers, in storage bins, in attics, and in one's room. If a child did not follow this code of conduct, punishment was meted out invariably in the same way. Bedtime would occur without the usual good supper. The tone of the punishment was never harsh. The mother was always loving and forgiving, and the child was always repentant.

In "Two Little Runaways" (January 1880) the mother "carries both the darlings off to sleepland." In "The Bad Boy" the boy says, "she told me to put on my dress and go to bed. I feel very bad, for it will be a long time till dark, and I must eat bread and milk, and the rest will have cake and tarts."[3] In "A Sail in a Tub" the punishment was "and put them to bed right away. They had only bread and butter for their supper. Peggie and Pollie think they will never go sailing again."[4] Even in poetry such as "Two Naughty Chicks" the poems ends: "Children don't run away. 'Tis bad to disobey."[5] Across the ocean some twenty years later a famous little disobedient rabbit was put to bed without bread and milk and blackberries but instead, camomile tea. Early bedtime and light suppers must have had a rehabilitative effect on nineteenth-century disobedient and runaway children, for invariably they asked forgiveness and vowed never to be bad again.

Kindness to animals was an important theme in *Our Little Ones*. Animals protected small children from drowning, being lost, being lonesome, and being attacked by other animals. More than three-fourths of the stories are about animals and pets. Children loved their pets and took care of them. If the animals were undomesticated, such as squirrels, the children usually realized that the animals were better off if set free so that they could live as nature intended. Sometimes loyal pets died. Occasionally, people were the cause of an animal's death. In "Mopsie's Walk" (November 1880) the mice are killed by a woman in a brutal way, and Mopsie goes home to tell her mother "about the poor little mice who lost their mother and died of grief."[6] The author adds that this is a true story— so as to reinforce the moral. In the "Wire House" (May 1887) a mouse dies in a mouse trap.

However, people never die in *Our Little Ones*. A mother may express her fear of death in the poem "Beth and Faye" while she sits by the bed of her two little girls.

> Closer now I lean above them,
> To be sure I feel their breath,—
> So like is their heavy slumber
> To the sleep that we call death.
>
> And I think of the empty homes,
> And the empty hearts, to-night,
> And of playthings used no longer,
> And of cribs put out of sight

Then I thank the God who gave them,—
Dear little Faye and Beth,—
That I touch their warm, soft fingers,
And feel their baby breath.[7]

For the readers of *Our Little Ones*, it was a safe, comfortable world, surrounded by loving parents, faithful friends and servants, and loyal pets. A bounteous nature made up the world that they enjoyed. People outside of this cozy world might be children who lived only a few miles away in large cities, the South, or foreign lands. Stories of such people sounded like fairy stories or tales of fantasy—so remote did they seem. "The Little Snow Shoveler" (February 1881), "The Italian Apple Girl" (March 1881), "The Little Peanut Boy" (May 1881), and "The Organ Grinder" (August 1881) were stories of boys and girls living in vastly different circumstances. They might go to bed hungry but not as a punishment. Their hunger was a fact of life.

The attitudes of the upper-middle class toward minorities appear thoughtless rather than intentionally unkind. In "Four Little Boys" (February 1881), four mischievous little black boys made a shamble of the school room and refused to learn. In "Weezy's Sambo" (June 1881), a little black doll was mistreated. In "Selfish Sambo" (November 1885), we read about a black pony who was selfish. In "Little Red Sukey" (June 1881), a little Indian girl has to beg for a living. "Denny O'Toole" (July 1881) is a poem about a "tattered but jolly Irish boy." "Alaska's Children" is about a trip to Alaska, and the author said, "Alaskan children are not very pretty, but they are good-natured."[8] Writers for *Our Little Ones* often showed more sensitivity in writing about animals than they did when they wrote patronizingly about children who were different from their readers.

Nature was an integral part of the content of *Our Little Ones*. On the first page of each issue was a seasonal illustration. Many articles were devoted to natural history topics such as orioles' nests, butterflies, or fire beetles. Some accounts described how animals help or hinder each other's survival. In "The Crocodile's Dentist" (April 1886), the reader is told how important the plover is in keeping a crocodile's teeth clean and strong. On the other hand, in "The Whale's Foe" (July 1886), the whale thrasher is described as a fish whose sharp tail can slash a whale to pieces. Many poems and stories feature anthropomorphic raindrops, calla lillies, or peach trees.

A few stories about travel appeared, especially in the last years of *Our Little Ones*. In the early issues articles about the West Indies often appeared, but in later years they dealt more with Europe and parts of Asia, such as China and India.

In 1892 Adams relinquished the editorship of *Our Little Ones* to Lawrence Elkus, who continued in that role until 1896. In March 1899 the magazine merged with *Little Folks*.*

Notes

1. Richard L. Darling, *The Rise of Children's Book Reviewing in America, 1865-1881* (New York: R. R. Bowker, 1968), 34-39.

2. Cornelia Meigs, ed., *A Critical History of Children's Literature* (New York: The Macmillan Co., 1969), 236.

3. *Our Little Ones and the Nursery* 1 (November 1880), 31.

4. Ibid., 1 (April 1881), 176.

5. Ibid., 1 (June 1881), 231.

6. Ibid., 1 (November 1880), 27.

7. Ibid., 1 (May 1881), 200-201.

8. Ibid., 6 (August 1886), 314.

Information Sources

BIBLIOGRAPHY

Siri Andrews, ed., *The Hewins Lectures, 1947-1962* (Boston: Horn Book, 1963); Gene Gleason, "Whatever Happened to Oliver Optic?" *Wilson Library Bulletin* 49 (May 1975); 647-50; Eleanor Weakley Nolen, "Nineteenth Century Children's Magazines," *Horn Book* 15 (January-February 1939), 55-60; "Oliver Optic," *The Critic* 787 (April 3, 1897), 242-43; Elizabeth Pullar, "Oliver Optic—The Prince of Story Tellers," *Spinning Wheel* 35 (October 1979), 20-23; Elva Sophronia Smith, *The History of Children's Literature* (Chicago: American Library Association, 1980).

INDEX SOURCES

None.

LOCATION SOURCES

Scattered issues are in many universities and major public libraries.

Publication History

MAGAZINE TITLE AND TITLE CHANGES

Our Little Ones and the Nursery: Illustrated Stories and Poems for Little People (November 1880-March 1899).

VOLUME AND ISSUE DATA

Our Little Ones and the Nursery: Illustrated Stories and Poems for Little People (vol. 1, no. 1-vol. 19, no. 5).

PUBLISHER AND PLACE OF PUBLICATION

Russell Publishing Co., Boston (1880-1899).

EDITOR

William Taylor Adams (1880-1892); Laurence Elkus (1893-1899).

Mary Kelly Isbell

OUR YOUNG FOLKS: AN ILLUSTRATED MAGAZINE FOR BOYS AND GIRLS

The first issue of *Our Young Folks* appeared in January 1865 as the war that had exacted so horrifying a toll for five years was drawing to a close. The West was still a country for pioneers but an urban America was rapidly growing on the earlier rural, agrarian world of villages and small towns. Yet the image of that world remained powerful and is perhaps with us still, carrying with it the romantic and wistful belief that life is better, simpler, truer, nobler, when lived under the wide sky and in the pure air of the country. It was a fruitful time for children's periodicals.[1] No other significant magazine appeared in 1865, but 1867 saw *Our Boys' and Girls' Magazine (Oliver Optic's Magazine*)*, the *Riverside Magazine for Young People*,* and *Frank Leslie's Boy's and Girl's Weekly*.*

Our Young Folks: An Illustrated Magazine for Boys and Girls was published in Boston by Ticknor and Fields, an established firm that also published *Every Saturday, The Atlantic Monthly*, and *The North American Review*. Most of the major children's periodicals of the period were brought out by well-known houses (Ticknor and Fields was to become Fields, Osgood and Co. and later Houghton Mifflin). *Our Young Folks* ran from 1865 until 1873, when it was absorbed by *St. Nicholas*.* Its publishers described it as "the best juvenile magazine ever published in any land or language" whose editors rejected "dull and trashy articles as alike worthless," taking "all possible care to procure reading that shall furnish entertainment and attractive instruction."[2] John Townsend Trowbridge, Gail Hamilton, and Lucy Larcom were the original editors; Hamilton (pseudonym for Mary Abigail Dodge) dropped out by 1868, following a disagreement with Fields. Trowbridge was in Washington, D.C., at first, and "Miss Larcom handled the periodical's major editorial responsibilities, for which she received an annual salary of \$1,200."[3] All three editors wrote for the magazine. Larcom frequently published poetry and stories. Hamilton wrote both fiction and nonfiction. Trowbridge contributed some forty items, including a number of serials, some of which later appeared in book form; his "Jack Hazard and His Fortunes" seems to have been especially popular. When *Our Young Folks* ceased publication, Trowbridge went to *St. Nicholas* as a staff member.

The magazine, a monthly costing \$1.50 a year, was a sixty-four-page octavo. It carried no advertising; circulation eventually exceeded 75,000.[4] Alice Jordan called it the "[first] of the modern type of magazine for boys and girls" and described its "gay orange paper covers with the names of its editors surrounding a well-clad Minerva complacently seated on the front."[5] The contents included fiction, nonfiction, poetry, some illustrations, and regular monthly features at the back of the magazine. "Round the Evening Lamp" consisted of charades, arithmetical puzzles, illustrated rebuses, music, plays, and pantomimes. "Our Letter Box," begun in January 1866, carried not only letters from readers but the comments and response of the editors and occasionally of writers. The department ran competitions and printed prizewinning entries. Readers submitted so many compositions that in July 1870 "The Letter Box" announced a new section, "Our Young Competitors." In some issues as many as eight pages were given to this department although it more often ran to four or five pages. From

March 1871 to May 1872 the column "Mutual Improvement Corner" provided a place for readers to find pen pals.

To judge from their letters and contributions, the readers of *Our Young Folks* ranged in age from about ten to eighteen. This is certainly the audience toward which the articles and stories were directed, although occasionally an issue might carry an item specifically intended for younger readers—for example, "The Mouse and His Friends: A Little Story for Little Readers" by Annie Moore (October 1871). Sometimes in the later years the magazine ran what it called a picture-story: usually, a two-page spread divided into four frames and showing without words some humorous event that youngsters of all ages could enjoy. Although *Our Young Folks* was often New England in flavor and certainly northern in its pro-Union, antislavery sympathies, it was read by young people throughout the country and even abroad. Letters and contributions came, for example, from the New England states and the Eastern Seaboard, from Indiana, Illinois, Kansas, Missouri, Iowa, Kentucky, Alabama, Colorado, and California, from Hamilton and Toronto in Canada, and from American children living abroad. These readers must have been middle class and upper middle class, well educated, mostly Protestant. The tone of the magazine indicates that they were being reared to assume their share of responsibility toward family and society in cheerful and sometimes courageous performance of duty. They were encouraged to pity those less fortunate and to exercise appropriate charity. Excessive display of materialism was frowned upon; yet it was not expected that these young people would be ascetic or puritanical. Poverty was usually presented in *Our Young Folks* (as in much of the writing for children at this time) as physically hard but morally uplifting. For example, in "The Inequalities of Fortune" (January 1866) Gail Hamilton wrote, "poverty seems to be favorable to the best mental and moral training of a vast majority of persons. Remember that this is not universally true. . . . But I think you will find that a large majority of those who are eminent for their talents, their virtues, and their usefulness were not born in costly homes, did not wear rich clothes in their childhood, and were not provided with numerous servants, elegant carriages, and expensive toys."[6] Although many of the characters in *Our Young Folks'* fiction are middle-class, admirable people—both adults and children—respect the poor; successful characters, whether poor or comfortably off, display moral and physical energy of the kind suggested by Hamilton.

Throughout its nine years of publication, *Our Young Folks* maintained a high standard of quality. Contributors for 1865 included Thomas Bailey Aldrich, Harriet Beecher Stowe, John Greenleaf Whittier, Louisa May Alcott, Mayne Reid, and Henry Wadsworth Longfellow. Aldrich's "Story of a Bad Boy" ran as a serial from January 1869 through December of the same year. "Holiday Romance" by Dickens was published in four parts in 1868; the second installment, "From the Pen of Miss Alice Rainbird," is the story we know as "The Magic Fishbone." Serials were frequently published later as books: for example, Trowbridge's "The Adventures of Jack Hazard"; Lucretia P. Hale's "The Peterkin Papers''; Mrs. A.D.T. Whitney's ''A Summer in Leslie Goldthwaite's Life'' and ''We Girls: A Home Story''; and Mrs. A. M. Diaz' ''William Henry's Letters for His Grandmother.'' Many of the writers whose names appear in the table of contents, often with great frequency, are no longer familiar and are not read by young people any more; some of the writing seems now to be marred by sentimentality, springing from a view of the world we no longer share. Nevertheless, even pieces by the most obscure contributors were frequently written by authors who shared the editors' wish to bring material of consistently high quality to the magazine's readers. Similarly, the artwork met demanding standards; *Our Young Folks* included a number of fine illustrations by Winslow Homer. When the magazine began to run music, the editors chose not only pieces by now-forgotten composers but works by Mozart, Beethoven, and Schumann.

Each issue of *Our Young Folks* includes a mixture of fiction and nonfiction, poetry, and pieces that can be characterized as education and as entertainment, such as the ''Lessons in Magic'' series and the charades and plays for readers to perform. There is perhaps slightly more fiction than nonfiction. A small percentage of the fiction is historical, and an even smaller proportion is fantasy. There are some stories of foreign origin (for example, Persian, Egyptian, German), an occasional myth and folktale. Most of the fiction, however, is realistic and American: family stories, adventure tales, stories that reflect the world the readers know or wish they could enter.

A number of pieces fall between fiction and nonfiction into a kind of subgenre of each; in them, the writer uses a fictional narrative framework to present information. Generally, an older person is giving the information to an eager group of listeners, as for example in the serial ''Farming for Boys'' (January 1865 and following issues) and in ''Lawrence's Lesson'' (December 1866), which gives instruction about how to save a drowning person.

Straightforward nonfiction includes many nature articles, often based on personal experience. A number are by Harriet Beecher Stowe; in the February 1865 issue, for example, she described the creatures—snake, woodchuck, bullfrog, flying squirrel—that she and her family had watched near their new house (''Our Country Neighbors''). ''The little lady who started the Civil War'' was also a careful observer of the natural world. Lucretia P. Hale, best known today as a humorist, had a series called ''The Four Seasons, and a Little About Their Flora'' (February 1866 and following issues). C. A. Stephens, whose work first appeared in ''Our Young Contributors,'' wrote frequently from Maine about events in both the human and animal worlds.

Other nonfiction is wide ranging and varied. For example, Thomas Bailey Aldrich contributed a series of essays called ''Among the Studios'' (September 1865 and following issues), which describes the studios and work of contemporary artists. There are pieces about physical science, occasional biographical sketches (often to accompany a portrait reproduced in the magazine), essays about young heroes and heroines, pieces about explorers, and historical material bringing readers information about the ancient and medieval worlds and the

American past. "Round-the-World Joe" is a serial describing the Far East (February 1867 and following issues). "The Schoolmistress in Siam" is about Mrs. Leonowens who was governess to the wives and children of the king of Siam for six years (November 1872). Elizabeth Agassiz, wife of the noted scientist, wrote a number of pieces under the title "The World We Live On" (January 1869 and following issues). Readers can learn how ice is cut, how glass is made, how coal is mined, and who first used the mariner's compass, and they can follow a series on seasonal sports. "Our Letter Box" often includes a section describing and recommending new books.

Some of the nonfiction pieces seem very specifically directed toward the improvement of readers. The first issue, for example, carried a piece by Dio Lewis, "Physical Health: To the Young People of America." After a stirring opening ("The great war will end. Then what magnificent expansion! But what immense responsibilities! Soon they must rest upon you,—your manhood and womanhood. God and the nations will watch you"), the author went on to describe the poor physical condition of American youth with their "great heads, beautiful faces, brilliant eyes; but with that attenuated neck, thin, flat chest, and languid gait."[7] He then demonstrated poor and desirable habits and posture, accompanying his text with illustrations. "A Few Plain Words to My Little Pale-Faced Friends" (September 1865) by Lewis describes the benefits to children of daily sunbathing. Edward Everett Hale contributed the series "How to Do It" (how to talk, write, travel, read). "How to Write" (July 1869) gave rise to correspondence between readers and Hale. He had advised young writers to use their own language, to choose short words in preference to longer ones, fewer words rather than more; in "Our Letter Box" for January 1871 he answered controversy over his advice to young Americans never to use the words *presume* and *commence*. A series by Charles A. Barry, "How to Draw" (July 1870 and following issues), is composed as letters to a little girl and instructs youngsters in drawing.

The Civil War ended four months after the first number of *Our Young Folks* appeared. Not surprisingly, the issues of the first years contain many pieces, both fiction and nonfiction, that reflect that terrible struggle, the events leading up to it, and its aftermath. Although the concentration of such items diminished, as late as September 1873 there is a story called "Patty's Responsibility" about two little girls sold into slavery in Africa, one of whom ended up in Salem and was owned by the writer's great-grandfather. Most of the pieces emphasize the absolute righteousness of the northern cause. For example, "The Boy of Chancellorville" (September 1865) by Edmund Kirke describes General Lee as "the man who neither smokes, drinks, nor chews tobacco; who has, in short, none of the smaller vices, but all of the larger ones; for he deliberately, basely, and under circumstances of unparalleled meanness, betrayed his country, and, long after all hope of success was lost, carried on a murderous war against his own race and kindred."[8] Kirke could, however, grant a common humanity to the combatants, saying in the same story, "After all—after even the atrocities the

Rebels have committed,—it is true that the same humanity beats under a gray coat that beats under a blue one.''[9] In the serial "Three Days at Camp Douglas" (April 1865 and following issues), Kirke described a prison camp near Chicago, giving details to show how well the camp is run and comparing conditions and mortality rates with those found in southern prisons. The good southerners for Kirke are not found among the upper classes but among the ordinary people. Moreover, he said,"[at] least one quarter of the whole number confined at Camp Douglas are truly loyal men, who were forced into the Rebel ranks, or have seen the error of their ways, and desire to return to their allegiance."[10] In "The Turning of the Leaf" by Trowbridge (June 1865), Uncle Rodman explains to two children the causes, goals, and results of the Civil War just ended. "In a word, children, slavery was the cause of the war; and God permitted the war in order that slavery might be destroyed.... The rebellion was a stupendous piece of folly as well as stupendous wickedness." Lincoln and those who elected him, says Uncle Rodman, did not want "to interfere with the 'peculiar institution' in the States where it existed four years ago. Unjust and unwise as it was to keep human beings in bondage, they did not feel that the law gave them any right to take slaves away from their masters by force." But slaveholders "became so violent, unreasonable, and wicked in their opposition to all who thought slavery wrong, in their hatred of free institutions, and in their attempts to carry slavery into new States. . .that a few believed. . .that it was right to resist force with force and to go with arms to rescue negroes from the hands of their masters."[11]

The heroes of the Civil War pieces published in *Our Young Folks* are simple soldiers (as in the serial "Winning His Way" by Carleton, January 1865 and following issues) and twelve-year-old drummer boys (as in "The Little Prisoner" by Edmund Kirke, January 1865 and following issues). Even infants and small children could exert an influence over adults involved in the war. Annie in "The Baby of the Regiment" by T. W. Higginson (February 1865), "had not the slightest prejudice against color, and did not care in the least whether her particular friends were black or white."[12] Taken back by her mother to their home in the North, Annie dies, but "her little life, short as it seemed, was a blessing to us all, giving a perpetual image of serenity and sweetness, recalling the lovely atmosphere of far-off homes, and holding us by unsuspected ties to whatsoever things were pure."[13] In Alcott's story "Nelly's Hospital" (March 1865), the little girl makes a hospital for injured wildlife, a project that affects positively both her own development and the recovery of her older brother, wounded in the war.

Trowbridge wrote four postwar pieces in 1866. "A Visit to Mt. Vernon" (February 1866) describes his conversation with a black girl scrubbing clothes in the washhouse. In "The Battle-Field of Fredericksburg" (March 1866) he talks to several southerners; one young man thinks that Lee was too humane to press to victory, but he is satisfied with the outcome of the war, because if the South had won, "this would have been the worst country, for a poor man, under the sun, because there would have been no chance for white labor—blacks would have done it all.''[14] In ''Richmond Prisons'' (May 1866) Trowbridge records his conversation with a southerner who, sympathetic to the northern cause, had helped prisoners. In ''A Tennessee Farm-House'' (June 1866) Trowbridge visits a family who describe the depradations suffered at the hands of both armies.

As might be expected in a publication of these sympathies, writers of both fiction and nonfiction in *Our Young Folks* view black people with compassion for their suffering. Adult blacks are seen as self-sacrificing and noble. Katy, the ''aged negress'' in ''The Little Prisoner'' (April 1865) who finds the wounded drummer boy, has held onto her belief in the efficacy of prayer throughout all of the tragedies of her life. Poor and uneducated, Katy and her suffering brothers and sisters are seen to have God and right on their side. In ''The Colored Mammy and Her White Foster-Child: A True Story'' by Dolly Dixie (March 1868), a black slave is given a sickly white baby to nurse: ''So she willingly put away her own dark baby, and nursed the little white one with the tenderest care.''[15] Nothing more is said of the fate of the black child, but the white one grows up feeling that it is wrong to sell people and eventually frees her own slaves.

Black children often share the saintly characteristics of the adults. The heroine of ''How June Found Massa Linkum'' by Elizabeth Stuart Phelps (May 1868) is a child who is worked as hard and treated as miserably after the war as she had been when she was a slave. She sees Lincoln, runs away to find him, and dies on the way. The writer imagines her entering heaven and finding Massa Linkum, who has preceded her and who leads ''her gently to that other Face, that thorn-crowned Face, of which poor little June had known nothing in all her life.''[16] The little runaway slave in ''Tobe's Monument'' by Elizabeth Kilham (February 1872) is killed by Rebel soldiers, because he won't give up the boots his protector, the Captain, has charged him to take particular care of. In addition to this story, Kilham contributed a number of pieces based on her experience teaching newly freed black children in Virginia. She saw most of these youngsters as bright, eager, and attentive despite their poverty and their harsh past, and she described their antics and responses with amusement and sympathy even when writing about a wild boy who continually disturbed her school (''Old Nick,'' July 1873).

All of the black children in these pieces, indeed all of the black characters, speak in pronounced dialect, which the writers attempt to render phonetically. Even the slave child who grows up in a Salem household with the writer's grandmother in ''Patty's Responsibility'' (September 1873) speaks as if she had been raised by old Katy in the South. There is perhaps just a hint of condescension in the treatment of black figures. On the one hand, the writers recognize their suffering and the extent to which they have been victimized by white oppressors, but they distance blacks by making them saintly or, as in the case of Old Nick and some of the other Virginia children, endearing rascals and by giving them a different speech. Northern blacks, who might be presumed to be more like the writers in experience and language, seldom appear in these pieces.

Indians are treated in a handful of *Our Young Folks* articles, usually with sympathy tinged with condescension. "Burton and the Baby" by Helen C. Weeks (February 1870) is, said the author, the true story of the Sioux massacre in Minnesota in 1862. After listing some of the causes of the outbreak, Weeks said, "Terrible wrongs had been done them [the Indians], and they avenged them even more terribly."[17] In the two-part serial "One Little Indian Boy: And How He Became a Medicine-Man" (July 1871 and following issues), Weeks used a narrator who tells two children about the life of a Sioux from infancy to maturity. One of the children says he will go to see the Indians some day and maybe they'll be civilized. Uncle John replies,

> I doubt if the Sioux ever will. . . . They are almost too fierce and warlike. But when you are older I do mean you shall go with me and see the real civilization among the Choctaws and Chicksaws in the Indian Territory. There is the surest answer to those people who declare extermination the only course to be pursued. . .your pennies in the mission-box might better go to the home than the foreign heathen, and perhaps some day people will realize what might, could, and should be done with these unfortunate children of our common Father. On the whole, Bert, I had, with you, almost rather be an Indian than one of the whites who have wronged them.[18]

"The Little Sac's Revenge" ("Theodora," January 1873) mentions "The lazy stoicism so natural to the Indian race" and another story by the same author ("Pap Chippewa and the Wolves," December 1873) presents Indians as dissipated inferior creatures who practice deception. In "The Two Winogenes" (September 1868) a white mother in northern Michigan gives her baby an Indian name. When the two Winogenes meet at about the age of six, the author makes a pointed comparison of their appearance, lives, and future, with the white child much the more attractive.

In April 1868 a curious poem appeared in the magazine, "The Little Jew: A True Story," signed The Author of "John Halifax, Gentleman." It begins: "We were at school together,/The little Jew and I./He had black eyes, the biggest nose,/The very smallest fist for blows,/Yet nothing made him cry."[19] The speaker describes the teasing to which the Jewish child is subjected and his meek response and remarks, "He never lied nor cheated,/Although he was a Jew." The teasing comes to a head when the speaker attempts to force an apple on the other child who has confessed hunger but, looking at the setting sun, says he can wait to eat; in anger, the speaker pinches and punches the boy and thus extracts the information that "It was their solemn fast-day. . .I mocked; he only wept:/ 'What father does, I do.'" The speaker goes home to tell the story to his father, a minister, expecting "that he would laugh outright/At the poor silly Israelite" and is astonished to be given a stern lecture: " 'Would God that you may ever be/As faithful unto Him—and me—/As he you hold in scorn!' " Next day, the speaker begs the little Jew's pardon, and they become friends for life.[20]

Most of the readers of *Our Young Folks* probably had limited contact with blacks, even more limited experience of Indians, and rare firsthand knowledge of Jews. Although hardly representative of the growing diversity of the country, at least these pieces did indicate to the magazine's audience that not all people in the nation mirrored their own image.

In keeping with an attitude to be found in other writing of the period, pieces in *Our Young Folks* sometimes sentimentalized infancy and early childhood, particularly—as might be expected—when dealing with the death of children. Stories like "Freddy's New Year's Dinner" (L. Maria Child, July 1865), the early part of Harriet Beecher Stowe's serial "Little Pussywillow" (September 1866 and following issues), and "How a Letter Went to Papa" (Annie Clyde, July 1872) perpetuate the picture of childhood as a time of sweet innocence. "The Beautiful Gate" (Helen Wall Pierson, January 1869) is the sentimental story of the death of a slave boy. At the same time, the reader could find healthy correctives to this view. The children in "William Henry's Letters to His Grandmother" (Mrs. A. M. Diaz, October 1867 and following issues) are energetic, appealing, and believable. Thomas Bailey Aldrich's autobiographical novel "The Story of a Bad Boy" (January 1869 and following issues) is narrated in a humorous, sometimes self-mocking voice and is distinguished by sharply observed detail.

The editors of *Our Young Folks* took their readers seriously and there is little condescension toward them. Implicit in the articles and stories is the belief that even young children can become competent, that older children can make valuable contributions to their families and to society, that children matter. This belief is seen in its most banal and hackneyed form in Horatio Alger, Jr.'s story "How Johnny Bought a Sewing Machine" (August 1866), which, like all Alger stories, relies heavily on luck and has an unbelievably virtuous hero. "Helping Father" (William L. Williams, February 1867), although not particularly distinguished, at least shows a more realistic solution of a family's financial problems; the boy Daniel takes over household chores that his father has previously paid others to do and thus saves these wages for the family exchequer. Princess Alicia in Dickens's "The Magic Fishbone" (part 2 of "Holiday Romance," March 1868) flies round and organizes the whole palace with skill and good humor, supplying a lighter version of the theme of the helpful child. The twelve-year-old drummer boys in Civil War stories like "The Little Prisoner" (January 1865 and following issues) and "The Boy of Chancellorville" (September 1865) are thrown into a violent and tragic adult world. Although they come to seem sentimental clichés, they remind us that children have often, willingly or unwillingly, been thrust into activities beyond their emotional and physical strength. In "A Clean Sweep" (Caroline Augusta Howard, February 1870), a wretched little sweep is rescued and sent to live in the country. However, there, too, he will have a job; it will be pleasanter work under a kind employer, but it will be work, and he is still a child. In "Cash," also by Howard (January 1868), a boy who supports his widowed mother is rescued from difficult work in a similar way and removed to the country where he continues to work, but in better circumstances.

To help its readers develop their capabilities, *Our Young Folks* ran articles like "Farming for Boys" (January 1865 and following issues) and Edward Everett Hale's series "How to Do It" (March 1869 and following issues). Fiction such as the "Little Pussy Willow" series (Harriet Beecher Stowe, September 1866 and following issues) emphasized that happiness comes when one does the work at hand cheerfully and well; the fifth installment, for example (January 1867), contrasts the energetic industry, good nature, and competence of country-reared Little Pussy with the fretful discontent of rich Emily.

Fiction by Elizabeth Stuart Phelps, however, shows young women who rebel against the domestic mode and insist on finding their work in unconventional areas. In "More Ways Than One" (April 1871) a young woman who hates taking care of the baby and helping her sickly mother sells electroplating door-to-door so that she can hire a servant to work at home in her place and thus free herself to do what she really wants. Jemima in "The Girl Who Could Not Write a Composition" (August 1871 and following issues) goes home to the Midwest after failing miserably at an "awful Massachusetts boarding-school." She could not write a composition—and her attempts to do so are amusingly rendered. But she joins her father in his furniture business, and after his death, to everyone's astonishment, she takes over the business and makes a success of it, supporting her mother and younger brother. "Our Little Woman" (November 1872 and following issues) and its sequel "Hannah Colby's Chance" (October 1873 and following issues) contrast two young women, distant cousins. Hannah lives a comfortable if rather pointless life with her mother and sister—a life that she has never questioned until she watches her cousin Lois nurse a dying mother, go back to work in a shoe shop, and then put herself through medical school. Lois has been influenced in this choice by her mother's wistful remark about the lack of women doctors at the hospital, and she says to Hannah, "If there's a better or greater or nobler thing for a woman to do in this year 1872 than the thing I am going to do, I should like to see it!"[21] When Hannah's mother loses her money (in part because, considering investments no business of a woman, she has left it all to a male adviser), Hannah refuses all the usual employments offered to impoverished gentlewomen and goes into the picture-framing business.

Like much of the writing for children and young people of the period, *Our Young Folks* has its share of didactic, moralistic pieces. Trowbridge's "Father Brighthopes" series (August 1865 and following issues), "Kitty. A Fairytale of Nowadays" by "Aunt Fanny" (January 1869), and Hamilton's essay "Little Things" (April 1866) are examples. Adults of all periods and all cultures try to teach their children what they consider important and to make certain standards of behavior and certain goals admirable, whether they do so in explicit lessons or in other ways. From both the frankly didactic and the more subtle writing in the pages of *Our Young Folks*, we can derive some notion of the ideals being held up to readers. Children should be honest and courageous; faithful to family, friends, and country; industrious and competent; good-humored and cheerful. They should respect their parents. When necessary, they should contribute to the economic support of the family. They should behave with charity and generosity to those less fortunate. City life is important to the functioning of the nation, and so are business and industry, but country life is pure, good, old-fashioned; it can act as a restorative and a counterbalance to the potential and actual dangers of urban living. Success is desirable, although the question of how it is to be defined is sticky; clearly, worldly success is not enough, although it is not to be despised. Girls should be womanly, boys manly, and yet feminist notes are being sounded, notably in work by Phelps. Children and adults alike should rest their trust in God, believing with old black Katy in "The Little Prisoner" (April 1865) that the Lord hears their prayers and will send the angels to help. The twelve-year-old drummer boy of "The Little Prisoner" can draw on moral courage in the face of violent threats because he has fully learned two truths: "That God is Infinite Right, and cannot do wrong; and that he governs all things."[22] He has been taught this lesson by his poor widowed mother on her bended knee. "And what this truth gave to James, it will give to every little boy and girl who reads this. No matter how poor you may be. . .if this truth is in your heart, you are rich."[23] The children who die young in the pages of *Our Young Folks* have this courage and truth; in dying, they go home to God, leaving their example to guide those who survive them. Attention to the moral stance of the magazine should not, however, obscure for us the fact that it was devoted to the entertainment as well as the education of its readers. Every issue carried items like plays, puzzles, games, music, and stories whose primary aim was to give pleasure.

The correspondence in "Our Letter Box" and the stories, essays, and poems printed in "Our Young Contributors" give ample evidence that the subscribers to *Our Young Folks* read their magazine with attention and enthusiasm, apparently absorbing the aesthetic standards and internalizing the moral stance presented to them. The level of writing skills is astonishing, even in the youngest contributors. We know that many of the young people who were published in the "Young Contributors Department" of *St. Nicholas* went on to become well-known writers. Although this does not seem to be true of the contributors to *Our Young Folks*, their capabilities give evidence of the standards being upheld in at least some of the nation's schools, since presumably ordinary youngsters were able to express themselves with such command of vocabulary, syntax, and style.

The post-Civil War period saw the publication of many children's magazines of varying types and degrees of excellence, all the way from the Sunday school magazine to the blood-and-thunder thriller. *St. Nicholas* was to lead this field and has become the symbol of excellence in magazine publishing for young people. In its nine years of existence, *Our Young Folks* achieved a standard that makes it a worthy associate of *St. Nicholas*, with which it merged in 1874. It offered to its readers entertainment, instruction, and inspiration; expecting much of them in attention and performance, it rewarded them by believing them capable of responding to the best the editors could publish.

Notes

1. For a discussion of developments and changes in the publication and content of children's periodicals at this time, see R. Gordon Kelly, *Mother Was a Lady* (Westport, Conn.: Greenwood Press, 1974), 1.

2. As quoted by John Morton Blum in the Introduction to *Yesterday's Children* (Boston: Houghton Mifflin, 1959), xiv.

3. Kelly, *Mother Was a Lady*, p. 20.

4. Ibid., p. 19, based on material in Betty L. Lyon, "A History of Children's Secular Magazines Published in The United States from 1789 to 1899" (Ph.D. diss., Johns Hopkins University, 1942).

5. Alice M. Jordan, *From Rollo to Tom Sawyer* (Boston: Horn Book, 1948), 123.

6. *Our Young Folks* 2 (January 1866), 14.

7. Ibid., 1 (January 1865), 38.

8. Ibid., 1 (September 1865), 603.

9. Ibid., 608.

10. Ibid., 1 (May 1865), 298.

11. Ibid., 1 (June 1865), 399.

12. Ibid., 1 (February 1865), 104.

13. Ibid., 109.

14. Ibid., 2 (March 1866), 167-68.

15. Ibid., 4 (March 1868), 137.

16. Ibid., 4 (May 1868), 279.

17. Ibid., 6 (February 1870), 96.

18. Ibid., 7 (August 1871), 488.

19. Ibid., 4 (April 1868), 238.

20. Ibid., pp. 240-41.

21. "Our Little Woman," ibid., 8 (December 1872), 736.

22. *Our Young Folks* 1 (July 1865), 464.

23. Ibid.

Information Sources

BIBLIOGRAPHY

Jane Benardete and Phyllis Moe, eds., *Companions of Our Youth: Stories by Women for Young People's Magazines, 1865-1900* (New York: Frederick Ungar, 1980); John Morton Blum, *Yesterday's Children: An Anthology Compiled from the Pages of OUR YOUNG FOLKS, 1865-1873* (Boston: Houghton Mifflin, 1959); R. Gordon Kelly, *Mother Was a Lady* (Westport, Conn.: Greenwood Press, 1974); Alice M. Jordan, *From Rollo to Tom Sawyer and Other Papers* (Boston: Horn Book, 1948); Cornelia Meigs, Anne Thaxter Eaton, Elizabeth Nesbitt, and Ruth Hill Viguers, *A Critical History of Children's Literature* (New York: Macmillan, 1953); Frank Luther Mott, *A History of American Magazines, 1865-1885* (Cambridge: Harvard University Press, 1938), vol. 3.

INDEX SOURCE

Joann L. Taylor, *Index to OUR YOUNG FOLKS* (unpublished manuscript, Elizabeth Nesbitt Room, School of Library and Information Science, University of Pittsburgh).

LOCATION SOURCES

Bound volumes are in many university, public, and historical society libraries; some libraries have incomplete sets. Vols. 1-9 (complete set) are available on microfilm from University Microfilms International, Ann Arbor, Mich.

Publication History

MAGAZINE TITLE AND TITLE CHANGES

Our Young Folks: An Illustrated Magazine for Boys and Girls (1865-1873).

VOLUME AND ISSUE DATA

Our Young Folks: An Illustrated Magazine for Boys and Girls (vol. 1, no. 1-vol. 9, no. 12).

PUBLISHER AND PLACE OF PUBLICATION

Ticknor and Fields, Boston (1865-1868); Fields, Osgood, Boston (1869-1870); James R. Osgood, Boston (1871-1873).

EDITORS

John Townsend Trowbridge, Lucy Larcom, and Gail Hamilton, pseudonym for Mary Abigail Dodge (1865-1867); John Townsend Trowbridge and Lucy Larcom (1867-1873).

Joan Brest Friedberg

P

THE PANSY

Begun in 1874, *The Pansy* was the first venture into the juvenile periodical field by Daniel Lothrop, an established Boston publisher of children's books, who subsequently established *Wide Awake** (1875) and *Our Little Men and Women** (1880). "Pansy" was the pseudonym of Isabella Macdonald Alden, who was already widely known by 1874 for her "Pansy" books for Sunday school libraries. The wife of a Presbyterian minister (Gustavus R. Alden), she sought to "make religion attractive to young people and the observance of the Golden Rule a pleasure."[1] Alden and her husband taught Chautauqua assemblies, and *The Pansy* was, as were other Lothrop periodicals, associated closely with the Chautauqua movement.

The Pansy was a weekly nondenominational Sunday school paper. Monthly cumulated issues were sent to mail subscribers. Each monthly issue had, in addition to fiction, nonfiction articles, poetry, a list of Bible readings for the upcoming month, news items, a letter from "Pansy," and letters from children who were members of the Pansy Society. Annual cumulations of *The Pansy* were also available. They omitted the monthly list of Bible readings, news items, and the letters from "Pansy" and members of the Pansy Society.

The Pansy Society had as its objectives the rooting out of besetting sins and the teaching of right conduct. Each member signed a pledge against a sin and reported progress in conquering it to "Pansy." Local chapters of the Pansy Society held meetings that frequently combined religious services with needle-work sessions. As of December 1889 there were more than 5,000 Pansies.[2] The Pansy Society later merged, at least in some areas of the country, with the Christian Endeavor Society. "*The Pansy* is for children not quite old enough to read *Wide Awake*. It contains stories of child life the world over, with pictures to match. 'Pansy,' the children's favorite, is its editor, and her writings must teach just the lessons they need."[3]

This description of the purpose and audience of *The Pansy* appeared in advertisements run in *Babyland** and other Lothrop juvenile periodicals. Material included in *The Pansy* was chosen for audience interest as well as its edifying and informative qualities. Emphasis was placed on Christian values.

Fiction in *The Pansy* was didactic. White middle- and upper-class families were the norm. Alden's stories usually began with a biblical text, and biblical texts were quoted frequently in them. One continued story, "The Little Card" (November 1891), concerned the evils of liquor and what young people could do to combat this pernicious influence. A major theme of this and other stories in *The Pansy* was that the sweet innocence of children could make a difference in the lives of even the most depraved adults, a theme that appeared in much of the fiction of the time, including the immensely popular *Elsie Dinsmore* books.

Besides Alden, most of the writers for *The Pansy* were regular contributors to *Babyland, Our Little Men and Women*, and *Wide Awake*.

Nonfiction in *The Pansy* included both single-issue and series articles to inform young readers about a variety of topics. One of these series, which began in 1892, discussed famous authors, both British and American. Another described various cities in the United States by asking children who lived in or who had visited these cities to send their opinions, observations, and so on. A series about foreign cities was written by adult contributors who had visited the cities discussed.

Illustrations in *The Pansy* ranged from full-page prints to small sketches illustrating the stories. Some of the illustrations were placed several pages before the work they illustrated to arouse interest in the rest of the magazine. The cover of the monthly issue was a wreath of purple pansies with the title enclosed. An inside title page was illustrated with a print representing the season or the theme of the issue.

Both the monthly issues and the annual volumes included a section of advertisements both for products and for other Lothrop publications. The monthly issues offered premiums to boys and girls who sold subscriptions to Lothrop periodicals.

Fiction and some nonfiction from *The Pansy* were periodically compiled into separate books and published by Lothrop. These titles include *An April Walk, and Other Stories from The Pansy* (1890); *A Day at Grandpa Bogart's, and Other Stories from The Pansy* (1888); *A Friend in Need, and Other Stories from The Pansy* (1887); *A Happy Summer Day, and Other Stories from The Pansy* (1886); *Harry's Invention, and Other Stories from The Pansy* (1887); *In Vacation, and Other Stories from the Pansy* (1885); *Jerusalem, and Other Sketches from The Pansy* (1888); *A Light from Persia, and Other Stories from The Pansy* (1886); *Miss Doctor Bellby, and Other Stories from The Pansy* (1888); *The Mission of a Gray Sock, and Other Stories from The Pansy* (1887); *A Morning Ride, and Other Stories from The Pansy* (1886); *A Package for Rose, and Other*

Stories from The Pansy (1887); *Railroad Building, and Other Stories from The Pansy* (1887); and *Who did It, and Other Stories from The Pansy* (1884).

Notes

1. "Alden, Isabella Macdonald," *National Cyclopedia of American Biography* (New York: James T. White & Co., 1909), 10:405.
2. "The P.S. Corner," *The Pansy* 17 (December 1889), 4.
3. *Babyland* 13 (January 1889), n.p.

Information Sources

BIBLIOGRAPHY
Frank Luther Mott, *History of American Magazines*, 5 vols. (Cambridge: Harvard University Press, 1938-1968); *National Cyclopedia of American Biography* (New York: James T. White & Co., 1909).
INDEX SOURCES
None.
LOCATION SOURCES
No early volumes have survived in major library collections. Library of Congress has the most extensive collection.

Publication History

MAGAZINE TITLE AND TITLE CHANGES
The Pansy (1874-1896).
VOLUME AND ISSUE DATA
The Pansy (vol. 1, no. 1-vol. 23).
PUBLISHER AND PLACE OF PUBLICATION
D. Lothrop and Co., Boston (1874-1896).
EDITOR
Isabella Macdonald Alden (1874-1896).

Carol J. Veitch

PARLEY'S MAGAZINE: FOR CHILDREN AND YOUTH

No author of children's books enjoyed wider popularity in the United States of the 1830s and 1840s than Peter Parley, the kind-hearted, gouty old storyteller who was in reality the literary creation and persona of Samuel Griswold Goodrich. An extraordinarily prolific and ambitious self-styled moralist, historian, naturalist, and travel writer—his tales of America (1827), Europe (1828), Africa (1830) and Asia (1830) were followed, also in 1830, by *Parley's Sun, Moon and Stars*—Goodrich had firmly established his triple career as writer, editor, and publisher when in 1833 he inaugurated a juvenile biweekly. *Parley's Magazine* immediately achieved an impressive circulation of 10,000. Addressed primarily to a mixed urban and rural nonsectarian Christian audience, *Parley's* sought to inculcate the conventional values of prudence, honesty, industry, moderation, love of country, and faith in machine-age progress, as it experimented with various means of rendering learning pleasurable rather than arduous. Not the least of these devices was the implied presence in the magazine, like that of a benevolent parent or god, of Peter Parley himself. Although Goodrich soon withdrew from the project due to failing health, the ideas concerning childhood education that Parley personified and embodied continued to dominate the magazine throughout its twelve-year history. Certain of these ideas also influenced the course not only of later children's magazines but of American grade-school education.

Born in Ridgefield, Connecticut, in 1793, of a family of distinguished Congregationalist clergymen and lawyers, Samuel Goodrich received his early education in makeshift local schools where he showed himself to be more of a wandering than a bookish cast of mind. His parents, having judged him unsuited to either of the family men's traditional callings, arranged a clerkship for him in a Hartford business office. This experience, which proved on the whole disagreeable to him, nonetheless led, through acquaintances he made, to the awakening of his lifelong interests both in writing and publishing. In 1826, after a number of business and personal setbacks, and after much reading and an inspiring encounter with the English writer Hannah More, Goodrich moved to Boston, then the hub of literary America, and audaciously installed himself in an office at Washington and School streets, directly above the venerable Old Corner Bookstore—the hub of the hub. Before long he occupied the building's entire second floor and had fixed his reputation as a champion of new American writers (he would later become the first major publisher to take an interest in Hawthorne) and as a shrewd businessman with a keen sense of the market.

In *Recollections of a Lifetime* (1856), his copious memoirs, he referred to *Parley's* only once, in an appendix to the final volume: "This work," he said of the magazine, "was planned and established by me but after about a year I was obliged to relinquish it, from ill health and an affection of my eyes. It was conducted, without interest or participation on my part, for about twelve years, when it ceased."[1]

In 1832, a year before *Parley's* first number appeared, Goodrich, overworked and prone to fainting spells, had traveled to England in search of medical treatment for a heart ailment (that may have been psychosomatic) and to look into the many fraudulent Peter Parley books being published abroad without his consent. (As a leading publisher of his day, Goodrich himself was typical in engaging from time to time in such piratings; he retaliated against his British rivals by reprinting some of *their* Parley titles in the United States, pocketing the profits.) Such abuses against the good Parley name suggest the considerable popularity that Goodrich's books enjoyed abroad. When in 1839 Daniel Webster returned to the United States from England, he reported that of all Americans, English children most eagerly demanded news of Peter Parley.

A publisher's notice at the head of *Parley's* first issue grandly presented readers with a point-by-point summary of the magazine's proposed contents:

I. Geographical Descriptions, of manners, customs, and countries; II. Travels, Voyages, and Adventures, in various parts of the world; III. Interesting Historical Notices and Anecdotes of each State, and of the United States, as well as of foreign countries; IV. Biography, particularly of young persons; V. Natural History, as birds, beasts, fishes, etc.; as well as plants, trees, flowers, etc.; VI. A familiar description of the Objects that daily surround Children in the Parlor, Nursery, Garden, etc.; VII. Original Tales, consisting of Home Scenes, Stories of Adventure, etc., calculated to stimulate the curiosity, exercise the affections, and improve the judgment; VIII. An Account of various trades and pursuits, and some branches of commerce. IX. Cheerful and Pleasing Rhymes, adapted to the feelings and comprehension of youth.[2]

This formidable list, the publisher asserted, was merely a partial overview, meant only to "convey some idea of the intentions of the conductors," whose full breadth of purpose and design was "too various to be enumerated."[3]

One is reminded by such puffery that Goodrich was a contemporary of P. T. Barnum (a fellow Connecticut Yankee who at various times in his own career combined, although in different proportions from Goodrich, the moralist, showman, and popularizer of knowledge); that midnineteenth-century Americans loved rhetoric and spent a considerable portion of their leisure time attending public lectures on philosophical, scientific, religious, and other themes; that popular admiration of fancy speech represented but one evidence, in an intensely mobile, economically expanding, society, of a widespread felt need and demand for education; and that *Parley's Magazine*, like virtually every publication in which Goodrich had a hand, responded to that need and demand with remarkable energy and skill.

Parley's had three owners during its twelve-year operation. Its first publisher, Lilly, Wait and Company of Boston (Goodrich himself edited but did not publish the magazine), was transformed, by early 1834, into Samuel Colman: successor to Lilly, Wait, also of Boston, with a long complement of secondary distributors from Portland, Maine, to New Orleans. The following year it became the property of the brothers Francis, Joseph H. of Boston and Charles S. of New York, both sons of the celebrated first American publisher of *Mother Goose*.

Goodrich's successor as editor of *Parley's* was a member of a family already well known in 1834 for its intense interest in childhood education. Dr. William Alcott, Bronson's cousin and close friend, had previously taught school, earned a license to practice medicine, and edited the *Juvenile Rambler*. Whether or not he knew Goodrich personally is uncertain although likely. Goodrich made no reference to him (or to any of the Alcotts) in *Recollections*, but their paths must have crossed at least occasionally even before William became involved in *Parley's*. Goodrich was erratic about sharing credit with collaborators and about acknowledging influences on his work; by not mentioning Alcott even briefly he may have been attempting once more to hoard the limelight.

What makes the Goodrich-Alcott connection so interesting, with respect to *Parley's*, is their apparent mutual debt, by whatever means arrived at, to the educational theories of the Swiss writer and teacher Johann Pestalozzi (1746-1827). In certain important respects, *Parley's Magazine* and the various schools the Alcotts founded and ran represent some of the earliest American experiments with the Pestalozzian method, which from the late nineteenth century to the present has exercised a major influence on American grade-school education.

In *Parley's* first issue Goodrich expressed the unconventional (Pestalozzian) idea that education ought to encompass training the body as well as the mind. Beginning in December 1840 the magazine presented a full program of gymnastics, complete with elaborate stick-figure diagrams. Pestalozzi had advocated the introduction of music and art lessons into the grade-school curriculum. A drawing course appeared in *Parley's* in 1839. From 1835 to 1842 every issue carried the music and lyrics of a song, and at various times the magazine published related articles of musical instruction.

Goodrich did not refer to Pestalozzi either in *Recollections*, although the probability of some influence, however indirect, is great. Alcott left *Parley's* at the end of 1837 and his successor is unknown; it can be fairly speculated, however, that the Swiss writer's ideas continued to effect the magazine's editorial outlook until its demise.

Goodrich's style as a writer reveals an affinity with, if it did not take a direct lead from, Pestalozzian theory. Pestalozzi had said that children might best master conceptual thinking by building on accurate observations of their immediate physical surroundings. Goodrich, for example, introducing the concept of the points of the compass, asked readers to locate the north wall of the room in which they were sitting at the moment.

Goodrich was an inexhaustible master of the odd fact, the startling, evocative detail. He seems to have savored these choice morsels of reality partly for their own sake: the storyteller in him was at times almost prepared to gain the upperhand—although never for long—over the moralist-educator. Bees, *Parley's* reported, when massed inside their poorly ventilated hives, "have recourse to the same instrument which ladies use to cool themselves, when an apartment is overheated. . . . The little creatures unite their wings so as to form a very proper sort of fan, and move them so rapidly that they can hardly be seen."[4] The analogy, leading from the familiar to the unfamiliar, was among Goodrich's (and Pestalozzi's) most favored teaching devices; readers suddenly found themselves gazing into the bees' forbidding inner sanctum as though into their own homes.

From an item called "Boys' Marbles," the first article to appear in the magazine, one learned that the Emperor Augustus, as a boy, "spent many hours" playing an ancient precursor of the well-known children's game. "This trifling circumstance," Goodrich observed with ponderous high spirits, "presents us with a pleasing trait in the juvenile character of the greatest of all the Roman emperors.''[5] In "Red Snow," one of many explorers' travel accounts published in *Parley's*, Captain Parry, the "celebrated English navigator" who "made several attempts to effect a north-western passage round America to Asia," encountered a "peculiar kind of red snow, which he saw at various times in those cold northern regions. This singular color is supposed to be occasioned by a multitude of very small insects. The number of these insects in a drop of water was calculated, by the aid of a magnifying glass, at more than 12,000.''[6]

One detects in this last piece a trace of the sanguine hurdy-gurdy believe-it-or-not mentality of a Barnum sideshow or a Ripley's compendium. Goodrich fastidiously restrained but could not always banish such theatrical impulses from his writing, toting up the morals to be drawn from, and insisting on the literal truth of, the stories he told, however bizarre they sometimes also were:

"The Electrical Eel"

There are some fishes which possess the wonderful power of being able to stun their prey by what is called an electric shock. The most remarkable of these is the electrical eel, which inhabits some of the ponds and marshes of South America.

A specimen of this eel was lately exhibited in Paris. Most people were satisfied by a single touch, that it possessed the power of electricity. But one doctor, either too credulous, or too rash, seized the fish with both hands. He quickly had reason to repent his folly. The animal imparted to him the most violent shocks, which forced him to leap about and utter the most piercing screams. He then fell into convulsions, in consequence of being unable to shake the fish from his grasp. In this situation he remained some time and would probably have died, had not some one plunged his hands in water, which caused the eel to drop off. The doctor has since been dangerously ill. The following is a picture of this singular fish.[7] (A woodcut appears directly below.)

Readers of this anecdote not only learned of the existence of an exotic sea creature and were advised how to behave in its presence; they were also treated to a frightening—or for beefier tots, merely tantalizing—bit of sensationalism. Most interesting perhaps about this tale, considering the period in which it was published, is the fact that the foolish victim was not a disobedient child but a full-grown and, as one would infer from his occupation, respected adult. Such willingness to acknowledge the shortcomings of persons old enough to be the readers' own parents set *Parley's* apart from an earlier tradition of American children's literature, exemplified by the *New England Primer* and the writings of ~~Jacob~~ John Abbott, which placed strict emphasis on the child's absolute need to obey and revere his or her elders. In the character of Peter Parley, the kindly old storyteller who surrounded himself with curious children, Goodrich established with the reader a familiarity and rapport like that observed to exist, in many cultures around the world, between members of the oldest and youngest of the three principal generations alive at any time, an affectionate bond so rooted in mutual respect that certain rules of decorum might be safely dropped from time to time and fun be had at the middle generation's expense.

Goodrich, it must not be doubted, believed with sober determination in the importance of discipline in a child's education. It may be significant, in terms of the impression of adult behavioral standards that he meant the eel story to convey to his young readers, that the incident occurred in Paris; a French (or other foreign) doctor, in Goodrich's estimate, was somewhat more likely to engage in hair-raising acts of folly than was an American doctor. But reading *Parley's*, one is struck at least part of the time by the respect shown readers even when they were being taught a lesson. Children, Goodrich believed, were "beings full of sensibility to hope and fear, to pleasure and pain, to sorrow and to joy, who have undertaken a long and hazardous journey."[8]

Nor did *Parley's* publish child obituaries, which other contemporary juveniles like the popular *Youth's Companion** regularly printed, romanticizing the pious deaths of obedient children and bemoaning the less seemly demises of those who had acted badly in their brief life on earth. It seems likely that many readers would have felt cheered by the omission, if not grateful.

Readers were apt to gain from *Parley's* an exuberant sense of the vastness of the material world, the variousness of its resources and peoples, and an unspoken but ironclad assurance that humankind, and most especially Americans, were well on their way to mastering the physical, if not always the moral, impediments to the attainment of a civilization unequaled in all history. The 1800s, *Parley's* implied, was an American century. Goodrich himself, in *Lights and Shadows of American History* (published in 1844 as volume 7 of *Parley's Cabinet of American History*), asserted: "The glory of Europe is behind them and ours is just beginning. In a few instances our standard of civilization might be lower than Europe's, but in considering all the elements we come out higher in education, art, science, comfort, religious toleration and in our physical, moral, and mental make-up."[9]

Most numerous among the magazine's nonfiction pieces were articles concerning various aspects of natural history. The United States remained a largely rural nation throughout *Parley's* history; accounts of American birds, field animals, and plants corresponded to readers' interest in their familiar surroundings while also reaffirming patriotic pride in the natural bounty of the country as a whole. A great many other articles, describing more geographically remote flora, fauna, and natural occurrences—"Eruption of Mt. Vesuvius" (August 3, 1833), "The Guava" (September 14, 1833)—extended readers' awareness of the dimensions of their world and encouraged them to consider all such phenomena, however apparently farflung on their maps and globes, within the ken of their inquiring intelligence.

Animal behavior was viewed in *Parley's* as having a moral dimension. "The Pike" (1844), for example, was described as being a ravenous cannibal lacking not only in fellow-feeling for others of its species but in affection even for members of its own family. "He will eat...brothers and sisters, father and mother, provided he can conquer them....If any escape him, it is not owing to friendship or favor....He knows none." But the article concluded, "we know that all things are made for good purposes."[10] Thus nature was to be regarded above all as a demonstration of the divine order, a plan never to be understood solely in human terms.

Parley's acknowledged the growing economic and social importance of the nation's eastern cities. A piece comparing Boston in 1775 and 1840 (November 1840) called attention to improvements in the means of transportation and to other technical advances that rendered the contemporary city a more congenial place to live in than had been the city of the founding fathers. Certain consequences of urbanization, and community building generally, were revealed in articles not directly concerned with cities. "Wolves in America," it was observed in a nature piece, "as the country becomes thickly settled, gradually disappear, or are destroyed."[11] As with its natural history articles, *Parley's* presented readers both with the familiar and the exotic in its accounts of urban life. In "The Forum, a Splendid Ruin of Rome" (1844), achievements of a past civilization were both extolled and contrasted to certain superior accomplishments of the present day— "In ancient times, when there was no printing..." and so on.

The articles "Money" (June 22, 1833) and "Commerce" (July 20, 1833) prepared readers for future roles in the marketplace while again emphasizing the advantages of present-day arrangements over those of the past. "Shipbuilding" and "The Art of Making Pins" (both August 31, 1833) traced familiar objects to their sources in industry and the handicrafts. Parley's account of the celebrated "Automaton Chess Player" (June 22, 1833), which toured the United States in 1833, assumed the apparatus to be some sort of fake; all mysteries of man-made origin were susceptible of rational explanation. Reason, according to *Parley's*, was power, an immense fund of strength for personal happiness and human progress.

Parley's publisher stated in the first issue that he had "made arrangements to have the work abundantly illustrated with spirited engravings."[12] Goodrich as editor and writer considered illustrations essential for children's learning. A picture, he believed, after Pestalozzi, might relieve a child's doubts concerning the meaning of a difficult passage; illustrations thus contributed to the clarity and concreteness of the child's sense of the world. Attractive artwork also delighted children, Goodrich observed, thus making learning itself more appealing to them. In a number of surviving copies of the magazine one finds that woodcuts have been brightly hand colored by the original readers, evidence of the fascination the images must have held for the children and of Goodrich's success at engaging their attention.

Every issue of *Parley's* presented eight or nine woodcuts, varying as widely in subject matter as the articles they accompanied and ranging in size from spot illustrations occupying the space of a newspaper filler to full page. Sinclair

Hamilton in *Early American Book Illustrations and Wood Engravings* considered it likely that many cuts used in *Parley's* had already appeared in other publications. Good woodcuts were costly and to be taken advantage of by an enterprising publisher; articles were probably written at times around an illustration that happened to fall into the editors' hands.

Most illustrations published in *Parley's* were unsigned, but it is known that certain leading engravers were among its contributors. Notable among them was Dr. Alexander Anderson of New York, the "father" of American woodcut engraving, sometimes also called the "American Thomas Bewick." Anderson at his best was a master of lively characterization and composition. More than fifty illustrations in *Parley's* bear his name or initials.

Among the other artists represented were Boston's Asa Bowen, an engraver almost as admired as Anderson, and several of Bowen's students, Alonzo Hartwell, George T. Devereux, and others. The July 1841 issue included one splendid full-page engraving after a painting by John James Audubon. Audubon frequented the Broadway bookshop of *Parley's* New York publisher Charles S. Francis, and the appearance of this beautiful illustration suggests that Francis, one of the city's most respected bookmen, may have played an active editorial role in the magazine, perhaps even replacing William Alcott after the latter's departure in 1837.

Virtually none of *Parley's* hundreds of illustrations was humorous in intent; with perhaps three exceptions (at least two or them the work of Anderson), one finds nothing in the magazine's pages remotely comparable to the whimsical cartoon fantasies of Palmer Cox and W. W. Denslow, published in *St. Nicholas** a half century later.

Under William Alcott's editorship, *Parley's* offered periodic instructions on the "proper use" of the magazine's art, with readers encouraged not merely to enjoy the illustrations but to "study" them, examine facial expressions, identify implied actions or plots, determining in each instance the artist's "meaning" (April 12, 1834). These editorial directives, dreary though they seem today, aimed at involving children more actively as readers and at promoting class discussions—both Pestalozzian goals—in schools where the magazine was used as a supplementary text. It seems likely that William's cousin, Bronson, would have read *Parley's* with his students at his Temple School, which when it opened in Boston in 1834 was probably the most progressive experimental grammar school in the United States.

In 1839 *Parley's* undertook another experiment in reader involvement, serializing what the editor described as a "complete Drawing Book for young children," a planned home (or school) course of instruction, with model drawings to be imitated or traced over and with detailed assignments. Three years later it carried out its most ambitious use, from a design standpoint, of visual art, a series of "Hieroglyphic Amusements," elaborate rebuses requiring scores of individual woodcuts (many no doubt recycled). Although the messages spelled out in these puzzles were not particularly lighthearted, the "Hieroglyphics" represented a guarded yet unmistakable attempt at turning learning into play. Although *Parley's* editors were never prepared to credit their readers' amusement as an adequate reason for printing any article or picture, some issues revealed a piecemeal tolerance for sheer fun. The publication of occasional riddles, ''conundrums,'' and other word and picture games established patterns that later children's magazines, especially *St. Nicholas*, greatly enlarged on.

In its last two years of independent existence, *Parley's* assumed a somewhat drabber appearance graphically, with virtually no smaller woodcuts inserted to break the monotony of the double columns of type. By this time the publisher was feeling the discouraging effects of competition from Goodrich's own new juvenile periodical venture, *Merry's Museum* (with which *Parley's* finally merged in 1844), and probably needed to limit operating expenses. In launching his rival magazine, Goodrich, with characteristic shrewdness and appreciation of the persuasive power of visual art, commissioned a frontispiece engraving calculated to win his reader's hearts. Kindly old Peter Parley was known by millions of children to walk with a limp; kindly old Robert Merry sported nothing less than a peg-leg! Readers' sympathies and subscription dollars shifted in favor of the more exaggerated infirmity, as planned. Such was Goodrich's remarkable understanding of his audience.

Scarcely more humor can be detected in *Parley's* articles and poetry than in its illustrations. Wit had a place where it carried in its wake some lesson in right conduct. Thus under the head ''Good Book-Keepers,'' readers learned that: ''Sir Walter Scott, in lending a book to a friend, cautioned him to be punctual in returning it. 'This is really necessary,' said the poet in apology; 'for though many of my friends are bad *arithmeticians*, I observe almost all of them to be good book-keepers.' ''[13] A reader today cannot help but be surprised upon discovering that ''Holyday Time'' (December 1841), the story accompanying a whimsical Anderson engraving in which a small band of wayward schoolboys are seen making a shambles of their classroom, is not a lighthearted account of youthful mischief but a sober criticism of incorrect behavior.

Above all, the name of Peter Parley became synonymous in midnineteenth-century America with a disdain for nursery rhymes, fairy tales, and juvenile fantasy generally, which Goodrich believed were misleading, nonsensical, and at times unnecessarily terrifying. Goodrich did not so much originate as Americanize this view, which influential didactic English children's book authors such as Sarah Trimmer, Maria Edgeworth, and Lucretia Barbauld were already advocating when he started out as a publisher and writer. These English writers in turn traced their inspiration to Jean-Jacques Rousseau, whose theory of ''natural'' childhood development seemed to them to preclude any role for ''unnatural'' fantasy in the child's education.

Goodrich himself wrote at length on this matter in *Recollections of a Lifetime*, recalling how as a boy of ten he had received from his father a book of *Mother Goose* rhymes as well as copies of two popular illustrated chapbooks, *Goody*

Two Shoes and *Gaffer Ginger*. "These were a revelation," he recalled. "Of course I read them, but I must add with no relish."[14]

Perhaps Goodrich had received the books too late in his childhood to have enjoyed them. One gathers, though, from both the tone and substance of his remarks, that this circumstance alone could not have accounted for his extreme loathing of the rhymes and tales.

It is significant that he became aware of the books through his father, who, as a pious Congregationalist minister, presumably entertained the most stringent religious standards of his time concerning the appropriateness of imaginative literature for the young. Similarly, when somewhat later in his childhood Goodrich balked at a collection of Perrault's fairy tales that friends had put into his hands, it was his stalwart mother who reassured him that such stories were mere fictions meant to amuse the reader. " 'Well, they don't amuse me!' " he recalled having replied.[15] It was not, then, his family religious training that caused him to feel as he did about fantasy.

Goodrich's childhood reaction to "Little Red Riding Hood" will strike some readers today as no different from their own. "Though it seized strongly upon my imagination," he said of the tale, it "excited in me the most painful impressions. I believed it to be true. . . . I imagined that what happened to the innocent child of the cottage might happen to me. . . . On going to bed, I felt a creeping horror come over me. . . . I soon seemed to see the hideous jaws of a wolf coming out of the bedclothes . . . ," and so on.[16] Perhaps his objection to fairy tales, then, was a matter of temperament.

But young Goodrich was not a timid soul. His quarrel with fantasy literature is best understood in philosophical terms; as he also observed in *Recollections*: "That such tales should be invented and circulated in a barbarous age, I can conceive; . . . But that they should be put into the hands of children, and by Christian parents, and that too in an age of light and refinement—excites in me the utmost wonder."[17] To Goodrich, then, fairy tales and kindred nonsense were morally backward, anachronistic; they represented an obstruction to education and so to the progress of the age.

Fiction printed in *Parley's* did not deviate from Goodrich's point of view. In 1835 William Alcott, in attempting to stir readers into critical reflection on a certain short story, felt dutybound to specify the exact extent to which the work before them was indeed fiction: "Well, readers," he ventured, "how do you like the story? Before you reply, I suppose you will ask the question; 'Is it true?' Now, then, I must tell you that it is *not* true. . . . But it is exactly such a thing as *might* have happened."[18]

Stories served as pretexts for imparting useful information and for rehearsing cherished values and beliefs. In "I'd Be a Butterfly" (May 25, 1833), a story possibly written by Goodrich himself, a boy named Harry tells his father he would rather play all day than go to school. Harry's father surprises him by granting him his wish; the boy, on his own, suffers a series of misfortunes, decides at last that he would be better off behind his school desk, returns, and, self-motivated for the first time, gradually works his way to the head of the class. Thus *Parley's* encouraged the young to think and act for themselves while implying that good children were apt to share common goals where their education and social and moral conduct were concerned. "Tell you a story, Mary?" a bewildered, well-meaning aunt muses, in a tale that echoes with canny precision a scene from Goodrich's own life story. "Indeed, love, I hardly know what kind of story to tell you. Shall it be about a frog—or a fairy—a giant?" Mary replies: "Dear, dear, aunt—not such silly stories, please—something sensible—I don't like nonsense!"[19]

Nearly all of *Parley's* fiction was unsigned; none, alas, is memorable. Poetry in the magazine was equally undistinguished, although several contributors in this department were admired in their day. Lydia Signourney (the "sweet singer of Hartford"), Hannah F. Gould, and Grenville Mellen were among the Americans presented in *Parley's*; English poets Richard and Mary Howitt and S. C. Hall also contributed verse. A child's evening prayers was a common theme of these quaintly sentimental versifiers, as was the safety and warmth of one's family home, the mutual love of parent and child, the ephemeral beauty and divine orderliness of nature. "Sing for the Oak Tree,/The monarch of the wood;/ Sing for the Oak-Tree,/That groweth green and good."[20] Thus crooned Mary Howitt in "The Oak-Tree," a fair and sufficient sampling of *Parley's* verse.

In its November 1925 number *St. Nicholas*, by then the leading American children's periodical for more than fifty years, ventured a nostalgic backward glance at the juvenile magazine it considered its most respected and imaginative precursor. In " 'Uncle' Peter Parley," a certain amount of erroneous information was passed along (*Parley's* was confused with Goodrich's later effort, *Merry's Museum*, which was incorrectly called the "first children's magazine"), but *Parley's* overall tone and range of subject matter were fairly and accurately described.[21]

Most striking about the *St. Nicholas* piece, especially perhaps to a reader lately immersed in the pages of *Parley's*, is its author's puckish wit, his easy familiarity with the reader, the mingling in the voice of admiration for past achievements and pride in being a part of a more advanced and knowing enterprise and age. If *Parley's Magazine* did not always live up to *St. Nicholas* standards, readers of 1925 were told, the earlier work was not to be sneered at. Its founder and editors had done the best job that had been possible in their bygone day. Thus the myth of modern progress, which Samuel Griswold Goodrich had been so vigorous an exponent of, had become within three generations' time the popular measure of his own, and Peter Parley's, legacy.

Notes

1. Samuel Griswold Goodrich, *Recollections of a Lifetime*, 2 vols. (New York and Auburn, Ala.: Miller, Orton and Mulligan, 1856), 2:543.
2. *Parley's Magazine*, March 16, 1833, (Specimen number), inside front cover.
3. Ibid.

    4. Ibid., p. 7.
    5. Ibid., p. 6.
    6. Ibid., March 16, 1833, p. 10.
    7. Ibid., p. 15.
    8. Ibid., p. 5.
    9. Samuel Griswold Goodrich, *Lights and Shadows of American History*, cited in Rita Podell, "Samuel Goodrich or Peter Parley" (M.A. thesis, Columbia University, 1939), 76.
    10. *Parley's Magazine*, 12 (1844), p. 228.
    11. Ibid., p. 670.
    12. Ibid., March 16, 1833, inside front cover.
    13. Ibid., September 16, 1833, p. 16.
    14. Goodrich, *Recollections*, pp. 166-69.
    15. Ibid., 1:167.
    16. Ibid., p. 166.
    17. Ibid., p. 169.
    18. *Parley's Magazine*, 3 (1835), p. 20.
    19. Mrs. S. C. Hall, "Holyday Time," *Parley's Magazine*, 9 (December 1841), 381.
    20. Ibid., 6 (September 1838), p. 287.
    21. " 'Uncle' Peter Parley," *St. Nicholas* 53 (November 1925), 79.

Information Sources

BIBLIOGRAPHY

James C. Derby, *Fifty Years Among Authors, Books and Publishers* (New York: G. W. Carleton and Co., 1884); Samuel Griswold Goodrich, *Recollections of a Lifetime* 2 vols. (New York and Auburn, Ala.: Miller, Orton and Mulligan, 1856); Sinclair Hamilton, *Early American Book Illustration and Wood Engravings* (Princeton, N.J.: Princeton University Press, 1968); Alice M. Jordan, *From Rollo to Tom Sawyer* (Boston: Horn Book, 1949); Frank Luther Mott, *History of American Magazines*, 5 vols. (Cambridge: Harvard University Press, 1938-1968): Rita Podell, "Samuel Goodrich or Peter Parley" (M.A. Thesis, Columbia University, 1939); Daniel Roselle, *Samuel Griswold Goodrich, Creator of Peter Parley: A Study of His Life and Work* (Albany, N.Y.: State University of New York Press, 1968); William Oliver Stevens, " 'Uncle' Peter Parley," *St. Nicholas* 53 (November 1925), 78-81.

LOCATION SOURCES

A complete set of bound volumes is in Teachers College Library, Columbia University, New York. New York Public Library; New York Historical Society, New York, N.Y.; Brooklyn Public Library, Brooklyn, N.Y.; Vassar College Library, Poughkeepsie, N.Y.; and Sterling Library of Yale University, New Haven, Conn., all have incomplete sets. Available on microfilm in the American Periodical Series from University Microfilms International, Ann Arbor, Mich.

Publication History

MAGAZINE TITLE AND TITLE CHANGES
Parley's Magazine: For Children and Youth (1833-1844).

VOLUME AND ISSUE DATA
Biweekly (1833-1836, 1839); semimonthly (1837-1838); monthly (1840-1844). Quarterly
    issues containing three months' issues also published (1840-1844). Regular annual
    volumes.
PUBLISHER AND PLACE OF PUBLICATION
Lilly, Wait and Company, Boston (1833); Samuel Colman, Boston (1834); Joseph H.
    Francis, Boston; and Charles S. Francis, New York (1835-1844).
EDITOR
Samuel Griswold Goodrich (1833); William Alcott (1833-1837); Charles S. Francis?
    (1838-1844).

Leonard S. Marcus

PLAYS: THE DRAMA MAGAZINE FOR YOUNG PEOPLE

Emerging as a leading center for the publication of children's periodicals during
the nineteenth century, the city of Boston continued to serve this legacy well
into the twentieth century and in September 1941 became the home base for still
another new journal for American young people, *Plays*. This periodical dedicated
itself to making entertaining and enlightening drama available to schoolchildren,
and with minor changes in format and some subtle shifts in emphasis that reflect
educational attitudes and cultural events at work in the larger American society,
it continues to pursue this goal today.

Plays: The Drama Magazine for Young People originally sold for 30¢ an issue
or $3 a year, averaging ninety-six pages an issue. The original plan to publish
monthly September through June was cut back after the first year to an eight-
issue plan, October through May, to meet better the needs of teachers using
Plays in the classroom. S. Emerson Golden was credited as editor of the first
volume, with A. S. Burack as managing editor and Richard D. Whittemore as
circulation manager.

From the beginning a basic structure characterized *Plays*. Drama for the entertainment, edification, and performance of young people was presented and
grouped according to reading levels. At the front of each issue would be several
plays recommended for junior and senior high school students, followed by a
similar number for intermediate-level students, grades four through six. After a
third section intended for children in grades one through three, the rest of each
issue would be devoted to one, two, or three special-interest plays—often radio
plays, in the first two decades of publication. Since it met many of the same
needs, *Plays* absorbed a weaker journal, *One Act Play Magazine and Radio-
Drama Review*, in October 1942.

Different emphases characterize the three levels. Although most of the plays
were not overtly didactic, they all sought to strengthen certain values and traditions while affording the participating readers or actors an enjoyable exercise
in drama. Most of the plays for younger students adapted legends, fables, fantasies, and fairy tales. Robert St. Clair's "Miss Muffet's Wish" (December

1941) and Lucy Kennedy's "The Pied Piper of Hamelin" (November 1941) are self-explanatory titles from the first volume, and the genre has continued its predominance until the present.

Older students were initially offered a preponderance of biographical plays—thirty-five in the first volume alone—which held up statesmen, scientists, inventors, musicians, and authors as role models worthy of emulation. Bernard J. Remies's "Clara Barton, Lady of Mercy" (May 1942), Robert Bedford's "Louis Pasteur" (November 1941), and Philo Higley's "First Freedom" (October 1941)—a radio play about printer John Peter Zenger—all exemplify this type of dramatization.

Plays for holidays and special occasions reminded readers of accepted traditions and valued modes of behavior and could be found in every issue. October brought Columbus Day; November, Thanksgiving; December, Christmas; and so on throughout the year. Primary, intermediate, and older students could all count on plays devoted not only to the major religious and national holidays but also to lesser occasions such as Armistice Day, Arbor Day, St. Patrick's Day, and Mother's Day, each with its own highlighted virtues to emphasize in dramatic form.

Aside from the radio plays, which included instructions for sound effects so students could simulate an actual performance in a radio studio, the special plays at the back of each issue often reflected didactic concerns. A series called "Vocabulary Builders" provided definitions for phrases such as "Achilles' heel" or "pyrrhic victory" (September 1941); Jack Steele's series of courtesy plays in volume 1 dealt with errors in etiquette that the audience was to evaluate and correct. In January 1942 the publisher announced a new section, "Plays for Defense," that would be presented for the duration of the war to instill in the readers, among other things, "safety procedures, conservation of our resources, examples of alertness, confidence, loyalty and courage . . . the role that the young American citizen can play during the war."[1] Many of these "Victory Plays" promoted war bonds and stamps, including Alice Very's "Victory for Liberty" (January 1943), in which primary students were to dress as giant bonds and stamps, delivering exhortations of their patriotic worth.

Volume 2 ushered in a new editor, A. S. Burack, who was to publish and edit *Plays* for the next thirty-two years. "Production Notes"—hints for staging—began to appear at the back of each issue, and "vocational guidance plays" by Samuel S. Richmond became a regular feature. Stressing the many career opportunities available, each of these plays selected one for emphasis, such as law: "On Trial" (February 1946); farming: "Born to the Soil" (December 1944); journalism: "Cub Reporter" (March 1945); teaching: "We But Teach" (April 1945); and stenography: "Wanted—A Stenographer" (November 1942).

Richmond was just one of a regular group of contributors to *Plays*. Burack drew heavily on a core team of writers that changed gradually over the years; in the 1940s playwrights regularly credited included Helen Louise Miller, Helen

L. Howard, Alice Very, Graham Du Bois, Lindsey Barbee, and the husband and wife team of Mildred Hark and Noel McQueen.

In September 1945 a short column, "Spotlight on Books," debuted. This collection of brief book reviews, rarely consisting of more than a short paragraph, remained the only column in *Plays* throughout its history. After V-J Day the need for victory plays disappeared, and the precariousness of life in the new Atomic Age was nervously confronted in Marcus Konick's "The Atom and Oak Ridge, Tennessee" (May 1946), a play revealing in its attempt to accept not only the deeper meanings of the attack on Hiroshima but the need for cautious coexistence with Russia.

By the end of the 1940s a gradual shift could be seen in *Plays* toward more comedies and away from biographies in favor of adapted literary classics. Volume 8 (1948-1949) listed in its index five patriotic plays, twelve biographical or historical plays, twenty-two legend and fairy-tale plays, and twenty-five comedies. Ten years later the biographical and historical plays had decreased to nine and the legend and fairy tales to nineteen, but the comedies had increased to thirty-seven.

Replacing the biographies were adapted literary classics, often written as radio plays, such as Alexander Dumas's "The Three Musketeers" (April 1953). Literary giants such as Jonathan Swift, Jules Verne, Mark Twain, Robert Louis Stevenson, Nathaniel Hawthorne, and William Shakespeare were made accessible to *Plays* readers in this manner.

Throughout the 1940s and 1950s, and into the 1960s and 1970s, productions concerning holidays continued to be integral to Burack's conception of *Plays*. Occasions such as Book Week, American Education Week, and Fire Prevention Week afforded opportunities for the promotion of important cultural values; similarly, Red Cross Day and Pan-American Day were honored with skits and plays. A few science fiction plays began to appear in the 1950s, such as Claire Boiko's "The Marvelous Time Machine" (May 1959). This interest, reinforced perhaps by Sputnik and America's entry in the space race, could be found in the 1960s as well, as America worked to put a man on the moon. Deborah Newman and Claire Boiko joined Miller, Hark, and McQueen as *Plays*' most regular contributors in its second decade of publication. The practice of reprinting previously published plays gradually increased.

During the 1960s dramatized classics continued to be popular, and melodramas and mysteries increased in number. Puppet plays were introduced for primary grade students in 1966. Occasionally, political issues found their way into the pages of *Plays* in the late 1960s: "Beware the Genies" (January 1969) was an antipollution play by Claire Boiko; "Dinnetah" (May 1969) by Barbara Winther showed true concern for Amerindian rights.

A growing interest in other cultures is evident in *Plays* during these years. In volume 30 (1970-1971) *Plays* published fifteen works concerning other cultures, compared with eleven adapted literary classics. Included among regular contributors in this period were Earl J. Dias, John Murray, Anne Coulter Martens, Adele Thane, and the prolific Claire Boiko and Helen Louise Miller.

In the mid-1970s holiday themes were gradually giving way to improvisations (a series called "Creative Dramatics"), drama workshops, skits and spoofs, pantomimes, and musical programs. In May 1973 the division of drama by reading levels was further simplified to two categories: plays for junior and senior high school students and plays for grammar school students. Aileen Fisher, who had earlier written pageants for *Plays* lionizing the pioneers and the settlement of the West, now turned her attention to ecology with a calvacade for conservation, "What Now, Planet Earth?" (April 1974). The women's movement also received a voice in works such as Boiko's "The Fastest Thimble in the West" (April 1974) and Miller's "Shirley Holmes and the FBI" (March 1974). Although literary classics still held importance, such as Juliet Garver's "Elizabeth" (October 1977), a dramatic monolog based on the work of Elizabeth Barrett Browning, there was also room for "The Trouble with Tribbles" (October 1977), a *Star Trek* episode by David Gerrold.

Plays never enjoyed wide circulation; it hovered around 28,000 at the end of 1977.[2] The following June, Burack died. His wife, Sylvia Kamerman, had helped him on the magazine (and on its companion book publishing venture, Plays, Inc.) for thirty-seven years, as associate editor through most of it. She succeeded him as editor, vowing to maintain his standards and editorial policies. A typical issue from May 1979, for instance, included a play about a dating machine and an adaptation of Horatio Alger, Jr., for the older students, works on Snow White and Johnny Appleseed for the younger students, a humorous skit based on *60 Minutes*, and a dramatization of *Jane Eyre*.

Over forty years old, *Plays* continues to provide entertainment. While trying to transmit a sense of the richness that awaits one who reads great literature, it urges growth through creative dramatics, pantomime, and musical programs. The traditional importance of holidays, civic responsibility, and a sense that Americans have a multicultural heritage remain important themes in the magazine. The technology of the modern world, the influence of mass media, and the problems of adolescence are also confronted, as *Plays* continues to publish drama for American students, drama intended not only to entertain but to enlighten and, more subtly, to instruct.

Notes

1. *Plays: The Drama Magazine for Young People* 1 (January 1943), i.
2. Ibid., 37 (December 1977), 96.

Information Sources

BIBLIOGRAPHY
None.
INDEX SOURCES
Reader's Guide (April 1953-February 1978).

LOCATION SOURCES
Bound volumes are in many major public and university libraries.

Publication History

MAGAZINE TITLE AND TITLE CHANGES
Plays: The Drama Magazine for Young People (1941-).
VOLUME AND ISSUE DATA
(vol. 1, no. 1-).
PUBLISHER AND PLACE OF PUBLICATION
Plays, Inc., Boston (1941-).
EDITOR
S. Emerson Golden (1941-1942); A. S. Burack (1942-1978); Sylvia Kamerman Burack (1978-).

Scot Guenter

R

RANGER RICK'S NATURE MAGAZINE

Ranger Rick's Nature Magazine, published monthly since 1967 by the National Wildlife Federation, is available only through membership in Ranger Rick's Nature Club ($10.50 a year, 1981). The purpose of the publication is "to give boys and girls a year-round program of activities, adventure and knowledge which will help them appreciate and enjoy nature; to help them know and respect all things that grow and creatures that move, that all may desire to conserve and wisely use the vital natural resources of the world."[1]

The magazine takes its name from Ranger Rick, a raccoon, whose purpose is to help children identify with the world of nature. This is accomplished through "Ranger Rick and His Friends," a regular monthly feature that treats various aspects of ecology: game management (February 1974); encroachment of subdivisions on nature (March 1974); dredging of swamps (March 1978); city trees in trouble (July 1981); and trail bikes (August 1981). The January 1979 issue repeated Adventure #1, "How Rick's Rangers Came to Be," providing a new generation of readers with the *raison d'être* for the group and introducing the entire cast of characters who banded together originally to clean up Shady Pond but soon saw the need for a permanent patrol to keep Deep Green Woods clean, safe, and fun.

Other recurring departments include "Hollow Oak Book Nook," featuring short reviews of books about nature that may be purchased at a discount through the magazine; "Dear Ranger Rick," a section containing letters from members telling of their adventures in nature study; "Who-o-o Knows," a page of questions from readers answered by Wise Old Owl; "Happy Bee," short current-event items dealing with nature; the "Useta-Think Twins," a feature aimed at correcting popular misconceptions about animals and other forms of wildlife; and "Ollie Otter's Fun Pages," containing a variety of amusements each month, such as riddles, quizzes, coloring games, dot-to-dots, and crossword puzzles, all about topics from nature studies and often related to other topics in the issue. Frequently appearing is "Ranger Rick's Wild Alphabet," each time dealing with unusual creatures whose names begin with the same letter of the alphabet: A— agama, aardwolf, alpaca, abalone, aphid, and albatross, each accompanied by an illustration, pronunciation guide, and brief description (April 1977).

The magazine devotes a large amount of space to children's creative activities in literature and art. "Little Chipmunk" (July 1974) was written by a young contributor; a contest for writing a story ending is conducted annually: "Where Do We Go from Here?" (September 1977); "Cria—a Young Vicuna" (June 1979); and "Pixie" (March 1980). "Dear Ranger Rick" often contains verse submitted by young readers, accompanied by the children's pictures. Children's artwork is also accepted through this feature and through various contests such as the one for bird drawings in June 1975. The October 1975 issue featured children's inventions similar to those of Arnold Lobel in "Ice Cream Cone Coot" (December 1974)—tire bird, tufted telephone, mixadee, pickledee, and plug-a-chug.

The crafts section of each issue presents challenges to adults as well as to children through enticing subjects such as animal-shaped Valentines (February 1974); creature kites (August-September 1974); candy-cane puppets (December 1974); merry window panes (November 1975); snowflakes to make (December 1976); painting with yarn (November 1979); and painting snow figures (December 1979).

Ranger Rick's Nature Magazine makes even the most informative articles exciting and entertaining. This is the result of publishing contributions from distinguished writers, artists, and photographers. Each issue is profusely illustrated. Approximately 80 percent of the pictures are in full color. These dramatic color photos produced by "top wildlife photographers/contributors" relate to all aspects of wildlife identification and observation.[2] Some particularly intriguing subjects have been "Wandering Continents" (February 1974); "Weeds in the City" (March 1974); "All the Better to 'Ear You With" (April 1974); "Animal Warning Signals" (August-September 1976); "Nature's Holiday Colors" (December 1977); "Totem Poles" (February 1978); "PaPa Parents" (December 1975); and "Superswimmers" (July 1981).

Certain issues of the magazine have been devoted completely to special topics: Hawaii (February 1974); the Amazon (November 1974); Japan (November 1976); Canada (February 1978); and the USSR (October 1978). In the issue on Japan, articles treated bamboo, the mandarin duck, rubber, Japanese toys, silk spinners, Tanuki the raccoon dog, crickets, and the Japanese folktale "The Magic Teakettle" (November 1976).

Frequently, *Ranger Rick* contains stories about nature in serial form: "Maple Magic" (February 1978 and following issues); "A Place for the Children"

(August-September 1975 and following issues); "The Lawn That Went Wild" (May-June 1976 and following issues); "Tamara's Trip" (March 1980 and following issues); and "Backyard Bandit" (August 1981 and following issues). Folktales are sometimes included such as the Russian tale "The Sly Fox" (October 1978); the Mayan tale "King of the Birds" (November 1979); and the Indian legend "Star of the Lake" (July 1974).

A substantial amount of verse is found in the pages of this nature-oriented magazine—much of it high-quality submissions by children but also many poems especially selected to accompany a subject emphasis: "If I Were a Mouse" (March 1974); "A Bird Party" (November 1975); "Seaside" (February 1976); "After-Dark Poems" (August 1981). The August-September 1974 offering in poetry was devoted to limericks about animals.

At times even music has been the subject of articles: "Plant a Seed"—its words and music (May-June 1974); "Bravo, Charley Crow"—with its music (February 1977); and "Ranger Rick's Recycled Junk Band"—an ecology song with its music (May 1977).

Two areas of social studies that are very adroitly brought under the nature-studies umbrella are biography and history. Biographical sketches of naturalists and others concerned with the natural sciences have appeared: Audubon (January 1976), "The Tree that George Washington Planted—the Tulip Tree" (May-June 1976), "Dr. Edwin James, Plant Hunter of the Old West" (June 1979), and Jean-Henri Fabré (January 1980). Historical subjects have been treated in "Life on the Prairie" (February 1974), "The Welcome Bird—a Historical Story" (May-June 1974), "Growing Up in Old New England" (January 1976), and "Liberty Tree—A Story of the War for Independence" (July 1976).

Aspects of Indian culture have been featured in the magazine: Kachina dolls of the Hopi Indians (October 1976); dogs of the Indians (July 1976); and a Mayan maze (November 1979). Eskimo materials are found in the "Naput" stories dealing with Eskimo life, animals, and nature in the Arctic (December 1974; January 1979; and April 1977).

Information about prehistoric creatures has been a frequent inclusion in articles like "Mary and the Monster"—the Ichthyosaur in Lyme Regis, England (March 1974); the unicorn (January 1976); "Graveyard of Giants—the Brontosaurus" (January 1979); and "Dinosaurs in Our Every Day Life" (September 1981).

Bird studies have included penguins (January 1975, February 1977, and December 1978), berry birds (December 1979), birds of prey (March 1974), whooping cranes (February 1976), and the white stork (March 1978); ducks received special treatment in "Quacker Quiz" (March 1980).

Articles about a variety of creatures have treated diverse topics such as the Andean condor (August-September 1976), the osprey (February 1974), camels (April 1976), the jaguar (November 1974), the timber wolf (December 1974), and salamanders (December 1974); bears were the subject of "Grin and Bear It"—a collection of "bear" cartoons (March 1980).

Most issues of the magazine contain some material about the seashore and water life. Articles of unusual quality and appeal discussed ocean forests (December 1975), sharks (January 1977), sponges (February 1977), the nautilus (January 1978), sand dollars (January 1977), and dolphins (April 1974, August 1975).

A sampling of pieces about astronomy and space included "Pictures in the Sky"—constellations (January 1977); "Mars Is a Maybe" (October 1977); and "Super-Sights—Aurora Borealis" (February 1978).

Articles about energy for the young are bound to be in evidence in an energy-conscious nation: "Warm House" (February 1974), "Cool House" (May-June 1974), "Solar Energy" (December 1974, December 1975), "Warm Tips for Winter" (December 1979), and "Solar Car" (August 1981). The September 1981 issue contained the feature "Ranger Rick's Energy Board-Game."

The lively content, information-packed pages, and inclusion of all aspects of natural history—animals, plants, geology, and weather—make *Ranger Rick's Nature Magazine* popular with both children and adults. Trudy Dye Farrand, editor, identified the secret of its success when she stated that it "treats its readers as intelligent young people who should not be talked down to or patronized."[3] *Ranger Rick* aims to "tell it like it is. The sooner children learn how nature works, the better. We don't shy away from the fact that all living creatures must eat to live, and that many animals are predators preying on smaller creatures. We also provide a basis for understanding of sex by treating animal procreation in a very natural way."[4]

Children who have experienced nature studies through the stories, photographs, and activities of *Ranger Rick's Nature Magazine* are ready subjects to sign and live out the Ranger Rick pledge: "I give my pledge as a member of Ranger Rick's Nature Club / To use my eyes to see the beauty of all outdoors / To train my mind to learn the importance of nature / To use my hands to help protect our soil, water, woods and wildlife / And by my good example, to show others how to respect, properly use, and enjoy our natural resources."

Notes

1. Lavinia Dobler and Muriel Fuller, *The Dobler World Directory of Youth Periodicals*, 3rd ed. (New York: Citation, 1970), 51.
2. Howard Chapnick, "Markets & Careers," *Popular Photography* 79 (August 1976), 22.
3. Ibid., 120.
4. Ibid., 120.

Information Sources

BIBLIOGRAPHY
Alyce Joyce Chambers. "Recent Trends in Children's Periodicals" (M.A. thesis, East Tennessee State University, 1975); Howard Chapnick, "Markets & Careers," *Popular Photography* 79 (August 1976), 16-22; Lavinia Dobler and Muriel Fuller, *The Dobler Directory of Youth Periodicals*, 3rd ed. (New York: Citation, 1970.);

Bill Katz, ed., *Magazines for Libraries*, 2nd ed. (New York: R. R. Bowker, 1972); Nancy Larrick, "Classroom Magazines: A Critique of 45 Top Sellers," *Learning* 7 (October 1978), 60-67; Selma K. Richardson, *Periodicals for School Media Programs* (Chicago: American Library Association, 1978).
INDEX SOURCES
Subject Index to Children's Magazines.
LOCATION SOURCES
Library of Congress and several other state, university, and public libraries around the United States.

Publication History
MAGAZINE TITLE AND TITLE CHANGES
Ranger Rick's Nature Magazine (1967-).
VOLUME AND ISSUE DATA
Ranger Rick's Nature Magazine (vol. 1, no. 1-).
PUBLISHER AND PLACE OF PUBLICATION
National Wildlife Federation, Washington, D.C. (1967-).
EDITOR
Trudy Dye Farrand (1967-).

Mary D. Manning

THE RIVERSIDE MAGAZINE FOR YOUNG PEOPLE

Horace Elisha Scudder (1838-1902), although not a first rate writer, was one of the most important American literary figures of the nineteenth century. He served as an editor for the distinguished Boston publisher Houghton Mifflin and its predecessor Hurd and Houghton for more than thirty years, culminating in his editing *The Atlantic Monthly*, then owned by Houghton Mifflin, from 1890 to 1898. His accomplishments, which included considerable involvement with children's literature, merit much more study than they have so far received.

Scudder's greatest contribution to children's literature was the establishment in 1867 of *The Riverside Magazine for Young People*, the most important children's magazine to emphasize literary merit to be founded in America before *St. Nicholas** in 1873. As far as literary merit is concerned, *The Riverside* is arguably the most important children's magazine to be published in America, although financially, and probably in popularity among young readers, it was a failure.

Ellen Ballou, who used the publisher's archives to write the official history of Houghton Mifflin's early years, divided the credit for originating *The Riverside* between Scudder and Henry Houghton.[1] Houghton was the proprietor of the Riverside Press, a Cambridge, Massachusetts, printing house, as well as partner in Hurd and Houghton, a New York publishing house that was soon to open a Boston office, as befitted a firm that was to make its reputation as the publisher of New England writers. Ballou indicated that Hurd and Houghton had decided by 1865 to publish a magazine, probably because almost all major trade publishers were doing so. That Houghton entered periodical publishing with a magazine for young people indicates not only the growth in acceptance achieved by children's literature during the preceding decade but also that such magazines, in the view of a practical businessman, had potential for profit. In addition, Houghton had on his staff a young man named Horace E. Scudder, who had already published a book for young readers and who was greatly interested in children's literature.

By the mid-1860s there had developed a clear need for magazines for children that stressed literary value rather than obtrusive morality. The first of these magazines was *Our Young Folks*,* begun by Ticknor and Fields in Boston (1865) as a sister magazine of *The Atlantic Monthly*. *Our Young Folks* is clearly the model on which Scudder and Houghton based *The Riverside Magazine* when they founded it two years later. *The Riverside Magazine*, however, was no mere imitator; in quality, it quickly surpassed the older publication. Important as *Our Young Folks* was, it was also, as the first of a new type of children's magazine, fumbling; side by side with major literature, it had its full share of didacticism. It was unwilling to relinquish entirely the formulas that had brought success to children's magazines such as *The Youth's Companion** during the half-century before the Civil War. Scudder and Houghton had no such qualms.

According to Ballou, the final decision to begin *The Riverside Magazine* was reached in May 1866; the first issue appeared in January 1867. The format was handsome, with an attractive cover and many internal illustrations, and reviewers were impressed. Although both Scudder and Houghton lived and worked in Boston or its environs, the magazine was published from New York under the Hurd and Houghton imprint.

Despite Scudder's youth—he was only twenty-eight when the magazine began—he proved an excellent editor, able to deal tactfully with both his authors and his publishers and skillful at attracting talent to the magazine. Frank R. Stockton is sometimes called one of Scudder's discoveries, and that is true as far as Stockton's involvement with children's literature is concerned; he had, however, earlier published in other magazines, including the old *Southern Literary Messenger*. Many other authors contributed to *The Riverside Magazine*, including Mary Mapes Dodge, Lucretia P. Hale, Rose Terry (Cooke), Rebecca Harding Davis, Sarah Orne Jewett, and Scudder himself.

Scudder's most significant literary coup was enlisting Hans Christian Andersen as a contributor of original fairy tales, a victory of major proportions because Andersen had failed to respond to Scudder's early letters and because the Danish author's painful shyness made it difficult for the editor to approach him personally. Andersen became both a contributor to *The Riverside Magazine* and an author for Hurd and Houghton.

There is little doubt that *The Riverside Magazine* was a major influence in the development of *St. Nicholas*. Mary Mapes Dodge, the first editor of *St. Nicholas*, and Frank R. Stockton, her associate editor, not only were aware of Scudder's magazine, they also wrote for it. Yet *The Riverside Magazine* was a financial failure, and in December 1870, after only four years of publication, it was absorbed into *Scribner's Monthly*, a new adult magazine founded to compete with *Harper's*. Clearly, the failure of *The Riverside Magazine* was not seen by other publishers as indicative of the future for the literary children's magazine; the publishers of *Scribner's Monthly* (later called *The Century*) themselves founded such a magazine in 1873: *St. Nicholas*. Why did *The Riverside Magazine* fail, when its predecessor, *Our Young Folks*, outlasted it by three years and its successor, *St. Nicholas*, died—lingeringly—in 1943? The obvious answer is that Hurd and Houghton never achieved enough circulation for the magazine so that income would cover expenses. But that answer begs the important question of why the magazine did not achieve real popularity. That question can never be fully answered, but I suggest that part of the answer lies in editorial personality, that is, the persona created, consciously or unconsciously, as a means of addressing and, of course, attracting an audience for a magazine. In this respect, the impression one gains of *The Riverside Magazine* is one of brilliance, but it was a cold brilliance, of the sort that made it unlikely that the magazine could create the sort of affection among its readers that *St. Nicholas* developed early and maintained even during its slow decline. This aspect of *St. Nicholas* can be credited to Mary Mapes Dodge, who not only gave the magazine literary quality but also charm through a personal column called "Jack–in–the–Pulpit" included in each issue during the magazine's early years. Skilled editor though he was, Scudder was not able to give *The Riverside Magazine* the warmth and informality that Dodge gave *St. Nicholas*. We might speculate that Scudder associated informality with the occasional sentimentality that afflicted *Our Young Folks*; yet the coldness of *The Riverside* is absent from Scudder's own books for children.

After the cessation of *The Riverside Magazine* Horace E. Scudder continued his distinguished career with Hurd and Houghton and Houghton Mifflin, editing not only *The Atlantic Monthly* but also the famous Cambridge editions of standard poets. Although the *Riverside's* failure must have been a blow to its young editor, he did not abandon his interest in children's literature: between 1876 and 1884 he published his books about the traveling Bodleys, including material he had originally published in *The Riverside Magazine* as part of his editorial duties, and in 1894 he published *Childhood in Literature and Art*.

Unlike *St. Nicholas, The Riverside Magazine* has been forgotten. Yet in production, illustrations, and literary quality—everything, in fact, except popular success—it set a standard that has seldom been equaled.

Note

1. Ellen B. Ballou, *The Building of the House: Houghton Mifflin's Formative Years* (Boston: Houghton Mifflin, 1970), 110-28.

Information Sources

BIBLIOGRAPHY

Ellen B. Ballou, *The Building of the House: Houghton Mifflin's Formative Years* (Boston: Houghton Mifflin, 1970); Ellen B. Ballou, "Horace Elisha Scudder and the Riverside Magazine," *Harvard Library Bulletin*, 14 (Autumn 1960) 426-52. Alice M. Jordan, *From Rollo to Tom Sawyer* (Boston: Horn Book, 1948); R. Gordon Kelly, *Mother Was a Lady* (Westport, Conn.: Greenwood Press, 1974); Horace E. Scudder, *Henry Oscar Houghton* (Cambridge: Riverside Press, 1897).

INDEX SOURCES

None.

LOCATION SOURCES

Portland Public Library, Portland, Me.; Minnesota Historical Society, St. Paul; Brown University Library, Providence, R.I.; Teachers College Library, New York.

Publication History

MAGAZINE TITLE AND TITLE CHANGES

The Riverside Magazine for Young People: An Illustrated Monthly (January 1867-December 1870).

VOLUME AND ISSUE DATA

The Riverside Magazine for Young People: An Illustrated Monthly (vol. 1, no. 1-vol. 4, no. 12).

PUBLISHER AND PLACE OF PUBLICATION

Hurd and Houghton, New York (January 1867-December 1870).

EDITOR

Horace E. Scudder (January 1867-December 1870).

David L. Greene

ROSE BUD

On a July evening in 1832, when the Gilman family was gathered in their home in Charleston, South Carolina, one of the children suggested to Caroline Howard Gilman "how pretty it would be" to have a newspaper "in which children could write." Whether or not the idea had occurred to Gilman previously, the child's remarks evidently inspired action. That night she proposed that the title of the periodical for children be the *Rose Bud* and that its caption be a quotation from Walter Scott's *Lady of the Lake*: "The Rose Is Fairest When Tis Budding New." "A wiser head"—presumably her husband, Dr. Samuel Gilman—contributed the subtitle *Youth's Gazette*. Subsequently, on August 11, 1832, the first issue of the *Rose Bud; or Youth's Gazette* was published. The paper, consisting of four pages with three columns to a page, began as a weekly, appearing every Saturday for its young readers.[1]

In the "Editor's Address" in this first issue Gilman described the contents she had planned for the paper: "It will contain original prose and poetry, notices of new books and toys, extracts from children's works that are not common,

and many other interesting things which cannot be detailed here.''[2] She also
informed her ''Young Friends'' that, through the paper, she hoped to do ''something'' for their ''pleasure and improvement.''[3] It is in this statement that readers
can still find the essential purpose of the *Rose Bud*. Gilman composed and selected
tales and verse whose chief purpose was the improvement of her reader's characters. Improvement of their intellects, however, was clearly the aim of many
of the feature articles as well. That the editor of the *Rose Bud* was bent upon
improving humanity is not surprising, for the children's literature of the time
was generally didactic. What is surprising is that her efforts in behalf of ''pleasure'' occur as often as they do—sometimes overtly and at other times through
her adoption of a lively tone. She introduced humorous verse and anecdotes
occasionally as well as conundrums, charades, and enigmas.

On the second page of this first issue appears the column ''For My Youngest
Readers.'' It is set in larger type than is used elsewhere in the paper, the
vocabulary is elementary, and the words are carefully divided into syllables.
This column became a standard feature of the *Rose Bud*, although the distinctive
type and syllabication were soon dropped. The subject of this first column is a
bizarre account of a cat killing rats that have invaded a flour barrel, but, happily,
later columns treat tamer activities.

On this same page Gilman announced that she intended to include in future
issues news of happenings in Charleston as well as in foreign countries. She did
indeed report news of the city, most consistently the deaths of children. A child's
obituary occurs in the second issue of the paper, and others appear throughout
the life of the paper. Foreign news is reported occasionally, and in her second
issue she began this service with an account of the efforts of Dona Maria, the
fourteen-year-old queen of Portugal, to regain her throne from a ''wicked''
uncle.[4] ''Notices of College and School Examinations'' and ''Reports and Transactions of Juvenile Societies,'' also projected for publication in the *Rose Bud*,
play little or no part in future issues.

This first issue includes reviews of two children's books, along with the names
of their booksellers. In later issues book reviews and booksellers' advertisements
appear frequently. Most of the titles are no longer generally familiar, although
Mary and Charles Lamb's *Tales from Shakespeare* and one of the editions of
Mother Goose published in Boston by Munroe and Francis are two exceptions.

Dominating the third page of this initial issue are two letters to the editor.
One is purportedly from Hexandria, a wild flower that recognizes the superiority
of country life, having been transplanted from ''a retired bank in the country to
a gay panterre in town.''[5] The second is from Sally Hatebook, whose name
clearly reflects her attitude toward learning. Later issues of the paper publish
letters from actual subscribers, although Sally Hatebook reappears in brief moral
narratives as do other stereotypes with names such as Dickey Bluff, Lucy Dash,
Polly Saunter, and Patty Positive.

On the last page of the *Rose Bud's* first issue are poems that well represent
the two kinds of verse favored by Caroline Gilman. ''The Little Boy's Complaint

About Butter'' is a humorous account of a child who looks forward to the time when he can eat what he pleases; in fact, his house will be a pie: "As soon as I become a man, / I'll have a pie as tall as you, / With doors and windows like a house, / And lin'd with plums all thro' and thro'. . . ./My windows all with jelly made / Like Boston glass shall glisten bright, / And sugar candy for the frames, / At every turn shall greet my sight." The second poem treats a serious subject sentimentally. In "Mother, What Is Death?" the mother explains immortality to her daughter by drawing an analogy between the dead baby, who "will rise / More beautiful than now" and a "wither'd worm" emerging from the cocoon with "wings of starry gold."[6] Although her verse appears throughout the periodical and was published separately as well, Gilman acknowledged her limitations as a poet in "My Autobiography," where she describes herself as "only a versifier."[7]

The original prose promised children in the periodical's statement of purpose was often contributed by the editor herself in the form of domestic fiction. Her characters regularly conform to the type of "gentry figures" who embody those values considered essential to the moral order of early nineteenth-century America.[8] "The Planter's Son" is a story that opens with William Ashley berating Jim, a small black boy who serves as the groom for the Ashleys' horses. At the height of his anger, young Ashley raises his whip; his brother Henry, trying to stop him, is struck instead. Henry recovers, and it is a chastened William who comes to understand that "if we cannot control our language, we cannot control our temper."[9] A second story, "The Old Frock," is one in which Mrs. Alger admonishes her daughter Jane not to dress for "display," warning her that if such is her purpose for attending parties, she should stay at home.[10] Still another is "The Young Mathematician," whose central character is Laura Sinclair, a young woman born to wealth. In due time, however, her "perplexed and harassed" father loses his fortune, and only her skill as an accountant enables the family to enjoy economic recovery.[11] Interestingly, this is not the only time in the *Rose Bud* that Gilman attributes to a woman certain responsibilities and skills that stand in marked contrast with the conventional role of women in the early nineteenth century.

The most important nonfiction prose published during the life of the paper— a series of letters of Eliza Wilkinson—appears in the first two volumes. Not really intended for children, these letters were written by a "connexion" of the Gilman family during the British invasion of Charleston in 1779.[12] The first of the letters is printed in the December 1, 1832, issue, and they continue intermittently into volume 2. These letters, edited by Gilman, were later published as a separate volume, as was some of Gilman's own work, notably the novels *Recollections of a Housekeeper* and *Recollections of a Southern Matron*.

In her autobiographical essay Caroline Gilman erroneously identified the *Rose Bud* as "the first juvenile newspaper, if I mistake not, in the Union."[13] However, in her newspaper of October 13, 1832, she recognized two predecessors: *The Youth's Temperance Lecturer*, a monthly published in New York, and *The*

Juvenile Rambler, a weekly published in Boston. Then in the issue published October 21, 1832, Gilman called her readers' attention to still another New England periodical for children, one having *Rose Bud* as *its* title. As a consequence, in the prospectus for the periodical's second volume, published August 17, 1833, the editor made the following announcement: "Since the publication of the Rose Bud, papers of a similar character have increased so rapidly at the North, as to induce the Editor to change its title."[14] Beginning with the first issue of volume 2, the *Rose Bud* bears the title the *Southern Rose Bud*. But more significant than the name change—and not reflected in that change—is another decision announced in this prospectus: "The Southern Rose Bud...will be adapted in many points to mature readers, though not relinquishing the juvenile department."[15]

From volume 2 on, Caroline Gilman's newspaper is less and less a children's periodical and increasingly one for adults. The prospectus for volume 3, published on July 26, 1834, states that future issues will be adapted to "family reading," and the taste of young people of "maturer years will be carefully studied."[16] Furthermore, it was announced that issues comprising the third volume would be published every other week rather than weekly. The prospectus for the fourth volume, published in the *Southern Rose Bud* of August 22, 1835, recognizes that the paper's title must again be changed, this time to reflect changes of content and audience: "The Rose Bud, at the close of the third volume, is well entitled by its age, its patronage, the literary character of its contributors, and the advanced years of its early subscribers, to change its title to *The Southern Rose*."[17] Henceforth, until the final issue of August 17, 1839, the periodical is called the *Southern Rose* in recognition of its adult audience.

Any evaluation of the paper must take into account its evolution: "one must separate the first volume, which she stated was to be purely for children, from the second and third, which are in the developmental stage toward the adult magazine of volumes four through seven, which are avowedly for adults."[18] Although one critic believes that "in many ways volumes IV, V, and VI were the most successful ones," the earlier volumes, and especially the first, are the concern of this essay.[19] Volume 1, in the opinion of the author of a full-length study of Caroline Gilman's work, "carried out Mrs. Gilman's stated intention of providing both entertainment and instruction"; the *Rose Bud*, despite its didacticism, appealed to children, largely because of the editor's "knowledge of and affinity for children."[20] The editor herself perceived that her greatest strength as a writer lay in her work for children: "My only pride is in my books for children....I know that I have learned the way to youthful hearts, and I think I have originated several styles of writing for them."[21]

The reason for the demise of the *Southern Rose* was probably two-fold. Pleas for subscription payments in later issues suggest financial difficulties, in spite of claims to the contrary in the "Editor's Valedictory Address," which was published in the paper's final issue. More importantly, by 1839 Caroline Gilman had found the deadlines of periodical publication onerous. In her farewell remarks she explained that "she would prefer some mode of publication less exacting than the rigorous punctuality of a periodical work."[22] Indeed, her preference was expressed for much of the rest of her life in the publication of books of prose and poetry, some representing new work and others consisting of material that had first been published in her periodical.

Notes

1. For the circumstances surrounding the decision to publish the periodical, see *Rose Bud*, October 20, 1832, p. 30. Although the first issue of the paper appeared August 11, the second issue was not published until September 8; subsequently, the *Rose Bud* adhered to a weekly schedule.

2. Ibid., August 11, 1832, p. 1.

3. Ibid.

4. Ibid., September 8, 1832, p. 6.

5. Ibid., August 11, 1832, p. 3.

6. Ibid., p. 4.

7. Caroline H. Gilman, "My Autobiography," in *The Female Prose Writers of America*, ed. John S. Hart (Philadelphia: E. H. Butler, 1852), 56.

8. R. Gordon Kelly, *Mother Was a Lady* (Westport, Conn.: Greenwood Press, 1974), 57.

9. *Rose Bud*, September 29, 1832, p. 17.

10. Ibid., June 1, 1833, p. 158.

11. Ibid., December 15, 1832, p. 61.

12. Ibid., December 1, 1832, p. 55.

13. Gilman, "Autobiography," p. 55.

14. *Rose Bud*, August 17, 1833, p. 204.

15. Ibid.

16. *Southern Rose Bud*, July 26, 1834, p. 191.

17. Ibid., August 22, 1835, p. 206.

18. Janice J. Thompson, *Caroline Howard Gilman—Her Mind and Her Art* (Ann Arbor, Mich.: Xerox University Microfilms, 1975), 201.

19. William S. Hoole, "The Gilmans and the Southern Rose," *North Carolina Historical Review* 11 (1932), 122.

20. Thompson, *Caroline Howard Gilman*, p. 201.

21. Gilman, "Autobiography," p. 56.

22. *Southern Rose*, August 17, 1839, p. 416.

Information Sources

BIBLIOGRAPHY

Caroline H. Gilman, "My Autobiography," in *The Female Prose Writers of America*, ed. John S. Hart (Philadelphia: E. H. Butler, 1852), 49-57; William S. Hoole, "The Gilmans and the Southern Rose," *North Carolina Historical Review* 11 (1934), 116-28. R. Gordon Kelly, *Mother Was a Lady* (Westport, Conn.: Greenwood Press, 1974); J. M. Smith, "Rose Bud: A Magazine for Children," *Horn Book*, 19 (1943), 15-20. Janice J. Thompson, *Caroline Howard Gilman: Her Mind and Her Art* (Ann Arbor, Mich.: Xerox University Microfilms, 1975).

INDEX SOURCES
None.
LOCATION SOURCES
The seven volumes appear in *American Periodical Series, 1800-1850*, Ann Arbor, Mich.,
    University Microfilm, Reel 688. Libraries holding original issues of the periodical
    are noted in the *Union List of Serials of Libraries in the United States and Canada*.

Publication History

MAGAZINE TITLE AND TITLE CHANGES
Rose Bud; or Youth's Gazette (1832-1833); *Southern Rose Bud* (1833-1835); *Southern
    Rose* (1835-1839).
VOLUME AND ISSUE DATA
Rose Bud; or Youth's Gazette (vol. 1, no. 1-vol. 1, no. 52); *Southern Rose Bud* (vol. 2,
    no. 1-vol. 3, no. 26); *Southern Rose* (vol. 4, no. 1-vol. 7, no. 26).
PUBLISHER AND PLACE OF PUBLICATION
The periodical was always published in Charleston, S.C., but by several publishers: J.
    S. Burges (1832); William Estill (1832-1833); J. S. Burges (1833-1835); E. J.
    Van Brunt (1835-1836); Burges and Honour (1836); J. S. Burges (1836-?); B.
    B. Hussey (1838-1839).
EDITOR
Caroline Howard Gilman (1832-1839).

Lalla N. Overby

S

ST. NICHOLAS

In the poet's world, the child is father of the man, but in the publishing world, as in that of biology, the child is sum and synthesis of its parents. Nowhere is this principle clearer than in *St. Nicholas*, the best known of nineteenth-century American juvenile periodicals. A product of Scribner & Co. (later The Century Co.), publishers of *Scribner's Monthly* and *The Century*, *St. Nicholas* reflects in every issue the influence of its adult-oriented counterparts. The same authors and illustrators appear in both magazines; the same conceptual and structural patterns control both; and the same broad editorial goals characterize both. In these parallels is perhaps the lasting significance of *St. Nicholas*, for as it presents high-quality entertainment to a juvenile audience, it communicates as well the style, attitudes, and values of an established, secure, upper-middle-class culture, creating a sociointellectual pattern that touched several generations of readers.

Scribner's Monthly, first published in November 1870, was the creation of Dr. Josiah Gilbert Holland, Roswell Smith, and Charles Scribner. Their intention was to develop a high-quality competitor for *Harper's Monthly* and the *Atlantic Monthly*, and they succeeded. Reflecting Holland's awareness of middle-class conservatism as well as the more liberal and artistic concerns of its associate editor, Richard Watson Gilder, the new magazine "was not merely a miscellany..., but was founded in conviction, open-mindedness, ambition for leadership, and a determination to be of public service. The main idea of the editors was to discover what was best and then to exploit it."[1] To this end *Scribner's Monthly* quickly developed a pattern of publishing fiction, essays, and a scattering of poetry. These contents were accented by a group of regular departments: "Topics of the Times," an editorial page; "The Old Cabinet," a section of lighter editorial comment; "Etchings," devoted to light verse; "Culture and Progress," concerned with literature and the arts; a short-lived "Nature and Science" column; and a regular discussion of current events, "The World's Work." Successful from the outset, *Scribner's Monthly* and *The Century* endured for sixty years, coming to be regarded as a consistent advocate for "the highest aesthetic and moral ideals" and "often an effective force in political and social reform."[2]

The acceptance of *Scribner's Monthly* encouraged Roswell Smith to pursue his plan for a similar magazine for children. As early as 1870, he had approached Mary Mapes Dodge with the idea of such a magazine; in 1873 he hired her as editor. Building upon *The Riverside Magazine*,* which Scribner & Co. had acquired in 1870, and upon authors already associated with *Scribner's Monthly*, *St. Nicholas* appeared for the first time in November 1873 in an edition of 40,000 copies. That the two magazines were to parallel each other is plain. An unsigned blurb in the November 1873 *Scribner's Monthly* called attention to the new publication, remarking: "Whether we shall lead the little child, or the little child shall lead us, remains to be seen; but it will be pleasant to have him at our side, to watch his growth and development, and to minister, as we may, to his prosperity....Wherever 'SCRIBNER' goes, 'ST. NICHOLAS' ought to go. They will be harmonious companions in the family, and the helpers of each other in the work of instruction, culture and entertainment."[3]

The early years of *St. Nicholas* were fruitful. The magazine expanded from forty-eight to ninety-six pages an issue, and the circulation stabilized at approximately 70,000 issues a month. Aiding in this growth was the publisher's acquisition of other juvenile magazines, which enabled *St. Nicholas* to add new authors as well as new subscribers: *Our Young Folks** and *The Children's Hour** were absorbed in 1874, *The Schoolday Magazine* and *The Little Corporal** in 1875, and *Wide Awake*,* the last to be taken over, in 1893. The transition of Scribner & Co. to The Century Co. in 1881 had no significant effect, and *St. Nicholas*, like its parent magazines, flourished. With the backing of a prosperous publishing house, Mary Mapes Dodge was able to pay substantial sums to contributors (Kate Douglas Wiggin received $150 for her first story, "Half a Dozen Housekeepers," published in 1878), making the magazine a highly regarded market for writers and illustrators throughout the country.

Dodge directed *St. Nicholas* for thirty-two years, leaving an indelible imprint upon the magazine and upon American juvenile publishing. After her death, in 1905, William Fayal Clarke, who had worked closely with her during the last years, assumed the editorship. Clarke's twenty-two years as editor brought little change, beyond an expansion of the departments to keep pace with modern interests. Changes of another sort, however, marked the start of *St. Nicholas*'s decline. Shaken by administrative turmoil as well as by the advent of low-priced, mass-market magazines, The Century Co. attempted to regain its strength by altering the nature and scope of *The Century*. Changed from a monthly to a quarterly in 1929, it was sold in 1930 to the Forum Publishing Co.[4] *St. Nicholas* fared no better. A succession of short-term editors after Clarke's retirement did nothing to establish continuity or build circulation, and the parent company decided to cut its losses. *St. Nicholas* was sold in 1931 to the American Education Press and in 1935 was transferred to the Educational Publishing Co. With volume 67 (1940) it changed format, appearing in a soft-paper, large-type, picture-book version, rather than in the slick-paper format of its past. This change did not halt the decline, and the last issue appeared in February 1940. An effort was made in 1943 to revive the magazine after the model of its early days, but the attempt failed after only four issues, ending at last the enterprise begun seventy years before.

When Mary Mapes Dodge assumed the editorship of *St. Nicholas* in 1873, she was an established writer for children, an experienced editor, and a person with definite ideas of what a children's magazine should be. Under her guidance *St. Nicholas* took shape, following the pattern laid down by *Scribner's Monthly* and reflecting from the outset an enduring commitment to quality. Drawing upon the Scribner's stable of authors, Dodge gave the early issues a selection of notable names that might otherwise have been absent. She exercised absolute control over the magazine, from its content to its makeup, regulating not only what was said, but how it was said. Most significantly, she was able to put into practice her ideas about children's reading.

Dodge's experience in writing and publishing was extensive. Widowed in 1858, she turned to writing to support her two young sons, and quickly produced a number of well-received works. Of them, the best known is *Hans Brinker; or The Silver Skates* (1865). During the same period, she worked with her father, James Mapes, in the editing of his magazine, the *Working Farmer*. In 1868 she became an associate editor of *Hearth and Home*, a weekly edited by Donald Grant Mitchell and Harriet Beecher Stowe, where she remained until invited to *St. Nicholas*.[5]

The editorial philosophy that Dodge brought to *St. Nicholas* she outlined in "Children's Magazines," published in *Scribner's Monthly*, July 1873. Two ideas in particular stand out in this essay. First is her assertion that an ideal juvenile magazine must be natural and entertaining: "The child's magazine needs to be stronger, truer, bolder, more uncompromising than [an adult periodical]. Its cheer must be the cheer of the bird-song, not of condescending editorial babble. If it *mean* freshness and heartiness, and life and joy, and its words are simply, directly, and musically put together, it will trill its own way."[6] With this argument she justified the uncompromising awareness of style and morality that permeates the magazine, just as it did *Scribner's Monthly*.

Second, and more significantly, the magazine must be unabashedly didactic; that is, it must convey—albeit subtly—a definite system of ideals and values:

Doubtless a great deal of instruction and good moral teaching may be inculcated in the pages of a magazine; but it must be by hints dropped incidentally here and there; by a few brisk, hearty statements of the difference between right and wrong; a sharp, clean thrust at falsehood, a sunny recognition of truth, a gracious application of politeness, an unwilling glimpse of the odious doings of the uncharitable and base. In a word, pleasant, breezy things may linger and turn themselves this way and that. Harsh, cruel facts—if they must come, and sometimes it is important that they should—must march forward boldly, say what they have to say, and go.[7]

Just as its parent publications strove to be a forum for open-minded yet principled discussion of public and literary issues, so would *St. Nicholas* strive to inform, entertain, and educate its young readers. As it did so, it was to aim at preparing them for ''life as it is''—reality as perceived by a well-educated, well-established segment of upper-middle-class American society.[8]

In seeking to implement these goals Dodge faced two problems. One was mechanical: the building and retaining of an audience, for a juvenile readership is transient. To this end she employed a technique already proven in *Scribner's Monthly*—scheduling regular departments in each issue of the magazine. Some were short lived; others endured. All, however, focused on one or more groups of readers or on clearly identified interest groups. Some were determined by age, such as ''For Very Little Folk'' (1873-1899), a page of simple stories set in large type. Others served as an editorial page, as in Dodge's column ''Jack-in-the-Pulpit'' (1873-1896), in which she wrote about matters of taste, behavior, and morality. Some focused attention on contemporary affairs, as in the transient ''Curiosity Shop'' (1896-1897) and ''Current Events'' (1898-1899). Still others sought to inform or equip the readers with other resources, as did the ''St. Nicholas Treasure-Box of Literature'' (1880-1882), reprinting notable works from the past; ''Work and Play for Young Folk'' (1883-1886), concerning recreation and games; and ''Nature and Science for Young Folks'' (1900-1930), focusing upon the varieties of science and technology. These departments, like those in the parent magazine, provided continuity from issue to issue.

Also helpful was deliberate reader involvement. ''The Puzzle Box'' posed riddles, mathematical problems, and word games, solutions to which the readers could send in for judging. ''The Letter-Box,'' begun in 1874, published letters from readers, as did ''Young Contributors' Department,'' begun in 1876. The best-known and longest-lasting devices for reader involvement, though, are ''The Agassiz Association,'' begun in 1885, and ''The St. Nicholas League,'' begun in 1899. The first of them is a conservation group, developed to awaken readers to the natural world and the problems facing it through the encouragement of local nature-study groups. The second, conducted for its first ten years by Albert Bigelow Paine, solicited and published reader contributions—drawings, photographs, verse and prose—with awards of certificates and medals going to the winners. A popular and highly esteemed department from the outset, the League served to stimulate readers' interest in publication and attracted work from many youngsters who later became recognized authors; its lists of winners include Ring Lardner, Robert Benchley, William Rose Benet, and William Faulkner.

The other problem was the need for contributions that would meet the magazine's stated artistic and intellectual standards. The degree to which Dodge succeeded is one of the reasons for the magazine's enduring reputation, for in the fiction and nonfiction of *St. Nicholas*, she assembled a body of material well suited both to her own editorial intentions and to the prevailing sentiments of her audience. In attempting to carry out the stated aims, *St. Nicholas* presented to its readers the traditional values of middle-class America. As it did so, however, it also presented a view of the world oriented toward certain realities of the present: urbanization, mechanization, and the increasing complexities of the modern world.

The nature of *St. Nicholas* is handily summarized by a comment appearing in one of its articles. Brander Matthews, comparing Benjamin Franklin and Ralph Waldo Emerson (January 1895), remarked that the two together "give us the two sides of the American character. Franklin stands for the real and Emerson for the ideal. Franklin represents the prose of American life, and Emerson the poetry.... Self-reliance was at the core of the doctrine of each of them, but one urged self-help in the spiritual world and the other in the material."[9] The same dualism characterizes *St. Nicholas*. Its nonfictional contents argue for personal knowledge of the material world, its fiction argues for a moral world, and both genres advance the message of individual competence and self-reliance.

The nonfiction of *St. Nicholas* falls into five major categories. The first (and smallest) of them is the travel or geographical article. Telling of exotic, faraway places in matter-of-fact fashion, these essays present to their young readers the diversity of the world. Including titles such as Mary Hallock Foote's " 'Muchacho' of the Mexican Camp" (December 1878), John Keiller's "Latitude One Hundred and Eighty" (March 1880), George Washington Cable's "New Orleans" (December 1893), and Bertha Runkle's "Child Life in China and Japan" (January 1905), the articles suggest the importance of an awareness of the peoples, geography, and phenomena of the physical world.

Ranking second among the nonfiction is the biographical article, giving glimpses into the life of the great and near-great, past and present. Most of these pieces, not surprisingly, deal with figures from American history; others, though, include diverse figures such as Edward Jenner, Hans Christian Andersen, and Queen Victoria. Two tendencies appear in these articles. They deal, as much as possible, with current or recent celebrities; thus one finds Noah Brooks's remarks about President James A. Garfield in "A Noble Life" (November 1881), Tudor Jenks's "Admiral George Dewey" (October 1899), and Annie Isabel Willis's "In a Poet's Workshop" (September 1890), relating a visit with Oliver Wendell Holmes. In addition, they try to show the "human" side of their subjects, so Noah Brooks referred to Abraham Lincoln as a father in "A Boy in the White House" (November 1882), and Dr. Charles Alexander Eastman wrote about his Indian boyhood in "Recollections of the Wild Life" (December 1893 and following issues).

Emphasized throughout is the importance to the person discussed (and, by implication, to the reader) of self-reliance, industriousness, and open-mindedness. If the biographies are informative, they are instructive as well.

Third among the nonfiction is the historical article, discussing events and ideas drawn from the entire range of human history. Like the biographies, most of these pieces focus upon American and British topics; however, numerous other areas of history appear. From world history come essays such as Charles C. Abbott's "How the Stone-Age Children Played" (April 1878) and G. T. Ferris's "The Olympic Games" (April 1896). Hezekiah Butterworth's "The Black Douglas" (February 1876) and Maurice Thompson's "The Story of Robin Hood" (May 1883) draw upon British sources; American history is the source for F. N. Doubleday's "An Early American Rebellion" (July 1882), dealing with Bacon's Rebellion; Charles F. W. Mielatz's "A Boy's Recollection of the Great Chicago Fire" (October 1898); and Helen L. Coffin's "How We Bought Louisiana" (January 1904). All suggest that learning of the past is pertinent to the present. These are the events, the authors imply, that have generated the present; from them one may learn the enduring lessons (notably industry, fortitude, and faith), so as to have a fuller understanding of one's own times.

A still larger class of nonfiction is the scientific article, supplying insights into the operations of the natural world and a broad exposition of the mechanics of modern technology. Many of these essays focus on technological advances and their workings; among them are J. A. Judson's "Gunpowder" (July 1877), including a detailed formula for black powder; Tudor Jenks's "About Flying-Machines" (April 1896), a long and thoughtful discussion of aircraft possibilities; and George Ethelbert Walsh's investigation into energy sources and possibilities, "What a Lump of Coal Could Do" (October 1904). All implicitly make the point that humankind has turned technology to its own advantage, showing how from precise, scientific knowledge comes the ability to deal competently with the devices that characterize the present.

Other offerings deal with natural science. Some are general: for example, W. K. Brooks's "Something About Birds" (April 1877), C. F. Holder's "How Some Animals Become Extinct" (August 1887), and Dan Beard's discussion of the comparative anatomy of the vertebral column, "Mother Nature and the Jointed Stick" (October 1902). Some are specific: typical are Richard Rathbun's "The Giant Squid" (February 1881) and Ernest E. Thompson's essay on the partridge, "The Drummer on Snowshoes" (April 1887). A few are concerned with geology, astronomy, or other branches of science: among them are Ernest Ingersoll's "Placer and Gulch Mining for Gold" (August 1880), Irene Brown's "A Glimpse of Saturn" (October 1900), and Julian Ralph's "An Indian Village" (July 1903). All, though, emphasize knowledge for the sake of knowledge, suggesting that this is how one comes to grips with all of the varied manifestations of the world.

Among all nonfictional articles, the largest group is the one dealing with practical matters. This group consists of works intended to give the reader a command of the organization and operation of his or her society, suggest certain skills and accomplishments that may prove desirable, and convey facts designed to instill in the reader the skills necessary to function effectively in the modern world. The subjects of these articles are varied. Some discuss physical fitness, arguing for a sound body as well as a sound mind: among them are Washington Gladden's "A Talk with Girls and Their Mothers" (May 1880) and Walter Camp's "Intercollegiate Foot-Ball in America" (November 1889 and following issues). Others are how-to-do-it articles: typical are J. H. Hubbard's "How to Make an Ice-Boat" (January 1878), Leo H. Grindon's discussion of chemistry for entertainment, "Parlor Magic" (October 1878), and William A. Eddy's "Reaching a Great Height with Kites" (April 1892).

Most of the articles in this category, however, discuss the nature of the urban world, implying that since the United States is an urban nation, one must know fully all that constitutes it. Teresa A. Brown's "The Story of a Life-Saving Station" (January 1896) and Walter Kenyon's "A Little Talk About the Big Panama Canal" (October 1905) examine the ways in which society makes existence safer and easier. Some articles give insights into the workings of city life: among them are W. A. Linn's "Telegraph-Boys" (December 1879) and Patti Lyle Collins's "The Dead-Letter Office" (February 1894). Others reflect the same sociological consciousness that permeated *Scribner's/Century*, speaking to the problems of the less advantaged classes of the city. Washington Gladden wrote "The Disadvantages of City Boys" (March 1880); Charles L. Brace wrote about the pernicious influences of the city streets in "Wolf-Reared Children" (May 1882); and Charles Barnard examined the training of immigrants for domestic service in "Fräulein Mina Smidt Goes to School" (September 1884). Although these articles convey numerous details about the facts of the world, they present these details from the perspective of the upper middle class.

If the nonfiction of *St. Nicholas* aims at equipping readers for life "as it is," the fiction seems intended to equip them for the world as it ought to be. The stories, to be sure, exist, first, as entertainment. Varied in length, style, and nature, they possess well-rounded, satisfying plots; they present situations that most of the readers might appreciate and identify with; and they present characters who are generally well drawn and sympathetic. As they do this, however, they exist, second, as instruction, conveying to their readers ideals, standards, and models that ostensibly will be useful in organizing their lives.

Like the nonfiction, the fiction of *St. Nicholas* falls readily into several categories. The smallest of them is technical fiction, stories that either use a fictional format to convey scientific information or, like science-fiction, base their plots upon extrapolations from established scientific principles. Into the first group fall tales such as Ella Bertha Bradley's "Burning Peaches" (May 1876), which uses the making of the confection, peach leather, to impart the principles of oxidation, and Lloyd Wyman's "Johnny's Lost Ball" (May 1878), discussing buoyancy and the determination of volumes as a boy uses a bucket of water to float a ball out of a drainpipe. The second group includes works such as Rossiter

Johnson's "Phaeton Rogers" (December 1880 and following issues), relating the comic adventures of an inventive youngster, and Clement Fezandie's "Through the Earth" (January 1898 and following issues), describing a shuttle tube between the antipodes and incorporating matters such as atmospheric resistance, weightlessness, and telemetry. In many ways these stories bridge the gap between fiction and nonfiction, since they overtly deal with matters of technical fact, yet do so through characters and situations resembling those found in the more traditional fiction.

A larger category is fantasy. Freed from the necessity of hewing to a strict scientific framework, these stories are more flexible in structure and more imaginative. They also attract a number of more significant authors, so fantasy became a staple of St. Nicholas and a remarkably high-quality one. The first issue includes Rebecca Harding Davis's "The Enchanted Prince" (November 1873). A later issue has Sarah Orne Jewett's "The Pepper-Owl" (June 1876), telling of an animated pepper-shaker; Frank R. Stockton's familiar "The Griffon and the Minor Canon" (October 1885 and following issues); Rudyard Kipling's "How the Camel Got His Hump" (January 1898), as well as other Just-So Stories; and L. Frank Baum's "Queen Zixi of Ix" (November 1904 and following issues), a work unduly overshadowed by the better-known Oz tales. The stories are unfailingly entertaining, but they manage to convey a message: courtesy, generosity, and optimism are desirable, even necessary qualities if one is to make one's way in the world. The message is sometimes overt, more often subtle, but present nonetheless.

Historical fiction, the third major category, constitutes a still larger group. Set against a backdrop of historical events or periods, and frequently incorporating historical personages into their action, these stories fall into a generally repetitive pattern. A young person, between ages ten and eighteen, comes into contact with events or persons that exert an influence upon him or her and through this contact learns something of human nature, the times, or the world. Some of the stories take their topics from around the world: Sarah Keables Hunt's "Latifa" (March 1876) deals with adventures in Arabia; Samuel Scoville's "A Boy of Galatia" (April 1900) describes a Greek youth's preparation for the Olympic Games; and Gensai Murai's " 'Kibun Daizin'; or From Shark-Boy to Merchant Prince" (July 1904 and following issues) relates a seventeenth-century Japanese boy's rise to fame and fortune. Others focus upon England and Europe. Among them are Hezekiah Butterworth's tale of Cromwell, "The Greyhound's Warning" (January 1877); Sidney Lanier's "King Arthur and His Knights of the Round Table" (December 1880); and Elbridge S. Brooks's Napoleonic story, "A Boy of the First Empire" (November 1894 and following issues).

Most of the historical stories are devoted, as one might suspect, to American history. Of them, many deal with predictable events in predictable ways: Charles Barnard's story of the War of 1812, "Rebecca, the Drummer" (July 1874); Mrs. E. G. Carter's "A Little Boston Girl of 1776" (November 1876); and Christine Chaplin Brush's "Sally's Soldier" (May 1880), involving Decoration

Day, need little explication. Others, however, go beyond these subjects to deal with events and circumstances that have left their mark upon the nation's thought and feelings: Noah Brooks's account of the way West, "The Boy Emigrants" (November 1875 and following issues), followed by "The Boy Settlers" (November 1890 and following issues); Frances C. Baylor's "Juan and Juanita" (November 1886 and following issues), exploring Indian life in the American Southwest; Thomas Nelson Page's memorable Civil War tale, "Two Little Confederates" (May 1888 and following issues); Joel Chandler Harris's "Daddy Jake, the Runaway" (March 1889), telling of antebellum slave life; and Howard Pyle's "Jack Ballister's Fortunes" (April 1894 and following issues), a swashbuckling account of piratical adventure in American coastal waters. All serve the same end: they acquaint their readers with diverse facets of American history, and they do so through the actions of a person with whom the reader can identify.

All of the historical fiction, whatever its setting, aims at a common goal: to use the appeal of history and historical events to convey contemporary ideas. If they attempt to communicate something of the flavor of Arthurian England or Revolutionary America, the stories attempt also to convey the importance of duty, industry, independent thought, and individual integrity. Drawing their analogies from the great and near-great of history, they imply that the values and attitudes making these persons significant are values closely paralleling the genteel, middle-class attitudes of the *Scribner's/Century* readership.

Largest of all of the fictional categories of *St. Nicholas* is that dealing with reasonably ordinary persons under reasonably ordinary conditions—the domestic story. These stories have, as a rule, settings contemporaneous with their publication. The characters, too, are contemporary: parents are clerks, military personnel, professional men (and, occasionally, women), or housewives; children attend school, do chores, earn money with odd jobs, form clubs, and play games. Equally familiar and timely is the status of these characters: although members of the upper and lower classes occasionally appear, the central characters are predominantly middle class, possessing sufficient money for their needs and a few luxuries, but persons who are not wealthy. The effect, therefore, is to present a body of literature whose cast resembles the readers for whom *St. Nicholas* was intended and that echoes, in many ways, the attitudes prevalent in that group.

The stories in this category, like those constituting the historical fiction, are varied. Some deal with school life—Edward Eggleston's "The Hoosier School-Boy" (December 1881 and following issues), focusing upon rural life and education; Frances Hodgson Burnett's "Sara Crewe" (December 1887); and Jessie M. Anderson's "Three Freshmen: Ruth, Fran, and Nathalie" (January 1895 and following issues), discussing life at Smith College. Some are adventuresome: the dime novelist Edward S. Ellis's "Swept Away" (May 1883), involving a flood on the Mississippi, and Jack London's "The Cruise of the 'Dazzler' " (July 1902) are typical. A few are comic, as are Lucretia P. Hale's "The Peterkins Celebrate the Fourth of July" (July 1877) and Mark Twain's "Tom Sawyer

Abroad'' (November 1893 and following issues). Some, inevitably, are blatantly didactic, including J. G. Holland's temperance lecture, ''My Friend, Colonel Backus'' (March 1877), and Mary Hallock Foote's homily upon obedience, ''A Visit to John's Camp'' (April 1890).

Most, however, concern familiar facets of daily life: the obtaining of jobs, the responsible handling of money, the facing of obligations, and the relationship of children to parents. Some are rural in setting, most are urban, and all provide an attractive central character whose words and actions establish a thoroughly acceptable model. In this group are works such as Louisa May Alcott's ''Eight Cousins'' (January 1875 and following issues) and ''Jack and Jill'' (December 1879 and following issues); Frances Hodgson Burnett's ''Little Lord Fauntleroy'' (November 1885 and following issues); Sarah Orne Jewett's ''A Bit of Color'' (April 1889 and following issues), published in book form as *Betty Leicester*; and Kate Douglas Wiggin's ''Polly Oliver's Problem'' (November 1892 and following issues). Accepting the need for conscientious mastery of commonplace matters, these stories suggest ways in which steadfast adherence to forthrightness, duty, industry, and reliability will pave the way for the reader as it has for the protagonist.

Throughout the fiction of *St. Nicholas* one finds two traits: a variety of subject matter and a consistency of theme. The subject matter varies according to the type of fiction involved, offering a wide selection for the reader; there is no monotonous, obviously repetitious pattern of topics. Nor is there any overt catering to juvenile attitudes or juvenile vocabulary. The ideas and the language are as varied as the story types, acquainting the readers with new ideas and new—even adult—modes of expression as well as with a broad range of fictional types and subtypes. More significant, though, is the consistency of theme. Whatever the story type involved, the protagonists embody traits deemed important by their creators and by their readers: they respect duty, keep an open mind, are unquestionably honest, are thrifty and industrious, and, above all, are unwaveringly self-reliant. Exercising these qualities, they make their way in a world that strikingly resembles that of their readers, so the import is clear. If the fictional characters can prevail by adhering to the values of the American upper middle class, so, too, can the readers. Whatever else the fiction of *St. Nicholas* may have done, it advanced the ideals embraced by its parent publication.

The significance of *St. Nicholas* as a document of nineteenth-century American life is difficult to overestimate. A well-conceived, carefully edited, lavishly produced magazine throughout most of its existence, it influenced the form of later juvenile periodicals, most notably *Cricket** (1973-). It provided American children with the work of the most notable writers of the past and the present. It succeeded in its stated mission of combining tacit instruction with entertainment. Tellingly, it served in a time of turmoil as a powerful force in striving to maintain a degree of cultural continuity in American life. Dedicated as it was to the creating and maintaining of an informed populace, *St. Nicholas* advanced a consistently genteel, principled, upper-middle-class view of life, tacitly seeking to perpetuate the values and attitudes of this class in the next generation. Whether it succeeded in this undertaking is uncertain. What is certain, though, is that *St. Nicholas*, even as it lived up to Dodge's literary goals, was in every way a proper child of the parent *Scribner's/Century*, a literate, principled, conservative, yet open-minded voice of the nineteenth-century American elite.

Notes

1. Robert Underwood Johnson, *Remembered Yesterdays* (Boston: Little, Brown, 1923), 87.
2. Frank Luther Mott, "Scribner's Monthly—The Century Magazine," *A History of American Magazines, 1865-1885* (Cambridge: Harvard University Press, 1938), 3:459-60, 480.
3. *Scribner's Monthly*, November 1873, p. 115.
4. Samuel C. Chew, *Fruit Among the Leaves* (New York: Appleton-Century-Crofts, 1950), 122-23.
5. Henry Steele Commager, "Dodge, Mary Elizabeth Mapes," *Notable American Women, 1607-1950*, ed. Edward T. James et al. (Cambridge: Belknap Press of Harvard University Press, 1971), 1:495.
6. "Children's Magazines," *Scribner's Monthly*, July 1873, p. 352.
7. Ibid., p. 354.
8. "Fifty Years of St. Nicholas," *St. Nicholas* 51 (November 1923), 20. See also Frank Luther Mott, "St. Nicholas," *History of American Magazines*, 3:500-505.
9. *St. Nicholas*, January 1895, pp. 205-6.

Information Sources

BIBLIOGRAPHY
Samuel C. Chew, *Fruit Among the Leaves* (New York: Appleton-Century-Crofts, 1950); Henry Steele Commager, ed., *The St. Nicholas Anthology* (New York: Random House, 1948); Fred Erisman, "The Utopia of *St. Nicholas*: The Present as Prologue," *Children's Literature*, vol. 5 (Philadelphia: Temple University Press, 1976); R. Gordon Kelly, *Mother Was a Lady* (Westport, Conn.: Greenwood Press, 1974); Mary June Roggenbuck, "*St. Nicholas Magazine*: A Study of the Impact and Historical Influence of the Editorship of Mary Mapes Dodge" (Ph.D. diss., University of Michigan, 1976); Florence Stanley Sturges, "The *St. Nicholas* Years," *The Hewins Lectures, 1947-1962* (Boston: Horn Book, 1963).

INDEX SOURCES
Anna Lorraine Guthrie, *Index to St. Nicholas, 1873-1918* (New York: Appleton-Century-Crofts, 1919). Vols. 28-36 are indexed in *The Children's Catalog* (New York: H. W. Wilson, 1909).

LOCATION SOURCES
Bound volumes are in many university and major public libraries. Vols. 1-20 are available on microfilm from Micro Photo Division, Bell & Howell, Wooster, Ohio.

Publication History

MAGAZINE TITLE AND TITLE CHANGES:
St. Nicholas: Scribner's Illustrated Magazine for Girls and Boys (1873-1881); *St. Nicholas: An Illustrated Magazine for Young Folks* (1881-1930); *St. Nicholas for Boys and Girls* (1930-1940; 1943).

VOLUME AND ISSUE DATA

St. Nicholas: Scribner's Illustrated Magazine for Girls and Boys (vol. 1, no. 1-vol. 8, no. 12); *St. Nicholas: An Illustrated Magazine for Young Folks* (vol. 9, no. 1- vol. 56, no. 12); *St. Nicholas for Boys and Girls* (vol. 57, no. 1-vol. 67, no. 4; vol. 70, no. 1-vol. 70, no. 4).

PUBLISHER AND PLACE OF PUBLICATION

Scribner & Co., New York (1873-1881); The Century Co., New York (1881-1930); American Education Press, Columbus, Ohio (1930-1934); Educational Publishing Corporation, New York and Darien, Conn. (1934-1940); St. Nicholas Magazine, Inc., New York (1943).

EDITOR

Mary Mapes Dodge (1873-1905); William Fayal Clarke (1905-1927); George F. Thompson (1927-1929); Albert Gallatin Lanier (1929-1930); May Lamberton Becker (1930-1932); Eric J. Bender (1932-1934); Chesla Sherlock (1934-1935); Vertie A. Coyne (1936-1940); Juliet Lit Sterne (1943). During the 1934-1940 period it was not unusual for several issues in succession to appear without an editor's name being given.

Fred Erisman

THE SCHOOLMATE: A MONTHLY READER FOR SCHOOL AND HOME INSTRUCTION OF YOUTH

The Schoolmate: A Monthly Reader for School and Home Instruction is typical of midnineteenth-century children's periodicals that subordinated entertainment and aesthetic values to instruction and practical values. It was established in February 1852 to provide supplementary textbook material for the classroom as well as to be a "fireside companion" for youth. Published by George Savage, a textbook publisher, *Schoolmate* was edited by A. R. Phippen, who was assisted, in the language of the times, by "eminent practical teachers."

The inside cover of each volume reprints "The Speakers Chart," depicting a variety of conventional gestures to be used while making a speech. Each gesture is numbered for ease of subsequent reference. The second section of every issue consists of speeches, primarily by American orators, such as Henry Clay's "Ambition," Thomas H. Benton's "Oregon Question," and a supposed speech by an Ottawa chief. Each is interspersed with numbered references to the illustrated gestures appropriate to a given point or passage. In addition to the illustrations of gestures, eleven "Rules for Speaking" provide instruction on tone, inflection, intonation, stance, dress, and the proper way to execute a bow.

Parallel to "The Speaker's Chart" at the front of the issue, is "The Reader's Chart" on the inside back cover, which illustrates correct and incorrect positions for reading and offers "The Four Important Rules for Reading." These stress the importance of correct posture and pronunciation, the need for understanding the text, and the necessity to be natural in the act of reading. Twenty "Rules for the Pauses, Tones, Inflections, Emphasis, and Manner of Reading" explain the meaning of symbols used in the text to describe the basics of oral interpretation. *Circumflex inflection*, for example, indicates that the voice should rise and fall on that word, while the notation "——" indicates slow movement in reading the passage. The editor stated that students should memorize all of the signs and points in order to recognize them and to be able to use them in the reading exercises and speeches, which were doubtless chosen primarily for their adaptability to elocution practice.

The first article in each issue is approximately one page long and relates to the underlying purpose of the magazine, "How to Become a Good Reader." There are twenty lessons, and when the cycle has been completed, the lessons are simply repeated. Titles such as "Natural Use of Voice," "The Pauses to be Observed in Reading," and "The Exclamation Mark" exemplify the didactic nature of this section.

The Schoolmate gained some recognition as an instructional aid. In the third volume *The Albany Evening Atlas* was quoted as saying: "The Schoolmate is an Educational Miscellany of rare excellence and usefulness, and we heartily commend it to teachers and schools."

Aesthetics were not ignored in *The Schoolmate*. An average of six or seven engravings were reproduced in each issue, and the main lessons and stories were closely related to a stylized vignette. The cover page of the first volume bore a delicate, intricate, stylized engraving of three young children reading together under a grape arbor in view of the schoolhouse. The artist, Jocelyn of New York, also developed a composite drawing for the covers of volumes 2, 3, and 4 that portrayed a child standing on a stump practicing a speech, one young boy using a telescope, a schoolhouse, young ladies playing musical instruments, and other children engaged in scholarly activities so as to represent "a complete picture of all the objects for which this work was intended."

Some poetry was printed in each issue, and original music, both words and notation, appeared, in the back of every issue. Lessons about becoming a good reader are followed by stories, items about general education and natural science, speeches, music, and eventually, news items and puzzles to be solved.

"Chapter of News" always appeared on the 30th and 31st pages of the issue: international events, national occurrences, human interest stories, and obituaries completed the contents of this section. Children learned of the marriage of Emperor Louis Napoleon III to the Countess Teba after a very short courtship, of the possibility of a tunnel under the Hudson River, of the story of a white man captured by a band of Chippewa, and of the death of Daniel Webster: "Another of our Mighty Men has gone."

The section "Teacher's Desk" contained letters from the editor to the children, word and drawing puzzles, and anagrams. This, the editor tells his reader, "is the fun part—This part of the magazine belongs to you." Through the "Teacher's Desk" Phippen solicited letters from children. "You must all write as often as you can," he encouraged. "Give us a description of some natural curiosity in your own neighbourhood or some historic event or anecdote not generally known."

Through "Teacher's Desk," too, he made frequent appeals for increased sub-scriptions. "We should like the assistance of every boy and girl." "Show this magazine to your companions...." In the last issue of the second volume, he offered premiums—free books to clubs or classrooms of subscribers. A further inducement was a reduction to 75¢ from the regular price of $1 a year or 10¢ for a single issue.

Although the magazine was published on the Eastern Seaboard, its influence was felt as far west as Kentucky and north to Ohio. Frank Luther Mott, in *A History of American Magazines*, perhaps had *The Schoolmate* in mind when he stated that the influence of these early magazines was probably far greater than was indicated by the number printed or circulated.[1] *The Schoolmate* sought to extend and publicize its influence by publishing several letters to the editor as well as newspaper reviews and testimonials. The Portmouth, N.H., *Gazette*, for one, wrote: "This publication is designed to supply what we have considered a positive want in our schools."

In 1855 *The Schoolmate* joined forces with the *Student* and *Family Miscellany* (formerly the *Student*) to form a magazine entitled *The Student and Schoolmate** of Boston. Thus the goals of *The Schoolmate*, to entertain and instruct young people as well as to encourage virtue and piety, lived on through another publication.

Note

1. Frank Luther Mott, *A History of American Magazines* (Cambridge: Harvard University Press, 1938), 2:151.

Information Sources

BIBLIOGRAPHY
James Cephas Derby, *Fifty Years Among Authors, Books and Publishers* (New York: G. W. Carleton Co., 1884); Frank Luther Mott, A History of American Magazines, 5 vols. (Cambridge: Harvard University Press, 1938-1968).
INDEX SOURCES
None.
LOCATION SOURCES
Incomplete volumes are in the Library of Congress; Boston Public Library; Houghton Library, Harvard University, Cambridge, Mass.; Providence Public Library, Providence, R.I.; New York Teachers College.

Publication History

MAGAZINE TITLE AND TITLE CHANGES
The Schoolmate: A Monthly Reader for School and Home Instruction of Youth (1852-1854).
VOLUME AND ISSUE DATA
The Schoolmate: A Monthly Reader for School and Home Instruction of Youth (vol. 1, nos. 1-9-vol. 4).
PUBLISHER AND PLACE OF PUBLICATION

George Savage, New York (1852-1853); George Savage, New York; and Morris Cotton
    & Co., Boston (1853); A. R. Phippen, New York (1854).
EDITOR
A. R. Phippen (1852-1854).

Mary Lou McKeown

SENIOR SCHOLASTIC

When *The Western Pennsylvania Scholastic* came off the press on October
22, 1920, its editor, Maurice R. Robinson, founded a publishing empire. This
eight-page weekly newspaper, mostly about high school sports in the Pittsburgh
area, was to become in 1922 the national high school magazine called *Scholastic*
and then in 1943 *Senior Scholastic*. Increasing in circulation "from 2700 as a
local paper, to 9000 in the first year of the national magazine, to 27,000 in 1923,
to 42,000 in 1925,...to over 100,000 before 1930," and to more than 250,000
in 1945, this magazine was, and is, the heart of the Scholastic empire.[1] But
starting in 1931 the Scholastic Publishing Company added numerous other magazines and services, becoming the Scholastic Corporation in 1932, Scholastic
Magazines, Inc., in 1956, and finally Scholastic, Inc., in 1980. By 1970, when
the corporation was at its peak productivity, it published thirty-five magazines
for 12.5 million subscribers in the fifty states, Canada, and some schools abroad;
operated five book clubs for elementary and secondary schools; and produced
"a wide range of instructional materials—from paperback books to records, from
wall maps to filmstrips—plus the annual Scholastic Awards program."[2] With
inflation, especially the rising cost of paper, the 1970s were hard times for
magazines, and Scholastic suffered. But on its 60th anniversary it still published
thirty-one magazines with a circulation of more than 10 million, and its ventures
into book clubs, textbooks, and other educational services continued to ensure
the solvency of its magazines. Scholastic, Inc., in other words, survives, and,
therefore, so does *Senior Scholastic*. Furthermore, although its content and format, even its title, may change—as they have over the years—some form of
Scholastic's high school magazine will surely be around in 2000 and after.

One would not have dared such a prediction in the early days of the magazine.
Begun in Robinson's spare time with the help of his high school principal and
a co-worker, Raymond Mc Partlin, the magazine (or newspaper) was first published by the Western Pennsylvania Interscholastic Athletic League and carried
no general news. The teachers' enthusiastic response to this innovation in educational printing encouraged Robinson to pursue plans for the magazine he
really wanted to publish. So in 1922 he set up the first *Scholastic* exhibit at the
National Education Association's Convention, sold subscriptions, secured a charter
of incorporation from the state of Pennsylvania, and went national. September
1922 saw the publication of the first volume (numbered volume 3) of *Scholastic*,

a biweekly high school magazine of thirty-two pages, in slick paper about 8 1/2 by 11 inches, with a cover in two colors.

During the 1920s *Scholastic* contained a short story in every issue (by Willa Cather, Ring Lardner, and William C. Morrow, for example); often a biographical sketch of the story's author; articles on literature (Elmer Kenyon's "William Shakespeare vs D. W. Griffith," September 13, 1924), art (Eugenia Eckford's "Young Etchers," February 2, 1929), and geography (Roy Chapman Andrews's " 'Wind Devils' of the Gobi," September 24, 1924); student-centered items (for example, articles about sports, debate, and composition—often about how to do something—and jokes, puzzles, and film reviews); as well as "The News Caldron," the current events department. With the exception of the material for students and "The News Caldron," much of each issue was reprinted from and reminiscent of other good-quality magazines of the day. Thus Robinson appealed to concerned adults while also offering high school students something new. His purpose was to "do for the life and literature of today what textbooks did for the past."[3] But if *Scholastic* was a forerunner of what is now called "relevancy in classroom materials," these first steps were small. The content of the magazine was largely contemporary material, but the tone and implied values of this content were clearly those of educated, upper-middle-class adults.

Throughout the 1920s and 1930s Robinson worked to increase the magazine's circulation. He was assisted by his business partner, G. Herbert McCracken, who also secured wealthy investors and wrote sports articles, working during the early years of the magazine as head football coach at Allegheny and then at Lafayette Colleges. When in 1925 Robinson began the Scholastic Awards, prizes and scholarships for students' original writing (eventually also for art and photography), he gained great reader involvement, and the magazine's circulation nearly doubled. The magazine's success enabled Robinson to increase his editorial staff. Besides McCracken, also assisting Robinson during these years were four other writers, most importantly, Kenneth Gould who, as Robinson took over the publishing side of the business, was to be managing editor from 1926 until 1944 and then editor-in-chief until his retirement in 1960.

Gould's influence on *Scholastic* was as major as one might expect of thirty-four years of work. Under his editorship *Scholastic* grew and established itself as the magazine it was to become: *Senior Scholastic*. Greatly instrumental in developing and nurturing the Scholastic Awards, Gould made the magazine a major force in support of artistic creation by young people, giving many (such as Maureen Daly) their start by publishing their winning entries in the last May issue of each year.[4] Just as significant was his continuing, judicious selection of short stories appealing to adolescents.[5] Looking for stories about young men and women and their problems, he published a body of adolescent literature before the concept of such a literature had occurred to most adults. Indeed, throughout his years as editor, the magazine displayed an increasing attention to audience— to high school students' interests, attitudes, and concerns. Hired originally to write "The News Caldron," however, Gould displayed his greatest interest in and influence on the current events section. As the Scholastic Publishing Company added new magazines to cover subjects once handled by *Scholastic* (or *Senior Scholastic*), for example, *World Week* in 1942, *Practical English* in 1946, and *Literary Cavalcade* in 1948, current events became increasingly the content of *Senior Scholastic*.

But to begin with, the magazine under Gould differed very little from what it was like under Robinson. Then in 1931 it absorbed *Magazine World*; in 1932, *Current Literature, World News*, and *Current Topics*. To handle the increased information to be included, Gould reorganized the magazine's format into four sections, one on literature, one on art, and two on social studies. He also introduced teachers' pages, one for English and one for social studies teachers. But increased circulation and content seemed to warrant a weekly—begun September 23, 1933. It had only three sections, for English, social studies, and students. The English section was similar to what earlier issues offered, including the book reviews by May Lamberton Becker (begun in 1932). The other two sections were larger and different. There were, for instance, articles of several pages analyzing current or historical events, a feature called "Who's Who in the News," "The Round Table" (student writing), and "Student Forum" (letters to the editor). The first teacher edition in 1936 added several pages at the beginning for teachers and were to combine with similar pages in *Senior Scholastic* to become *Scholastic Teacher* in 1946. Between 1938 and 1948 the magazine was published in a "combined edition," uniting the English, social studies, and teacher editions. The year 1936 also began "Boy Dates Girl" by Gay Head, continued until 1961 when it became "Talking It Over." "On the Air" (about radio) and "Sharps and Flats" (about music) were also added under Gould. What all of these changes and additions yielded was a successful magazine with considerable respect for its audience and a heavy emphasis on current events.

World War II altered *Scholastic's* appearance and contents. The soft newsprint used until the late 1970s replaced the slick paper of the early days; war stories and events occupied a large portion of each issue; patriotism was even more heavily stressed than it had been; and from September 1942 until February 1944 no table of contents or editorial page appeared. Beginning March 8, 1943, the magazine bore the title *Senior Scholastic*, with no explanation of the change. Then on February 14, 1944, Jack Lippert was identified as managing editor. Despite these changes, however, Gould's influence prevailed. No strong editor emerged during the 1940s; the responsibility was passed from hand to hand and often shared. But maintaining its regular features and continuing its evolution toward becoming a current events magazine, *Senior Scholastic* survived—indeed, prospered. Gould's editorship proved a secure foundation.

As the Scholastic empire mushroomed, during the next twenty years, *Senior Scholastic* had two strong editors, Eric Berger in the 1950s and Roy Hemming in the 1960s. Under their editorship the magazine continued to evolve along the lines established by Gould. By 1970 *Senior Scholastic* focused on students and social studies (largely, current events). First, the pages of student writing and then the short story were eliminated, erasing all evidence of the old English section. Next, serious and lengthy news articles became common. Finally, in the late 1960s efforts to attract and hold students strengthened. Berger and Hemming, in other words, developed the focus and tone that Gould's editorship began.

Berger contributed only to the first half of this task, gradually improving the quality of news coverage and shaping a format for the magazine's future. In tone the magazine reflected the prevalent adult attitudes of the 1950s. Traditional values were never seriously questioned. For example, sex roles, family, communism, and America were conventionally treated. The fiction was especially revelatory. One example, Eileen Tighe's "Father Knows Best" (November 1, 1950) portrays a father-son relationship plagued by disagreement, the father an intelligent businessman concerned about foreign affairs, the son a successful athlete unable to use his head very wisely. Although sympathetic to the son, the story crystalizes its message in its title. If, as editor, Berger did little to change the tone and values implicit in the contents, he greatly improved the intellectual quality of the magazine. His years offered several interesting series, most notably, first, Henry Steele Commager's "American History in Literature," book reviews of works such as Benjamin Franklin's autobiography (November 4, 1950), Mark Twain's *Roughing It* (January 3, 1951), and William Allen White's autobiography (April 25, 1951); and second, Isaac Asimov's "Breakthroughs in Science" (1958-1959), articles about key scientists and their discoveries. The insights, variety, and complexity found in articles in these series were also present in regular social studies features such as "Forum of the Week" and "Understanding the News." Rather than narrowing the focus, the magazine under Berger attempted to broaden and deepen students' knowledge of the world. The means for doing so was the two-or-more-page article rather than the brief report. Eventually, Berger's preference for the article established a new format, one still used by *Senior Scholastic*. Each week saw the discussion of a debatable issue ("Forum Topic of the Week"), an article about national affairs, one about world affairs, sometimes one about history or a critical issue or event, a current events section, and the usual items for students.

Hemming retained essentially this format throughout his editorship. As inflation began, the short stories disappeared, and the issue shrank to twenty-four pages. But articles lengthened and deepened, and some excellent series appeared, for example, "The Different Drummers," about men and women who changed American history, and "Critical Issues," several-paged analyses of things such as Nixon's election and black power. More striking, though, than Hemming's continuing efforts to improve the magazine's intellectual content and focus was his response to the social unrest of the late 1960s. In keeping with the times, the adult tone of the magazine, which was sometimes overtly patronizing in the 1950s, began to fade away. In language and content articles revealed writers' efforts to be "relevant." There emerged uncertainty, tolerance, and considerable objectivity in tone, and many articles dealt with aspects of students' lives or addressed topics from a point of view similar to that of students. Student rebellion, the drug culture, activities of the civil rights movement—all received sympathetic coverage if not unequivocal support.

After Hemming's retirement in 1969 no subsequent editor had as significant an impact as Robinson, Gould, Berger, or Hemming had had. The magazine reflected Scholastic's efforts to combat inflation without prohibitive losses. The struggle was recorded in the frequent change in editorship, in the merger of *Senior Scholastic* first with *World Week* and then *American Observer* in 1972, and finally in the magazine's return to biweekly publication in 1975. The thirty-four-page issue then reappeared and survived, sometimes reaching more than fifty pages in the late 1970s—to be cut by four pages in 1980. In 1978 a slick paper replaced the newsprint used since the 1940s.

Despite these changes, however, the trends begun under Gould, Berger, and Hemming continued to develop, the format becoming one almost entirely of articles carefully directed to the student reader. Perhaps an excessive concern with readership characterized *Senior Scholastic* during the late 1970s. Polls (most notably the National Institute of Student Opinion Poll) were developed to determine students' interests in and attitudes toward the magazine. Special features were designed to "reach" students. "Senior Serial: The Halls of Haywood High," for instance, was a continuing play about various students' lives, suggesting in its action the positive and negative possibilities involved in certain responses to problems teenagers typically face. Also nearly every issue included an article on teenage pregnancy, drug abuse, crime, or some other prevalent social problem. Even articles on national and world affairs often approached their topics as they related to their readers, as for example, in "Teenagers and the Disappearing Dollar: Far Away Events Can Affect Us All" (November 16, 1979).

In the 1980s *Senior Scholastic* evidenced less concern with its readers, having gone far in catering to them in the 1970s. Surveys continued to be taken of readers' opinions of the magazine, and teenagers' interests continued to be addressed in articles such as "Lowering the Legal Wage for Teenagers—Will It Create More Jobs?" (April 3, 1981). But most articles explored a national or world event in the tradition of Berger and Hemming—in some depth and with respect for (if little pampering of) its readers. Indeed, in 1981 there were fewer items of the joke and puzzle variety than there had ever been; the news was the center of emphasis.

The history of *Senior Scholastic* is thus one of sharpening its focus on readership and content. As the Scholastic empire grew and its educational publications became essential to classrooms around the world, its high school magazine became increasingly oriented to the concerns of high school readers. Scholastic expanded but *Senior Scholastic* narrowed and enriched its content, eventually presenting national and world problems in depth and with complexity—without either patronizing or pampering its teenage readers.

Notes

1. Kenneth Gould, "Scholastic: A Record of 25 Years," *Senior Scholastic*, October 22, 1945, p. 4.
2. This quotation and the preceding paraphrased sentence are from Richard Pawelek, "50 Years...Oh You Kid!" *Senior Scholastic*, October 26, 1970, p. 3.
3. Gould, "Scholastic: A Record," p. 4.
4. Some of the best stories are reprinted in Kenneth Gould and Joan Coyne, eds., *Young Voices: A Quarter Century of High School Student Writing Selected from the Scholastic Awards* (New York and London: Harper & Brothers, 1945).
5. For examples see Ernestine Taggard, ed., *Here We Are: Stories from Scholastic Magazine* (New York: Dodd, Mead, 1952).

Information Sources

BIBLIOGRAPHY
May Lamberton Becker, *Reading Menus for Young People: Chats about Much Loved Books Old and New* (New York: Scholastic Corporation, 1935); *Best High School Writing, or Saplings...Verse, Short Stories, and Essays Selected from Manuscripts Written by High School Students in Competition for the Scholastic Award*, a series (New York: Scholastic Corporation, 1926-1940); Kenneth Gould and Joan Coyne, eds., *Young Voices: A Quarter Century of High School Student Writing Selected from the Scholastic Awards* (New York: Harper & Brothers, 1945); Grant Overton et al., *Enjoying the Arts: A Group of Essays on Appreciation* (reprinted from Scholastic) (Pittsburgh: Scholastic Corporation, 1933); *Scholastic, Congress at Work: A Graphic Story of How Our Laws Are Made and of the Men Who Made Them* (1939; rev. ed., Pittsburgh: Scholastic Corporation, 1945); *Scholastic, 1944: America Votes: A Non-Partisan Handbook of the 1944 Presidential Election* (New York: Scholastic Corporation, 1944); *Scholastic, The War for Freedom: Background Facts to Help You Understand the War* (Dayton: Scholastic Corporation, 1942); Ernestine Taggard, ed., *Here We Are: Stories from Scholastic Magazine* (New York: Dodd, Mead, 1952).

INDEX SOURCES
Subject Index to Children's Magazines; Abridged Readers' Guide to Periodical Literature; Readers' Guide to Periodical Literature.

LOCATION SOURCES
Bound volumes are in many university and major public libraries. Vols. 3-113 are available on microfilm from University Microfilms International, Ann Arbor, Mich.

Publication History

MAGAZINE TITLE AND TITLE CHANGES
The Western Pennsylvania Scholastic (1920-1922); *Scholastic* (1922-1932); *Scholastic Combined with Magazine World, Current Literature, World News, and Current Topics* (1932-1933); *Scholastic: The High School Weekly* (1933-1943); *Senior Scholastic* (1943-1972); *Senior Scholastic, Now Including World Week* (1972); *Senior Scholastic, Now Including World Week and American Observer* (1972-1978); *Senior Scholastic* (1978-).

VOLUME AND ISSUE DATA

The Western Pennsylvania Scholastic (vol. 1, no. 1-vol. 2, no. 32); *Scholastic* (vol. 3, no. 1-vol. 20, no. 9); *Scholastic Combined with Magazine World, Current Literature, World News, and Current Topics* (vol. 21, no. 1-vol. 22, no. 9); *Scholastic: The High School Weekly* (vol. 23, no. 1-vol. 42, no. 5); *Senior Scholastic* (vol. 42, no. 6-vol. 100, no. 4); *Senior Scholastic, Now Including World Week* (vol. 100, no. 5-vol. 100, no. 9); *Senior Scholastic, Now Including World Week and American Observer* (vol. 100, no. 10-vol. 110, no. 18); *Senior Scholastic* (vol. 111, no. 1-).

PUBLISHER AND PLACE OF PUBLICATION
Western Pennsylvania Interscholastic Athletic League, Pittsburgh (1920-1922); The Scholastic Publishing Company, Pittsburgh (1922-1932); The Scholastic Corporation, Pittsburgh (1932-1943), Dayton (1943-1956); Scholastic Magazines, Inc., Dayton (1956-1980); Scholastic, Inc., Dayton (1980-).

EDITOR
Maurice R. Robinson (1922-1926); Kenneth M. Gould (1926-1944); Jack Lippert (1944-1947); Jean Coyne and Margaret Hauser (1947); Herbert L. Marx (1948-1950); Eric Berger (1950-1959); Roy Hemming (1960-1969); Ed Sparn (1970-1972); George Nikolaieff (1972-1975); Virginia Sims (1975-1977); Jim Brownell (1977); Elizabeth Dowling, Peter Jones, and Richard Pawelek (1978); Tad Harvey (1978-1979); Michael Cusack (1979-).

Virginia L. Wolf

SEVENTEEN

For nearly four decades, since its beginning during World War II, *Seventeen* has held a nearly constant vision of itself and its audience. Although the young female reader of the 1940s would hardly recognize the young female reader of the 1980s as a contemporary, *Seventeen* has veered little from its original intent. *Seventeen News*, a publication by the magazine's Public Relations Department, claims: "Today, the grandaughters of these girls [original readers] are still buying the magazine in record numbers. *Seventeen's* current circulation is 1.5 million, with a pass-along readership of 6.4 million—nearly half the nation's population of teenage girls."[1] Thus, the adolescent passage *Seventeen* successfully navigates is transgenerational and it seems that the magazine is still responding to a felt need present in today's under-twenty female population.

The premiere issue of *Seventeen* was in September 1944. This was actually a transition issue between the new *Seventeen* and an original intention, a screen magazine called *Stardom: Hollywood's Most Exciting Magazine*, begun in February 1942 and edited by Wade Nichols and Carl A. Schroeder.

The first issue of *Stardom* appeared in what the editors referred to as a "troubled and tumultuous world," shortly after the "jackals of the Orient lashed out at America." Even with paper restrictions and other shortages resulting from the war effort, the editors promised a "higher standard screen magazine."[2] The initial organization of *Stardom* was simple and would remain so; it was divided into articles, fiction, and photographs, all either about or by famous Hollywood personalities. The "articles" section was the most important, and some typical selections include: "Jean Harlow's Last Interview" (February 1942), "The Love Story of Hedy Lamarr" (July 1942), and "Dear Captain Gable" (February 1944). The "fiction" pieces were always "by the stars" and would include efforts such as "Love at Work" by Ann Sheridan (February 1942) and "Wild Life Lover" by Rita Hayworth (July 1942). The highlight of the "photos" section would be the natural-color portraits of stars such as Gene Tierney, Hedy Lamarr, and Joan Bennett. Compared to the other, more slick and sensational fan magazines, *Stardom* offered peaceful and sometimes even courageous portraits of America's favorite media figures, particularly Humphrey Bogart, Mickey Rooney, Gene Tierney, Cary Grant, and the ever-popular Lana Turner and Clark Gable.

The May 1944 issue of *Stardom* was the last to be subtitled *Hollywood's Most Exciting Magazine*. A shift was in progress away from an adult screen magazine, first to a women-only and then to a teenage-girl format. The June 1944 issue was called *Stardom: Hollywood's Magazine for Women*, with the editorial statement: "In the new *Stardom*—redesigned from cover to cover—readers will find all the exciting, exclusive Hollywood stories they've always found. . . . But from here in, Hollywood will be interpreted from a new vantage point—from the standpoint of a woman's most vital concerns—her home, her future, her career."[3] In July of that year it was resubtitled *With Young Fashions*, with half of this issue dedicated to fashion and beauty aids for young girls. The August 1944 issue was *Stardom's* finale. In their last message to the readers the editors wrote: "Beginning with the next issue, *Stardom* will be changed into a new fashion of young magazine . . . full of ideas on fashion and beauty, movies, music and Personalities—in fact, everything of current interest to young people. It will be called *Seventeen*."[4]

Seventeen, with its roots in *Stardom*, has always been tightly tied to popular culture, and this is immediately obvious from even a cursory glance of any randomly selected issue. To the non-initiate *Seventeen* may seem to be only an advertising medium—pushing upon young teenage girls, their hands stuffed with their parents' dollars, page after page of new fashions, new personal-care products, and every sort of new entertainment form available. The magazine could easily be dismissed, by the outsider, as an advertising rip-off that covers itself with a few articles and fiction entries. But that would be to miss the mass appeal of *Seventeen*. *Seventeen* must be understood from its audience's point of view if it is to be given any cultural significance. The average reader is 16.7 years of age. Most are urban or suburban, fairly affluent, and conversant in the language of popular culture, for whom the reading of *Seventeen* is an invitation to participate in an easily gained, popularly understood, identity. If they choose they can adopt, or adapt, the *Seventeen* way of life and turn to the periodical and its auxilary publications not only for advice on what to wear and how to be well mannered in every possible situation but also for dialogs and answers to common teen problems, interpretations of world events, and even for inspiration.[6]

Seventeen, for its part, has taken seriously this role in the lives of so many young American females. Edited by a string of cautious, conservative, and responsible women, the magazine has been up front with information for its readers. Although *Seventeen*'s pages of glamorous fashions and beauty guides have twisted with the tides of popular convention, underneath all of this has stood the *Seventeen* girl: independent, yet supportive, directed, and, above all, confident in herself.

There are nearly 500 extant issues of *Seventeen*, and it would take an essay of heroic proportions to discuss every minor shift the magazine has taken. But because *Seventeen* has been so consistent in its self-image, it is possible to discuss broader trends and concrete changes.

Under the editorship of Helen Valentine (1944-1950) *Seventeen* got off to a good start in the fall of 1944.[7] The first issue welcomed the audience to the new publication with *"Seventeen* Says Hello!" where it announced: *"Seventeen* is your magazine, High School Girls of America—all yours! It is interested only in you—and in everything that concerns, excites, annoys, pleases or perplexes you."[8] The first issue was divided by a table of contents that would be modified and refined over the years: "What You Wear" "How You Feel," "Getting Along in the World," "Your Mind," and "Having Fun." The articles and photo spreads grouped under "What You Wear" have always remained standard fare— the locales, models, fashions, and hairdos change, but basically the formula has remained a constant throughout the decades. The 1940s had features such as: "Good to Be in Fall Clothes" (September 1944), "Dress Rehearsal—Curtain at 8:30" (December 1944), "Make Your Separates Cotton" (April 1948), and "Bewitching Study Hours" (September 1949). The "How You Look" articles included the popular monthly column "Dressing Table Talk," where readers would seek the magazine's advice on issues such as how they should cut their hair, what is the proper way to apply nail polish, and how much makeup is appropriate for school, job, date. The "Getting Along in the World" offerings concentrated basically on guiding teens through the crises of interpersonal relationships, with staple columns such as "For Seniors Only," usually authored by Alice Beaton, and "Why Don't Parents Grow Up?" by either a staff writer or a teen contributor. The "Having Fun" entries were consistently light in spirit and concentrated on entertainment; it was in this section that Edwin Miller, an associate editor, began his columns on popular media figures and trends, which has continued, with various titles, to this day.

Probably the most interesting articles in *Seventeen* in the 1940s were found under the rubric "Your Mind"; certainly, this is where the topical problems of the day were explored and worked out. The November 1944 issue, for instance, had a very pro-Russia photo-essay that stated: "If you walked down the street of a Russian village, America wouldn't seem so far away. In every village American jazz pours through the loud-speakers of the public radio."[9] Other selected titles include "After Surrender...What?" (November 1945), "Take a

Look at Cancer'' (April 1948), ''You Can Understand Jet Propulsion'' (September 1948), and ''Psychology Is All About People'' (February 1949).

In July 1945 *Seventeen* published an unsigned article, ''Contest Winner,'' concerning its search for the typical American teenage girl. In lieu of a ''winner,'' which they said would obscure the diversity of American girls, they published ''Winner's Code,'' a set of guidelines by which a winner lives. Some selections from this mixed bag include:

> Our typical American girl is frequently...not to say incessantly...convinced that Bill or Henry or Slats is the most *wonderful* boy in the world; she doesn't believe in poaching on the preserves of friends; she never betrays her family's privacy; she will defend members of her family...against unkindness or maliciousness or snobbish discrimination; she's no genius; she's superbly curious about the world, and she's eager and ambitious to take her place...to do a prideful job on everything she tackles.[10]

Seventeen, from its inception, took it as a goal to educate young women by giving them facts. For example, as early as 1945 it presented an enlightened and appropriately admonishing article about ''Drinking and Smoking'' (November 1945). A controversy arose in the ''Your Letters'' column in May 1947 after the publication of ''Sex...The Life Force'' in March of that year. ''Sex...The Life Force'' was a responsible, cautious article about sex and reproduction that appears archaic by today's standards. Yet it prompted a multitude of responses from the audience. *Seventeen*, in its editorial stance of presenting both sides of reader response, printed a letter from a mother of a teenage girl from Brooklyn who was angered that ''Sex...The Life Force'' was ''out of place in a magazine which makes its appeal to the teen-age group''; and one from a father (also from Brooklyn) who delighted in writing, ''I feel that this article should be reprinted and distributed to every teen-age school student in the United States as a public service.''[11]

In January 1945 *Seventeen* incorporated a ''Fiction'' section into the formula of the periodical that would be a mixture of professional and amateur (that is, reader) selections. The solicitation by the magazine for reader-written short stories and poems led to the Annual Short Story and Poetry contest.[12]

Two other events marked the life of the magazine in the 1940s. The first, in June 1947, was the advent of the yearly ''It's All Yours'' issue, in response to reader suggestions for columns and articles.[13] This immensely popular yearly issue featured teens taking over the regular columns, doing all of the fiction writing, and providing photographs and illustrations. The second event, closely tied to the first, was the establishment of ''specialty'' issues that tried to tie all aspects of the magazine—fashion, food, fiction—to one special theme. A selection from one year included ''The Golden Anniversary of New York City'' (June 1948), ''Girl Meets Boy'' (April 1948), ''Birthday Issue'' (July 1948), and "You and Your School" (October 1948). Some of the special issues were repeated yearly, and some were discarded. The most popular of the theme issues, "Back to School," premiered in August 1948 and has remained the August issue.

By the end of the decade of the 1940s *Seventeen* had settled into a comfortable groove. The division of information had remained fairly constant, as had indeed the type of information it had chosen to communicate.

The 1950s saw *Seventeen* plant itself very squarely in the comfortable lap of the American middle class. An important shift in editors occurred in 1954 with the appointment of Enid Annenberg Haupt as editor-in-chief. She remained in that spot until 1970. It was also in the early 1950s that *Seventeen* tried to refocus its image away from the young teenagers to the more sophisticated older girl. For instance, the May 1950 issue was an "It's All Yours" month with the older teens supplying the material, and yet there are traces of the subteen audience with selections such as "Decorating Our Dollhouse."

To the staff of *Seventeen* the 1950s was a decade to focus reader energy on trying to come to terms with a few important issues: boys, domestic details, and the beginning concerns of female and male sexuality. A very popular column was begun in June 1950, "From a Boy's Point of View" by Peter Leavy. (Leavy wrote this column until late 1955 when it was taken over by Jimmy Wescott who carried it well into the 1960s). "From a Boy's Point of View" basically served, tongue-in-cheek, to let young women know just how a boy thinks and "feels" about, for instance, the way a young lady dresses, modulates her voice, wears makeup, flirts, and even kisses.

The domestic influence also grew in importance, and this is reflected in the increase of recipes and decorating tips provided. The "Food and Home" department grew over the decade and included articles such as "What Is a White Sale?" (August 1950), "Sewing Is so Easy" (June 1951), "How Do Your Houseplants Grow?" (March 1951), "Table Decorations" (March 1952), "Picnic Partners" (July 1953), "The Favorite Recipe Contest" (September 1955), "Valentine's Cakes" (February 1956), "This Is the Way We Care for Tableware" (October 1958), and "Paint Your Room with Sunshine" (September 1959).

An interesting debate between the sexes began in July 1958 with the article "What Every Girl Should Know," a panel discussion by six boys about sex and girls. Set up in a question and answer format it prompted some interesting answers to questions about things such as premarital sex:

A. There is only one girl I want to have sex with and that's my wife.

A. Gee, if you say that premarital sex relations are all right for women, for men—have a little fun, get a little experience before you're married—you'll have a prostitute on every block.[14]

One year later in July 1959 a response to the previous summer's all-boy panel produced "What Girls Think About Sex." The girls were asked similar types of questions and gave much the same sort of replies:

Q. Do you think girls are afraid of sex?

A. Many girls, because of the way they received their sex educa-tion...are very much afraid of sex. They're afraid of getting involved with a boy, of something happening when they're out on a date.

A. You don't have to be afraid, you just have to realize its wrong and not what is done in our society.[15]

In September 1959 a column began, which also survived the whims of fancy, called "Looking Ahead to College," which would every month spotlight a particular college and career choice. Although this column would also undergo name and format changes, it is another good place to look in *Seventeen* for changes in attitudes about a female in the workplace.[16]

From a certain point of view the most interesting single issue of the 1950s might be that of the specialty issue of September 1958: "The FUTURE." In this issue the young reader was promised to be "Heiress to the modern world."[17] In an editorial (unsigned, as an overwhelming majority of *Seventeen* editorials are) the audience was told that not only men, but women, would be on the moon within ten years; that in a few years they would have at their disposal atomic-powered cars, live telecasts to Europe; that a jet plane ride from New York to Paris would take 1 hour. In a high-tech dream of the future the girls were not promised a release from their traditional responsibilities, just a rewriting: "Prom-ised for the future: a wonderland of glassed-in cities circling in space, private 'flying platforms' and electronic genies to do your work—to cook and clean and at the push of a button wash and dry your clothes while they hang in the closet!"[18] As the importance of science grew in their lives they would, of course, witness the cure to cancer, the common cold, and acne.[19]

Historians, when writing an official history of any era, have long had to cope with the problem of "periodization"—how to organize large quantities of in-formation into compact departments. When writing about the history of a pe-riodical, the same problem arises. It seems that a decade such as the 1960s, which has already gained mythic proportions, would be easily handled in a neat compartment; but examining issues of a magazine like *Seventeen* reminds the writer how the lines between decades blur very easily.

The early 1960s saw *Seventeen* retain its traditional divisions of the magazine: "What You Wear," "How You Look and Feel," "Fiction," "You and Others," "Home and Food," and "Having Fun." Seemingly, these topic headings cov-ered all of the articles and photos they wanted to display in an effective and efficient manner. Throughout the 1960s several monthly columns routinized, including: "College and Careers," "Curl Up and Read," "Hear Your Heros,"

"Young Living," "Teens in the News," "Teens Are Listening to...," "*Seventeen* Salutes 4-H in Action," "The Hollywood Scene," "Teen Travel Talk," and "In My Opinion." Some of these columns, such as "*Seventeen* Salutes 4-H in Action," survived only for a short period, but by and large, with only minor retitling, most would survive the decade.

Two of these columns probably get at the subjective reality of the *Seventeen* reader most closely. "Young Living," by Abigail Wood was a question and answer column that, almost always, responded sensitively to the romantic and interpersonal problems vexing young readers. Judging from the length and intensity of her answers, it appears that Wood took her role as a problem solver very seriously. The range of questions, although edited and somewhat narrow, does seem to get at the domain of adolescent concerns: "Is He Too Old for Me?" (February 1960), "How Can I Say I Don't Love Him?" (March 1960), "Should a Girl Fall for a Line?" (August 1960), "How Can I Get Over My Helpless Crush?" (June 1962), "Sometimes I Hate Myself" (October 1963), "I'm Poor...and It Hurts!" (December 1963), "Why Can't My Mother Grow Up?" (June 1965), and "My Parents Are So Narrow-Minded" (March 1967).

The second column, "In My Opinion," begun in January 1963, is also important for its subjective, reader-initiated nature. These columns were long editorials, usually written by older teens, male and female, expressing opinions on popular national-level issues. In the mid-1960s the teens would write about issues such as "Laws Against Teen-Age Drinking Defeat Their Purpose" (July 1965) and "Teachers Who Rely on 'Objective Tests' Are Cheating Their Students" (June 1966). "In My Opinion" stretched into the 1970s when the teens took on even more complex issues: "We Must Stop Multiplying" (May 1970), "Let's Revamp Scientific Priorities..." (February 1972), and "Amnesty for War 'Exiles' Will Bring Us Together" (April 1972). An anthology of "Young Living" columns that stresses personal problems, combined with the "In My Opinion" editorials for their broader applications, would probably come as close as any sociological survey toward an understanding of the 1960s experience for the American teenager.

Seventeen would not be left behind by other national magazines in its quest to cover the "important issues" of the decade. As a responsible publication dedicated to exposing its readers to the concerns being worked out in the wider culture, it offered selections such as "*Seventeen* Special Report on Drinking" (July 1960), "The Beats Like I Think I Know Them" (October 1960), "Teens Talk About Religion" (March 1963), "Your Letters: The Assassination of J.F.K." (February 1964), "Bit by the Beatles" (March 1964), "What You Can Do for Human Rights in Your Home Town" (May 1965), "Come Take My Hand: Project Head Start" (December 1965), "Report from Vietnam... Mississippi...Appalachia" (January 1966), "Twiggy: New Top Model" (March 1967), "Face to Face with a Vietnamese Girl in New York" (May 1967), and "Marijuana: Just How Harmless Is It?" (May 1968). In some way, in issues not cited, *Seventeen* reported on most of the major events of the decade in its usual cautious, dedicated manner.

It is important to remember, however, that no matter how eager *Seventeen* was in the 1960s to educate and guide its audience, it remained, and remains, primarily an image maker. Although it was committed to the widening of awareness, *Seventeen* never relinquished its goal to get girls to look good and feel good about themselves. Fashion consciousness was of overriding importance; the *Seventeen* girl did not wear cut-up blue jeans but rather recast current taste to the middle-class model. The magazine grew in length during the 1960s, and to get to every important issue, the reader passed over page after page of fashion tips and advertisements for the newest, most interested, consumer appetites. The *Seventeen* of this decade also retained the speciality issue, as well as the three yearly issues "Back to School," "It's All Yours," and "Christmas."[20]

As many other periodicals would do, *Seventeen* began the decade of the 1970s with a look to the future. The article "Soar into the '70's" found *Seventeen* soaring "into the future—as far as the mind can comprehend" and finding a similar kind of mixture of images as it had in 1958. Some of these visions included discothèques on jet planes, temperature-controlled clothing, liberal arts coming to the fore again, eighteen year olds voting, artificial hearts transplanted with ease, and a cure for cancer.[21]

An important event for *Seventeen* occurred in December 1970 when Enid A. Haupt stepped down as editor-in-chief, a position she ably held for sixteen years. For the next six years, until January 1976, with the appointment of Midge Turk Richardson, *Seventeen's* chief editorial position would be held, for short periods, by a succession of women and one man, Ray Robinson. The 1970s also saw the magazine pare its jumbo issue length to about 150 pages and even reduce its physical dimensions.[22]

The approach *Seventeen* had taken to its audience in terms of information it wanted to present remained much the same in the 1970s, much of it, in fact, inherited from the 1950s format. The topic headings still included "Fashion," "Fiction," "How You Feel," "Beauty," and "Articles" of topical interest. Many of the same columns, often written by the same people (for example, Abigail Wood and Edwin Miller), stayed intact, although they were renamed. However, three new directions were pursued. An increase in health and fitness appears early in the decade with an emphasis on exercise and healthier foods and diets aimed at making the reader look like a cover girl model. A sports consciousness is evident as early as May 1973; a "Sports" column was added in January 1977; and a "Sports" special theme issue was published in April 1978. An irregular column, "Young Americans," was begun in May 1973 that spotlighted the various life-styles of girls around the country. The "mini-mag" was inserted into the formula in April 1975. A "magazine-within-a-magazine," the "mini-mag" format was to present breezy, very short articles and suggestions on a potpourri of issues: how to call a boy, black skin care, how to find a dentist, and so on. The 1970s also saw an increase in the popular "make-over" selections, where a reader was transformed from an ordinary teenage girl into a beauty with a new hairdo, wardrobe, and makeup routine (for instance, June 1970 and July 1979).

With a loosening of social conventions *Seventeen* could, in the 1970s, present a variety of issues in which it could respond in a more forthright presentation than ever before. Seemingly, almost every social and personal issue was selected. Some include "The Growing Menace of Pep Pills" (May 1970), "My Visit to Vietnam" (June 1970), "Prejudice" (December 1970), "Questions You Ask Most About Birth Control" (January 1971), "New Ways to Combat V.D." (April 1972), "I Was a Teen Alchoholic" (May 1973), "What Every Young Woman Should Know About Rape" (May 1975), "What Teens Think About Violence and Sex on TV and in Movies"(June 1977), "Getting Together for Womens' Rights" (March 1978), and "Women in the Military" (July 1979).

Again, it must not be assumed that *Seventeen* saw itself as a public-issues forum; it did not. It still maintained its traditional mix of fashion, beauty, and decorating articles. If anything, the 1970s saw *Seventeen* in a quest for a balance between old and new. For all of the new information it presented on life-styles, there was still time to continue, for instance, its mission to find out what makes boys "tick" (see "Exclusive National Survey: What Boys Look for in Girls," March 1978). Also, with an awareness by the *Seventeen* Research Department that "half of all first brides are girls under twenty," the periodical has tried to service that sector with articles such as "One + One" (February 1972) and a special bridal issue in February 1977.[23]

Seventeen, in the early 1980s, has remained a quick-paced, lively, sleek publication. Although it has responded to the conventions of 1980s magazine presentation, it basically has retained the same direction in terms of the image it wishes to project. In fact, a 1981 publication by *Seventeen* promotes the motto put forth in the original September 1944 edition: "to cover everything that concerns, excites, annoys, pleases and perplexes young women."[24]

The division of the magazine has settled into the following formula, which, by now, must be viewed as a minor shift in taste: "Fashion," "Beauty," "Decorating/Crafts," "Food," "Fiction," "Articles," "Regular Features," "Mini-Mag." Abigail Wood is still responding to teenage problems in a column called "Relating," which is reminiscent of the old "Young Living" column she wrote for so many years (see, for instance, "My Mom Is Impossible," November 1982). Edwin Miller is still covering popular media figures in his "Spotlight" monthly feature. The "Articles" section is still presenting to the audience issues of current concern, such as "Are You Obsessed with Your Weight?" (July 1982), an article about teenage eating disorders, and "Why Teens Join Cults" (November 1982). The magazine still gives heavy emphasis to fashion trends, college decisions, and, of course, boys (February 1983).

In an interesting departure, the July 1982 issue contains an "Open-Letter" to *Seventeen* readers and their parents. It is of interest for both its subject matter and editorial self-consciousness. For the first time in thirty-eight years *Seventeen* began, in August 1982, a column called "Sex and Your Body" devoted solely to the "sexual concerns" of its readers. In wishing to state their editorial policy of helping teenage girls figure out their lives and problems and to state their own motivations, the editors wrote:

> ... for it was not with wild editorial impulse or a desire to sensationalize our magazine that directed the decision. Rather, it is our purpose to inform and enlighten you, our readers, in a prudent, discreet manner, so that you may better cope with the time in which you live. We want to fulfill your need to respect and understand your bodies, so that you can deal responsibly, as teens and adults, with your sexuality. These days many young people don't seem to be doing that.[25]

Every magazine, to survive the perils of the publishing industry and a whimsical reading audience, must have a clear self-image and must project this self-image in a consistent manner. *Seventeen* is a stellar example of a successful publication, because it has been so consistent in its message and expertly edited and published. Although the specific reader will almost certainly abandon the teenage needs *Seventeen* serves, there is another in the generational train right behind her. *Seventeen*, now in its fourth decade, has in one sense been passed from mother to daughter. Female adolescence is a confusing and stressful period as any comprehensive survey of a periodical like *Seventeen* bears out. With its specific focus on the issues concerning young women, *Seventeen* does indeed provide a needed service. As the teenager passes into adulthood and leaves *Seventeen* behind, its message and identity suggestions will remain with her. But for the young female between the ages of thirteen and twenty *Seventeen* must still be responding to some felt needs, and if its Public Relations Department and circulation numbers are correct, it will continue to do so for some time.

Notes

1. "*Seventeen* Magazine," *Seventeen News*, May 1981, p. 1.
2. "Message-to-the-Readers," *Stardom: Hollywood's Most Exciting Magazine*, February 1942, p. i.
3. Ibid., *Stardom: Hollywood's Magazine for Women*, June 1944, p. 1.
4. Ibid., *Stardom: With Young Fashions*, August 1944, p. 1.
5. "*Seventeen* Magazine," *Seventeen News*, May 1981, p. 4.
6. See, for instance, *The Seventeen Book of Decorating* (New York: David McKay, 1961); *The Seventeen Book of Etiquette and Entertaining* (New York: David McKay, 1963); *The Seventeen Cookbook* (New York: Macmillan, 1964); *The Seventeen Book of Prayer: An Anthology of Inspirational Prose and Poetry*... (New York: Macmillan, 1965); *The Seventeen Guide to College Choice* (New York: Macmillan, 1969).
7. *Seventeen News*, May 1981, claims that the initial issue was read by 400,000 teens.
8. "*Seventeen* Says Hello," *Seventeen*, September 1944, pp. 32-33.

9. "This Is Russia," Ibid., November 1944, p. 46.

10. "Contest Winner," Ibid., July 1945, p. 47.

11. "Thank You for Your Letters," Ibid., May 1947, p. 4.

12. A list of randomly selected titles of short stories and poems would be meaningless in this context. For a cross section, see *Nineteen by Seventeen: Stories from Seventeen Magazine* (Philadelphia: Lippincott, 1952) and *Prize Stories from Seventeen* (New York: Macmillan, 1968), which is a selection of the contest winners from 1959 to 1968.

13. Although "It's All Yours" first appeared in a June issue, within a few years it would become a regular January feature.

14. "What Every Girl Should Know," *Seventeen*, July 1958, p. 59.

15. "What Girls Think About Sex," Ibid., July 1959, pp. 75-76.

16. See the columns that appear throughout the 1950s by Dr. Charles A. Bucher and later by Joan Hawkes and David Kline. For a more recent view, see Sally Platkin Koslow's "55 Jobs You Should Know About," Ibid., October 1978, pp. 130-ff.

17. "Heiress to the Modern World—YOU!" Ibid., September 1958, p. 109.

18. Ibid.

19. Ibid., p. 130.

20. The placement of these specialty issues in the calendar year has remained a constant into the 1980s.

21. "Soar into the '70's," *Seventeen*, January 1970, p. 48.

22. In the 1960s *Seventeen*'s average issue size was usually well over 200 pages. The August 1965 "Back-to-School" edition was 402 pages. The magazine was shortened considerably after 1975.

23. "*Seventeen* Magazine," *Seventeen News*, May 1981, p. 2.

24. Ibid., p. 1.

25. "An Open Letter," *Seventeen*, July 1982, p. 16.

Information Sources

BIBLIOGRAPHY
None.
INDEX SOURCES
Reader's Guide to Periodical Literature.
LOCATION SOURCES
Bound volumes are in many major public and university libraries. The Library of Congress possesses the complete series beginning with *Stardom* (vol. 1, no, 1).

Publication History

MAGAZINE TITLE AND TITLE CHANGES
Stardom: Hollywood's Most Exciting Magazine (1942-1944); *Stardom: Hollywood's Magazine for Women* (1944); *Stardom: With Young Fashions* (1944); *Seventeen* (1944-). *Seventeen* has had various subtitles, the most recent, *Seventeen: Young America's Favorite Magazine*.
VOLUME AND ISSUE DATA
Stardom: Hollywood's Most Exciting Magazine (vol. 1, no. 1-vol. 3, no. 5); *Stardom: Hollywood's Magazine for Women* (vol. 3, no. 6); *Stardom: With Young Fashions* (vol. 3, no. 7-vol. 3, no. 8); *Seventeen* (vol. 3, no. 9-).
PUBLISHER AND PLACE OF PUBLICATION
Triangle Communications, Inc., New York (1942-).

EDITOR
Wade Nichols and Carl A. Schroeder (1942-1944); Helen Valentine (1944-1950); Alice
    Thompson (1950-1954); Enid A. Haupt (1954-1970); Ray Robinson (1971); Rose-
    mary McMurty (1972); Carolyn Gottfried (1972-1973); Rubye Graham (1974-
    1975); Midge Turk Richardson (1976-).

                                                                    JoEllen Laissue

SLAVE'S FRIEND

The *Slave's Friend* was a publication of the American Anti-Slavery Society
and an important part of the abolitionist movement during America's Great
Revival. Founded in 1833 by the reformer William Lloyd Garrison and the
wealthy philanthropists Lewis and Arthur Tappan, the American Anti-Slavery
Society sought to abolish slavery immediately regardless of political consequences or of the constitutional guarantees of the slaveholders. At their annual
meeting of 1834 Lewis Tappan proposed that the society begin a series of four
monthly journals to flood the nation with the abolitionists' message: *Human
Rights*, the *Anti-Slavery Record*, the weekly *Emancipator*, and, for children, the
Slave's Friend.

The *Slave's Friend* was a sixteen-page monthly that was first published in
1836 from the society's New York headquarters on the corner of Nassau and
Spruce streets. The periodical was edited by Lewis Tappan and published by R.
G. Williams.[1] A variety of very short stories, poems, discourses, statistics, and
illustrations presented young readers with a horrible picture of the condition of
slaves in America. The periodical took pains to show the wickedness of slaveholders, the nobility of the black race, and the hypocrisy of a nation that called
itself Christian but permitted one human being to own another.

The unsigned articles presented vignettes that dramatized the conditions of
slavery. Black infants were stolen from their mothers' arms in Africa and forced
to endure horrible conditions on slave ships. Once they reached American shores,
slaves might be sold by the pound along with livestock and household goods.
But most terrible of all, slaves were denied the liberty and justice due all people.

The telling of most stories was melodramatic and sentimental, but young
readers were presented with the immediacy of the condition of slaves in America.
Tales were direct, and they challenged children to imagine themselves in the
position of unfortunate slaves.

The first issue of the *Slave's Friend* began with the poem "The Golden Rule":
"Be you to others kind and true,/As you'd have others be to you;/And neither
do nor say to them/Whate'er you would not take again."[2]

The *Slave's Friend* denounced slavery from all points of view. Stories of the
bondage of Moses and the Jews in Egypt and the story of Joseph being sold into
slavery by his brothers condemned slavery from the Bible's religious point of
view. Quotations of Patrick Henry and Thomas Jefferson gave American patriots

cause to denounce slavery. The anecdote of George Washington bowing to a black man so that no one would be more polite than himself showed the former slaveholder's respect for men regardless of the color of their skin. Numerous stories of caged birds and butterflies showed slavery to be imprisonment contrary to the laws of nature.

Advertisements of slaves for sale, taken from contemporary newspapers were reprinted in the *Slave's Friend*, and they were always followed with editorial comments by society members. Readers were advised about proper treatment of blacks: "never call one a Negro, Blackey or Darkey...never call a colored man a boy."[3] The *Slave's Friend* showed slavery to be a national shame. Articles described other countries that had rid themselves of the backward institution, even as it continued in the otherwise progressive United States.

A few articles of general interest were included in the *Slave's Friend*, but they, too, were used to convey its antislavery message. A description of the printing press, for example, stresses how the printing media was important for spreading messages, messages such as the evils of slavery.

The physical appearance of the *Slave's Friend* was simple and handsome. Illustrations from wood engravings were well conceived and executed, and often the same cuts were used again and again for similar articles. Well-used favorites included a black man bound with the chains of slavery, a black woman crying out to heaven before being taken by slave traders, and two girls, one black and one white, reading together unaware of the differences of their color.

Three frontispieces were used during the magazine's publication, and their imagery symbolized its philosophy. The first showed an enlightened Christian gentleman teaching a group of children. With volume 2 in 1837 it was changed to show three children reading and flanked by columns bearing the figures of Justice and Freedom resting on two books: the Bible and the Declaration of Independence. The Eye of God floated above these symbols. Finally, with volume 4 the frontispiece was simplified to show a monumental female personification of Freedom.

The *Slave's Friend* was one aspect of the active pamphlet campaign of the abolitionist movement. The Anti-Slavery press also published sermons, addresses, reports, and memoirs of runaway slaves. The price of the *Slave's Friend* was listed as 1¢ an issue, 10¢ a dozen and 80¢ a hundred, but few were actually sold. "Only a few were printed to sell; most of them were distributed gratis by strewing the wayside, the parlor, the bar room, the stage coach, the rail car and the boat dock, and by sending them haphazardly through the mails to such addresses as could be secured from published lists."[4]

The publication was financially supported by the Tappan brothers who were the "financial angels" of the Great Revival.[5] It is estimated that between 25,000 and 50,000 copies of each of the four publications of the American Anti-Slavery Society were published each month.[6]

By 1837 the *Slave's Friend* asked readers to form their own Juvenile Anti-Slavery Societies, which would be auxiliaries of the American Anti-Slavery

By 1837 the *Slave's Friend* asked readers to form their own Juvenile Anti-Slavery Societies, which would be auxiliaries of the American Anti-Slavery Society. Directions, advice, and a suggested constitution for juvenile societies comprised one issue of the *Slave's Friend*. Subsequent issues noted the many juvenile societies that sprang up, as well as the contributions they made to promote the movement.

The *Slave's Friend* disappeared abruptly in 1838 with volume 4, no. 2. Its subject had been a volatile issue in America, and much of the country was vehemently opposed to receiving abolitionist propaganda. Anti-slavery societies began to find themselves victims of violent attacks. Moreover, the financial backing of the Tappan brothers ran dry after they lost their fortunes in the financial Panic of 1837 and could no longer sponsor the publications of the American Anti-Slavery Society. The demise of the society itself soon followed. "By the summer of 1839, the Society had ceased to embody a movement; it was fast becoming an organization without a constituency; in a year it was to be little more than a name."[7]

Notes

1. Bertram Wyatt-Brown, *Lewis Tappan and the Evangelical War Against Slavery* (Cleveland: The Press of Case Western Reserve University, 1969), 143.
2. *Slave's Friend* 1 January ([?] 1836), i.
3. Ibid., 1 (July 1836), 4-5.
4. Gilbert H. Barnes, *The Anti-Slavery Impulse, 1830-1844* (Gloucester, Mass.: Peter Smith, 1973), 100.
5. Ibid., p. 107.
6. Wyatt-Brown, *Lewis-Tappan*, p. 144.
7. Barnes, *Anti-Slavery Impulse*, p. 160.

Information Sources

BIBLIOGRAPHY
Gilbert H. Barnes, *The Anti-Slavery Impulse, 1830-1844* (Gloucester, Mass.: Peter Smith, 1973); Bertram Wyatt-Brown, *Lewis Tappan and the Evangelical War Against Slavery* (Cleveland: The Press of Case Western Reserve University, 1969).
INDEX SOURCES
None.
LOCATION SOURCES
Available on microfilm from Greenwood Press, Westport, Conn.

Publication History

MAGAZINE TITLE AND TITLE CHANGES
Slave's Friend (1836-1838).
VOLUME AND ISSUE DATA
Slave's Friend (vol. 1, no. 1-vol. 4, no. 2).
PUBLISHER AND PLACE OF PUBLICATION
R. G. Williams for the American Anti-Slavery Society, New York (1836-1838).

EDITOR
None listed, but publications of the American Anti-Slavery Society were the work of
     Elizur Wright and Lewis Tappan.

John R. Edson

SOUTHERN BOYS' AND GIRLS' MONTHLY

Founded in Richmond, Virginia, *Southern Boys' and Girls' Monthly* published
its first issue in January 1867 and its final one in July 1868. In the Salutatory
the editors stated the reasons that induced them to enter upon their work. The
Monthly was intended to be "wholly literary" and the correspondents were all
to be Southern. In refining the definition of "literary," the editor stated: "But
a true literature in a Christian land is based on the principles of sound morality
and redolent of the perfumes of the Holy Scriptures. And nothing is worthy of
the name of literature for the young which does not teach them lessons of correct
principles, and lead them in paths of Christian virtue."[1]

In confining itself to the contributions of southern writers, the *Monthly* saw
itself furnishing "the means of developing that native talent which is lying
dormant among us.... Too much have we been disposed to rely on other sections
of the land and other countries of the world to supply us with literature for the
old and young.... Talent is here in abundance, but active exertion is wanted."
In this vein an invitation was extended to "cultivated scholars of both sexes to
enter the ranks of literature and cope with the writers of the world for the palms
of success."[2]

The format of the *Monthly* was "thirty-two pages, octavo, printed on clear
white paper, making a yearly volume, title page and index included, of nearly
400 pages." Terms were listed as follows: "Single subscribers, $1.50. Any one
sending the names of five subscribers will be entitled to a sixth copy gratis."[3]

The contents of the magazine were projected to encompass "stories to interest
and instruct the young, historical and biographical narratives, anecdotes illustrative of great and virtuous character, instructive and entertaining articles explanatory of the principles of science, nature and art; in fine, everything which
will entertain and instruct the young, and lead them in the ways of truth, usefulness and honour will always be acceptable."[4]

Representative of the "stories to interest and instruct the young" were cautionary tales such as "Playing with Fire" (April 1868), "Prascovia Lopouloff:
or, The Siberian Exiles" (May 1868), "The Raven's Feather" (December 1867),
and "Ellen Roby," a serialized boarding-school story (May 1868).

Instructive articles, which appeared in each issue, covered a variety of subjects:
"Lighthouses" (January 1867), "Trades and Professions of Animals" (April
1868), "Russian Caravans in China" (May 1868), and "Uncle Frank and His
Nephews and Nieces," which told of customs in distant cultures (April 1867).

Historical and biographical narratives were featured in the magazine as promised: "Dickens" (May 1868); "The Saracenic Well," an anecdote from the life of Mahommed [sic] (April 1868); and "One Way of Crossing the River," describing Dr. Livingstone's travels (December 1867).

Interspersed through each issue were verses, always didactic, but dealing with a variety of subjects: "The Wishing Cap," "But One Pair of Stockings," and "Old Times"(May 1868). Usually, verses were listed as "selected," but a few appeared under the names of now obscure writers.

"Anecdotes illustrative of great and virtuous character" were usually fillers such as "The Tiger and His Victim" and "Don't Use Angry Words" (May 1868).

Special features of *Southern Boys' and Girls' Monthly* were designed for reader participation. In this respect it resembled several other of its contemporaries that solicited correspondence, enigmas, anagrams, puzzles, and Bible questions from its readers. In the section "Editors' Monthly Chat" are comments on answers received for the puzzles as well as rules governing the submission of items to the magazine. In some issues this section was called "Editorial Bureau," where questions from readers were answered and lengthy admonitions were directed at readers regarding their correspondence with the *Monthly*: "We desire the improvement of our young readers a great deal more than the money we receive from them for this magazine; and hence we feel it right and necessary some times to instruct and some times to reprove a little."[5] Following this, nearly two pages of the October 1867 issue were devoted to the relationship of letter writing to character building.

The *Monthly*'s masthead in each issue proudly proclaimed: "It is illustrated with numerous fine drawings." So it was. The cover illustration remained the same throughout the two volumes—a group of children under a tree enjoying a book. Many articles were decorated with highly embellished initials or a drawing of a bird or an animal to relieve the monotony of the solid page.

A few of the issues of the *Monthly* carried advertisements, usually religious. For example, a half-page of the May 1868 issue announced the *Southern Pulpit and Pen*, a monthly "devoted to Religious Literature and Science, containing one sermon from some eminent Southern divine, essays from Southern authors on religious, literary, and scientific topics, reviews and editorial notices of current publications." A quarter-page announced *The Young Marooners...* by F. R. Goulding, which was heralded as "the most successful book of entertainment for the young written since the days of DeFoe and his 'Robinson Crusoe.' "[6]

Incorporated in the back of the April 1867 issue were several "notices of the press"—comments about the *Monthly* that had appeared in periodicals such as the *Baltimore Sun, Danville (Virginia) Register, The Deaf and Dumb Casket* (Raleigh, North Carolina), *The North Carolina Presbyterian*, and *Christian Observer* (Richmond, Virginia). Probably the most glowing recommendation was the one from the *New Orleans Picayune*, which said "this monthly gives some little more of moral and religious instruction than do others, and a large class of patrons will desire this magazine above all others for their children. It will be recollected that it is in no respect denominational, while it does inculcate, in pleasing tales, Christian morality."[7]

Problems, some of which led to the demise of the *Monthly* in July 1868, were evident earlier in its history: "Failures in the Post Office Department" assured the Baltimore subscribers that their failure to receive previous issues was in no way the fault of the magazine. "As it never reached Baltimore at all, it is a matter of conjecture where it went." Further problems with the postal service were cited: a subscriber in Arkansas received no copies from April to August; another reported receiving the March issue with a piece cut out of page 79; a third complained that it took four weeks for his copy to travel 100 miles within the same state; and a clergyman in Georgia reported that he had received only "every fourth number, no more." The editors' response was to place the blame on the postal service, saying, "the many failures of the United States Post Office to fulfill its important trusts in the Southern States is becoming a very serious matter to publishers and businessmen." A further inconvenience to subscribers was described in the same issue: in the course of making improvements to the magazine, a new power press was secured "whose arrival in Richmond was delayed about ten days longer than expected." This item concluded by saying that "cuts designed for this number" failed to arrive in time to be included, but that arrangements had been made "whereby all these matters will be regulated and our young friends will not be subjected to these annoying inconveniences."[8]

Thus plagued by transportation problems and shortages of equipment and materials symptomatic of Reconstruction, the *Southern Boys' and Girls' Monthly* ceased publication with the July 1868 issue. In its short life it had apparently, according to its "notices of the press," made "an entertaining and instructive journal for the benefit of youth, giving them substantial knowledge and directing their thoughts in right channels" and had fulfilled its proclaimed objective of meeting the "wants of that particular section of the country where it was expected to circulate."[9] In the pages of the *Monthly* one not only experiences the religious literature for the young of the period but also comes to recognize the sectional political and economic problems facing the nation, especially the South, following the Civil War.

Notes

1. *Southern Boys' and Girls' Monthly* 1 (January 1867), 1.
2. Ibid., pp. 1-2.
3. Ibid., 1 (April 1867), inside front cover.
4. Ibid., 1 (January 1867), 2.
5. Ibid., 1 (October 1867), 348-49.
6. Ibid., 1 (May 1867), 201.
7. Ibid., 1 (April 1867), 129.
8. Ibid., 1 (October 1867), 349-50.
9. Ibid., 1 (April 1867), inside front cover.

Information Sources

BIBLIOGRAPHY
Gertrude C. Gilmer, ed., *Checklist of Southern Periodicals to 1861* (Boston: F. W. Faxon, 1934), where *Southern Boys' and Girls' Monthly* is dated from 1853 to 1867 (?). The material in the periodical, however, contradicts this beginning date.
INDEX SOURCES
None.
LOCATION SOURCES
Tulane University, New Orleans; Duke University, Durham, N.C.; Historical Foundation, Montreat, N.C.; University of North Carolina, Chapel Hill, N.C.; Virginia State Library, Richmond, Va.; College of William and Mary, Williamsburg, Va.

Publication History

MAGAZINE TITLE AND TITLE CHANGES
Southern Boys' and Girls' Monthly (January 1867-July 1868).
VOLUME AND ISSUE DATA
Southern Boys' and Girls' Monthly (vol. 1, no. 1-vol. 2, no. 7).
PUBLISHER AND PLACE OF PUBLICATION
White and Howard, Richmond, Va. (1867-1868).
EDITOR
Rev. E. Thompson Baird and Professor William Logan Baird (1867); Baird & Brother (1868).

Mary D. Manning

STONE SOUP: THE MAGAZINE BY CHILDREN

Stone Soup is a magazine founded in 1973 with two purposes: to publish only the works of children and to publish them in a well-designed format that is usually found only in fine-press publishing or in ephemeral publishing. But by 1981 *Stone Soup* had a circulation of more than 8,000, with a readership of approximately 80,000; it attracts school and library audiences but also has individual subscriptions; and it receives more than 2,000 submissions a year from children. Its subscription list and submissions envelopes reveal the names of more than 31 states, Canada, Japan, Ireland, and Oman; thus *Stone Soup* reaches a national and even an international audience. The magazine attracts readers not only by its unique orientation but also by its fine appearance. It is 6 by 8 3/4 inches; contains forty-eight pages; is printed on heavy, white paper; and is bound pamphlet style, with a heavier paper cover featuring a full-color painting by a child.

Stone Soup contains many types of writings by children such as letters to the editor, stories, poems, descriptive passages, jokes, autobiographical accounts, and book reviews. Its artwork includes drawings made in ink, pencil, and crayons; cartoons; and paintings in watercolor, poster paint, and finger paint. Comparing each of these works to similar works by children in other media reveals one strong impression: a true variety of material. For example, in the letters-to-the-editor section, the letters discuss events in children's lives, their praise or suggestions for *Stone Soup*, and reactions to their own material published in the magazine. Occasionally, adults' letters have been published also, but the editors now say they will probably not publish any more material by adults, preferring to keep the focus on children's work rather than divert attention to adult research interests and professional comments. In general, the magazine's contents reveal a wide diversity. No single regional, political, economic, social, or intellectual bias predominates. The artwork is equally diverse. Many pieces are lavishly detailed and strongly imaginative. The magazine appeals not only to children but also to those interested in children's artistic productions.

Stone Soup was founded in 1973 by students at the University of California at Santa Cruz who were involved in a children's art program. The Editorial Board, composed of five members, was aided by three advisors. Their initial editorial expressed a "deep interest in the work of young children. Rather than seeing children's writings and illustrations as transitional works to be passed over, we came to see the works as finished statements in themselves having an intrinsic value that could be appreciated by adults as well as children."[1] Their aim was to present "a high quality anthology that is readily accessible to children through their schools, libraries, and eventually bookstores." They further announced that children would review children's books as a unique addition to the criticism of children's books. The first issue was hospitable to adult work as well, but this emphasis was soon dropped.

The founding of *Stone Soup* can be seen as an unusual, but not unforeseen, offshoot of the extraordinary interest in children, children's art, and spontaneous home and school activities of the late 1960s and early 1970s. The editors followed their manifesto with a retelling of the folktale "Stone Soup," which emphasizes cooperation, survival in the face of problems, and good ingredients for a wholesome product. The first children's contributions included an alphabetical acrostic, a play, one-paragraph stories or passages, several poems, and writings in Spanish and Japanese with English translations. Thirteen pages were devoted to "The Golden Eagle," a book by an eight-year-old boy from Carmel, California. The first issue was printed in black and white, with the subtitle *A Journal of Children's Literature*. The cover bore an adult's drawing of an old woman and an ex-soldier cooking stone soup. The issue was favorably reviewed by the American Library Association, *San Francisco Chronicle, Detroit Free Press*, and other newspapers.

Within a short time, Gerry Mandel and William Rubel took over as editors, and the magazine was reconstituted as the publication of the Children's Art Foundation, a nonprofit, tax-exempt foundation directed by the two editors. The Children's Art Foundation collects artwork by children throughout the world and maintains files of this material, which it circulates in sets to libraries and schools for a small fee. To further develop the collection, the directors occasionally solicit artwork about topics such as "People Working" (1979) or "Interiors" (1981).

In a similar way the Children's Art Foundation also collects children's writing. From the more than 2,000 submissions a year, only 0.5 percent are published. Most submissions come at the end of school years, often in envelopes containing forty or more works written as class assignments. The editors choose very little such material which is frequently repetitive and accept only the material that strikes them as honest, unusual, open, and suffused with the writers' personality and excitement. Their policies have occasionally cost them cancellations, letters of protest from adults, and attempts at censorship; for example, a story about childbirth was protested. Together with their insistence on original and honest material, the editors believe in payment for work. They pay $20-40 a story, $5 a picture, and $10 for a book review. They often commission illustrations for stories, and they assign books to their file of book reviewers. Book-review assignments are made for books that they believe are of above-average interest.

The goals for the magazine remain substantially the same, although the magazine has improved in appearance and design, and children are now paid for their work. The magazine demonstrates that children are capable of better work than is often thought. The editors insist that adult's ideas for children's stories are often too narrow. They refute the common idea that young children cannot write long works. Children have more sophisticated vocabularies than expected, although often their natural language is naive. More can be done to encourage good writing by children, they believe, although their goal is not necessarily the development of a professional career for children but to encourage the excitement, the joy, of having something to say and saying it. The editors' files of 10,000 pieces of writing plus approximately 25,000 unfiled pieces are available to researchers in children's writing.

New developments in *Stone Soup* and The Children's Art Foundation are special issues and "Little Books." A special issue of works by Lee Tandy Schwartzman, aged seven, of Seattle, Washington, contains "Crippled Detectives; or The War of the Red Romer" (November-December 1978), a 48-page story illustrated with nineteen drawings. Basically, the story is of four sisters and a brother "who take it upon themselves to save the world from an evil villain, Red Romer, and his gang." Red Romer is "fierce" and "had stoled money from the hospital."[2] Sections of verse; dialogue dramatized like a play; letters; notes; schoolroom lessons on the alphabet, numbers, and common shapes; and interpolated "stories of our ancestors" round out the story, which ended in the time-honored way: "Everyone bad died and was buried in a rain the mirror and moon had caused. So our comrades packed and went home well but tired, and somehow Lee knew that Black Romer was still roaming looking for evil to do."[3]

The second new type of publication is the "Little Book," written by children five through twelve years of age. Currently, seven "Little Books" which measure 3 by 4 inches, are offered at 50¢ each: *The Great Wild Egg Hunt, The Bee That Could Never Be Killed, Wildest Horse in America, Frankenstein Locks Himself*

Out, Little Dog, The Beautiful Puppy, and *Amy Goes to the Moon*, a story of a young stowaway on Apollo 17.

In 1977 the editors of *Stone Soup* published *The Editors' Notebook*, a forty-page pamphlet in the format of the magazine. The handbook, a guide to teaching writing and art to children, consists of five main parts. The Introduction briefly directs itself to teachers "who are interested in refining and developing their creative arts programs." The first chapter, "Poetry," claims that the "first language of childhood is the language of the poet," simple, rhythmic, direct, and innovative. But poetry written by children is usually "fundamentally uninteresting," because it is "filtered through strict formulas."[4] William Rubel gave examples of poor poems and contrasted them with good ones. The second chapter, "Writing," suggests that writing programs often "become sidetracked with projects and attitudes which tend to encourage writing which resembles in form but not in substance genuine creative work." Rubel not only gave an example of this formulaic writing, in this case the "tough, but . . . interesting" life of a garbage can, but he also claimed that this stiff, predictable writing is varied only by conventionalized material from the mass media. He recommended teaching children, instead, to write by drawing on their own experiences, dreams, fantasies, and beliefs, so that writing becomes a "means of exploration, as a means of growing and gaining control over his or her own ideas and observations."[5] In the next chapter Rubel cautioned against using children's pictures "as windows through which to peer at the inner child" or as the catchall term *children's art*.[6] Even after seventy years of study, most people do not have a good system of analysis for children's art, according to Rubel. He hoped for more naive, personal art from children rather than copies of adult models. Finally, in the last section of the pamphlet, Rubel concentrated on achieving what is "essential" in the Creative Arts Program: the quality of the relationship between the child and the teacher and the quality of the relationship of the children to each other. "What is essential is the strength with which the entire class is working toward a unified set of goals."[7]

The editors have succeeded in making *Stone Soup* a distinctive publication in terms of design and content. The variety of material published contrasts with more ordinary single-issue publications. Warm mentions of family life, gentle irony, strongly juxtaposed emotions, and neologisms outweigh conventional responses to nature, to emotional traumas, such as death and the births of siblings, and to holidays. Family relationships are carefully presented: "Now I know what changed inside me when Paul yelled at me. It was my heart, because he *is* my brother and I love him. He loves me too" (Kellie O'Benar, age eleven.)[8] "I am very involved with Mom and this baby" (Jewel Cousins, age ten).[9] Titles such as "At Least I Don't Talk to Fried Eggs" and "Charlotte Little: Master Novelist" poke gentle fun at the self and an imagined self (January-February 1980). In 1981 a black girl entering school asked, "What Happened to the Real Me?" In 1981 stories also discussed stays in hospitals, the firing of a teacher, and memories of a grandfather. Nancy Weiland, age eleven, wrote, "Candy was a SKYN-

ABOOBARIS. If you don't know what that is, she is a rare kind of bird. She is the only one left of her kind.''[10] Other word coinage involves "The Silverburg Theory of Seesawtivity," invented by Sarryl Reeves, age eleven, in that same issue. Finally, an unusual series is "The Amy Books," a multichapter series written by the Shields sisters, of Dayton, Washington, and published in volume 4, no. 3. In contrast to the usual newspaper submissions these are both long, multichaptered works and the personal responses to books which they contain: "I thought it was sad but not too sad.... You know, I had tears in my eyes," wrote Kristen Swanson, age eleven, in 1973, about *Tell Me About Death, Tell Me About Funerals* by Elizabeth Adam Corley.[11]

More children's writing and more artwork is published in each issue of *Stone Soup* than in any comparable magazine. For example, *Cricket** prints three poems from a poetry contest, twelve letters to the editor, and five pictures in a contest for imaginary musical instruments.[12] *Stone Soup* typically publishes thirteen to twenty-eight artworks, fourteen stories or poems, and three or four book reviews. It offers support to children thinking of themselves as writers and artists; by printing such material it shows its readers the lives and versions of life available to those who want them.

Created in a time of intellectual and cultural ferment, *Stone Soup* has been carefully developed and continues to offer an outlet to creative children while retaining a strong interest in the work of ordinary children with naive, excited, personal points of view. Many of its issues and "Little Books" are in short supply, foretelling a possible collectors' interest. Like *St. Nicholas** and the Canadian *All About Us—Nous Autres*, *Stone Soup* is a valuable collection of children's art and writing.

Notes

1. Editorial, *Stone Soup*, 1 (May 1973), vii.
2. *Stone Soup* 7, no. 2 (November-December 1978), 7.
3. Ibid., p. 48.
4. "Poetry," *The Editors' Notebook*, 1977, p. 9.
5. "Writing," ibid., p. 17.
6. Ibid.   ·
7. Ibid., p. 29.
8. *Stone Soup* 6, no. 4 (March 1978), 8.
9. Ibid.
10. Ibid., 2, no. 1 (November 1973), pp. 10-11.
11. Ibid., p. 68.
12. *Cricket* 3, no. 5 (1976).

Information Sources

INDEX SOURCES
None.

LOCATION SOURCES
A full file is maintained by the Children's Art Foundation and in university libraries such
     as that of San Jose State University, San Jose, Ca.; Northwestern University
     Library, Evanston, Ill.; or the Contemporary Culture Collection of the Temple
     University Library, Philadelphia, Pa. Full files may also be found in libraries like
     the Donnell Center, Children's Room, New York Public Library.
BIBLIOGRAPHY
Steven Winn, "A Magazine Kids Write Themselves," *San Francisco Chronicle*, February
     18, 1981, p. 57.

Publication History

MAGAZINE TITLE AND TITLE CHANGES
Stone Soup: A Journal of Children's Literature (May 1973-January 1975); *Stone Soup:
     A Magazine by Children* (March 1975-May 1977); *Stone Soup; The Magazine by
     Children* (September 1977-).
VOLUME AND ISSUE DATA
Stone Soup: A Journal of Children's Literature (vol. 1, no. 1-vol. 3, no. 3); *Stone Soup:
     A Magazine by Children* (vol. 4, no. 5-vol. 5 no. 5); *Stone Soup: The Magazine
     by Children* (vol. 6, no. 1-).
PUBLISHER AND PLACE OF PUBLICATION
Stone Soup, Inc., Santa Cruz, Ca. (1973-1975); Children's Art Foundation, Santa Cruz,
     Ca. (1976-).
EDITOR
Lee Christy, Laura Garcia, Richard Hof, Gerry Mandel, Gretchen Rendler, and William
     Rubel (1973-1975); Gerry Mandel and William Rubel, co-editors (1975).

Bernice O. Zelditch

STORY FRIENDS

Story Friends is a weekly Mennonite Sunday School paper for the youngest
readers. (See also *Words of Cheer*,* *Youth's Christian Companion*,* and *With*.*)
It began December 24, 1905, as *Beams of Light*, "a four-page illustrated paper
for children of the home and Sunday School," and was first published by the
Gospel Witness Company of Scottdale, Pennsylvania.[1] It printed stories, poems,
short articles, and correspondence from its young readers. For the first two years
of publication the two inside pages contained a discussion of the current week's
Sunday School lesson. After April 1908 the paper was published by the Mennonite Publishing House of Scottdale and edited by a succession of Mennonite
writers and editors. Beginning with the first issue of 1958 the name was changed
to *Story Friends*.

As its title suggests, *Story Friends* has been a cheerful paper with pleasant,
inviting stories and illustrations. It has carried poems; short stories, mostly by
Mennonite authors; and articles about things to do, home and school life, and
missions, written for children from ages four to eight. Series such as "Our

Missionary Friends'' told about everyday events in the lives of missionary children in Ethiopia, Tanganyika, and Luxemburg, among other places. Nature features, activity ideas, picture stories, and puzzles appeared frequently.

A typical poem is the following:

SICK IN BED
By Eileen Gingerich

My tummy aches—so does my head;

So all day long I've been in bed.
My mother read and sang to me;
She brought me trays of toast and tea.
The doctor checked my tummy-ache,
And gave me little pills to take.

The pills will take away the pain,
And God will make me well again.[2]

Story Friends was the first in a triad of youth publications for Mennonite children and young people, the second and third (in ascending order of age-group) being *Words of Cheer* and *Youth's Christian Companion*. All taught the Christian virtues and sought to reinforce home and church life through moral instruction and edification. In 1976 editor Alice Hershberger wrote:

> The over-arching purpose of [*Story Friends*] is to magnify Jesus Christ and His way in terms a child can grasp. Children of this age group are full of questions about God and Jesus, the Bible, prayer, church doctrinal practices. Stories of everyday experiences at home, at church, in school, at play help provide some answers. Of special importance are relationships: patterns of forgiveness, respect, honesty, trust. Emphasis is on spiritual values, but not from a purely humanistic viewpoint; rather, recognizing Jesus Christ as a source of power to live out "goodness."[3]

Quite a few Mennonite artists associated with the Mennonite Publishing House have produced illustrations for *Story Friends*. Among them are Ruth Eitzen, Esther Rose Graber, and Pauline Cutrell. The circulation in 1979 was 13,600. In 1958 it was about 22,500.

Notes

1. *The Mennonite Encyclopedia* (Hillsboro, Kans.: Mennonite Brethren Publishing House, 1955-1959), 1:254-55.

2. *Story Friends*, October 23, 1960, p. 4.

3. *Writer's Market '77*, ed. Jane Koester and Paula Arnett Sandhage (Cincinnati: Writer's Digest, 1976), 434.

Information Sources

BIBLIOGRAPHY

John A. Hostetler, *God Uses Ink* (Scottdale, Pa.: Herald Press, 1958); *The Mennonite Encyclopedia* (Hillsboro, Kans.: Mennonite Brethren Publishing House, 1955-1959); *Writer's Market '77* (Cincinnatti: Writer's Digest, 1976).

INDEX SOURCES

None.

LOCATION SOURCES

Bound volumes are in most Mennonite libraries, including those at Goshen College, Goshen, Ind.; Eastern Mennonite College, Harrisonburg, Va.; and the Lancaster Mennonite Historical Society archives, Lancaster, Pa.

Publication History

MAGAZINE TITLE AND TITLE CHANGES

Beams of Light (1905-1958); *Story Friends* (1958-).

VOLUME AND ISSUE DATA

Beams of Light (vol. 1, no. 1-vol. 52, no. 52); *Story Friends* (vol. 53, no. 1-).

PUBLISHER AND PLACE OF PUBLICATION

Gospel Witness Company, Scottdale, Pa. (1905-March 1908); Mennonite Publishing House, Scottdale, Pa. (April 1908-).

EDITOR

Daniel Kauffman (1905-April 15, 1906); D. H. Bender (April 22, 1906-June 23, 1907); A. D. Martin (June 30, 1907-June 20, 1909); H. F. Reist (June 27, 1909-May 9, 1920); anonymous (May 16, 1920-October 23, 1921); J. A. Ressler (October 30, 1921-1937); Lina Z. Ressler (1937-1946); Helen Trumbo (1955-1961); Jane Lind (1962-1965); Alice Hershberger (1966-March 1977); Marjorie Waybill (April 1977-).

John Daniel Stahl

STORY PARADE

Story Parade was begun in 1936 by a group of educators known as the Association for Arts in Childhood (AAC) who felt the need for an excellent literary magazine for children. With its handsome appearance and high literary standards, *Story Parade* became a leading juvenile periodical of its day, providing a showcase for the work of new artists and writers for nineteen years until it ceased publication in 1954.

Story Parade was an important periodical for many reasons. Initially, it represented a revival of quality in juvenile periodical literature. Second, it encouraged juvenile book publication, since many of the stories it published eventually became hardcover books. Finally, in retrospect, *Story Parade* provides a reflection of the changing attitudes and styles of nineteen years of American popular culture.

In the first issue *Story Parade* editors explained the purpose and high hopes for their new publication:

This new literary magazine for boys and girls is designed to give children the best in stories, verse, and plays by contemporary writers. In addition, there will be presented foreign and other material of value not easily accessible to young readers. The qualities sought in illustration and decoration are simplicity and artistic value. In one department, 'Our Own,' we will print writings of literary merit by children. Published by a membership group, *Story Parade* is in no way a commercial enterprise. Its object is the wide distribution of good literature for children in an attractive form and at a low price.[1]

With the decline of *St. Nicholas*,* no existing juvenile periodical met the standards of *Story Parade* editors. In the 1930s *St. Nicholas* bore little resemblance to earlier issues. Its pages were cluttered with advertising, and its stories generally lacked literary merit.

In 1935 the sponsors of *Story Parade* (librarians, teachers of children, school supervisors, college teachers, and editors) "recalled their own childhood delight in certain story magazines no longer existent or sadly changed; they deplored the lack of such periodicals for young children; and then they decided to make such a magazine."[2] They formed the nonprofit Association for Arts in Childhood, Inc., and launched *Story Parade*. Members of the AAC "had to guarantee with their own money that the magazine would be able to pay an editor, to assure a printer's contract, and to keep the organization going until subscriptions would be sufficient to carry the load. For several years, while the magazine was coming to be known, they would have to keep it going from their private contributions."[3]

The Advisory Board of the AAC included representatives of leading cultural institutions. Katherine F. Lenroot, chief of the Children's Bureau; Bess Goodykoontz, assistant commissioner of education, and Margaret Mead of the American Museum of Natural History met with eight other representatives of libraries and educational institutions.

The Editorial Board of *Story Parade* was headed by Lockie Parker and Barbara Nolen who served as literary editor. Nolen held that position throughout the publication history of the magazine, and Parker remained chief editor for a period of eighteen years until he was replaced by Lucille Ogle in May 1953. Ruby Warner served as children's editor and Howard Simon was the first art editor.

The Association for Arts in Childhood had other projects in conjunction with its new magazine. The organization sought to cooperate with other groups wishing to foster appreciation of the arts among children in the fields of music, dance, theatre, radio, and literature. With the Columbia Broadcasting System's School of the Air, the AAC co-sponsored an annual series of radio programs for children known as "Tales from Near and Far," featuring noted storytellers such as Ruth Sawyer. The AAC also published booklists of recommended new titles and a series of bulletins such as "Arts in Childhood," which included articles about the visual art interests of young children.

The 1930s was a time of development in the field of early childhood education and juvenile publishing. As described by Barbara Bader in *American Picture-books*, "The years 1935-40 which brought to a climax the first period in modern picturebook publishing, also brought into the field new blood and new talent, new signers and publishers, and some were all three."[4]

This new talent supplied the material for *Story Parade*. Authors who wrote regularly included Elizabeth Coatsworth, Charles J. Finger, Ellis Credle, Glen Rounds, and Wilfred Bronson. Regular *Story Parade* illustrators were Fritz Eichenberg, Lois Lenski, Kurt Weise, and Henry C. Pitz.

Literary excellence distinguished *Story Parade* from its competitors. Readers were offered new tellings of old epics, serialized stories from new books, old and new poetry, articles about natural history, and many reviews and discussions of new books recommended for themselves. Children might find the story of Cuchulain, "The Terrible Stranger," or Wanda Gag's interpretation of Emily Dickinson's poem "Snow" in issues of 1936. The lengthy, chatty book reviews by editor Barbara Nolen discussed both recent publications and old favorites.

Many stories of enduring quality first appeared in early issues of *Story Parade*. "The Seven Simeons" by Boris Artzybasheff was serialized beginning with the issue of March 1937, and it appeared with different black and white renderings of the books's splendid color illustrations. "The Great Geppy" by William Pène du Bois appeared in 1939, and the "Five Chinese Brothers" by Claire Huchet Bishop appeared in October 1938. The issue of September 1944 featured the story of misunderstanding and compassion, "The hundred dresses" by Eleanor Estes, with illustrations by Louis Slobodkin.

The literary strength of *Story Parade* lay in its stories describing and celebrating the varied patterns of contemporary regional American life. *Story Parade* authors were familiar with their subjects, be it Ann N. Clark's "Happy Days," a story about a Hopi Indian village; Glen Round's "Whitey Looks for a Job," a tale of a boy's adventure in a lumber camp; or Cornelia Meigs's "Mother Makes Christmas," describing the holiday in rural Vermont. These stories and thirteen others about life in modern America formed the "Roundabout America" series that was subsequently published as the book *Children of America*.

By 1937 *Story Parade* led the trend for stories of regional Americana. The genre was the mainstay of the work of Lois Lenski in her own "Roundabout America" series and in the many tales of rural mountain life written by Ellis Credle.

By its second year of publication, *Story Parade* had six times as many subscribers as the 1,600 with which it began in 1936. The best stories of its first banner year were reprinted for those who had missed them in the *Story Parade Red Book*. This first compilation was followed by four others: *The Blue Book, The Green Book, The Silver Book*, and *The Gold Book*. Material from *Story Parade* had been too good to be lost as old magazines were discarded; in book form the material could be properly preserved. Material in the *Red Book* included

Walter de la Mare's story, "Mr. Bumps and His Monkey"; "First Fair Days" by Elizabeth Coatsworth, will illustrations by Helen Sewell; "Wreck Asho-o-ree" by May McNeer, with illustrations by her husband Lynd Ward; and "Beanstalk Jack," a poem written and illustrated by Lois Lenski.

Stories from the magazine were published in the new series of *Story Parade Picture Books*, and they created a new look for popular, mass-produced children's books. Barbara Bader, in her history of American picture books, writes:

> Many of the stories, through a hook-up with the Artists' and Writers' Guild, found their way into books. Published by Grosset & Dunlap and dubbed *Story Parade Picture Books* (a second, slightly older series was called *Story Parade Adventure Books*), they were equally picturebooks and story books. Thin and flat, they were not tall or oblong, large or small, the marks—stigmata—of a picturebook; designed like picturebooks, so that the whole page was illustrated and plentifully provided with color, they retained from story books consecutive paragraphs of type. They were slender and inviting but they didn't look "babyish," they had lots of reading but they didn't look "hard."[5]

In addition to the stories about regional Americana *Story Parade* included stories about contemporary children in foreign lands. Magazine covers pictured the stories' locations, and special issues such as the Pan-American issue of April 1939 were devoted to stories, poetry, songs, games, and crafts from a geographical region. *Story Parade* attracted subscribers from around the world, and the magazine attempted to widen the horizons of its readers and to promote a feeling of international understanding, which was one of its major themes, at least until the outbreak of World War II.

Several animal characters appeared regularly in *Story Parade*. The story "Oscar the Trained Seal" by Mabel E. Neikirk created a new and regular visitor to *Story Parade*. Oscar eventually appeared in his own books and became a good friend of Peter Penguin, the official mascot of *Story Parade*, who spoke through editorials, "Peter Penguin Talking," and who founded the Penguin Club for international pen pals.

Story Parade's literary appeal was complemented by its fine illustrations and handsome design. Early years of *Story Parade* featured covers lithographed in two colors as well as a wide variety of black and white illustrations within. Wide areas of white space set off both illustrations and text. Illustrations were done in a variety of techniques, mostly the techniques of drawing. Black and white drawings were the leading style of American illustrators of the 1930s who used this idiom of reportage to depict life as they saw it. Handsome and stylish black and white drawings eliminated "the high costs and uncertain results of color printing." Moreover, "Drawing itself is a good, a line has its own personality, a drawing in line makes its own statement."[6]

The variety of black and white drawings in *Story Parade* encompassed the witty line work of Fritz Eichenberg, the humor of Robert McCloskey, the sketchy and textured vignettes of Helen Sewell, and the simple and childlike outlines of Lois Lenski. Also worthy of note were the clear diagrams and illustrations of animals by Wilfrid Bronson, which accompanied his regular articles on natural history.

The two-color lithographic covers of *Story Parade* were a logical step beyond its black and white illustrations. One color could replace the structure of black line, and another could be added for its decorative value. *Story Parade* covers set the mood for the contents of an issue, and collections of the covers were frequently offered for sale as nursery decorations.

As with the rest of the world at the outset of World War II, the appearance and content of *Story Parade* began to change, and by the end of the war, the magazine had been almost entirely transformed. When regular contributors went off to war, *Story Parade* had to continue without their talents. Glen Rounds left the magazine in 1942 but sent the cover design, "He's in the Army," for January 1944, showing himself in uniform with a bayonette and surrounded by children and dogs.

With wartime shortages *Story Parade* was condensed to conserve paper and printing materials. Its paper was thinner and its size was reduced from about sixty to forty-eight pages. Text was arranged into two columns a page, and borders became narrow, with less white space between the lines of type.

More distressing than these physical changes was the wartime change of attitude that displaced the call for international understanding and brotherhood that had been so long the philosophy of *Story Parade*. A new monthly series, "Victor" by Dorothy and Nils Hogner, showed a dog named Victor and a cat named Puss discuss proper conduct for children during wartime. They echo Uncle Sam's motto, "Save, serve, conserve," as they explain how children could donate copper pennies to be converted into ammunition and how they might help their mothers save kitchen fat that could be made into glycerine for use in explosives. A poem, "Waste Fats," was contributed by a child and seemed to mark the beginning of the end of literary quality for *Story Parade*.

With the tenth volume (1945) the appearance of *Story Parade* changed again. This time, full-color illustrations printed in halftone were introduced, first on the covers, then on alternating pages, and finally throughout the magazine. Several pages of advertising were added, and the serious look of the 1930s began to be replaced by the cute look of the 1950s.

Ads for the newly developed Golden Books filled entire pages and the new series "Meet the Artist" introduced members of the Artists' and Writers' Guild who illustrated the Golden Books. Golden Book artists became the illustrators of *Story Parade*, including Feodor Rojankovsky, Gustaf Tenggren, and Richard Scarry. Bright colors and rosy smiles gave *Story Parade* a look that tried hard to be sweet and popular with the ever-increasing membership of the baby-boom generation.

When paper dolls became a regular feature in 1947, little girls could cut out smart fashions designed by Hilda Moche, and *Story Parade* had become more of a plaything than a literary magazine. Once the paper dolls had been cut out, it could be discarded, since it was no longer a fine magazine to be reread. In 1949 the summer issues were deleted, Disney stories were serialized, and crafts became a new feature of the magazine. *Story Parade's* self-image had changed, and its issues featured stories, pictures, comics, puzzles, cutouts, and recipes.

During the 1950s popularity and mass appeal were the qualities *Story Parade* sought for itself. Cartoons were regularly included, featuring the mascot Peter Penguin or the zany "Merry Mice." Full-color advertisements for Disney comics, Lionel trains, and other symbols of that decade filled several pages of each issue, whereas in its early years *Story Parade* had included only sedate ads for new books.

Even with its new format *Story Parade* did not continue long into the 1950s. In May 1953 general editor Lockie Parker was replaced by Lucille Ogle, an associate of Golden Books. Helen Jo Jasper assumed the new position of educational editor in November 1953. When *Story Parade* ceased publication in December 1954, its appearance and content were completely different from what they had been in 1936. But for its nineteen years of publication, *Story Parade* had featured the work of many authors and artists and distributed this work to a wide audience, making its mark on both the creators and the audience of children's literature.

Notes

1. *Story Parade*, January 1936, inside front cover.
2. Lou Labrant, "And She Did," *Elementary English Review* 20 (December 1943), 332-33.
3. Ibid.
4. Barbara Bader, *American Picturebooks from Noah's Ark to the Beast Within* (New York: Macmillan, 1976), 212.
5. Ibid., p. 148.
6. Ibid., pp. 140-41.

Information Sources

BIBLIOGRAPHY
Barbara Bader, *American Picturebooks from Noah's Ark to the Beast Within* (New York: Macmillan, 1976); Alice Dalgliesh, "Improvement in Juvenile Books," *Publishers Weekly* 118 (October 25, 1930), 1970-73; N. Edwards, "The Arts in Childhood," *Elementary School Journal* 47 (March 1947), 368-69; Lou LaBrant, "And She Did," *Elementary English Review* 20 (December 1943), 323-33.
INDEX SOURCES
Six-month indexes are in the June and December issues for volume 2 (1937) until volume 8 (June 1945).

LOCATION SOURCES
Bound volumes are in major public libraries, but final years of the periodical are difficult
to locate.

Publication History

MAGAZINE TITLE AND TITLE CHANGES
Story Parade (January 1936-December 1954).
VOLUME AND ISSUE DATA
Story Parade (vol. 1, no. 1-vol. 19, no. 10).
PUBLISHER AND PLACE OF PUBLICATION
Association for Arts in Childhood, New York (1936-1945); Story Parade, New York
(1946-1954).
EDITOR
Lockie Parker (January 1936-April 1953); Lucille Ogle (May 1953-December 1954).

John R. Edson

THE STUDENT AND SCHOOLMATE

The merger in 1855 of *The Student and Young Tutor*, which had begun publication
in 1846 under the editorship of N. A. Calkins and J. S. Denman, with *The Schoolmate*,* established in 1852 by A. R. Phippen, formed *The Student and Schoolmate
Magazine*. Its subtitle, *A Monthly Reader for School and Home Instruction*, "containing original dialogues, speeches, biography, history, travels, poetry, music,
science, anecdotes, problems, puzzles, etc.," accurately described the content emphasis pursued until the magazine's demise in 1872. Calkins and Phippen stated in
the editorial policy that their new publication would:

> provide teachers and scholars with a magazine that each month supplies
> fresh reading matter...to instruct young people how to read aloud. Not
> one in a dozen youth who graduate from public or private schools can
> read...[he] may be able to pronounce in monotonous succession, but that
> is not reading....A good reader must understand and feel the subject and
> make the printed page speak with the meaning of its author...not in a
> lifeless, unnatural way as to make the hearers yawn, but so as to cheer
> the weary hours of an invalid...causing him to forget all pain in the
> pleasure of following the reader through the maze of important news,
> terrible catastrophes, thrilling stories, business matters, comicalities and
> advertisements.[1]

To accomplish these goals *The Student and Schoolmate* contained in each
monthly issue, almost without fail, two unique features—a declamation and a
dialog. The declamations, selected from the best speeches of the day, were
accompanied by a chart of directions for practicing "Emphasis, Tone, Inflection,
and Gesture." A two- or three-page dialog, or play, helped students not to

become actors but to learn to read effectively by assuming the role of a fictitious character. Speaking was considered a useful and necessary exercise for boys, and the two features gave them an opportunity to win elocution prizes at contests. These features also provided writers with the opportunity to reflect on events in the world outside the schoolroom while instilling certain moral and patriotic beliefs in their youthful readers.

Declamation titles ("The Two Armies" by Oliver Wendell Holmes, "The Martyrdom of Perpetua" by Rev. S. G. Bulfinch, "The Union" by Daniel Webster) and dialog subject matter (patriotism, grammar, short-hand parsing, astronomy, nature, secession) reflect the editorial influence of William T. Adams after he became sole editor in 1857. From time to time Adams, who seems to have written many of the dialogs, received criticism of his selections, but he defended them, and although he respected the opinions of the complainers, he asked to be pardoned "for using his own judgment in the matter."[2]

Later dialogs acknowledged female students and courted their readership with titles such as "The Sewing Lesson," "The Model Husband," and "The Widow and Her Son." One of the most unusual dialogs appeared in April and May 1860 under the title "One Hundred Years Hence." The main character, Miss Rip Van Winkle, while conducting a class in phrenology (a reflection of the popularity of the fad), discussed with her students the two primary head bumps of progression and locomotion. Boys were later invited into her class to answer questions about future events in the country. Their prediction was that "one hundred years hence" Madam Hesperiana Bloomero would be president of the United States, succeeding ten previous lady presidents. The population would reach 700 million in the twentieth century, and 10 trillion boxes of Russia Salve would have been sold! This brief excursion into futurism was unique for *The Student and Schoolmate*. The focus of almost all other stories, poems, essays, biographies, and occasional pieces was on the practical, materialistic world and how the student could become an honest, hardworking citizen.

Although the first editors believed "every 'student' likes to have a 'schoolmate' and all 'schoolmates' should be good 'students,' " they also expected their magazine "to cheer. . .the fireside by their friendly visits and pleasant instruction."[3] Consequently, home subscriptions were welcome, even if no attempt was made to publish material particularly for parents or very young children.

Throughout the years *The Student and Schoolmate* changed little in size or format. Unlike *The Youth's Companion*,* *Merry's Museum*,* and *Oliver Optic's Magazine*,* the pages, with the exception of "The Teacher's Desk and Our Museum," were not divided into columns, and the number varied only from thirty-two in 1855 to forty-eight in 1872. The print was small, with the density of the page relieved by an occasional crude, two- to three-inch engraving, sometimes placed on its side. More frequent and larger illustrations are found in later years, but no color was ever used in them. The editor explained, in the October 1861 issue, the technique of engravings (copper, steel, wood, or stone) "by which the magazine is made more pleasing" but did not give credit to the artists who furnished the illustrations. He believed that "interesting reading matter was most desired" by readers; therefore, illustrations by Thomas Nast, F.O.C. Darley, Gaston Fay, John La Farge, and Gustave Doré, found in other magazines of the period and even in *Oliver Optic's Magazine*, do not appear in *The Student and Schoolmate*. Significant improvements in printing made possible an 1864 "steel portrait" of Oliver Optic and a "much-awaited photogravure of Paul Revere" frontispiece for the May 1869 issue. Subscription costs also varied little—from $1.00 for twelve issues in 1855 to $1.50 in 1866. Claiming to be "the only magazine to do this," at the end of the year subscribers could return their nonsoiled copies to the magazine office and, for 25¢, 45¢, and, later, $2.00, receive "an elegantly bound volume in neat cloth, with gilt backs."[4]

The Post Office Act of 1852 transferred postage costs from subscriber to publisher, resulting in lower rates and greater convenience but creating other problems. Subscribers sometimes failed to give notification of change of address or to pick up their copies from the post office, "leaving the publisher to pocket the loss and an insult besides."[5] The editor blamed no reader for being poor, but he believed that none was so poor that he could not inform the publisher of the inability to pay.

Explaining magazine delays, Adams, in his monthly chat with readers, would apologize for "a freshet which delayed the manufacture of our paper," or "the difficulty of procuring suitable paper," or a "severe and fatal illness in the family of the Boston editor." In words familiar even today, irregular magazine delivery was the fault of the post office, not the magazine office. Complaints about "former transactions of business affairs" were answered by an affirmation that "books are kept with a scrupulous air, which scarcely admits of a mistake."[6] A terse reply was given to a correspondent with these words: "Your insulting message on the cover of the March number does not inform us where you live."[7]

As is true of almost all children's magazines, circulation figures are either unavailable or unreliable. Adams reported a rapid increase in circulation in 1864 and in 1867 aimed to secure a circulation of 100,000 but did not tell if his efforts were successful. It seems that, for a time, agents contacted individual subscribers. But, again, the results are unknown. It also appears that the premium method of enlisting subscribers was tried during the early 1860s but abandoned in favor of the cash system of commissions for clubs. Since the premium lists were often printed on the magazine covers and the covers were not bound with the inside pages, it is difficult to determine the types of prizes and the conditions for earning them. However, the November 1866 issue shows that a reader could earn a seven-octave piano with carved legs and case for 500 new subscriptions and $625, a gold watch for 150 subscriptions and $130, and a color portrait of General Grant for 50¢ and 1 new subscriber. In 1871 the editor reaffirmed the policy of "no especial prizes for subscriptions" but rather the "design to give the worth of your money in the magazine."[8]

Authors who wrote for *The Student and Schoolmate* were, for the most part, almost unknown in the literary world. It was the editorial policy not to present a long array of names celebrated in other departments of literature but to encourage teachers and others who had a ''special fitness'' for a subject area. Except for serializations by Jacob Abbott and Sophie May and an occasional story or piece by L. Alcott, Grace Greenwood, Gail Hamilton, Jane Austin, E. Kellogg, Lucy Larcom, Catherine Trowbridge, and Caroline Hewins, most authors (for example, Christie Pearle, Lizzie Wood, H. Clay Preuss, Aitchpee, Myra Shattuck, Peter Pencil) are not represented even in other magazines of the period. A poem by Whittier, Longfellow, or Lowell broke with the stated goal of including only matter written expressly for *The Student and Schoolmate*.

However, two of its more prolific authors were to become famous: Horatio Alger, Jr., and editor William T. Adams. It is in *The Student and Schoolmate* that we find the original serialization of Alger's *Ragged Dick* (January 1867). Alger ended each monthly episode with a cliff-hanger, and Adams informed readers that ''Mr. Alger writes for no other juvenile magazine but the *Schoolmate*, exclusively.''[9] (Such practices must certainly have been helpful in assuring subscription renewals.) Only here could readers follow further adventures of Ragged Dick in ''Fame and Fortune'' (January 1868), ''Rough and Ready'' (January 1869), ''Rufus and Rose'' (January 1870), and ''Paul the Peddler'' (January 1871). Shorter Alger stories—including ''The Worst Boy in School,'' ''Sam's Adventures,'' ''The Rivals,'' ''Harry Lynch's Trip to Boston,'' and ''The King of the Playground''—and an occasional dialog preceded *Ragged Dick*. All were moralistic, but the middle-class Protestant values of piety, submissiveness, and diligence were gradually being replaced by the belief that success could be achieved through competition, aggressiveness, and perseverance (aided by the fortuitous arrival of a rich uncle or friend). Alger's writing style was flat and the dialog superficial, but he was a good storyteller.

Author William T. Adams (or ''Oliver Optic,'' as he signed most of his stories) found his magazine a useful outlet for his literary pursuits and for his self-imposed motto: first God, then country, then friends.[10] By 1859 the first feature in each issue was usually a serialized story by him. Clearly a prelude to the Alger stories and written primarily for boys, they included ''The Magic Lantern; or Winter Evening Lessons'' (January 1859), ''The Young Philosopher'' (January 1860), ''Frank Howard's Journey in the United States'' (July 1859), ''The Young Travelers''(January 1861), ''The Widow and Her Son: A New Year's Story'' (January 1862), the life adventures of Paul Clifford in ''Live and Learn'' (January 1863), ''Onward and Upward'' (July 1863), ''Trials and Triumphs'' (January 1864), ''Work and Play'' (July 1864), and ''Out in the World''(January 1865). The protagonist was often a young man who overcame personal difficulties or followed the example of an upright adult in order to become responsible and respectable. Although the girls in his stories were likely to be simple, faithful, and self-sacrificing, staying at home, praying for their brothers' safe return from war, and eagerly waiting to hear about their adventures, the girls who read the stories may have labored beside their brothers and father in a factory, on the farm, or in a cottage shop that day. In addition to the stories and dialogs, Adams wrote some of the essays (about military matters, travel, chemistry, lying, deceit, immigrants, and so on), biographies, and "filler pieces," which were brief prose articles varying in subject matter from "How the Japanese Fish" to the dangers of the careless use of firecrackers.

Adams is important to the history of children's periodicals for the use he made of *The Student and Schoolmate*. Through the selection of dialogs and speeches, music and poetry, essays and serialized stories, he molded the attitudes and minds of young readers subtly but firmly and effectively. It was in his chatty "Teacher's Desk and Our Museum" column (later to be called "Tangled Threads and, still later, "At Our Desk") that Adams extolled the proud men who "shouldered the musket in defence of the Flag of the Union" and informed readers of the progress of the Civil War.[11] From the time he saw events transpiring that could "deluge the country with blood" until the day he wrote "slavery is no more,"[12] the editor urged readers to be patriotic and to fight, not necessarily against the "barbarous institution" of slavery but "for the right to think and act like men."[13] One of the most unusual essays, written by Paul Creyton, was "More About Ants" (July 1861). Slavery was shown to exist even among various species of ants, where there were warriors and cowards as well as black ants who favored slavery no more than did humans. A curious but fascinating engraving, appropriately called "The Institution," accompanied the essay.

Adams firmly believed that the war would revive public virtue, and he did his utmost to instill in the minds of his "students" the courage necessary for the triumph of principles that, to him, were born of God and could not perish. No one was exempt from the duties of the hour of war: girls should sew, boys should carry wood and water, and all were to visit the orphans and widows. Especially sensitive to the historic character bequeathed by his forefathers, Adams hoped his readers would be "equal to the days that were trying men's souls."[14]

The titles of poetry ("The American Flag," "Battle of Bull Run," written by a twelve-year old boy), of songs ("The Dove of Peace," "Our Soldier Boys"), of dialogs ("Courage," "The Comedy of Secession," "Avoiding the Draft"), and of speeches ("Our Union Must Be Preserved") show how all-pervasive was the theme of patriotism. Few other secular or Sunday school magazines of the time were so editorially dedicated to a cause.

Concurrent with the emphasis on patriotism was Adams' commitment to temperance. One long poem was as much an exercise with words as it was a speech about temperance, using moderation, renovation, intoxication, ruination, deprivation, profanation, inebriation, persuasion, imitation, continuation, exultation, and so on—until its final consummation. In the dialog "The Demons of the Cup," Rushington, already intoxicated, enters a room demanding more whiskey. Fairy Little Toty tries to convince him of the evils of his ways and shows him Poverty and Crime at the bottom of the glass. Rushington sees the legion of demons and the error of his ways and asks instead for a temperance pledge— all within only three pages (December 1862). Subtle molding of malleable minds permeated most of the so-called literature for children in the nineteenth century. One would find it, too, in *The Student and Schoolmate* in stories such as "Corss and the Indians" by Francis Lee (September 1861), where the Indian "is a sly savage"; and "John Chinamen in California" by B. W. Putnam (June 1864), in which John was one of the "strange beings" of the Mongolian race, "a very funny creature who was always small and always yellow but industrious and orderly."[15]

Throughout the "Teacher's Desk" column, students learned items of news (Panama Canal progress, that boys could not coast on the streets of Grand Rapids in the winter, a Polar expedition, peace between Prussia and Austria, the assassination of Lincoln), discoveries (new planets, sixty-five chemical elements), and inventions (electric telegraph). Teachers were supplied "the rare and curious in literature and art" along with puzzles, enigmas, problems, conundrums, and other diversions common as evening entertainment in the homes of the nineteenth century. Although news details were omitted, readers of *The Student and Schoolmate* learned more about the world beyond the schoolroom than readers of most other magazines of the period. (*St. Nicholas** was to continue the practice in its "Watch Tower" column.)

In July 1860 Adams bemoaned the increase in the number of books being published. Horace Scudder, seven years later, was to echo the concern that people had too much rather than too little to read. Adams recommended that trashy books be avoided altogether and a good book be read attentively if it was worth reading at all. Skimming was considered "a pernicious habit."[16] To promote good reading, then, beginning in 1863 he devoted a portion of his editorial comments to "Our Book Table Page," reviewing Sophie May's *Little Prudy* and the Horatio Alger, Jr., books as well as *Helps to Education in the Homes of our Country* and Scott's *Ivanhoe* and the Waverley novels.

One other feature of *The Student and Schoolmate* is worthy of special attention. Early editors Phippen and Calkins believed there should be singing in school every day "to cheer our spirits, rest our minds, and purify and elevate our feelings."[17] They printed a series of music lessons in the original *Student*, and Adams, sharing the emphasis on music as "a welcome guest, in every society," continued to publish a song or piano piece in most monthly issues of *The Student and Schoolmate*. During the Civil War period, songs were patriotic; at other times the music reflected seasons of the year (spring, Christmas, vacation time, the New Year) or general interests (Sabbath Day, peace, wisdom, temperance, hope). Occasionally, an original, solo piano piece was printed, sometimes sideways on the page, presenting considerable problems for the young pianist. Music included a polka for the New Year, a duet to celebrate spring, a sleigh-bell march, Oliver Wendell Holmes's words sung to the tune of "My Country 'Tis of Thee" by 1,200 Boston schoolchildren at the Musical Festival on October 18, 1860, in honor of the visit of the Prince of Wales; the music was as varied as the composers represented (L. H. Southard, Alexander Clark, E. C. Howe, E. R. Blanchard, G. J. Webb, Thomas Magoun). Even more unusual was the inclusion in the editor's column of lists of recent music published by the O. Ditson Music Publishing Company.

Readers were encouraged to send for titles such as "The Cornflower Waltz," "L'Aspiration," "Keep the Ball a-Rolling," "O Sing Unto the Lord," and "The Milk-Maid in the Morning." What is noteworthy about this magazine feature is not the reputation of the composers or the quality of the music but the fact that Americans had money to spend on pianos and organs and leisure time in which to enjoy singing or playing a musical instrument.

Some interesting observations emerge from a careful scrutiny of *The Student and Schoolmate*. The magazine addressed itself primarily to a male student readership with series about travel, military matters, practices of the business world, themes of patriotism and temperance, and the emphasis on public speaking. Yet it included an unusual amount of poetry, even though it was poetry of instruction and admonition. Humor is lacking except in occasional witticisms such as "Noah Webster is the great Enchanter whose *spells* will never cease to affect our literature."[18] Absent also is literature of the imagination, the literary fairy tale (H. C. Andersen's tales were being printed in *The Riverside Magazine** between 1867 and 1870), the domestic tale, mythology, and correspondence from readers. The index to each volume reflected the editor's lack of concern for authors; titles were given but not until 1867 was the name of the writer included.

Adams, a traveler and always the master teacher, was determined in his attempt to reform his student readers, inculcating in them a humanitarian concern for society and an awareness of the contribution they might make to it. According to the *Dictionary of American Biography*, Adams relinquished his editorship in 1867 (when *Oliver Optic's Magazine** began publication);[19] however, nothing in either the "Teacher's Column" or on title pages confirms that fact. Reasons for the cessation of publication were not given by the editor, although in December 1871 he stated that his time was occupied as a juror in a criminal court, and he apologized for not outlining the course of the magazine for 1872. Reverting in the last issues to the original title, *The Schoolmate*, the magazine left its unique imprint on the middle or transition period of children's periodicals.

Notes

1. *The Student and Schoolmate Magazine* 1 (November 1855), 2.
2. Ibid., 10 (December 1861), 454.
3. Ibid., 1 (November 1855), 2.
4. Ibid., 8 (December 1859), 210.
5. Ibid., 14 (November 1864), 157.
6. Ibid., 9 (April 1860), 144.
7. Ibid., 15 (April 1865), 126.
8. Ibid., 27 (January 1871), 53.
9. Ibid., 23 (May 1869), 243.
10. *Cyclopaedia of American Literature*, ed. M. Laird Simms (Detroit: Gale Research Co., 1965), 2:878.

11. *The Student and Schoolmate Magazine* 10 (August 1861), 315.

12. Ibid., 15 (May 1865), 158.

13. Ibid., 10 (June 1861), 237.

14. Ibid., 12 (February 1863), 61.

15. Ibid., 13 (June 1864), 143.

16. Ibid., 9 (July 1860), 253.

17. Ibid., 1 (November 1855), 33.

18. Ibid., 8 (October 1859), 142.

19. *Dictionary of American Biography* (New York: Scribner's, 1928), 1:103. *American Authors 1600-1900: A Biographical Dictionary of American Literature*, ed. Stanley Kunitz and Howard Haycraft (New York: H. W. Wilson, 1938), 12.

Information Sources

BIBLIOGRAPHY

Betty L. Lyons, "A History of Children's Secular Magazines Published in the United States from 1789-1899" (Ph.D. diss., Johns Hopkins University, 1942); John Tebbel, *From Rags to Riches: Horatio Alger and the American Dream* (New York: Macmillan, 1963).

INDEX SOURCES

Indexed by volume (titles only through 1866; author and title thereafter).

LOCATION SOURCES

Vols. 1-28 (with the exception of vol. 5, nos. 3-5, and vol. 6, nos. 1-6) are in the Children's Literature Research Collection, University of Minnesota Libraries, Minneapolis; Vols. 1-30 are in the Library of Congress and Houghton Library, Harvard University, Cambridge, Mass.

Publication History

MAGAZINE TITLE AND TITLE CHANGES

The Student and Schoolmate Magazine: A Monthly Reader for School and Home Instruction (1855-1865); *The Student and Schoolmate, and Forrester's Boy's and Girl's Magazine* (1865-1866); *The Student and Schoolmate: An Illustrated Monthly, for All Our Boys and Girls* (1866); *The Student and Schoolmate: An Illustrated Monthly for Our Boys and Girls* (1867-1870); *The Student and Schoolmate: An Illustrated Monthly for Youth* (1871); *The Schoolmate: An Illustrated Monthly for Boys and Girls* (1872). (Caption title and title page are not always the same.)

VOLUME AND ISSUE DATA

The Student and Schoolmate Magazine: A Monthly Reader for School and Home Instruction (n.s. vol. 1, no. 1-vol. 14, no. 6); *The Student and Schoolmate, and Forrester's Boy's and Girl's Magazine* (vol. 15, no. 1-vol. 16, no. 6); *The Student and Schoolmate: An Illustrated Monthly, for All Our Boys and Girls* (vol. 17, no. 1-vol. 18, no. 6); *The Student and Schoolmate: An Illustrated Monthly for Our Boys and Girls* (vol. 19, no. 1-vol. 26, no. 6); *The Student and Schoolmate: An Illustrated Monthly for Youth* (vol. 27, no. 1-vol. 28, no. 6); *The Schoolmate: An Illustrated Monthly for Boys and Girls* (vol. 29, no. 1-vol. 30, no. 4).

PUBLISHER AND PLACE OF PUBLICATION

Robinson & Richardson, Boston; Calkins and Stiles, New York (1855-1856); James Robinson & Co., Boston (1857-1858); Robinson, Greene & Co., Boston (1859);

Messrs. Galen James & Co., Boston (1860-1862); Joseph H. Allen, Boston (1863-1872).

EDITOR

N. A. Calkins (1855-1857); N. A. Calkins (May 1857-November 1857); N. A. Calkins (December 1857); William T. Adams (January 1858-October 1872?).

Harriett R. Christy

SUNSHINE FOR YOUTH: ALSO FOR THOSE OF ALL AGES WHOSE HEARTS HAVE NOT WITHERED

The title *Sunshine for Youth: Also for Those of All Ages Whose Hearts Have Not Withered* might lead the reader to infer that the publisher, Edward Charles Allen of E. C. Allen and Company, was a sentimental man. However, publishing history reveals him as a man with an astonishing amount of hard-headed acumen. After devising a soap formula that he parlayed into thousands of dollars by an unusual distribution device, he went into publishing and succeeded by selling to the public what it wanted. When he started publishing *Sunshine*, he was already publishing two successful periodicals: *People's Literary Companion* and *National Farmer and Home Magazine*. Both of these papers were used to advertise Allen's mail-order soap business and to sell advertisements of companies that sold their products by mail.

On March 3, 1887, the postal act provided second-class mailing privileges to magazines of this sort. This decade was a propitious time to start another periodical, this one with a new audience in mind—juveniles. *Sunshine* began publication in 1886 as a monthly, selling for 50¢ a year, or 25¢ for new subscribers, or 5¢ for a single copy.

Sunshine started out boldly and confidently in its bid for young readers. In one of its first issues the rules for writers for the periodical were spelled out: "1. Be sure you have something to say. 2. Say it. 3. Then stop—short. Also remember that you must write up—not *down* to the intelligence of the bright American boys and girls."[1] In addition, the publisher solicited the aid of teachers: "A word to teachers. *Sunshine* wants your help and means to be worthy of your friendship. Say a good word for it when you honestly can; and why not use it as a reader in your school occasionally."[2]

Inducements to young readers were offered for continued reading. Club premiums that would be given for getting new subscribers were announced. This had proved to be a great money getter ever since the Civil War. Authors of prominence who would appear on the pages of *Sunshine* were announced. They were not writers well known for their writing for juveniles, but they were known in the newspaper and magazine business. Some of these people were Thomas F. Willson, editor of the *New York Weekly World*; Will K. Norton, Mrs. Margaret Hamilton; and J. W. Burgess. Testimonials were also included. Mary E. Vandyne, former editor of *Harper's Young People*,* was quoted as saying, "This bright little *Sunshine* will be popular and permanent.''[3] Another quote, probably from the publisher himself, was, "Every boy and girl who can read English will find something interesting in the October *Sunshine*.''[4]

Columns, departments, and adventure-packed serials began that would sustain reader interest. ''Uncle Ned's Easy Chair'' department announced that $5 would be awarded to the boy or girl who submitted the best letter about the best and worst thing that George Washington had ever done. The reader was told that the contest was limited to subscribers; however, if the entry was accompanied by 25¢, the letter would be considered. In addition, money would be awarded for solutions to puzzles that would appear regularly. Some of the regular departments that appeared were ''History Made Easy,'' ''Stamps and Coins,'' ''Familiar Astronomy,'' and ''Boys Who Began on the Farm.'' The latter featured men whose early life began on farms and who as adults achieved spectacular success. Some of them were Horace Greeley, Robert Burns, Andrew Jackson, Daniel Webster, and Abraham Lincoln, who according to the writer, ''took a newspaper regularly, paid for it in advance, and got a vast amount of comfort and benefit out of it.''[5]

Underlying most stories, features, and nonfiction was the premise that hard work can lead to success, particularly for farm boys. This philosophy was most prominent in the ''Boys Who Began on the Farm'' series, but much of the filler material, including poetry, also underscored this philosophy. P. T. Barnum wrote a letter to *Sunshine* outlining how to get ahead. The editor gave examples of success and salaries; however, the editor reminded his readers, ''remember success is accomplished by hard work, sterling honesty to yourself and to your fellow man.''[6] Just in case some boys weren't sure of the avenue to success, the editor ran an advertisement that said, ''I was at work on a farm for $20 a month. I now have an agency for E. C. Allen and Co.'s publication and often make $20 a day.''[7]

When success came to a farm boy, he would be prepared for life by features such as ''What Millionaires Eat.'' So it was that E. C. Allen, the entrepreneur, promulgated the philosophy that the way to success could be achieved by anyone with hard work, honesty, and so on. In so doing, he made money from both *Sunshine* and his mail-order business.

Most of the material in *Sunshine* was unsigned or written by its staff although well-known names appeared occasionally in its pages. Some reprints and some original material by notables such as John Trowbridge, Lucy Larcom, Edward Everett Hale, Emily Huntington Miller, Margaret E. Sangster, Eugene Field, and Henry W. Longfellow appeared. Some writers who were connected with national and international newspapers were also contributors: Foster Coates, managing editor of the New York *Mail and Express*; and Henry Hanie, Paris correspondent of the *Boston Herald*. Artists who contributed were F. A. Feraud of the New York *Graphic* and Mrs. Jessie Shepherd of *Harper's Young People*. The writer of whom *Sunshine* seemed to be most proud was Rose Elizabeth Cleveland, sister to the president of the United States. Each time her name appeared, the statement of her relationship to the president always appeared, which would lead one to suspect that the quality of her writing was not the most significant thing about her publication.

During the first year of *Sunshine's* publication the slant seemed to be toward adolescent rural boys, but during the second year more material appeared that would interest girls and women. A new contest was begun, "What is a Lady?" and "What is a Gentleman?" This had proved to be a popular contest with *Our Young Folks,** and *Sunshine* was using all of the formulas that had proved successful with juvenile periodicals of the preceding two decades. Some of the articles that would interest female readers were "A Venerable Woman Teacher," "She Didn't Go to the White House," Spain's Baby King's Sister," and "Fashions for the Fair."

Articles that would appeal to older females were about household management and fashions: "Worth Remembering Household Hints," "No More Birds in the Bonnet," "Etiquette of Calling Cards," "Homey Kitchens," "Homey Kitchen Art of Dishwashing," "The Indispensable Boa," and "Women Wage Earner."

The articles reflect the social history of the United States at the end of the nineteenth century. The patronizing attitude toward the Irish was revealed in "Molly" by Frank Sweet, a story about an Irish maid trying to save money for her family. Another story was "Wah Fing," about a Chinese boy who lived in Chinatown in a large western town. The author said, "The chinamen seemed never to have wasted any time in the praiseworthy occupations of 'Cleaning up their houses.'[8] Attitudes toward the South are revealed in stories such as a "Noble Southern Boy" and "Johnny Reb." In the Thanksgiving issue of that first year was a large cartoon showing people of various nationalities eating Thanksgiving dinner at the same table.

The role of women at that time was in a state of flux. Articles and features reflected the ambiguity of women's role in American society. Household, fashion, and etiquette hints appeared regularly; however, the column "About Women" indicated that women, too, could achieve success. The how-to-achieve success formula was never spelled out in detail for women, but instances were cited of women entering business and the professions: "Miss Helen Gould has read law and did she desire, could pass the examination entrance to the New York bar." "Lady Randolph Churchill, who was Miss Jerome, of New York, is about to start a quarterly journal." "Miss Caroline Hazard, the new President of Wellesley College, is herself not a college graduate. She is forty-two years old." "Miss Sara Bernhardt is highly ecstatic over her Hamlet which she says is entirely her own creation."[9] Such items, juxtaposed with articles about how to set a nice table and under what circumstances a woman should leave a calling card, reflected the gradually widening opportunities for women at the turn of the century.

With the August-September issue of 1894 *Sunshine's* publisher E. C. Allen and Company was taken over by S. W. Lane and Co. On the first page the new publishers announced that they had purchased *Daughters of America* and that *Sunshine* would be sent to the subscribers of *Daughters of America* for the remainder of the subscription. Lest the agents and subscribers worry about the future of *Sunshine*, the new editor and publisher ran the following advertisement:

> E. C. Allen and Co., who formerly were publishers in this city, retired from the business world—amassing property worth one million dollars. S. W. Lane, resident of Augusta for nearly 30 years, has held many offices in the city, was city treasurer and collector for a number of years, twice elected mayor, almost unanimously, against his expressed wishes. He now represents the city in the State legislature. He was the first to gain confidence and personal friendship of the late E. C. Allen, the founder of *Allen's Lists*, at the very beginning of his famous career.[10]

In this issue a full page was devoted to fashion for the first time. A notable woman appeared on the first page of a number of issues. Articles on fine ironing, the culture of flowers, discontented children, and the making of lace multiplied, and stories and articles for youth began to disappear.

A new kind of writer began to be advertised in forthcoming issues. Serialized stories of Mrs. E. Burke Collins, Ella Stratton, Sylvanus Cobb, and Charlotte Braeme (sometimes under the pseudonym of Bertha M. Clay) started appearing. They were excessively sentimental, dramatic stories with illustrations to match the content. A typical example is Ella H. Stratton's "Starved." The last paragraph reads, "Tearful faces encircled the form of the little heroine, but Hetty did not heed them. She had found that for which her lonely heart had hungered, and was at rest. Hetty was dead, and mother and child were reunited."[11]

Many stories had as their theme women who had to fend for themselves because of selfish, drunken, or deceased husbands. Margaret Burnham in "Broken Down Wives" said, "husbands don't realize the hard work women do."[12] In one article the classes of husbands are listed as "some of the poor bargains in the matrimonial treadmill," and the author went on to say that "if I had my way, a law should be passed that no woman could marry before she was 26 years old."[13] In Sarah E. Gannett's story "The Lost Rent Money" the readers find "in two rooms— 8 people—a drunken father, a hard-working overburdened mother, and six little children."[14] The portrait of the father as a less noble character than the mother had long been a staple of juvenile literature.[15]

In the last ten years of *Sunshine* new columns were added. Some of them were "Bed and Bedding," "The Library," "The Garden," "The Home," "Farm and Garden." Occassionally, the editors would publish a short story and poem for boys and girls. At times a full page would be a piece of sheet music with titles such as "My Old New England Home" and "Don't Take Away My Little Home." The editor had a column in which he addressed problems of education, morals, and current events. *Sunshine* had become a household magazine.[16]

Reader involvement was encouraged in "Letters from Home Workers" and popularity contests between the serials. Subscription rates were reduced to 10¢

a year. Club premiums now were the kind that would appeal to readers of the sensational reading of the time. The books of Charlotte Braeme and Charles Garvice were offered free with two new subscriptions.

New serial adventure storywriters appeared—some original and some reprints. They included serials by Frank Stockton, Col. Prentiss Ingraham, Oliver Optic (pseudonym of William T. Adams), Roger Starbuck (pseudonym of Augustus Comstock), and Horatio Alger. *Sunshine* now numbered about twenty-five pages with at least nine of them devoted to advertisements.

The last two years of *Sunshine's* life were frenzied in its frantic appeal to subscribers. Advertisements increased in number and vulgarity. An example is one for Wolcott's Pain Paint. The rhyme that accompanied the advertisement was the E. C. Allen and Horatio Alger philosophy in its most blatant form:

GET AHEAD

> The greatest curse is poverty
> The torment to the mind
> I want to earn quick money
> Some honest wealth to find
>
> To work and dig I'm willing
> And strike a manly blow
> If so I win a fortune
> And get my share of dough.[17]

The bill that Congress passed in 1907 that excluded mail order periodicals whose subscriptions were not paid in advance sounded the death knell for periodicals such as *Sunshine*.[18] What had started out as in interesting although not distinguished periodical for youth and adult rural lower-income readers had deteriorated into a cheap story paper for a mail-order house.

Notes

1. *Sunshine for Youth* 1 (January 1887), 4.
2. Ibid.
3. Ibid., 1 (September 1887), 6.
4. Ibid.
5. Ibid., 2 (April 1888), 4.
6. Ibid., 1 (August 1887), 6.
7. Ibid., 1 (April 1887), 2.
8. Ibid., 7 (January 1893), 9.
9. Ibid., 13 (September 1829), 12.
10. Ibid., 8 (August-September 1894), 15.
11. Ibid., 9, (November 1895), 1.
12. Ibid., 13 (June 1899), 11.
13. Ibid., p. 12.
14. Ibid., 13 (March 1899), 1.

15. Ann Scott MacLeod, *A Moral Tale: Children's Fiction and American Culture, 1820-1860* (Hamden, Conn.: Archon Books, 1975), 130.

16. *American Newspaper Directory* (New York: G. P. Rowell and Co., 1907), 1484.

17. *Sunshine for Youth* 16 (October 1902), 11.

18. Theodore P. Greene, *America's Heroes* (New York: Oxford University Press, 1970), 62.

Information Sources

BIBLIOGRAPHY

Jane Bingham and Grayce Scholt, *Fifteen Centuries of Children's Literature* (Westport, Conn.: Greenwood Press, 1980); R. Gordon Kelly, *Mother Was a Lady* (Westport, Conn.: Greenwood Press, 1974); Ann Scott MacLeod, *A Moral Tale: Children's Fiction and American Culture, 1820-1860* (Hamden, Conn.: Archon Books, 1975); Frank Luther Mott, *A History of American Magazines*, 5 vols. (Cambridge: Harvard University Press, 1938-1968); Mary Noel, *Villains Galore* (New York: Macmillan, 1954); Selma K. Richardson, ed., *Research About Nineteenth-Century Children and Books: Portrait Studies*, monograph no. 17 (Urbana-Champaign, Ill.: University of Illinois, Graduate School of Library Science, 1980); John Tebbel, *The American Magazine* (New York: Hawthorn Books, 1969).

INDEX SOURCES

None.

LOCATION SOURCES

Vols. 1-21 are in the Library of Congress and at Bowdoin College, Brunswick, Maine. Vols. 1-21 are available on microfilm from Greenwood Press, Westport, Conn.

Publication History

MAGAZINE TITLE AND TITLE CHANGES

Sunshine for Youth: Also for Those of All Ages Whose Hearts Have Not Withered (1886-1907).

VOLUME AND ISSUE DATA

Sunshine for Youth: Also for Those of All Ages Whose Hearts Have Not Withered (vol. 1, no. 1-vol. 21, no. 10).

PUBLISHER AND PLACE OF PUBLICATION

E. C. Allen and Company, Augusta, Maine (1886-1894); S. W. Lane and Co., Augusta, Maine (1894-1897); Lane's List Incorporated, Augusta, Maine (1897-1907).

EDITOR

Samuel W. Lane (1886-1894); none listed (1894-1907).

Mary Kelly Isbell

T

'TEEN MAGAZINE

'Teen Magazine began monthly publication in June 1957. From a beginning circulation of about 300,000 and a subscription price of $3, 'Teen has grown to a circulation of slightly less than 1 million and a subscription price of $9. Catering to teenage girls (thirteen to eighteen), the magazine has been described by Bill Katz and Barry Richards's *Magazines for Libraries* as "popular, well done, and recommended for most collections" and "one of the best teen-age magazines on the market today."[1] The periodical seeks to be both informative and entertaining. The editors' philosophy acknowledges the reader's integrity; the editorial choices demonstrate a desire to provide guidance in keeping with conventional mores and the expanding choices open to women today while stressing individual responsibility for one's own life.

Since fashion and beauty are among the major interests of most teenage girls, articles about these subjects make up roughly one-third of the magazine. At least one article about fashion trends or fashion use, exercise, or diet is included in each issue. Other self-improvement explanations treat topics like hair care, makeup application, and individual analysis of physical attributes. The content of these core articles has remained relatively unchanged throughout the years, variety being provided by superficial shifts in fashion and the introduction of new products. Although freelance contributions are solicited, nearly all of the feature articles are staff written. All reflect careful research.

Feature articles frequently build on these basic themes of fashion, exercise, and diet. An article might, for example, explore one facet of the way diet influences health. Medical subjects of primary interest to women (toxic shock syndrome, for instance) are included frequently and presented honestly and straightforwardly, written to be accessible even to the younger audience without being condescending. Emphasis is on clear information and taking responsibility for one's own health and behavior.

Feature articles often parallel those of magazines aimed at adult women audiences. The intermittent "Buy Wise," for instance, outlines shopping considerations for a particular appliance, like stereo equipment or hair dryers, thus serving a consumer education function. Dealing constructively with strong emotions is a recurring topic: jealousy, loss of a friend, anger—these emotions can be as strong in teenagers as adults. The same social themes featured in adult magazines find their place here too; quality of life and mainstreaming the handicapped affect teenagers sometimes even more than they affect adults.

Other feature articles are more clearly aimed at a teenage audience. "Career Classified," a recurring feature, describes an occupation, its attractions for particular personalities and talents, and the educational requirements for entering the profession. Articles aimed directly at nurturing the intellect are likely to be focused on practical and immediate applications like study habits or on personal benefits from "academic" pursuits like writing poetry or keeping a diary. General adjustment topics, like adapting to a new environment, are given a setting geared specifically to teens, like adjusting to changing school and how to behave as "the new girl."

Since fashion plays such a large part in the magazine, photography is a key element. Photographs to accompany freelance articles are solicited, but every photograph included meets professional standards.

One of the magazine's most appealing features is the emphasis on responding to reader requests and publishing reader contributions. Several "Dear—" columns offer one avenue of reader expression. "Dear Beauty Editor," for example, invites reader questions on personal grooming and dress. Questions included in the column are those likely to be of interest to a sizeable segment of the readership and those that can be answered briefly. Sometimes the answers refer to specific products. "Dear Jack" and "Dear Jill" columns done singly sometimes and sometimes together respond to reader questions about behavior and relationship problems. These answers are usually limited to the obvious advice, but when a problem is especially serious or complex, Jack and Jill do not hesitate to recommend seeking more specific aid from a trusted counselor, clergyman, or other professional. "Dear Doctor" answers the predictably recurring questions about a young woman's maturing body and also queries about diseases of all sorts from the common cold to cancer, various kinds of treatments from bed rest to surgery, and health maintenance from megavitamin therapy to frequency of medical examinations.

"We Get" letters to the editor is another constant call for reader response. Both praise and blame are included along with readers' general comments about current events as they affect their lives. From time to time a questionnaire asks readers to speak out on a subject of broad impact. The topics range from personal, such as attitudes toward and information about families, to controversial issues, such as abortion. The results of the questionnaires are reported in a later issue.

Another reader-controlled spot is the guest editor column, which replaces the earlier practice of the cameo article on a "Terrific Teen." In this column the young woman's accomplishments are summarized, and she is invited to speak for herself to the readers. Usually, she explains how she got started in her special interest and suggests ways others can achieve similar satisfaction.

"Rhyme and Reason" presents original poetry from readers. Quality of the verse varies enormously. The column provides a good demonstration of the versatility of poetry as teens express their feelings and opinions in verse about everything from the meaning of life to food preferences.

Other occasions are found to celebrate individual readers. The search for a 'Teen Model of the Month/Year, through photographs submitted by readers, gives an opportunity to highlight many girls. Outstanding achievements of teens are sometimes made the focal point of an article. A teen's substantial weight loss, for instance, serves to inform and to inspire readers.

One short story is included in each issue. From the outset, consistently good fiction has been one of the highlights of the magazine. As a former 'Teen fiction editor remarked, "We take only top quality fiction. Our readers deserve the best."[2] Early suggestions to potential contributors stressed sound plot construction and variety. Later editors added encouragement to consider controversial ideas and to experiment with form. The changes in young adult literature since the 1950s are mirrored in 'Teen. Themes include the standard interests in boy-girl and parent-teen relations, but they also include characters grappling with problems of divorce and death. Plots involve the decisions young women must make. Denouements frequently point toward traditional choices, but more recent outcomes show a broader range of options considered available.

The " 'Teen Inquirer" section focuses on entertainment personalities. Articles about stars of movies and television shows answer fans' questions about the real person behind the screen image. Two things reflect the specific audience here: the youth of the stars most often featured and the air time of the television shows featured (after school). Musical entertainers are usually from the popular field and are obviously young. This relatively small section of the magazine (marked by a change in paper quality from slick to pulp) further draws the movie-magazine audience by including a section of addresses for fan mail to be directed to individual stars.

'Teen has other standard features. The monthly horoscope begins with a general personality profile of the dominant sign. For people born under each zodiac sign, specific predictions and recommendations for the month follow.

Advertising is a predictably constant aspect of the magazine. "Flea Market" compiles special short ads of products and services of the sort included in many women's magazines. Regular advertisers include those aimed at a general audience, like record clubs. Most advertise fashion, grooming, and feminine hygiene products. Although topics such as premarital sex and use of controlled substances like alcohol and tobacco are candidly discussed in the magazine, the absence of advertisements associated with these products reflects both the general editorial policy and the legal implications of the ages of the intended audience.

Notes

1. Bill Katz and Barry G. Richards, *Magazines for Libraries*, 3rd ed. (New York: R. R. Bowker, 1978), 838.
2. Personal interview with fiction editor Betty Price, December 31, 1966.

Information Sources

BIBLIOGRAPHY
None.
INDEX SOURCES
Biography Index, Readers Guide to Periodical Literature.
LOCATION SOURCES
Bound volumes of the last decade are in many public libraries. All issues are available on microfilm from University Microfilms International, Ann Arbor, Mich.

Publication History

MAGAZINE TITLE AND TITLE CHANGES
'Teen Magazine (1957-).
VOLUME AND ISSUE DATA
'Teen Magazine (vol. 1, no. 1-).
PUBLISHER AND PLACE OF PUBLICATION
Petersen Publishing Company, Los Angeles (1957-).
EDITOR
Since the inception of the magazine, the editor, managing editor, and/or publisher (variously titled) has been either Robert Petersen or Robert Macleod. Others serving as editor include Charles Laufer (1960-1965); Cathie Mann (1973-1977); and Roxanne Camron (1977-).

Dixie Elise Hickman

TIP TOP WEEKLY: AN IDEAL PUBLICATION FOR YOUTH

"It Tops Everything" as a slogan for *Tip Top Weekly* was most appropriate, since the first issue of Street and Smith's new half-dime weekly for juvenile readers sold out completely. The immediate success of the thirty-two-page magazine may be attributed in part to its accessibility on newsstands via wide distribution by railway, its attractive format and price, and the appealing title; however, the introduction of Frank Merriwell, a fine student and a natural athlete, was foremost in making this publication so popular.

Tip Top Weekly retained some of the basic characteristics of the dime novel, for it was a weekly library (series) with each issue containing a complete story about the same hero. Beginning with issue no. 1 on April 18, 1896, reader interest in *Tip Top Weekly* focused on the continuous, developing role of Frank Merriwell; such character portrayal and development was unusual in this type of periodical. Frank excelled in all sports during his years at a prep school, at Yale University, and on his worldwide travels. These school-sports stories intrigued thousands of American youth each week for sixteen years as they followed the adventures of Frank, his brother Dick, and eventually his son Frank Merriwell, Jr.

Tip Top Weekly became a most profitable business venture for the well-established New York publishers, Street and Smith; and their selection of Gilbert Patten as the author of the series was most fortunate. In a letter to Patten on December 16, 1895, O. G. Smith, one of Street and Smith's owners, outlined the framework for a new series for boys and requested that Patten consider writing it. He stressed that the series should include a hero with a catchy name, concern a young man at boarding school (military or naval academy), and have some minor characters who speak in dialect. After episode twelve, the hero must leave school, attain some money and travel, and be accompanied by a school friend and a professor. A romantic interest was acceptable but not essential. Later the hero was to enter college (perhaps Yale University) and then travel again.[1]

An experienced writer of dime novels, Gilbert Patten accepted the assignment. In deciding on a suitable name for the hero, Patten stated in his autobiography: "And then, suddenly, I had it—Frank Merriwell! The name was symbolic of the chief characteristics I desired my hero to have—*Frank* for frankness, *merry* for a happy disposition, *well*, for health and abounding vitality."[2]

Although he complied with O. G. Smith's specifications for the new series, Patten was a capable, imaginative writer. In his autobiography he discussed his own goals in creating the weekly stories.

> As the first issues were to be stories of American school life, I saw in them an opportunity to feature all kinds of athletic sports, with baseball, about which I was best informed, predominating.
>
> Such stories would give me an opportunity to preach—by example— the doctrine of a clean mind and healthy body. And also, unlike the old dime novel writers, I would attempt to present even minor characters in such a manner that the readers could visualize them clearly. With me, plot would be secondary to character depiction as far as I could make it and still write a story of interesting action and suspense.[3]

The publishers accepted the first story, "Frank Merriwell; or First Days at Fardale," in which Frank begins his adventures as a cadet at the military academy but stated that they would not start the library until they had ten numbers and were assured of adequate material; and they reminded Patten that the name of Frank Merriwell was to be one of their copyrights.[4]

Patten chose the pseudonym Burt L. Standish and used it exclusively with *Tip Top Weekly*. For sixteen years he wrote almost all of the 850 issues of the magazine. When he had another assignment, he continued to supervise each issue of *Tip Top*.[5]

Unfamiliar with life at a military school or university, Patten did a great deal of research to make each of Frank's experiences as realistic as possible. The stories must have seemed authentic enough to readers, for by the third month of publication, circulation was 75,000.[6] In regard to later circulation figures for the long-lived magazine, Charles Bragin stated: "Publishers never revealed their sales, but we estimate that the *Tip Top Weekly* Merriwell stories had a circulation up to a million copies weekly, with Buffalo Bill, Nick Carter, and Diamond Dick series not far behind."[7]

Each story title was compound and indicative of a specific adventure with an added clue about plot, location, or character. Each of the 850 titles (1896-1912) reveals the progressive activities of the Merriwells. Examples of titles are no. 45, "Frank Merriwell's Great Run; or Trouncing the Tigers" (1897); no. 279; "Frank Merriwell's Twirler; or Dick Merriwell's Jump Ball" (1901); no. 795, "Dick Merriwell's Commencement; or The Last Week at Yale" (1911). At the conclusion of each story, the title of the next issue was announced, undoubtedly to ensure good sales for the following week. Also, this device served as a transition between episodes and added continuity to the entire series.

Written in a lucid, simple style, each series episode of about 20,000 words teamed with action, mystery, interesting characters, and entanglements. The character given the most depth was Frank, a born leader who demonstrates good sportsmanship and unsurpassed athletic prowess. Most perceptive in making judgments, he can deal with human relations successfully whether at home or in a foreign land. Throughout the series Patten emphasized the importance of integrity and self-esteem, the worth of the individual, and personal achievement. These values, conveyed through the attitudes and conduct of the Merriwells, gave credibility to the characters, heroic stature to the American sports figure, and a distinct identity to *Tip Top Weekly*.

Because the majority of the stories occurred during the terms of the school year, readers were aware of Frank's age. If the author permitted Frank to graduate from Yale, *Tip Top Weekly* might lose many younger readers and loyal sports fans. To vary the series, Patten had Frank leave Yale after his third year, travel extensively, discover an unknown half-brother, Dick, and then return to Yale as a senior.[8] To retain the school and sports scenes, Patten had Dick Merriwell, a superior athlete, repeat the Fardale-travel-Yale pattern. Frank was the hero in the first 274 issues; Dick appeared in no. 275; and the "Dick Merriwell at Fardale" series began with no. 285 (August 17, 1901). To comply with reader demand *both* Frank and Dick were featured in the rest of the series.

There was not a consistent scheme in using either of the titles *Tip Top Weekly* and *Tip Top Library* on the cover and on the first page of the first forty-five numbers. Because of an increased postal rate for *library* weeklies, the word

Library was dropped; and only *Tip Top Weekly* was used in subsequent issues. The subtitle on all numbers was *An Ideal Publication for Youth*. Author credit varied; some issues indicated "By Burt L. Standish," but others specified "By the Author of Frank Merriwell." Often the two forms were used interchangeably in the same issue. Copies of *Tip Top Weekly* were sold at newsstands or by mail subscription, and readers could purchase individual back issues or buy *Tip Top Quarterly*, which had thirteen issues bound together.

Only nominal changes were made in the its format over the years. *Tip Top* remained 7 by 10 inches until no. 265 (May 4, 1901), when it became 8 by 11 inches.[9] All covers, from the earliest editions in blue and white and later issues in full color, were illustrated with a crucial scene from the story. Although there were no illustrations in the text, later numbers had small designs (often portraits of the main characters) adjacent to the title on page 1.

Eventually, some regular departments were included on pages following the weekly story. "Applause" gave readers the opportunity to laud the merits of the magazine and Frank. Another popular form of reader involvement was Professor Fourmen's column in which inquiries could be made about physical fitness. Many contests oriented toward the interests of sports-minded boys offered substantial prizes to individuals and teams for athletic skills and records. Literary competition involved suggesting a plot for an issue of *Tip Top* or writing an essay about a favorite character other than Frank.

Gradually, the magazine began to decline, however. Frank had married Inza, the girl he met during his days at Fardale; and he and Dick were no longer active in college sports. As the characters matured, readers lost interest. The last issue of the sixteen-year run of the magazine was no. 850 (July 27, 1912), "Dick Merriwell's Marathon; or How the Last Olympic Mile Brought Victory. The next week the first issue of *New Tip Top Weekly* appeared, featuring Frank Merriwell, Jr., a new cadet at Fardale Academy. Gilbert Patten did not write this series, however.

Although *Tip Top Weekly* was replaced by other popular literature that reflected the interests and values of a different era, Frank was not forgotten. New generations continued to read the many books that contained reprints of the Merriwell stories. For years, Gilbert Patten received thousands of letters concerning Frank, and a number of correspondents claimed that the stories had influenced them to attend college.[10] Contemporary writers marvel at the fictitious Frank's great triumphs at Yale, and sports announcers refer to a brilliant, winning last-minute play as a "Frank Merriwell finish." The legend of the All-American hero from *Tip Top Weekly* lives on.

Notes

1. Gilbert Patten, *Frank Merriwell's "Father": An Autobiography by Gilbert Patten ("Burt L. Standish")*, ed. Harriet Hinsdale and Tony London (Norman, Okla.: University of Oklahoma Press, 1964), 174-76.

2. Ibid., p. 177.

3. Ibid., pp. 178-79.

4. Quentin Reynolds, *The Fiction Factory; or From Pulp to Quality Street* (New York: Random House, 1955), 90.

5. Gerald J. McIntosh, "More Books and Stories by Gilbert Patten," *Dime Novel Round-Up* 37 (March 15, 1968), 25.

6. James M. Cain, "The Man Merriwell," *Saturday Evening Post* 199 (June 11, 1927), 129.

7. Charles Bragin, *Bibliography: Dime Novels, 1860-1964* (New York: Privately printed, 1964), [2].

8. Cain, "Merriwell," p. 132.

9. Floyd L. Beagle, *"Blood and Thunders"; or Dime Novels of the 80's and 90's* (n.p., n.d.), n.p.

10. Gilbert Patten, "Dime Novel Days," *Saturday Evening Post* 203 (March 7, 1931), 60.

Information Sources

BIBLIOGRAPHY

Floyd L. Beagle, *"Blood and Thunders"; or Dime Novels of the 80's and 90's* (n.p., n.d.); Charles Bragin, *Bibliography: Dime Novels, 1860-1964* (New York: Privately printed, 1964); James M. Cain, "The Man Merriwell," *Saturday Evening Post* 199 (June 11, 1927), 12; Kenneth L. Donelson and Alleen Pace Nilsen, *Literature for Today's Young Adults* (Glenview, Ill.: Scott, Foresman, 1980); Stewart H. Holbrook, "Golden Boys of Pulp Fiction; Frank Merrriwell, Pride of Old Eli," *The South Bend Magazine* October 22, 1961, p. 6; Albert Johannsen, *The House of Beadle and Its Dime and Nickel Novels*, 3 vols. (Norman, Okla.: University of Oklahoma Press, 1950); Roy Nuhn, "Tip Top's Frank Merriwell— an 85 Year Old Legend," *Hobbies* 86 (April 1981), 100; Russel Blaine Nye, *The Unembarrassed Muse: The Popular Arts in America* (New York: The Dial Press, 1970); Gilbert Patten, "Dime Novel Days," *Saturday Evening Post* 203 (February 28, 1931), 6; and (March 7, 1931), 33; idem, *Frank Merriwell's "Father": An Autobiography by Gilbert Patten* ("*Burt L. Standish*"), ed. Harriet Hinsdale and Tony London (Norman, Okla.: University of Oklahoma Press, 1964); Quentin Reynolds, *The Fiction Factory; or From Pulp Row to Quality Street* (New York: Random House, 1955).

INDEX SOURCES
None.
LOCATION SOURCES
Private collections. Special collections are in universities and major public libraries.

Publication History

MAGAZINE TITLE AND TITLE CHANGES
Tip Top Weekly: An Ideal Publication for Youth and *Tip Top Library: An Ideal Publication for Youth,* interchangeably (no. 1, April 18, 1896-no. 45, Feburary 20, 1897); *Tip Top Weekly: An Ideal Publication for Youth* (no. 46, February 27, 1897-no. 850, July 27, 1912).

VOLUME AND ISSUE DATA
Tip Tip Weekly: An Ideal Publication for Youth and/or *Tip Top Library: An Ideal Publication for Youth* (no. 1-no. 45); *Tip Top Weekly: An Ideal Publication for Youth* (no. 46-no. 850).
PUBLISHER AND PLACE OF PUBLICATION
Street and Smith, New York (1896-1912).
EDTIOR
None listed.

Marion J. Mulholland

W

THE WEEWISH TREE: A MAGAZINE OF INDIAN AMERICA FOR YOUNG PEOPLE

The civil rights movement of the 1960s created a receptive climate within the United States for independent expressions from ethnic groups. *The Weewish Tree*, which began publication in November 1971, was one such expression. The American Indian Historical Society was responsible for this unique juvenile magazine. The society was and is an all-Indian organization of young and adult native Americans from all walks of life including scholars, historians, and traditionalists. Before the advent of *The Weewish Tree*, the society had achieved success in publishing *The Indian Historian*.

The Weewish Tree: A Magazine of Indian America for Young People was designed to provide authentic information about American Indians, past and present. The editors did not assign a specific grade level to the magazine but suggested that it would be appropriate for young people from the age of six to sixteen. "It could be used for reading aloud, for information, and for games and crafts anywhere in the elementary grades; for information in junior high, if history units include Indian history and culture; and on a very different level of interest in senior high school for ethnic studies and for art."[1]

This educational "nourishment" was symbolized in the title *The Weewish Tree*. "The word 'Weewish' is an Indian word, used by the Cahuilla (Kah-wee-ah) Indians of Southern California. It means 'acorn food.' It is made from the nut of the mighty oak tree.... This remarkable food, which is more nutritious than wheat or corn, can be cooked into a gruel, a soup, bread, pancakes, or biscuits. It is called 'Weewish.' And so we have the name that means so much to so many people: The Weewish Tree!''[2] Just as "Weewish" provided bodily nourishment, so *The Weewish Tree* provided food for thought. "And thought is what's needed today as never before."[3] This explanation of the title, variously modified, appeared at the beginning of each issue.

The group of editors responsible for the preceding statements and for the contents of the magazine varied in number throughout the years. One name has stood out by always being listed first and finally being listed alone in the last few issues. Jeannette Henry must be given a great amount of credit for the authenticity and success of this cultural endeavor.

By 1980 the magazine had grown to an estimated circulation of 11,000, according to *Ayer Directory of Publications*. Sold by subscription, *The Weewish Tree* cost $6.50 a year, with reductions for longer periods or for bulk subscriptions. The first volume contained six issues, but later volumes were increased to seven. The period covered by a single volume varied from a calendar year, January through December, to the school year, September through May.

The physical format of the magazine changed only slightly during its nine years of existence. Initially, page size was 9 by 6 inches in the first two volumes. Thereafter, pages measured 8½ by 5½ inches. The number of pages in an issue varied from twenty-four to forty-eight, with thirty-two being the usual number.

The covers were usually gold, occasionally orange, and printed on heavy-weight paper. The first two issues and the most recent issues had lightweight, off-white covers, however. The covers were always attractively decorated with earth-colored drawings or stylized sketches that were noteworthy representations of Indian art. The first cover design was done by John Wasson, a Nez Percé, but other cover artists were seldom acknowledged. Covers were rarely closely tied to specific articles.

Authentic Indian drawings or designs and photos typically accompany the articles and decorate the magazine's margins. The contents of the magazine vary, but each issue contains a selection of stories simply told and a number of brief articles on Indian customs, history, social life, and legends. A sampling of titles illustrates the range of topics: "Two Feathers," "Indians of Today," "Cheyenne Dances," "The Fine Art of Indian Quill Work," "How to Make a Clapper," "The Ponca Shinny Game," "The Common Seal," "The Cherokee Alphabet, Hoopa Alphabet," and "How Kodoyampe Created Man." All of the articles were written by Indians; for example, "Running Bear" in the first issue was contributed by a fourteen-year-old Maliseet girl in New Hampshire.

In addition to the explanation of the title described earlier, the one feature that was sustained throughout all eight volumes was "Books to Read." One or two books about Indians were reviewed in each issue. The books represented various types and interests such as *Maria Tallchief* by Marion Gridley, a biography of a ballet dancer, and *Navajo and Hopi Weaving Techniques* by Mary Pendleton.

Other features included "The Weewish Dictionary," which provided definitions of unfamiliar words used in the magazine. "Questions and Answers" provided answers to readers' questions in many early issues. Writing contests, recipes, pen pals, and letters appeared repeatedly but less frequently than the above. Some word games and exercises invited the active participation of the child readers.

Two special issues of *The Weewish Tree* appeared in September 1975 and 1976. "O Wai Ya Wa" (1975) was edited by John White and produced by Indian students in Chicago. The title was the name of a special elementary school program for American Indian children begun in September 1973 to combat the high dropout rate of Indian students and to increase school achievement. The curriculum of this program concerned Native Americans and helped students understand living in two cultures. This special issue reflected the purposes of that program through the contributions of its participants.

"The Qualla Cherokees of North Carolina" (1976) was the title of the second special issue. Chief editors were Laurence French and Richard Crowe, but the contents were written and produced by the young people of the Eastern Cherokee Tribe. Photos by Jim Hornbuckle and by courtesy of the Department of the Interior added interest and authenticity. Articles provided information about past and present, government and education, festivals and foods, poetry and the arts, and distinguished leaders.

After eight volumes, covering more than a nine-year period of time, *The Weewish Tree* ceased publication. The last issue was dated November-December 1980. The editor explained that "the rising costs of printing and mailing have made it impossible to continue. Since this magazine does not accept advertising, the problem is even more serious."[4] Delayed postal delivery was another problem that plagued the publisher for several years. In the final issue the editor hoped to resume publishing in 1982.

In the meantime four children's books have been planned for *Weewish* readers. The first, *A Thousand Years of American Indian Storytelling*, was published in the fall of 1981. The others, *A Child's History of the American Indian*, one containing biographies, and one relating to sports, will follow. Separate guides are planned to aid in their use. These four books will contain some new articles and information along with a collection of articles previously published in *The Weewish Tree*. All will aid in the fulfillment of the original educational purpose of the periodical.

Notes

1. Marian H. Scott, comp. and ed., *Periodicals for School Libraries: A Guide to Magazines, Newspapers and Periodical Indexes* (Chicago: American Library Association, 1973), 243.

2. The Editors, "The Mighty Oak," *The Weewish Tree* 1 (November 1971), 2-3.

3. The Editors, "To the Parent, To the Teacher," ibid., p. 40.

4. Jeannette Henry, "Important Notice," ibid., 8 (November-December 1980), 31.

Information Sources

BIBLIOGRAPHY
"The Weewish Tree," *Periodicals for School Libraries* (Chicago: American Library
    Association, 1973).
INDEX SOURCES
Subject Index to Children's Magazines.
LOCATION SOURCES
Bound volumes are in the Iowa State University Library, Ames, Ia.

Publication History

MAGAZINE TITLE AND TITLE CHANGES
The Weewish Tree: A Magazine of Indian America for Young People (1971-1980).
VOLUME AND ISSUE DATA
The Weewish Tree: A Magazine of Indian America for Young People (vol. 1, no. 1-vol.
    8, no. 6).
PUBLISHER AND PLACE OF PUBLICATION
The American Indian Historical Society, San Francisco (1971-1980).
EDITOR
Jeannette Henry (1971-1980).

Rosalind E. Engel

WIDE AWAKE

If it is true that "more than any other class of literature, children's books
reflect the mind of the generation that produced them," then surely *Wide Awake*
reflects the preoccupation with child nurture that characterized late nineteenth-
century America.[1] The evolution of the magazine from its precursors, the history
of its own editorial policy as it derived from the ideology of its creator Daniel
Lothrop, and the account of its merger with a rival publication, *St. Nicholas*,*
illustrate the dynamics of an industry, that, by the end of the century, was to
become increasingly associated with a youth-centered democracy. As the economy of the country stabilized during the affluent period of the Gilded Age, the
American middle class was able to afford the leisure time and money to indulge
its children.

One of the first juvenile periodicals to focus on the particular needs of American
children, *Wide Awake* emphatically stressed the concept of selfhood for youth.
Daniel Lothrop wanted his magazine to appeal to the integrity and independence
of the child and to provide him or her with a guide to "true good living."[2] The
publisher's life was a model example of the self-starting businessperson who
puts moral ideas into successful practice; his background, like that of many
prominent in the publishing world, derived from the responsible eastern elite
who had a strong sense of mission concerning the cultural and social ideas they
had to transmit. After a modest start in the drugstore business, Lothrop established
his publishing firm in Boston and built his success on the trade of juvenile books

sold to schools and libraries. Edward Everett Hale, Lothrop's biographer, described the two guiding principles of Lothrop's work: "1. Never to publish a book purely sensational, no matter what the chances of money it has in it. 2. To publish books which will make for true, steadfast growth in right living."[3] Lothrop's rapid rise in the business was based on strong, close relationships with his authors and solicitous advance planning of his publications. In fact, this close supervision of both manuscripts and writers allowed him to use the publishing office as a moral pulpit. Lothrop's ambition to publish material to guide the populace was especially directed at the community of youth, which he "segmented" as a social group by publishing four specialty magazines for them: *Wide Awake, Babyland,* * *Our Little Men and Women,* * and *The Pansy,* * a strategy that suggests some manipulation of the reading interests of the young as well as considerable business acumen. Of the four publications, *Wide Awake* had the longest life, from 1875 to 1893, when it was absorbed by *St. Nicholas*. Ella Farman Pratt, a children's writer, and Charles Stuart Pratt were chosen to edit the magazine in strict accordance with Lothrop's views.

Wide Awake opened its first issue with a feature of self-promotion called "Opinions of the Press," which underscored the publication's intention to act as a corrective to bad models of juvenile publication: "Magazines like the *Wide Awake* are good for young folk, and contain nothing of the "run-away-to-sea" style for boys, or the "elope-and-be-happy" incentive for girls, which are greatly cried against by parents now-a-days."[4]

The magazine's use of advertisement was critical to its survival in this period, since the financial crisis of 1873-1875 brought hard times to many publications in the form of inflated costs for material and low circulation rates. An important feature of the advertising was to encourage "good" (that is, tasteful and morally uplifting) reading through the column "Literary Gossip"; since many of the books promoted were published by Lothrop himself, he was able to combine commercial profit with educational idealism and moral responsibility.

The new "celebration of the child" espoused by *Wide Awake* was projected through adult eyes; the early issues of the magazine were preponderantly filled with romantic poems and stories that were formulaic both in content and in structure. Ella Farman, the co-editor, focused on the problems of New England gentry; "How Miss Chatty Earned a Living" (March 1876) describes the plight of genteel poverty for a spinster left destitute by her parents' death. Louise Chandler Moulton's stories frequently dealt with the economic and social ordeals of the same class. "Jessie's Neighbour" (January 1876), for example, uses the confrontation between the rich and the poor merely as a backdrop for a tale of the moral education of a spoiled young girl. Many writers tried to emulate the success of *Little Women*, and Adeline Dutton Whitney's stories of New England girlhood have been compared to Alcott's work. But even in adventure stories like "The Little Savages of Beetle Rock" (January 1878), the female protagonists are portrayed in traditional roles. If there was a single writer who exemplified the values of *Wide Awake*, it was "Pansy" (Isabella Macdonald Alden), a member of the Women's Christian Temperance Union and, for a short period, editor of her own magazine, the *Pansy*—"For Jesus' Sake." Like Lothrop, Pansy dedicated her life to the guidance of youth to the "right paths" and soon became involved in the activities of the Chautauqua movement.

Many other minor writers contributed to the periodical as well as numerous authors identified only by initials. Major writers of the century were most often the subjects of panegyrics such as the "Series on Poets' Homes" (1875-1878), written by Hezekiah Butterworth, Richard Stoddard, and others. These essays stress the virtue of traditional American values and express a romantic nostalgia for America's beginnings. Side-by-side with the sentimental view of the past there co-existed a future-oriented cult of the child. Verses like Louis Chandler Moulton's "Wide Awake," which opened the first issue, and Samuel Duffield's "Parvulus" (January 1876), celebrate the freedom and naturalness of the child, an especially appealing image for America, a young republic. At the same time, much of the material in the magazine stresses the innocence and vulnerability of the child. Several informational pieces drew attention to proper child nurture, as in "How to Amuse the Babies" (February 1875), and the special status and needs of the very young were recognized through the "Easy Reading" feature, written in helpful "syl-la-bic" spelling. In its early issues, *Wide Awake*'s concern for the children of the poor was from the point of view of the comfortable, middle-class observer; the series "Child-Toilers of the Boston Streets" (January 1878), for example, describes in graphic detail lives of degradation and want; yet no practical suggestions are made for the alleviation of such neglect. A concern for the spiritual and imaginative needs of the young was the hallmark of a special British contributor and close friend of Lothrop, George MacDonald; several issues featured work written for the periodical ("A Double Story," July 1875) and a novel published as a separately paged supplement (*Warlock o' Glenwarlock*, 1881).

One of the most important factors in the change in editorial policy of the magazine over the next several years was the marital and professional relationship of Daniel Lothrop and Margaret Sidney (Harriet Mulford Stone). Sidney had begun her writing career late in life; her major work, *The Five Little Peppers and How They Grew*, was serialized by *Wide Awake* in 1878 and published in book form in 1881. In 1880 Sidney married her publisher, and as one critic observed, this made "success by her own efforts. . . less important."[5] She shared and promoted many of Lothrop's interests, such as the Chautauqua movement and the American Institute of Civics, and actively participated in his social causes, such as efforts to rehabilitate the American Indian. Most of her work, with the exception of the "Peppers" series, consists of minor, didactic pieces that present heavily stereotyped characterization, as in "Cousin Sally's Wedding Slippers" (May 1881).

Sidney's first *Peppers* novel was a significant departure from other children's books of that period, however, in its treatment of the daily realities of economic want, and the work was soon followed by a stream of regional stories describing the small details and uncertainties of everyday life from many levels of the social spectrum. The monopoly of New England authorship was broken as more contributions to *Wide Awake* came from writers in the Midwest and the South. Mary Catherwood of Ohio researched her stories of the French settlers with great care, and her contemporary tales of bayou life are filled with vivid details of local color and accurate dialect. A focus on the small features of rural living was the stamp of Sarah Orne Jewett's stories. She studied closely the models of French and Russian realism—Flaubert, Zola, and Tolstoy—and applied the lessons of their incisive observation to her sketches of Maine life, such as "The Church Mouse" (February 1883). The work of Susan Coolidge (Sarah Chauncey Woolsey) depicted contemporary life in various settings; "Who Ate the Pink Sweetmeat?" (January 1884), for example, is a combination of fantasy and the realistic description of a Dutch immigrant family's adjustment to life in London. Coolidge's adventure stories were matched in liveliness by the tales of "Charles Egbert Craddock," whose real identity as Mary Murfree was not discovered for many years. "Down the Ravine" (December 1884 and following) is a good illustration of her exciting tales of the Tennessee Mountain folk; her descriptions of their rugged environment and dangerous sport could easily be mistaken for the work of contemporary male writers like Mark Twain and Dan Beard.

It was during the years of Lothrop's involvement in the Chautauqua movement that *Wide Awake* began to focus closely on social issues. Under scrutiny came charitable institutions such as "The Chinese Mission School" (February 1880) and "The Philadelphia Newsboys and their Annual Fourth of July Dinner" (July 1880). These articles emphasized the source of the philanthropy, and the descriptions of the activities were often to the detriment of the poor and the social outsider. The growing social consciousness of the cultural elite was especially directed toward the "Indian problem" and the process of Americanization of the native. Margaret Sidney visited the Carlisle School for Indian Pupils in 1883, and her description of the institution was featured in an extensive article in the March 1884 issue of *Wide Awake*. Sidney emphasized the claim of Indian rights upon the white man and the dignity of Indian culture, but her praise of the efforts of the white philanthropists betrays the fear and ethnocentrism of her race. "Think of it! . . . children rescued by this noble womanly effort from savage degradation to grow up into great citizenship."[6] An article about another institution, "The Ramona Indian Girls' School" in New Mexico, appeared in a later issue of the magazine (September 1888). The analysis, written by a resident chaplain, was more objective than Sidney's description but also more chillingly rigid in its doctrinaire views: "Education alone can clear their minds of superstitions, and free them from foolish and cruel observances. . . . The teepee and hogan must be educated out of the Indian mind."[7] A more positive and romantic picture of the integration of the Indian was portrayed by Theodora Jenness in the series "Piokee and her People" (December 1892 and following issues).

The concern with the indoctrination of the Indian into the mainstream of American society was related to a broader preoccupation with education at the end of the nineteenth century. The Chautauqua movement resulted from a near-mystical belief in the benefits of self-improvement and from a reaction to Anthony Comstock's attacks on the vices of reading trash. Lothrop promoted the interests of the movement and profited from the publication of works that were part of its syllabus. In 1881 the Chautauqua program was incorporated as part of *Wide Awake* with the establishment of the Chautauqua Young Folk's Reading Union (CYFRU) Supplement. The course of reading was planned far in advance and included practical material directed to the interests of its middle-class audience: "Magna Carta Stories," "The Travelling Law School," and "Behaving: Papers on Children's Etiquette." The Chautauquans followed the dictum of *mens sana in corpore sano* (sound mind, sound body) and thus space in the supplement was devoted to features like "Health and Strength Papers," which hotly debated the pros and cons of discarding corsets and high-button boots for loose clothing and sensible shoes (1882 CYFRU Supplement). When the activities of the organization deteriorated to tent entertainment, and "the sale of culture at so much a pound," the movement lost much support, and by 1890 *Wide Awake* had dropped "The Juvenile Side of Chautauqua."[8]

In its mature years *Wide Awake* grew more sophisticated in format and content, reflecting the increased cosmopolitanism of the country. The settings of many stories were cities rather than rural areas. A. M. Diaz's "Polly Cologne" (July 1881 and following issues), an earlier series, had used an urban background in a manner strongly reminiscent of Lucretia Hale's *Peterkin Papers*, and in the 1887 issue a series called "My Uncle Florimond" by Sidney Luska (Henry Harland) presented a sympathetic picture of Jewish community life in New York. *Wide Awake*'s broader cultural sources in these years included foreign authors like France's Alphonse Daudet ("The Last Day at School," March 1888) and immigrant writers like Hjalmar H. Boyesen, who wrote of the folklore and culture of his native land in stories such as "Inge, the Boy King" (December 1888). Later issues featured many writers now considered the most stylistically innovative of the period; Kate Chopin, for example, contributed brilliant sketches in which she recreated the exotic atmosphere and speech of Cajun country, as in "How the Lilies Work" (April 1893). In earlier years *Wide Awake* had published mostly sentimental verse and the work of established poets like James Whitcomb Riley and classics like "The Land of Used-to-Be" (August 1881). By the last issue the magazine featured the work of experimental poets like Bliss Carman, who displayed bold innovation in the use of unusual meters and irregular verse structure in "The Marching Song" (August 1893).

Throughout its life *Wide Awake* had been known for its tasteful format and consistent technical excellence, outstanding even in an age of numerous juvenile periodicals of high quality. Its art soon evolved beyond the limitations of early woodcuts and engravings. Later issues featured work that showed the influence of Howard Pyle's elaborate technique and the lively, fluid style of art such as Stanley Bodfish's illustrations for the adventure story "Queer Company Home" (January 1882). The magazine used artists like Alfred Brennan and W. T. Smedley, who contrasted greatly in style, to express a wide range of moods. Brennan's rococo pen-and-ink lines captured the fantasy of a poem like Mary Wilkens's "Castles in Spain" (August 1883), whereas Smedley's skillful technique of steel engraving expressed all the nuances of the human countenance for the "Benny" series: for example, "Benny's Disappearance" (September 1883). John Derwent's playful feature "Floral Fantastics" (December 1892) combined the stylishness of art nouveau with imaginative whimsy to subvert forever the saccharine incarnation of nature typical of early artwork in children's magazines.

When Daniel Lothrop died in 1892, *Wide Awake* quickly followed. In the last issue "The Story of *Wide Awake*" (August 1893) presented a tribute to the publisher's entrepreneurship and to the magazine's success in a fairy-tale fashion. The takeover by *St. Nicholas* was explained and justified in terms of a "mission fulfilled." The truth was that Lothrop's guiding hand was sorely missed after his death; efficient management had been the basis of his success, and his wife, who tried to carry on alone, lacked his business skill and direction. In addition, there were economic and sociological factors that spelled the doom of a publication like *Wide Awake*. Lothrop's magazine never built its circulation rate beyond 25,000, or 20-30 percent of that of *St. Nicholas*; *Wide Awake*'s appeal to the narrow audience that shared its ideology curtailed its growth and economic survival. Used as an ideological instrument by the publisher, *Wide Awake* died, the emblem of a vanishing culture and the product of a genteel publishing tradition.

Notes

1. A.S.W. Rosenbach, Introduction to *Early American Books* (Portland, Maine: Southworth, 1933), xxvi-xxvii.
2. Edward Everett Hale, "An American Publisher," *Lend a Hand* 9 (1892), 263.
3. Ibid.
4. *Wide Awake* (Boston: Lothrop, 1875), preface.
5. Richard L. Darling, *The Rise of Children's Book Reviewing in America, 1865-1881* (New York: R. R. Bowker, 1968), 29.
6. *Wide Awake*, March 1884, p. 236.
7. Ibid., September 1888, pp. 219-20.
8. Frank Luther Mott, *A History of American Magazines* (Cambridge: Harvard University Press, 1938-1968), 4:204.

Information Sources

BIBLIOGRAPHY
Edward Everett Hale, "An American Publisher," *Lend a Hand* 9 (1892), 253-63; Alice M. Jordan, *From Rollo to Tom Sawyer* (Boston: Horn Book, 1948); R. Gordon Kelly, *Mother Was a Lady* (Westport, Conn.: Greenwood Press, 1974); Frank Luther Mott, *A History of American Magazines* (Cambridge, Mass.: Harvard University Press, 1938-1968), vol. 4.

1069 WITH

INDEX SOURCES
John F. Sargent, *Reading for the Young: A Classified and Annotated Catalog* (Boston: American Library Association, 1890), indexes 1875-1889.
LOCATION SOURCES
Several university and large public libraries have complete sets of bound volumes.

Publication History

MAGAZINE TITLE AND TITLE CHANGES
Wide Awake: An Illustrated Magazine for Boys and Girls (1875-1893); title pages from 1875 to 1881 bear the title *Wide Awake Pleasure Book* (subtitle varies slightly).
VOLUME AND ISSUE DATA
Wide Awake: An Illustrated Magazine for Boys and Girls (vol. 1, no.1-vol. 36, no. 12; vol. 37, nos. 1-3); October 1881—each number includes the *CYFRU Supplement* (Chautauqua young folks' reading union supplement).
PUBLISHER AND PLACE OF PUBLICATION
D. Lothrop & Co., Boston (1875-1893).
EDITOR
Ella Farman Pratt (1875-1891); Ella Farman Pratt and Charles Stuart Pratt (1891-1893).

Diana Chlebek

WITH

With magazine has been a paradox and something of a daring venture from its inception to the time of this writing. It is a jazzy teen-oriented contemporary monthly published by a conservative religious denominational publishing house that depends on a religious, still mostly rural constituency for its support. *With* has generated a lot of reaction from its readers; its editors have been under pressure to change their editorial policies more than once; the continued publication of the magazine has been in doubt—not only for financial reasons—but the venture is still alive.

With took sides in an emerging generational struggle: it chose the young people's side, very much in the style of the 1960s, of which it is a product. Sex, drugs, the war in Vietnam, protest marches, long hair—all of these familiar cliché themes have appeared in *With*, but with a difference. Editors, writers, and readers have been Mennonite, that is, predominantly rural, conservative, pacifist Christians, generally of Swiss-German background.

The style of *With* has deceived many into thinking that it is advocating "sex, drugs, and rock-and-roll." In fact, although occasionally irreverent, *With* challenges its readers to think for themselves about those and other matters, from a Christian perspective. The flashy graphics, the "hip" subjects, and the catchy slogans of *With* are the medium but not all of the message.

It began in 1964 as an idea for a successor to the "youth page" of *The Mennonite* (a General Conference Mennonite Church publication) and to *Youth's Christian Companion.** By 1967 an editor, J. Lorne Peachey, and a title had been chosen, authors and photographers contacted. The first issue appeared on June 24, 1968. The first controversy blew up about "I Loved a Girl," Walter Trobisch's frank, thoughtful series of letters about sexual involvement. By December 1968 Peachey noted, "Editor finds himself backed into a corner at church meetings, being lectured on how to put out a 'decent' magazine for young people. 'Our youth are tired of this hippish, wild, sexy stuff you've been feeding them.' "[1] In a rather staid, literal-minded denomination, few souls over thirty took kindly to calendar graffiti (January 1970) such as "Spill the Offering Sunday" and "Listen to the Beatles Day."

If the older readers had been reading carefully, however, they would have discovered that beneath the surface of irreverence, satire, and irony, *With* was by no means preaching irresponsibility. It could be frivolous on small questions, but on the important issues it was eminently reasonable—and faithful to faith in God and the church.

One of the biggest explosions of reaction from its reading public was caused by an anonymous article by a Mennonite pastor—the subject: masturbation. The author said it was not wrong, not bad, not harmful. To the younger generation, that is, *With*'s readers, that view may still have sounded risky, but to many in the older generation, it was a bold attack on fundamental morality. Actually, the article was a remarkably well-balanced and insightful statement of the author's personal experience, the evolution of his thoughts on the subject, and some theological options.

Calls for the impeachment of the editor and a halt to *With* were heard at church assemblies, but strong support for *With* also emerged, especially from many of its readers.

With has not been all controversy. The whole folk culture—the counterculture—of the 1960s was reflected in *With*, refracted through the eyes of young Mennonites, historically pacifist, service oriented, modest, and relatively unsophisticated, but newly adventuresome. *With* printed exciting fiction; photojournalism about contemporary lives; poetry; articles about rebellion, love, sex, coffeehouses, race relations, Vietnamese society, an underground high school newspaper, the Gaza strip, and death; many features about courtship and marriage; and scenes from the activities of youth, such as "Outspokin'," the bicycle-excursion groups. Movie and book reviews emphasized culture and the arts (new to many conservative Mennonites), and a novel gimmick was a regular in-fold calendar with humorous graffiti. A song-book issue collected some contemporary folk and religious music and made it accessible to many beginning strummers. J. Lorne Peachey and his successor Richard Kauffman (better known as Dick) have made *With* a Mennonite youth magazine that looks at the world from the perspective of contemporary American youth. Its flaws have been over-responsiveness to fads and cheap shots; its strengths, above all, are frankness and the willingness to face difficult issues, searching for moral and spiritual integrity without legalism.

Note

1. "A Short, Concise, Updated History of the Development of a Magazine for Menno Youth Called *With*," *With* 7, no. 4 (May 1974), 5.

Information Sources

BIBLIOGRAPHY
See *With* 7, no. 4 (May 1974), 4-5, for a chronology of the development and history of the magazine.
INDEX SOURCES
None.
LOCATION SOURCES
Bound volumes are in most Mennonite libraries, including those at Goshen College, Goshen, Ind.; Eastern Mennonite College, Harrisonburg, Va.; and the Lancaster Mennonite Historical Society archives, Lancaster, Pa.

Publication History

MAGAZINE TITLE AND TITLE CHANGES
With (July 1968-).
VOLUME AND ISSUE DATA
With (vol. 1, no. 1-).
PUBLISHER AND PLACE OF PUBLICATION
Mennonite Publishing House, Scottdale, Pa. (July 1968-).
EDITOR
J. Lorne Peachey (June 1968-April 1974); Richard Kauffman (May 1974-).

John Daniel Stahl

WORDS OF CHEER

Words of Cheer, the longest-published children's paper of the Mennonite Church in America, took the middle place of three Mennonite children and youths' periodicals published for readers approximately nine to eleven years old. (See also *Story Friends** and *Youth's Christian Companion.**) For decades it was a major source of enjoyment and instruction for (mostly Mennonite) girls and boys, presenting Christian faith in its Mennonite incarnation through fiction, poetry, articles, and other features. The editors maintained a level of literary quality worthy of respect.

Henry A. Mumaw, a medical doctor, publisher, and the founder of Goshen College, Goshen, Indiana, founded *Words of Cheer* in 1876, when he was twenty-six, ten years before he graduated from a medical school in Chicago. Mumaw was born near Winesburg, Ohio, on January 27, 1850. He planned, edited, printed, and published the paper at Orrville, Ohio, where the first issue appeared in April 1876. It contained short articles, poems, stories, Bible queries, an explanation of the Sunday School lesson, and letters from the editor. In his first issue he wrote: "I want to bring something especially prepared for you; something that will meet your wants, and help you to live right and to do your part well in life. . . . I shall do my best to entertain you, and to help you bear your little crosses and cares and trials. . . . That is what I am come for, to cheer you. . . . You will need words of cheer, and they are to be had in abundance.''[1] He encouraged his readers to find new subscribers: ''We believe that a large majority of our little readers are willing to work for *Words of Cheer*, because it is a good work, and look for their reward when this life is past, and they shall receive the reward of the faithful in heaven.''[2]

Before he sold the publication to the Mennonite Publishing Company in Elkhart, Indiana, two years later, *Words of Cheer* had carried advertisements. Landis from Lancaster County advertised a folding clothes dryer; a company on Broadway, New York, advertised stereoscopes and magic lanterns; and Mumaw recommended a microscope with which the viewer could see the eye of a fly. The paper was then sent postpaid at the rate of 25¢ for one copy for one year or 15¢ a year if a church bought fifty a year. Anyone sending in a new subscription received a premium.

Joseph Summers, known to his readers as ''Uncle Joseph,'' became the editor for the next fourteen years until his death August 21, 1892. As a young man Summers had traveled to California twice, once driving a team of horses through the western frontier. During the period of his editorship *Words of Cheer* was an eight-page monthly designed to be read by boys and girls at home.

The next editor, Abram B. Kolb, made the change from monthly to weekly publication. Kolb, or ''Cousin Abe,'' was born near Kitchener, Ontario. For a while he taught in Kent County, Michigan, where two of his pupils were Orville and Wilbur Wright. Kolb's health failed in 1904, and he was succeeded by D. H. Bender, who also briefly edited *Beams of Light* (see *Story Friends*). He served for two years and was followed by Phoebe Funk Kolb, who edited the paper (although her name did not appear as editor) for two further years.

In 1908 ownership of the paper was transferred to the Mennonite Publishing House, Scottdale, Pa., and A. D. Martin served as its first editor there for a brief time until his health also failed. In 1909 *Words of Cheer* called itself ''a weekly illustrated paper for the home and Sunday School'' (Sunday School was a relatively new and in some areas still controversial innovation among Mennonites at the time). The front page displayed, as it did for many years to follow, a banner title with a scene of shepherds at the Annunciation. The first page usually featured an etching, lithograph, or photograph as well as text. One issue (January 3, 1909) had, among other things, ''Men of the Bible'' by Daniel Kauffman; ''Cheerfulness,'' a short essay by Lillawah Carter; ''He Gave Out That Hymn for Me,'' an anecdote about the hymn ''Just as I Am.'' It also included a section on the Sunday School lessons; a poem, ''What the Bird Says''; a mnemonic device for learning the number of books in the Bible; and several short essays about moral and religious topics. To indicate the geographical spread and rural location of its readership: in one issue *Words of Cheer* readers wrote in from McCall Ferry, Pennsylvania; Inman, Kansas; Cherry Box, Missouri;

East Scottdale, Pennsylvania; Windom, Kansas; Canton, Ohio; Wayland, Iowa; and Johnstown, Pennsylvania.

H. Frank Reist was the next editor, from 1909 to 1912. Breaking the spell of the short-term editors was J. A. Ressler, "Uncle J. A.," who with his wife, who was known as "Aunt Lina," edited the paper for twenty-four years, from 1912 to 1936. A representative sample of the combination of religious and moral wisdom to be found in *Words of Cheer* during the editorship of "Uncle J. A." is the following series of maxims from the January 2, 1921, issue:

Do You Know—That love lightens labor? That obedience is the test of love? That a gentle boy is likely to be a gentleman? That the greatest battles are fought out in human hearts? That the only safe guide to follow is the Lord Jesus Christ? That the greatest victory under heaven is when one conquers himself? That the boy who takes his mother's advice will not be likely to go far astray? That he who asks God's help to do right will not need to ask God's mercy for doing wrong? That the spirit in which a task is done counts for as much as the work itself? That the best way to do a better job is to do better the job you already have? That the time spent in acquiring a good education is the best investment you can make?[3]

A tradition that established itself in *Words of Cheer* was the editor's comments after "Readers Write" letters—pithy, kind, often witty. Readers' letters often requested pen pals and sometimes sparked lifelong friendships. "Printer's Pie" was a feature that challenged readers to unscramble the jumbled letters in a verse.

Ellrose D. Zook edited the paper from 1936 to 1949, followed by Elizabeth Showalter, widely known throughout the church as "Aunt Beth." Under her direction the paper acquired a new typeface for the title and a cleaner, more modern layout. In this period artists Ivan Moon and Jan Gleysteen, among other Mennonite illustrators, produced much graphic work of high quality for *Words of Cheer*. Larger photographs came into use. Despite the stylistic changes, the themes remained essentially the same. Features in this period included "Stories About Juniors in Other Countries," for example, "African Rain Maker"; serial fiction such as "Lucila's Search"; stories with Bible settings; picture issues that told about church activities or travel ("We Enter Japan"); and Photographer Jim stories ("Billy Packs His Bag"). A number of series promoted activities, "junior projects" such as "The Hundred Pennies," "What You Can Do to Help—New Clothes for Your Twin," and "Things to Make and Do—Putting on an Indian Sari." Missions abroad and at home ("Mennonite Youth Village") and articles and stories about nature vied with puzzles and contests such as the photo identification of missionaries series, "Know Your Church." The "Know Your Church" contestants provide an illuminating glimpse of the readership of *Words of Cheer* in 1950. Of the 283 reported respondents, almost 40 percent were from Pennsylvania. Ohio was second with 10 percent, followed by Ontario, 10 percent; Indiana and Virginia, 6 percent; Illinois and Michigan, 4 percent; Oregon, 3.5

percent; Delaware, Iowa, and Kansas, 3 percent each. The vast majority of respondents were between the ages of nine and fourteen.[4]

After Elizabeth Showalter, Helen Trumbo edited *Words of Cheer* (as well as *Story Friends*) for a year and a half. In August 1961 Paul M. Schrock became the 11th editor. Helen Alderfer presided over the final months of *Words of Cheer*, which was superseded by *On the Line*, a similar publication. In her last editorial in *Words of Cheer* she summarized the changes that had occurred since 1876: "The first readers of *Words of Cheer* either read by candle or kerosine light in the evening, walked or rode to church in a horse-drawn buggy. For them the telephone was one year away, Thomas Edison's carbon lamp four years away, mass production of cars (425 gasoline autos built by Olds) 24 years away, and the first regular commercial broadcast by radio 45 years away. From only a few copies at first the subscription went as high as 27,119. It would take a large building to hold all of the readers of *Words of Cheer* since its beginning."[5]

It is worth noting that the influence of *Words of Cheer* continued to be strong, with an eager reading audience of Mennonite children, through the 1960s, since the overwhelming majority of their parents did not have television in their homes, for reasons of conscience and church policy.

Notes

1. Quoted in *Words of Cheer*, December 27, 1970, p. 8.
2. Ibid.
3. Ibid., January 21, 1921, p. 3.
4. Ibid., June 4, 1950, pp. 3, 6.
5. Ibid., December 27, 1970, p. 8.

Information Sources

BIBLIOGRAPHY
John A. Hostetler, *God Uses Ink* (Scottdale, Pa.: Herald Press, 1958); *The Mennonite Encyclopedia* (Hillsboro, Kans.: Mennonite Brethren Publishing House, 1955-1959).
INDEX SOURCES
None.
LOCATION SOURCES
Bound volumes are in most Mennonite libraries, including those at Goshen College, Goshen, Ind.; Eastern Mennonite College, Harrisonburg, Va.; and the Lancaster Mennonite Historical Society archives, Lancaster, Pa.

Publication History

MAGAZINE TITLE AND TITLE CHANGES
Words of Cheer (1876-1970).
VOLUME AND ISSUE DATA
Words of Cheer (vol. 1, no. 1-vol. 95, no. 52).

PUBLISHER AND PLACE OF PUBLICATION
H. A. Mumaw, Orrville, Ohio (April 1876-February 1878); Mennonite Publishing Company, Elkhart, Ind. (March 1878-April 1908); Mennonite Publishing House, Scottdale, Pa. (April 26, 1908-December 27, 1970).
EDITOR
Henry A. Mumaw (April 1876-February 1878); Joseph Summers (March 1878-July 1892); Abram B. Kolb (August 1892-January 1904); D. H. Bender (February 1904-February 1906); Phoebe Funk Kolb (March 1906-April 1908); A. D. Martin (April 1908-June 1909); H. F. Reist (June 1909-February 1912); J. A. Ressler (February 1912-September 1937); Ellrose D. Zook (October 1937-September 1949); Elizabeth A. Showalter (October 1949-January 1960); Helen Trumbo (January 1960-July 1961); Paul M. Schrock (August 1961-1969); Helen Alderfer (1969-1970).

John Daniel Stahl

WORLD OVER

World Over is one of the best-known Jewish children's magazines. It was begun in 1940 under the editorship of Israel Goldberg. Its sponsoring organization was the Jewish Education Committee of New York. (The sponsorship has remained the same, although the name of the sponsor was changed in 1970 to the Board of Jewish Education of Greater New York.)

In the first year six issues of eight pages each were published; in the second, sixteen issues of eight pages; and in the third, fifteen eight-page issues. Subsequently, fifteen issues of sixteen pages each were published every two weeks from October to May.

The magazine began with a tabloid format (15½ by 10½ inches) and has continued as a large magazine (10¾ by 8½ inches) since the first issue of volume 4 (October 30, 1942). The first volumes did not use color but were printed in sepia and then in black on an off-white stock. Two-color printing was introduced with volume 5. During the first few years the type size was fairly standardized, and the spacing was bold and attractive. There were attractive photo-essays, relating to current news events and Jewish art and history, in the first three volumes. By volume 4, when the page size decreased, the layout of the magazine became cluttered—probably in an effort to compress all the material into the smaller size page—but was still friendly and inviting. The use of both two- and three-column pages helped vary the appearance of the text.

The magazine, "for Jewish boys and girls," was designed as a tool for pleasurable Jewish educational enrichment in a religious school atmosphere (generally, synagog schools meeting after public school hours during the week and on Saturday and/or Sunday mornings). Youngsters featured in photographs seem to range in age from early elementary to junior high school students. Cartoon features (the most prominent and longest lasting of which is "Joey and His Friends," inaugurated by Herb Kruckman in the first issue of volume 2) seem geared to young readers. The articles, however, were designed for older students.

They were printed in fairly small type and were not stimulating. One article began, "Joyously hailed by Jews the world over, the Balfour Declaration of 1917 came as the climax of twenty years of Zionist activity."[1] "Do You Know" (later called "Now You Know"), consisting of miscellaneous Jewish information, was begun by Lillian Port in volume 2, number 7 (January 1942). Also among the regular features of *World Over* were cartoon stories. The earliest dealt with famous Jews involved in critical moments of Jewish history. It was prepared by Lillian Port and began with the first issue of volume 3 (October 31, 1941). Sholem Aleichem's story about the young scamp Mottel was adapted and presented in serialized cartoon form by Ezekiel Schloss in the issues of volume 4. Herb Kruckman also did an issue-by-issue series of moral tales in the same volume.

Mazes, rebuses, and other similar puzzles and a Bible quiz, stamp column, and occasional craft projects were offered in the first volumes of the magazine, as were various writing and photography contests that invited reader response. In volume 4 the focus of the light material was on cartoons, and the games and crafts were dropped. Since the subject of the cartoons and cartoon features was invariably thinly veiled educational information, students had no option but to learn—or not read. Current news events still received wide coverage and heavy emphasis. Word puzzles returned to the pages of *World Over* with volume 5 (was the experiment in unabashed didacticism a failure?) and a double spread of games, puzzles, and cartoons (including, for a time, a female—if not feminist—counterpart to "Joey and His Friends," called "Debby," drawn by Shirley Knoring) was subsequently a regular part of the periodical. Articles about music and songs, complete with notes and words, appeared from time to time.

Many stories, some written specifically for *World Over*, others taken from previously published sources (like the stories of I. L. Peretz, Sholem Aleichem, Joseph Gaer, Judah Steinberg, Sadie Rose Weilerstein, and others) appeared with increasing frequency in the pages of the magazine. They were, on the whole, of high quality. Sometimes they were printed in a larger font than the informational material. Often they were serialized over several issues. Occasionally, the magazine published a poem by a famous Jewish poet like Saul T. Chernichovski (November 12, 1943) Philip M. Raskin (May 17, 1946), and Nathan Alterman (January 10, 1947) or by a non-Jew writing on a Jewish theme (like Longfellow's "Judas Maccabeus," November 27, 1942). The language and subject matter of the stories and poems seem suitable for children fourth grade and above. When "Reader's Corner" was established, the contributions were primarily by youngsters aged ten to twelve.

In the first years most of the factual material was written by the editors. It may not always have been interestingly written, but it was not beyond the ability of most young readers—particularly with the guidance of a teacher, a reasonable expectation since the periodical was designed for distribution in religious schools for classroom or supplemental enrichment reading (probably, one suspects, a euphemism for "homework"). Excellent articles on the war and the activities of the Jewish and general underground resistance movements appeared in the 1943 and 1944 issues, some as special features, others as part of the current events sections.

By the time Deborah Pessin became editor, in 1944, almost every article had a by-line. The endless cartoon stories were no longer as prominent as they had been earlier. There were new story features, such as "The Solomon Legends" by Chaim N. Bialik, "translated freely" by Jacob S. Golub in the issues of volume 7. From time to time there were outstanding features about Jewish art, such as the series known as "The Language of Art" (begun in volume 8) and photographic essays such as "The Vanished World" (December 27, 1946), with pictures by Roman Vishniac. The overall tone of the periodical was uneven in both quality and appeal. Yet *World Over* included something for everyone in the audience for which it was designed. At this stage it was an exciting magazine with a great deal to offer.

By the early 1950s Ezekiel Schloss and Morris Epstein had become co-editors (with the start of volume 11; Schloss had been art advisor and director and Epstein had been managing editor for several years before their joint editorship). The magazine was printed on good paper; the cover showed imaginative use of color. Many sizes of type were used, with a sense of purpose: the largest print served for simple stories; small print appeared on some captions and in the puzzles, as well as for much of the informational matter. The editors were conscious of the need to package a magazine in a manner appealing to the ages of the children in the desired audience, and by and large, at this stage of *World Over*'s history, they succeeded very well.

Many illustrations, primarily by Schloss, sought to capture pictorially the highlights of the stories. Sometimes they were successful; at other times they merely decorated the page. The very predictability of Schloss's style created a welcome sense of familiarity—until it became wearisome. Photographs and "The Language of Art," an excellent selection of reproductions of Jewish fine art and artifacts, still graced occasional issues of the magazine. This feature offered two-page spreads about artists such as Jakob Steinhardt (April 18, 1952), Bernard Picart (December 28, 1951), and Marc Chagall (January 18, 1957) or about ritual Judaica (for example, "The Seder Plate," April 4, 1952). The only quibble with the feature is that the reproductions in this series and in most of the other picture features were generally disappointingly small and sometimes muddy. (There were exceptions. One was the fine "Scissors Scenes from the Book of Genesis," a double-page feature about paper cutouts in the December 15, 1953, issue. "Paper Cut-Outs," January 29, 1960, was not equally successful.)

The layout had become much cleaner and better balanced. The alternation of two- and three-column pages worked effectively. A visual problem closely related to the readability of the nonfiction was (and continues to be) a lack of subheads in the body of an article. Their presence would not only have lessened the impression that each piece was inexhaustibly long but would also have drawn the eye and mind down the page with a sense of anticipation.

World Over's reading audience spanned the Hebrew school years, approximately second to seventh grades. Its primary appeal, however, was to children in fourth through sixth grades. Reader contributions, mostly poetry, reflected an interest in the magazine from children between the ages of six and thirteen who lived in all parts of the United States and Canada. Most of the cartoons were unbelievably corny ("Joey..." by Herb Kruckman and later "Dot N' Dan" by Gabe Josephson); but however silly they may now seem to adults, they were the first things many children turned to. The games were easy and the crossword puzzle relatively difficult. A famous-person guessing game, "Who Am I," was challenging and informative. Most of the craft projects were well conceived and provided clear directions. A cartoon feature, "In Legendland," retold *midrashim* in a broadly appealing format.[2]

Holiday stories, historical fiction, and modern Israel were all subject matter for *World Over*. Adventure stories, stories that held some suspense and mystery, and stories that offered a sense of excitement in the encounter with Jewish tradition were the most successful. Fictionalized treatment of the marvels associated with the building of the fledgling State of Israel often fell into the "adventure" and "suspense" categories. Many stories were serialized. The issues of November and December 1951, for instance, included installments of a story about the Jews of Rome and Pompeii by Harry Wedeck; "Forbidden Frontier" by Yehuda Haezrahi; "In Those Days," excerpted from the book of the same title by Judah Steinberg; a simple Hanukkah story by Judith Ish Kishor; and a radio playlet by Robert Garvey (November 2, 1951). Almost half of each issue was devoted to stories. In volume 14 readers were exposed to excellent literature in stories by famous writers such as Sholem Aleichem and S. Y. Agnon and to excerpts from the newly published *Anne Frank: The Diary of a Young Girl*.

Poetry, as usual, received less consistent treatment. In one issue (November 30, 1951), a two-page spread honored Jewish book month with rhymed couplets by Morris Epstein. Another issue contained no poetry at all. From time to time the work of a noted Jewish poet was featured, as in a spread on Yehuda Halevi (December 11, 1953) and an issue devoted to the great poet Ch. N. Bialik (February 5, 1953).

The nonfictional material was written with no attribution, presumably by the editors or by guest authors whose "expertise" was often justly proclaimed with pride (an article about the Jews of North Carolina, part of a series on Jews in American communities, by Harry Golden, May 16, 1952; a photo-essay in the previous issue, featuring the Jerusalem Zoo, prepared by the famous photographer Werner Braun). The authors may have been competent authorities in the fields about which they wrote (as, for example, Sidney B. Hoenig, professor of Jewish history, Yeshiva University, who wrote "The Synagogue Through the Ages," May 14, 1954), but they were not all accomplished writers for children. The articles hardly ever seem to have been worth reading for the pleasure of learning but give the impression instead of being a species of educational medicine.

Among the informational features were short biographies of famous living Jews, called "People in the News"; a summary of current events of Jewish interest; one photograph in each issue entitled "Pictures of the Past"; the believe-it-or-not of Jewish information called "Now You Know"; book reviews, a stamp corner, and a feature about either a holiday or a special Jewish theme. In addition, each issue's carefully chosen cover was explicated in a mini–essay in tiny print on the magazine's inside front cover.

The material was carefully chosen, covering the widest possible range of Jewish history, culture, ceremony and custom, literature, and current events of Jewish concern. From time to time an entire issue was dedicated to a holiday; a famous Jewish scholar, writer, or artist; or a topic such as "The Synagogue in America" (December 13, 1957) and "Jewish Life in the Middle Ages" (October 7, 1960). Throughout the pages of *World Over* children were exposed to architecture, archeology, rabbinic texts, famous personalities, and, above all, world issues of vital concern when they were topical. On the whole, therefore, *World Over* was an outstanding educational tool and an excellent magazine during the 1950s.

World Over in the 1960s looked exactly as it had from the late 1940s through the 1950s. Schloss and Epstein still served as the magazine's editors. There were no new regular features or exciting innovations. The puzzles, games, crafts, and cartoons held no real surprises. "In Legendland" had been replaced with a classic comic feature, "Highlights of History," that did not capture the essence of its material in this format as well as the legends presentation had done. Many of the stories were well written, charming, and appealing, but far fewer pages were now devoted to fiction in each issue. The art features were still well selected. However, the poor quality of the magazine's reproduction and the crowding of many overly small pictures on a single page sometimes made the result appear muddy, considerably reducing the effectiveness of the art displayed.

An increasing number of special issues devoted to in-depth exploration of single topics was published. The excellent January 18, 1963, issue about Latin America offered broad coverage and variety. The use of "special" issues seems to demonstrate some editorial awareness of a need for innovation in *World Over* as well as the usefulness of focusing all material in a single issue on one theme.[3]

By the late 1960s most children's magazines had begun to pitch to selected rather than broad age groups, because what appealed to a second or third grader was highly unlikely to have any attraction for an incipient adolescent. *World Over*'s intended audience, in the early 1970s, is difficult to determine. The cartoons and the style of the line drawings and illustrations seem to have been appropriate for readers as young as first to third grades. They are juvenile, unsubtle, and very dated. Schloss and Herb Kruckman were still producing work identical to what they had done two to three decades before. In fact, craft features (and perhaps other material) were sometimes reprinted without change (or acknowledgment) from earlier issues. The editors clearly counted on new young readers being interested in the same things that had appealed to earlier generations of readers. But the new readers had different tastes and responded to different external stimuli and challenges. For example, "Now You Know" and the games and puzzles were designed to appeal to the middle-level reader, who might have found the crossword puzzle too difficult. The rebus presented an additional problem, since it was not well drawn. It is hard, in reviewing the magazine, to determine what words the pictures were supposed to represent. The stories, on the whole, were perhaps frustratingly challenging to most fourth graders but not beyond the ability of fifth and sixth graders. However, the verbal texture and format of the informational articles had become sufficiently detailed and complex to frustrate even sixth and seventh graders—who would not have been interested in a magazine that seemed so clearly intended for a younger audience. The few items published in each "Reader's Corner" nevertheless showed that material was submitted by students from first to seventh grades, although there is obviously no way of determining in what proportion they were received by the magazine or how directly they were solicited. "Highlights of History" demonstrated most vividly the stagnation of the magazine: the drawings showed no cognizance of changes in cartoon style; the dialog was dull, with no sense of pace; and the sketchy information it provided was neither sufficient in itself nor interesting enough to entice students to look further. Nor was any bibliographic information ever provided, in the unlikely possibility that someone would actually be motivated to find out more about the person or event being highlighted.

Some of the special-feature issues, such as the Soviet Jewry issue of December 20, 1974, and the fine PLO questionnaire contained in the issue of January 30, 1976, were welcome exceptions to the drabness of *World Over*.

In 1974 Ezekiel Schloss assumed sole editorship.[4] Edith Lazaros Honig is listed as his assistant and Sigmund Laufer as associate art editor. The magazine, despite the new staff members, did not improve greatly. The pages continued to have a dull uniformity of presentation, with no contemporary flavor. Gabe Josephson's illustrations and cartoons were flat, humorless, and stale. The main current-events feature, "The News," was fairly well balanced, with headings large enough to attract some interest and articles short enough to maintain it. *World Over* still used the same printing techniques and styles of its earlier years, making it a competent but boring fossil at a time when secular children's magazines had become exciting and innovative—and television had robbed all but the most intrepid of any motivation to read at all.

In the autumn of 1976 a potential competitor to *World Over* appeared on the scene. *Levana Monthly*, "a wealth of information," was published in Philadelphia.[5] Stephen Schaffzin was publisher, Linda K. Schaffzin senior editor, and Susan Wall, editor. *Levana Monthly* used a tabloid-size newspaper format that radiated enthusiasm and energy. Each issue had eight pages, with three wide columns well divided among text, illustration, photographs, and bold headings. A monthly calendar in each issue unified many of the features, which celebrated, explained, or recalled holidays, anniversaries, and other events of importance to Judaism that were marked during the month. The first issue included many

short articles on the fall holidays, such as how to use a *lulav* and *etrog* for
Sukkot, Simhat Torah in the *Soviet Union, yizkor* (the memorial service on Yom
Kippur), and the *piyyut* (medieval poem) "Like Clay in the Hands of the Potter."
The periodical contained letters to the editor, called "Levana Responsa." "Havi
Nashira" presented the words and music of a relevant song, with additional
notes about the composer and the significance of the music chosen. "Tillie
Tayahvone" (from *bi'tayavon*—"hearty appetite"—yet another of many puns)
offered recipes for a "Tishre salad" and a "Shanah Tovah shake." The first
"Projects for 10 Fingers or 2 Hands" called "The Tree of Life, or How to give
life to a tree. The Adventures of Hayyim Aytz" gave directions for making
puppets. The back page of the magazine included a crossword puzzle, a word
unscrambler, and "Wordsworth Learning," a Hebrew-English column. Volume
1 also introduced a cartoon called "Souper Chicken" that incorporated many
of the gimmicks and wry tongue-in-cheek humor of Superman and Electric
Company's Letterman.

A potential problem with *Levana Monthly* was its consistently self-conscious
use of puns on Hebrew words and traditional lines, involving a wink to the adults
in its audience. Children are often mystified by and resentful of jokes they know
have a level of meaning they are not expected to understand or can't appreciate
without explanation.

The editor's goals—a joyous and intelligent celebration of Jewish life and
information for young people—were well on the way to realization in the first
volume. The quality of contemporary relevance, visceral celebration of Judaism,
and hipness that characterized *The Jewish Catalogue* were evident in this magazine. An outstanding "Teacher's Edition" accompanied each issue. The supplement contained suggested lesson plans using the magazine's material, with
discussion guides, bibliographical information on subjects covered in the magazine, and sources for additional enrichment (films, slide presentations, and so
on). The editors of *Levana Monthly* also solicited input from teachers on the
response of their students to the special features and topics covered in the magazine.

When Ezekiel Schloss retired, in the spring of 1977, Stephen and Linda
Schaffzin were invited to become the new editors of *World Over*. They moved
their base of operations to the New York offices of *World Over*, retained *World
Over*'s Laufer as associate art editor, and incorporated into the old magazine
most of the features and writers of their short-lived monthly.

The new *World Over* came into existence with volume 39, no. 1 (October
14, 1977). It continued to be a biweekly for another two years, with one of its
highlights a two-week calendar giving dates of celebrations and anniversaries.
Volumes 41 and 42 contained ten issues, and volume 43 appeared in eight issues,
making the periodical essentially a monthly rather than a biweekly publication.
Most of its time-worn departments are gone. There is a letters-to-the-editor
feature called "POB." For a while there was also a second letter column,
"Responsa," where a question by a reader was answered by "Millie and Eli"
(whose names derive tortuously from the Hebrew title of the periodical, *Olam*

u-mi-lo-o) "and the rest of the gang at *World Over*." Current events are covered in *Etmol* (an asterisk directs readers to the bottom of the page, where the word is translated—*etmol* means "yesterday"—and explained as "*World Over's* news in review"). "Watch Out" is a compendium of future features in the magazine, special events (including minireviews of television programs, movies, and books), and important calendar dates.

Several feature articles are presented in each issue. Some suffer from a sense of condescension and are heavily flavored with pedagogic intensity. Legends and occasional stories appear to have been reprinted from old issues of *World Over*, and other fiction is extracted from full-length books. The most recent volumes have included a story in each issue. Occasionally, issues contain a story in Hebrew, with a few of the words considered too advanced for young readers of Hebrew translated in footnotes.

In many issues, "Arty Craft" presents competent directions for creating projects, and "Sidney Seudah" provides recipes. Cartoons include "Betman and Robin Yood" and "Joey" by Herb Kruckman. Puzzles, some submitted by readers, and the "Wordsworth Learning" feature from *Levana Monthly* have appeared in most issues, together with other games, under the rubric "Strain Your Brain." The music feature of the Schaffzin's original magazine is not usually presented so directly in *World Over*, but words and music for Jewish songs find their way into many articles.

The graphics in *World Over* now have a very contemporary appeal and a variety that the old *World Over* had lacked for many years. The use of two shades of a color in addition to black is creative and includes employing color as borders and backgrounds on many pages. Individual pictures and reproductions are much larger now, giving each print better definition and more prominence. The result is a less cramped and more interesting layout. There is a nice integration of Hebrew in the body of the magazine and in the titles of the departments, although it may be intimidating for children with limited or no knowledge of Hebrew.

World Over has renewed vitality. Real imagination, goodwill, and humor are evident in the conception and execution of the magazine. Its layout and design are creative. The rigid adherence to symmetry, congealed in the old format, is gone. The covers have vibrancy and appeal, although they are not all equally well realized. Space is nicely used. *World Over* has been positively influenced by jazzy contemporary secular children's magazines in its use of headings, marginal quips, layout, and illustration. Articles have not only by-lines but a capsule biography of each author on the page, giving readers a sense that the material is written by real people. The contents seem geared best to children of the middle grades. The various typefaces used in each issue are large enough for youngsters of this age group, without being so big as to seem babyish. They are, at the same time, sophisticated enough to ensure their appeal.

The magazine broadcasts many requests for contributions from readers. Contests, invitations to be "stringers" for *World Over* (and the material submitted

by the stringers), code offers, letters to the editor, and so on all make it clear
that the magazine is intent on developing reader involvement.[6]

What of the future? The most recent issues of the magazine have a more
"settled" quality than earlier Schaffzin issues did. There is less clutter—and,
correspondingly, somewhat less of a sense of spontaneity. The consistent pattern
of the current layout threatens a possible return to rigidity. That would be too
bad. Some of the gimmicks are self-consciously clever and overly coy. They
may not wear well. It is, however, still too early to draw any conclusions other
than positive ones from the new *World Over*. The magazine has come back to
life and promises to give a new generation of youngsters the same positive
exposure to issues and events in Jewish life that readers of *World Over* in its
earliest decades were privileged to enjoy.

Notes

1. *World Over* 4 (October 30, 1942), 6.
2. Rabbinic homilies that interpret the verses of the Bible and their implications, God's
relationship to human beings, and so on. They are probably the earliest "sermons."
There are more than 100 collections of *midrashim*.
3. *Keeping Posted*, which is now exclusively a minicourse in the style of a magazine,
did not begin its special-subject issues until somewhat later.
4. Morris Epstein died at the end of 1973. The first Schloss issue was vol. 35, no. 8
(January 11, 1974).
5. *Levana*, which means "moon"—that is, "month"—in Hebrew, was of course an
instantly recognizable pun for Hebrew speakers.
6. There is now a separate "Teachers' Edition," which is identical to the students'
edition except for additional "marginal notes with points of discussion, suggested questions and other ideas," and an "Insert" with "expanded ideas, projects, resources and
other tidbits of interest to the Jewish teacher" (vol. 42, no. 1, p. 8a). The "Insert" also
has an annual index in the final issue of the year. The categories included in the index
for vol. 41, no. 10 (May 30, 1980), are Arts and Crafts; Bar Mitzvah; Book Reviews;
Calendar; Drama; Ecology and Nature; Hebrew; Holidays; Holocaust and Anti-Semitism;
Immigration; Israel; Israel: Personalities and Calendar Items; Kashrut; Music; Oral History; Recipes; Soviet Jewry; Sports; Stamps; Stories; Stringers; Tzedakah.

Information Sources

BIBLIOGRAPHY
Naomi Patz, "The Jewish Children's Periodical: Study, Evaluation and Proposal" (M.A.
        thesis, Hebrew Union College-Jewish Institute of Religion, New York, 1979).
INDEX SOURCES
Annual index from vol. 41 (1979-1980) included as part of the "Teacher's Edition"; by
        subject, in *Index of Jewish Periodicals* (Cleveland: College of Jewish Studies
        Press, June 1963-January-June 1977), from that publication's inception through
        vol. 14, nos. 3-4.
LOCATION SOURCES
Library of Congress, Boston University, New York Public Library, Ohio State University,
        among others. Bound volumes of *World Over* are in major Judaica collections

around the country, particularly in colleges of Jewish studies; in the libraries of the rabbinical schools (Hebrew Union College-Jewish Institute of Religion, New York; and Jewish Theological Seminary, New York); and in the library of the Board of Jewish Education of Greater New York, *World Over*'s publisher.

Publication History

MAGAZINE TITLE AND TITLE CHANGES

World Over / olam oo'mi-lo-o [with the Hebrew equivalent in Hebrew characters] (March 15, 1940-). The subtitle on the masthead first was *A Pictorial Magazine for Children and Youth*. Vol. 3, no. 11, (March 20, 1942) gained a superscript over the title—"America's Leading Magazine for Jewish Boys and Girls"—and the masthead subhead was dropped. With vol. 4, no. 1 (October 30, 1942), the subhead became "*A Magazine for Jewish Boys and Girls.*" This changed with vol. 12, no. 1 (November 3, 1950), to "*A Magazine for Boys and Girls.*" By vol. 25, no. 12 (March 13, 1964), it read: "*A Magazine for Youth.*" With vol. 33, no. 1 (October 1971), the subtitle became *A Magazine for Young People*. With vol. 39, no. 1 (October 1977), the subhead was again dropped, and the Hebrew title of the publication was given equal billing with the English title.

VOLUME AND ISSUE DATA

World Over / olam oo'mi-lo-o [in Hebrew characters]: *A Pictorial Magazine for Children and Youth* (vol. 1, no. 1-vol. 3, no. 10); *World Over / olam oo'mi-lo-o*, "America's Leading Magazine for Jewish Boys and Girls" (vol. 3, no. 11-15); *World Over / olam oo'mi-lo-o*, "A Magazine for Jewish Boys and Girls" (vol. 4, no. 1-vol. 11, no. 15); *World Over / olam oo-mi-lo-o*, "A Magazine for Boys and Girls" (vol. 12, no. 1-vol. 25, no. 11); *World Over / olam oo-mi-lo-o*, "A Magazine for Youth" (vol. 25, no. 12-vol. 32, no. 15); *World Over / olam oo-mi-lo-o: A Magazine for Young People* (vol. 33, no. 1-vol. 38, no. 15); *World Over / olam oo'mi-lo-o* (vol. 39, no. 1-).

PUBLISHER AND PLACE OF PUBLICATION

Jewish Education Committee of New York, Inc, (1940-1970); Board of Jewish Education, Inc., New York (1970-).

EDITOR

Israel Goldberg (1940); Maurice L. Spector (1940-1944); Deborah Pessin (1944-1947); Morris Epstein, Managing Editor, Norton Belth, editorial director (1947-1949); Ezekiel Schloss, Morris Epstein (1949-1973); Ezekiel Schloss (1974-1977); Stephen Schaffzin and Linda K. Schaffzin (1977-).

Naomi Patz

Y

YOUNG JUDAEAN

The *Young Judaean* began formal publication in 1910.[1] It is the oldest Jewish children's magazine continuously published in this country. Volume 1, no. 1, appeared in October 1910. Lotta Levensohn was the editor, according to a letter to readers from the editor, although there was no masthead. In her "greetings," Levensohn wrote: "We intend to publish stories and essays and poems and games—all of them Jewish, of course; and you will do your share by taking part in the prize competitions for essays and poems. . . . And I am very anxious that you write and tell me what you think of the things we publish, and what you would like to have us publish. And we must never, for one minute, forget that we are doing this to make ourselves always more Jewish."[2]

The first issue contained a poem, "The New Year" by Emma Lazarus, on page 1; a story by Sholem Aleichem; and four pages of news of Young Judaea clubs and other Zionist organizations and activities, including athletic leagues. There were no illustrations, but the back cover was filled with advertisements. The periodical was approximately 9 by 6 inches and the first issue contained eight pages printed in black on white, with text divided into two columns a page.

The second issue, twelve pages long, had a poem by John Greenleaf Whittier (about autumn) on the first page; an editorial by Judah L. Magnes; a personal account of the observance of Sukkot by Ruth A. Schechter, age sixteen, whose father was the great Jewish scholar Solomon Schechter; and four pages of Hebrew text. Readers were invited to submit essays about "Zionism" or poems about "Zion," with specific prizes stipulated for the winning entries.

The third issue (now advertised at $1 a year rather than the 50¢ of the initial issues) contained no advertising, was twenty-four pages long, and was printed on coated stock. It contained a poem by Emma Lazarus and a short play in verse form about Judas Maccabeus by Henry W. Longfellow, an article about the "Trendel" (*dreidl*), a historical piece reprinted directly from the work of the Jewish historian Heinrich Graetz (listing volume and chapter numbers), stories, games, suggested readings about "Chanuckah," and the words and music for a song. The only illustration was a pious engraving.

The fourth number presented more illustrations, most of them still stylized engravings. The layout alternated double and single columns. The periodical was clean, neat, and not at all juvenile in appearance. The contents were clearly geared to youth (if not to children) and did not sound condescending. Many of the stories and informational articles were reproduced from earlier sources. Authorship is given for new material, but there is no indication who the identified writers are. Although all may have been well known to their readership, none has had lasting fame.

The first masthead of any sort appeared on page 17 of volume 1, no. 6: *The Young Judaean: Official Organ of Young Judaea, a League of the Nationalist Jewish Youth*. The organization's New York address completed the masthead information.

Volume 2 indicates that it is available at $1 a year or 10¢ an issue—a bargain for newsstand readers, since only seven issues seem to have appeared in 1911-1912. A full masthead finally appears in the third issue of that year (December 1911), with David Schneeberg named as editor and Sundel Doniger as associate editor. The magazine contained poems and stories by well-known writers, many of which had appeared elsewhere or were translated from Hebrew (with the translator's name included in the credits); "Topics of Current Jewish Interest" such as "The Turko-Italian War" and "Russian Passports Question" (December 1911); and "Cousin Judith's Corner," which reprinted some letters to the editor and commented on others. There were no games or puzzles except for a request for readers to identify the theme of an engraving of a biblical scene.

"Puzzledom, Wit and Humor" was introduced in volume 3 (1912-1913), "a page of puzzles which we hope to make a permanent department of our magazine."[3] The hope was not fulfilled, because many subsequent issues contained neither. At this point the issues of the *Young Judaean* were consistently interesting, informative, varied, well written—and very serious by modern standards. A sense of the increasing Jewish presence in Palestine and the concomitant hopes for a Jewish future in the "homeland" infused its pages with subjects as varied as Aaron Aaronsohn's discovery of wild wheat, the Bezalel School of Art in Jerusalem, the assumption of guard duty in the Galilee by a group of Jewish volunteers known as the *shomrim*, and a visit to Palestine by the "benefactor" Baron Rothschild. The magazine now printed many photographs, most of them faces and places associated with the upbuilding of Jewish Palestine, as well as old-fashioned engravings by a few recognized Jewish artists and many unknowns.

Volume 4 contains no mastheads. Levensohn's name appears as the author of many feature articles, and Schneeberg makes one significant appearance: In the seventh issue of volume 4 (April 1914), "Editor's Chat" bearing his name announces the experimental participation of various young Zionist clubs as guest editors and adds: "I know from the many kind letters and words received that The *Young Judaean* has won its way into the hearts of thousands of our boys and girls. But we should not be content until our monthly is the equal of any of the many fine periodicals that our gentile friends publish—*Youth's Companion,** *St. Nicholas,** or *American Boy—Open Road.** We have not their resources, but we possess an even more valuable asset, the keen spirit of fellowship."[4]

After Schneeberg moved from editor of the magazine to executive director of the Young Judaea organization, Emanuel Neumann became editor.[5] The basic format and features of the magazine (news, holiday notes, stories, and so on) were retained, and a special feature by Schneeberg, "Young Judaea Official Notices"—recounting the activities of the various Young Judaea clubs around the country—was added. By volume 6 (1915-1916) the graphics and use of space in the magazine were more interesting, and the separate cover for each issue was more ambitious than its predecessors (but not as exotic as the covers beginning with volume 7, which use unusual colors on white stock: mauve, olive, rose, lavender, and on on). The Judaean Press, Inc., was listed on the cover as issuer of the magazine, which may account for its new sophistication in color and layout. An annual index appeared, including the categories "Fiction," "Informational," "Poetry," and "Illustrations."

Volume 8 (1917-1918) saw two- and three-color covers; consecutive page numbering through the volume (362 pages that year); the introduction of "Current Topics: A Monthly Review of Jewish Events" by Lotta Levensohn, complete with explanatory maps; "The Junior Judaean," a special section designed for younger children, edited by Cousin Judith and "Conducted by Members of Cousin Judith's Club"; the serialization of Theodor Herzl's "Oldnewland" (*Altneuland*), translated by Levensohn (and continued into volume 9); and "Sense and Nonsense—Jokes and Anecdotes of Jewish Life."

J. H. Neumann followed Emanuel Neumann as editor. His name disappeared from the masthead with the first issue of volume 9, and although the magazine continued to function well, no editor is listed in volumes 9 and 10. (This phenomenon occurs repeatedly throughout the magazine's seventy-year history.) The organization, and with it the magazine, seem to have gone through a difficult period that culminated with the discontinuation of the Department of Education of the official Zionist movement. The Young Judaea organization was one of the activities of the department. Young Judaea determined to become self-supporting. The continued publication of the magazine was a symbol of the intention to survive independently. At the bottom of each page of volume 11, no. 4, (December 1920) are the words "The Work of Young Judaea Must Go On."

By volume 12 (1921-1922) *Young Judaean* had a glossy cover of heavy coated stock. It was printed in colored ink on white paper or in black ink on colored paper. The body of the journal still contained no color. The type varied in size and style within single issues; some fonts were exceedingly small. The quality and quantity of the artwork and illustration were inconsistent. Some issues were filled with fine reproductions of pictures by Ephraim Lilien, old engravings, and photographs; others had a dull, businesslike feeling totally at variance with what a children's magazine in the third decade of the twentieth century was already expected to look like. The number of pages was not the same for each issue: some had as few as twelve pages, and others were twice that size. The consecutively numbered pages totaled 378 for the volume.

There was again an editor (again Lotta Levensohn). The magazine declared itself dedicated to preparing "the Zionists of tomorrow...for your great tasks of the future."[6] These future Zionists were mostly members of the Young Judaea clubs around the country and were youngsters between the ages of eleven and fifteen. The magazine was geared to this age group far more successfully, by modern standards, than any of its American Jewish predecessors. The *Young Judaean* benefited from the exciting innovations in general children's works and was influenced by both the virtues and failings of its Jewish forebears.

When Levensohn became editor, she issued a request for stories, poems, essays, compositions, and drawings by readers, since "the *Young Judaean* is your own magazine"[7] and asked for readers to design logos for the department headings. They included categories such as "Jewish News," covering current events items that occasionally dealt with sports and reports on the progress of musical prodigies; "Books"; and "Young Judaean Club News." The emphasis of the informational articles was on Zionism and Israel. There was no specific letters-to-the-editor feature, perhaps since the club news contained information on activities of groups and individuals throughout the country.

Each issue contained at least one story or serialized segment of a longer work. Rufus Learsi, Saul Cohen, and Shulamith Ish Kishor were among the most prolific storywriters for the magazine. The subjects of their stories were usually adventure filled, dealing with Jews around the world, with the problems attendant on the development of Palestine, and with fictionalized renditions of Jewish historical themes. They were, on the whole, well written and interesting. Unfortunately, most of the poetry that appeared was either too difficult for young readers to appreciate or overly simple, and, consequently, banal. Louis I. Newman, P. M. Raskin, and Jesse Sampter poems were frequently featured on the poetry page. The language of the periodical was suitable for teenage readers, with children at the bottom end of the age range no doubt having to make an effort to understand some of the news and informational material in each issue. But the magazine was filled with energy, excitement, and a sense of purpose, making it very attractive.

Numerous advertisements appeared on its pages, including diverse sponsors such as Jr. Literary Guild Book Club, Ex-Lax (chocolate and fig flavored), New York City banks and hotels, Atlantic City hotels, Cunard Steamship Lines, and the Jewish Institute of Religion and the Jewish Theological Seminary (the non-Orthodox rabbinical schools in New York). The ads were located on the inside front cover, on full pages toward the end of the magazine, and across the bottom and on side columns of continuation pages.

During the 1920s there were a number of changes. The magazine followed the secular rather than the Jewish calendar (making January, rather than September or October, the first issue), and the normal number of issues a year was reduced from twelve to nine. After 1924 pagination ceased to be consecutive; most issues contained thirty-two pages, although the October 1929 issue ran forty pages. By 1923 the magazine's dimensions had been enlarged (to 10 by 12 inches). A fine glossy paper was used for the inside of the magazine as well as for the cover. Color printing was still reserved for the cover only and had been increased to two and three colors on white stock, again in odd combinations: lavender and yellow, blue and orange, blue and lavender. There were many photographs, sophisticated illustrations, and very attractive logos. The work of Gustave Dore, Saul Raskin, and Rosfeld-Ress appeared often.

Nevertheless, the magazine was visually still more functional than inviting. As before, type size was fairly small. An occasional piece was printed in a larger size type, whether for the encouragement of younger readers or simply for variety is not at all clear. The general appearance of the magazine, although very clean, was still too grown up for its readership, at least according to today's standards. The age group the magazine was attempting to reach had been broadened to ''as large a list...as there are Jewish children in your city.''[8]

By the end of the decade the contents of a typical issue included editorials and club news, a short humorous story, a serialized adventure tale, biographical sketches, a feature about early Zionist activities, three or four more pages on the difficulties of Zionism and *halutziut* (pioneering), and other ''Current Topics.'' The stories were usually historical fiction or fictionalized Zionist memoirs of a sentimental or adventurous tone. Almost all of the stories were well written, and most were by professional writers, rabbis, and Judaica scholars.

The magazine seems to have gone through some troubled times in the early 1930s, as evidenced by the course of volume 21. There were to be four issues in 1932; yet June 1934 is listed as issue number 14 of volume 21. Although no editor is named for any of these issues, caring hands continued to manage the periodical and even tried to introduce new life from time to time. In February 1934, for instance, ''Our Contributors Page'' was announced: ''If you have written anything that you think worth printing...we invite you to send it to us.''[9] The column ''Did You Know That? Oddities in American Jewish History'' also began to appear, as did a renewed ''Young Judaean News,'' an essay contest, and (small wonder, given world events) an expanded news section: ''Current Topics / A Monthly Review of Jewish Events.'' The news—which dealt primarily with the rise of nazism and the increasingly beleaguered plight of Europe's Jews, with Jewish settlement and development of Palestine, and with domestic issues that were (or, at least, should have been) of concern to young Jews—provides a fascinating capsule picture of the difficult years of the 1930s. (A sad controversy is revealed in the many short references to internecine struggles among Jewish leaders over the relative merits of working on two fronts: the Middle East, for the establishment of Israel, and Europe, to help the Jews there; or temporarily abandoning the Zionist goal to concentrate on the efforts to save Europe's Jews— all of this, of course, before Hitler's genocidal plans were known or perhaps even formulated.)

Aubrey Mallach became editor of *Young Judaean* in 1937. One of his first editorial acts was to update the appearance of the magazine and invite readers' involvement: ''Some of our readers have criticized the (logos) and we have been told that anyone could draw better ones. If any reader. . .can improve on the heads that we use. . .$5. for every one accepted.''[10] Most other reader activities were channeled through the clubs, but letters and poems by readers began to appear in the journal. The *Young Judaean* became brighter, livelier, and more attractive. An entire issue, June 1939, was prepared by the members of various Young Judaea clubs as coordinated by the editor of the regular readership-involvement column ''Hora.''

Despite the horrors headlined in the current-events column (now featured on the inside front cover), the feeling of the magazine was mostly upbeat. Reality was not kept from the pages, however, as shown by the ''In Memoriam'' prominently placed in the April 1939 issue to recall the six ''scouts and guides who gave their lives for our country (Palestine) in the year 1938.''[11] One was twenty-three; the others were all between eleven and sixteen. Some were killed on intercity roads; the rest died in the ''Tiberias Massacre.''

In 1941 Aharon Kessler and Deborah Pessin became editors of the *Young Judaean*. Suddenly, the magazine began to look like a *children's* magazine: large print; double-page features and stories; and clear, attractive, simple headings. The contents, too, shifted: the focus now was directed far more toward holidays, stories, crafts, and songs than to Zionist activities and information. A cartoon feature highlighted Jewish historical heroes and events. It was drawn by Herb Kruckman (who later became identified with and inseparable from *World Over*. Pessin, too, later became editor of *World Over*.

Physically, the magazine's coated stock was of good quality, and artwork reproduced well on its pages. The cover was printed on the same paper as the rest of the magazine. The entire magazine was printed in black ink on white paper. A single additional color and its wash decorated, with only a fair amount of success, the undistinguished illustrations it was intended to enhance. Many drawings were by the art editor or by Jane Bearman. There were some photographs. The effect was reasonably attractive but not stimulating. Although type size was still small, the general appearance of the periodical accorded well with contemporary concepts of child-oriented magazines. Each of the eight issues for that year numbered twenty pages.

The tone set in the early 1940s continued through the decade. A look at the issues for 1949 reveals some new features, all consistent with this focus: arts and crafts projects (making a Hanukkah menorah, a model of the Tower of David, a lanyard bracelet, and so on); creative writing contests (won by children aged eleven and twelve); odd facts about Judaism (in the column "Do You Know"); jokes and scrambled word puzzles; dance and song instructions; and poems by subscribers. "Shalom Haverim" continued the old "Young Judaea News." Three or four very short stories were now printed in each issue. Their subject matter was modern Israel, Hasidic legends, and general Jewish content (such as holiday observances). The names of the writers of most of the material are not well known. Some of the stories were taken, with acknowledgment, from other sources. There were rarely serialized stories. The only poetry in the magazine was submitted by young readers, and its quality was no better than might be expected. The overall tone of the periodical was pleasant and nicely geared to children in the sixth through eighth grades. There was no longer any advertising.

A major change had occurred, however, in the goals of the magazine. The editorial concern now seemed as much directed toward producing an acceptable magazine for youngsters as toward the goal of inculcating within them "a burning faith in the future."[12] Theoretically, such a consideration should have brought improvements. In practical terms, however, although the magazine may have become slightly more polished and slick, it also became much more mundane and routine. It was no longer vibrant, impassioned, and exciting, as it had been in the years before the establishment of the State of Israel. The *Young Judaean* seems to have lost its individuality and become, instead, a conscious competitor of *World Over*, which by this time was the leading Jewish children's magazine.[13]

The most radical change that took place during the 1950s was the reduction of the size of the periodical—to 6½ by 9½ inches—making it again approximately the size it had been in its earliest years (the change took place with volume 42, no. 1, October 1953).

Toward the end of the decade a change in editor brought even more simplification: *Young Judaean* was visually cleaner and more attractive, but it contained even less material, and the implied readership age was clearly younger than ever.

In 1963 yet another editor, Doris B. Gold, shifted the focus back. During her nine years with the periodical, there was more informational material about Israel and a greater sense of the existence of world Jewry than there had been for many years. There was also less emphasis on literature and general Jewish culture.

During the 1970s the most exciting part of *Young Judaean* was its covers, some of which consisted of well-reproduced art and interesting photographs, all of appropriately eye-catching size. The contents of the magazine, however, contained very little of real interest or broad appeal. There were, of course, brighter moments, but they were the exception to the drab norm.

Young Judaea had opened its membership to younger children, and this may partially account for the change: the editors do not seem to have realized that less complex writing and concepts did not mean greater banality. A letter to the editor (the column "Yours—Judaeanly," on page 14 of the November 1978 issue, volume 67, no. 1) complained that "the stories are a little juvenile." The editor responded, "some members of Young Judaea are only eight or nine years old, and our magazine has to be enjoyed by them as well as older members of the movement.'' Many puzzles and games have been included in the issues of the last twenty years. They seem consistently too hard for the ability of many of the readers and possibly confusing. The artwork has been uninspiring, as has the use of color.

As has been the case throughout the life of this Zionist-oriented youth magazine, the material dealing with Israel and Zionism (rather than general Jewish or secular matters) has had the greatest appeal and has usually been the most carefully written. This is true for fiction, poetry, informational articles, and illustrations.

In the early 1980s the magazine has again become a large-format publication. There are no other positive changes. Sadly, the *Young Judaean* has moved from an ambitious, energetic magazine that competed with the best of secular children's periodicals in its desire to stimulate the interest of young Jews in political Zionism and has become instead a nondescript house organ for Young Judaea, no longer involved in competitive journalism.[14]

Notes

1. The Young Judaea youth organization was formed in 1909; publishing the magazine was one of its first projects. Several issues appeared in 1909, containing news of the recently founded Jewish youth movement, but when the October 1910 issue appeared, it was indicated as "Volume 1, No. 1."

2. *Young Judaean* 1, no. 1 (October 1910), 2.

3. Ibid., 3, no. 1 (October 1912), 22.

4. Ibid., 4, no. 7 (April 1914), 14.

5. Neumann was one of the founders of Young Judaea, president of the Zionist Organization of America, and later a member of the Jewish Agency Executive.

6. *Young Judaean* 12, no. 1 (November 1921), 1.

7. Ibid., 12, no. 12 (November 1922), 313.

8. Ibid., 19, no. 1 (January 1929), 1. The same editorial states that the magazine "aims to express Young Judaea's policy of Zionist education for the Jewish youth of America. It furnishes this in an interesting and entertaining way. Reading the *Young Judaean* keeps you abreast not only of what happens in Young Judaea, but to the Jews of the entire world. It supplies you with fascinating stories and charming illustrations, and is as satisfactory a gift as can be desired."

9. Ibid., 21, no. 10 (February 1934), 9.

10. Ibid., 25, no. 6 (February 1937), 10.

11. Ibid., 27, no. 7 (April 1939), 3.

12. Ibid., 40, no. 1 (October 1951), 3.

13. *Young Judaean* was the same size as *World Over*, had almost identical use of color and style of cover and artwork, similar features and double-page art and ritual objects, spreads, crafts, a stamp column, and games. The focus was more intensely but not exclusively on Israel.

14. In the November-December issue of 1981 (vol. 70, no. 1, p. 2) the editor celebrated the 70th year of the magazine's publication and recalled the early years of the magazine

that was once the "only illustrated magazine devoted exclusively to the interests of the Jewish Youth" and promised that "Like our earliest predecessors, *YJ* at 70 will still be bringing you" the wide range of stories, articles, features, poetry, and reader contributions for which the magazine was once famous. Would that today's *Young Judaean* did meet the standards and achievements of the early volumes.

Information Sources

BIBLIOGRAPHY
Naomi Patz, "The Jewish Children's Periodical: Study, Evaluation and Proposal" (M.A. thesis, Hebrew Union College-Jewish Institute of Religion, New York, 1979).
INDEX SOURCES
Annual index from vol. 6 (1915) to vol. 17 (1927); by subject, in *Index to Jewish Periodicals*, since vol. 52, no. 1 (November 1963).
LOCATION SOURCES
Bound volumes of *Young Judaean* are in the Zionist Archives and Library, New York; New York Public Library; Library of Congress; Jewish Theological Seminary; Hebrew Union College-Jewish Institute of Religion, Cincinnati; and various Judaica and university libraries around the country.

Publication History

MAGAZINE TITLE AND TITLE CHANGES
Young Judaean (October 1910-).
VOLUME AND ISSUE DATA
Young Judaean (vol. 1, no. 1-).
PUBLISHER AND PLACE OF PUBLICATION
Young Judaean Organization, New York (1910-1915); The Young Judaean Press, sponsored by the Young Judaea Organization, New York (1915-1922); The Young Judaean Press, New York (1922-1942); American Zionist Youth Commission, New York (1942-1953); Zionist Organization of America and Hadassah, New York (1953-1967); Hadassah, the Women's Zionist Organization of America, New York (1967-1969); Hadassah Zionist Youth Commission, New York (1970-).
EDITOR
Lotta Levensohn (1910-1911); David Schneeberg (1911-1914); Emanuel Neumann (1914-1915); J. H. Neumann (1915-1918); none listed (1918-1920); Leon S. Lang (1920); Julian M. Drachman (1920); Saul J. Cohen (1921-1922); Lotta Levensohn (1922-1923); Norman N. Gerstenfeld (1923-1924); J. H. Neumann (1924-1925); D. Leonard Cohen (1925?-1927); Sidney Wallach (1928; none listed for nos. 4-9 of that year); D. Leonard Cohen (1929; none listed for nos. 6-9 of that year and the first nine issues of the following year); Ellis Radinsky (1931); Leo W. Schwarz (1931-1932); none listed (April 1932-1935); Racille Srolovitz (1936); Rabbi Leon Spitz (1936-1937); Aubrey Mallach (1937-1941); Aharon Kessler and Deborah Pessin (1941-1944); Aharon Kessler (1944); Aharon Kessler and Anne Green

(1944-1946); Anne Green (1946-1949); Norman Schanin (1949-1952); Millicent Rubenstein (1952-1957); Ahron Gelles (1957-1961); Steve Friedman (1961-1963); Doris B. Gold (1963-1972); Barbara Gingold (1972-1982); Mordecai Newman (1982-).

Naomi Patz

YOUNG MISS

Young Miss, throughout its forty-year history, has exemplified the white, middle-class view of preteens and teenagers. It has attempted to keep pace with changes in the social role of women while retaining an emphasis on fashion, beauty, celebrities, and dating.

The magazine currently known as *Young Miss* was first published in July 1941 by Parents' Magazine Press and entitled *Calling All Girls*. It was introduced as "a brand new magazine for girls and sub-debs with 32 pages of girl comics and stories and other features."[1] Speaking through a representative girl, Susan, the editors wrote, "Most of the comic magazines are filled largely with comics that boys like better than girls, but *Calling All Girls* is going to have what we want and nothing else."[2] Each issue offered several biographical comics of heroines, including Princess Elizabeth, Juliette Lowe, Eleanor Roosevelt, Jackie Cochran, Margaret Bourke-White, and Marion Anderson. The "Yorktown Younger Set" and "Air Hostess No. 1," renamed "Judy Wing" in issue number 10, were serialized comics in each issue.[3] Historical stories featuring women were also presented in colored comic-strip format. Other features in *Calling All Girls* included "Girls in the News," "Fashions," "Good Looks," "Good Manners" by Eleanor Boykin, "Junior Housekeeping," "Let's Talk Things Over" by Alice Barr Grayson, "Movies," fiction, and poetry. Fiction included a mystery serial, "Mayor Martin's Daughter." Contests were a continuing feature. "Gadgets for Girls," renamed "Tricks for Teens" in April 1944, and "Susan Says" were monthly contest columns for readers. Famous teenagers acted as junior advisory editors and included the Moylan Sisters, Judy Garland, Gloria Jean, and Shirley Temple. Senior advisory editors included Dorothy Canfield Fisher and Osa Johnson. The president of Parents' Magazine Press, George J. Hecht, offered "Thirteen Ways Girls Can Help in the National Defense" in the first issue.[4] This emphasis on helping the country by cheerfully doing without continued throughout the war years. In volume 3 (March 1943) "The Yorktown Younger Set" was retitled "The Victory Club." Volume 3 (June-July 1943) began the practice of combining issues to comply with war regulations, a policy that was retained after the war. Authors who contributed fiction during the war years included Carolyn Keene, Margaret Sutton, and Adele De Leeuw.

Volume 5 saw the start of Calling All Girls clubs and a weekly radio program, "Calling All Girls Club of the Air," featuring fashion editor, Nancy Pepper, Jenny Jabberwocky, and dramatizations of stories from *Calling All Girls*. The clubs and radio program were sponsored by department stores in large cities. New columns, "Record Raters" and "Jabberwocky and Jive" by Nancy Pepper, were offshoots from the radio show.

With the end of World War II the focus of *Calling All Girls* shifted dramatically. Emphasis on independent women gave way to a preoccupation with dating and fashion. The color comics, dropped owing to postwar newsprint shortages, were not reinstated as promised. In 1946 several new features were begun, including "Personalities," an article in each issue about a male star that included an autographed picture. Featured stars included Peter Lawford, Perry Como, Bing Crosby, Gregory Peck, and Henry Fonda. Before 1946 the features had been about women. A readers' letter column was begun, called for the first two issues "Your Pen in Hand" and then retitled "From You to Us." Other new departments included "Calling All Girls Club News," "Careers," "Dope on Decorating," and "Good for Giggles." With issue number 52 (August 1946) page size was increased to make *Calling All Girls* comparable to *Time*, *Good Housekeeping*, and most of the movie magazines.

The beginning of 1947 saw an increase in pages, much of which was devoted to advertisements. New departments included "As You Wrote It" and "Utterly Fantastic," which were reader contributions, and "Puzzlers' Post." The Junior and Senior Advisory Boards were removed from the masthead with the issue of December 1947.

By 1948 the editors had switched the emphasis from preadolescent to high school girls. New features included a pictorial visit to a college campus and a complete novelette or condensed novel, one of which was *Big Doc's Girl* by Mary Medearis. Authors of fiction included Adrien Stoutenberg, Dorothy K. Aldis, James L. Summers, Amelia Elizabeth Walden, Elizabeth Goudge, and Edna Ferber. "Let's Talk It Over," the reader-problem page written by Alice Barr Grayson, now had famous parent-daughter "guest conductors" in each issue.

Issues in 1949 included a story by Phyllis Whitney, *And Both Were Young* by Madeleine L'Engle, an article by Margaret Bourke-White, a poetry contest judged by Joseph Auslander, and the new reader contribution column "Hi-Ways." In October 1949 *Calling All Girls* was renamed *Senior Prom*, "the complete magazine for teens, debs & co-eds."[5] New columns included "Counter Cues," "Sports Lights," "Prom's Girl of the Month," "The Mail Shopper," and "Prom Compliments." All mention of the Calling All Girls Club and its activities disappeared. Issues in 1950 included fiction by Gladys Taber, Dorothy Canfield, and Robert A. Heinlein and *Winter Wheat* by Mildred Walker. New columns included "Book Talk" by Phyllis A. Whitney and "Picture Prom."

The last issue of *Senior Prom* was March 1951 (volume 11, number 107). Evidently *Parents' Magazine*'s attempt to appeal to the older teen failed, because no more issues were published for two years. In the spring of 1953, volume 1, number 1, of *Polly Pigtails' Magazine* for girls, published by "21 Publishing Corporation," a subsidiary of *Parents' Magazine*, appeared. Its editor-in-chief was "Polly Pigtails," reminiscent of "Susan" in the first issue of *Calling All Girls*, who was pictured as a blonde with braided pigtails tied with ribbons. George Hecht, who had been president and publisher of *Senior Prom*, was *Polly Pigtails' Magazine*'s new president and publisher. The new magazine was digest size with 132 pages and was printed on light green "eye-ease" paper as were *Humpty Dumpty's Magazine** and *Children's Digest*,* also published by *Parents' Magazine*. *Polly Pigtails' Magazine* was geared to the eight to twelve-year-old preteen girl with "stories, comics, things to do, fun, fun, fun."[6] Biographical comics of women, successful in the early issues of *Calling All Girls*, were continued in *Polly Pigtails' Magazine*, many reprinted from *Calling All Girls*, but in limited color. Regular features included "Polly in the Kitchen" and "Adventures of Polly Pigtails," both in comic format; "Polly Reads the News," which was a contest feature; "Polly's Party Ideas"; "Polly's Beauty Hints"; "Polly Likes to Sew"; and "Polly's Crossword Puzzle."

The 1954 issues included a new feature, articles about forming chapters of Polly Pigtails' Club, complete with an official membership and club charter in each issue. In 1955 "Adventures of Polly Pigtails" was in prose rather than comic format. Polly was featured on all covers with her dachshund, Finnegan. Issues included more jokes, riddles, and ideas for activities. Fiction authors included Zoa Sherburne and Mabel Leigh Hunt.

With volume 2, number 14 (October 1955), the title *Calling All Girls* was resumed. Polly's name was removed as editor-in-chief, and "The Editor's Page" was signed by Betty Sears, because "Polly is so busy with school and all her other activities."[7] "The Adventures of Polly Pigtails" was retitled "The Adventures of Polly and her Friends." New comics about Penny and Tizzie were included. White paper replaced the green to facilitate photo reproduction, but most articles still dealt primarily with beauty, parties, fashion, and etiquette.

In 1956 Polly and Finnegan were removed from the cover at the beginning of the year and replaced with photographs of stars. By the end of the year, however, Polly and Finnegan were back. A single-frame cartoon, "Emmy Lou," began as a regular feature, and the comic strip biographies were discontinued. Also introduced were mystery serials; "*Calling All Girls* Fashion Notes"; "Was My Face Red!" which was contributed by readers; "Have You Heard These?" and a new series about pet care. As a regular feature star interviews with a photo included stars such as Doris Day, Hayley Mills, Shari Lewis, Annette Funicello, and Connie Francis.

In 1958 "Polly in the Kitchen" was dropped and replaced with "*Calling All Girls* Recipes of the Month." Fiction authors included Zoa Sherburne, Ruth F. Chandler, Margaret H. Bacon, Mabel Leigh Hunt, and Gertrude Bell. During the next five years the magazine changed little. Many articles were reprinted from earlier issues, and Betty Sears, editor, and Rubie Saunders, associate editor, were regular contributors. Article topics included letter writing, weight loss, baton twirling, camping, ice skating, boating, and popularity. Crossword puzzles were a regular feature.

In the January 1964 issue a new column, "From You to Us," in which editor Sears answered readers' letters, began in response to reader request. The covers, drawn by Freeman Elliott for seven and a half years, featuring Polly and Finnegan, were discontinued for covers that illustrated a featured story. By 1965 the covers were changed to photographs. In 1966 the fashion section was expanded at the request of readers and a "Good Looks" section was begun. "Tizzie" was discontinued, and a new column, "The Bookshelf" by Barbara Nolen, was begun, again due to reader request.

As of the November 1966 issue, *Calling All Girls* was renamed *Young Miss*, "fun, fashions, and good looks."[8] The editorial stated, "We changed the name of your favorite magazine to *Young Miss* because now you are real swingers!"[9] The emphasis of the magazine was now on fashion, beauty, and boys. As a consequence there were fewer stories.

In 1967 "Penny" was dropped. "Laugh It Up," formerly entitled "Giggles Galore," and "The Babysitter" were regular humor features. The covers now featured celebrities, often popular musical groups, including the Beatles, the Lovin' Spoonful, the Monkees, Petula Clark, the Beach Boys, and Sally Field. "The Adventures of Polly and her Friends" and serialized stories were discontinued. Helpful tips were no longer liberally scattered throughout the magazine, although a few were included under the page filler "Did You Know . . . That . . ." Most of these tips were reprints from the old contest column "Tricks for Teens." Regular columns included "Beautiful Buys," "*Young Miss* in the Kitchen," "Fashions for the Young Miss," "Beauty for the Young Miss," and "Riddle Dee Dee." "From You to Us" became an advice column edited by Dorothy Gordon.

The year 1968 saw a continuation of popular music groups as cover features. A regular column about careers was begun. The magazine changed little during the next seven years. Celebrities continued to be featured on the covers. Emphasis was on fashion and beauty. Many articles and stories were reprinted from past issues. Article topics included bike manners, new television shows, temper, hobbies, drugs, VD, women's liberation, menstruation, guitars, and backpacking. In 1976 new columns were "Special People-Great Ideas," "Celebrity Scene," and "Youth Beat," a column for reader response to controversial subjects, such as "pot" legalization and the Equal Rights Amendment. "Especially for You," a letter from the editor, became a sporadic feature. Issues contained less fiction and more nonfiction articles.

In 1979 *Parents Magazine* was acquired by Gruner & Jahr, U.S.A. Covers now featured teen models with ordering information for their makeup and clothes. "Special People-Great Ideas" was dropped, and a new column, "Rock 'n Roll Express," began. In 1980 "From You to Us" was retitled "Letter by Letter." "Youth Beat" was dropped. "We Speak Out," "Back Talk," "What Would You Do?" short quizzes, and contests were regular features. Most issues contained only one fictional story.

In 1981 volume 28, number 268, appeared in two editions. The March 1981 edition was in the traditional digest-size format with the typical newsprint pages and regular features. The spring 1981 edition was a pilot issue for the new *Young Miss*. It was larger and published on glossy paper, with splashy graphics, color, and advertisements throughout the magazine. It had ninety-six pages compared with sixty-six pages in the old-style edition. The emphasis was still on fashion, beauty, and movie stars. The only regular features retained were "Was My Face Red!" and "Letter By Letter." New features included "Face to Face," "Excuse Me," "Dear Beauty Editor," and "The Doctor Is In." April, May, and June-July 1981 issues continued in the former digest format.

With the August 1981 issue a new format was adopted. A new feature "Up-front," includes the columns "His Side," "At the Movies," "The Pet Shop," "Was My Face Red!" "Book Beat," "How To," "Celebrity Hotline," "The Record Department," and "Going Places." Other new features include "Star Tracks," "Keeping Fit," "On the Job," and "It's Your Turn." Newly appointed editor-in-chief Phyllis Schneider commented in her new column, "From Your Editor": *Young Miss* has 'grown up'—it's bigger, it's better, and it's jam-packed with what you've been asking for."[10] Readers are invited to apply for the *Young Miss* Round Table, a national committee of 300 male and female teens, who will keep the "editors up-to-date on trends, happenings, hobbies—anything of interest to teens."[11] The September 1981 "Heroes & Heroines" features Brooke Shields. Previously, issues had been numbered consecutively beginning with *Polly Pigtails' Magazine*, but the September 1981 issue is numbered volume 29, number 2. *Young Miss* seems to be changing to appeal to the older reader. However, unlike *Senior Prom*, which became more difficult to read than *Calling All Girls*, the new *Young Miss* may attract more readers because it is more spacious and attractive.

Notes

1. *Calling All Girls* 1 (September 1941), front cover.
2. "Susan Says," ibid., 1 (September 1941), inside front cover.
3. "Judy Wing," ibid., 1 (September 1942), 9.
4. George J. Hecht, "Thirteen Ways Girls Can Help in the National Defense," ibid., 1 (September 1941), 20.
5. *Senior Prom* 9 (October 1949), front cover.
6. *Polly Pigtails' Magazine* 1 (Spring 1953), front cover.
7. Betty Sears, "The Editor's Page," ibid., 2 (October 1955), 5.
8. *Young Miss*, 13 (November 1966), front cover.
9. Rubie Saunders, "From You to Us," ibid., 29 (August 1981), 8.
10. Phyllis Schneider, "From Your Editor," ibid., 29 (August 1981), 8.
11. "Join the *YM* Round Table," ibid., 29 (August 1981), 94.

Information Sources

BIBLIOGRAPHY

Liz Austrom, "Magazines for Young People," *Emergency Librarian* 7 (July-August 1980); G. E. Cawood and M. J. Greenlaw, "Juvenile Magazines in the U.S.A.:

A Compleat Overview with History and Trends,'' *Top of the News* 34 (Summer 1978); Lavinia G. Dobler and Muriel Fuller, *The Dobler World Directory of Youth Periodicals*, 3rd enlarged ed. (New York: Citation, 1970); Philip H. Dougherty, ''*Young Miss* to Change its Look,'' *New York Times*, February 6, 1981; T. D. Horn, Audrey Fisher, and J. L. Lanman, ''Periodicals for Children and Youth,'' *Elementary English* 43 (1966); Elizabeth Johnson, ''Magazines for Home Purchase,'' *Top of the News* 21 (June 1965); idem, ''The Magazine Rack-Children,'' *Top of the News* 24 (April 1968); W. A. Katz and B. G. Richards, *Magazines for Libraries*, 3rd ed. (New York: R. R. Bowker, 1978); Nancy Larrick, ''Classroom Magazines: A Critique of 45 Top Sellers,'' *Learning* 7 (October 1978); Christy Marshall, '' '*Young Miss*' Updates Look,'' *Advertising Age*, July 6, 1981; J. Mathews, ''Magazines and Newspapers for Children,'' *Childhood Education* 50 (April 1974); Selma K. Richardson, *Periodicals for School Media Programs* (Chicago: American Library Association, 1978); Marian H. Scott, *Periodicals for School Libraries*, rev. ed. (Chicago: American Library Association, 1973); Dorothy Spoerl, ''Magazines and Newspapers for Children,'' *Childhood Education* 38 (1962); Janice C. Stewart, ''Content and Readership of Teen Magazines,'' *Journalism Quarterly* 41 (Autumn 1964), 580-83; K. L. Walsh, ''Indexed Periodicals: Children's Magazines for Schools,'' *Serials Review* 4 (October 1978); ''Warner Takes on *Parent's* [*sic*] & *Young Miss*,'' *CPDA News* (June 1981); Barbara H. Will, ''The Teenage Magazine,'' *Library Journal* 103 (December 1978); Roland E. Wolseley, *The Changing Magazine: Trends in Readership and Management* (New York: Hastings, 1975); Sylvia H. Wright, *Magazines Recommended for Use with Children, Grades K-12: A Comparative Survey of Six Basic Lists Compiled by Librarians and Educators*, 2nd ed. (Teaneck, N.J.: Franklin Square-Mayfair Subscription Agency, 1969, ERIC Document 029 873).

INDEX SOURCES
Subject Index to Children's Magazines.
LOCATION SOURCES
Bound volumes of *Calling All Girls, Senior Prom, Polly Pigtails' Magazine*, and *Young Miss* are in the Library of Congress. *Calling All Girls*, vol. 1 (1941), through *Senior Prom*, vol. 11 (1951), are in the Free Library of Philadelphia. Los Angeles Public Library and Enoch Pratt Library, Baltimore, have vols. 3-11 of *Calling All Girls/Senior Prom*. Arizona State University, Tempe, Ariz., has issues beginning with *Polly Pigtails' Magazine* (vol. 1 is incomplete) to the present. *Young Miss* is available on microfilm, vol. 13 (1966-) from University Microfilms International, Ann Arbor, Mich.; and on microfiche, vol. 23 (1976-) from University Microfilms International and vol. 22 (1975-) from Micro Photo Division, Bell & Howell, Wooster, Ohio.

Publication History

MAGAZINE TITLE AND TITLE CHANGES
Calling All Girls (1941-1949); *Senior Prom* (1949-1951); *Polly Pigtails' Magazine* (1953-1955); *Calling All Girls* (1955-1966); *Young Miss* (1966-).
VOLUME AND ISSUE DATA
Calling All Girls (vol. 1, no. 1-vol. 9, no. 89); *Senior Prom* (vol. 9, no. 90-vol. 11, no. 107); *Polly Pigtails' Magazine* (vol. 1, no. 1-vol. 2, no 13); *Calling All Girls* (vol. 2, no. 14-vol. 13, no 124); *Young Miss* (vol. 13, no. 125-).

PUBLISHER AND PLACE OF PUBLICATION
Parents' Magazine Press, New York (1941-1949); Teen Institute, Inc., a subsidiary of
    Parents' Magazine, New York (1949-1951); "21" Publishing Corporation, a
    subsidiary of the publishers of *Parents' Magazine*, Concord, N.H. (1953-1962);
    The Better Reading Foundation, New York (1962-1968); Parents' Magazine Press,
    Bergenfield, N.J. (1968-1979); Parents' Magazine Enterprises, Inc., a subsidiary
    of Gruner & Jahr, U.S.A., Bergenfield, N.J. (1979-).
EDITOR
Frances Ullmann (1941-1947); (1947-1949); Claire Glass (1947-1951); Polly Pigtails
    (editor-in-chief, 1953-1955); Betty Sears (1953-1963); Rubie Saunders (1963-
    1979); Lois Cantwell (editor-in-chief, 1979-1980); Suzanne Kennedy Flynn (ed-
    itor-in-chief, 1980-1981); Faith Garrett Vosbrinck (1981); Phyllis Schneider (ed-
    itor-in-chief, 1981-).

Gayle Keresey

YOUTH'S CABINET

In his January 1846 introduction to the new series of *Youth's Cabinet*, editor
Francis C. Woodworth explained that the publication was not a new work, nor
was it "a Phoenix rising from the smoldering ashes of a starved periodical."[1]
It was merely an old favorite in a new dress. For the preceding eight years
Youth's Cabinet had been published semimonthly in quarto form and resembled
a paper rather than a magazine.[2] Woodworth, believing the time had come for
a change in the form of the *Cabinet*, instituted a monthly magazine that would
emphasize "History, Biography, Sketches of Travelers All Over the Globe,
Natural History (new and interesting facts in the vegetable and animal kingdoms),
Poetry, Enigmas, some Stories and some strains of Music."[3] A little humor
would even be allowed occasionally. Believing there were enough other literary
poisons for young people to read, the Presbyterian minister intended to furnish
reading matter that would "instruct the intellect, refine the taste, bind stronger
the golden chains of domestic and social life, aid parents, teachers and ambas-
sadors of the cross...to raise higher the standard of morality and virtue, purity
and holiness and to exert a healthful influence in the education of the young for
this world and for heaven."[4] Those who preferred an unnatural and unhealthful
diet of reading matter were advised to go elsewhere. His magazine would interest
the "mere child as well as the youth of a riper intellect" and would be, he
hoped, all a well-regulated family could desire.[5]

The subtitle for early issues, *A Repository of Gems for the Mind and Heart*
was later changed to *A Book of Gems for the Mind and Heart, Beautifully
Embellished*. Although the editor drew the attention of readers to both the quality
and quantity of the engravings used in the magazine, he failed to identify the
artists who had furnished the embellishments. Only the titles of illustrations were
listed under the index heading "Embellishments" or, later, "Engravings." (Titles of essays, stories, and poems were indexed separately, also without giving

recognition to the author.) In spite of the generous use of engravings, the magazine was no more or less attractive than other magazines of that period.

For $3 subscribers received the *New York Evangelist* along with the original *Youth's Cabinet*, until the end of 1845, when the *Sabbath School Monitor*, a semimonthly sheet, was substituted for the *Evangelist*. After 1852, when the size of *Youth's Cabinet* was reduced and the cost lowered to $1, a two-column format was abandoned. An attempt to make the pages more attractive by using a garland border was short-lived, as was the increase from thirty-two to forty-eight pages.

D. Austin Woodworth was his brother's only publisher, with the editorial office located at 118 Nassau Street, on New York City's publishers' row. An extensive essay in volume 1 (January 1846) describes the publishing world of 1846 and lists fifty-one publishing houses then located on Nassau Street. Both known and unknown titles are among their publications: *New York Daily Telegraph, Youth's Temperance Gazette, Farmer's Library and Journal of Agriculture, Home Missionary, Mother's Magazine, Knickerbocker Magazine, American Phrenological Journal, The National Preacher, New York Sun, The Tailor's Magazine and Report of Fashions*. Woodworth lamented in the essay that some magazines were not what they should be and ''went abroad carrying poison that takes hold of the soul and does its work of death there.''[6] Besides envisioning his magazine as a higher ''Gem,'' Woodworth knew the art of printing. In the longest essay of the magazine's life, he wrote a history of printing and described the composing stick; how to set captions; the fonts used, as well as the use of solid or leaded matter; types of ink; and cylinder presses; and he included illustrations of various machines and printing offices—a valuable historical record of the state of the art in 1850.[7]

Both a paternalistic and an ecclesiastical concern for his readers is expressed in the opening fireside talk with readers (January 1846) and in a variety of ways throughout the life of the magazine. An engraving of a man in an armchair, holding a magnet, adorned the cover of early issues. With all too obvious symbolism, Woodworth, from his editorial chair, compared the magnetism of a loadstone to his ability to attract readers and to interest them in preparing their souls for eternity. Under the pseudonyms ''The Man with the Magnet,'' ''Theodore Thinker,'' and ''Uncle Frank,'' Woodworth seems to have written the majority of the magazine's essays, biographies, and stories. His interest in words and language resulted in brief lessons on the use of alliteration, illative and causative propositions, the three syntactical combinations, the Latin sentence ''Rex rectus regnum regit'' (which illustrated several important principles, he stated) and even a defense of the use of the contractions *ain't, don't, won't,* and *can't.* His contest for a brief English sentence using all letters of the alphabet and all parts of speech brought in 211 entries, all of which he later published. (The winning sentence was ''Oh, just go from me! Why vex and quiz a poor black man?'') Because Woodworth believed deeply in the importance of good literature in the household, he devoted a section of each issue to ''Notices of

New Publications.'' Published in very small print, various titles were noted and recommended: *The Vicar of Wakefield*, a new edition of the *New England Primer*, *A History of the Hat*, *The Musical World*, *Eutaxia; or The Presbyterian Liturgies*, *The Escaped Nun*, and *The Autobiography of Alfieri*.

Woodworth's use of both singular and plural first-person narrative, and his repeated use of "Dear Reader...," "Will it be agreeable to you, reader...,"and "Would you care to...kind reader" illustrate his efforts to ingratiate himself with his young subscribers. The practice resulted in a lack of both objectivity and literary sophistication. However, he did believe a writer needed to understand the mind of a child and should obey the laws of good taste, whether in writing a nursery song or an epic poem.

Among the subjects for the biographies he wrote were Robert Fulton, Mary Queen of Scots, Nicolo Poussin, Harriet Martineau, John Spurzheim the phrenologist, Jenny Lind, William Cowper, and the magazine itself. Stories (including occasional fables "for Little Folks and Great Ones too") were often completely in dialog form and taught the folly of selfishness, pride of birth, conceit, lying, as well as the importance of honesty, the dangers of strong drink, and the beauty of animal and plant life.

Since many readers would never visit New York City, Woodworth introduced them to the Gothic architecture of the city—the original building of the University of the City of New York, the French Church on Franklin Street, the Harlem Tunnel, Carmine Street Presbyterian Church, the Park, City Hall and its famous fountain, and many other places of interest to him. Engravings that accompany the descriptions are a historical tribute to a city no longer remembered or experienced.

Contact with readers was sustained through "Uncle Frank's Monthly Table Talk.'' Here were gathered together the "Off-Hand Notes and Queries,'' the gentle warnings to pay overdue subscription fees ("When you fail to be punctual in your payments, you cripple us in ours"[8]), and responses to children's letters (from Iowa, the Arkansas Territory, Illinois, Georgia, Wisconsin, and Michigan, in addition to the eastern states). "Table Talk'' also included personal comments about the editor's illnesses; travels (to Boston where it was a pleasure to have a policeman tap a "segar"-smoking pedestrian on the shoulder to tell him he was breaking a city ordinance); attendance at concerts by the Hutchinson family, William Bradbury, and other musicians of the time; and the opening of the Crystal Palace, at which President Pierce was guest speaker. Although the monthly chat often exceeded two or three magazine pages, readers were insulated from the real-life events of westward expansion, slavery, statehood, Indians, the discovery of gold, new inventions, and so on. Even after the magazine merged with its next-door friendly rival at 116 Nassau Street, *Merry's Museum*,* Woodworth invited readers to send their correspondence directly to him at the old address. His paternalistic instinct was not easily suppressed or relinquished.

The material not written by Woodworth varied from "Superstition Connected with Sneezing," "The Eye, and How to Abuse it," and "The Oyster's Enemies" to "An Apology for Hogs" and "The Drolleries of Santa Claus." Many of these pieces were reprinted from other magazines (*Mother's, School Friend, Inverness Courier, Youth's Penny Gazette*) or were written by T. S. Williamson, E. A. Comstock, William Oland Bourne, William Alcott, M.D., Lydia Baxter, and others. L. Maria Child, T. S. Arthur, Lydia Sigourney, Kate Cleveland, and Felicia Hemans were frequent contributors to this and other magazines of the period. The omission of serialized stories was a policy decision. For some reason Woodworth rejected the practice that other editors used to retain subscribers. Remaining adamant in his view, Woodworth refused to print Frank Rambler's "Letters from the Country."

Poetry; music; pages of puzzles; charades; enigmas; historical, biblical, arithmetical, and geographical questions (submitted by children); and "fillers" (such as "Beware of little sins," "Better waste money than time," and "A good book and a good woman are excellent things to those who know how to value them; but there are many who judge of them both only by their covering")—all embodied the editor's purpose: "amusement our means—instruction our end."[9]

In December 1855 Woodworth announced that Francis Forrester, editor of *The Boys' and Girls' Magazine, and Fireside Companion** would become assistant editor of *Youth's Cabinet*. Ill health was forcing "Uncle Frank" Woodworth to be absent from his office more frequently; "Aunt Sue" was responsible for writing his monthly column. The magazine began its third series in January 1857. In April, without announcement to its readers, *Youth's Cabinet*, which some time earlier had annexed *The Mentor* (1851?), merged with *Merry's Museum, Parley's Magazine,** and *Schoolfellow*, giving it a circulation "far beyond that of any other young people's magazine in the world," according to the editor—an assertion that cannot now be verified.[10] Francis Woodworth's name appeared with Robert Merry and Hiram Hatchet as co-editors of *Merry's Museum* in 1858 and 1859; "Uncle Frank" wrote an occasional "Monthly Talk" column, and *Merry's Museum* carried *Woodworth's Cabinet* on its masthead even as late as 1867, but the magazine was no longer *Woodworth's Youth's Cabinet*.

Youth's Cabinet was neither a distinctive nor an innovative magazine. No department or feature was particularly unusual or imaginative. Satisfied with supplying much of the material himself and rewarded with laudatory correspondence from his readers, Woodworth did not find it necessary to cultivate large numbers of authors. Although there is reference to Bible lessons, religious training, and proper cultivation of the soul for eternity, the influence of Rev. Francis Woodworth is more evident as author-editor than as minister. He wrote for young boys and girls who thought and read for themselves. To exert a healthful influence; to create pure minds, pure hearts; to remind readers that all are "humble voyagers, O'er life's dim, unsounded sea"—such were the noble aims of *Woodworth's Youth's Cabinet*.[11]

Notes

1. *Youth's Cabinet* 1 (January 1846), v.
2. Woodworth, when *Youth's Cabinet* was published in "paper" format, joined forces with Eliza Follen, editor of *Child's Friend*,* and Lydia Maria Child, editor of *Juvenile Miscellany*,* in attacking editorially the evils of slavery. For a more complete discussion of the subject, see John C. Crandall, "Patriotism and Humanitarian Reform in Children's Literature, 1825-1860," *American Quarterly* 21 (Spring 1969), 12-18.
3. *Youth's Cabinet* 1 (January 1846), vi.
4. Ibid.
5. Ibid., p. v.
6. Ibid., 1 (May? 1846), 144.
7. Ibid., n.s. 3 (March? 1852), 71-84.
8. Ibid., n.s. 6 (January? 1855), 244.
9. Ibid., n.s. 3 (January? 1852), title page.
10. Ibid., series 3, no. 3 (April? 1857), 124.
11. Ibid., 1 (December? 1846), 356.

Information Sources

BIBLIOGRAPHY
None.
INDEX SOURCES
None.
LOCATION SOURCES
The holdings of the Children's Literature Research Collections, University of Minnesota
        Libraries, Minneapolis, are almost complete and include: vols. 1, 2, 3, 5, 6 (1846-
        1851); n.s. vols. 3, 4, 5, 6, 7, 8 (1852-1856); 3rd series, nos. 1, 2, 3 (1857).

Publication History

MAGAZINE TITLE AND TITLE CHANGES
Youth's Cabinet: A Repository of Gems for the Mind and Heart (1846-1851); *Woodworth's
        Youth's Cabinet* (1852-1856); *Woodworth's Youth's Cabinet: Comprising Both a
        Treasury of Knowledge and a Gallery of Amusement* (1857).
VOLUME AND ISSUE DATA
Youth's Cabinet: A Repository of Gems for the Mind and Heart (vol. 1, no. 1-vol. 6,
        no. 12); *Woodworth's Youth's Cabinet* (n.s. vol. 1, no. 1-vol. 8, no. 12); *Wood-
        worth's Youth's Cabinet: Comprising Both a Treasury of Knowledge and a Gallery
        of Amusement* (series 3, nos. 1, 2, 3).
PUBLISHER AND PLACE OF PUBLICATION
D. Austin Woodworth, New York (1846-1857).
EDITOR
Rev. Francis C. Woodworth (1846-1857); name appeared on masthead in 1858 and 1859,
        after merger with *Merry's Museum*.

Harriett R. Christy

THE YOUTH'S CASKET

The Youth's Casket was a monthly magazine for boys and girls published in Buffalo, New York, from 1852 to 1857. This modest magazine was the first publication of Erastus F. Beadle, who later made his mark on American publishing with the dime novels that he, his brother Irwin, and their partner Robert Adams began to produce in the 1860s.

Beadle was descended from pioneer stock, and the publication of *The Youth's Casket* was one small part of his life of enterprise and adventure. He was born in 1821 in Otsego County, New York, and took his first job as a miller's apprentice at the age of seventeen. Legend has it that Beadle carved letters from pieces of wood and used this "type" to label sacks of grain. He traveled from farm to farm labeling whatever needed to be labeled before he settled in Cooperstown, New York, where he met the printer Elihu Phinney who took Beadle as his apprentice. From this master printer, Beadle learned the trades of typesetting, stereotyping, printing, and binding.

Beadle tried his hand at wood engraving also, and at the age of twenty-one he sent examples of his work to a New York publisher who saw promise in it, but who suggested that he not settle in New York City where the wood-engraving profession was already too full.[1]

In 1847 Beadle moved to the village of Buffalo and worked as a stereotyper for Jewett, Thomas & Co., publishers. The first printing press had been brought to Buffalo in 1811, and the first newspaper began in 1812. By 1851, with a population of more than 42,000, the city was ready for its first juvenile magazine.

In 1850 Beadle's brothers, Irwin and James, joined him in Buffalo, and they began the firm of Beadle & Brother's Stereotype Foundry. Their publication, *The Youth's Casket*, first appeared in December 1851. Its title refers to a jewel box or repository of good reading material. Besides its reading material, a good midnineteenth-century juvenile magazine needed illustrations. So to publish *The Youth's Casket* the Beadle Brothers formed a partnership with a Buffalo engraver, Benjamin Vanduzee. Vanduzee produced engraved plates from original illustrations created by himself and other Buffalo artists, and the Beadles stereotyped the text for printing.

It appears that Erastus Beadle wrote a substantial portion of the early issues of his magazine, although many of his biographers claim he was only a publisher and not a writer.[2] Almost every early issue of the magazine contains an article written by "E.E.B." Although these are not the exact initials of Erastus F. Beadle, articles by this author profile the interests, travels, and life of Beadle. In the article "A Burning Village" (January 1852) E.E.B. related the story of Indians burning the village of Cherry Valley in Otsego County, New York, which was the county where Beadle was born. In the story "My Grandfather and the Boy Soldiers" (October 1852) E.E.B. wrote about how his grandfather fought in the Revolutionary War, losing a leg in battle. Benjamin Beadle, the grandfather of Erastus was a veteran of this war, although it is doubtful that this thrice-married father of twenty-three children lost a leg in battle. E.E.B. wrote travelogs throughout New York State, New England, and the West. His lengthy "Trip to the Falls" (August 1852) with varied wood engravings of Niagara Falls was published in book form as "Emily and Clara's trip to Niagara Falls" authored by "the Editor of Youth's Casket."

E.E.B. also wrote about more exotic excursions, such as "China and the Chinese" (February 1853), "Scenery in South America" (December 1852), and "Icebergs and Ships" (January 1853). Although these articles have more ambitious subjects than the author's treatments of topics from his own backyard, they lack the detailed and convincing style and seem derived entirely from guidebooks.

E.E.B. was not the only pseudonym of an author who wrote for *The Youth's Casket*. The editor of the first twelve issues is listed as Harley Thorne, although no such person appears in contemporary Buffalo city directories. It has been assumed that the second editor, James O. Brayman, who also edited the daily *Commercial Advertiser*, used this pseudonym rather than link his name with a fledgling juvenile magazine.[3] Even after the nonexistent Harley Thorne left his editorial offices, he continued to contribute articles such as "Samuel Sober's Temperance Speech" and "Father Wiley's Chats" (both February 1853) and "Painters and Painting" (March 1853). Rather than assuming that Harley Thorne was James O. Brayman, one cannot help but wonder if this also was a pseudonym of Erastus Beadle. Whatever the case, Brayman became editor of *The Youth's Casket* in 1853 and served in that capacity until he went west in 1855.

The physical appearance of *The Youth's Casket* was modest but handsome. It contained between sixteen and thirty-eight pages an issue and sold for an annual subscription rate of 50¢. It was first issued in white wrappers printed with red-orange ink and later in tan wrappers printed in black. *The Youth's Casket* measured 8½ by 5⅜ inches, and articles were printed two columns a page. All pages were stereotyped, and the publisher advertised that he could reprint past issues, should someone order a back copy. Beginning in 1856 an attractive pictorial cover shows eight vignettes of children at play and at home. Children are shown on horseback, receiving advice from their elders, bathing at a swimming hole, reading, flying a kite, and pushing one another on a swing. Illustrations throughout *The Youth's Casket* are numerous and handsome. Decorative borders and vignettes enliven most lengthy articles, and most seem to have been created especially to illustrate an article's subject, although a few illustrations seem more general purpose.

In the introduction to the first issue of *The Youth's Casket*, publisher Beadle explained the purpose of his new magazine. It was being produced for "amusement and instruction" and promised a "variety of historical, scientific and philosophical information... and a pleasant variety of tales, and articles relating to sports, pastimes, &c." More illuminating than this general statement, Beadle described what he himself wished to accomplish with his new business venture: "We frankly confess that, in part, we labor that we may obtain money; but in return for the money which you send us we shall exert ourselves to do you good, and to repay you with that which will be really of more value to you than that which you paid with."[4]

The Youth's Casket contained much that was written originally for it, but an equal amount was gleaned from various works of literature, natural history, and science. The first volume included a story by Hans Christian Andersen, "There Is a Difference" (June 1852), about an apple tree blossoming in a ditch. This story somehow found its way to Buffalo, even though it was first published that same year (1852) in the *Danish People's Almanac*.[5]

More predictably, the first volume initiated the staple of a series of biographies for children, the first being "Portraits of the Presidents," beginning with Washington and ending fourteen months later with the incumbent Franklin Pierce. In its second year of publication, a new series, "Portraits of Men of Science and Literature," took up when "Presidents" had run out. With the third volume of 1854, a six-month series, "A Few Chapters on Stereotyping, Printing, Paper-Making, Bookbinding, &c," explained in fairly technical terms a great deal that a young reader might want to know about these subjects. This series was written by the editor James O. Brayman, and it included many full-page engravings of contemporary machinery to explain every step in the production of a publication like *The Youth's Casket*.

The Youth's Casket always welcomed and printed articles and poems from young readers as well as their letters, which were featured in the column, "The Editor's Monthly Talk with His Friends." So many of these letters to the editor lavishly praise *The Youth's Casket* and point out its reasonable price that the reader cannot but wonder if the publisher himself used this column as a form of advertising.

Throughout the magazine, readers were encouraged to seek out new subscribers, and they were offered premiums, including sets of plates and books and the grand prize of a Melodeon. In 1855 the grand prize was won by a young man who sold 107 new magazine subscriptions.

During 1855 great changes took place in *The Youth's Casket*. By this time Beadle had sold his stereotyping business but had acquired sole ownership of his publishing business. Still, one monthly juvenile magazine did not keep this energetic man occupied, nor did it generate enough income to suit his needs. In January 1856 Beadle's new monthly ladies' magazine, *The Home: A Fireside Companion* was issued. This magazine was edited by Harriet E. G. Arey, who had just taken over the editorship of *The Youth's Casket* after James O. Brayman went west. Arey had contributed poetry to *The Youth's Casket*, and as editor she continued to write poetry and serialized stories. With the help of her associate, Mrs. C. H. Gildersleve (later Mrs. Rachel Longstreet), the women wrote a large portion of the magazines she edited. Under her editorship *The Youth's Casket* expanded again and offered a wide variety of articles. Each month it contained a lengthy article about its zodiac sign as well as a discussion of the historical events that had occurred during that month. The column "Nuts to Crack" presented puzzles, scientific questions, and enigmas that readers were challenged to answer. Under the editorship of Arey, *The Youth's Casket* took on a more feminine and domestic tone. A monthly "Floral Department" written by "Aunt

Hatty" and the "Scripture Sketch" of "Aunt Mary" replaced the adventurous stories of pioneer life that had been printed two years earlier. Illustrations of mothers and children became a staple, and numerous moralistic poems were included in each issue. Education was not neglected, and "Uncle Philo" gave monthly lessons in astronomy, botany, history, and natural science.

With Arey in charge of his magazines, Erastus Beadle left Buffalo and went to Omaha, Nebraska, to seek his fortune as a speculator in the land boom in the Kansas Territories. He arrived there in 1856, too late to get rich in western real estate, and returned a poor man to Buffalo that same year.

In 1857 *The Youth's Casket* ceased publication. Its final editions noted that the publishers needed to devote more time to their other magazine, *The Home*. The last two issues indicate that *The Youth's Casket* was to be combined with a Boston magazine *Forrester's Boys' and Girls' Magazine, and Fireside Companion.**

Before it ceased publication, a series of books, "The Casket of Juveniles," was issued in six volumes, each available in either green paper wrappers or a uniform blue binding. The books were composed of stories previously printed in *The Youth's Casket*: "Leonard Barton, the Blind Boy," "Emily and Clara's Trip to Niagara Falls," "The May-Day Ramble," "The Burning Village," "The Book of Animals," and "The Book of Birds."

In 1858 Erastus Beadle, his brother Irwin, and their new partner Robert Adams left Buffalo for New York, where they began publishing handbooks on a variety of subjects that sold for 10¢ each. Their dime songbooks, housewive's guides, and baseball guides found a ready market in New York City. Shortly thereafter, the Beadle brothers and Robert Adams moved the publication of *The Home* to New York, leaving Arey and Gildersleve without a magazine to edit. They, with their husbands, founded a rival, but similarly titled, magazine of their own called *The Home Monthly*.

In spite of any rival publications from now far-off Buffalo, the publishing success of the firm of Beadle Brothers & Adams began at this point. In 1860 they began to produce their dime novels, which were written to appeal to masses of Americans. Although their literary quality was questioned, the Beadle Dime Novels proved an extraordinary popular success. But it had all begun in Buffalo with the publication of *The Youth's Casket*. This modest and short-lived publication had given Erastus and Irwin Beadle their first practical experience in serial publication.

Notes

1. *The Beadle Collection of Dime Novels* (New York: New York Public Library, 1922), 76.

2. Della T. Lutes, "Erastus F. Beadle: Dime Novel King," *Proceedings of the New York State Historical Society* 39 (1940), 152.

3. Albert Johannsen, *The House of Beadle and Adams and Its Dime and Nickle Novels: The Story of a Vanished Literature* (Norman, Okla.: University of Oklahoma Press, 1950), 20.

4. *The Youth's Casket* 1 (January 1852), v-vi.

5. Hans Christian Andersen, *The Complete Andersen* (New York: Heritage Press, 1942), xxiv.

Information Sources

BIBLIOGRAPHY

Erastus F. Beadle, *To Nebraska in '57: A Diary of Erastus F. Beadle* (New York: New York Public Library, 1923); *The Beadle Collection of Dime Novels* (New York: New York Public Library, 1922); Albert Johannsen, *The House of Beadle and Adams and Its Dime and Nickle Novels: The Story of a Vanished Literature* (Norman Okla.: University of Oklahoma Press, 1950); Della T. Lutes "Erastus F. Beadle: Dime Novel King," *Proceedings of the New York State Historical Society* 39 (1940), 147-57; Frank Luther Mott, *A History of American Magazines* (Cambridge: Harvard University Press, 1938), vol. 2; Frank H. Severance, "Bibliography: The Periodical Press in Buffalo, 1811-1915," *Buffalo Historical Society Publications* 19 (1915), 177-312.

INDEX SOURCES

None.

LOCATION SOURCES

New York Public Library (vols. 1-6); Buffalo & Erie County Public Library, Buffalo, N.Y. (vols. 1-5).

Publication History

MAGAZINE TITLE AND TITLE CHANGES

The Youth's Casket: An Illustrated Magazine for Children (January 1852-December 1854); *The Youth's Casket: An Illustrated Magazine for the Young* (January 1855-December 1857).

VOLUME AND ISSUE DATA

The Youth's Casket: An Illustrated Magazine for Children (vol. 1, no. 1-vol. 3, no. 12); *The Youth's Casket: An Illustrated Magazine for the Young* (vol. 4, no. 1- vol. 6, no. 12).

PUBLISHER AND PLACE OF PUBLICATION

Beadle & Vanduzee, Buffalo, N.Y. (January 1852-March 1853); Beadle & Brother, Buffalo, N.Y. (April 1853-November 1853); E. F. Beadle, Buffalo, N.Y. (December 1853-December 1855); Beadle & Adams, Buffalo, N.Y. (January 1856-December 1857).

EDITOR

Harley Thorne (1852); James O. Brayman (1853-1854); Harriet E. G. Arey (1855-1857).

John R. Edson

YOUTH'S CHRISTIAN COMPANION

Youth's Christian Companion, along with its sister publications for younger readers, *Story Friends** and *Words of Cheer*,* was a unifying and guiding force, of high literary standards, for young people in the Mennonite Church for nearly fifty years (1920-1968), during which time the cultural differences between the

Mennonite Church and American society diminished. American Mennonites, as a small but strong religious and ethnic community settled mostly in the rural eastern United States (especially Pennsylvania, Ohio, Indiana, and Virginia), faced the challenge of training their children and young people in the faith and way of life they had sustained and developed during two centuries in the New World from roots in the Anabaptist Reformation of sixteenth-century Holland, Switzerland, and Germany. Although in many ways like other Christian denominations, most Pennsylvania and Virginia Mennonites at the time of the founding of *Youth's Christian Companion* dressed distinctively in plain clothes (the prayer veiling or "covering" for the women, the "plain coat," a straight-cut jacket without a tie, for the men). They had been reviled, jailed, and sent to work camps for their biblical pacifism during World War I. *Youth's Christian Companion* began as a means of educating and engaging Mennonite young people to keep alive their parents' and forebears' faith and vision. The memory of religious persecution in Europe and America was very fresh.

Clayton F. Yake, the first editor of *Youth's Christian Companion* and its editor for thirty-five years, had a childhood typical of Mennonites of his generation. He was born in the fertile farmland of Lancaster County, Pennsylvania, November 25, 1899, and later wrote, "as a youth I often watched cows to pasture them by the roadside; I was a mere farm lad from a lowly home, acquainted with hard toil and frugality."[1] He went to school in a red brick schoolhouse by the side of the road, where he was inspired by the teaching and life of H. Frank Reist, later president of Goshen College, Goshen, Indiana. Reist, Yake wrote, "led me to Christ at the age of sixteen," and it was Reist who as editor of *Christian Monitor* accepted Clayton's first "pen product" and encouraged him to write. "I had been teaching school ever since the age of seventeen, except when I was attending school myself, although most of my summers were spent on the farm." Yake married Martha Eby of Lititz, Pennsylvania, in 1918 and moved with her to West Liberty, Ohio, to work on the farm of the Orphans' Home there, "after the door to the occupancy of one of the best Lancaster County farms had been literally spiked shut."[2]

It was at West Liberty, Ohio, that Aaron Loucks, general manager of the Mennonite Publishing House of Scottdale, Pennsylvania, came to ask Yake to become the editor of a new young people's paper. Accepting this request as the calling of God, Clayton and Martha Yake moved to Scottdale, where he assumed what became three and a half decades of duties as the prime shaper of a periodical that was an intrinsic and influential part of the life of Mennonite Church youth. Although he was a Lancaster County native, Yake took a broad, nonprovincial approach that eventually caused members of the Lancaster Mennonite Conference to consider him too liberal and to found another youth paper (*Youth Messenger*) to supplant *Youth's Christian Companion* in their churches.

Yake's eight-page illustrated weekly was sent to Sunday School superintendents and distributed by them on Sunday mornings (and thus was often read furtively or longingly glanced at during the sermon). *Youth's Christian Com-*

panion was meant for readers who during a later decade would be called "teens," but an older and a younger audience read it as well. *YCC*, as *Youth's Christian Companion* came affectionately to be called, featured missionary reports, short stories, articles, poems, quizzes, and Sunday School studies, which were interpretations of biblical texts. Missionaries sent in sketches of life in India, China, North Africa, and other places. India was one of the earliest fields of American Mennonite missions and thus was reported on in special detail by well-known missionaries such as Fannie Lapp and George J. Lapp in the serial "Lessons from India Life," in his memoirs, and by Wilbur and Velma Hostetler.[3] Science was also an important area of interest in *YCC*. Features such as "Molecules and Atoms," "Radio Waves," and "Beyond the Solar System" in the series "Spiritual Truths Revealed in Science" brought general knowledge in readable form, by H. Harold Hartzler, Goshen College professor of math and astronomy. M. T. Brackbill, professor of physics, mathematics, and astronomy at Eastern Mennonite College, Harrisonburg, Virginia, in the late 1940s and early 1950s authored the series "Stars from Starrywood," giving seasonal information on the skies interspersed with discussions about God, immortality, and heaven.

Youth's Christian Companion, besides presenting interesting information from science, Bible knowledge, and mission activities, sought to inculcate an attitude toward life that reflected the character and ideals of the Mennonite Church and of the editor. This was an attitude of high, earnest moral striving. Although it taught one to set modest goals in daily life and promoted humility in work and relationships, it also valued taking satisfaction in a job well done and finding joy in family and friendships. The paper did not reflect a pronounced class consciousness, but it did show signs of American middle-class values, with important exceptions. Although there was frequent discussion of professions and types of work, there was no emphasis on career or success as goals in themselves. In the first few decades of its history there was no overt and almost no implied political point of view and comment other than obedience to the government, except in cases where the government demanded actions contrary to conscience and the teachings of the church, which were based on what was, to the believers, God's will. As World War II approached, *Youth's Christian Companion* published articles calling young men in the church to obedience to Jesus' commandment to love one's enemies and to the Old Testament commandment against killing, which in practical terms, for Mennonites, meant refusal to serve in the military in any capacity. Prominent Mennonite scholar Guy F. Hershberger wrote "To Keep Alive our Scriptural Peace Testimony" in the January 7, 1940, issue. In "The Youth Movement of the Nations," Sanford G. Shetler critically examined the Hitler Youth and youth movements under Stalin and Mussolini (February 16-April 13, 1941). After the war Yake published articles about Mennonite relief workers who went to Europe as volunteers to help rebuild war-ravaged countries.

In *YCC* good citizenship in family, school, church, and community led first to good citizenship in the kingdom of heaven and second to good citizenship in the nation-state of America; not that disrespect or disloyalty to the government was taught—on the contrary. But the government was primarily appreciated for permitting religious freedom and for its laws and institutions; otherwise, allegiance was absent. Government was to be obeyed, but within limits: the highest allegiance was to God. The church's historical stand on separation of church and state prevented involvement in politics and prohibited members from voting.

Saved and unsaved, Christian and non-Christian, were the major divisions of humanity. The theological issues of pacifism and its foundation in biblical interpretation and history were set forth in detail as World War II approached. Within the less-disputed Christian realm the principal forms of experience were exercising the Christian virtues such as gentleness, meekness, forbearance, charity, honesty, faith, and hope. Obedience to parents was stressed. Witnessing to others through word and deed were important duties of the Christian. Growth in relationship to God was explored in essays, articles, and fiction. Common themes were conviction of sin, repentance, submission and acceptance of forgiveness, the striving to discern God's will through study of the Bible, receptiveness to counsel from brother and sister Christians, and the act of listening to God through prayer and inner silence. Stories of conversion such as "How a Skeptic Was First Made to Think of Christ," by an unknown author in the January 5, 1930 issue, were frequent.

Perhaps the most favored plot in the short stories, as in "Old Acquaintance" by Esther Eby Glass (December 26, 1954), was the temptation of a "good" young man or woman, usually by a worldly companion from school, someone who typically wore flashy clothes and saw nothing wrong in going to the movies or dancing. ("Inside Hollywood" by Dorothy Clark Haskin, a serial begun in November 1954, presented accounts of scandals and conversions in Los Angeles.) The rejection of parents' ideals as the young person strayed into worldly habits would be followed by disillusionment, loneliness, and disgust. If nothing calamitous occurred such as a smashup in a sports car, a lesser crisis usually brought about repentance, forgiveness (by God, family, and church), and the exalted feeling of being cleansed and ready to begin anew. In "Old Acquaintance," Paul, a star football player until a serious football accident, calls his debonair girlfriend Sue on New Year's Eve to tell her he has lost their theater tickets. Sue takes the chance to brush him off in favor of Rod Bentley, the new football star and one of the country club set. A chance glimpse of an old diary with Paul's New Year's resolutions from a few years earlier reminds him of his abandoned discipline of faith, and he resolves to join his parents at the watchnight service, where he knows he is being prayed for. Moralistic as it sounds—and is—the story is nonetheless well written and vivid. Stories such as this one reflected the Mennonites' perpetual struggle during the middle decades of the twentieth century against being overwhelmed by mainstream American mores. Mennonite educational institutions were promoted in *YCC* as part of that endeavor, especially the church colleges—Goshen, Eastern Mennonite, and Hesston—which were featured in many articles such as "Prepare for the Future at a Church School" by Fannie Schrock (April 27, 1941).

Yake regularly addressed his readers in his dignified, individual style. Although he upheld and promoted a standard of gentlemanliness and ladylikeness for young men and women, the central ideal of *YCC* was spiritual integrity. That was inextricably linked to identification with the Mennonite community.[4] But the range of themes covered in *YCC* was admirably broad, from alcoholism to archeology, church history, Holland, Korea, public speaking, Savonarola, the solar system, Yale University, and zeal. *YCC* reported on and promoted the activities of the Mennonite Youth Fellowship (MYF). "With Negroes in the Deep South" by Edwin L. Weaver, which appeared in several parts from May to August 1950, spoke of a growing interest in the social issues of race and economic justice.

One of Yake's great talents as editor was the discovery and cultivation of talented young writers. He earned the loyalty and appreciation of many writers whose work he published and whom he helped through encouragement and criticism. Among them are Christmas Carol Kauffman, one of the most prolific of American Mennonite authors, whose books *Not Regina* and *A Search to Belong* first appeared serialized in *YCC* and are still in print. Other authors who got their start or a good push ahead in *YCC* were Esther Eby Glass (*The Miller Five*), Omar Eby (*A Covenant of Despair, How Full the River*), Elaine Sommers Rich, and Robert J. Baker.

Beginning with the January 2, 1955 issue, C. F. Yake was succeeded by Urie A. Bender, a Canadian teacher and author. Bender had served as assistant editor of *YCC*, as Ethel Yake Metzler, Yake's daughter, had before him. (Ethel Yake Metzler edited the paper during a period of her father's illness.) Bender continued Yake's policies, giving a bit more prominence to fiction and dropping the proverbs, moral sayings, and Bible verses that Yake used as fillers at the bottom of nearly every page. Africa became a focus of interest as missions and political unrest increased in scope there. In 1955 Edwin L. Weaver wrote an extensive series of articles on political and religious change in Africa. With the first issue of 1957 Bender changed the format of the paper from eight pages, 9 by 11½ inches, to sixteen pages, 5¼ by 8½ inches. Circulation had steadily increased throughout the years of Yake's editorship to 33,000 in 1954.

Urie Bender spoke to his readers through his editorial column "Just Talking." "With your suggestions and prayer support we want to make the paper a down-to-earth, interesting, looked-for, regular visitor and friend," he wrote in the January 6, 1957, issue.[5] Alternate service for conscientious objectors continued to be a subject of interest. The graphics and layout became more "modern" and reflected a 1950s aesthetic. Already begun during Yake's editorship was the series "Choose Your Career," now expanded to include that of weatherman, math major, stenographer, veterinarian, agronomist, food specialist, and medical-pharmaceutical researcher. Melvin Gingerich wrote columns of thoughtful advice, "It Seems to Me," and Elaine Sommers Rich continued "Thinking

With . . ." The same themes appeared, with a style of writing adapted to the faster pace and less formal outlook of the 1950s.

With the first issue of 1962 Willard E. Roth took over the editorship. A young minister with a bachelor of arts degree from the School of Journalism at the State University of Iowa and a bachelor of divinity from Goshen College Biblical Seminary, he brought several years of experience as an editor and journalist to the job. He retained the existing format but introduced cartoons and more dramatic photographs and graphics. Departures from the past in content reflected a generation of Mennonite young people more affluent than their parents had been as youth, distantly touched by the emerging turmoil over American military involvement in Vietnam, and open to new possibilities. In 1941 YCC had still carried the article "Why Mennonite Young Men Should Choose Farming as a Vocation" by Harry C. Swarr, "an intimate friend and old-time pal of the editor's" (June 8-15, 1941). A generation later, the September 13, 1964, issue carried "Christian Youth Encounter a Technological Age," with new fields (for Mennonites) such as "In Industry," "In Finance," and "In Law." Lester Groff wrote: "We are no longer like grandfather, who took his eggs to the store to exchange them for sugar and sold his excess milk from the family cow to the neighbors. Today we do things big. We buy our 1964 Tempests right out of high school, pay our savings down, and pay the balance over four years. We are handling lots of money, mostly other people's."[6]

Although most of YCC's readership (even young people) did not vote for doctrinal reasons, political issues began to be addressed directly, as the 1964 election between Barry Goldwater and Lyndon Johnson came up for discussion in "Election Issues as I See Them" (October 18, 1964), a query of sixteen randomly chosen readers of Companion. "Teenagers" had come into existence, and their problems were explored in quizzes, articles, and photo-essays. Although he continued to publish serialized fiction, articles on faith and missions, poems, and essays, Roth increasingly turned to the topical and contemporary. A popular figure such as Joan Baez was portrayed in "She Speaks to Her Generation," the pros and cons of smoking were aired, and new authors appeared on the list of contributors. P. R. Tedesco (a pen name for Phyllis Reynolds Naylor) became a prolific, comic contributor with the column "1st Person Singular." Ken Reed, I. Merle Good, and other promising young Mennonite writers of a new generation entered the stage. The draft, the war in Vietnam, sexual involvement, and identity crises had joined features such as "Handel—The Man Behind 'The Messiah' " and "Beethoven—Philosopher of Music."

In 1968 the history of Youth's Christian Companion came to an end with the decision to replace YCC with the monthly youth magazine With.* YCC had played a central role in training and shaping the world view of Mennonite young people from the 1920s through the 1960s. At the same time it reflected changes in the Mennonite Church, whose youth were always at the cutting edge of activity and innovation in translating the tradition of Mennonite faith into specific lives in twentieth-century America.

Notes

1. "From the East Room—FAREWELL," *Youth's Christian Companion*, (December 26, 1954), p. 412b.
2. Ibid.
3. For an indication of the importance of reports from India in church youth papers to the development of Mennonite missions in India, see John A. Lapp, *The Mennonite Church in India, 1897-1962* (Scottdale, Pa.: Herald Press, 1972).
4. See John Daniel Stahl, "Conflict, Conscience, and Community in Selected Mennonite Children's Stories," *Mennonite Quarterly Review* 55 (January 1981), 62-74.
5. *Youth's Christian Companion*, January 6, 1957, p. 4.
6. "In Finance," ibid., September 15, 1964, pp. 7-8.

Information Sources

BIBLIOGRAPHY

John A. Hostetler, *God Uses Ink* (Scottdale, Pa.: Herald Press, 1958); John A. Lapp, *The Mennonite Church in India, 1897-1962* (Scottdale, Pa.: Herald Press, 1972); *The Mennonite Encyclopedia* (Hillsboro, Kans.: Mennonite Brethren Publishing House, 1955-1959); John D. Stahl, "Conflict, Conscience, and Community in Selected Mennonite Children's Stories," *Mennonite Quarterly Review* 55 (January 1981), 62-74; Clayton F. Yake, "From the East Room—FAREWELL," *Youth's Christian Companion* 35 (December 26, 1954), 412b-12c.

INDEX SOURCES

Youth's Christian Companion is indexed in each December issue by topic and, beginning with 1954, by author.

LOCATION SOURCES

Bound volumes are in the historical libraries of Bluffton College, Bluffton, Kans.; Eastern Mennonite College, Harrisonburg, Va.; Goshen College, Goshen, Ind.; and the Lancaster Mennonite Historical Society archives, Lancaster, Pa.

Publication History

MAGAZINE TITLE AND TITLE CHANGES

The Youth's Christian Companion (1920-1950); *Youth's Christian Companion* (1950-1968).

VOLUME AND ISSUE DATA

The Youth's Christian Companion (vol. 1, no. 1-vol. 31, no. 5); *Youth's Christian Companion* (vol. 31, no. 6-vol. 49, no. 52).

PUBLISHER AND PLACE OF PUBLICATION

Mennonite Publishing House, Scottdale, Pa. (1920-1968).

EDITOR

Clayton F. Yake (1920-1954); Urie A. Bender (1955-1961); Willard E. Roth (1962-1968). During 1952 Ethel Yake Metzler, nominally assistant editor, carried out the editor's responsibilities during a period of her father's illness while he was in Florida.

John Daniel Stahl

THE YOUTH'S COMPANION

More than half a century after its demise, *The Youth's Companion* remains one of the two best-known periodicals for the young published in America. Its financial success, great popularity and longevity—it died at the age of 102—make it one of the most significant of all American magazines. During much of its long life (1827-1929), it was uncannily successful in reflecting the dominant trends about the sort of literature children should read.

The *Companion* grew out of the religious ferment of early nineteenth-century New England. Among Boston intellectuals of the period, liberal Protestantism was dominant, culminating in the establishment of the American Unitarian Association in 1825; many of the oldest New England churches, including the first and second churches of Boston, moved from orthodox Congregationalism to Unitarianism. It would be difficult to claim that those who considered themselves orthodox continued in any real sense the intellectual rigor of Puritanism, although they thought that they did; it is, instead, more accurate to see the orthodox as those who attempted to hold on to the evangelical fervor of the Great Awakening of the mid-eighteenth century, something early Puritans would have seen, negatively, as enthusiastic and possibly smacking of antinomianism.

The career of Nathaniel Willis (1780-1870), the founder of *The Youth's Companion*, may best be understood as part of the orthodox reaction to religious liberalism in New England. During his early adulthood he became a political journalist and printer, and after his conversion to what the *Dictionary of American Biography* accurately calls "his lifelong devotion to the letter of Christian law," he founded in Boston in 1816 one of the most important religious newspapers of the age, the *Recorder*, a journal that maintained its influence until it was merged into the *Congregationalist* in 1867.[1] (In 1858 Willis engaged in a controversy over whether he, the *Recorder*'s publisher, or Sidney E. Morse, its first editor, founded "the first religious newspaper" in the world, a futile dispute since there were religious newspapers founded before 1816.)

The Youth's Companion grew out of Willis's religious newspaper. In his words: "We had a regular children's department in the *Recorder*. We found all the children and youth were interested in it. This suggested the idea of a child's paper. We issued proposals for the *Youth's Companion*, and the number of subscribers which came in induced us to commence it in June, 1827."[2] The *Companion* did, in fact, begin to appear regularly with the issue for June 6, 1827; it was preceded by a specimen number dated April 16.

To the modern child or adult, the early *Companion*—indeed, the magazine for nearly half a century—is forbidding. For much of this period it consisted of only four or eight small-folio pages and featured edifying stories and articles, all in miniscule type. Its origin in a religious newspaper is obvious. Despite educational reformers influenced by Rousseau and other enlightenment figures, secular education in New England during the *Companion*'s early years was rooted in the values and concerns of seventeenth-century Puritanism. To the Puritan the purpose of education was to increase the moral and spiritual awareness of children, especially of their own depravity; literacy was important, because to understand God's word, one must be able to read it. Fortunately, Puritanism stressed the value of the intellect, and this emphasis continued even after New England orthodoxy had surrendered intellectual vigor to Unitarianism.

To attempt to distinguish between morality, religion, instruction, and entertainment in the early *Youth's Companion* is artificial. It may be said, in fact, that although much that was moral and religious in the magazine could not have been entertaining even when it first appeared, there was nothing intended to be entertaining that did not have a moral or religious theme. What makes *The Youth's Companion* stand out from other early children's magazines is that Willis did at least attempt to entertain his readers. Yet Willis's periodical was more akin to tracts published by the American Sunday-School Union than it was to later magazines for children. Despite some contributions by Willis's son Nathaniel Parker Willis, there is little of literary value in the early *Companion*. As much as he may have tried to sugar-coat the message—and he seldom tried at all—Willis's main purposes were plain: he wanted to edify his young readers, to instill high (if simplistic) moral principles, and to save their souls.

Nathaniel Willis sold *The Youth's Companion* in 1857 to Daniel S. Ford and John W. Olmstead, and although Willis's name was retained as "senior editor" for another five years, he essentially withdrew from any role in the affairs of the magazine he had founded. From 1857 until his death in 1899 Ford edited and managed the periodical, bringing it to the greatest prosperity of any American magazine for children. Olmstead and Ford used the name "Olmstead & Co." until the partnership dissolved in 1867, Ford keeping the *Companion*. From that time until the magazine ceased publication, it was published by "Perry Mason & Co."—the ampersand was later dropped—a name invented by Ford and one that became nearly as famous among young readers of the period as it did to adult readers of a later generation when Erle Stanley Gardner used it as the name of his fictional lawyer-detective.

By retaining Willis's name on the masthead and, more importantly, by continuing to fill the pages of the *Companion* with tales of repentant infants, Ford at first seems to have intended no major alteration in the magazine. But gradually the old paper began to change. By the late 1860s there was less emphasis on didacticism, and Ford began to try to attract significant writers. By 1872, two years after Nathaniel Willis's death, the *Companion* looked as forbidding as ever, but religiosity had been relegated to occasional articles. Sentimentality was present in strength, to be sure, but there was an increasing emphasis on adventure and humor for their own sake. *The Youth's Companion* was, in fact, hesitatingly trying to discover what its young readers wanted to read, rather than what adults thought was appropriate for them.

Ford was not essentially an editorial innovator; his genius was rather in promoting his magazine. He was, however, extraordinarily responsive to the interests of the reading public. As Ford realized, a successful magazine for children could no longer be primarily a supplement to the lessons of the public and church schools. Children's magazines could still continue to teach lessons but they could not do so as blatantly as Nathaniel Willis had for so many years. With extraordinary success, Daniel Ford pushed *The Youth's Companion* with the market.

During the twenty years from 1860 to 1880 there were two main developments in periodicals for the young, developments that, in very different ways, were reactions to earlier children's literature. One was the success of magazines that emphasized literary value in their offerings for children and deemphasized, more or less successfully, conscious didacticism. The earliest of these magazines was *Our Young Folks** (1865-1873), issued by the publishers of *The Atlantic Monthly*. The other development was the growth of the dime novel, beginning in the 1850s and reaching a peak of popularity in the 1870s and 1880s.

It is easy to see dime novels as a reaction to religiosity and didacticism. Dime novels were printed at low cost and sold cheaply; they featured—in lieu of theme, character, or, indeed, literary distinction of any sort—exciting stories of action and adventure. They were read widely, primarily by adolescents, and provided an escape not only from the everyday world but also from the lugubrious didacticism featured in the early *Companion* and its contemporaries. Even the sentimentality of dime novels, in which the hero wins out against extraordinary odds, is opposed to the view of life held by New England religious orthodoxy.

Daniel Ford took advantage of both the demand for literary quality and the desire for action and excitement. In 1872 the *Companion* absorbed *Merry's Museum*,* a children's magazine that had tried for literary quality in the late 1860s by hiring Louisa May Alcott as editor. More importantly, significant writers began appearing in the pages of the *Companion* itself. During the rest of the nineteenth century, Mary E. Wilkins, Frances Hodgson Burnett, L. Frank Baum, J. T. Trowbridge, and Jack London, among many others, can be found in *The Youth's Companion*, but generally with less important examples of their work—in the case of Baum, with an outrageously sentimental story. The *Companion* did not, as a rule, feature stories of character and theme; adventure was its forte, but it was high-class adventure, seldom with the absurdities, either in sentiment or character, found in dime novels. Despite the major authors who wrote for it, the *Companion*'s most typical, and most popular, author was C. A. Stephens. Much of what Stephens wrote characterizes the fiction, by whatever author, published in *The Youth's Companion* during most of the Ford period: it was discriminating enough to satisfy parents and exciting enough to entertain young readers.

The *Companion*'s nonfiction during the later Ford years was impressive. In issues of the early 1870s, nonfiction was primarily factual accounts of science, geography, and history, usually dull and sometimes condescending; it was, in fact, a continuation of the concerns of Nathaniel Willis and the early *Youth's Companion*. But within a few years, important names began to appear in the *Companion* over significant nonfiction. Among these names are those of William Gladstone, Francis Parkman, Thomas Huxley, Edwin Godkin, Woodrow Wilson, and many others, including some famous in their own time but forgotten today. Most of them succeeded in presenting their articles in ways that did not con-

descend to their readers; indeed, they were so uniformly successful in doing so
that one wonders whether the *Companion*'s editorial office should be considered
a silent collaborator in some of the articles.

Daniel Ford's *Youth's Companion* was, in fact, a heterogeneous mix, a fact
that helps explain its wide appeal. During a month of weekly issues, the magazine
was certain to include science and history, puzzles, at least one famous writer,
and both serial and and short fiction, all well illustrated. Each issue contained
eight to sixteen small-folio pages, and at one point, the *Companion* claimed that
it published each year the equivalent of some 2,000 book pages, all for $1.50.

Throughout this period, Daniel Ford and his successors managed to rope many
of their young readers into selling subscriptions by offering premiums, primarily
toys, games, and sports equipment. The premiums were so numerous and their
quality so high that the annual premium issue of the *Companion* was eagerly
awaited.

One of Ford's most interesting experiments was an attempt to solve a problem
faced by all magazines for children: its audience quickly outgrows it. Unlike
adult periodicals, which may find loyal readers who will subscribe indefinitely,
a children's magazine over the course of, say, five years loses almost entirely
one group of readers and must replace it with another. To some extent Ford was
successful in overcoming this problem by suggesting that his magazine was, as
its running title stated, "The Companion for All the Family." To make it even
more obvious that the *Companion* was a general magazine for all ages, he
included a separate "Children's Page." Some discussions of the magazine have
been misled by the campaign, for *The Youth's Companion* remained essentially
a children's magazine throughout its long career. Ford, however, did build up
a readership more stable than that of most periodicals for the young, probably
by convincing adult readers that they were reading something suitable for the
entire family when they were actually reading children's literature.

Daniel Ford's uncanny ability to give readers what they wanted and then to
promote it to the hilt made *The Youth's Companion* one of the most successful
magazines in the country. Frank Luther Mott stated that the *Companion*'s circulation was 4,800 when Ford and Olmstead purchased it in 1857.[3] In 1882 it
claimed 263,000 in Ayer's *American Newspaper Annual*; in the late 1890s it
reached a half-million. Mott placed it as having the highest magazine circulation
in the country in 1885, and it was always greater than the most important
contemporary magazines for adults: *Harper's, The Century, Scribner's,* and *The
Atlantic Monthly*. Among other children's magazines, there was none with a
circulation anything like that of the *Companion. St. Nicholas,** for example,
seems never to have reached the 100,000 mark.

Daniel Sharp Ford died on December 24, 1899, aged seventy-seven, five years
older than the magazine he had nurtured for more than forty years. *The Youth's
Companion* by the time that Ford died had become not only a highly profitable
publication, it was also to many of its readers an institution.

Ford's associates continued the *Companion* nearly without change. It remained highly compartmentalized; it continued to offer nonfiction by famous names and serials and short stories by C. A. Stephens and others; it still billed itself as a general magazine for the entire family. In 1892 Ford had issued a special number for the Columbian Exposition, with front and back covers elaborately lithographed in colors, an issue that is said to have been printed with greater sophistication than that attempted by any other magazine of the period. Ford's successors began to print one cover a month in colors, and the magazine continued to be very attractive.

Ford's associate, Edward Stanwood, succeeded him as editor and retained that position until 1911; he was succeeded by Charles M. Thompson, who had also been with the magazine for many years. Circulation remained high for a decade or so after Ford's death and then began a gradual decline.

Despite danger signals, the magazine's editors continued the Ford formula without change. Most striking during the post-Ford years were probably the patriotic covers published during World War I. The *Companion* stressed its age more than it had done before, and the covers of its anniversary issues were nearly as striking as those for the war effort. The *Companion*'s emphasis on its antiquity was legitimate: few major magazines were older. But the emphasis also indicates that the *Companion*'s owners were not paying enough attention to the interests of current readers, a mistake never made by Daniel Ford.

The continuity of the *Companion*'s editorial mix and the continued presence of writers such as C. A. Stephens gave readers few indications that the magazine was in trouble. Even the 1921 reduction of page size would not have suggested such difficulties, for the old small-folio format was being abandoned throughout the magazine industry.

Then in 1925 *The Youth's Companion* was purchased by Ellery Sedgwick, owner of *The Atlantic Monthly*. Sedgwick had been on the staff of the *Companion* some thirty years before. When he purchased the magazine that had employed him so many years earlier, Sedgwick was in the process of building a minor magazine empire. In addition to purchasing *The Atlantic* from Houghton Mifflin in 1908, Sedgwick owned *House Beautiful* (which he had purchased in 1913) and the venerable *Living Age* (founded as *Littell's Living Age* in 1844 and bought by Sedgwick in 1919). Although the *Companion*'s readers may well have been unaware of its problems, the Boston publishing community could not have been ignorant. Undoubtedly, sentiment was involved in Sedgwick's decision to purchase the ailing magazine. In addition, he had been successful in revitalizing *The Atlantic Monthly* without sacrificing the literary quality of what was arguably America's most important magazine; he undoubtedly hoped to duplicate his success with *The Youth's Companion*.

The *Companion*'s new editor was Harford Powel, Jr. Powel abandoned the now-hoary pretense that, despite its name, *The Youth's Companion* was a general magazine for the entire family and aimed at the adolescents who had always been the magazine's primary readers. In 1928 the *Companion* became a monthly, very much in editorial policy and appearance like *American Boy—Open Road** and *Boy's Life*,* although the emphasis on significant nonfiction continued; C. A. Stephens was still a contributor. In 1929 Sedgwick gave up, and after its September issue *The Youth's Companion*, at the age of 102, was merged with the *American Boy*, which, even though it continued the *Companion*'s volume numbers and made the name of the older magazine a minor part of its own, was the surviving periodical.

Why did *The Youth's Companion* die? Part of the answer must be that its last owner was unwilling to commit himself or the other magazines he published to the long-term losses that continuing the *Companion* would have entailed. In hindsight we can postulate that restoring the magazine to profitability would probably have been impossible during the Depression.

The real question, however, is not why Ellery Sedgwick was unwilling or unable to support the magazine for longer than the four years he had owned it but rather why it had declined so greatly during its final two decades. The decline was not one essentially of quality but rather of popularity and profitability. It was, after all, an institution that, like *The Saturday Evening Post* some forty years later, seemed almost impregnable.

The answer lies in the fact that it was, indeed, an institution, and that meant that it had acquired traditions that were as important to its management as they were to readers, even when readership had begun to dwindle. Some declining magazines that have become institutions save themselves by acquiring managements who are willing to make the necessary changes. Two of the most important nineteenth-century magazines, both major institutions, managed to do so: Sedgwick built on the extraordinary prestige of *The Atlantic Monthly* when he turned it into a modern magazine of intelligent discussion; the owners of *Harper's Magazine* in 1925 dropped its illustrations and inhibitions and—obviously with an eye on what Sedgwick had done—turned it into a periodical of intellectual, and frequently very liberal, investigation.

At least until Sedgwick bought it, *The Youth's Companion* did not have such a management. Daniel Ford was succeeded by long-time associates who had deep respect for the magazine that he had developed but who did not have his extraordinary ability to gauge the market. Some commentators have suggested that Ford's *Companion* went largely to rural households; America became steadily more urban after Ford's death, but his successors did nothing to redirect the magazine. Nor did they cease their emphasis on the *Companion* as a general magazine even though it placed it in competition with periodicals such as *Collier's* and *The Saturday Evening Post*. Regrettably, what had made *The Youth's Companion* extremely successful in the 1880s and 1890s became hallowed traditions to be maintained even when they hastened the magazine's decline.

Throughout most of its long career, *The Youth's Companion* was unequaled in reflecting current fashions and trends in children's literature. During the many years it was owned by Daniel Ford, it was unequaled in popularity and not substantially lower in literary quality than even magazines such as *The Riverside*

*Magazine** and *St. Nicholas*. No children's magazine has educated and entertained its readers for a longer period, and when *The Youth's Companion* ceased publication, probably no other magazine was mourned so widely.

Notes

1. *Dictionary of American Biography*, 20:306-9.
2. "Autobiography of a Journalist," in Frederic Hudson, *Journalism in the United States from 1690 to 1872* (New York: Harper & Brothers, 1873), 293.
3. Frank Luther Mott, *A History of American Magazines* (Cambridge: Harvard University Press, 1938-1958), 2:266. See also 4:17.

Information Sources

BIBLIOGRAPHY
Dictionary of American Biography, entries for Daniel Sharp Ford and Nathaniel Willis; Frederic Hudson, *Journalism in the United States from 1690 to 1872* (New York: Harper & Brothers, 1873); Frank Luther Mott, *A History of American Magazines*, 5 vols. (Cambridge: Harvard University Press, 1938-1968); Lovell Thompson, ed., *Youth's Companion* (Boston: Houghton Mifflin, 1954).
INDEX SOURCES
Richard Cutts, *Index to the Youth's Companion*, 2 vols. (Metuchen, N. J.: The Scarecrow Press, 1972).
LOCATION SOURCES
Library of Congress; Yale University; University of Minnesota, Minneapolis; New York Public Library; Brown University, Providence, Rhode Island, have the most complete collections.

Publication History

MAGAZINE TITLE AND TITLE CHANGES
Youth's Companion (April 16, 1827-August 2, 1834); *Youth's Companion and Sabbath School Recorder* (August 9, 1834-May 13, 1836); *The Youth's Companion* (May 20, 1836-September 1929).
VOLUME AND ISSUE DATA
Youth's Companion (vol. 1, no. 1-vol. 8, no. 11); *Youth's Companion and Sabbath School Recorder* (vol. 8, no. 12-vol. 9, no. 52); *The Youth's Companion* (vol. 10, no. 1-vol. 102).
PUBLISHER AND PLACE OF PUBLICATION
Nathaniel Willis and Asa Rand, Boston (1827-1830); Nathaniel Willis, Boston (1830-1856); Olmstead & Co., Boston (1857-1867); Perry Mason (&) Co., Boston (1867-1929), the latter owned by Daniel S. Ford and his successors, 1867-1925; by the Atlantic Monthly Co., 1925-1929.
EDITOR
Nathaniel Willis (1827-1856); Daniel S. Ford (1857-1899); Edward Stanwood (1899-1911); Charles M. Thompson (1911-1925); Harford Powel, Jr. (1925-1929).

David L. Greene

YOUTH'S DAYSPRING

Youth's Dayspring was a publication of the American Board of Commissioners for Foreign Missions, which issued it from their Boston headquarters for the six years from 1850 until 1855. The periodical aimed at "disseminating intelligence and awakening interest" about the work of Christian missionaries throughout the world.[1] The uplifting topic of missionary work and the exotic subjects of foreign lands and peoples guaranteed the periodical its wide interest for young readers in midnineteenth-century America.

The American Board of Commissioners for Foreign Missions was founded in 1810 by the Congregational Church, and it became interdenominational in 1812. In its earliest years the board began sending young, devoted missionaries to the South Pacific Islands. In 1818 it began to publish its main periodical, *Missionary Herald*, which brought news of its worldwide missionary activities to supporters in the United States. By the 1850s missionaries had established churches, schools, and printing presses in distant points throughout the world. In 1850 the board began to publish *Youth's Dayspring*, first using material from the *Missionary Herald*, which was "adapted to the use of those who have little leisure for reading, and for youth."[2]

As the periodical developed, much of the prose and poetry was written especially for it, and many articles stress the relationship of the missionary movement to children. Readers were told how young "heathens" were converted, how the children of missionary parents fared in their strange surroundings, and, finally, how children safe at home in the United States might work to aid the missionaries abroad. Many lively articles telling of the strange and exotic customs of non-Christian peoples were written by missionaries afield. Typical profiles described the Hindoo blacksmiths who worship their tools, the gamblers of Madras, the Fakeer holy men of India, and the Whirling Dervishes of Constantinople. Although articles are always concerned with the salvation of foreign souls, the subjects of *Youth's Dayspring* are not unlike the literary genre of the travelogs popularized by Jacob Abbott in his "Rollo" travel series of the same period.

As the board saw it, appropriate material consisted of "selections and compilations from the correspondence of missionaries; in other words...of their travels, labors and observations in many countries...describing countries and climates, routes, means and modes of travel and transportation; tribes, races and nations; their characteristics, physical, mental and moral; their social condition and habits; their institutions of religion, education and government; their industrial pursuits, and the means of subsisting and preserving health among them."[3]

Throughout its articles, the strange and fascinating habits of native peoples were described at the point in history when ethnic cultures were being influenced by Western visitors. Missionaries were among the first Westerners to live among ethnic peoples as they quickly followed explorers and traders who had made initial discoveries and contacts. Often missionaries were met by natives whose encounters with traders had left them suspicious of intruders. In their articles for *Youth's Dayspring* missionaries told of the hardships they faced in foreign lands and the sacrifices and sufferings they endured in their work. Almost every issue contained a story or poem about the death of a missionary or a missionary's child.

Throughout the *Youth's Dayspring* an attitude of intolerance toward non-Christian religions is most apparent. Native peoples were described as savages living in darkness and deprived of the light of Christianity through which their souls might be saved. This attitude is just the opposite of the romantic notion of the "Noble Savage" that ascribed purity to the natural state of peoples unspoiled by the evils of Western civilization. In the series "A Missionary Lesson" different religions of the world were considered, and the fundamental "errors" of each was pointed out for the reader's benefit. Young readers were told again and again of the validity of Christianity and of the errors of every other way of life.

The physical appearance of *Youth's Dayspring* resembled many other publications of Sabbath Day Societies. The monthly issues measured 6 by 4 inches and contained sixteen pages of prose, poetry, letters, religious instruction, and illustrations from wood engravings. The engravings vary in size from decorative vignettes to full-page illustrations for an article. Full-page engravings successfully depict light and shadow, three-dimensional roundness, texture, perspective, and some personality in the faces of figures. As the editor described them, the engravings "show you how the people look in these distant countries, or what hideous idols they worship, or what strange looking objects are found there, or some scene in which missionaries were in peril. . . . The object of all of them is to let you know more about the 'world which lieth in wickedness,' that you may be moved to help save it."[4] The exotic scenes beyond a reader's imagination were brought to life in the illustrations of the *Youth's Dayspring*.

The meaning of the title of the magazine was explained at length by its editor. *Dayspring* refers not only to the light of dawn spreading sunlight onto the world but also to the Christian gospel "sending its gladdening rays over the benighted nations of the earth."[5] The cover illustration depicted the sun rising over mountains, lighting a fallen idol and a group of children. One child directs the attention of another to the light, symbolizing how a missionary must dispel the darkness of paganism by showing the light of the Christian religion.

Youth's Dayspring was edited by four individuals during its six-year span. The first editor was H.G.O. Dwight, who had served as a missionary in Constantinople. He was followed by Mr. Stoddard of the Nestorian mission, who served as editor for a few months before returning to Western Asia. Rev. Nathan Dole became editor and served for four years until his death in June 1855. After his death an unnamed secretary of the board edited the periodical until the end of the year.

The December 1855 issue announced the termination of *Youth's Dayspring*. The publication had cost the board more than $3,000 a year, and since its inception many other religious publications for children had begun. The board decided to merge *Youth's Dayspring* with the *Journal of Missions* to form the

Journal of Missions and Youth's Dayspring. About one-fourth of each issue of this periodical was to be devoted to material for young readers.

Youth's Dayspring remains a testimony to the activities of the devoted Christian missionaries, as well as a record of both the negative and beneficial effects the missionaries had on the civilizations they sought to change. For its young readers the periodical must have fostered an awareness of the infinite diversity of peoples of their expanding world, even if it did so only to condemn those differences as heathenish faults.

Notes

1. *Commemorative Volume in Connection with the Seventy-fifth Anniversary of the American Board of Commissioners for Foreign Missions, Held in Boston, October 13-16, 1885* (Boston: American Board of Commissioners for Foreign Missions, 1885), 88.

2. *Memorial Volume of the First Fifty Years of the American Board of Commissioners for Foreign Missions* (Boston: American Board of Commissioners for Foreign Missions, 1861), 373.

3. Ibid., p. 371.

4. "About the Dayspring," *Youth's Dayspring* 5 (December 1855), 177.

5. "The Dayspring," ibid., 5 (February 1854), 27.

Information Sources

BIBLIOGRAPHY
Commemorative Volume in Connection with the Seventy-fifth Anniversary of the American Board of Commissioners for Foreign Missions, Held in Boston, October 13-16, 1885 (Boston: American Board of Commissioners for Foreign Missions, 1885); *Memorial Volume of the First Fifty Years of the American Board of Commissioners for Foreign Missions* (Boston: American Board of Commissioners for Foreign Missions, 1861); Graeme Kent, *Company of Heaven: Early Missionaries in the South Seas* (Nashville and New York: Thomas Nelson, 1972).
INDEX SOURCES
None.
LOCATION SOURCES
Library of Congress; Yale University; University of Iowa; Brown University, Providence, Rhode Island; Massachusetts Historical Society, Boston; Williams College, Williamstown, Mass., Bowdoin College, Bowdoin, Me.

Publication History

MAGAZINE TITLE AND TITLE CHANGES
Youth's Dayspring (1850-1855).
VOLUME AND ISSUE DATA
Youth's Dayspring (Vol. 1 no.1-vol. 6, no. 12).
PUBLISHER AND PLACE OF PUBLICATION
American Board of Commissioners for Foreign Missions, Boston (1850-1855).

EDITOR

H.G.O. Dwight (1850-?); Mr. Stoddard (1850-1851); Rev. Nathan Dole (1851-June
    1855); none listed (June-December 1855).

John R. Edson

THE YOUTH'S EMANCIPATOR

Abolitionists in pre-Civil War America used many weapons. Very significant
was the periodical press, which forwarded the cause through *The Genius of
Universal Emancipation*, the *Liberator*, *The Anti-Slavery Standard*, the *Emancipator*, *The Charter Oak*, *The Abolitionist*, *The Herald of Freedom*, the *Anti-
Slavery Bugle*, and hundreds of other publications. Of particular interest to
students of children's literature are the few juvenile antislavery periodicals. The
Slave's Friend,* for instance, appeared monthly between 1836 and 1839, and
the less specialized *Youth's Cabinet, Devoted to Liberty, Peace, Temperance,
and Religious, Moral, Intellectual, and Physical Education* ran weekly between
1837 and 1845.

A less known yet vigorous children's antislavery periodical was *The Youth's
Emancipator*. Printed in a four-page octavo format by F. Cowdery and published
from the office of *The Oberlin Evangelist* in Oberlin, Ohio, this newspaper lived
a short but stormy existence, going through nine issues. The first number appeared
in May 1842. Because the editors then waited until a sufficient number of readers
agreed to subscriptions of 25¢ a year, the second issue did not appear until
August 1842. Thereafter, the newspaper appeared monthly until it ceased publication in March 1843.

The circumstances of its publishing and editing lie today in shadows. However,
we can piece together evidence suggesting dissension and other problems. From
May 1842 through January 1843 *The Youth's Emancipator* was published by the
executive committee of the Oberlin Youth's Anti-Slavery Society. This group
may be identical to the Oberlin Young Men's Anti-Slavery Society, which "was
in existence at least as early as 1842, and was reorganized in 1851."[1] Or perhaps
there were two antislavery societies competing for young abolitionists' support.
In any case, something went wrong, for the February 1843 issue curtly announced, "This paper is no longer to be published by the Youths' Anti-Slavery
Society, nor to be edited, as heretofore, by a member of that society."[2]

Through the first five numbers J. H. Livingston and J. G. Jennings shared
editorial duties; Livingston handled the next two issues alone, and the editor of
the two final issues remained anonymous. The editor of the first issues can
perhaps be identified as Jasper Hull Livingston, from Jamaica, West Indies, an
Oberlin student from 1839 to 1844. The editor of the final issues is most likely
John Giles Jennings, an Oberlin student from 1842 to 1844, who later made a
fortune selling land in Cleveland. His leaving the editorship may be explained
by his youth (he was born in 1825); his poor health, which forced him to leave

the college before graduation; and, perhaps, his own priorities—he was not an enthusiastic supporter of Oberlin president Asa Mahan's aggressive style.[3]

The fervor and energy permeating *The Youth's Emancipator* derive largely from its being published in Oberlin. Founded less than a decade before the first issue of the periodical, the colony and the college stressed a zealous sense of Christian mission and an uncompromising reform spirit that together gave Oberlin a national reputation. Early colonists signed a covenant "Lamenting the degeneracy of the Church and the deplorable condition of our perishing world," by which they vowed "to maintain deep-toned and elevated personal piety, to provoke each other to love and good works...and to glorify God in our bodies and spirits, which are His."[4] Here women and blacks could attend college, Christian revivalism could promise new life, temperance could flourish, later peace activists of the 1860s could argue the immorality of war, fugitive slaves could find refuge, and strong-willed Congregationalists could argue for moral reform of a nation beset with evil.

At Oberlin many forceful personalities—among them Charles G. Finney and John J. Shippherd—helped mold a great nationwide movement that converted the energy of the evangelistic revivals of the 1820s and 1830s into the energy of social reform. Even their rhetoric comes from evangelists' sermons. Starting from the importance of individual regeneration, they argued that repentance of the sin of slavery would regenerate first each individual and then America as a whole.[5] Oberlin graduates carried such rhetoric into the founding of Michigan colleges with decided antislavery foundations, support of abolitionist politicians like Ohio's Joshua Giddings, and publication of *The Youth's Emancipator*.

The greatest strength of *The Youth's Emancipator* resides in its positive faith in youth. Major reform movements in antebellum America successfully recruited numbers of young people, whose years were seen as no barrier to participation: "Y is for Youth—the time for all/Bravely to war with sin;/And think not it can ever be/Too early to begin."[6] Completely in line with contemporary abolitionist psychology, the editors of *The Youth's Emancipator* several times explained their hope. For instance, in the "Prospectus" they emphasized "how easily the mind may be swayed in youth, when every tender feeling is alive and every chord of sympathy vibrates at the touch of suffering."[7] The editors' assessment of their potential effect upon the child rings psychologically true: "In childhood he will be the friend, in youth the advocate, and in manhood the unflinching supporter of Anti-Slavery. And when the story of wrong calls the pitying tear to the eye of the innocent prattler, then will his heart be fashioned for virtue and goodness."[8]

As might be expected of nearly all abolitionist periodicals, *The Youth's Emancipator* sticks to one central aim, to inspire action against an evil that has caused most of the nation's ills. However, again as we find in other abolitionist literature, the pages offer many distinct supporting points. We read, for instance, that slaves are by nature able, generous, noble, kind, loving, faithful; are not born slaves; have souls; enjoy family life; have the right to flee slavery; and would not voluntarily choose servitude. Slaveholders, meanwhile, treat people as property, inflict unspeakable physical and emotional cruelties, debase themselves, teach children moral viciousness, control the national power structure, and fear righteous opposition. White nonslaveholders aid the owner, for they assume that they deserve better treatment than do blacks, condone unjust prejudice, and break promises made to blacks. Readers thus must avoid despair, love their neighbors, aid fugitive slaves, and observe the law of moral right.

The editors used a variety of persuasive techniques. Especially in the earlier issues, titles seem deliberately framed to pique curiosity. A title like "Yankee Ingenuity *vs*. Southern Slavery," "The Fugitive's Farewell to His Country," or "Have the Negros [*sic*] Any Minds?" might inspire an otherwise reluctant reader. Unfortunately, with the departure of Jennings and Livingston, titles mostly became uninspiring phrases like "Canada Schools" or "Interesting Anecdote."

More important is the variety of genres through which contributors (usually identified by initials) attacked slavery. They had the least success with two belletristic forms, dramatic dialogs and poems. The few dialogs are essentially lectures with named speakers. For instance, in "Stealing Slaves" (September 1842) young Samuel gives his friend Henry many paragraphs of antislavery logic interspersed by Henry's periodic "Certainly" or "Certainly not."

Writers conveyed stronger emotions through poems that vary greatly in technical skill. Much of the poetry is little more than versified polemic set to rhyme. A child asks, for instance: "And is it not, mother, a sinful thing,/The bosoms of others with pain to wring—/To bid them go labor and delve the soil,/And seize the reward of their weary toil—."[9] However, the poetry sometimes resounds with heightened emotion, as when a slave, who must leave the verdant land, laments: "Land of the noble spirit's grave—/Land of the tyrant, and the slave—/Land of my birth—farewell—farewell."[10]

Generally more effective is the straightforward prose of the editorials, essays, and letters. Most editorials, especially in the earlier issues, glow with moral self-confidence. Jennings assured his young readers of success in their crusade: "Then, fellow youth, let us go on, fearing not the threats of the enemies of justice, and caring not for the objections any weak-hearted ones may throw in our way; but putting our trust in that God who will avenge the oppressed, let us continue our efforts until He shall crown them with victory."[11] Essays and letters likewise assail the major faults of slaveholding with an unswerving belief in the cause. Although nearly all of these pieces sound alike and the style does not always flow, each has the merit of driving straight to its point with little verbiage, a journalism of direct usefulness.

The most persuasive writing in *The Youth's Emancipator* comprises narratives recounting experiences of slaves and freed blacks. Especially striking are the narratives purportedly authored by the blacks themselves. In the narratives we find many dramatic recreations of chases and hairbreadth escapes and physical and emotional cruelties. We see, for instance, the inhumanity of wealthy Mr. G—, whose "poor slaves always looked miserable and half starved, and even his house servants were often seen with the bleeding gash in the cheek, on the arm, or the neck, while doubtless their backs would have revealed a wretched tale.''[12]

One central fact about the periodical cannot be overlooked. About 90 percent of its most significant material consists of reprints from other publications: verses from *The Poetical Works of Elizabeth Margaret Chandler* and extracts from periodicals such as the *Western Christian Advocate*, the *Slave's Friend*, the *Genius of Universal Emancipation*, and the Cincinnati *Philanthropist*. The editors borrowed most heavily from *Charter Oak: An Anti-Slavery Family Newspaper* and *Biographical Sketches and Interesting Anecdotes of Persons of Color* by Abigail Mott, the New York abolitionist and women's rights advocate. Meanwhile, the most convincing evidence against slavery comes from *American Slavery as It Is*, Theodore Weld's massive gathering of eyewitness accounts, judged by Dwight Lowell Dumond "the greatest of the antislavery pamphlets; in all probability, the most crushing indictment of any institution ever written.''[13]

While the editors reprinted telling abolitionist material, two problems arose from their heavy dependence on other sources. Most obviously, the very fact of massive borrowing suggests that the editors had little new to say. A second difficulty concerns the age of most sources. For instance, the *Slave's Friend* ceased publication in 1839, and all quotations from the *Genius of Universal Emancipation* are at least three years old. Weld's exposé was published in 1839, Chandler's poems in 1836, and Mott's *Sketches* in 1826. Perhaps the young Oberlin abolitionists believed their cause was timeless, but their use of familiar sources, and to such a degree, must have vitiated the impact of their periodical.

We find some fragmentation in the way features are written. Since *The Youth's Emancipator* is essentially an anthology, the style of the featured contents varies from artless simplicity to awkward ineptness to sophisticated reflection. Even the editorial rhetoric greatly changes with the switch in editors. Jennings and Livingston addressed readers as equals, but the last editor instructed "My Young Friends" (February 1843) not to expect baby talk and to ask elders about difficult words—the tone becomes patronizing.

Nervousness permeates *The Youth's Emancipator* as the editors struggle to sustain the periodical. Every issue reminds its readers that the subscription fee is payable "*always* in advance." The prospectus in the first issue asks that youth sustain the effort, but by the fourth issue it is clear that too few paying subscribers have come forward. By the time Jennings and Livingston had departed, the venture had collapsed. The editor of the penultimate issue chided reluctant contributors, "You are bound to take enough interest in the welfare of the slave to overcome both your indolence and your modesty.''[14] Elsewhere, he complained of insufficient revenue to meet expenses. Hoping to postpone the inevitable, he proposed to reduce the price if 5,000 readers would subscribe. He made one last attempt, in March, to find readers: "Now every copy of the *Youth's Emancipator* is a floating battery and plays with resistless power upon the walls of ignorance and prejudice. And shall it now be sustained?''[15] But by now the quality of work had deteriorated markedly, and the same issue suggested chaos at the office, for the staff had unwittingly dunned paid subscribers. Not surprisingly, publication soon quietly ceased.

The Youth's Emancipator clearly died quickly because of insurmountable problems: it presented already familiar moral arguments without addressing changed political realities, it relied heavily upon reprinting other sources, its business operations faltered, disagreement eroded its staff, and perhaps most importantly, it misconceived how to capture the interest of young people—unlike the *Slave's Friend*, for instance, it never used illustrations. However, in transmitting a sense of urgency and importance of mission, *The Youth's Emancipator* testifies to the integrity and moral fervor of the youthful evangelical fervor of Oberlin.

Notes

1. Robert Samuel Fletcher, *A History of Oberlin College from Its Foundations Through the Civil War* (Oberlin, Ohio: Oberlin College, 1943), 1:237. Thanks are also due W. E. Bigglestone, Oberlin College archivist.

2. *The Youth's Emancipator*, February 1843, p. 2.

3. *Memorial Record of the County of Cuyahoga and City of Cleveland, Ohio* (Chicago: Lewis Publishing Co., 1894), 113; Fletcher, *History*, pp. 476-86. Neither Livingston nor Jennings contributed further abolitionist material; the Oberlin College collection of antislavery propaganda contains nothing by either one. Nancy Farnsley and Charles Farnsley, eds., *Lost Cause Press Microcard Collection: Anti-Slavery Propaganda in the Oberlin College Library November, 1968* (Louisville, Ky.: Lost Cause Press, 1968).

4. Fletcher, *History*, p. 110.

5. See Gilbert Hobbs Barnes, *The Antislavery Impulse 1830-1844* (New York and London: D. Appleton-Century Co., 1933); Anne C. Loveland, "Evangelicalism and 'Immediate Emancipation' in American Antislavery Thought," *The Journal of Southern History* 32 (1966), 172-88.

6. *The Anti-Slavery Alphabet* (Philadelphia: For the Anti-Slavery Fair, 1846), 16.

7. *The Youth's Emancipator*, May 1842, p. [1].

8. Ibid., May 1842, p. [3].

9. Ibid., October 1842, p. [4].

10. Ibid., May 1842, p. [4].

11. Ibid., September 1842, p. [3].

12. Ibid., October 1842, p. [4].

13. *Antislavery: The Crusade for Freedom in America* (Ann Arbor, Mich.: University of Michigan Press, 1961), 249.

14. *The Youth's Emancipator*, February 1843, p. [2].

15. Ibid., March 1843, p. [2].

Information Sources

BIBLIOGRAPHY
Robert Samuel Fletcher, *A History of Oberlin College from Its Foundation through the Civil War* (Oberlin, Ohio: Oberlin College, 1943), 2 vols.
INDEX SOURCES
None.

LOCATION SOURCES
Extant copies are extremely rare. The American Antiquarian Society Library, Worcester, Mass., has a complete run.

Publication History

MAGAZINE TITLE AND TITLE CHANGES
The Youth's Emancipator (May 1842-March 1843).
VOLUME AND ISSUE DATA
The Youth's Emancipator (vol. 1, no. 1-vol. 1, no. 9).
PUBLISHER AND PLACE OF PUBLICATION
The Executive Committee of the Oberlin Youth's Anti-Slavery Society, Oberlin, Ohio (May 1842-January 1843); none listed, Oberlin, Ohio (February 1843-March 1843).
EDITOR
J. H. Livingston and J. G. Jennings (May 1842-November 1842); J. H. Livingston (December 1842-January 1843); none listed (February 1843-March 1843).

Avon Jack Murphy

YOUTH'S FRIEND AND SCHOLAR'S MAGAZINE

The arrival of a new century, in 1800, heralded an era of change and concern in the United States, particularly in religion and education. To many greeting the new century, religion appeared to be endangered by progress, commerce, and the impact of Enlightenment ideas.

Faced with these threats, many Protestant clergymen resorted to the vigorous, emotional techniques of revivalism to lead people back to the churches. "The Great Revival kept the country in religious ferment for twenty-five years...for the first time bringing a majority of Americans into the Protestant churches."[1] One outgrowth of this religious fervor was the establishment, by the various churches, of Sunday schools for both adults and children and the formation of a comprehensive philosophy of religious education.

During the last quarter of the eighteenth century there had been great concern expressed, in England, for the condition of childhood among the industrial classes, a concern that gave rise to various industrial and Sunday school movements intended to teach reading to underprivileged children. What began in England as an educational charity for factory children spread quickly to the United States and was imitated not only by American factory owners but also by the churches. However, in the United States the stress was not on reading; "the Sunday school movement in early nineteenth century America...was primarily concerned with religious instruction."[2]

On January 11, 1791, a constitution was adopted for the First Day, or Sunday School Society of Philadelphia, the first permanent Sunday school organization in the United States. This and other smaller Sunday school organizations were influenced by Sunday schools being formed in England, especially those created by Robert Raikes, a printer and publisher of Gloucester, England.

The intent of the First Day, or Sunday School Society of Philadelphia was "to confine [their teachings] to reading and writing from the Bible and such other moral and religious books as the society from time to time might direct . . . to cultivate charity among those of different names [denominations] . . . to give more effect to Christian exertion in general; and encourage and strengthen each other."[3] By the 1820s children, both rich and poor, were being sent to Sunday schools across the nation, and quantities of moralistic publications were being produced to supplement instruction from the Bible.

In 1817 the Philadelphia Sunday and Adult School Union was formed from a merger of the First Day, or Sunday School Society with other groups. Out of this, in turn, was created the American Sunday School Union on May 16, 1824, to coordinate the efforts of the various Protestant Sunday school movements. It grew with astonishing speed, and "within eighteen months there were 400 branches of the organization in twenty-two of the twenty-four states and territories."[4] In 1907 the American Sunday School Union joined the World Sunday School Association, which in 1947 became the World Council of Christian Education.

One of the many aims of the American Sunday School Union (ASSU) was "to disseminate useful information, circulate moral and religious publications in every part of the land."[5] The result was a flood of books and periodicals, described by one recent historian as a "glutinous mixture of morality and 'applied Christianity.' "[6] Frederick Adolphus Packard (1794-1867), editor of publications for the American Sunday School Union, and, later, Dr. John Seely Hart (1810-1877), editor of periodicals, set the tone for the ASSU publications. "ASSU books were carefully nonsectarian. Every book issued . . . was reviewed by a board of laymen representing the major evangelical sects. . . . As a result, the children's stories lacked all traces of the inner conflicts of early nineteenth century Protestantism . . . and the message conveyed by most Sunday school stories was more broadly moral than specifically religious."[7] The children's publications issued by the American Sunday School Union frequently followed the didactic tradition epitomized in James Janeway's *Token for Children* (1771) in which young readers are exhorted to pious ways lest they die young. The various books published by the ASSU dealt with subjects such as obedience, punctuality, and ways of improvement. Similar didactic topics were staple items in the children's periodical published by the American Sunday School Union, *Youth's Friend and Scholar's Magazine*.

In 1823 the American Sunday School Union began publication of two periodicals. The first, the *American Sunday-School Magazine* (1823-1832), was for teachers. The second was produced for children, the *Teacher's Offering; or Sabbath Scholar's Magazine* (1823-1825), retitled the *Youth's Friend and Scholar's Magazine* (1825-1864), a magazine of sixteen pages, which sold for 25¢ a year and reached a circulation of 10,000 by 1827.[8]

Modeled on British periodicals such as Dorothy and Mary Kilner's *Youth's Magazine or Evangelical Miscellany* (1816), the *Youth's Friend* contained brief religious essays, anecdotes, and moral platitudes illustrated by a scattering of woodcuts. "Too large a proportion of doctrinal matter," the *American Journal of Education* noted in an 1827 review of *Youth's Friend*, but added, "The editing of this publication indicates, on the whole, much acquaintance with the habits and disposition of children."[9]

For parents and educators, the *Youth's Friend and Scholar's Magazine* supported conventional wisdom concerning the education and protection of childish innocence current at the time. The protected child, it was thought, could be guided by proper religious and moral instruction. The child's innocence provided the foundation for adult morality. With its religious exhortations and moral tales, the *Youth's Friend* seemed ideally suited to this purpose.

Children found the *Youth's Friend* appealing for that "acquaintance with the habits and disposition of children" pointed out by the *American Journal of Education*. At the time of the initial appearance of the *Youth's Friend* there were few children's magazines that attempted to entertain as well as instruct the child. The feeble and (in retrospect) stilted attempts at entertainment by the *Youth's Friend* found a favorable audience in children denied the inexpensive weeklies then published or the genuine fun seen later in magazines such as *St. Nicholas,** *The Riverside Magazine,** and *Harper's Young People.**

During the century religious enthusiasm declined, superseded by the drive for industrial development and the vexing issues of midcentury, particularly that of slavery. Education, under the influence of a more pragmatic turn of mind, lessened its stress on religious and moral instruction. The shift was from pure, moralistic instruction to entertainment coupled with learning. In the face of changing emphases many evangelical periodicals disappeared, among them the *Youth's Friend and Scholar's Magazine*, which ceased publication in 1864. In its publishing lifetime, however, it had influenced the development of numerous other Sunday school periodicals for children and had initiated a change among such periodicals in the direction of a less didactic approach to writing for children.

Notes

1. Charles Sellers and Henry May, *A Synopsis of American History* (Chicago: Rand McNally & Co., 1963), 151.

2. Mary Cable and the Editors of *American Heritage, American Manners and Morals* (New York: American Heritage Publishing Co., 1969), 184.

3. Alice B. Cushman, "A Nineteenth Century Plan for Reading: The American Sunday School Movement," *The Hewins Lectures, 1947-1962*, ed. Siri Andrews (Boston: Horn Book, 1963), 206-7.

4. Anne MacLeod, *A Moral Tale: Children's Fiction and American Culture, 1820-1860* (Hamden, Conn.: Archon, 1975), 22.

5. Cushman, "Nineteenth Century Plan," p. 209.

6. Cable, p. 184.

7. MacLeod, *Moral Tale*, p. 23.

8. Frank Luther Mott, *A History of American Magazines* (Cambridge: Harvard University Press, 1938), 1:144.

9. *American Journal of Education* 2. (February 1827), 127.

Information Sources

BIBLIOGRAPHY

M. F. Alstetter, "Early American Magazines for Children," *Peabody Journal of Education* 19 (November 1941), 131-36; Mary Cable, and the Editors of *American Heritage*, *American Manners and Morals* (New York: American Heritage Publishing Co., 1969); Alice B. Cushman, "A Nineteenth Century Plan for Reading: The American Sunday School Movement," *The Hewins Lectures, 1947-1962*, ed. Siri Andrews (Boston: Horn Book, 1963); Mary K. Eakin, and Alice Brooks McGuire, "Children's Magazines Yesterday and Today," *Elementary School Journal* 49 (January 1949), 257-60; Sheila A. Egoff, *Children's Periodicals of the 19th Century* (London: The Library Association, 1951); Alice M. Jordan, *From Rollo to Tom Sawyer and Other Papers* (Boston: Horn Book, 1948); Ann Scott MacLeod, *A Moral Tale: Children's Fiction and American Culture, 1820-1860* (Hamden, Conn.: Archon Books, 1975); Frank Luther Mott, *A History of American Magazines* (Cambridge: Harvard University Press, 1938).

INDEX SOURCES

None.

LOCATION SOURCES

No complete collection of *Youth's Friend and Scholar's Magazine* seems to exist. The following issues and volumes are in existence, however, at these locations: American Antiquarian Society, Worcester, Mass. (vols. 1, 3, 4 [partial], 5, 6 [partial]; issues are available from 1830, 1831, 1832, 1835, 1838, 1840, 1841, and 1844); Historical Society of Pennsylvania, Philadelphia (issue of June 1830); Library Company of Philadelphia (issues of January, April, May, and July, 1829: vol. 6, nos. 1, 4, 5, 7; and January through December 1827: vol. 4, nos. 1-12); University of Pennsylvania, Philadelphia (issues from 1828 [complete], 1838 [partial], 1839 [partial], 1841 [partial], and 1843 [complete]).

Publication History

MAGAZINE TITLE AND TITLE CHANGES

Teacher's Offering; or Sabbath Scholar's Magazine (1823-1825); *Youth's Friend and Scholar's Magazine* (1825-1864).

VOLUME AND ISSUE DATA

None.

PUBLISHER AND PLACE OF PUBLICATION

American Sunday School Union, Philadelphia (1823-1864).

EDITOR

None listed.

Anne D. Jordan

YOUTH'S INSTRUCTOR

The first half of the nineteenth century was a period of religious ferment and innovation in the United States. Both the new sects and the more established denominational churches were concerned with the religious and ethical education of the young. As a consequence, numerous Sunday and Sabbath schools were established and a number of religious periodicals created to supplement religious education. Among the longest-lived of these periodicals was the *Youth's Instructor*, first published in 1852 by the Seventh-day Adventist Church and still in circulation today under the title *Insight*.

The Seventh-day Adventist Church, which grew out of the Millerite movement of the 1840s, was organized as a union of existing Adventist sects in 1863 by Ellen Harmon White and her husband, James White. The name derives from the conviction that Saturday is the seventh day of the week and therefore the true Sabbath, according to *Genesis* 2:1-3 and *Exodus* 20:8-11, and the Adventists' belief in the second coming of Christ. *Youth's Instructor* was a part of the Adventist's extensive missionary and educational programs and was originally conceived by James White as a method of religious instruction for children and a vehicle for establishing Sabbath schools.

James White had been a schoolteacher in Maine before he met Ellen Harmon, his future wife, and they, together, organized the Seventh-day Adventist Church. Maintaining his interest and concern in the education of children after their organization of the church, he turned his attention to the religious needs of Adventist children, who he believed had been neglected by the movement until then. In the July 8, 1852, edition of the Seventh-day Adventist paper, the *Review and Herald*, White announced:

We design publishing a small monthly paper, containing matter for the benefit of the youth. And we are satisfied that our brethren and sisters will agree with us, that something of the kind is very much needed. The children should have a paper of their own, one that will interest and instruct them.

. . . We trust that such a paper as we design publishing will interest such children, and also be the means of waking up their parents, or guardians to a sense of their important duty. On them rests the awful responsibility of training souls for the Kingdom of God. But it is a lamentable fact that many of their children are left without suitable instruction.—We feel more on this subject than we can express. . . .

We intend to give four or five lessons, in the form of questions and answers, in each number, one for each week for Sabbath School lessons. These schools can be held where there are but two or three children as well as where there are more.[1]

The first issue of the *Youth's Instructor* was published from James White's home in Rochester, New York, in August 1852. At that time the magazine was a monthly, priced at 25¢ a year to those who could pay and distributed free to children who could not afford the subscription price. There was no declared editor, but the magazine was under the direction of James White, assisted by

Annie Smith, an Adventist follower. For the year 1854 Anna White, James White's sister, assumed the editorship.

In the first issue of the *Youth's Instructor*, James White prepared a "series of nineteen Bible lessons on the main points of the faith. While these were designed for the children and youth—an omnibus assignment—they served also, in the absence of other Sabbath school material, as the lesson studies for adults. These first lessons were followed by seventeen others selected from a non-Adventist paper. Eight lessons on the sanctuary followed, and then the momentum was exhausted."[2] Busy with other church matters, White allowed the *Youth's Instructor* to languish for eight months until Roswell F. Cottrell, a corresponding editor for the *Review and Herald*, took it upon himself to prepare a year's course of weekly lessons, later published in book form under the title of *The Bible Class*.

In 1855 James and Ellen White moved the Seventh-day Adventist publishing headquarters to Battlecreek, Michigan, where it remained until 1903 when both the General Conference (the Adventist organizational headquarters) and the Review and Herald Publishing Association, which issued the *Youth's Instructor*, moved to Washington, D.C. Following its move to Battlecreek and the death of Annie White, the *Youth's Instructor* became somewhat disorganized under the editorship of G. W. Amadon. Originally, each monthly issue contained Bible lessons for an entire month, but for several years they appeared only intermittently, and in 1861 and 1862 an exacting and didactic department was instituted instead under the title "Questions for Little Bible Scholars," which demanded an extensive knowledge of biblical minutiae.

This unorganized and eclectic type of Bible study ended in 1863, when Adelia Patten (Van Horn) furnished a two-year series of lessons to the *Youth's Instructor*, published under the title "Bible Knowledge for Little Children," and, a year later, assumed the post of editor of the periodical. Under her direction the lessons were organized into convenient weekly units, their content was structured and adapted for children, and an attempt was made to entertain as well as instruct young readers.

In 1870, under the editorship of Professor G. H. Bell, a pioneer in Seventh-day Adventist educational and Sabbath school work, *Youth's Instructor* began publication on a biweekly basis to stimulate Sabbath school interests. The *Youth's Instructor* was advanced to weekly publication in 1878 and remained as a weekly until its demise in 1970.

During this period the *Youth's Instructor* was aimed at both young children and adolescents. In 1890, however, under the editorship of Winnie E. Loughborough (Kelsea), the decision was made to limit the *Youth's Instructor* to older children and a paper designed for younger children was established under the title *Our Little Friend*, published by Pacific Press. "This, besides stories and general matter fitting the little child, carried the primary and kindergarten Sabbath school lessons; and thus the *Youth's Instructor* was released to a role wholly befitting its name."[3]

The *Youth's Instructor* continued to satisfy the needs of Adventist young people until superseded by *Insight* in 1970. In addition to continuing to provide instruction in biblical and Adventist doctrine, it also contained general articles and columns of interest to young people. Counseling service was provided in the column "Answers to Correspondents" from February 5 through August 13, 1907, followed by a similar column, "Questions and Answers," which appeared three times between 1907 and 1910. Lora E. Clement, editor from 1923 to 1952, wrote an extremely popular advice column, "Let's Talk It Over," which dealt with problems and issues young people were likely to encounter in daily life.

The *Youth's Instructor* also served as a medium in which various interests of the Seventh-day Adventist Church could be presented. During the period from May 14, 1907, through March 17, 1931, for example, several temperance issues were published. From 1908 until 1914 *Youth's Instructor* also contained a column devoted to promoting the Young People's Missionary Volunteer Society, a responsibility later transferred to the *Church Officer's Gazette* so that "the *Youth's Instructor* [could] devote itself to more general matters of spiritual and cultural interest to youth."[4]

To adapt to the changing needs of young people and to the times, the Review and Herald Publishing Association ceased publication of the *Youth's Instructor* in 1970, replacing it with *Insight*, a periodical more contemporary in design, format, and content. *Insight* has replaced the stress on instruction seen in *Youth's Instructor* with a blend of feature articles, essays, narratives, short stories, poetry, and how-to-do-it articles.

Notes

1. *Review and Herald*, July 8, 1852, p. 37.
2. Arthur W. Spalding, *Origin and History of Seventh-day Adventists* (Washington, D.C.: Review and Herald Publishing Association, 1962), 2:63.
3. Ibid., p. 73.
4. Ibid., 3:127.

Information Sources

BIBLIOGRAPHY

Cecil Coffey, *The Church God Built* (Washington, D.C.: Review and Herald Publishing Association, 1972); Emma Howell Cooper, *The Great Advent Movement* (Washington, D.C.: Review and Herald Publishing Association, 1968); Anne D. Jordan, *The Seventh-day Adventists: A History* (St. Louis: Concordia Publishing House, forthcoming); Nathaniel Krum, *The Church Triumphant* (Washington, D.C.: Review and Herald Publishing Association, 1972); C. Mervyn Maxwell, *Tell It to the World* (Mountain View, Calif.: Pacific Press, 1977); Arthur W. Spalding, *Origin and History of Seventh-day Adventists* (Washington, D.C.: Review and Herald Publishing Association, 1961, 1962), vols. 1, 2, 3, and 4; Mary Trim, *"Tell Me About Ellen White"* (Washington, D.C.: Review and Herald Publishing Association, 1975); Richard Utt, *A Century of Miracles* (Mountain View, Calif.: Pacific Press, 1963); Ellen G. White, *Testimonies for the Church* (Mountain View,

Calif.: Pacific Press, 1948), vol. 1; idem, *Testimony Treasures* (Mountain View, Calif.: Pacific Press, 1949), vols. 1, 2, and 3.

LOCATION SOURCES

Review and Herald Publishing Association, Washington, D.C. (all volumes); American Antiquarian Society, Worcester, Mass. (issues from vols. 7, 10-11); Library of Congress (vols. 52-63, 82, 84-); New York Public Library (vols. 2-3, 6-13, 19, 46, 47-55 [partial], 81 [partial]-84).

Publication History

MAGAZINE TITLE AND TITLE CHANGES

Youth's Instructor (1852-1970); *Insight* (1970-).

PUBLISHER AND PLACE OF PUBLICATION

Review and Herald Publishing Association, Rochester, N.Y. (1852-1855); Review and Herald Publishing Association, Battlecreek, Mich. (1855-1903); Review and Herald Publishing Association, Washington, D.C. (1903-).

EDITOR

James White (1852-1853, 1855-1857); Anna White (1854); G. W. Amadon (1858-1864, 1867-1869); Adelia P. Patten (Van Horn) (1864-1867); G. H. Bell (1869-1871); Jennie R. Trembley (1871-1873); Jennie A. Merriam (1873-1875); Minerva J. Chapman (1875-1879, 1884-1889); Mary K. White and V. A. Merriam (1879-1880); V. A. Merriam (1880-1881); Eva Bell (Giles), (1882-1883); Eva Bell Giles, Adolph B. Oyen, Winnie E. Loughborough (1883); none listed (1884-1889); Winnie B. Loughborough (Kelsea) (1890-1891); none listed (December 30, 1891-August 30, 1894); however, in his last editorial (December 20, 1894), p. 400, N. W. Lawrence, calling himself "the present editor," mentioned laying down the responsibilities he had carried "during the three years just passed"; J. H. Durland and M. E. Kelloff (1895-1896); J. H. Durland (1897); W. H. McKee and J. C. Bartholf (1897-1899); Adelaide B. Cooper (Evans) (1899-1904); Fannie M. Dickerson (Chase) (1904-1922); Lora E. Clement (1923-1952); Walter T. Crandell (1952-April, 1970); Mike Jones (May? 1970-1975); Donald John (1976-).

Anne D. Jordan

YOUTH'S MAGAZINE

Youth's Magazine began monthly publication in May 1860 in Nashville, Tennessee, under the editorship of George C. Connor and "Aunt Alice." Its title page described it as "solely devoted to the Interests of the Youth of the South." This publication superseded another Nashville juvenile, *The Children's Book of Choice and Entertaining Reading for the Little Folks at Home* (1855-1860).* The content of *Youth's Magazine* was to be "forty-eight pages of choice and entertaining reading from the pen of its editors, contributors, and current literature; thus giving the reader 576 pages of a book for the small sum of one dollar."[1]

In comparison with similar periodicals, the format of *Youth's Magazine* was particularly attractive for the period. A double-lined box outlined the text, with a short title at the top of the page. The cover bore an engraving of a decorative, leafy garland in which were enclosed the title, date, and editor's name. The advertisement stated that each number would contain a "beautiful electro-plate engraving, numerous wood engravings, as well as four beautiful steel-plate engravings during the year."[2]

In the December 1860 editorial *Youth's Magazine* praised the benefits of extensive reading by young people, stating: "There are no pleasures within the reach of mortals, apart from those of religion and virtue, which tend so much to elevate and satisfy our nature as those connected with a love of reading and the pursuit of knowledge." However, "reading" is *not* to be "confused with the perusal of novels," which "is now too general to need to be stimulated." Because there are so many books that convey instruction while they please and interest, "there is little to excuse or even palliate the perverted taste that would reject them in favor of trashy fiction."[3]

In this light it is easy to see why the large portion of stories and anecdotes were presented in *Youth's Magazine* aimed at character-building. In most cases the titles suffice to indicate their purpose: "Eighteen Tests of Good Breeding" (October 1860); "Member of the Try Company" (September 1860); "Deeds of Kindness" (September 1860); "Don't Be Foolhardy" (October 1860); and "Trust Not Appearances" (July 1860).

Although the verse in *Youth's Magazine* conformed generally to the pattern of didacticism prevalent at the time, a few exceptions can be found: "Uncle Sam" by R. H. Tewkesbury, a patriotic piece containing the names of all *thirty-three* states in its stanzas (August 1860); "My Little Boat" (October 1860); and "A Song for October" by T. W. Parsons (October 1860).

Numerous selections dealt with the death of a child: "The Dead Baby" (July 1860), "Going Home" (June 1860), "The Little Boy That Died" (September 1860), "My Boy in Heaven" (March 1861), "Sent to Heaven" (April 1861) and "My Darling's Shoes" (June 1860).

"Paltering in a Double Sense" was a "trick" poem about the Revolutionary War, which could be read variously, depending on the punctuation (September 1860); but conventional, moralistic verse was the rule: "Not in Vain" (December 1860), "The Orphan" (April 1861), "Will You Be There?" (March 1861), and "Do the Best You Can" (December 1860).

Youth's Magazine carried some interesting informational articles: "Names of the Months" (July 1860), "Origins of Plants" (July 1860), "Occupations of Animals" (September 1860), and "Names of Steamships Lost in Crossing the Atlantic" (May 1860).

Natural science articles covered topics such as oysters (June 1860), alligator eggs (December 1860), the inauguration of a queen bee (December 1860), the panther (February 1861), the butterfly's eye (February 1861), and the eagle (February 1861).

Articles about historical and geographical topics came from far and near: the first issue contained articles about "Morocco" and "Lake Lucerne" as well as a piece about "The Mammoth Cave" (May 1860). Other titles were "The Destruction of Jerusalem" (November 1860), "The Heroine of Fort Henry" (August 1860), "The Last Charge of Napoleon's Old Guard" (August 1860), and "John Hardeman's Trap—An Indian Encounter on the Border of North Carolina and East Tennessee" (March 1861).

Biographical sketches, which were numerous in the magazine, for the most part concerned American heroes like George Washington (August 1860), John Paul Jones (April 1861), Ben Franklin (December 1860), Roger Sherman (February 1861), and Henry Clay (March 1861).

Although music played only a minor role in the contents of *Youth's Magazine*, two pieces need to be mentioned: "The Children's Hosanna," three verses with the musical accompaniment (July 1860), and "Cradle Song," a "beautiful duet for two young ladies" giving detailed instructions for the tone and movements to accompany the singing of it (June 1860).

The regular features in *Youth's Magazine* offered many of the same items found in other periodicals of the day: puzzles, quizzes, conundrums, enigmas, and charades about biblical topics. "Wit and Wisdom," a department at the back of each issue, contained anecdotes and items thought to be of general interest borrowed from other publications.[4] "The Little Folks Department," usually attributed to "Uncle George" during his editorship and later to "Uncle John," consisted principally of admonitions or Bible stories. A page of "New Publications" was contained in early issues, announcing titles such as *Virginia Baptist Ministers* (May 1860), *Hester and I*; *or Beware of Worldliness* (June 1860); and *Mary Bunyan, the Dreamer's Blind Daughter* (July 1860), which were usually published by Sheldon & Co. and distributed by Graves, Marks & Co., Nashville, publishers of the magazine.

The editors encouraged letters from the young readers and devoted space to replies to questions "relating to studies, trials and troubles of youth" in the section "Queries and Answers."[5] In one instance the question was asked if the editor believed "in dancing and parties." The answer, delineating the folly of such worldly diversions, led to further advice on language suitable for youth: the avoidance of slang such as *howdy* and *reckon*, which were described as "lazy usages"—not of their original meanings whatsoever.[6]

Editorials were confined to a section at the back of each issue called "Our Country," the contents of which varied considerably: in "Our Bow" the magazine was called a "frail bark launched upon the troubled waters of the literary ocean."[7] "Our New System" was a "scheme for keeping little folks out of mischief" by teaching them the telegraphic alphabet.[8] The story of gaining independence from England was retold in the editorial of July 1860; and the selection in November 1860 dealt with the death of nine-year-old Luella Graves, daughter of the printer of *Youth's Magazine*, who "had reached a level of purity and happiness in her Father's house in Heaven. Be ye also ready!"[9] In March

1861 the editor stated that "some readers have advanced beyond childhood and are capable of appreciating writings which interest and instruct those who are advancing to the condition of young men and women." A new biographical series was begun for them, recognizing "them as moral and intellectual beings."[10]

In September 1860 when "Uncle John" assumed editorship, he encouraged his readers to "write about any and every thing that interest you; but write it in prose, don't write poetry.... We do not think this is by any means a useful exercise for young people, for 'rhyming' is too often taken for poetic talent." In writing prose young people were encouraged to work for *ideas* and to learn to read well, spell correctly, and reason vigorously. With patience and industry and a good teacher they "will work wonders" and "neither lack thoughts nor an ability to express them."[11]

In "Our Country" in April 1861 the editor noted that that issue completed the first volume of the publication. He expressed the hope that interest would be "not only sustained but augmented in future issues." Here the issue, the volume, and even the magazine itself closed with the expectation of having "each number of *Youth's Magazine* for the next year issued at the proper time. We do not expect to be *behind time* any more."[12]

Thus ended the life of *Youth's Magazine* after one short year of publication. As *The Children's Book of Choice and Entertaining Reading*, the magazine had experienced five years of successful production, but following the decision to reach an audience of older readers, it survived only one year, experiencing two editorships during that time. Both the format and content of *Youth's Magazine* were superior to most religious periodicals of this period, and in its early days it gave promise of being a successful and continuing publication. Almost certainly, the problems facing magazine publishers in the war-torn Confederacy contributed more to its demise than did any literary or editorial difficulties.

Notes

1. *Youth's Magazine* 1 (May 1860), inside back cover.
2. Ibid.
3. Ibid., 1 (December 1860), 382.
4. Publication from which stories, articles, and fillers were taken for *Youth's Magazine* include *Life Illustrated* (June 1860), *Charleston Courier, Sunday School Times, Le Journal des Enfants, Atlantic Monthly, Historical Magazine* (all September 1860); *Philadelphia Press* (November 1860); *The Companion* (December 1860); *Exchange Magazine* (February 1861); and *London Morning Chronicle* (October 1860).
5. *Youth's Magazine* (May 1860), 54. In this section of correspondence with readers, letters were included from points as far as Arkansas; Sweet Home, Texas; and Philadelphia, Mississippi; and as near as Trenton, Bolivar, and Winchester, Tennessee.
6. Ibid., 1 (May 1860), 45.
7. Ibid., p. 44.
8. Ibid., 1 (July 1860), 139.
9. Ibid., 1 (November 1860), 335.
10. Ibid., 1 (March 1861), 527.

11. Ibid., 1 (September 1860), 236.
12. Ibid., 1 (April 1861), 573.

Information Sources

BIBLIOGRAPHY
Gertrude C. Gilmer, ed., *Checklist of Southern Periodicals to 1861* (Boston: F. W.
    Faxon, 1934).
INDEX SOURCES
None.
LOCATION SOURCES
Duke University, Durham, N.C.; University of North Carolina, Chapel Hill, N.C.

Publication History

MAGAZINE TITLE AND TITLE CHANGES
Youth's Magazine (May 1860-April 1861).
VOLUME AND ISSUE DATA
Youth's Magazine (vol. 1, no. 1-vol. 1, no. 12).
PUBLISHER AND PLACE OF PUBLICATION
Graves, Marks & Co., Nashville (1860-1861).
EDITOR
George C. Connor (May 1860-August 1860); "Uncle John" (September 1860-April
    1861), who is never identified. An advertisement also lists "Aunt Alice" and
    "Uncle Robin," who are not identified either.

Mary D. Manning

THE YOUTH'S NEWS PAPER

In the first years of the American Republic children lived amid a sometimes
bewildering array of daily events: political, social, military, criminal, and domestic. Lacking access to today's many television programs, magazines, and
weekly readers designed to keep youngsters abreast of current events, children
had little to read that would explain current happenings in terms a child might
comprehend. An early attempt to meet this need was *The Youth's News Paper*.
Unfortunately, as laudable as the underlying intention may have been, the overall
inadequacy of execution guaranteed a quick demise. Publication ceased after six
issues.

The Youth's News Paper appeared in New York City in an eight-page octavo
format each Saturday for six weeks, running from September 30 to November
4, 1797. The publisher initially hoped to sell it for $3 a year, as advertised in
the first issue. Subsequently, however, he lowered the price to $2, still high
compared with rates for adult weeklies of the time.

The masthead announced that the paper was printed "for the EDITOR, and
C. Smith." Almost certainly, however, Charles Smith was both editor and
publisher. Smith was already an experienced editor, having produced pocket

almanacs since 1794 and *The Monthly Military Repository* from 1796 to 1797. Moreover, he customarily published almost all of his own books; the technique of assimilating other people's work, seen in *The Youth's News Paper*, also characterizes Smith's geographies and military writing, and the preface to his *Universal Geography Made Easy* (1795) sounds very much like the preface "To the Youth" in *The Youth's News Paper*. Finally, *The Youth's News Paper* reproduces some of the more original scientific material of *Universal Geography Made Easy*. George L. McKay, while not providing supporting evidence, also concluded that Smith was the editor.[1]

The first issue of *The Youth's News Paper* opens with a preface clearly stating the editorial policy. Addressing *"My Dear Young Friends,"* Smith asserted that children cannot profit from reading adult newspapers, because "the size of these large papers, the perplexity of the stile, [sic] the multiplicity of the matter they contain, and the number of advertisements which have no relation at all to your concerns, deter you." He also feared pernicious effects of contemporary newspapers upon "tender minds." However, since all must travel through this world toward the next, Smith proposed "a news-paper, wholly dedicated to you and suited to your capacities" to serve as "a treasure of knowledge" about the contemporary world.[2]

Smith did not invite outside contributors to submit material to his paper. Rather, probably doing all of the writing himself, he relied almost entirely on the technique of analysis and expansion familiar to readers from listening to sermons based upon biblical texts and similarly organized. He typically reprinted from an adult newspaper the lead paragraph(s) in a recent article, which contained several key words. He went on to discuss those words, providing moral and religious instruction, social and political commentary, geographic information, and scientific explanation.

The contents of the articles that Smith selected suggest he did not intend to create an overly optimistic view of the world for his young audience. In fact, unlike the newspapers from which he appropriated his lead paragraphs—including the *New York Gazette*, the *Gazette of the United States, and Philadelphia Advertiser*, the *Boston Mercury*, the *Boston Gazette*, and *Claypoole's American Daily Advertiser* (sources are seldom named)—*The Youth's News Paper* presented its readers with a difficult and dangerous world. Except for a half-dozen entries on topics such as the launching of the frigate *Constitution* and the creation of a New York county, the lead paragraphs are overwhelmingly negative. They describe mad dogs and hydrophobia (three times), the ravages of yellow fever (twice), trials and sentencing of seventeen assorted criminals, a girl's burning to death, nine drownings, a youthful suicide, quarrelsome couples, death by lightning, Lafayette's shameful captivity, several deaths during a political fray, a discovered corpse, a fatal tumble down stairs, storm damage (twice), barn arson, French spies, theft of public property, a capsized schooner, and devastating earthquakes (twice).

A seven-paragraph item in the October 28, 1797, issue illustrates the typical structure of the periodical's contents. The first two paragraphs constitute the basic news account of how the schooner *Tacy* capsized while en route to Baltimore and how the passengers were rescued. In paragraph three Smith began his expansion with a geographical description of Baltimore. He devoted the fourth paragraph to more information as he taught the names of several kinds of ships, including unusual ones like zebecs and polacres. The item concludes with admonitions to remember man's powerlessness before God's will, to recognize the dreadfulness of the sea's violence, and to prepare for eternity when sailing.

The editor accepted as one of his prime responsibilities making children God-fearing citizens. Reference to the Almighty is made in nearly every selection. God is said to preserve or destroy man without his knowing God's motives. Readers could recognize God's planning in physical occurrences such as tides, could fear His retribution for arson or suicide, and could thank Him for living in an area not subject to earthquakes. Above all, readers were asked to see that an irreligious education during childhood would almost certainly destroy them. We find, not surprisingly, frequent reminders to remember and speak to God, as when Smith provided a prayer for recitation by children wishing not to become orphans (September 30, 1797).

Spiritual nurturing simultaneously involves a strong moral nurturing. Smith repeatedly taught the traditional values, warning children to forsake drunkenness, dueling, and suicide, while exhorting them to cultivate love, benevolence, and philanthropy. True morality was based upon a right relationship with God, as Smith suggested in this reflection upon drinking: "But does the drunkard bestow service on God: does he pray, hear the Word of God, partake of Gods ordinances; all these things are mockery and blasphemy; for they, who in such corrupt minds are unworthy to converse with man, cannot be worthy to walk with God."[3]

One specialized moral point is the child's responsibility to love the other members of the family, especially parents. Smith averred dryly, for instance: "Early godliness and a filial and tender attachment to the parents will commonly assure a full measure of days."[4] His doctrine of such a duty waxes a bit strained when children are counseled to beware of fire not so much to save themselves from burning to death as to spare the feelings of their "tender parents" (September 30, 1797).

The editor's personal opinions were particularly pronounced when he touched on politics. His pages swell with faith in the republican spirit of the new America. Assailing the vanity of noble titles, he boasted, "The United States of America do exceedingly well without a king and without nobility," for "Liberty and equality...is a maxim worthy of the dignity of man. Nobility proceeds from merit."[5] Although he never delivered his promised definition of *republicanism*, he was in awe of its fermentative influence: "What great things and changes have we lived to see in the world! The greatest kingdom of Europe [France] converted into a republic: new republics in Italy created.... America independent and rising: the form of government changed in Venice, Genoa, Holland''—like earthquakes, such convulsions presage the Resurrection.[6]

Even as he applauded revolutionaries, however, Smith hardly showed himself a radical egalitarian. To those who would alter the Constitution to remove its defects, he replied with a rhetorical shudder, preferring ''to preserve the constitution and avoid a revolution.''[7] More than once he pointed out the sort of political balance that makes America work so well: here neither despotic rulers nor anarchical liberty holds sway. Thus he wrote with the same temper as the Founding Fathers, a conservative republicanism.

The pages of *The Youth's News Paper* also reflect the contemporary interest in geography. In the 1790s Jedidiah Morse, Caleb Bingham, Nathaniel Dwight, William Guthrie, Enos Weed, and others published books filled with geographical information to satisfy Americans' optimistic curiosity about the world before them. Smith himself published two geographies, *The American Gazetteer; or Geographical Companion* (1797) and, as noted earlier, *Universal Geography Made Easy*. In *The Youth's News Paper* he provided within nearly every item a capsule description of at least one locale. We hear, for instance, of New Haven's location, its university, and its 500 houses. Most are descriptions of localities in the United States, for, as he said in a description of New York State, ''It is useful and pleasant for young people, to have as perfect a knowledge of their country as possible.''[8] In his description of New York, Smith provided a chart indicating the names and populations of the state's counties as of 1790, its five new counties, and statistics on its population growth (November 4, 1797). Although atypical in its length, such description illustrates Smith's belief, shared by most of his contemporaries, that by saturating children with masses of geographical details, author-teachers can help children begin to know the great world.

The most ambitious pages in *The Youth's News Paper* feature scientific discussions. The editor assumed his young readers had the necessary curiosity to follow explanations of various phenomena, such as hydrophobia, lightning, storms, and tides. Today some of these theories sound quaint, as when we learn that ''subterraneous'' fires cause all earthquakes or that yellow fever endangers people because ''Vessels therefore in the human body, the pores of which are not large enough, that elastic air, or earthly, or even watery particles could penetrate them, are perforated by fixed air, enwrapt in particles of fire, and the vessels by thus violently enlarging the pores, are by degrees rendered unfit to contain and preserve, what they ought to preserve for the formation of the blood.''[9] For the most part, Smith was merely repeating the accepted scientific thought of his time. But he actually became excited as he introduced the electrical theories of Benjamin Franklin, for many scientific popularizers a symbol of the restless and optimistic American sense of inquiry. Throughout his periodical, Smith displayed a faith in science as a sign of an enlightened age.

Unfortunately, Smith's enthusiasm failed to assure the success of his project. One reason is undoubtedly his literary gracelessness. He created a mundane, serviceable style, much as he did in the dull pages of his gazetteer and in his translations of Baron Kotzebue's comedies. Awkward planning may also have contributed to the paper's limited appeal. Too often items lose their focus, and the final paragraph bears little connection to the earlier paragraphs. For instance, an article on the theft of hospital supplies leads to a reminder that true religion abhors dishonesty but inexplicably ends with an account of recent frosts (October 28, 1797). Another source of annoyance may have been Smith's practice of ending each issue at precisely the bottom of its eighth page often without finishing the last item, which was left to be completed in the next issue.

Finally, it may be said that Smith's sense of children's interests was deficient. It is difficult to imagine how some selections could have interested many youthful readers, for example, a long account of a Swedish politician's relish for solitude.

On November 4, 1797, *The Youth's News Paper* ceased publication. Its intent of explaining current events to children was laudable, but Smith adopted limited methods to realize a very ambitious goal; he had no predecessor's work on which to build, and he was hardly a notable literary stylist. However, this ill-fated venture did not destroy him, for Smith was at heart a businessman always ready for new ventures. For the last ten years of his life he busied himself with several projects as author, translator, bookseller, and publisher; but except for a second edition of *Universal Geography Made Easy*, he never again wrote for children.

Notes

1. "A Register of Artists, Booksellers, Printers and Publishers in New York City, 1781-1800," *Bulletin of the New York Public Library* 45 (1941), 496.
2. *The Youth's News Paper* 1 (September 30, 1797), 1-2.
3. Ibid., p. 7.
4. Ibid., 1 (October 21, 1797), 32.
5. Ibid., 1 (October 7, 1797), 16.
6. Ibid., 1 (October 21, 1797), 30.
7. Ibid., 1 (October 7, 1797), 11.
8. Ibid., 1 (November 4, 1797), 43.
9. Ibid., p. 48.

Information Sources

BIBLIOGRAPHY
None.
INDEX SOURCES
None.
LOCATION SOURCES
Complete runs are at the American Antiquarian Society, Worcester, Mass.; the New York Historical Society,; and the New York Public Library.

Publication History

MAGAZINE TITLE AND TITLE CHANGES
The Youth's News Paper (September 30, 1797-November 4, 1797).
VOLUME AND ISSUE DATA
The Youth's News Paper (vol. 1, no. 1-vol. 1, no. 6).

PUBLISHER AND PLACE OF PUBLICATION
Charles Smith, New York (September 30, 1797-November 4, 1797).
EDITOR
Charles Smith (September 30, 1797-November 3, 1797).

Avon Jack Murphy

YOUTH'S TEMPERANCE ADVOCATE

In 1839, because there was no juvenile periodical "directly calculated to arrest the attention, gain the hearts, and guide the habits and practices of the young," the *Youth's Temperance Advocate* was established by the American Temperance Union.[1] Believing that their "chief reliance" was on the "rising generation," the founders of the paper thought the *Advocate* should be "entirely adapted to the juvenile mind, and so cheap that it can easily be furnished by parents and friends of temperance to the thousands of youth in our great Republic."[2] This four-page newspaper contained lectures and anecdotes, with "true stories," temperance songs, and a scattering of jokes and poems. It sold for 75¢ per 100 and was distributed the first Sunday of each month in many Sunday schools; neither its format nor its price changed during its lifetime. In September 1858 the title—at least on the inside pages—changed to the *Youth's Temperance Advocate and Band of Hope Record*. Despite John Marsh's claim in 1866 that the *Advocate* "has never missed a number in its regular issues to the close of the year 1865,[3] no American library lists issues dated after December 1860.

The emphasis of the paper is on *temperance*, by which the editors meant abstinence from alcohol in any form. Readers were encouraged to shun medicinal alcohol and even mince pies, unless the mincemeat was prepared with something other than the traditional cider or wine (December 1841). Gin, rum, and whiskey are proscribed, as are wine and beer. Cider, too, the "Nest Egg of Intemperance" (June 1845), is condemned for its alcohol content as is root beer, for, they cautioned, "into root beer is sometimes put a good deal of whiskey."[4] Even coffee and tea—doubtless because they are stimulants—are frowned upon. The truly temperate are to drink nothing but water, because it is "the only element which 'God has given to nourish and invigorate his creatures and beautify his footstool.' "[5]

Later issues of the *Advocate*, while retaining the stand against alcohol, add prohibitions against smoking and overeating as well. Possibly because its editors were mindful of the paper's Sunday school affiliations, nontemperance themes such as "Seven Classes of Company to be Avoided" (November 1846?), the importance of living for others, and the sins of idleness begin to appear after 1845. Obedience to parents is also an important theme, with authors celebrating models such as the patient young man told to meet his father on London Bridge at noon, who cheerfully waits there in the cold for seven hours because his father is busy and forgets him until that evening (July 1858). A series of Bible lessons appeared in 1855.

From the very beginning, the *Advocate* is characterized by a high level of anonymity. No editor is ever designated, and very few of the pieces are signed. Occasionally, the author of a poem or story receives credit—Washington Irving is one, for "The Ruined Family," reprinted from an unidentified source. Most of the pieces seem to have been culled from other temperance publications and, occasionally, from newspapers or books such as the *Presbyterian*, the *Temperance Almanac, Spirit of the Age, Merry's Museum*,* the *Cincinnati Morning Star*, and even *Scientific American*. The *Advocate* cannibalizes even itself, for it appears that if a piece seemed especially popular, it was reprinted over and over. Irving's "The Ruined Family" is one such piece; a few long pieces and many short anecdotes are also reprinted.

Not only does the prose lead a double life, the illustrations do too. Some of the engravings were provided by Robert Sears, a New York engraver. Because not all of the illustrations have temperance themes, creativity is often exercised in the accompanying prose to make the illustration appropriate. Thus it is that a depiction of Prometheus having his liver torn by the vulture appears as "The Vulture and the Drunkard," to accompany a piece describing the imaginary agonies of a drunk who hallucinates that a vulture is mutilating him (September 1845). The Pool of Bethesda becomes symbolic of the temperance movement, for as the pool cured those who entered it, so do joining the movement and the signing of the pledge cure many (October 1843). A piece below a cut of the tunnel beneath the Thames celebrates the tunnel, which will add something to the wealth of London but not as much as would removing all of the grogshops and brewhouses (September 1844). Illustrations are also used over and over. The pyramidal "Progress of Drunkenness" in issue 6 (May 1840?) becomes "The Drunkard's Up Hill and Down Hill" in issue 76 (March 1846). A scrawny nag appearing to the side of a cut illustrating "The Drunkard's Home" (January 1845) is featured alone above the poem "Petition of a Drunkard's Horse" (June 1846?) and again above a piece revealing that "Even the Horses Have Changed" since their drunken owners became temperate (April 1855).

Despite its moral themes the *Advocate* is surprisingly lively. Lectures are numerous, but the didacticism is couched in anecdotes, jokes, stories, and conversations. There are the continuing conversations of "The Temple Family"— who discuss at great length and with much thoroughness topics such as the number of drunkards in America, the effect of alcohol on the body, and whether or not a drunkard's body might actually go up in flames. Temperance humor about drunks avoiding water and drinkers made to look silly by their families abound. Anecdotes about Indians also appear: presented as reformed drunkards who avoid alcohol, they serve as examples for the reader. Examples, too, are animals, which either do not touch alcohol or get drunk once and learn their lessons.

The paper has as its motto "Hearken unto me, o ye children, for blessed are they that keep my ways," and its editors took this to heart, aiming their main thrust at children up to courting age. Adults were also expected to read the *Advocate*, as attested by pieces such as "A Word for Mothers" (May 1849) and "Good Done by the *Advocate*" (August 1841), in which an intemperate adult who reads the paper reforms. But the emphasis is on children not only as readers but in the pieces themselves, as victims, examples, or moral influences.

The victims include those who learned to enjoy alcohol as children and grew up to be drunkards, those whose parents are drunks, and those who die after drinking whiskey or rum. A typical tale is that of "Poor Charles," who is given gin-sling as a child, grows up to become a drunkard, kills another drunk, and is hanged after delivering a speech in which he blames his parents for making him a drunk (October 1846?). The children of drunkards are routinely held up as objects of pity and examples of misery, whom readers are encouraged to help rather than spurn. Legion are examples in the *Advocate* of children from age four to eleven who drink hard liquor and drop dead or die later of fits.

The children who exert moral influence are usually the children of drinkers who, through their artless prattle or active temperance work, win their parents to temperance. Six-year-old Anne, who innocently makes her father "The Inebriate" realize that he is making his family suffer (January 1845), exemplifies the type, as do the two children who keep their father away from the local tavern by preparing a little cold-water tea and reading to him from the Bible.[6] The temperate child of an intemperate father is to be like the fisherman's son who guided his father through the fog by the sound of his voice (September 1860). The exemplars tend to be temperate children of great personal beauty or temperate children who work hard for the cause. An example of the former is "The Boy Nye," the sole survivor of a shipwreck, who survives because his devotion to total abstinence has preserved a good constitution (May 1856). Examples, too, are the children raised in total abstinence who grow up "like Daniel and his companions, ruddy, healthy, and beautiful" (March 1849). "Master Henson," a fourteen-year-old temperance speech maker, is to be emulated (March 1846), as is a nameless little girl who gathers ninety signatures on temperance pledges (December 1845).

The *Advocate* is a curiosity now; its importance lies chiefly in its place in history as a manifestation of an important nineteenth-century reform movement. Not always particularly well-written and insistently didactic, the *Advocate* hammered away at a single message, although the ways in which it is presented are as varied as possible. The *Advocate* does not "intend to equal in humor Peter Parley's Magazine and Robert Merry's Museum," for it "deals too much in sober realities"; but with its stories of drunkards reformed, sober Indians, and teetotaling animals, it tries to "catch the attention and rivet the heart."[7]

Notes

1. *Youth's Temperance Advocate* 1 (December? 1839), 1.
2. Ibid.

3. John Marsh, D.D., *Temperance Recollections* (New York: Charles Scribner & Co., 1866), 65.

4. *Youth's Temperance Advocate* 89 (April 1847), 355.

5. Ibid., 19 (September 1858), 35.

6. Ibid., 19 (July 1858). It is hoped that they edited judiciously as they read: Psalm 103, which was one they chose, praises God for water and then for the "wine that maketh glad the heart of man."

7. Ibid., 20 (January 1859), 2.

Information Sources

BIBLIOGRAPHY

American Temperance Union, *Report of the Executive Committee of the American Temperance Union* (New York: American Temperance Union, 1842, 1843, 1844, 1848); John Marsh, *Temperance Recollections* (New York: Charles Scribner & Co., 1866).

INDEX SOURCES

None.

LOCATION SOURCES

American Antiquarian Society, Worcester, Mass.; Boston Public Library; Detroit Public Library—Burton Historical Collection; Library Company of Philadelphia; New York Public Library; Rutgers University, New Brunswick, N.J.; University of Minnesota, Minneapolis; Yale University, New Haven.

Publication History

MAGAZINE TITLE AND TITLE CHANGES

Youth's Temperance Advocate (1839-1860?). On inside pages, *Youth's Temperance Advocate* (1839-1858); *Youth's Temperance Advocate and Band of Hope Recorder* (1858-1860?).

VOLUME AND ISSUE DATA

Youth's Temperance Advocate (no. 1-no. 96; vol. 9, no. 1-vol. 20, no. 12?). On inside pages, *Youth's Temperance Advocate* (no. 1-no. 96; vol. 9, no. 1-vol. 19, no. 8); *Youth's Temperance Advocate and Band of Hope Recorder* (vol. 19, no. 9-vol. 20, no. 12?).

PUBLISHER AND PLACE OF PUBLICATION

American Temperance Union, New York (1839-1860?)

EDITOR

None listed.

Pat Pflieger

Selected Bibliography of American Children's Periodicals

Acanthus, Atlanta, Ga., 1877-1884

Action Age: The Magazine for the Young, Detroit, Mich., 1967-1969?

Advance: A Magazine of Inspiration for Young People, Birmingham, Ala., 1904-

Adventure Trails for Boys and Girls, Putney, Vt., 1943-

Amateur Press. See *Youth's Press*.

American Boy—Open Road, Boston, Mass., 1919-1954

American Boy's Magazine, Philadelphia, Pa., 1870-1872

The American Girl, New York, N.Y., 1917-1979

American Newspaperboy, New York, N.Y., 1927-

American Sunday-School Magazine, Philadelphia, Pa., 1824-1832

American Young Folks, Manchester, N.H., 1875-1885?

American Youth, Chicago, Ill., 1889?-1898?

American Youth, New York, N.Y., 1912-1921

American Youth, New York, N.Y., 1935-

Apples of Gold, Boston, Mass., 1872-1917

Association Boys, New York, N.Y., 1902-1911

Babyland, Boston, Mass., 1877-1898

The Baptist Union, Chicago, Ill., 1890-1904

Bee, Albany, N.Y., 1844-1845

Belles and Beaux, New York, N.Y., 1874

Benziger's Magazine: An Illustrated Catholic Family Monthly, New York, N.Y., 1898-1921

The Boy, Columbus, Ohio, 1909

Boy Citizen, Fort Wayne, Ind., 1924-1926

Boyland. See *Trailmaker*.

Boys and Girls, Philadelphia, Pa., 1897-1906

Boys and Girls, Nashville, Tenn., 1909-1941?

Boys and Girls: A Nature Study Magazine, Ithaca, N.Y., 1903-1907

Boys' and Girls' Journal: A Magazine for the People and Their Children, Philadelphia, Pa., 1848-1853?

Boys' and Girls' Literary Bouquet, Philadelphia, Pa., 1842-1846
Boys' and Girls' Magazine, Boston, Mass., 1843?
The Boys' and Girls' Magazine, and Fireside Companion. Boston, Mass., 1848-1857.
Boys' and Girls' Monthly Bouquet. See *Boys' and Girls' Literary Bouquet*.
Boys' and Girls' New Monthly Magazine, n.p., 1868?
Boys' and Girls' Newspaper, New York, N.Y., 1935
Boys' and Girls' Own Magazine, New York, N.Y., 1859-1860?
Boys' and Girls' Penny Journal. See *Boys' and Girls' Journal: A Magazine for the People
    and Their Children*.
Boys and Girls Quarterly, Cincinnati, Ohio, 1902?-1925?
Boys and Girls World, Los Angeles, Calif., 1938-1939
Boy's Best Weekly, Cleveland, Ohio, 1909-1910
Boys' Brigade Bulletin, San Francisco, Calif., 1892-1893
The Boys' Champion, New York, N.Y., 1881-1883
Boys' Holiday. See *Holiday Magazine for Children*.
Boy's Home Weekly, Cleveland, Ohio, 1908
The Boys' Leader: A Journal of Fact, Fiction, History and Instruction, New York, N.Y.,
    1878-1879
Boys' Ledger, n.p., 1872
Boys' Life, Boston, Mass., 1911-
The Boys' Magazine, Smethport, Pa., 1910-1920
Boys' Monthly Gazette, Charlestown, Mass., 1857-1858?
Boys' Monthly Magazine, Cleveland, Ohio, 1927-?
Boys of Albany, New York, N.Y., 1877-1878?
Boys of New York: A Paper for Young Americans, New York, N.Y., 1875-1894
Boys of the World: A Story Paper for the Rising Generation, New York, N.Y., 1875-
    1877
Boys of Today, Elgin, Ill., 1920-1925?
Boys' Own, Boston, Mass., 1873-1874
Boys' Own, Boston, Mass., 1877?
The Boys' Own Story Teller: Rich, Spicy, and Entertaining, New York, N.Y., 1875-
    1878
Boys' Star Library, New York, N.Y., 1887-1896?
Boys Today, Nashville, Tenn., 1941-1952?
The Boys' Week-day Book, n.p., 1832
The Boys' World, Elgin, Ill., 1902-1935
The Brownies' Book, New York, N.Y., 1920-1921
Bubble, New York, N.Y., 1849?
Burke's Weekly for Boys and Girls, Macon, Ga., 1867-1871
Calling All Girls. See *Young Miss*.
Cargo: A Magazine for Boys and Girls, Nashville, Tenn., 1936-1939
The Catholic Boy, Minneapolis, Minn., 1932-1970
Catholic Young People's Friend, Chicago, Ill., 1974-
Catholic Youth's Magazine, Baltimore, Md., 1857-1861
Chautauqua Young Folks' Journal, Boston, Mass., 1884-1890
The Child at Home, Boston, Mass., 1863-1873
Child-Garden of Story, Song and Play, Chicago, Ill., 1892-1903
Child Life, Chicago, Ill., 1921-

Child-Life: A Theosophic Magazine Published in the Interests of All Children, Brooklyn, N.Y., 1896-1897

Child Lore, Brooklyn, N.Y., 1910-1912

Childhood: The Juvenile Magazine of the Pacific Slope, San Francisco, Calif., 1914?-1923?

Children of the United States, Omaha, Neb., 1900-1907

Children's Activities for Home and School, Chicago, Ill., 1934-

The Children's Book of Choice and Entertaining Reading for the Little Folks at Home, Nashville, Tenn., 1855-1860

Children's Digest, San Francisco, Calif., 1937?

Children's Digest, Chicago, Ill., 1950-

Children's Friend, Nashville, Tenn., 1859-1873?

Children's Friend, Dayton, Ohio, 1860?-1863

Children's Friend, Richmond, Va., 1862-1915

The Children's Friend, Salt Lake City, Utah, 1902-1970

The Children's Friend: A Monthly Magazine Devoted to the Best Interests of the Young, West Chester, Pa., 1866-1875?

Children's Guide, Macon, Ga., 1863-1865?

The Children's Hour, Philadelphia, Pa., 1867-1874

Children's Leader, Philadelphia, Pa., 1925-1939

The Children's Magazine: Calculated for the Use of Families and Schools, Hartford, Conn., 1789

Children's Magazine, New York, N.Y., 1829-1874

Children's Magazine, New York, N.Y., 1903-1913

Children's Magazine, Stamford, Conn., 1904?

Children's Missionary, Nashville, Tenn., 1894-1906

Children's Museum, New York, N.Y., 1881-1882?

Children's New Church Magazine, Boston, Mass., 1880-1891?

Children's Playmate, Cleveland, Ohio, 1929-

The Children's Playtime, Cleveland, Ohio, 1930-1932

Children's Star Magazine, Washington, D.C., 1907-1910?

Children's Work for Children. See *Missionary Mail for Boys and Girls*.

Child's Cabinet, New Haven, Conn., 1832

Child's Companion, Skaneateles, N.Y., 1838-1839

The Child's Companion, St. Louis, Mo., 1937-

Child's Companion and Youth's Friend, Philadelphia, Pa., 1846?-?

Child's Delight. See *Kind Words*.

The Child's Friend, Boston, Mass., 1843-1858

Child's Garden, San Francisco, Calif., 1923-1928

Child's Gazette, Boston, Mass.? 1835-?

Child's Magazine, New York, N.Y., 1827-1846?

Child's Magazine, Portland, Maine, 1857-1858?

Child's Monthly, n.p., 1877

The Child's Paper, New York, N.Y., 1852-1897?

Child's World, Philadelphia, Pa., 1862-1871

Christian Endeavor World, Boston, Mass., 1886-

Clark's School Visitor, Philadelphia, Pa., 1857-1875

Classmate: A Paper for Young People, New York, N.Y., 1895-1959?

Cobblestone, Peterborough, N.H., 1980-
Cold Water Army, Boston, Mass., 1841?-1843
Comrade, Philadelphia, Pa., 1909-1914
Cricket: The Magazine for Children, LaSalle, Ill., 1973-
Current Events, Springfield, Mass., 1902-
Demorest's Young America, New York, N.Y., 1866-1875
Ebony Jr! Chicago, Ill., 1973-
The Encourager, New York, N.Y., 1846
Epworth Era, Nashville, Tenn., 1894-1931
Epworth Herald, Chicago, Ill., 1890-1940
Epworth Highroad, Nashville, Tenn., 1932-1941
Every Youth's Gazette, New York, N.Y., 1842
The Family Pioneer and Juvenile Key, Brunswick, Maine, 1830-1837
Family and School Visitor, Bangor, Maine, 1839?
Favorite, n.p., 1852
Florence Crittenton Magazine, Washington, D.C., 1899-1917
The Fly; or Juvenile Miscellany, Boston, Mass., 1805-1806?
Forest Garland, n.p., 1853-1854
*Forrester's Boys' and Girls' Magazine, and Fireside Companion. See Boys' and Girls'
       Magazine, and Fireside Companion*
Forrester's Play-mate, Boston, Mass., 1854-1867?
Forward, Philadelphia, Pa., 1882-1939
Forward for Young People, Philadelphia, Pa., 1940-
Four and Five, n.p., 1918-?
Frank Leslie's Boy's and Girl's Weekly, New York, N.Y., 1866-1884
Frank Leslie's Boys of America, New York, N.Y., 1873-1878?
Frank Leslie's Chatterbox, New York, N.Y., 1879-1887
Frank Leslie's Children's Friend, New York, N.Y., 1866?
Girls, Alexandria, Va., 1898-1917. Continuation of *Florence Crittenton Magazine*.
Girls and Boys of America. See Munro's Girls and Boys of America.
The Girls' Companion, Elgin, Ill., 1902-1949
Girls of Today: A Mirror of Romance. See New York Mirror.
The Golden Argosy, New York, N.Y., 1882-1888
The Golden Book Magazine, New York, N.Y., 1925-1935
Golden Days for Boys and Girls, Philadelphia, Pa., 1880-1907
Golden Hours: A Magazine for Boys and Girls, Cincinnati, Ohio, 1869-1880
Golden Rule, Albany, N.Y., 1841-1842?
Golden Rule, Boston, Mass., 1875-1886?
Golden Weekly, New York, N.Y., 1889-1891
Good Times and Popular Educator, Boston, Mass., 1877-1884?
Good Words for the Young, Philadelphia, Pa., 1865-1870
Happy Days, New York, N.Y., 1894-1924
Harper's Round Table. See Harper's Young People: An Illustrated Weekly.
Harper's Young People: An Illustrated Weekly, New York, N.Y., 1879-1899
Highlights for Children, Columbus, Ohio, 1946-
Highroad, Nashville, Tenn., 1941-
The Hive: A Juvenile Paper, Salem, Mass., 1828-1830
Holiday Magazine for Children. See Children's Magazine (1903-1913).

Humpty Dumpty's Magazine, New York, N.Y., 1952-
Infant's Delight, n.p., 1870
Infant's Magazine, Philadelphia, Pa., 1829-1842
Ingenue, New York, N.Y., 1959-
The Instructor. See *The Juvenile Instructor*.
Jack and Jill, Philadelphia, Pa., 1938-
John Martin's Book: The Child's Magazine, Garden City, N.Y., 1912-1933
Judy, New York, N.Y., 1846-1847?
Junior Astronomy News, New York, N.Y., 1933-?
Junior: A Juvenile Paper by Young Writers, Dorchester, Mass., 1893-1897
Junior Munsey, New York, N.Y., 1897-1902
Junior Natural History Magazine, New York, N.Y., 1936-1963
Junior Naturalist: For the Preservation of Wildlife, San Francisco, Calif., 1938-?
Junior Naturalist Monthly, Ithaca, N.Y., 1899-1907
Junior Scholastic, Pittsburgh, Pa., 1937-
Juvenile Gazette, Providence, R.I., 1819-1820?
Juvenile Gazette, Boston, Mass., 1848
The Juvenile Gazette: Being an Amusing Repository for Youth, Providence, R.I., 1827-
    1828
The Juvenile Instructor, Salt Lake City, Utah, 1866-
Juvenile Key, Brunswick, Maine, 1830-1831?
The Juvenile Magazine, Philadelphia, Pa., 1802-1803?
The Juvenile Magazine, Philadelphia, Pa., 1811-1813?
The Juvenile Magazine, Utica, N.Y., 1827-1828
Juvenile Magazine, and Youth's Monthly Visitor, New York, N.Y., 1831-1832?
Juvenile Mirror; or Educational Magazine, New York, N.Y., 1812?
The Juvenile Miscellany: For the Instruction and Amusement of Youth, Boston, Mass.,
    1826-1836
The Juvenile Monthly, Amherst, Mass., 1829
Juvenile Museum, Mt. Pleasant, Ohio, 1822-1823
Juvenile Olio, Philadelphia, Pa., 1802
The Juvenile Port-Folio and Literary Miscellany, Philadelphia, Pa., 1812-1816
Juvenile Rambler, Boston, Mass., 1832-1833
Juvenile Repertory, Philadelphia, Pa., 1828-1829?
The Juvenile Repository, Boston, Mass., 1811
The Juvenile Repository, Providence, R.I., 1830
The Juvenile Repository, Boston, Mass., 1833-1834?
Juvenile Repository: Containing Lessons and Stories for the Young, New York, N.Y.,
    1842-1845?
Juvenile Temperance Watchman, n.p., 1854
Juvenile Weekly Gazette, New York, N.Y., 1850-1851?
Keeping Posted, New York, N.Y., 1955-
Kind Words, Greenville, S.C., 1866-1891
Kings' Treasuries. See *Pioneer for Boys*.
Knapsack, Cincinnati, Ohio, 1892-1897?
Little American, West Point, N.Y., 1862-1864
Little...Bee: A Catholic Gatherer of Amusement and Instructive Reading, Chicago, Ill.,
    1884-1885

Little Bouquets. Superseded by *Lyceum Banner*.
Little Chap: A Journal of Education and Literature, Holyoke, Mass., 1896
Little Chief, n.p., 1868
Little Christian, Boston, Mass., 1871-1904?
Little Chronicle. See *World's Chronicle*.
The Little Corporal, Chicago, Ill., 1865-1875
Little Folks: An Illustrated Monthly for Youngest Readers, Boston, Mass., 1897-1926
Little Forester, Cincinnati, Ohio, 1854-1855?
Little Gleaner, Fredericksburg, Va., 1868-1869?
Little Joker, New York, N.Y., 1863-1866
The Little Messenger, Philadelphia, Pa., 1868-1873
Little Ones at Home, n.p., 1878-1881
Little People: An Illustrated Journal for Girls and Boys, Detroit, Mich., 1875
The Little Pilgrim, Philadelphia, Pa., 1853-1867
Little Traveler: A Monthly Paper for the Youth, Waynesville, Ohio, 1853-1855
The Look-Out: A Monthly Magazine for Young People, Boston, Mass., 1889-1891?
Lyceum Banner, Chicago, Ill., 1868-1872?
The Mentor: A Magazine for Youth, Philadelphia, Pa., 1850-1851?
Mentor and Youth's Instructive Companion, New York, N.Y., 1830-?
Merry's Museum, New York, N.Y., 1841-1872
Message Bird: A Monthly Literary Periodical. Supersedes *Little Traveler*.
Missionary Mail for Boys and Girls, Philadelphia, Pa., 1876-1958
Monthly Instructor and Fireside Companion. See *Forrester's Play-mate*.
Mt. Vernon Enterprise, New York, N.Y., 1847-?
Munro's Girls and Boys of America, New York, N.Y., 1873-1877?
My Weekly Reader, Columbus, Ohio, 1929-
National Little Corporal's School, Chicago, Ill., 1870-1874
The New Church Magazine for Children. See *Children's New Church Magazine*.
New Horizons for Youth, New York, N.Y., 1960-1964
New York Boys, New York, N.Y., 1877-1878
New York Mirror, New York, N.Y., 1875-1876
News Citizen, n.p., 1941-
The Nursery, Boston, Mass., 1867-1881
Oliver Optic's Magazine, Boston, Mass., 1867-1875
Onward, New York, N.Y., 1869-1870
Our Boys, New York, N.Y., 1875-1878
Our Boys and Girls, Kansas City, Mo., 1894-1895
Our Boys and Girls. See *Boys and Girls*, 1897
Our Boys and Girls, Ridley Park, Pa., 1899-1901
Our Boys' and Girls' Own: An Illustrated Catholic Monthly. See *Benziger's Magazine: An Illustrated Catholic Family Monthly*.
Our Boys' Magazine, Booneville, Mo., 1908-1909
Our Leisure Moments, Buffalo, N.Y., 1870
Our Little Friend, Mountain View, Calif., 1871?-?
Our Little Granger, Cincinnati, Ohio, 1880-1890?
Our Little Men and Women, Boston, Mass., 1880-1900
Our Little Ones and the Nursery: Illustrated Stories and Poems for Little People, Boston, Mass., 1880-1899

Our Young Folks: An Illustrated Magazine for Boys and Girls, Boston, Mass., 1865-1873

Our Young Folks' Illustrated Paper, Augusta, Maine, 1871-1873

Our Young People, Philadelphia, Pa., 1880-1898?

Our Youth, New York, N.Y., 1885-1890

Pacific Youth, San Francisco, Calif., 1874

Packard's Monthly: The Young Men's Magazine, New York, N.Y., 1868-1870

The Pansy, Boston, Mass., 1874-1896

The Parents' Gift: Youths' Magazine, Philadelphia, Pa., 1830-1831?

Parley's Magazine: For Children and Youth, New York, N.Y., 1833-1844

Pictorial Gallery for Young People, n.p., 1878-1893

Pictures and Stories, Nashville, Tenn., 1870-?

Pictures and Stories, n.p., 1941-1958?

The Pilgrim: A Magazine for the Home, Battle Creek, Mich., 1899-1907

Pilgrim Highroad. Supersedes *The Wellspring: For Young People.*

Pioneer: Devoted to the Boys, Roxbury, Mass., 1857-1858

Pioneer for Boys, Philadelphia, Pa., 1915-1950

Play Mate. See *Children's Playmate.*

Plays: The Drama Magazine for Young People, Boston, Mass., 1941-

Portal. See *Sunday School Advocate.*

Quaker. See *Junior Munsey.*

The Raindrop: A Monthly Miscellany, Turtle Creek, Pa., 1879-1880

Rally. See *The American Girl.*

Ranger Rick's Nature Magazine, Washington, D.C., 1967-

The Riverside Magazine for Young People, New York, N.Y., 1867-1870

Rose Bud. See *Southern Rose.*

The Sabbath School Treasury, Boston, Mass., 1828-1851?

St. Nicholas, New York, N.Y., 1873-1943

Satchel, Philadelphia, Pa., 1846-1847

Scattered Seeds, Philadelphia, Pa., 1869-1935

The Scholar's Gazette, Philadelphia, Pa., 1831-1832

The Scholar's Penny Gazette, Boston, Mass., 1848-1850?

Scholar's Weekly Gazette. See *The Scholar's Gazette.*

School Weekly, Oak Park, Ill., 1898-1908

The Schoolfellow: A Magazine for Boys and Girls, Athens, Ga., 1849-1857

The Schoolmate: A Monthly Reader for School and Home Instruction of Youth, New York, N.Y., 1852-1854

Senior Scholastic, Pittsburgh, Pa., 1920-

Service. Superseded *Baptist Union.*

Seventeen, New York, N.Y., 1942-

Slaves's Friend, New York, N.Y., 1836-1838

Southern Boys' and Girls' Monthly, Richmond, Va., 1867-1868

Southern Rose, Charleston, S.C., 1832-1839

Spare Hours, Boston, Mass., 1866-1867?

The Standard-Bearer: An Illustrated Magazine for the Young, New York, N.Y., 1851-1863?

Star Monthly, Oak Park, Ill., 1894-1908

Stone Soup: The Magazine by Children, Santa Cruz, Calif., 1973-

Stories for the Little Child, Nashville, Tenn., 1935-1941
Stories from Many Lands: A Monthly Publication for Catholic Youth, New York, N.Y., 1906-1907?
Story Friends, Scottdale, Pa., 1905-
Story Parade, New York, N.Y., 1936-1954
Story World, Philadelphia, Pa., 1872-1931
Student: A Family Magazine and Monthly School Reader, New York, N.Y., 1846-1850?
The Student and Schoolmate, Boston, Mass., 1855-1872
Sunday Digest, Elgin, Ill., 1887-?
Sunday School Advocate, New York, N.Y., 1841-1921
Sunday School Journal and Advocate of Christian Education. See *Sunday School Times*.
Sunday School Times, Philadelphia, Pa., 1859-
Sunshine for Youth: Also for Those of All Ages Whose Hearts Have Not Withered, Augusta, Maine, 1886-1907
Target. See *Sunday School Advocate*.
Teacher's Offering; or Sabbath Scholar's Magazine, Philadelphia, Pa., 1823-1843?
'Teen Magazine, Los Angeles, Calif., 1957-
'Teens. Supersedes *The Youth's World: A Paper for Boys*.
Tip Top Weekly: An Ideal Publication for Youth, New York, N.Y., 1896-1912
Trailmaker. See *Boyland*.
Treasure Trove: An Illustrated Magazine, New York, N.Y., 1877-1893
The Tutor, Philadelphia, Pa., 1842
Wee-Wee Winkie: The Children's Magazine, Rochester, N.Y., 1912-1913
Wee Wisdom, Kansas City, Mo., 1893?-
Weekly Magpie, Edgewood, Md., 1859
The Weewish Tree: A Magazine of Indian America for Young People, San Francisco, Calif., 1971-1980
The Wellspring: For Young People, Boston, Mass., 1844-?
What Not, n.p., 1859-1860
Wide Awake, Boston, Mass., 1875-1893
With, Scottdale, Pa., 1968-
Words of Cheer, Orrville, Ohio, 1876-1970
Work and Play, Springfield, Mass., 1870-1872
Work and Play: An Illustrated Magazine for Girls and Boys, New York, N.Y., 1874-1876?
World, Washington, D.C., 1975-
World Over, New York, N.Y., 1940-
World's Chronicle, Chicago, Ill., 1900-1919
Young America, West Chester, Pa., 1857?-1858?
Young America, New York, N.Y., 1900-1901
Young America Monthly Magazine, Boston, Mass., 1858-1859?
Young America: Stories and Pictures for Young People, Boston, Mass., 1886-1890
Young America: The National News Weekly for Youth, New York, N.Y., 1935-1944?
Young American, Brookline, Mass., 1857-1858?
Young American, New York, N.Y., 1874-1876
Young American: Devoted to the Amusement and Instruction of the Young, Buffalo, N.Y., 1869
Young Americans, Albany, N.Y., 1867-1904

Young American's Magazine of Self-Improvement, Boston, Mass., 1847

Young Calvinist, Grand Rapids, Mich., 1920-1929

Young Catholic's Guide, Chicago, Ill., 1867-1871

Young Christian: A Magazine for Universalist Sunday Schools and Families, New York, N.Y., 1851-1854?

Young Christian Soldier, New York, N.Y., 1867-1868?

Young Churchman's Miscellany, New York, N.Y., 1846-1848?

Young Citizen: A Magazine for Supplementary Reading in the Public Schools, Cedar Falls, Ia., 1901-1908?

Young Democracy: A Journal of the New Generation, New York, N.Y., 1919-1921

Young Evangelist, St. Louis, Mo., 1865-1906?

Young Folks Circle, Springfield, Ohio, 1882-1885?

Young Folks' Magazine. See *Youth: An Illustrated Monthly Journal for Boys and Girls.*

Young Folks' Monthly, Chicago, Ill., 1870-1883

Young Folks News, Philadelphia, Pa., 1868-1873?

Young Folks' Rural, Chicago, Ill., 1870-1881

Young Glory: Patriotic War Stories, New York, N.Y., 1898

Young Idea: A Monthly Juvenile Magazine for the Youth of Our Land, Belvidere, Ill., 1887-1890?

Young Israel, New York, N.Y., 1871-1909?

Young Israel, Cincinnati, Ohio, 1908?-1940

Young Israel: Devoted to the Jewish Home, Detroit, Mich., 1907-1911

Young Judaean, New York, N.Y., 1910-

Young Knight, Garrett, Ind., 1908-1914?

Young Lutherans' Magazine: An Illustrated Juvenile Monthly, St. Louis, Mo., 1902-1939?

Young Men of America, New York, N.Y., 1877-1889?

Young Miss, Concord, N.H., 1941-

Young New Yorker: A Boys Story Paper and World of Sport, New York, N.Y., 1878-1879

Young People, Philadelphia, Pa., 1880-?

The Young People's Book; or Magazine of Useful and Entertaining Knowledge, Philadelphia, Pa., 1841-1842

Young People's Journal of Science, Literature and Art, New York, N.Y., 1848

Young People's Leader, Philadelphia, Pa., 1925-1939

Young People's Magazine, New York, N.Y., 1846

Young People's Magazine, Boston, Mass., 1894-1895?

Young People's Magazine, Chicago, Ill., 1901-1902?

The Young People's Mirror, New York, N.Y., 1848-1849

Young People's Service, Chicago, Ill., 1904-1925

Young People's Weekly. See *Sunday Digest.*

Young Pioneer, New York, N.Y., 1923-1931

Young Reaper, Boston, Mass., 1844-1855?

Young Reaper, Philadelphia, Pa., 1857-1908?

Young Socialists' Magazine, Chicago, Ill., 1908-1920

Young Southron: A Magazine for Boys and Girls, Atlanta, Ga., 1897

Young Virginian, Mt. Clinton, Va., 1874-1876

Youth: An Illustrated Monthly Journal for Boys and Girls, Philadelphia, Pa., 1902-1906

Youth Temperance Visitor, Rockland, Maine, 1863-1870?

Youth Today: The Month's Best Reading for Young People, Concord, N.H., 1938-1941

Youth's Cabinet, New York, N.Y., 1846-1859

Youth's Cabinet: Devoted to Liberty, Peace, Temperance, & Religious, Moral, Intellectual, & Physical Education, Boston, Mass., 1837-1845

The Youth's Casket, Buffalo, N.Y., 1852-1857

Youth's Christian Companion, Scottdale, Pa., 1920-1968

The Youth's Companion, Boston, Mass., 1827-1929

Youth's Companion, and Weekly Family Visitor, New York, N.Y., 1832-1834

Youth's Comrade. See *Youth's Realm*.

Youth's Dayspring, Boston, Mass., 1850-1855

The Youth's Emancipator, Oberlin, Ohio, 1842-1843

Youth's Friend, Cincinnati, Ohio, 1846-1857?

Youth's Friend and Scholar's Magazine, Philadelphia, Pa., 1823-1843?

Youth's Galaxy, New York, N.Y., 1853

Youth's Guide to Piety and Virtue, and Literary Casket, Poughkeepsie, N.Y., 1836-1837?

Youth's Instructor, Rochester, N.Y., 1852-

Youth's Instructor and Guardian, New York, N.Y., 1823-1832?

Youth's Journal, New York, N.Y., 1828-1829?

Youth's Journal, Pittsburgh, Pa., 1892-1895?

Youth's Literary Gazette, Philadelphia, Pa., 1832-1833

The Youth's Literary Messenger, Philadelphia, Pa., 1837-1839

Youth's Lyceum, New Lisbon, Ohio, 1837

Youth's Lyceum and Literary Gazette, Xenia, Ohio, 1835-1836?

Youth's Magazine, Cincinnati, Ohio, 1830?-1838?

Youth's Magazine, Nashville, Tenn., 1860-1861

Youth's Magazine: A Monthly Miscellany, New York, N.Y., 1838-1841

Youth's Magazine; or Spirit of the Juvenile Miscellany, Boston, Mass., 1830

Youth's Medallion, Boston, Mass., 1841-1842

Youth's Mental Casket and Literary Star, Jersey City, N.J., 1839-1842?

Youth's Monitor, Portland, Maine, 1840-1842

Youth's Monthly Magazine, Boston, Mass., 1850-1851?

Youth's Musical Companion, Sharon, Pa., 1924-1926?

The Youth's News Paper, New York, N.Y., 1797

Youth's Penny Gazette, Philadelphia, Pa., 1843-1858

Youth's Press, Troy, Pa., 1888-1891

Youth's Realm, Boston, Mass., 1896-1906

Youth's Repository of Christian Knowledge, New Haven, Conn., 1813

Youth's Outlook, Boyne City, Mich., 1905-1913?

Youth's Temperance Advocate, New York, N.Y., 1839-1860

Youth's Temperance Banner, New York, N.Y., 1866-?

Youth's Temperance Enterprise, Albany, N.Y., 1842-1844?

Youth's Treasury, Nashville, Tenn., 1885

The Youth's Visitor, Boston, Mass., 1864-1872?

The Youth's World: A Paper for Boys, Philadelphia, Pa., 1907-1939

Zion's Young People, Salt Lake City, Utah, 1900-1902

Zoonooz, San Diego, Calif., 1926-

APPENDIX 2
Chronological Listing of Magazines

1830	*The Juvenile Repository*
1830	*Mentor and Youth's Instructive Companion*
1830	*The Parents' Gift: Youths' Magazine*
1830?	*Youth's Magazine*
1830	*Youth's Magazine; or Spirit of the Juvenile Miscellany*
1831	*Juvenile Magazine, and Youth's Monthly Visitor*
1831	*The Scholar's Gazette*
1832	*The Boys Week-day Book*
1832	*Child's Cabinet*
1832	*Juvenile Rambler*
1832	*Southern Rose*
1832	*Youth's Companion, and Weekly Family Visitor*
1832	*Youth's Literary Gazette*
1833	*The Juvenile Repository*
1833	*Parley's Magazine: For Children and Youth*
1835	*Child's Gazette*
1835	*Youth's Lyceum and Literary Gazette*
1836	*Slaves's Friend*
1836	*Youth's Guide to Piety and Virtue, and Literary Casket*
1837	*Youth's Cabinet: Devoted to Liberty, Peace, Temperance, & Religious, Moral, Intellectual, & Physical Education*
1837	*The Youth's Literary Messenger*
1837	*Youth's Lyceum*
1838	*Child's Companion*
1838	*Youth's Magazine: A Monthly Miscellany*
1839?	*Family and School Visitor*
1839	*Youth's Mental Casket and Literary Star*
1839	*Youth's Temperance Advocate*
1840	*Youth's Monitor*
1841?	*Cold Water Army*
1841	*Golden Rule*
1841	*Merry's Museum*
1841	*Sunday School Advocate*
1841	*The Young People's Book; or Magazine of Useful and Entertaining Knowledge*
1841	*Youth's Medallion*
1842	*Boys' and Girls' Literary Bouquet*
1842	*Every Youth's Gazette*
1842	*Juvenile Repository: Containing Lessons and Stories for the Young*
1842	*The Tutor*
1842	*The Youth's Emancipator*
1842	*Youth's Temperance Enterprise*
1843	*Boys' and Girls' Magazine*
1843	*The Child's Friend*
1843?	*The Youth's Penny Gazette*
1844	*Bee*
1844	*The Wellspring: For Young People*
1844	*Young Reaper*
1846?	*Child's Companion and Youth's Friend*

1859	*Boys' and Girls' Own Magazine*
1859	*Children's Friend*
1859	*Sunday School Times*
1859	*Weekly Magpie*
1859	*What Not*
1860?	*Children's Friend*
1860	*Youth's Magazine*
1862	*Children's Friend*
1862	*Child's World*
1862	*Little American*
1863	*The Child at Home*
1863	*Children's Guide*
1863	*Little Joker*
1863	*Youth Temperance Visitor*
1864	*The Youth's Visitor*
1865	*Good Words for the Young*
1865	*The Little Corporal*
1865	*Our Young Folks: An Illustrated Magazine for Boys and Girls*
1865	*Young Evangelist*
1866?	*Frank Leslie's Children's Friend*
1866	*The Children's Friend: A Monthly Magazine Devoted to the Best Interests of the Young*
1866	*Demorest's Young America*
1866	*Frank Leslie's Boy's and Girl's Weekly*
1866	*The Juvenile Instructor*
1866	*Kind Words*
1866	*Spare Hours*
1866	*Youth's Temperance Banner*
1867	*Burke's Weekly for Boys and Girls*
1867	*The Children's Hour*
1867	*The Nursery*
1867	*Oliver Optic's Magazine*
1867	*The Riverside Magazine for Young People*
1867	*Southern Boys' and Girls' Monthly*
1867	*Young Americans*
1867	*Young Catholic's Guide*
1867	*Young Christian Soldier*
1868?	*Boys' and Girls' New Monthly Magazine*
1868	*Little Chief*
1868	*Little Gleaner*
1868	*The Little Messenger*
1868	*Lyceum Banner*
1868	*Packard's Monthly: The Young Men's Magazine*
1868	*Young Folks News*
1869	*Golden Hours: A Magazine for Boys and Girls*
1869	*Onward*
1869	*Scattered Seeds*
1869	*Young American: Devoted to the Amusement and Instruction of the Young*

1878	*Young New Yorker: A Boys Story Paper and World of Sport*
1879	*Frank Leslie's Chatterbox*
1879	*Harper's Young People: An Illustrated Weekly*
1879	*The Raindrop: A Monthly Miscellany*
1880	*Children's New Church Magazine*
1880	*Golden Days for Boys and Girls*
1880	*Our Little Granger*
1880	*Our Little Men and Women*
1880	*Our Little Ones and the Nursery: Illustrated Stories and Poems for Little People*
1880	*Our Young People*
1880	*Young People*
1881	*The Boys' Champion*
1881	*Children's Museum*
1882	*Forward*
1882	*The Golden Argosy*
1882	*Young Folks Circle*
1884	*Chautauqua Young Folks' Journal*
1884	*Little . . . Bee: A Catholic Gatherer of Amusement and Instructive Reading*
1885	*Our Youth*
1885	*Youth's Treasury*
1886	*Christian Endeavor World*
1886	*Sunshine for Youth: Also for Those of All Ages Whose Hearts Have Not Withered*
1886	*Young America: Stories and Pictures for Young People*
1887	*Boys' Star Library*
1887	*Sunday Digest*
1887	*Young Idea: A Monthly Juvenile Magazine for the Youth of Our Land*
1888	*Youth's Press*
1889?	*American Youth*
1889	*Golden Weekly*
1889	*The Look-Out: A Monthly Magazine for Young People*
1890	*The Baptist Union*
1890	*Epworth Herald*
1892	*Boys' Brigade Bulletin*
1892	*Child-Garden of Story, Song and Play*
1892	*Knapsack*
1892	*Youth's Journal*
1893	*Junior: A Juvenile Paper by Young Writers*
1893?	*Wee Wisdom*
1894	*Children's Missionary*
1894	*Epworth Era*
1894	*Happy Days*
1894	*Our Boys and Girls*
1894	*Star Monthly*
1894	*Young People's Magazine*
1895	*Classmate: A Paper for Young People*
1896	*Child-Life: A Theosophic Magazine Published in the Interests of All Children*
1896	*Little Chap: A Journal of Education and Literature*
1896	*Tip Top Weekly: An Ideal Publication for Youth*

1896   *Youth's Realm*
1897   *Boys and Girls*
1897   *Junior Munsey*
1897   *Little Folks: An Illustrated Monthly for Youngest Readers*
1897   *Young Southron: A Magazine for Boys and Girls*
1898   *Benziger's Magazine: An Illustrated Catholic Family Monthly*
1898   *Girls*
1898   *School Weekly*
1898   *Young Glory: Patriotic War Stories*
1899   *Florence Crittenton Magazine*
1899   *Junior Naturalist Monthly*
1899   *Our Boys and Girls*
1899   *The Pilgrim: A Magazine for the Home*
1900   *Children of the United States*
1900   *World's Chronicle*
1900   *Young America*
1900   *Zion's Young People*
1901   *Young Citizen: A Magazine for Supplementary Reading in the Public Schools*
1901   *Young People's Magazine*
1902   *Association Boys*
1902?   *Boys and Girls Quarterly*
1902   *The Boys' World*
1902   *The Children's Friend*
1902   *Current Events*
1902   *The Girls' Companion*
1902   *Young Lutherans' Magazine: An Illustrated Juvenile Monthly*
1902   *Youth: An Illustrated Monthly Journal for Boys and Girls*
1903   *Boys and Girls: A Nature Study Magazine*
1903   *Children's Magazine*
1904?   *Children's Magazine* (Stamford, Ct.)
1904   *Advance: A Magazine of Inspiration for Young People*
1904   *Young People's Service*
1905   *Children's Magazine*
1905   *Story Friends*
1905   *Youth's Outlook*
1906   *Stories from Many Lands: A Monthly Publication for Catholic Youth*
1907   *Children's Star Magazine*
1907   *The Youth's World: A Paper for Boys*
1907   *Young Israel: Devoted to the Jewish Home*
1908?   *Young Israel*
1908   *Boy's Home Weekly*
1908   *Our Boys' Magazine*
1908   *Young Knight*
1908   *Young Socialists' Magazine*
1909   *The Boy*
1909   *Boy's Best Weekly*
1909   *Boys and Girls*
1909   *Comrade*

1910   *The Boys' Magazine*
1910   *Child Lore*
1910   *Young Judaean*
1911   *Boys' Life*
1912   *American Youth*
1912   *John Martin's Book: The Child's Magazine*
1912   *Wee-Wee Winkie: The Children's Magazine*
1914?   *Childhood: The Juvenile Magazine of the Pacific Slope*
1915   *Pioneer for Boys*
1917   *The American Girl*
1918   *Four and Five*
1919   *American Boy—Open Road*
1919   *Young Democracy: A Journal of the New Generation*
1920   *Boys of Today*
1920   *The Brownies' Book*
1920   *Senior Scholastic*
1920   *Young Calvinist*
1920   *Youth's Christian Companion*
1921   *Child Life*
1923   *Child's Garden*
1923   *Young Pioneer*
1924   *Boy Citizen*
1924   *Youth's Musical Companion*
1925   *Children's Leader*
1925   *The Golden Book Magazine*
1925   *Young People's Leader*
1926   *Zoonooz*
1927   *American Newspaperboy*
1927   *Boys' Monthly Magazine*
1929   *Children's Playmate*
1929   *My Weekly Reader*
1930   *The Children's Playtime*
1932   *The Catholic Boy*
1932   *Epworth Highroad*
1933   *Junior Astronomy News*
1934   *Children's Activities for Home and School*
1935   *American Youth*
1935   *Boys' and Girls' Newspaper*
1935   *Stories for the Little Child*
1935   *Young America: The National News Weekly for Youth*
1936   *Cargo: A Magazine for Boys and Girls*
1936   *Junior Natural History Magazine*
1936   *Story Parade*
1937?   *Children's Digest*
1937   *The Child's Companion*
1937   *Junior Scholastic*
1938   *Boys and Girls World*
1938   *Jack and Jill*

Geographical Listing
of Magazines

ALABAMA

Birmingham 1904 *Advance: A Magazine of Inspiration for Young People*

CALIFORNIA

Los Angeles   1938 *Boys and Girls World*
               1957 *'Teen Magazine*
Mountain   1871? *Our Little Friend*
  View
San Diego   1926 *Zoonooz*
San Francisco 1874 *Pacific Youth*
               1892 *Boys' Brigade Bulletin*
               1914? *Childhood: The Juvenile Magazine of the Pacific Slope*
               1923 *Child's Garden*
               1937? *Children's Digest*
               1938 *Junior Naturalist: For the Preservation of Wildlife*
               1971 *The Weewish Tree: A Magazine of Indian America for Young People*
Santa Cruz   1973 *Stone Soup: The Magazine by Children*

CONNECTICUT

Hartford   1789 *The Children's Magazine: Calculated for the Use of Families and Schools*
New Haven   1813 *Youth's Repository of Christian Knowledge*

	1832	*Child's Cabinet*
Stamford	1904?	*Children's Magazine*

DISTRICT OF COLUMBIA

Washington	1907	*Children's Star Magazine*
	1899	*Florence Crittenton Magazine*
	1967	*Ranger Rick's Nature Magazine*
	1975	*World*

GEORGIA

Athens	1849	*The Schoolfellow: A Magazine for Boys and Girls*
Atlanta	1877	*Acanthus*
	1897	*Young Southron: A Magazine for Boys and Girls*
Macon	1863	*Children's Guide*
	1867	*Burke's Weekly for Boys and Girls*

ILLINOIS

Belvidere	1887	*Young Idea: A Monthly Juvenile Magazine for the Youth of Our Land*
Chicago	1865	*The Little Corporal*
	1867	*Young Catholic's Guide*
	1868	*Lyceum Banner*
	1870	*National Little Corporal's School*
	1870	*Young Folks' Monthly*
	1870	*Young Folks' Rural*
	1884	*Little...Bee: A Catholic Gatherer of Amusement and Instructive Reading*
	1889?	*American Youth*
	1890	*The Baptist Union*
	1890	*Epworth Herald*
	1892	*Child-Garden of Story, Song and Play*
	1900	*World's Chronicle*
	1901	*Young People's Magazine*
	1904	*Young People's Service*
	1908	*Young Socialists' Magazine*
	1921	*Child Life*
	1934	*Children's Activities for Home and School*
	1950	*Children's Digest*
	1973	*Ebony Jr!*
	1974	*Catholic Young People's Friend*

Elgin	1887	*Sunday Digest*
	1902	*The Boys' World*
	1902	*The Girls' Companion*
	1920	*Boys of Today*
LaSalle	1973	*Cricket: The Magazine for Children*
Oak Park	1894	*Star Monthly*
	1898	*School Weekly*

INDIANA

Fort Wayne	1924	*Boy Citizen*
Garrett	1908	*Young Knight*

IOWA

Cedar Falls	1901	*Young Citizen: A Magazine for Supplementary Reading in the Public Schools*

MAINE

Augusta	1871	*Our Young Folks: Illustrated Paper*
	1886	*Sunshine for Youth: Also for Those of All Ages Whose Hearts Have Not Withered*
Bangor	1839?	*Family and School Visitor*
Brunswick	1830	*The Family Pioneer and Juvenile Key*
	1830	*Juvenile Key*
Portland	1840	*Youth's Monitor*
	1857	*Child's Magazine*
Rockland	1863	*Youth Temperance Visitor*

MARYLAND

Baltimore	1857	*Catholic Youth's Magazine*
Edgewood	1859	*Weekly Magpie*

MASSACHUSETTS

Amherst	1829	*The Juvenile Monthly*
Boston	1805	*The Fly; or Juvenile Miscellany*
	1811	*The Juvenile Repository*

1826	*The Juvenile Miscellany: For the Instruction and Amusement of Youth*
1827	*The Youth's Companion*
1828	*The Sabbath School Treasury*
1830	*Youth's Magazine; or Spirit of the Juvenile Miscellany*
1832	*Juvenile Rambler*
1833	*The Juvenile Repository*
1833	*Parley's Magazine: For Children and Youth*
1835	*Child's Gazette*
1837	*Youth's Cabinet: Devoted to Liberty, Peace, Temperance, & Religious, Moral, Intellectual, & Physical Education*
1841?	*Cold Water Army*
1841	*Youth's Medallion*
1843?	*Boys' and Girls' Magazine*
1843	*The Child's Friend*
1844	*The Wellspring: For Young People*
1844	*Young Reaper*
1847	*Young American's Magazine of Self-Improvement*
1848	*The Boys' and Girls' Magazine, and Fireside Companion*
1848	*Juvenile Gazette*
1848	*The Scholar's Penny Gazette*
1850	*Youth's Dayspring*
1850	*Youth's Monthly Magazine*
1854	*Forrester's Play-mate*
1855	*The Student and Schoolmate*
1858	*Young America Monthly Magazine*
1863	*The Child at Home*
1864	*The Youth's Visitor*
1865	*Our Young Folks: An Illustrated Magazine for Boys and Girls*
1866	*Spare Hours*
1867	*The Nursery*
1867	*Oliver Optic's Magazine*
1871	*Little Christian*
1872	*Apples of Gold*
1873	*Boys' Own*
1874	*The Pansy*
1875	*Golden Rule*
1875	*Wide Awake*
1877?	*Boys' Own*
1877	*Babyland*
1877	*Good Times and Popular Educator*
1880	*Children's New Church Magazine*
1880	*Our Little Men and Women*
1880	*Our Little Ones and the Nursery: Illustrated Stories and Poems for Little People*
1884	*Chautauqua Young Folks' Journal*
1886	*Christian Endeavor World*
1886	*Young America: Stories and Pictures for Young People*

	1889	*The Look-Out: A Monthly Magazine for Young People*
	1894	*Young People's Magazine*
	1896	*Youth's Realm*
	1897	*Little Folks: An Illustrated Monthly for Youngest Readers*
	1911	*Boy's Life*
	1919	*American Boy—Open Road*
	1941	*Plays: The Drama Magazine for Young People*
Brookline	1857	*Young American*
Charlestown	1857	*Boys' Monthly Gazette*
Dorchester	1893	*Junior: A Juvenile Paper by Young Writers*
Holyoke	1896	*Little Chap: A Journal of Education and Literature*
Roxbury	1857	*Pioneer: Devoted to the Boys*
Salem	1828	*The Hive: A Juvenile Paper*
Springfield	1870	*Work and Play*
	1902	*Current Events*

MICHIGAN

Battle Creek	1899	*The Pilgrim: A Magazine for the Home*
Boyne City	1905	*Youth's Outlook*
Detroit	1875	*Little People: An Illustrated Journal for Girls and Boys*
	1907	*Young Israel: Devoted to the Jewish Home*
	1967	*Action Age: The Magazine for the Young*
Grand Rapids	1920	*Young Calvinist*

MINNESOTA

| Minneapolis | 1932 | *The Catholic Boy* |

MISSOURI

Booneville	1908	*Our Boys' Magazine*
Kansas City	1893?	*Wee Wisdom*
	1894	*Our Boys and Girls*
St. Louis	1865	*Young Evangelist*
	1902	*Young Lutherans' Magazine: An Illustrated Juvenile Monthly*
	1937	*The Child's Companion*

NEBRASKA

| Omaha | 1900 | *Children of the United States* |

NEW HAMPSHIRE

Concord	1938	*Youth Today: The Month's Best Reading for Young People*
	1941	*Young Miss*
Manchester	1875	*American Young Folks*
Peterborough	1980	*Cobblestone*

NEW JERSEY

Jersey City	1839	*Youth's Mental Casket and Literary Star*

NEW YORK

Albany	1841	*Golden Rule*
	1842	*Youth's Temperance Enterprise*
	1844	*Bee*
	1867	*Young Americans*
Brooklyn	1896	*Child-Life: A Theosophic Magazine Published in the Interests of All Children*
	1910	*Child Lore*
Buffalo	1852	*The Youth's Casket*
	1869	*Young American: Devoted to the Amusement and Instruction of the Young*
	1870	*Our Leisure Moments*
Garden City	1912	*John Martin's Book: The Child's Magazine*
Ithaca	1899	*Junior Naturalist Monthly*
	1903	*Boys and Girls: A Nature Study Magazine*
New York	1797	*The Youth's News Paper*
	1812?	*Juvenile Mirror; or Educational Magazine*
	1823	*Youth's Instructor and Guardian*
	1827	*Child's Magazine*
	1828	*Youth's Journal*
	1829	*Children's Magazine*
	1830	*Mentor and Youth's Instructive Companion*
	1831	*Juvenile Magazine, and Youth's Monthly Visitor*
	1832	*Youth's Companion, and Weekly Family Visitor*
	1833	*Parley's Magazine: For Children and Youth*
	1836	*Slaves's Friend*
	1838	*Youth's Magazine: A Monthly Miscellany*
	1839	*Youth's Temperance Advocate*
	1841	*Merry's Museum*
	1841	*Sunday School Advocate*
	1842	*Every Youth's Gazette*
	1842	*Juvenile Repository: Containing Lessons and Stories for the Young*

1846   *The Encourager*
1846   *Judy*
1846   *Student: A Family Magazine and Monthly School Reader*
1846   *Young Churchman's Miscellany*
1846   *Young People's Magazine*
1846   *Youth's Cabinet*
1847   *Mt. Vernon Enterprise*
1848   *Young People's Journal of Science, Literature and Art*
1848   *The Young People's Mirror*
1849?   *Bubble*
1850   *Juvenile Weekly Gazette*
1851   *The Standard-Bearer: An Illustrated Magazine for the Young*
1851   *Young Christian: A Magazine for Universalist Sunday Schools and Families*
1852   *The Child's Paper*
1852   *The Schoolmate: A Monthly Reader for School and Home Instruction of Youth*
1853   *Youth's Galaxy*
1859   *Boys' and Girls' Own Magazine*
1863   *Little Joker*
1866?   *Frank Leslie's Children's Friend*
1866   *Demorest's Young America*
1866   *Frank Leslie's Boy's and Girl's Weekly*
1866   *Youth's Temperance Banner*
1867   *The Riverside Magazine for Young People*
1867   *Young Christian Soldier*
1868   *Packard's Monthly: The Young Men's Magazine*
1869   *Onward*
1871   *Young Israel*
1873   *Frank Leslie's Boys of America*
1873   *Munro's Girls and Boys of America*
1873   *St. Nicholas*
1874   *Belles and Beaux*
1874   *Work and Play: An Illustrated Magazine for Girls and Boys*
1874   *Young American*
1875   *Boys of New York: A Paper for Young Americans*
1875   *The Boys' Own Story Teller: Rich, Spicy, and Entertaining*
1875   *Boys of the World: A Story Paper for the Rising Generation*
1875   *New York Mirror*
1875   *Our Boys*
1877   *Boys of Albany*
1877   *New York Boys*
1877   *Treasure Trove: An Illustrated Magazine*
1877   *Young Men of America*
1878   *The Boys' Leader: A Journal of Fact, Fiction, History and Instruction*
1878   *Young New Yorker: A Boys Story Paper and World of Sport*
1879   *Frank Leslie's Chatterbox*

	1879	*Harper's Young People: An Illustrated Weekly*
	1881	*The Boys' Champion*
	1881	*Children's Museum*
	1882	*The Golden Argosy*
	1885	*Our Youth*
	1887	*Boys' Star Library*
	1889	*Golden Weekly*
	1894	*Happy Days*
	1895	*Classmate: A Paper for Young People*
	1896	*Tip Top Weekly: An Ideal Publication For Youth*
	1897	*Junior Munsey*
	1898	*Benziger's Magazine: An Illustrated Catholic Family Monthly*
	1898	*Young Glory: Patriotic War Stories*
	1900	*Young America*
	1902	*Association Boys*
	1903	*Children's Magazine*
	1906	*Stories from Many Lands: A Monthly Publication for Catholic Youth*
	1910	*Young Judaean*
	1912	*American Youth*
	1917	*The American Girl*
	1919	*Young Democracy: A Journal of the New Generation*
	1920	*The Brownies' Book*
	1923	*Young Pioneer*
	1925	*The Golden Book Magazine*
	1927	*American Newspaperboy*
	1933	*Junior Astronomy News*
	1935	*American Youth*
	1935	*Boys' and Girls' Newspaper*
	1935	*Young America: The National News Weekly for Youth*
	1936	*Junior Natural History Magazine*
	1936	*Story Parade*
	1940	*World Over*
	1941	*Young Miss*
	1942	*Seventeen*
	1952	*Humpty Dumpty's Magazine*
	1955	*Keeping Posted*
	1959	*Ingenue*
	1960	*New Horizons for Youth*
Poughkeepsie	1836	*Youth's Guide to Piety and Virtue, and Literary Casket*
Rochester	1852	*Youth's Instructor*
	1912	*Wee-Wee Winkie: The Children's Magazine*
Skaneateles	1838	*Child's Companion*
Utica	1827	*The Juvenile Magazine*
West Point	1862	*Little American*

OHIO

Cincinnati	1830?	*Youth's Magazine*
	1846	*Youth's Friend*

	1854	*Little Forester*
	1869	*Golden Hours: A Magazine for Boys and Girls*
	1880	*Our Little Granger*
	1892	*Knapsack*
	1902?	*Boys and Girls Quarterly*
	1908?	*Young Israel*
Cleveland	1908	*Boy's Home Weekly*
	1909	*Boy's Best Weekly*
	1927	*Boys' Monthly Magazine*
	1929	*Children's Playmate*
	1930	*The Children's Playtime*
Columbus	1909	*The Boy*
	1929	*My Weekly Reader*
	1946	*Highlights for Children*
Dayton	1860?	*Children's Friend*
Mt. Pleasant	1822	*Juvenile Museum*
New Lisbon	1837	*Youth's Lyceum*
Oberlin	1842	*The Youth's Emancipator*
Orrville	1876	*Words of Cheer*
Springfield	1882	*Young Folks Circle*
Waynesville	1853	*Little Traveler: A Monthly Paper for the Youth*
Xenia	1835	*Youth's Lyceum and Literary Gazette*

PENNSYLVANIA

	1802	*The Juvenile Magazine*
Philadelphia	1802	*The Juvenile Magazine*
	1802	*Juvenile Olio*
	1811	*The Juvenile Magazine*
	1812	*The Juvenile Port-Folio and Literary Miscellany*
	1823	*Teacher's Offering; or Sabbath Scholar's Magazine*
	1823	*Youth's Friend and Scholar's Magazine*
	1824	*American Sunday-School Magazine*
	1828	*Juvenile Repertory*
	1829	*Infant's Magazine*
	1830	*The Parents' Gift: Youths' Magazine*
	1831	*The Scholar's Gazette*
	1832	*Youth's Literary Gazette*
	1837	*The Youth's Literary Messenger*
	1841	*The Young People's Book; or Magazine of Useful and Entertaining Knowledge*
	1842	*Boys' and Girls' Literary Bouquet*
	1842	*The Tutor*
	1843	*Youth's Penny Gazette*
	1846?	*Child's Companion and Youth's Friend*
	1846	*Satchel*
	1848	*Boys' and Girls' Journal: A Magazine for the People and Their Children*

	1850	*The Mentor: A Magazine for Youth*
	1853	*The Little Pilgrim*
	1857	*Clark's School Visitor*
	1857	*Young Reaper*
	1859	*Sunday School Times*
	1862	*Child's World*
	1865	*Good Words for the Young*
	1867	*The Children's Hour*
	1868	*The Little Messenger*
	1868	*Young Folks News*
	1869	*Scattered Seeds*
	1870	*American Boy's Magazine*
	1872	*Story World*
	1876	*Missionary Mail for Boys and Girls*
	1880	*Golden Days for Boys and Girls*
	1880	*Our Young People*
	1880	*Young People*
	1882	*Forward*
	1897	*Boys and Girls*
	1902	*Youth, An Illustrated Monthly Journal for Boys and Girls*
	1907	*The Youth's World: A Paper for Boys*
	1909	*Comrade*
	1915	*Pioneer for Boys*
	1925	*Children's Leader*
	1925	*Young People's Leader*
	1938	*Jack and Jill*
	1940	*Forward for Young People*
Pittsburgh	1892	*Youth's Journal*
	1920	*Senior Scholastic*
	1937	*Junior Scholastic*
Ridley Park	1899	*Our Boys and Girls*
Scottdale	1905	*Story Friends*
	1920	*Youth's Christian Companion*
	1968	*With*
Sharon	1924	*Youth's Musical Companion*
Smethport	1910	*The Boys' Magazine*
Troy	1888	*Youth's Press*
Turtle Creek	1879	*The Raindrop: A Monthly Miscellany*
West Chester	1857?	*Young America*
	1866	*The Children's Friend: A Monthly Magazine Devoted to the Best Interests of the Young*

RHODE ISLAND

Providence	1819	*Juvenile Gazette*
	1827	*The Juvenile Gazette: Being an Amusing Repository for Youth*

1830   *The Juvenile Repository*

SOUTH CAROLINA

Charleston	1832	*Southern Rose*
Greenville	1866	*Kind Words*

TENNESSEE

Nashville	1855	*The Children's Book of Choice and Entertaining Reading for the Little Folks at Home*
	1859	*Children's Friend*
	1860	*Youth's Magazine*
	1870	*Pictures and Stories*
	1885	*Youth's Treasury*
	1894	*Children's Missionary*
	1894	*Epworth Era*
	1909	*Boys and Girls*
	1932	*Epworth Highroad*
	1935	*Stories for the Little Child*
	1936	*Cargo: A Magazine for Boys and Girls*
	1941	*Boys Today*
	1941	*Highroad*

UTAH

Salt Lake City	1866	*The Juvenile Instructor*
	1900	*Zion's Young People*
	1902	*The Children's Friend*

VERMONT

Putney	1943	*Adventure Trails for Boys and Girls*

VIRGINIA

Alexandria	1898	*Girls*
Fredericksburg	1868	*Little Gleaner*
Mt. Clinton	1874	*Young Virginian*
Richmond	1862	*Children's Friend*

1867   *Southern Boys' and Girls' Monthly*

NO PLACE

1832   *The Boys Week-day Book*
1852   *Favorite*
1853   *Forest Garland*
1854   *Juvenile Temperance Watchman*
1859   *What Not*
1868?   *Boys' and Girls' New Monthly Magazine*
1868   *Little Chief*
1870   *Infant's Delight*
1872   *Boys' Ledger*
1877   *Child's Monthly*
1878   *Little Ones at Home*
1878   *Pictorial Gallery for Young People*
1918   *Four and Five*
1941   *News Citizen*
1941   *Pictures and Stories*

Index

Contributors

Janice M. Alberghene is assistant professor of English at Bowling Green State University, where she teaches children's and adolescent literature. Her recent article, "From Frontier to Foreign Shores: Seeing Ourselves in the Thirties" (*Children's Literature Association Quarterly*, Fall 1981), looks at the patriotic projections of the Newbery Award books of the 1930s.

Jane Benardete is professor of English at Hunter College, CUNY. She is the author of *Realism: A Shape for Fiction* (Putnam's, 1972) and, with Phyllis Moe, *Companions of Our Youth: Stories by Women for Young People's Magazine, 1865-1900* (Ungar, 1981).

Carol Billman teaches at the University of Pittsburgh, where she is assistant professor of English and co-director of the Children's Literature Program. She has written about McGuffey's readers, Horatio Alger, and Nathaniel Hawthorne's writing for children.

Diana Chlebek is a doctoral candidate in comparative literature at Cornell University and specializes in prose fiction and folklore.

Harriett R. Christy is currently adjunct-instructor in the Department of Library Science and Media Education at the University of Wisconsin-Eau Claire, where she teaches courses in children's literature and literature for young adults.

Nancy Dahlstrom is a librarian at Oak Park and River Forest High School, Oak Park, Illinois.

Marguerite Davern, retired from elementary school teaching and administration, is a reviewer of adolescent literature for *Signal* and instructor of children's literature at the St. Clairsville Branch of Ohio University.

Patricia Demers is associate professor of English, University of Alberta, Edmonton, where she teaches courses in Renaissance literature and children's literature. She is the co-editor of *From Instruction to Delight: An Anthology of Children's Literature to 1850* (Oxford, 1982).

Alice Denham is associate professor of education at Texas Tech University and editor of the *Texas Tech Journal of Education*. She teaches graduate and undergraduate courses in adolescent literature, English teaching methods, and secondary education.

John R. Edson is a children's librarian at the Buffalo and Erie County Public Library, Buffalo, New York, and the proprietor of Reverie Press, a small private press that has published several juvenile titles.

Rosalind E. Engel, associate professor of child development, Iowa State University, specializes in teaching children's literature and has published extensively on books and reading for children.

Fred Erisman is professor of English at Texas Christian University in Fort Worth, Texas. A specialist in American Studies, he has published widely in the area of American popular literature; his writings on children's literature include studies of L. Frank Baum, Ralph Henry Barbour, Kate Douglas Wiggin, Laura Ingalls Wilder, *St. Nicholas Magazine*, and regionalism in American children's books. He is a member of the International Research Society for Children's Literature and currently serves on its Governing Board.

Joan Brest Friedberg holds a Ph.D. in English from the University of Pittsburgh. She is currently associated with the Carriage House Children's Center in Pittsburgh, where she works as a children's book specialist.

David L. Greene, chairman, Division of Humanities and Department of English, Piedmont College, Demorest, Georgia, founded the annual Conference on the Literary Aspects of Children's Literature in 1975 and from 1979 through 1982 served as book review editor for *Children's Literature* annual. He is working on a monograph about the development of nineteenth-century American historical journals.

Constance Gremore holds M.A. degrees in theatre arts and library science from the University of Minnesota, where she is completing a Ph.D. in theatre arts. She is currently a member of the community faculty at Metropolitan State University, St. Paul, Minnesota. Her publications include numerous reviews in *New Books for Young Readers* (1979-1982) and cumulative indexes to *Children's Literature* (1972-1976), *Children's Theatre Review* (1977-1978), and *Theatre Survey* (1960-1979).

Scot Guenter is a doctoral candidate in American Studies at the University of Maryland.

Dixie Elise Hickman is currently director of writing at the University of Southern Mississippi, Hattiesburg, Mississippi.

Nancy Lyman Huse is associate professor of English, Augustana College, Rock Island, Illinois. She has written about Tove Jansson's Moomintrolls and is currently doing research on politics and art in the criticism of children's literature.

Mary Kelly Isbell is a reference librarian in the Education/Psychology Division of Morris Library, Southern Illinois University. She is compiling a subject index to *Our Young Folks*.

Edward J. Jennerich is dean of the School of Library Science and Instructional Technology, Southern Connecticut State University, New Haven, Conn. He has taught courses in children's literature for the past decade and is a member of the Children's Literature Association. His publications include "Colonial Printing: Character and Distribution," "Perspectives on Teaching Children's Literature," and essays about "Esther Forbes," "Ludwig Bemelmans," and "Benjamin Harris" for *American Writers for Children* (Gale Research, in preparation).

Anne D. Jordan is a graduate of the University of Michigan, where she received awards for poetry and the short story in the Avery and Jule Hopwood Awards contest. In 1972 she founded the Children's Literature Association. Currently, she teaches writing at the University of Hartford and is an assistant editor with *The Magazine of Fantasy and Science Fiction* as well as a regular reviewer for The Children's Book Review Service.

Gayle Keresy is the media coordinator for East Arcadia School, Riegelwood, North Carolina. She is the magazine reviewer for *Voice of Youth Advocates* (VOYA).

Meredith M. Klaus holds the Ph.D. in comparative literature and is associate professor of English at Eastern Michigan University, where she has taught children's literature for the past five years.

Mary Lou Luttrell Kraft is supervisor of curriculum development for the English-Business Communications Program with the United States Department of Agriculture's Upward Mobility Program. She also serves as a lecturer with the Center of Adult Education, University College, and with the English Department, University of Maryland, College Park.

JoEllen Laissue is a doctoral candidate in American Studies at the University of Maryland.

Ruth K. MacDonald is associate professor of English at Northeastern University, Boston. She is the author of *Literature for Children in England and America, 1646-1774* (Whitston, 1982) and *Louisa May Alcott* (Twayne, 1983) and currently serves as president of the Children's Literature Association.

Roderick McGillis teaches in the Department of English at the University of Calgary.

Mary Lou McKeown is an associate professor, Faculty of Education, University of New Brunswick.

Mary D. Manning, assistant professor of English at East Tennessee State University, teaches courses in children's literature, American literature, and linguistics. She is currently treasurer of the Tennessee Folklore Society.

Leonard S. Marcus is a writer and a member of the Humanities faculty of the School of

Visual Arts, New York. He is editor of Dover's facsimile reprint edition of *New York Street Cries in Rhyme*, an early American children's chapbook, and is an editorial board member of *The Lion and the Unicorn*. His reviews and essays on children's literature and related matters have appeared in *The Washington Post Book World*, *Art in America*, *The Dictionary of Literary Biography*, and other publications.

Anne Menzies is agency head, Sprague Branch Library, Salt Lake City Public Library, and president of the Children's Literature Association of Utah.

Phyllis Moe is professor of English at Hunter College, CUNY, and chair of the department. Although her principal field of scholarship is medieval literature, she is also interested in children's literature. She has co-edited *Companions of Our Youth: Stories by Women for Young People's Magazines, 1865-1900* and written biographical entries about Abbie Farwell Brown, Helen Stuart Campbell, Eliza Lee Cabot Follen, Emily Clark Huntington Miller, and Sarah Chauncey Woolsey for *American Women Writers*.

Marion J. Mulholland is assistant professor of English, Central Michigan University, where she teaches literature for children and adolescents.

Avon Jack Murphy received his doctorate at the University of Wisconsin-Madison in 1971 and taught children's literature and other English courses at Ferris State College for twelve years. He is currently associate professor of English at Northeast Louisiana University where he coordinates the technical communication program.

Alleen Pace Nilsen is professor of education, Department of Educational Technology and Library Science, Arizona State University. She is co-editor of *English Journal* and co-author of *Books for Today's Young Adults*. Her articles and essays have appeared in *Top of the News*, *School Library Journal*, *Language Arts*, *The Reading Teacher*, and *Journal of Reading*.

Lalla N. Overby teaches at Brenau College, Gainesville, Georgia.

Naomi Patz is a writer and editor. She is a graduate of Barnard College and holds an M.A. in English Literature from Old Dominion University and an M.A. in Jewish religious education from Hebrew Union College, Jewish Institute of Religion.

Pat Pflieger is a Ph.D. student in American Studies at the University of Minnesota and has written *A Guide to Modern Fantasy for Children* (Greenwood, 1984).

Kathy Piehl is a writer with a strong interest in children's literature.

Martha Rasmussen is a free-lance writer and children's book reviewer. A 1957 graduate of the School of Journalism at the University of Missouri, she recently completed a master's degree in child development at Iowa State University. Her book reviews of children's literature appear regularly in the Des Moines Sunday *Register*.

E. Wendy Saul recently completed a Ph.D. at the University of Wisconsin. Her dissertation analyzes the school sports novel in America between 1900 and 1940.

Evelyn Schroth is associate professor of English at Western Illinois University.

John Daniel Stahl is assistant professor of English at Virginia Polytechnic Institute and State University at Blacksburg. He received a Ph.D. from the University of Connecticut, has written about Mennonite children's literature for *Mennonite Quarterly Review* and about children's literature and the media for the *Children's Literature Association Quarterly*, and he has served as editorial assistant for *Children's Literature*.

Beverly Talladay holds an M.A. in children's literature from Simmons College and is a school librarian in the Clarence Central School system in western New York State.

Carol J. Veitch is assistant professor of Library Science at East Carolina University, Greenville, North Carolina.

Janet Diana Vine teaches English and is English Department chairman at Kenmore East Senior High School, Kenmore, New York. She is the co-author of *English: A Comprehensive Review* (Cebco Standard Publishing, 1982) and *Discovering Literature, Reading Guide and Review Tests* and *Exploring Literature, Reading Guide and Review Tests* (Houghton Mifflin Company, 1968). In addition, she has had numerous articles and poems in national newspapers and literary magazines.

Mark I. West is completing a doctorate in American culture at Bowling Green State University. For his dissertation he is writing a historical analysis of controversies in American children's culture. He wrote the entries about Horace E. Scudder and Hezekiah Butterworth for the *Dictionary of Literary Biography* volume on American writers for children.

Virginia L. Wolf has studied, taught, and written about children's literature for nearly fifteen years. Beginning her work at the University of Kansas, she now is associate professor of English at the University of Wisconsin-Stout. She has taught literature for the young child, children's literature, writing for children, fantasy for children, censorship in children's books, and adolescent literature. Active in the Children's Literature Association since 1974, she has been a member of the Board of Directors and secretary and now serves as treasurer.

Bernice O. Zelditch currently teaches at Foothill College, Los Altos Hills, California. Her fields of specialization include children's literature, women writers, and nineteenth-century American literature.

About the Editor

R. GORDON KELLY is Associate Professor and Chairman of the department of American Studies at the University of Maryland. He is the author of *Mother Was a Lady* (Greenwood Press, 1974) and articles appearing in *Handbook of American Popular Culture* (Greenwood Press, 1982), *Children's Literature, American Quarterly, Phaedrus,* and *Twentieth-Century Children's Writers.*